Herbert Butterfield

C. T. McINTIRE

Herbert Butterfield

HISTORIAN AS DISSENTER

Yale University Press
New Haven &
London

Published with assistance from the Louis Stern Memorial Fund.

Set in Sabon type by Keystone Typesetting, Inc.
Printed in the United States of America by Sheridan Books.

LC Control Number: 2004040724
ISBN: 0-300-09807-3 (alk. paper)

A catalogue record for this book is available from the British Library.

The paper in this book meets the guidelines for permanence and durability of the Committee on Production Guidelines for Book Longevity of the Council on Library Resources.

10 9 8 7 6 5 4 3 2 1

About Butterfield

[He] brought to an end an epoch of historical writing.
— *Owen Chadwick, 1968*

. . . the most original historian of his generation.
— *Noel Annan, 1999*

He introduced me to the historical Jesus.
— *Eve Bogle, 1986*

Q. Did you ever meet Butterfield?
A. Yes.
Q. What did you think of him?
A. A likeable man.
Q. Did you read any of his books?
A. Not if I could help it.
— *Lord Dacre (Hugh Trevor-Roper), 1986*

By Butterfield

And nothing is more plausible to the unthinking than a past that has been made to appear like the world that they know in their own lifetime.
— *On the past, 1969*

[I]n the case of two brothers brought up in very much the same way, we have the one who becomes a nonconformist minister because his father was a nonconformist minister, while his brother becomes a militant atheist because his father was a nonconformist minister.
— *On historical explanation, 1971*

We can do worse than remember a principle which both gives us a firm Rock and leaves us the maximum elasticity for our minds: the principle: Hold to Christ, and for the rest be totally uncommitted.
— On certainty and flexibility, 1949

The twentieth-century situation seems to me to require what I have called the "insurgent" type of Christianity — not the kind which binds up its fortunes with the defence of the status quo. By "insurgent" Christianity . . . I mean the kind of Christianity which . . . is constantly ready to return to first principles, to make a fresh dip into the Gospels and the New Testament revelation.
— On dissent, 1956

Contents

Introduction   ix

Chronology   xxi

1   Aspirations   1

2   Art and Science   27

3   Reconciler   51

4   General Horizons   78

5   Patriotic History   102

6   Professor   133

7   Religion   164

8   Public Figure   202

9   On War and Historiography   235

10   Master and Aggression   270

11   World Ideas, World Politics   292

12   The Top and After the Top   319

13   Going Global   334

14   Nothing but History and Religion   363

Conclusion   403

List of Abbreviations   419

Notes   421

Bibliography   473

Index   493

Photos follow page 132

Introduction

"It was the fallacy of Whiggish history!" the student concluded her history essay triumphantly, and the professor, nodding in agreement, gave her the highest mark in the class. For decades the accusation resounded in colleges and universities throughout the English-speaking world. Little did most of the accusers know that they were evoking the rhetorical power of Herbert Butterfield.

Butterfield's little book *The Whig Interpretation of History* made his name as a historian. When he published it in 1931, he was a Fellow of Peterhouse, Cambridge, a lecturer in history in Cambridge University, barely thirty-one, slight of build, and very shy. The book, really just a rambling essay, was similarly unimposing. Readers found it difficult to fathom, yet somehow provocative and compelling. The oddness of the phrase "Whig interpretation of history" lodged it in the memory, and it came easily off the tongue. They recognized a fault they discerned in themselves.[1]

Butterfield identified an understanding of history that had dominated the culture of Europe and North America. As a way of viewing history, he charged, it committed the fallacy of reading the past wholly in the light of the present. He referred to the metanarrative that told of history as progress towards something approved in the present or for the hoped-for future. It involved the tendency to write history in a way that drew straight lines from people and events deemed desirable in the past to what we like most about our own culture, society, and religion. The effect was to write history as a success story, especially history that ratified, justified, even glorified the hegemony of the powerful in the world.

Butterfield had in mind the liberal Whig historians of the nineteenth and early twentieth centuries, champions of English liberty and opponents of the conservative Tories, who drew an ever-extending line of inevitability from the Magna Carta of 1215 to their own society. They were sure that their England embodied the fullness of civil and religious liberty. But Butterfield's readers realized that his observation readily transferred to other cases where they could see the fallacy operating: economic and political historians who justify the domination of the world by white capitalists, American historians who chronicle the sure rise of the United States to imperial power, social historians who document the triumph of the middle classes, and religious historians who embroider particular ecclesiastical traditions as direct fulfillment of Martin Luther or the apostles or Thomas Aquinas or John Wesley.

For countless historians, religious thinkers, and students, Butterfield's point represented one of the most significant historical insights gained in the twentieth century. They found the Whiggish fallacy everywhere — in books, at their universities, in institutional narratives, in special historical fields, in conversations, in the press, on Wall Street, in Parliament, at the White House, in Hollywood. The British Library placed the publication of *The Whig Interpretation of History* in its "Chronology of Modern Britain" as one of the most important cultural events of the twentieth century, one of only seven history books to receive the distinction.[2]

So complete was the stigmatization of Whiggish history that it became what Annabel Patterson called "one of the reigning conventions of the modern Anglo-American academy." Patterson, who felt troubled by the book — "his early tirade" — found herself adopting the culture of the duel as she threw down "a challenge" to this "orthodoxy" that is "most often associated with the name of Herbert Butterfield." She announced, "I propose to reinstate a 'whig interpretation of history,' in defiance of the historiographical orthodoxy that declares such an interpretation archaic and procedurally mistaken." She then thrust forward "a new whig interpretation of history."[3]

The Whig Interpretation of History was merely the most quotable of Butterfield's works. Denis Brogan adjudged that "there is none of his books, not even the earliest, which does not display an originality of approach and judgment."[4] Indeed, Noel Annan, not a person known to curry favour with anyone, regarded Butterfield as "the most original historian of his generation."[5] Virtually every one of his twenty-two books, and quite a few of his articles, left traces of the deep presence of his thought in the territories he inhabited, even among people who never heard of him. The epigraphs let us hear quickly about Butterfield from others, and from Butterfield himself on things that mattered to him.

Several of his books in particular enjoyed enormous influence, and this study gives them due attention: *The Whig Interpretation of History* for understanding history (1931), *Christianity and History* (1949) for the history of religion, *Origins of Modern Science* (1949) for the history of science, *Man on His Past* (1955) for the history of historical writing, and the combination of *Christianity, Diplomacy and War* (1953) with *International Conflict in the Twentieth Century* (1960) for the study of international relations. In the age of the Internet, Amazon.com offered continuing access to almost all his books, and a search for "Herbert Butterfield" yielded thousands of hits.

Butterfield's life-journey began in October 1900, during the final months of late Victorian England, in a low-income working-class Methodist family within the remote industrial village of Oxenhope in West Yorkshire, England. By the power of his academic achievements he constructed a path for himself from the worker's cottage in Oxenhope to the top of the high-standing culture of Cambridge University as well as to preeminence in the historical profession in the twentieth century, with a knighthood from the queen. He died in Sawston, a village south of Cambridge, in July 1979. The shift of his horizon from the village to the globe recapitulated the tale of the modern world as a whole.

His high marks in school examinations won him the scholarship money that catapulted him from Oxenhope to Cambridge. He entered Peterhouse as an undergraduate in 1919, along with hordes of others after the Great War in the largest new cohort in history. Here he studied history under the tutelage of Harold Temperley, already a luminary in the Cambridge scene and a figure of consequence in the peace settlements of the Great War just ended. Here, too, he encountered Lord Acton, the liberal aristocrat historian, by then long dead but very much a presence in historical discourse in Cambridge. He also encountered Leopold von Ranke, the German conservative master-historian, also long dead, but still hugely prominent in the intellectual milieu of Cambridge. Peterhouse kept Butterfield in Cambridge, electing him a Research Fellow, soon a full Fellow, and later, in 1954, the Master of Peterhouse. Within Cambridge University, on a parallel track, he became a lecturer in history, and then, in a society where professorships are few, he held consecutively two of the most prestigious chairs, Professor of Modern History from 1944 and Regius Professor of Modern History from 1963. In 1968 he retired to Sawston, where for another decade he continued to expand his horizons. The Butterfield chronology in this book gives the short story of his life, and the photographs let us see him, and two of his dwellings, at timely moments over the years.

During the sixty years of his life in Cambridge, he was surrounded by perhaps the most remarkable assemblage of historians in one spot in the world in the twentieth century. To name their names is enough to make the point, and we shall see them appearing in this study.[6] It is astonishing how many of them became the subject of a book and the recipient of a festschrift. Butterfield spent decades with many of these people. The pleasure of their company was no doubt mixed. With many he benefitted from the intellectual interaction. With a few he developed relations of deep and genuine affection. Among the whole, as within Cambridge generally, he experienced and no doubt partici-pated in what Maurice Cowling called the culture of "placid malice" inform-ing their human relationships.[7]

Looking at Butterfield we are struck immediately by the sheer range, the variety, and the oceanity of his interests. And what he said and wrote on virtually all the topics he touched made an impact. The festschrift presented to him after his retirement caught the point in its title, *The Diversity of History.*[8] He delighted in the problems of handling the complexity of general history. He defied the expectation then gaining ascendancy that the scholar and the teacher must specialize. At the same time, however, he placed upon himself the demands made upon the specialist, especially in the construction of his method. His library and research notes show that he worked up a reading knowledge of many languages over the years: Russian, German, Italian, Span-ish, and Latin to join his knowledge of French learned at school, some Dutch, and a start in Hebrew and Greek for reading the Bible. The interplay of the specialist and the generalist characterized his career. In this study we are able to watch Butterfield as he participates in the conversations of one field after another over many decades.

Prior to *The Whig Interpretation of History* Butterfield had already pub-lished *The Historical Novel: An Essay* in 1924, and with that little book he had made his entrance into the world of general thinking about history. He con-tinued over the length of his career to produce articles and books on historiog-raphy, historical thinking, and the history of historical writing. The most obvi-ously historiographical included *The Englishman and His History* (1944), *History and Human Relations* (1951), *Man on His Past* (1955), *George III and the Historians* (1957), and *The Origins of History* (1981). His career-long preoccupation with Lord Acton revolved around the theme of historical under-standing.

He had also published *The Peace Tactics of Napoleon, 1806–08* in 1929, a highly detailed work of research, focused on France and Russia, but spanning the continent. He eventually wrote a small book entitled simply *Napoleon* (1939). He traced out his interest in European international political history in two directions. One was a persistent emphasis on general European history. The topic surfaced in his lectures in the Cambridge Faculty of History as well as in his long-time desire to produce the *Concise Cambridge Modern History.* The other was the sustained treatment of international political theory. Among the pieces he produced were *Christianity, Diplomacy and War* (1953), *International Conflict in the Twentieth Century* (1960), and *Diplomatic Investigations* (1966). To this list we could add *The Statecraft of Machiavelli* (1940).

After *Whig Interpretation,* he turned to the history of England in the eighteenth century. The initial topic was the life of Charles James Fox, his aim being to write a detailed biography. This enlarged into an abiding interest in the reign of George III. His *Statecraft of Machiavelli* grew out of his questions about George III, as did *George III, Lord North, and the People, 1779–1780* (1949), *George III and the Historians* (1957), and a string of articles.

The history of science occupied his attention from the 1930s onwards, arising from his study of general European history. The yield on this topic included many articles, lectures, a couple of edited works, and above all *The Origins of Modern Science* (1949). Education was important to him, especially what goes on within universities. For two years, 1959–1961, he got to put his ideas into practice when he served as the highest executive officer of Cambridge University. His articles and lectures on education were numerous, with the most visible being *The Universities and Education Today* (1962). The history of ideas was always important to him, especially within European history. Late in life, he expanded well beyond Europe to examine the historical ideas of Islam, the Chinese, ancient Mesopotamia, and Egypt as well as Greece and Rome. *The Origins of History* (1981) was the most notable of the results.

The topic that especially animated him was religion, notably Christianity as a historical religion, and the attempt to understand the work of God in history. The topic of religion unavoidably connected with his concentration upon historiography and historical thinking. His most prominent work on religion was *Christianity and History* (1949), but there were also *Christianity in European History* (1951), *History and Human Relations* (1951), *Writings on Christianity and History* (1979), and a host of articles and lectures. Most of what he investigated beyond Europe in his later years connected in his mind with religion.

Besides this formidable range of topics we are also struck by the persistence of a number of intellectual questions that occupied Butterfield's mind. Certain issues concerned him deeply, and he sought to figure them out with intensity.

We have no doubt about the sincerity of his convictions and the authenticity of his quest. He raised most of his queries quite early, and he continued to consider virtually the same matters throughout his career. His questions touched upon history, politics, religion, morality, science, and war. It is uncanny how many of his concerns were also central questions of his times. Along with his generation, he experienced and responded to the collapse of Victorian society, the Great War of 1914–1918, the dominance of science, the achievements of technology, the Bolshevik revolution, the capitalist Depression, Hitler, Stalin, World War II, the bomb, the Cold War, consumer expansionism, impoverishment of the masses, decolonization, American world power, Viet Nam, and all the rest of the wonders, atrocities, and boredom of the twentieth century.

Butterfield's questions were many, but they can be referred to a number of groups of concerns. In this study we are able to track in detail how this historian gave himself to these issues over the course of a lifetime. Themes about history and religion predominate in this book, since he was a historian for whom religion mattered and a religious thinker for whom historical understanding was crucial. In historiography, he never gave up trying to understand historical study as a science. But at the same time he never let go of his interest in the effects of the historian's religion, politics, and personal orientation on historical writing. In diplomatic history and international relations, he queried the exercise of power among states. In eighteenth-century studies, he meditated on the early reign of George III and the right relations among political intentions and self-interest in the operation of public affairs. In the history of science, he thought about what happened when the big names of science were no longer the centre of the analysis. In education, he worried about how to support learning and originality when confronted by the unrelenting advance of the examination system. In connection with anything touching upon human affairs, he upheld the centrality of individual persons. In academic studies, he struggled with the question of the role of moral judgments made by the scholar or the analyst. In religion, he needed to know how the work of God, the operation of Providence, informed human history.

The theme of dissent runs through this book. Whenever something Butterfield proposed caught on he expressed surprise. And, as in the case of the Whig interpretation of history, when his ideas gained wide acceptance he expressed alarm. Butterfield seemed an unlikely figure to achieve dominance in anything. Everything about him, from his personality, physique, and social origins to his convictions about history, religion, morality, politics, and education represented counter-hegemony. Noel Annan called him an "iconoclast" and observed how he "scorned every orthodoxy." He also noted the adversative style of Butterfield's writings in which assertions were followed a few pages later by counter-assertions.[9] People commented on his twinkling eyes, his impish manner, his mischievous talk. They noticed how heartily he could laugh, even giggle, in any setting, especially the most august. Butterfield responded with intellectual and even bodily dissent from whatever prevailed. As we shall see, his criticism of the Whig interpretation of history proved to be merely one of his creative provocations of thought. He repeatedly pushed against the dominant modes of thought.

Butterfield was a lifelong, active Methodist, with a piety marked by contemplation, humane reverence for individual persons, tolerance, and devotion to God. In the most profound sense his Methodist spirituality animated his historical work. The term dissent, following upon the older term nonconformity, traditionally applied to Methodist resistance to the alliance of the Church of England with the English state. Long after English Methodists had made their peace with the Anglican establishment and had themselves come to form part of England's religious status quo, Butterfield continued to speak with the voice of dissent. In this study I use the notion of dissent, like nonconformity, in a way that is compatible with his usage. I do not reserve the term for the eye-riveting cases of yesteryear — those who went to the stake, got imprisoned, always voted no in Parliament.

Butterfield transvalued the notion of dissent into an ethic of living in tension with any established system, even, indeed especially, when he occupied a position of authority or privilege within the system. This entailed for him the practice of distancing himself from the requirements and expectations of the dominant powers in historical study, the university, religion, politics, and society. Butterfield deliberately used his thought to unsettle the thought of others. "As a teacher," Owen Chadwick has said, "he liked to disturb, even to shock; though never crudely nor as with a bludgeon." Edward Norman noted "the layers of his scepticism," and his "profoundly sceptical and subtle mind." Challenge to the ruling intellectual clarities marked his way of being in the world.[10]

People found it hard to figure out Butterfield's politics. A lineup of people counted him as a conservative. Noel Annan called him a radical conservative. Annabel Patterson associated him with the Tory views of Lewis Namier and David Hume. The neo-Marxist journal *Radical Philosophy* made him a reactionary.[11] But another lineup asserted the opposite. Maurice Cowling was sure that he was "never a figure of the Right." Cowling and J. C. D. Clark thought of him as an Asquithean Liberal, playing the fair-minded umpire, fixed in a version of progressivism represented by Herbert Asquith, the leader of a section of the Liberal party when Butterfield was coming of age.[12] Richard Acland felt that Butterfield might be close to socialism.[13] By contrast, still others acknowledged the difficulty of classifying Butterfield at all. Patrick Cosgrave observed about Butterfield that "although fascinated by politics, he could never have given — after his youthful flirtation with Asquith . . . — his complete allegiance to any party."[14]

The closest Butterfield himself came to clarifying the issue were a few categorical declarations now and then. For instance, near the end of his life he said point blank, "I have never been a Tory." And to Richard Acland, a Christian Socialist Member of Parliament in the mid-1950s, he said, "I would not feel able to call myself a socialist."[15] As we shall see, he complicated the issue of his politics many times over. Nonetheless, it is plausible to follow the lead of Charles Smyth, who, in 1931, read *The Whig Interpretation of History* and perceived therein Butterfield's attachment to the Whig tradition, but also his impulse to renovate the tradition. In that light, we may think of him as a twentieth-century New Whig. The term suggests a politics that is liberal, transformative, and progressive, but that flatly refuses to fit neatly into any of the going categories.[16]

It is the aim of this book to explore the work of Butterfield as historian. I cast the project as an intellectual biography, and as such it is a study in the history of historiography. The book is not a full-blown biography covering all aspects of his life, nor a memoir, nor a life of the man and his times. The casual reader will not a find a treasury of anecdotes that entertain. The voyeur will not be able to gaze on Butterfield's domestic and emotional life with the sort of material that filled perhaps a third of Jonathan Haslam's biography of E. H. Carr, Butterfield's contemporary and critic in Cambridge.[17]

The book is, rather, a close-up analysis of the life of the historian and the historian's intellectual career. I observe an intellectual at work at very close range, commencing before he is born and concluding after he dies. My quest is to understand how he became a historian and the sort of thinker he was, and how he worked out his vocation as historian. I deliberately keep my focus on his experience, activity, and discourse as historian, while ranging comprehensively throughout the whole of his nearly eight decades.

In the process we encounter, of course, his domestic world and emotional life. But the personal factors are there primarily as ingredients in the explanation of why and how he did what he did as an intellectual. We likewise meet the politics, the personal animosities, and the administrative machinations operating within Peterhouse and Cambridge University. But we delve into these only for the purpose of sorting out the impact they have on his historical work. We become involved as well with the historians and religious thinkers who came into his horizon, but these, too, appear in the analysis in so far as he interacted with them in the formation of his own thinking. We also engage, freely and often, the big events of the twentieth century, a century full of awesome and terrible things. But I glance at this wider world merely in order to serve our understanding of the history of his own intellectual life. All in all, his was the narrowly academic life.

My approach is what I might call radically historical. If I classify the book as an intellectual biography of a historian, I have in mind a study of an intellectual worker, someone whose vocation is to conduct historical analysis, reflect on religion, write and talk about religion and history, and promote historical and religious understanding. If as scholar, Butterfield generates historical and religious discourse, we need to examine his labour as well as the fruits of his labour. I want to explore the creative process by which he went about reading, thinking, lecturing, conversing, and writing as he did. I want to see what it was like for him to work as a historical and religious thinker, what he did from day to day and year to year, and how he came up with the things he had to say. We look at his work as it emerges and transforms, as it reaches or fails to reach publication, as it influences others or meets with opposition or falls into the abyss. The finished writings, especially his books, are crucial to this study, but I do not simply privilege them. I give virtually equal weight, sometimes even greater weight, to his unpublished work and occasional shorter writings, as I seek to understand the complex processes by which he practiced his work as historian and thinker. We look where necessary in order to discover the interweaving of his thinking with the thinking of others and the events of the wider world. With Butterfield, everything interconnects.

When we approach his work historically in this way, the questions multiply. What went on before a lecture was given and before a book was published? What was he trying to learn? What problems did he want to solve? What factors entered his thinking, consciously or not? With whom did he engage? What were the results, intended and unintended, in the lecture and the book? What were his arguments and the content of his thought? What were the things he took for granted or overlooked? When did he say something new, when did he repeat himself, and when did he display continuity in his thought? What did he accomplish? What responses did he evoke? What effects did he have?

This is a critical study of Butterfield's activity and achievement. I engage him in a kind of conversation about what he is doing. I perform a close exegesis of his texts, published and unpublished. I probe in order to feel that I am understanding what he is saying and what underlies what he is saying. I feel free to question him about what he writes and to comment on his work. I make no judgments about his personal life, a task outside the aim of the text. I do offer countless judgments about his intellectual projects and discourse, as I consider his method, ideas, arguments, writing, rhetoric, theses, published products, and so on. I read him in the light of his own work, to see how well he measures up to his own expectations and his own theory. I also consider how well he illuminates human history and helps us understand the study of history. My criticism appears within my historical examination of his work.

The bibliography displays what people have written about Butterfield, except for book reviews, since Martin Wight began the process in 1950. Among the most notable treatments are the essay by Denis Brogan in the festschrift prepared by J. H. Elliott and H. G. Koenigsberger, the various writings by Owen Chadwick, Maurice Cowling, and Kenneth Thompson, and the studies on special themes by Alberto Coll, Malcolm Thorp, Keith Sewell, and Michael Bentley. This study joins the list as the first general book on Butterfield as historian.[18]

What makes this kind of study possible are the resources Butterfield left us. The quantity and character of the materials available, both unpublished and published, permit an exacting look at the scholar and thinker at work. Butterfield's published output was considerable and diverse, both in genres and themes: monographic histories, religious explorations, published lectures, scholarly articles, philosophical reflections, historiography, theoretical essays, criticism, and reviews. The unpublished writings and other materials which he left behind are also vast and varied: typescripts and manuscripts of course lectures, unfinished book-length writings, beginnings of books, successive drafts of a general history, journal-sheets, thought-essays, diary pages, autobiography, memoirs, notes, correspondence, photographs, artifacts, a library, and a nearly complete run of fifty years of his *Cambridge Pocket Diary*. The list of works he projected doing or was invited to do is also vast.[19]

Besides all this, Butterfield agreed to discuss his work with me at length and, as it were, to create some made-to-order discourse. In 1975 and 1977 he devoted altogether some sixty hours to interviews with me, with about twenty of these hours recorded on tape. The first tangible outcome of these talks was my essay "Herbert Butterfield on Christianity and History," which introduced my edition of his writings on religion and history. The book appeared in New York in January 1979. He readily agreed to further talks in support of my expression of interest in expanding my essay into a more general historiographical study. We scheduled these talks for late July and early August 1979, but he went into hospital in early June and died in July, precisely during the time we had decided to meet.[20]

In December 1979, Lady Butterfield gave the vast majority of the Butterfield papers as a benefaction to the University Library at Cambridge, where they reside near the Lord Acton papers as Butterfield desired. At the same time she sent a file box of papers to Peterhouse. In February 1980 Peterhouse purchased about 700 volumes from his personal library for the college library.[21]

Butterfield gave me unrestricted access to his papers. These he kept in his study in his home in Sawston, near his baby grand piano and Harold Temperley's bust of the young Napoleon. There, with him facilitating my access, I freely read his diaries, letters, unpublished writings, and other materials. The exception to this grant of open use of his materials was the manuscript, which I read, which he described as "the very big Diary which covered the two years of my Vice-Chancellorship," and which, he said, "may contain a lot of material that isn't my own — e.g., accounts of confidential meetings, etc. . . . It doesn't really touch the historiographical side." Some of the papers I read remain with the family, and about 20 percent of the rest, those presented to Cambridge University Library, are withheld from researchers until the year 2030 because of their confidential character.[22]

Lady Butterfield was unfailingly kind in talking with me about her husband. She also granted me approval to read in his papers after his death and most generously provided me further access to the materials which remained with her. Eve Bogle, his long-time secretary, administrative aide, and research assistant, talked freely with me about him and his work and wrote me some of her reminiscences. Many colleagues in Peterhouse and the Faculty of History at Cambridge spoke with me quite candidly about him, some of them on tape. Many of his former research students very kindly shared their experiences of him with me as well.

For their timely help and kindness, each in different ways, I am especially grateful to Lady Butterfield, Peter Butterfield, Robin Butterfield, Eve Bogle, Brian Wormald, Maurice Cowling, and Edward Norman. I also thank others in and around Cambridge who generously gave their time to talk with me or write me about Butterfield: Owen Chadwick, Derek Beales, Gordon Rupp, C. R. Cheney, Joseph Needham, Geoffrey Elton, G. Kitson Clark, Denis Mack Smith, R. W. K. Hinton, Roger Lovatt, Celia Root, J. B. Quash, P. Pattenden, and three Masters of the college, Sir Graeme Clarke, Lord Dacre, and Professor Henry Chadwik. I thank the Fellows of Peterhouse for their generous hospitality on several occasions and for their assistance in many large and small ways. I thank the porters of Peterhouse for facilitating my visits to the college, supplying me with material on college history, and chatting engagingly with me about the Fellows and college life. I am grateful to the many people of Oxenhope, particularly Sidney Bancroft, who helped me become acquainted with the village where Butterfield was born and grew up, and to Ian Dewhirst of Keighley, who introduced me to the town where Butterfield went to school.

I thank the staff of Cambridge University Library for facilitating further research after Butterfield's death. I thank as well the staff of Peterhouse Library who helped me find the Butterfield papers and other relevant materials in their possession as well as the books from his library given to the college. I express my thanks, too, to the librarian of Wesley House, Cambridge, as well as to the staff of the library of the Faculty of History, Cambridge. I requested permission to consult the official records of Peterhouse during Butterfield's tenure as Master, but found that they were closed to researchers.

I acknowledge with much appreciation the support for my research provided by: the American Philosophical Society; the Social Sciences and Humanities Research Council of Canada; the Institute for Christian Studies, Toronto; and the University of Toronto.

I wish also to thank the editors of Yale University Press, especially Larisa Heimert and Nancy Moore, as well as Kay Scheuer and the readers of the manuscript for their enthusiastic support of the book and for their insightful suggestions.

I reserve my most special thanks for Rebekah Smick for all kinds of wonderful things. I want Matthias and Olivia to know that I appreciate their ways of showing interest in the book while in Rome and since.

My gratitude to Butterfield for his kindness to me personally is immense. I first met him at his Rede Lecture in the Senate House in Cambridge in November 1971. From that day forward, the generosity and candour with which he discussed his work with me over the years and the openness with which he made his personal papers available to me are a model of support for the freedom of historical inquiry. If what follows sometimes seems too critical or diverges too greatly from his self-understanding, I am confident that he would be the first to relish the differences.

Butterfield's work contributed to an extraordinarily creative period within historical study. In the pages that follow, we engage his unsettling thought and encounter the historian as dissenter. He continues to stimulate thought, even among those who disagree with him.

Chronology

1898

9 Apr Marriage, Albert Butterfield, a textile mill worker in Parker's Mill, and Ada Mary Buckland, a domestic servant and child caretaker in John Parker's house, at Wesleyan Methodist Chapel, West Drive, Oxenhope, West Yorkshire, England.

1900–1923

1900   7 Oct Herbert Butterfield born in a worker's cottage, Upper Town, Oxenhope, to Albert Butterfield and Ada Mary Buckland Butterfield. 9 Dec Baptism, Wesleyan Methodist Chapel, West Drive, Oxenhope.

1901   22 Jan Queen Victoria dies. King Edward VII. Father becomes a clerk in Parker's Mill, and family moves to 17 Woodhouse Road, later renamed 17 Keighley Road.

1903   17 Apr Edith Joyce (Pamela) Crawshaw born.

1905   Enters Council School, Oxenhope.

1910   6 May Edward VII dies. King George V.

1911   Enters Trade and Grammar School, Keighley.

1918   Jun Passes Advanced Level examinations: History, English, French. Jul Wesleyan Methodist Local Preacher (On Trial): first listing.

1919   Oct Matriculates in Peterhouse, Cambridge, lives in college.
1920   Essay: "Art Is History Made Organic," gets noticed in Peterhouse.
        Jun Cambridge Intercollegiate Exams: Class 1, Div 2.
1921   Jun Cambridge University History Tripos, Part 1: Class 1, Div 2:
        Economic History; Medieval History; English Constitutional History.
1922   Jun Cambridge University History Tripos, Part 2: Class 1, Div 1:
        English History 1714–1914; European History 1789–1914; Special
        Period: The Fall of Napoleon and the Reconstruction of Europe, No-
        vember 1813–November 1815.
        B.A., University of Cambridge.
        Elected: Hugo de Balsham Studentship, Peterhouse, for 1922–1923.
1923   Mar University Member's English Essay: "Charles Dickens."
        May LeBas Prize: "The Historical Novel."
        July Elected: Charles Abercrombie Smith Research Studentship, Peter-
        house, for 1923–1924.

        1923–1944

1923   Oct Elected Foundation Fellow, Peterhouse, continues to live in
        college.
1924   Feb Prince Consort Prize: "The Problem of Peace in Europe, 1806–8;
        Seeley Medal.
        The Historical Novel (Cambridge University Press): first book.
        Sep Visiting Fellowship, Princeton University (until May 1925).
1925   Director of Studies in History, Peterhouse (until 1931).
        Librarian, Peterhouse (until 1947).
        Father begins work as clerk in Merrall's Mill; father and mother move
        to 60 Rosebank Terrace, later renamed 60 Station Road.
1926   M.A., University of Cambridge.
        Elected Research Fellow, Peterhouse.
1927   "A French Minister at Vienna, 1806–7": first article.
        Independent lecturer to undergraduates on fee-paying basis.
1928   Acting Lecturer in History, Peterhouse (until 1930).
1929   Elected full Fellow, Peterhouse.
        Probationary Lecturer in History, Faculty of History.
        Begins Lectures on Modern History since 1490s (under various titles
        until 1959).
        The Peace Tactics of Napoleon, 1806–8: first academic history book.
        29 Jul Marries Edith Joyce (Pamela) Crawshaw, and moves to a flat on
        Fitzwilliam Road.

1930   University Lecturer in History, Cambridge University (until 1944).
1931   *The Whig Interpretation of History.*
        Ed., *Select Documents of European History,* vol. 3, *1715–1920.*
        Begins biography of Fox.
        Moves to a flat on Tennis Court Road.
        Peter Butterfield born, first child.
1933   "History and the Marxian Method."
1934   Giles Butterfield born, second child.
1936   King George V dies. King Edward VIII.
        10 Dec Edward VIII abdicates. King George VI.
1938   Editor, *Cambridge Historical Journal* (until 1952).
        Dec Lectures in Hitler's Germany: Berlin, Cologne, Bonn, Munster.
1939   Purchases and moves into a house, 89 Tension Road.
        Jul Temperley dies.
        Robin Butterfield born, third child.
        Napoleon.
        Contract for *Concise Cambridge Modern History.*
1940   *The Statecraft of Machiavelli.*
1941   "Napoleon and Hitler."
1942   "Capitalism and the Rise of Protestantism": first writing focused on religion.
1943   Proposes to write *Historical Geography of Europe.*
1944   *The Englishman and His History.*

1944–1948

1944   April Professor of Modern History (until 1963).
        The Study of Modern History: An Inaugural Lecture.
1945   Invited to edit (with G. N. Clark) *New Cambridge Modern History:* declines.
        Mrs. Eve Bogle becomes his personal secretary (until 1970).
1946   Two Acton articles. Proposes to edit Acton diaries.
1948   Lent term Lectures on the Origins of Modern Science.
        Michaelmas term Lectures on Christianity and History.

1949–1954

1949   Oct three books in one months, and fame: *George III, Lord North, and the People, 1779–80; The Origins of Modern Science, 1300–1800; Christianity and History.*

Fall term Institute for Advanced Studies, Princeton.
"Tragic Element in Modern International Conflict."

1950   Takes A. D. Peters as literary agent.
Begins extensive public lecturing: 65+ lectures for 1950 and 1951.
Council, Royal Historical Society (until 1953).

1951   Reissue of *Whig Interpretation of History* and wholly new readership.
History and Human Relations.
Apr "The Reconstruction of an Historical Episode": Historiography.
Jun "Scientific versus Moralistic Approach in International Affairs":
International Relations.
Aug "God in History": Integration of his thought.
Christianity in European History.

1952   24 Jan Father dies.
6 Feb George VII dies. Queen Elizabeth II.
Liberty in the Modern World.
Hon. Doctorate, Aberdeen University: first of 14 honourary doctorates.

1953   "The Role of the Individual in History."
Christianity, Diplomacy and War.

1954   15 Apr Giles Butterfield's suicide.
Misses Regius professorship, which goes to David Knowles.
Nov Vellacott dies.
Nov Belfast Lectures: "Man and His Past."
Dec Agrees to become Master of Peterhouse.

1955–1968

1955   17 Jan Master of Peterhouse.
Moves into the Master's Lodge, Peterhouse. Retains his house at 89
Tension Road.
Man on His Past.
President, Historical Association (until 1958).

1956   Hon. Doctorates, Columbia and Harvard Universities.

1957   *George III and the Historians.*
Draft, *England and the French Revolution, 1792.*

1958   Chair, British Committee on the Theory of International Politics (until
1968).

1959   Vice-Chancellor, University of Cambridge (until 1961).

1960   *International Conflict in the Twentieth Century.*
Administrative Board, International Assoc of Universities (until 1965).

1962   Hon. Doctorate, Sheffield University (first from an English university).
The Universities and Education Today.

1963   Oct Regius Professor of Modern History (until 1968).

1965   *The Present State of Historical Scholarship: An Inaugural Lecture.*
        Fellow, British Academy.

1965 & 1966   Gifford Lectures, Glasgow University.

1966   Ed., *Diplomatic Investigations.*

1967   Honourary Member, Royal Irish Academy.
        Foreign Honorary Member, American Academy of Arts and Sciences.

1968   Honorary Member, American Historical Association.
        Honourary Vice-President, Royal Historical Society.
        9 Jul Knighthood.

1968–1979, and After

1968   Jul moves into a Tudor house at 26 High Street, Sawston, Cambridge-
        shire, which he purchased.
        Oct Officially retires as Professor and Master. Honourary Fellow,
        Peterhouse

1974   Hon. Doctorate, Cambridge University.

1979   Jan *Writings on Christianity and History,* ed. C. T. McIntire.
        20 Jul Dies at Sawston.
        26 Jul Funeral in Peterhouse Chapel; ashes and memorial plaque in
        Peterhouse Chapel.

1981   *The Origins of History,* ed. Adam Watson.

1985   *Herbert Butterfield on History,* ed. Robin W. Winks.

1998   *Essays on the History of Science,* ed. Karl W. Schweizer.

Aspirations

Oxenhope and Keighley

Herbert Butterfield became a historian without intending it. It was unlikely, in any case, that as a child he knew what a historian was, let alone
fantasized about being one. He would have known even less what it meant to
be a religious thinker. His experience of becoming a historian, and living out
his life as a historian, illustrated a doctrine he proclaimed throughout his
career: history is a process of unintended consequences, or as he would say in
the religious language he loved, history is a process of learning to cooperate
with Providence.

Butterfield made it easy to cull certain kinds of information on his personal,
academic, and intellectual life, at least from his point of view. At various times
he drafted memoirs of his life and the lives of certain people close to him. He
also talked about his life in interviews from time to time in the 1960s and
1970s. It was his style to scatter autobiographical references throughout his
writings, published and unpublished, as he blended at least some aspects of his
personal life with his intellectual life as a historian. At the same time, he
seemed studiously to avoid reference to most of his nonacademic life, regarding it as irrelevant or inappropriate to mention.[1]

Late in life he remembered vividly that from about age eight he aspired to be
a writer. At that pristine age, from about 1909, he recalled, he wanted to write

something good. He tells of how as a youth he would begin long stories and novels about shipwrecks and coral islands in the furthest reaches of the British Empire. He kept starting over before the old piece was finished. His literary ambitions enlarged during his teenage years, during the Great War of 1914–1918. His taste in reading switched from *Treasure Island* and adventure in far-off lands to books newly placed on the family shelves — nineteenth-century novels by Charlotte and Emily Brontë, Sir Walter Scott, Victor Hugo, and Alexandre Dumas. His literary productions changed as well. From the safety of his retirement he admitted being very secretive about his youthful writing, not wanting anyone to catch him in the act.

About age twelve, he recounts, he felt a second aspiration, the desire to be a Methodist preacher. His father, Albert Butterfield, used to take him for long walks after dinner, night after night, whatever the weather, along the road in front of their house. His father would talk about life, the moors, the stars, religion, and his own aspirations to be a Methodist minister. Herbert would ask questions and listen. He testified that he felt the call to preach arise within him, transferred from father to son. The desire increased in his teenage years, and at the age of sixteen or seventeen he began to preach in the Methodist chapels around Oxenhope.

None of Herbert's youthful writing or sermons remain. He claimed he was too embarrassed to save them. Yet, he carried both desires, writer and preacher, with him in 1919 when at nineteen years of age he went up to Cambridge as a undergraduate at the end of the Great War.

Either vocation would have required the education that his father had missed and the leisure from manual labour that his father once lacked. His father, as the oldest son, had to leave school at about age ten to earn money for the family. He was a wool sorter, a child labourer in an Oxenhope textile mill, probably Parker's Mill, an industrial plant with about a hundred employees.

Oxenhope was an industrial village of about two thousand inhabitants, with three woolen mills located on the River Weir running through the village and another two or three on streams nearby. The village lay in a dale, surrounded above by the bleak Yorkshire moors whose level summits rose to 1,400 feet. Haworth, where the Brontë sisters once lived, was a short walk across the moors through sheep and cattle pastures. Ancient links connected Oxenhope with Bradford, nine miles to the south, but since the opening of the Worth Valley railway in 1867, the village reoriented towards Keighley, five miles to the north. The livelihood of the village depended on the success of the mill owners, who functioned as the local elite. They owed their social position to their relative wealth and economic hegemony in this little realm at the end of the railway.

Albert's father, Aquila Butterfield, had been a worsted wool weaver, most likely also in Parker's Mill. Aquila died when Albert was seventeen, and the wages Albert earned in the mill became even more necessary to sustain the family. Herbert never knew his grandfather or grandmother Butterfield. He grew up surrounded by his father's two younger brothers, Uncle Herbert and Uncle Frank. Like his father and grandparents on the Butterfield side, his uncles lived in Oxenhope until they died.

Herbert's mother, Ada Mary Buckland Butterfield, had left her home in Leominster, Herefordshire, at age fifteen to work as a domestic servant for John Parker, the mill master in Oxenhope. People usually called her Mary. She lived in the staff quarters of the Parkers' large house which occupied a prominent site in the centre of the village. Her job included caring for Dawson, the Parkers' blind son. At twenty-three she married Albert, age twenty-five, at the Wesleyan Methodist Chapel on West Drive in Oxenhope on 9 April 1898, and she became a wife at home. Her father, John Buckland, was a tailor, and she had one brother, Arthur Richard, and no sisters. Herbert was taken only rarely to Leominster to see his grandfather and grandmother Buckland and Uncle Arthur.[2]

Herbert was Albert and Mary's first child, born 7 October 1900 in Oxenhope. They brought him to baptism after two months, on 9 December 1900, at the large Wesleyan Methodist Chapel on West Drive. They named him for Uncle Herbert. His was the first entry in a new register of baptisms.[3] Within the next three and a half years his parents had a daughter, Edith Mary, named for Parker's daughter, and another son, Arthur, named for Uncle Arthur. Herbert's birthplace was the worker's cottage in Upper Town which his parents rented when they married, one in a row of old low two-storey stone dwellings, located up the hill within walking distance of the Methodist chapel in Lower Town. It was an enduring sign of his working-class roots that Herbert possessed only one given name. During the whole of his youth he lived in the shadow of his uncle, the older Herbert Butterfield. Not until he went up to Cambridge did he finally get his name to himself. Even then he was known in the academic world as "H. Butterfield." His full name, Herbert Butterfield, did not appear on the title pages of his books until the 1950s, after he had turned fifty years old. Little did the young Yorkshire Methodist boy know of the deep history of his name, which honoured St. Herbert, the obscure Anglo-Saxon Christian hermit from seventh-century England.

During the first nineteen years of his life Herbert attached himself strongly to his family and his little west Yorkshire world. His circumstances did not incline him towards individualism. People would say about him years later that he remained very proud of being an ordinary Yorkshireman. Yet, he enjoyed looking beyond Oxenhope. He found three outlets to the wider world; the first was the mill owners, the second the school, and the third the Methodist chapel.

The wealthy mill owners in their big houses became for him a symbol of superior civilization. They acted as the closest thing the village had to a gentry. They dominated the village society, economy, and culture. Because of their relations with the wider market, they could acquire distant goods which inspired awe and marked their position of power over the lower ranks in the village. They also evoked deference, a feeling Herbert's father and the family completely internalized and acted upon. For the Butterfield family, deference to their mill owner brought tangible rewards.

Before his marriage, Albert had worked at different jobs on the mill floor in Parker's Mill. He was a loyal and diligent worker. On the side, during the 1890s, he entered into a part-time business with Amos Dewhirst to run a modest shop—Messrs. Dewhirst and Butterfield—selling stationery, books, and sundries. The shop lasted from about 1893 to 1899. It occupied a little wooden building on West Drive opposite the large Methodist chapel.[4] John Parker, who disliked criticism from workers over wages and firings, took notice of Albert's loyalty and began to show him favour. He invited Albert into his big house and introduced him to Mary, his domestic servant and child caretaker. He then watched over the courtship that ensued. In due course, Parker gave approval for Albert to marry her, released her from domestic service, and allowed his daughter, Sarah Hanna, to act as witness for the marriage. About the time of Herbert's birth, Parker asked Albert to cross the line between capitalist and labour to work as a clerk in the mill owner's office. Part of Albert's new job was to deal with the workers on the owner's behalf, a duty Albert accepted readily. Later he became a bookkeeper of the mill's accounts and stock. The new position brought more money but not enough, which left an impression on his son. Butterfield carried with him throughout life the impression that he came from poverty. He wrote late in life, "I well remember, since my father was poor and often ill, how catastrophic the illness of the bread-winner was down to Lloyd George's insurance act of 1911."[5]

Albert and Mary managed to move the family to a bigger house, an appropriately lower bourgeois dwelling at 17 Woodhouse Terrace, later renamed 17 Keighley Road. This was the house in which Herbert grew up. The house belonged to a row of stone dwellings at the edge of the village. It was built on a slope, with two storeys in front and three behind, and a garden which ran down towards a stream called Leeming Water. The open fields lay beyond. The new setting allowed the boy to experience what he later called the sublimity of the encompassing hills and the desolateness of the moorlands. He remembered the weather as cold and dull, requiring a fire for warmth throughout the year. Befitting the minor rise in social status, Albert and Mary dressed the boy on Sundays like a little gentleman and perhaps on special occasions and for photographs like a little prince.

The mill owner gave the Butterfields the books and music he no longer wanted. This was the source of the adventure books and romantic novels that young Herbert read. The mill owner also gave them money to purchase an old upright piano. From about age ten Herbert took piano lessons and practiced on this piano, developing an attachment to playing which lasted throughout his life. At the mill owner's suggestion, and to further himself, Albert subscribed to *The Harmsworth Self-Educator,* and went through the fortnightly readings that came to the house, readings in all fields, including science. He purchased W. T. Stead's *Penny Poets,* a series of cheap editions of Victorian poetry. With his father's encouragement, Herbert read all these things when his father had finished. The mill owner's relationship with his father gave Herbert the model of social change that he came to embrace — the diffusion of socially higher culture downward to the working classes, those above lifting up those below.

Herbert's father evidenced proper gratitude towards the mill owner, but perhaps he shared the ambivalence suggested by a folktale common to the region. Butterfield later described the tale as the earliest fireside story he remembered, and he claimed that it and others of its kind aroused his interest in the past. The story recounted a near-calamity during the construction of the railway in the Haworth-Oxenhope area during the 1860s. The builder of the railway laid out the plans on the ground. Along came a cow, and when the builder turned his back, the cow ate the plans. The episode produced great laughter among the people, but soon evoked a different attitude when the people began to look on the loss of the plans as a disaster. The tale became a ballad, with the last verse singing:

> And then the local Haworth folk
> Began to think it was no joke,
> And wished the bloomen' cow might choke,
>   That swallowed the plan of the railway.

The social effect of the story would be multiple. It would reinforce the position of the industrial entrepreneurs, the class associated with the planning and continuing importance of the local railway as the link with the larger markets. At the same time, in the record of the cow's act, it would leave a hint of the people's resistance to the hegemony of the owners. In the end, however, the wish against the cow signalled the necessity of the people's deference to the owners.[6]

Herbert's father was demoted from his privileged place in the owner's office in Parker's Mill in the 1920s, when the mill owner gave the position to a relative. Then in 1925 he lost his job entirely when the owner closed the mill. The owner of Merrall's Mill, a bigger and still expanding woolen mill, absorbed many of Parker's workers, including Herbert's father. The new owner put him in charge of a larger staff and set him up in a bigger office. The position meant more money and higher local status. To match the move, his father took a bigger house, a finer looking, but still modest, Victorian brick terraced dwelling at 60 Rosebank Terrace, later known as 60 Station Road.

Herbert's second opening to the world beyond was provided by his schools and academic scholarships. He attended the local school run by the village council in Oxenhope from age five. It was here that he began to dream of writing, and when school was over for the day he would go home to compose his stories and novels. He recalls that he would sometimes watch the blacksmith or wheelwright at work, or enact imaginary stories, play marbles, and collect cigarette cards. He picked up the local dialect and retained a mildly noticeable Yorkshire accent throughout his long years at Cambridge. He knew how to drop his h's, as in Oxen'ope, and he enjoyed flaunting sentences like "Sam'er 'em oop an ugg'er 'em."

When he approached age eleven he faced a change of schools. Rather than send him to the nearest secondary school, his father encouraged him to try for a scholarship to the school with the reputation as the best in the region, the Trade and Grammar School in Keighley, a school for boys.[7] He won a Scott scholarship, and the money financed his first step out of Oxenhope. He often confessed in later years that he helped himself during the scholarship examination by glancing at another pupil's paper, and he would say, "I never lost the feeling that I had started out on my career with a piece of dishonesty."

To reach his new school in Keighley, Herbert traveled northward five miles early each morning on the steam railway through the Worth Valley. At midday when the other boys went home for dinner, he went to the newsagent's and tobacconist's shop which Amos Dewhirst now operated in Keighley not far from the school, and in a room in the back of the shop ate his dinner with the Dewhirst family. After the meal, when the other boys played sports, Herbert, who disliked sports, usually read. He would take the train home again late in the afternoon.

He attended Keighley from 1911 to 1918, during a particularly catastrophic period in world history. As he remembered it, he had grown up believing his childhood was uneventful, an ordinary kind of life in a ordinary world. He recalled receiving the first jolt to his complacency when he heard the news of the death of Tolstoy in 1910. "I realized that someone so great was alive in my time," he said. The second jolt was the outbreak of war between Italy and the

Ottoman Turks over Tripoli in 1911, a thing that seemed to him possible only because the Muslim Turks were the sort of people who operated "just outside the frontiers of civilisation." Then came jolt three, the beginning of the European war in 1914. He felt the wider world shake his little world, and he joined the countless others young and old who felt their old world collapse. He could remember with utter clarity where he was on 4 August 1914, the day the British declared war on Germany after the German invasion of Belgium. He was in Worcestershire, and he hoarded the newspapers blaring the war news in the headlines. There he listened to an old man recalling the Crimean War sixty years before, and suddenly everything in Europe seemed momentous and close at hand. He commented later in life that the Great War caused him much greater shock than the Second World War, even though the fury and reach of the second war were far greater. His shock had much to do with the ironic perception that the future of English liberty would depend on the defeat of Germany, the nation he had grown up believing was the cradle of English liberty. According to the interpretation of English history which he learned from his youth, the Anglo-Saxons, drawing on their Germanic origins, had achieved their rights and liberty and enshrined them in the ancient constitution of England, well before the Magna Carta and long before the Normans entered the land.

> I was brought up on the view that English liberty went back to the Teutonic forests, and that our parliamentary system was due to the Germanic elements in our constitution. Germany was associated with federation and free cities, as well as with Bismarck; associated also with the freedom of the Reformation — it was the Latin countries that had the papacy, the inquisition, and the Napoleonic despotisms. I heard the industrialists of the West Riding boast about the way in which their educational developments followed German models. I knew their sons, who so often, down to 1914, were sent to Germany (instead of going to our universities) to complete their education. British Protestantism was still under the leadership of Germany, and, as one German theological professor succeeded another in the seat of authority, I heard non-conformity taunted for having German professors as its virtual popes. I remember how often our toys were marked "Made in Germany," and a certain jealousy of German industrial success would appear spasmodically in the populace.[8]

He came to associate this germanophile reading of English liberty with the view promoted by Whig historians that "freedom had been perfect in Anglo-Saxon times," and that from time to time liberty needed only to be restored.[9]

The Keighley school had been founded by local merchants and manufacturers to educate their sons in science, mathematics, and commerce. The goal was to prepare them to take over their fathers' businesses and enlarge their economic profit. It was the duty of the headmaster, T. P. Watson, to guide the boys towards science and math. The environment was not congenial to Herbert's lower social origins or his propensity for the arts. He did show early academic promise, even winning an award for his studies in 1912–13. The prize was a book, C. H. H. Parry, *The Evolution of the Art of Music,* which he kept for the rest of his life.[10] But his marks in the ordinary level examinations which he took as he neared age sixteen, after four years in the school, were disappointingly low. He overheard one of his teachers comment, "Butterfield is played out." The words hardened in his head, and he confessed in later years that he heard the identical formula repeated by others from time to time throughout his career.

The misfit between Herbert and the school became serious after his poor examination results when the headmaster had to approve the three fields that Herbert would study for his advanced level examinations two years later. Looking back on the event, Butterfield repeated a tale of the way the headmaster pressed him. Only long afterwards did he regarded the experience as humorous. Watson wanted Herbert to study mathematics, in keeping with the purpose of the school, but Herbert wanted classics, as a literary field to help him become a writer. He and one other boy swore an oath together to oppose the headmaster until he permitted them to take classics. The other boy collapsed in the first interview with Watson and agreed to take natural sciences, but when his own turn came Herbert held firm in his refusal. Confronted with such unprecedented resistance, the headmaster proposed a compromise between classics and mathematics. Herbert would do history. Herbert never forgot his alarm: "I've always hated history, and besides, I can't remember dates." As he retold this story years later, long established as a historian, he would confirm that he still could not remember dates or even names, but he would highlight other experiences in his childhood which suggested an early delight with things historical. He would note that as a schoolboy he loved the rare occasion when he would walk alone within the walls of the old city of York, imagining all the people, the life, the battles that had animated the city over the centuries. He would emphasize that many of the novels he read in his teenage years were historical novels. It was only in retrospect, after the outcome was known — after spending years as a historian — that he came to think that what he hated was not actually history, but merely the history served up in the textbooks for the purposes of passing school examinations. He believed that he possessed from his youth a romantic love of things gone by, a love of the past.[11]

For the next two years Butterfield followed his lonely course and studied history, English, and French. He did not pursue science and math along with the sons of the mercantile class, nor did he study Latin and Greek as did the privileged youth in the elite schools of England. He followed neither the "modern" curriculum suitable for success in capitalist society, nor the "classical" curriculum for gentlemen and the aristocracy. The best he could expect from his nondescript historical curriculum might be a life consigned to teaching school.

As Herbert well knew, the immediate object of his studies was not to learn history but simply to pass the examinations that lay ahead. The shame of his low marks on the ordinary level examinations became a prod. His father pressed him hard, and Herbert quietly assumed the vicarious role of satisfying his father's unfulfiled aspirations. Education and scholarships would become the means of his advancement. He had to come out on top in the advanced level examinations, and he set to work with extraordinary single-mindedness. It would appear that his only noncurricular activity at school consisted of serving as student assistant prefect during his last year, a sign that his reputation with the headmaster must be rising.

Among his teachers at Keighley he remembered Edith Charnock, the formidable Nat Shearing, and especially F. C. Moore. Moore was the English teacher for the whole school. His interests rested securely in English literature, but he was the only one around who could handle the history. He had only two boys to teach at the advanced level, apparently one in English and Herbert in history. It had been Moore who uttered the remark that "Butterfield is played out," and Herbert felt certain that Moore disliked him. Herbert rebounded, in part, by submitting to Moore's influence in important ways. It was probably Moore who had urged him earlier to write poetry with emotional feeling, and throughout his last years at school Moore was the one who convinced him to write his papers with conscious attention to style and originality. Moore was enamored with the Romantic movement and probably led Herbert to break an attachment to impersonal and abstract ideas which Butterfield later remembered had appealed to him in his youth.[12] Moore's influence led apparently to Butterfield's first publication, a Romantic-style poem, reportedly published locally when he was seventeen.[13]

Moore was no historian, however, and he was not in touch with the issues that mattered to historians and history teachers. The chief history book used at Keighley was *A School History of England,* a textbook by Owen M. Edwards and others, supplemented by Edwards's *Notes on English History,* an outline of political events and personages, written in incomplete sentences. Herbert picked up the feeling from the school that he should never let anyone know he used so juvenile a resource. The Edwards books told the story of the great men of England and traced the rise of English liberty from ancient stirrings in the Teutonic forests to the triumph of Protestant religion in England, the achievement of parliamentary government, and coming of material progress and commercial greatness.[14] Herbert probably read no genuine history books at Keighley, and he probably wrote no high-level historical paper. He probably thought about no profound historical question. He had no dedicated history teacher to teach him, no fellow students interested in historical and intellectual debate, and no serious motivation of his own to study history. His preparation in history at Keighley was by any standard poor.

Herbert learned how to write exams, however. He scored high in the advanced level school examinations in the spring of 1918, although he recalls that he tended to spend too much time on one or two questions. His results allowed him to try for university admission and to sit for the county scholarship examinations that could bring him the funds to make university possible. In the summer of 1918 he succeeded in the county exams, and the authorities at Wakefield awarded him a Yorkshire West Riding Major Scholarship. He later told the story of an elderly woman on the examination committee who asked him what history of England he had read. Instinctively he remembered that he should not name the book they used at Keighley. He replied by muttering the name of J. R. Green's *History of England,* a book he had read from his father's shelves, probably a legacy from the mill master. She retorted, "Pretty old fashioned, isn't it?" He was devastated.

With Herbert's successes, the headmaster moved resolutely onto his side and suggested that he try for admission to one of the colleges in Cambridge University. It was probably Watson who recommended the entrance scholarship examination at Peterhouse, a college with a reputation for history. In January 1919 Herbert took the train to Cambridge to sit for the exams at Peterhouse. The man who examined him on behalf of the college was C. W. Previté-Orton, a medievalist of St. John's College. Herbert was petrified. He could remember only one date during the exam, an incorrect date at that, and he was certain he would fail the ordeal. He later heard via college gossip that a reference he made to Wordsworth's poetry turned the examiner in his favour. He won admission to Peterhouse, together with an entrance scholarship, and became the first student from Keighley Trade and Grammar School to enter Cambridge or Oxford.

Herbert's third opening from Oxenhope to the world was the local Methodist chapel. Butterfield always believed that his religion and even his politics, besides his social rank and lack of interest in the sciences, were silent factors creating the antipathy he had felt from his principal teacher. Moore was a pronounced sceptic, while Herbert was growing up to become a devout Methodist, like his father. Herbert often heard Moore utter remarks he perceived as antagonistic to Christianity, and he reacted not by drawing close to his teacher, but by refusing his teacher and becoming even more strongly attached to his faith. Herbert never explicitly revealed his religion around school, so Moore seemed not to know that Methodism was indispensable to his life outside. Moore also professed socialist views, to which Herbert responded by becoming a regular reader of the *New Statesman,* a politically liberal journal from London, and by adopting more self-consciously the politics of his father, the still traditional Methodist gravitation towards the Liberal party, particularly at the time to the progressive version represented by Herbert Asquith. In spite of these yawning differences with Moore, he supported his teacher vigorously when the headmaster quizzed him during an investigation of Moore's unorthodox views.

Herbert drew a clear line of demarcation between his world in Keighley and his world in Oxenhope, where the life of the Butterfields revolved around Methodist religion. They belonged to the Wesleyan Methodist Chapel which occupied a large, attractive, and prominent building that had opened on West Drive in 1891. With a membership of about two hundred, theirs was the largest of Methodist chapels in the circuit at the time. The mill owners were Methodists, and so were a large majority of the workers. The two Baptist chapels were tiny, and there were no Roman Catholics. The Parish of Oxenhope of the established Church of England seemed poor and unimportant. In a curious reversal of the religious structure of England, the Methodists supplanted the Church of England in Oxenhope as the dominant religion. Herbert grew up in what amounted to a Methodist village.

From childhood, Sundays for Herbert meant morning and evening services of worship, and morning and afternoon Sunday school. The chapel was the centre of his social life, where he found his friends and enjoyed social activities. Here he saw his first motion picture. Here, too, he encountered the music, the ideas, the history, and the experience of the Christian tradition. In the chapel he first heard Handel's "Messiah," listened to discussions of free will and predestination, Providence, sin, and salvation, became familiar with the Bible, and engaged the wider tradition of Methodist and medieval spirituality. Once, about age seven or eight, in response to an appeal by a visiting speaker from the "Band of Hope," he pledged himself to a life of abstinence from alcohol. He claimed later that his primary motivation for keeping the teetotaler pledge after he left Oxenhope was to please his father. Almost as a quirky sign of dissent, however, he took up smoking after he finished university, and became a chain-smoker of cigarettes.

At every turn during his first nineteen years, at each opening to the wider world, but especially in religion, Herbert found his father there with him.

Butterfield later testified that no one surpassed his father in the amount of influence he exercised over his life, no one in Oxenhope or Keighley or even Cambridge later on. Herbert even grew up to look much like his father. "Dad" was a slight man, about 5'8", with light red hair and pale complexion, often looking ill, and appearing very shy. Herbert grew to about 5'7½" in height, with a slight build and light complexion, a youthful look, and a shyness that easily rivalled his father's.[15]

His father achieved his hold over Herbert in a number of ways. The most direct channel was the walk they often took together in the evening from the time the boy was seven or eight to age thirteen or fourteen, when homework from Keighley consumed Herbert's evening hours. Herbert adored these walks. Late in life he likened his father's impact upon him to the influence the Jesuits used to exercise over the young. The second source of his father's impact was the Methodist "class" that his father led in place of his lost vocation as Methodist parson. A "class" was the Methodist version of a small religious cell. His class consisted of fifteen or so young men from the local chapel, probably workers from the mills, who met weekly in the Butterfield home for prayer, Bible study, and the cultivation of their inner life. His father encouraged them to wear dress suits for the meetings, as on Sundays, and to practice the social manners of the people who worked close to the mill master, manners which he regarded as more "civilized" than those of the workers on the mill floor. The young Herbert liked to sit on the edges of the class meeting during these evenings, and he picked up from his father a lasting sense of the importance of a life that was "civilized" as contrasted with "barbaric." The mode of his father's greatest influence, Butterfield believed, was his father's overall behavior and character which the young Herbert found utterly appealing. In his autobiographical reflections Butterfield later wrote: "My father was remarkable in his faith, his humility, and his extraordinary love and charity. His example (rather than his conscious formulations of the case) made me prize what I should call the theological values and gave me the firm conviction of the reality of spiritual things." His father's example shaped his basic ideals, character, and outlook on life, and oriented his life towards meditation, Bible reading, and a daily life that manifested Christian spirituality.

The influence of his father became even more colossal as the young Herbert's dislike of his mother stiffened. By the time he reached his seventies, Butterfield had constructed sharp, counterpoised images of his parents. His mother came from a family belonging to the religious group known as the Plymouth Brethren. In the milieu of Oxenhope she had turned Methodist and adopted what Butterfield remembered as a conventional and conservative attitude towards religion. This he found less attractive than his father's vivid religious impulses, and he began to dislike any attempts to tailor religion for those Christians who simply followed social expectations in religious practice. In contrast with the quietness of his father, young Herbert experienced his mother as loud and overbearing, a big woman. She dominated the household and would never stand for any nonsense. She had a temper which frightened Herbert and which she frequently directed against his father. Herbert felt she considered his father a weak figure, while he always experienced his father as a powerful personality. Decades later Butterfield could still recount with noticeable agitation the moment at about age eight when his father brought home his hard-earned weekly pay of one gold sovereign, and his mother hurled it back in his father's face. Butterfield professed that he then vowed secretly never to marry. Herbert witnessed the mildness of his father's responses to his mother and his nonjudgmental tolerance of his mother's aggressions, and admired his father all the more. Years later his father let Butterfield know that he bore her violence partly because he feared she would go out of her mind and commit suicide, like her brother, Herbert's Uncle Arthur. The episodes seemed to draw young Herbert more tightly to his father, and his father may have turned more intentionally towards the son to seek the recognition, consolation, and understanding that he did not receive from his wife. "We both discovered we had a rapport," Butterfield would say in later years.

Herbert never became particularly close to his sister and brother, who experienced less of the father's favour than he. Butterfield felt that his relationship with his mother improved in later life as he chided himself for his attitude towards her and managed to recognize her virtues, and he did marry after all, but his sense of the juxtaposition of the two personalities within the dynamics of the family affected him deeply. He came to extol certain virtues — humility, charity, self-restraint, nonjudgment of others — which he counted as Christian and which matched the shy and unassertive element in his emerging personality. He acknowledged near the end of his life, "[My father] was the person on whom I always most sought to model myself, though I never achieved the gentleness and humility in him . . . since nature seemed to saddle me with the hotter temperament of my mother."

His father was chief among those in Oxenhope who urged young Herbert to become a local preacher on the Haworth and Oakworth Methodist circuit, the jurisdiction that incorporated Oxenhope. Rev. H. Allen Riggall, the minister at Oxenhope from 1915 to 1918, guided him towards lay preaching. In later life Butterfield remembered preaching for the first time when he was about sixteen. He may have had opportunities to preach before the spring of 1918, when, at age seventeen, he formally passed the Methodist examinations which admitted him to standing as a lay preacher "on trial". He achieved full status one year later, in the summer of 1919, just before he left Oxenhope for Peter-house. The Methodist examinations tested his knowledge of the Wesleyan second catechism, the fifty-three *Standard Sermons* of John Wesley, and Wes-ley's *Notes on the New Testament*. Butterfield in his later years, looking back, located the source of the impulses that drove him into preaching: "My father also infected me with his passionate desire to 'preach the Gospel.'"[16]

Between the completion of secondary school in 1918 and his entrance into residence at Peterhouse in October 1919 Herbert had a full year free from formal study. He spent his time in Oxenhope with his father, reading, writing, and preaching on the local circuit. Sometimes on Sundays that year he walked to small chapels in the moorlands to take charge of morning or evening wor-ship. He had time to watch the final moments of the European war in the summer of 1918 and the beginning of the peace conference in Paris in January 1919. He heard the rising voices blaming the Germans, and he felt the pull of his youthful assumptions in favour of the Germans as the source of good things in English society. In the summer of 1919, he followed the news of the strike by police in nearby Liverpool and watched incredulous as Liverpool experienced an outburst of violence and looting on a scale never before seen in the city. He listened carefully to the debate about whether the violence and theft could be attributed to the existence of a larger population of criminals in the city than anyone knew about or to the ordinary population of respectable people whose public morals collapsed when the normal restraints of civilized society disappeared. He decided that the episode could not be blamed entirely on criminals, and he concluded that the civilized world was extraordinarily fragile. He meditated on Methodist spirituality and thought that perhaps the only genuine source of human stability lay deep within the inner life of each person. The First World War, the peace, and the Liverpool police strike all fixed themselves in his moral experience, and he referred to these three events again and again for the next sixty years.[17]

Peterhouse, Cambridge

Butterfield moved into residence in Peterhouse on his nineteenth birth-day, 7 October 1919.[18] He took with him the two aspirations of his youth — to be a writer and to be a Methodist preacher. He knew close to nothing about Peterhouse and had gone to the college only because he succeeded in winning a Peterhouse entrance scholarship in history. He professed that, because of the strength of his desire to be a writer, he would have selected English as his subject if there had been a scholarship available to him in that field.

The Peterhouse Butterfield entered boasted of three distinctions among the eighteen Cambridge colleges — it was old, small, and notable for the teaching of history. The college could claim to be the oldest in Cambridge. The founding year was 1284, when a number of male scholars attached to the bishop of Ely took up residence in buildings provided by Hugh de Balsham adjacent to St. Peter's Church outside Trumpington gate at Cambridge. Cambridge University reckoned this event as its foundation as well. In 1284, the number of scholars, known as Fellows, was something less than fourteen, the upper limit known to be set by regulation in 1344. There were no students analogous to the undergraduates of later centuries.[19] When Butterfield arrived in 1919 the college was highly conscious of its antiquity. The name of the principal student organization, the debating and literary society known as the Sexcentenary Club, reflected this historical interest by recalling the six hundredth anniversary of the college in 1884. The most prominent student publication in the college was society's magazine, *The Sex*.

In line with the huge influx of students after the Great War, the college in 1919 was larger than it had ever been before in its history, but with eight Fellows and a Master and 128 undergraduate students it remained among the smallest in Cambridge. The numbers rose to ten Fellows and a Master and 170 students in the following year, and during the 1920s settled down at around ten Fellows plus the Master and an average of about 150 students a year, making it permanently one of the smallest and most intimate colleges in Cambridge. Like Keighley, it was a male world, and Butterfield lived the next three years of his life in Peterhouse without the company of women. There had been women in Cambridge for decades, and women were admitted to degrees in the 1920s, but no women were admitted to Peterhouse until after Butterfield's death.[20]

The Peterhouse reputation for history was recent — the college had been renowned for the natural sciences — and was due entirely to the achievements of two men. The first was the aging Sir Adolphus Ward, then eighty-one, Master of Peterhouse since 1900. He was famous for his connection with Lord Acton, Regius Professor of Modern History at Cambridge until his death in 1902. Ward succeeded Acton as editor of *The Cambridge Modern History* and brought the huge project to completion. He also superintended the Cambridge historical series on English literature and foreign policy. He was known as a major figure behind the initiation and development of the Cambridge history curriculum and examination system, the Historical Tripos, dating from 1873, even though not resident in Cambridge at the time. The second was Harold Temperley, then forty, a product of the Cambridge Historical Tripos in 1900 and 1901, whom Ward brought in as a Fellow. He was already regarded as the most remarkable younger historian in the university and the leader of the junior historians group within it. He was promoted to Reader in Modern History in the university in 1919, just as Butterfield entered the college.[21]

Ward was known for his insistence that history should be studied for its own sake, and not for the sake of the present. It was a simple polarity in which he stood opposed to the position associated at Cambridge with J. R. Seeley, the Regius Professor of Modern History preceding Acton. Seeley had regarded history primarily as education for present politics, a view still reflected in the history curriculum when Butterfield came up to Cambridge. Within Peterhouse Ward placed unmitigated support behind Temperley, who professed the same view. Temperley had taken over responsibility for history in Peterhouse from Rev. T. A. Walker, an antiquarian and amateur chronicler of the history of the college, who was still around as a Fellow. Temperley's achievement was to establish history on a secure academic basis in the college and to attract first-class students. He exemplified, as John Fair noted, the transition towards a more professional and public style of historian.[22]

Butterfield was unprepared for Peterhouse. He felt he was a misfit, alienated from both Fellows and undergraduates. Surrounding him was the body of gentlemen scholars, old and young, who prided themselves on their traditions and their occasional associations with aristocracy and royalty. The bulk of the students came from well-to-do families, and many came from private schools for the social elite, like Harrow. By contrast, he was naive and unmannered, from a back Yorkshire village, with an accent that made the other students laugh. His family name, though common in Yorkshire, sounded strange in Cambridge, and people continually mocked him for it. Undergraduates unmercifully dubbed him "Buttercup" or "Butterworth."[23] He came from a school without tradition or academic reputation, and his education in history was astonishingly inferior. He could disguise neither his working-class origins nor the recent entry into the lower middle classes accomplished by his father. Later he would joke that he had no ability to "ape the manners or mimic the style" of those from the proper schools. He was a Methodist in an Anglican college, a local preacher forced to hide his calling from the learned Anglican clergy around him, and a pledged teetotaler amid wine-bibbers.

Years later Butterfield could laugh at how wildly he diverged from the prevailing style of Peterhouse in 1919. To symbolize the differences he would repeat a story about his first visit to the college, the day he sat for the entrance scholarship exams in January 1919. He came from a land where ordinary people rode in wagons pulled by horses and only the rich rode in automobiles. Upon arriving from Oxenhope at the Cambridge railway station, he surveyed the means of transportation awaiting him. Here the world of conveyances was turned upside down. Ordinary students took the automobile taxi, and the well-to-do took the horse-drawn hansom cab. He, of course, chose the horse wagon to take him to Peterhouse. He appeared at the college gate, in full view of the college porters, in the conveyance of the wealthy." I've been an imposter all the time," he could later comment with a smile.[24]

Temperley was aghast when he first met the new student Butterfield.[25] Late in life Butterfield recalled with good humor his first interview with Temperley, an episode which must have been excruciating for them both. As Butterfield tells it, Temperley asked the unpolished young man what history of England he had read at school. The unspoken warning from Keighley and the experience of the elderly examiner at Wakefield rushed over him. He responded with Cyril Ransome's *A Short History of England,* another book on his father's shelves from the mill owner's philanthropy. Temperley sputtered, "Ransome! The very name breathes poison!" and refused to take Butterfield for supervisions. Temperley sent him away to George Perrett, a coach outside the college, and Butterfield commenced his career at Peterhouse as an outcast.

The one who rescued Butterfield in his distress was Paul Vellacott, himself new to the college as a young Fellow that very year. The addition of Vellacott reflected policy to emphasize history in the reconstruction of the college after the war. The match between the new Fellow and the new pupil seemed hardly promising. Vellacott was a sportsman in cricket and hockey, fastidious in his dress, and was, as Cowling put it, a nonbelieving Anglican and a practical conservative. He was also a military man with a forbidding countenance, just returned from the war. The undergraduates called him Major. Yet he also felt a genuine love for poetry and artistry, and he loved to practice good manners. He had excelled as Temperley's best student at Peterhouse before the war. Butterfield came to know him as a person of great charity.[26]

Vellacott offered consolation and advice to the awkward outsider from Oxenhope. He tutored the young man in the manners, dress, and speech proper for the college and accelerated his restyling as a gentleman. He persuaded the novice to reveal his ambition to be a writer, and then encouraged him to improve his writing. Vellacott had so far written almost nothing, which the young student probably did not know. He never wrote much thereafter. He soon became for Butterfield like a father in the college. Until his death thirty-five years later, Vellacott remained Butterfield's most intimate confidant. In his autobiographical writings Butterfield acknowledged Vellacott's role as savior in Peterhouse: "I was so constructed that I was doomed not to be able to pass from the age of seventeen to the age of twenty-five without terrible turmoils and torments which I created for myself out of the seeming cauldron of my mind. I have often wondered how I should have passed through those years without the understanding and imaginative sympathy of Paul Vellacott."

Sometime during the first term in 1919 Butterfield wrote an essay on a topic set by Perrett, his coach in exile, entitled "Art Is History Made Organic." We do not know what he said, but we do know that the coach liked the essay and passed it on to a Peterhouse Fellow, possibly Temperley himself, if not Vella-cott, and the essay apparently circulated among other Fellows. Butterfield learned from leakage long after the event that the essay had revolutionized his reputation in the college. Relieved that they had not awarded a college en-trance scholarship to a fool, the gentleman Fellows swung to the opposite pole. They began to mentioned his name in their gossip about additions to their number. Temperley changed his mind as well. He summoned Butterfield to his rooms and agreed to become his supervisor straightaway.[27]

Temperley had reached the height of his powers as a historian and fully enjoyed playing an imposing role with the undergraduates. He had made his reputation with a biography of George Canning in 1905 and a diplomatic his-tory in 1915 on the relations between Prussia and the Hapsburgs, and he was known to be writing another diplomatic history on the foreign policy of Can-ning. During the war he made his name in government service in the Balkans, and he participated in the peace conference in Paris from the start. His practice of scholarship and patriotic service appeared heroic to Peterhouse Fellows and undergraduates alike. Butterfield learned quickly that Temperley had the repu-tation among students as the best history supervisor in Cambridge.[28]

Butterfield found Temperley literally overwhelming.[29] Like other super-visors, Temperley believed his duty was not merely to evaluate a student's formal written work, but to watch over the total intellectual development of each student assigned to him. The normal vehicle of this tutelage was the "supervision," the weekly hour-long meeting of the pupil with the teacher in the teacher's rooms. For many supervisors, the focus of each meeting was the paper prepared by the student on a topic set for the appointment, with the student doing most of the talking. As Temperley practiced the role, however, the supervision transformed into a Temperley monologue with the awestruck undergraduate looking on. Butterfield retained a vivid memory of Temperley and frequently narrated anecdotes symbolizing the experience. He bemoaned Temperley's "over exuberance" which took drastic measures to curb. He told of Temperley surveying his weekly essay by "taking in each whole page in a single glance, and dropping the successive sheets on the floor without a word of comment." Temperley would then embark on a tirade against Lloyd George, or brag about his work for the government. Butterfield depicted the image of Temperley standing "precariously on a small red chair, balancing a poker in his hand," all the while reciting passages from Swinburne. Such behaviour wrought terror in the speechless Butterfield. On top of this, Temperley ridiculed Butterfield's quiet questions about the examinations and mocked his faithful attendance at lectures. Butterfield wanted to learn about the rules and get advice about how to prepare. He remembered that Temperley instructed him abruptly "just to become a historian" and to let the exams take care of themselves. He tried to submit completely to Temperley's will. Butterfield survived this psychological brutality during the Lent and Easter terms that first year at Peterhouse. He felt himself converting to Temperley's view. Looking back, he would caricature his own behaviour: "I came with all the preoccupations of what we call a 'swot,' determined to mug things up for an examination, to find out what my teachers wanted me to say, and dish out the expected answers on all occasions."[30] He would also claim in later years that he found a device during his undergraduate studies to help him survive the process. He would try to follow what he called the humanist ideal about personalities and think of history as a thing about people, and not as a dead subject to be learned for examinations. For the rest of his career he denounced the practice of studying for the purpose of passing examinations and made the matter pivotal for his thinking about universities and historical study.[31]

The subjects he prepared during his first year included English economic history, English constitutional history since 1485, and medieval history. For the first time in his life he was able to hear historians discussing history, and some of the historians were among the best in the world. J. H. Clapham lectured on economic history that year, G. G. Coulton and Z. N. Brooke on medieval history, and D. A. Winstanley on English constitutional history. These were the lectures Temperley mocked him for attending.

In the first year intercollegiate examinations, Butterfield placed Class I, Division 2. The results brought Temperley's praise for "having done really well" and an uncharacteristically gentle nudge to improve in constitutional history. The college gave him the first year college prize for history and raised the amount of his scholarship. In the letter informing him of the increase Temperley added these words, revealing the assessment he had begun to form of the Yorkshire lad: "I hope it will be encouraging to you and it greatly pleases me that you are maintaining our traditions."[32]

From this moment onwards Temperley thought of Butterfield as his protege. Butterfield put himself completely under Temperley's power and deferred to him utterly. It is hard to overstate the dominance that Temperley exercised over him in the next nine years. Temperley virtually took over the direction of Butterfield's professional life, and ensured that he would emerge a historian.

Butterfield spent his entire second year without his protector, however. Temperley went away to Belgrade as a member of the European commission producing a Balkan settlement. Mentally, nonetheless, he remained utterly under

Temperley's domination. Vellacott took the supervisions that year, and Ward invited him often to the Master's Lodge for lunch. In keeping with the Cambridge tradition, he repeated his first year subjects for the second year, giving him two straight years of English economic history, general European history in the medieval period, and English constitutional history from 1485. In the examinations — the Historical Tripos, Part I — he ranked again Class I, Division 2, in a year when no one achieved a higher mark. He again won the college prize in history and again received a raise in the value of his scholarship.

When Temperley returned for Butterfield's third year, he adopted a new style with his young protege. As he sometimes did with others, he would come to Butterfield's room unannounced after dinner to talk history for hours at a time.[33] Butterfield at first found the new behaviour bewildering, but, to his surprise, he began to feel that Temperley might be talking to him as he would to another historian. Now more confident, Butterfield soon found the new intimacy congenial. Temperley still did most of the talking, but Butterfield was finding a way to mitigate the pain produced by his own awkwardness. He began to adopt a strategy for his role in social and academic conversations. He deliberately kept the attention off himself by asking the other person questions. The tactic became indispensable whenever empty spaces opened in a conversation. In later years, even after he had become undoubtedly the dominant figure, he invariably kept the focus of the conversation on the other person. He conveyed the feeling that he was genuinely interested in what the other person had to say. This style certainly worked with Temperley. In the end he overcame his fear of Temperley and professed a deep affection for his master teacher. In personality they remained polar opposites. Butterfield epitomized what it meant to be shy, whereas Temperley expressed "extraordinary exuberance." In religion Butterfield was the Christian, whereas, John Fair has suggested, Temperley exhibited a spirituality of nationalism and pagan romanticism.[34]

In his final year, Butterfield's subjects were new: English history 1714–1914, European history 1789–1914, and a "special period" with Temperley, "The Fall of Napoleon and the Reconstruction of Europe, November 1813–November 1815." He probably followed Winstanley's lectures on George III and the Whig Party, 1760–1771, and commenced therewith his engagement with English history in the eighteenth century and the early reign of George III. In the wake of Temperley's cynicism about lectures, he missed the lectures in modern European history and boasted ever after that he had done so. He lacked the courage to apply Temperley's doctrine to Temperley's own lectures on Napoleon, and Temperley, of course, excepted his own performances from the rule. Butterfield said he felt confident when he wrote Part II of the Historical Tripos at the end of the year. His old fault reappeared, he said, when he devoted too much time to the first questions and left no time for the remainder. The examiners that year were Temperley, G. P. Gooch, Geoffrey Butler, and R. R. Sedgwick. He learned much later that they fell out among themselves about his failure to finish. It was only after Gooch spoke urgently in his favour that the examiners agreed to award him the highest rank, Class I, Division 1. Forty years later he acknowledged his debt to Gooch.[35] One other student achieved that rank in history that year, G. R. Potter of St. John's College, who remained a lifelong friend.

Butterfield's repeated success in examinations visibly marked a monumental change occurring within him. He was modifying his aspirations to be a Methodist preacher and a writer. He believed, looking back, that the transition probably began around the end of his first year. It was apparently then that the previously implausible idea of becoming a historian began to seem like an option. In the tiny world of Peterhouse, the models were few, and, when a student achieved academic success like his, the pictures of an academic future easily came to mind. In later life he would say that at the time he heard of gossip among Peterhouse Fellows about making him a future Fellow. When Temperley's attitude changed towards him, and after he submitted himself to Temperley, he could readily imagine becoming a historian. Vellacott's care and praise enabled him to move towards the same end.

The community of aspiring gentlemen undergraduates in Peterhouse was at least as decisive as the Fellows in transforming Butterfield's social style and moving him towards historical interests. During his first year he threw himself into the Peterhouse Historical Society, newly resurrected by Temperley after the hiatus of the war. The organization's members soon boasted in *The Sex* that they were "probably the most virile society of its type in Cambridge."[36] Terms used by historical society members began to appear in his vocabulary. The secretary of the society wrote that its purpose was "to promote the growth of what may be called 'Historical-mindedness,'" and Butterfield made "historical-mindedness" one of his stock terms. The society discussed the topic of "the interpretation of history," and the concept began to appear in his own discourse. He was probably one of six students, in October 1920, during his second year, who led a discussion in the society under the title "The Interpretation of History."

Butterfield joined other college societies as well. He read a paper, his first paper on record, to the Peterhouse Theological Society in February 1921 on Savonarola, the dissenting Dominican friar who got himself burned to death in Florence in 1498 because of his challenge to both pope and government.[37] He became a prominent member of the Sexcentenary Club and participated actively as a debater. In his second year he argued against the motion that a supreme British Navy was essential for the future of England, and in favour of the motion that the discoveries of science have acted against the best interests of the people. In his third year he spoke in opposition to the motion that pure genius is unconscious, and for the motion that the family unit is socially indispensable. He served as editor of *The Sex* for the Lent issue in 1922. His leading article, entitled simply "Editorial," is the first extant publication attached to his name.[38]

Butterfield adopted two heroes, both historians, during his undergraduate years, and they remained his heroes for the rest of his life. The first was Lord Acton, a Roman Catholic, whose reputation for erudition was enormous. In class-conscious Cambridge, Acton's aristocratic title heightened the mystique, as it did Butterfield's admiration of him. Ward, as Master of Peterhouse, fostered the mystique by promoting his own reputation as the consummator of Acton's great project. Temperley got Butterfield reading Acton, probably about the time he took Butterfield on as a student. The historical society contributed to the mystique. During Butterfield's first year the members discussed Acton's famous inaugural address from 1895, which the secretary referred to as "the Breviary of all historians."[39] Butterfield read Acton's *Lectures on Modern History*, published in 1906 and reprinted just before he came up to Peterhouse. The volume contained the inaugural address and the letter Acton addressed to the contributors to *The Cambridge Modern History*. It is possible that he read Acton's inaugural during his first term at Peterhouse, or at least that he then became familiar with some of its language. The term "organic," which he used to his advantage in "Art Is History Made Organic," he may have lifted from Acton's inaugural. What Butterfield meant by organic has escaped us, but what Acton meant was the unity of history, the notion that life is an integrated whole and that in general history everything interrelates. In the context of Peterhouse, the term would have sounded as if it came from Acton. He also borrowed from Acton's letter to the contributors the image of a "rope of sand," which he used in just about everything he wrote for the rest of his life. The metaphor signified treatments of universal history that failed to see the continuous development of things over time. Acton became a fixture in Butterfield's discursive horizon.[40]

The second hero was Leopold von Ranke, the nineteenth-century historian from the University of Berlin, and a Lutheran. Ranke's recent presence in Cambridge came via Acton, who reinforced the earlier references to Ranke by Seeley, and in Peterhouse via the united front of Ward and Temperley, both of whom championed German historical scholarship. Temperley announced to his students that behind his approach to history stood Ranke, and his students adopted Ranke as well. And so did Butterfield. The more fully Butterfield gave himself to Temperley and Acton, the more he also gave himself to Ranke.[41]

If Butterfield felt attractions towards becoming a historian, he testified that his desire to be a writer did not simply wane. He continued to read poetry and novels, particularly at night. During these undergraduate years he began to experience difficulty falling asleep and, while lying in bed, he would read Thomas Hardy, Dickens, H. G. Wells, Tolstoy, and the like. His interest in historical novels received support from G. P. Gooch, whom he was coming to admire, who had recently called attention to the genre in an article in *Contemporary Review.* He also discovered to his delight that Temperley loved to read historical novels, and he gladly complied when Temperley loaned him the works of European novelists, especially historical novels by the Hungarian writer Mor Jokai. Temperley had written extravagantly about Jokai, and later published *Foreign Historical Novels* for the Historical Association.[42] Butterfield recognized how much of his own teenage reading included historical novels, especially Sir Walter Scott.

Butterfield also wrote, and wrote a lot. Virtually every week of three terms for three years he wrote an essay for his supervisor, not to mention numerous other pieces for other settings. He must have written at least a hundred essays as an undergraduate.[43] During the year he would show his best essays to Vellacott, and Vellacott liked his writing. Vellacott provided the link between writing and writing history. He was the one who suggested that Butterfield treat his history papers as writing, indeed as literary pieces. Butterfield composed poetry as well, mostly florid rhyming lines, but also a few experiments with free verse. He showed his poetry to no one.[44] In one essay he expressed the conventional romantic notion that "poetry expresses emotions and appeals to the feelings, whereas prose addresses itself more to the reason." He added, "Poetry is passion bubbling over, and the flame is imagination."[45] His editorial in *The Sex* for Lent 1922 showed him straining to unite the two genres, writing his prose in a poetic manner. Poetic prose became a permanent mark of his style of historical writing. He liked to play with words. In the editorial he took the name people used to mock him — Buttercup — and played a joke on himself. He played another joke on Vellacott's rule that proper writers should never end a sentence with a preposition. The final word of the editorial was "of." He played this joke in later writings as well.[46] His contemporaries appreciated his writing style and considered him eloquent in debates, and they said so repeatedly in *The Sex*. In following Vellacott's advice Butterfield found a way to blend his early desire to be a writer with his emerging aspiration to be a historian.[47]

Butterfield's desire to preach remained strong as well, even as he felt the drift

towards history. Aside from his participation in the Cambridge Literary Society, which for a time he served as secretary, it was his attraction to religion
which gave him connections outside the little world of his college. With his
newly acquired licence as a Methodist lay preacher, the Cambridge Methodist
circuit permitted him to preach. Throughout his undergraduate years he
would occasionally conduct services in the small Methodist chapels in the fenland around Cambridge. His general motivation towards religion continued
undiminished. He attended Wesley Methodist Church in Christ's Pieces, Cambridge, faithfully every Sunday when he was not preaching elsewhere. He read
the Bible and prayed in his room. He attended meetings of the liberal Student
Christian Movement (SCM) in the university. He also frequented gatherings of
the Cambridge Inter-Collegiate Christian Union (CICCU), the Protestant
evangelical society. In Peterhouse, he participated in the college theological
society. He also joined an SCM study group in the college for a while and
served on its committee. He sometimes worshiped in the college chapel where
he experienced the Anglo-Catholic tradition within the Church of England.
On occasion he received Holy Communion according to the rite the Church of
England, an act that must have been difficult for this young Yorkshire Methodist to let himself do.

He recalled later that his new experience of so many varieties of Christianity
affected him deeply. He could find something good in every one of the options,
but he found reason to dissent from every one of them as well. He experienced
the power of religious liberalism emanating from Germany, which the SCM
encouraged. He appreciated the CICCU's emphasis on the evangelical devotional life. He felt attracted to the liturgy of the Anglo-Catholics. He eventually quit the SCM in his third year because, he explained, he was disturbed
by a committee discussion about whether belief in God was necessary for
membership in the group. He stopped going to the CICCU when he began to
find them too constricted in their understanding of who was a Christian. He
found the Anglican liturgy too formal, but he continued to frequent the college
chapel and allowed the experience to act on him subtle ways. Among his
teachers he encountered Acton's Catholicism, Ward's Anglican Liberalism,
Vellacott's nonbelieving Anglican establishmentarianism, and Temperley's
pagan romantic sentiments. He found the Methodist sermons too intellectual,
but he continued to attach himself to Methodist practice and attended Wesley
Church because, he said, he wanted a place to praise God on Sundays.

It was becoming clear to him by the end of his third year that what mattered
most to him in religion was the inner life, his inner spirituality. He found that
he was coming through all his new experiences with a Methodist spirituality
remarkably close to the style he found so appealing in his father. In his inner

life he could unite his religious and literary aspirations and in doing so draw upon his newly forming historical inclination. In the days shortly before he took his final third-year examinations in 1922, he wrote in his diary, "it is in religion that life has reached its highest points throughout history—in religion, and perhaps in poetry, where the experience is akin to the religious."[48]

It was probably during his undergraduate years that Butterfield first responded to the political options available as he did to the alternatives facing him in religion. He saw good in each political position, but also saw reason to dissent from each. He came up to Cambridge with the political affinity for the Liberal party which, along with his Methodism, he had acquired from his father. He also had behind him his rejection of the vigorous socialist politics of his teacher at Keighley. Now in Cambridge he found left-wing politics very available. The timing was the aftermath of the Russian Revolution of 1917 and the triumph of the Communist party in the Soviet Union. It was also the moment of the rise of the British Labour Party in tandem with the decline of the Liberals. He also encountered eager supporters of the Conservative party in a university where the great majority of undergraduates arrived conservative. He would feel the appeal of each of these political positions. At the same time, he discovered, as he testified much later, "that the Left Wing as well as the Right Wing could lie and deceive." A memoir written late in life probably reflected something basic about his emerging politics of the early 1920s: "I had to make my own mind work more creatively, manufacturing my own picture of things out of the limited materials that were available. And—in politics, for example, I had to try to move to a stereoscopic vision, which might include something of both Left and Right, but also brought out new shapes, great masses that came in perspective—much of the resulting transformation having nothing to do with the conflict between Left and Right."[49] He did not take his thinking about politics very far as an undergraduate. With his growing attachment to history and the heightening of his convictions about the inner life, he seemed to have little impulse left to pursue something so contemporary and so mundane as politics.

During his three undergraduate years, the pulls and counter-pulls on Butterfield were manifold. He gave himself to Temperley and to the appeal of history. He affirmed the attractions of each of the religious and political options before him, and he adopted enough of the gentleman's manners and ethos of the college to allow him to fit in. But he also learned to dissent, to withhold himself from submitting to the demands and choices imposed on him by others. He began to turn his lack of fit into a doctrine and practice of dissent. Even as he gave himself to the influence of his master teacher in historical study, he kept himself from Temperley's pagan nationalism and romanticism. He retained his

youthful desires to preach as well as to write. He held on to his social simplicity, his Methodist religion, his teetotaling, and his loosely liberal politics. He
kept hold of the continuities with his youth and his father, while changing
himself, his perspective, his aspirations. By taking a stereoscopic view of the
new alternatives, he found a way to construct something entirely his own.

After winning the "double first," the exalted rank of Class I, Division 1, in
the historical examinations in his final year, Butterfield was admitted to the
B.A. degree of Cambridge University in June 1922. Undergraduates in Peterhouse admired him, and a biographical article about him in *The Sex* praised
him as a conquering hero.[50]

The Fellows praised him too. Temperley once again laid out Butterfield's
next step by arranging for Peterhouse to elect him to the Hugo de Balsham
Studentship for 1922–1923. Butterfield testified often over the years that the
election gave him a shock because he knew that staying at Peterhouse was
good for nothing except becoming a historian. He was not sure that he wanted
the historian's life. He had applied for jobs teaching school, and already held
in his hands the offer of a position at Lampeter in Cardigan County in Wales.
He still felt strongly about his desire to preach, or at least about his feeling of
obligation to his father to become a Methodist preacher, though he had started
to believe that he would not make a good Methodist parson. He sought the
advice of the Rev. H. M. Hughes, the principal of Wesley House, recently
founded as a theological school in Cambridge for the education of Methodist
ministers. He concluded that, although he might enjoy the preaching, he
lacked the social and pastoral skills to lead a congregation.[51] At the same time,
he was sure that settling down to teach in Lampeter would be dismal and
uninspiring and would be no help at all to his writing.

Butterfield trusted the judgment of others about him and accepted the research studentship at Peterhouse. He had an income at least for the coming
year. He turned down the job in Lampeter. It stretches the imagination to
contemplate the alternative life of Herbert Butterfield as the schoolteacher in
Wales. He took no steps towards becoming a Methodist parson. He could
easily have attended Wesley House. He said in later years that he feared he was
displeasing his father by abandoning his intention to be a preacher. He felt
the wrath of his mother, who considered him something of a failure because
he was still in school after completing his degree. The fissure between his
mother and him signalled the subtle rise in social class to which Cambridge
had treated the young man from Oxenhope. He was not certain, as he later
would admit, that he knew what his life would be like if he were to be a
historian, but he was sure that he was inadequate for what lay ahead.

2

Art and Science

New Vocation

The academic year 1922–1923 was traumatic for Butterfield. Within the intimacies of the college, Temperley took charge of him, like a master with an apprentice, and began to turn him into a historian. In the Cambridge of those years the importance of the college surpassed that of the university. In the humanities the college was the primary employer, and the writing of prize essays and election to a college fellowship were sufficient to set a person apart for the academic life. It was still unthinkable, indeed ungentlemanly, for a first-rate student in the humanities to study for the Ph.D., even though Cambridge had begun to offer such studies in history. In any case, the university organized no lectures or seminars for postgraduate research students. Amidst the tension within Cambridge created by the movement towards the professionalization of the discipline of history, Butterfield inhabited an ambiguous space. Temperley acted to make him into a professional historian while the college continued to make him into a gentleman.[1]

Very quickly Temperley bound Butterfield to a regimen of research on Napoleon in the years 1807 and 1808. Temperley was still giving specialized lectures for undergraduates on Napoleon in 1813–1815, the years surrounding the emperor's defeat, but he was also interested in the relations between France and Russia in 1807 when the two powers signed the Treaty of Tilsit.

Temperley was preparing another book on George Canning, and Tilsit was Canning's first ordeal after assuming office as British foreign minister. He seems to have gotten Butterfield interested in Tilsit quite soon after taking up the research studentship in Peterhouse. Guided by the master, Butterfield devoted himself to a detailed study of the events surrounding the Treaty of Tilsit. Temperley had him pursuing diplomatic history from published documents in the style of Ranke.[2]

At that moment Butterfield could feel as if he were entering the most thrilling and the most important field of historical study around. Diplomatic history was glowing with pride in England in the early 1920s, after the Great War, and he was attached to perhaps the master of the trade.[3] Temperley was a major reason for the ascendency of the field. After his *Life of Canning* (1905) and his *Frederic the Great and Kaiser Joseph* (1915), English historians awaited his new book on Canning's foreign policy, widely expected to display mastery of the British documents in London.[4] Simultaneously C. K. Webster, originally from Cambridge and now professor at the University of London, was writing a work on Lord Castlereagh, Canning's predecessor.[5] People classed the two historians together as heads of the Cambridge school of diplomatic history, even though the personal tensions between them were palpable. According to the dominant historiography, these two had the task of producing the definitive and permanent account of British diplomacy during the period of the Napoleonic wars, the Congress of Vienna, and the beginnings of the Congress System. That period was regarded as precisely analogous to the years surrounding the Great War of 1914–1919.[6] More than this, Temperley came out of the recent Great War as the preeminent expert on the diplomacy of contemporary European history. He was the one whom the victorious powers of Europe selected to direct the multivolume history of the Paris peace conference, and he was the choice of the British Foreign Office to assemble the definitive collection of British documents on the origins of the war.[7] Governments across Europe and in North America were publishing their papers relevant to the Great War and were simultaneously opening their archives still wider to historians for work on nineteenth-century topics. The sheer mass of documents newly available on issues felt to be extraordinarily crucial to modern life stimulated historians to go to work, especially aspiring historians. For diplomatic historians it was a moment of supreme confidence. Butterfield, the new research student, was there in the right place at the right time, and he caught the spirit of supreme excitement.[8]

Temperley no doubt also pushed Butterfield to enter the prize competitions mounted by the university, most of which he himself had won some twenty years before. In any case, going after the prizes was a thing even the students expected of their peers who scored high in examinations. First came the University Member's Prize for English Essay for 1922. The topic designated by the prize committee was "Charles Dickens," with the deadline set for mid-November. Next, with a slightly later deadline, came the LeBas Prize for 1923, with "The Historical Novel" as the assigned topic. Both subjects were regarded as essays in English literature, and, although Butterfield was in history, both topics coincided happily with his literary inclinations and even with his reading as a youth and at bedtime as an undergraduate. Temperley probably had a role in selecting the topic for the LeBas Prize, and he may even have had Butterfield in mind. The importance of the coincidence of the topic with Butterfield's interests is made clear when we note that the subjects set for the following two years would not have suited him well at all: "The Element of Irony in English Literature" and "The Commerce between the Roman Empire and India."[9]

Butterfield worked fast, first on Dickens and then on the historical novel. The experience must have perpetuated the ambivalence of his interests in history and literature. He won the first competition in March 1923 with a longish essay on the way Dickens straddled history and literature.[10] He won the second, more prestigious prize in May 1923 with an essay the length of a short book in which he juxtaposed historical novels, historical study, and the events of the past. The Peterhouse Historical Society had him give a reading from his essay during Michaelmas term 1923.[11]

Also about this time he wrote an essay, which remained unpublished, on G. K. Chesterton, the English Catholic writer of note, in which he showed himself entranced by Chesterton's idea that something new could occur at any moment in history, whether coming from God's action or human action. The effect of this possibility, Butterfield observed, was the contingency of history, and no matter how certain and predictable things might appear, we do not know what will happen tomorrow.[12]

The LeBas Prize brought with it publication of the winning entry by Cambridge University Press, and in due course, in 1924, Butterfield's work appeared as his first book, bearing the title *The Historical Novel: An Essay*. The result was a 113-page extended essay by a twenty-three-year-old which contained elements of both literary criticism and theoretical writing on historical knowledge and method. Given that he wrote to win a prize, we might expect him to say things to please the prize adjudicators, who included, no doubt, Temperley. If he did, no sycophantic tendencies are noticeable. We can take the book seriously as his first public statements about life and history. We can picture him using the theme to figure out his thinking about both literature and history, perhaps in the process reconciling two of the pulls upon his life.

We see him straining to write as if he were creating a piece of literature. At the same time we glimpse the beginnings of his microscopic research on the diplomatic events associated with Tilsit, to which he refers in the text. He is far from systematic in his treatment of the essay's theme, relying on repetition and metaphor instead of argument to carry his point. He illustrates the essay with the names of what amounted to a list of preferred writers from his youth and undergraduate days — Wordsworth, Stevenson, Hugo, Dumas, Jokai, and above all Dickens and Scott. Among the historians he names are Carlyle, Gibbon, and Gregorovius, but the unspoken name of Ranke lies behind everything he has to say about history.[13]

Butterfield's primary question in the book concerns the qualities of historical novels and the relationship of historical novels and history books to human history. His answer requires him to begin with, and make much of, the assertion that there was such a thing as "the past." The past, writes the young Butterfield, echoing the young Ranke at twenty-nine, is life "as it really happened, the thing that is the object of study and research." His metaphors, like Ranke's, suggest the interconnectedness of everything which composed the past — the past is a web woven of all that has gone on, a symphony with "each moment, each year, each age adding a new bar to the score, and carrying the architecture of the whole a little further." The past is separate from us, different from us, standing in need of recovery. History was the past.[14]

We gain access to the past, he continues, through "our idea of the past." Our idea of the past is a vague amalgam of images, an unsystematic understanding, of what went on long ago which contains much that is more or less wrong — such as that medieval England was the land of Robin Hood — and much that is more or less true — such as that King John signed the Magna Carta. We all carry our idea of the past around in our heads in the form of pictures and stories, with only a very few details fixed and verified. We get our idea of the past via many intermediaries. There are the traditions of our localities, the tales of our grandfather, ballads and operas, the speeches of politicians, ads in magazines, the school system, and hundreds of other ways. Historical novels and historical studies are two of the ways we use to recover the past and create our idea of the past. At the same time, our idea of history precedes and modifies any approach we take to the past via historical novels and historical studies. Butterfield's notion places his analysis on a wide and democratic terrain, appealing to our common experience of knowing something about our personal or collective past, whether or not we are readers of novels and history books.

His characterization of historical study gives some priority to the work of historians over novelists. He makes clear that he writes as a historian and not as a novelist, and that he approaches the delineation of the historical novel by way of contrast with historical method. He has to deal with the commonplace among at least historians that novels were somehow untrue while history books were true, mirroring the difference between fact and fiction. Yet, as an essential part of his analysis, he explicitly acknowledges that historical study has fundamental constraints upon it. In contrast with the reigning historicism of his day, he advocates the doctrine of the limits of historical study, or as he phrases it, "the impossibility of history."

He defines historical study as the "conscious" investigation of the past, a study which proceeds by means of research into "the accumulated facts" of the past in order to "build up" a memory that recaptures a bygone age. Historical study gathers "authenticated data" and gives attention to "strict accuracy of detail" and "fidelity to facts," and then engages in "the manufacture of history."[15] Other people use the facts of the past — the economist, the politician, the musician, the ecclesiastic, the philosopher, the architect — in order to further their present-day work in their special departments. The historian, by contrast, is interested in the past per se: "he loves the past for its own sake and tries to live in it, tries to live over again the lost life of yesterday, turning it back as one would turn back the pages of a book to re-read what has gone before; and he seeks to see the past as a far-country and to think himself into a different world." The historian nurtures "the regret for the things that are lost for ever."[16]

This is where the notion of the limits of historical study comes into his thinking. Historians cannot travel beyond the documents and other records that remain behind, and they cannot tell us more than the "facts" of history. As a result vast worlds are left out of our reconstruction of the past. Butterfield mentions as notable among these the lives of the vast population of ordinary people, the "hearts" of anyone, and the circumstances of most of what goes on in any "particular knot of human action at a given place and a given time." Historical study is best suited to give us certain aspects of the public actions of the elite. It offers much about politicians, military people, diplomats, economic statistics, the famous, but for most things it gives us only a "chart to the past." Historical study fails at the crucial point: "About the closest human things, history only tells us enough to set us guessing and wondering."[17]

Butterfield claims that the historical novel overcomes this feature of historical study, a feature which he regards as an "inadequacy in history itself." The historical novel fills the gaps in the evidence by means of the imagination, recovers the things which to history are irrecoverable, and brings us "near to human hearts and human passions," closer to the "heart of things." He writes: "In order to catch these things in the life of the past, and to make a bygone age live again, history must not merely be eked out by fiction, it must not merely be extended by invented episodes; it must be turned into a novel; it must be 'put to fiction' as a poem is put to music."

To a certain extent, he suggests, whenever any of us reads a history book we fill out the information we read by means of our imagination, so that we actually "see" Napoleon doing the action we are told he did. The historical novelist does this work far more completely for all of us. The novelist turns history into a picture, and then goes further to transform history even into a story. By turning history into a story, says Butterfield, the novelist, more completely than the historian, properly handles the way in which the people of the past actually lived their lives: "It is not enough to recover the facts of the lives that men lived long-ago and to trace out the thread of events; we must recover the adventure of their lives: and the whole fun and adventure of their lives, as of ours, hung on the fact that at any given moment they could not see ahead, and did not know what was coming. To the men of 1807 the year 1808 was a mystery and an unexplored tract; they saw a hundred possibilities in it where the modern reader only sees the one that actually happened."[18] In addition, by means of story, the novelist is able to go beyond the historian in recapturing what Butterfield calls "the whole experience of life." By this he means that every age of history, every generation, involves its own peculiar "set of historical conditions," a different complex of "problems and anomalies, and situations and combinations of circumstance," its own unique "entanglement of the individuals in these conditions."[19]

Butterfield makes it clear that at this stage in his life he regards the historical novel as superior to the history book. The reasons for this assessment take us to his basic assumptions about history and human life. First, he has bound himself to romanticism, a conviction he associates with "the love of the past for its own sake," attention to "the whole experience of life," and the use of imagination. His romanticism creates unrealistically high expectations about the human ability to achieve the complete reconstruction of life in the past, expectations which no historian and no history book could fulfil.

Second, however, he posits an overly constricted notion of historical study, a view we may call positivist, which ties it to the collection of facts and the manufacture of history from the facts, strictly interpreted, tightly adhered to. At the same time the romantic in him wants his historian to be "the romantic historian," to go beyond the mere facts, but his sense of the legitimate range of historical study prevents his historian from acting fully as the romantic. He does not delve into the notion of the "scientific historian" and history as "science." The term "the scientific historian" appears twice late in the essay, but without him giving it any attention. He does work with a view of "fidelity to facts" which would be more compatible with contemporary ideas of history as science than history as literature and romance.[20]

Third, he announces his allegiance to an idea of personality which goes beyond what his vision of historical study permits him to reach. For Butterfield, in this book, personality is a mystery, a unity of both observable exterior data and unobservable intimate matters of the heart. For him, historical study cannot penetrate into that mystery. Each personality is an individual and a sufficient end within history, and every person, and not just the kings and the generals, deserves to be recaptured. This task, in his view, historical study cannot do.[21] Only imagination can do what is needed, and because he believes that imagination pertains to literature, he claims that literature, and not history, reaches into the depths of the human heart and out to the completeness of the whole human experience.

Only occasionally in the book does Butterfield suggest that he might have misstated or overdrawn the difference between historical study and the historical novel. Once, for instance, he allows that the historian might use imagination to go beyond a bare-bones reconstruction of the most visible people of the past.[22] But, on the whole, in this book, he lives on the side of literature as supreme and regards history as relatively superficial. Is he catering to the adjudicators of a prize in English? Or has he not yet comprehended how historical study might validly engage whole personalities and whole situations of the past, and do more than dwell on the surface of the most prominent events and most visible elites of human history? He expresses no idea in the book of what the positive value of historical study might be, the sort of things he leads us to expect when he begins with the very intriguing proposal that historical study is one of many proper ways of approaching the past.

If his theory convinces us of his affinity with literature, and not with history, his writing style leaves no shadow of doubt. He wants so much to be the writer himself and to act as the romantic pictured by his ideal. We catch the point best just after he has quoted for us a lengthy passage from the opening chapter of Scott's *Ivanhoe*. Scott is his model, both for style of writing and for the genre of the historical novel.[23] But we should not blame Scott for the sentences throughout the book when Butterfield is most floridly romantic, saying the same thing two or three times with a different illustration, rhyme, and metaphor each time, as in the following passage: "But, most of all, the reason why we prize the book in the margins of which Coleridge himself scribbled pencil-notes of literary criticism, and keep a lock of Keats's hair, is that these things are like the stray flowers that cheat the scythe or like the last stars that out dare the morning sun; they are the few things that are saved from a shipwreck. The work of a historian is to reconstruct the past out of the debris that is cast up by the sea from the wrecks of countless ages."[24]

The book was not widely reviewed at the time, perhaps because, as the *New Statesman* suggested, historical novels were then a little-favored genre. Butterfield's literary sensibilities were fixed on Scott, Dumas, and the other romantics, and these sounded hopelessly obsolete next to James Joyce's *Ulysses* and T. S. Eliot's *Wasteland,* both published in 1922, and the writings of Virginia Woolf. The few reviews he did receive offered both polite praise and polite complaints. They applauded him for what the reviewers thought perhaps a generally sound analysis, but chided him for being too abstract and failing to engage the writings of any historical novelists in his discussion.[25] The literary journals took no notice of the book, and it soon went out of print. Fifty years later, in the 1970s, the work resurfaced in two reprint editions at a time when questions of literary criticism, narrative, and historical explanation became newly fashionable. Seventy-five years later, in 1999, Michael Bentley gave the book more attention than any other historical analyst in the twentieth century, noting especially the role of literary thinking at this stage in Butterfield's historical reflections. It was easy to find the critic who snickered at the thought of discussing the book at all, on the grounds that it was doubtful whether Butterfield himself was in deadly earnest in this piece. But such a cynical view is unwarranted when we read the book in connection with Butterfield's aspirations as a writer, his long-time attraction to historical novels, his relations with Temperley, and above all his theoretical awareness of multiple modes of knowing the past.[26]

Butterfield particularly relished two things he did in *Historical Novel.* He repeated the joke in his editorial in *The Sex* in Lent 1922 and closed the whole book with the word "about." It was another playful act of independence from Vellacott who had admonished him repeatedly to eliminate dangling prepositions. And he wrote a small work, an act of dissent from the prevailing prejudice for big books by historians, and an assertion in favour of his emerging taste for little books. Butterfield confessed in later years that when he had finished the project he was unable to make himself read another historical novel. Thereafter his late night reading switched to unexceptional detective novels.

In July 1923, after his achievements in the prize competitions, Peterhouse elected Butterfield to the Charles Abercrombie Smith Research Studentship for 1923–1924, and he knew he would stay at Peterhouse with an income for still another year. In the summer of 1923 he began to aim for another prize competition, the biennial Prince Consort Prize, which listed no assigned subject. Soon after, however, the college altered his plans dramatically. On 29 October 1923, Peterhouse gave him a shock for the second time by electing him a Fellow of the college, to be exact, a Foundation Fellow in history. He claimed long afterwards that, even at this late date, he would have preferred to be a Fellow in English if it had been possible. He accepted the position and resigned his research studentship. The move received hearty approval from undergraduates of Peterhouse.[27]

Butterfield's uncertain journey had brought him to what appeared to be a career as a college Fellow and historian, and the outcome surprised him. It now seemed that he would remain indefinitely in this society of gentlemen unlike himself, a world without women, and a setting that evoked both his loyalty and his dissent. The Peterhouse fellowship gave him all the legitimation he needed to be regarded as a scholar. Butterfield was Peterhouse's third Fellow in history, which, with Adolphus Ward, made four historians in Peterhouse out of nine Fellows and the Master, a deepening of the college's commitment to feature history. He still wanted to be a writer, and religion remained crucial for him. He could now envision history as a way to fulfil the literary desire, an avenue with an income. However, he felt tormented by uncertainties about how to fit religion into his new career as a historian. In social terms the fellowship in a Cambridge college confirmed his status as a gentleman, a status opened up to him in that era by his matriculation in Peterhouse and his admission to the Cambridge degree. Temperley and Vellacott gave a dinner in honour of his election as a Fellow. That evening, as if to signal that the social marks of a gentlemen held no great meaning for him, he kept his pledge as a teetotaler. While the others drank champagne, he drank ginger beer.

During 1923–1924 his new duties as Fellow absorbed a large portion of his time. He began teaching undergraduates in supervisions, about ten students a year, all young men, of course, and every week during term met with them individually. He became an examiner for the annual entrance examinations. He continued to reside in the college and participated actively in college life, including especially the historical society, the political science club, and the Sex Club.[28] The pages of *The Sex* report many papers on subjects of morality being given in college societies around this time, suggesting that moral questions were much on people's minds. He no doubt paid attention as Temperley kept the interest in Acton going around Peterhouse, and probably heard Temperley's paper to the college historical society in Lent 1924, "Acton's Philosophy of History."[29] His diary shows him wrestling with Acton in 1924 over the issue of moral judgments, stimulated perhaps by Temperley's presentation. In his diary he wrote that it was better for historians to have "a sympathy with human beings, and an understanding heart" than to act as judge of others.[30]

He also worked on his entry for the university Prince Consort Prize. He choose a topic he had begun under Temperley during the previous year, the diplomatic history connected with Napoleon's drive towards Russia and the events surrounding the Treaty of Tilsit between France and Russia in 1807. Working at a furious speed Butterfield submitted a typescript of several hundred pages with the title "The Problem of Peace in Europe, 1806–8."[31] He again put all his desire to be a writer into his style and the wording of his history. In February 1924 he won the prize, with the notation that his work warranted publication, and he received the Seeley Medal as well. The adjudicators for the prize included the elite of Cambridge history at the time — Temperley, Reader in Modern History; J. B. Bury, Regius Professor of Modern History; J. P. Whitney, Dixie Professor of Ecclesiastical History; and J. S. Reid, Professor of Ancient History. His reputation within Cambridge soared, as did his own self-confidence. With Temperley's encouragement he set to work to convert his essay into a book.

It seemed easier to him to refocus his ambitions as a writer than his ministerial intentions. His religious motivation and affinities remained. Now that his undergraduate days were finished he no longer frequented college or university religious societies, but he still faithfully attended Wesley Church. He also attended Anglican services in the college chapel and developed a friendship with Canon Charles Gillett, the Dean of Peterhouse chapel since 1922.[32] He lunched often with the Rev. W. E. Barnes, Fellow of the college, former college chaplain, and Huslean Professor of Divinity since 1901. Instead of recruiting him for the ministry, Principal Hughes had persuaded him to teach ecclesiastical history on the side to the young men who were preparing for Methodist ministry at Wesley House. He began in 1922. He gave no lectures, but instead met with the students one-on-one in the manner of the Cambridge supervision. The subject was the first four centuries of Christianity. In some sense he must have found the teaching of ministerial candidates a suitable substitute for becoming a minister himself. Above all during this period, he cultivated his own spirituality, what he understood as the well-being of his inner life.

It was probably during 1923–1924 that he asked to transfer his name to the list of lay preachers in the Cambridge Methodist circuit. He continued to take engagements one or two times a term as a local preacher in Methodist chapels around Cambridge and additional engagements between terms in the Oxenhope area when he would return home to see his parents. In his diary for 1924 he recorded going to Cottenham and Romsey Town during Lent term and Royston during Easter term. Between terms in Oxenhope, on three successive Sundays, he went to Streeton, Bridgehouse, and Lund Park. In the summer, again in Oxenhope, he went to Hermit Hole and a chapel in Keighley. We may suppose there were other occasions that went unrecorded. Sometimes he preached, sometimes he led a Bible class or the Sunday school. He wrote out all his sermons and Bible studies word for word, and, although none of his sermons survive, he recalled that he would usually select a moral or devotional theme rather than anything doctrinal or theological or exegetical.

It is possible that Vellacott, himself a sincere but unostentatious Anglican, knew something about Butterfield's activity in religion outside the college. However, the person at Peterhouse who knew most about his religious life was another young Fellow, Carey Francis, a mathematician and also a Methodist, who soon received confirmation as an Anglican. The two Fellows became intimate associates in religion until Francis left for Africa in 1928 to teach in an Anglican school for boys. Butterfield remembered him as "about the most wonderful man I ever met," and acknowledged that he was "utterly inspired by him." He regarded Francis as a man like his father who exemplified a spiritual Christianity.[33]

The one person who certainly knew nothing about his religious proclivity was Temperley, an agnostic toward Christianity at this time in his life, who would have thought it very improper for Butterfield to allow his religion to intrude upon his activities as a historian. Not knowing what else to do, Butterfield allowed a division to occur between his world as a scholar in Peterhouse and his religious world external to the college and within himself. It was a continuation of the divide he created between his Keighley life at school and his Oxenhope life at home and church. Nonetheless, in the context of Peterhouse, his decision to perpetuate his religious life as a Methodist, and not, like Carey Francis, to enter the Church of England, provided him with a mode of dissent from the ethos and society around him. His spirituality also gave him a region of dissent from the totalizing influence of Temperley.

Temperley was at least aware that his protege perhaps gave too much of himself to his college duties, and advised him to round off his education by taking a year abroad before it was too late. Cambridge University had a arrangement with Princeton University by which a member of Cambridge would spend a year at Princeton on a Jane Eliza Procter Visiting Fellowship. Butterfield applied, and won the award in May 1924, only one week before the deadline for a similar fellowship at Harvard University which he had intended to pursue. He decided for Princeton without applying to Harvard. Before he left for America, Ward died in June 1924, reducing the number of historians in Peterhouse to three. Butterfield participated in the election of the new Master, Baron Robert Chalmers, a former high-level civil servant, governor of Ceylon, and a Pali scholar who was sympathetic to history.[34] When a book appeared two years later honoring Ward, Butterfield reviewed it appreciatively for the local *Cambridge Review.*[35]

The academic year in the United States lasted from September 1924 to June 1925. Princeton was a long way from Oxenhope and Peterhouse. The fellowship included work as a teaching assistant for an undergraduate course on the Reformation, marking the papers of about sixty students. He also joined a graduate history seminar and participated in the world of the American doctoral student. He had time to work on Napoleon, and his diary shows him at work in mid-winter on chapter 2 of the book. He also had time to experience the America of the 1920s. He became engrossed in American history and sketched plans to write essays on the State Department and American relations with European governments during the revolutions of 1848–1849. He went off to Washington, D.C., for research in the John Clayton Papers in the Library of Congress and in the State Department papers for 1847–1853, the years when Clayton served as secretary of state. After building up a stack of notes, however, Butterfield stopped as quickly as he began, and the projects died.[36]

Much about life in America repulsed him, as his diary shows, and as an act of dissent he became perhaps even more attached to his Methodism. The war within American Protestantism between the fundamentalists and the modernists, then at its height, made him agitated. He particularly disliked what he regarded as the intolerance of the fundamentalists, and he meditated on toleration. He disliked even more the materialistic and acquisitive society which bombarded him in America, especially when it appeared to him that the interests of money dominated art, sex, and even religion. Too much in America reduced humanity to mere physicality. He wrote in his diary: "Less and less is sex being raised, organized, until it becomes love. All the spiritual and intellectual associations around love are being disentangled completely. Now the word love means purely the animal passion." The experience prompted him to collect his thoughts about life. He did not want to reject the material world, or simply to embrace spirituality. An important passage in his diary indicated the understanding he was coming to adopt. He took hold of the traditional notion that life was a duality of the material and the spiritual, and, rather than reject the one in favour of the other, or even to retain the two in polarity, he embraced their transformation into a higher unity: "And yet, tho' economic needs and animal instincts are the sub-structure of life, the whole point of life is to raise an intellectual and spiritual synthesis on top of these, so that these very things come out etherealised. Civilisation [is what] I would call this superstructure. It is determined first and foremost by material facts — by the fact that man is an animal who gets hungry and is moved by various instincts — but it gives these a spiritual significance and experience." He summarized his view succinctly: "The important thing is to turn the material fact, the economic necessity, into a spiritual opportunity."[37]

His American diary shows him contemplating the idea of personality. Personality represents the site within each person where the dualism of the material and the spiritual transposes into a higher unity. He recorded that one Sunday in March 1925 he took charge of the services in the Methodist Church in Princeton. The topic of his evening sermon was "On Personality." Butterfield and the minister had spent the week at the annual Methodist conference for the region, held at Asbury Park, New Jersey, then still a Methodist center. When the minister needed to stay at the conference over the Sunday, he invited Butterfield to fill the pulpit in his place. Butterfield agreed and wrote in his diary, "I felt too nervous, but I suppose I ought to do it if he can't get anyone to come from Asbury Park." When the episode was over he noted, "People seemed to be pleased with my services."[38]

In spite of his misgivings about America, some of his experiences stimulated his fantasies about being a writer. He told about going several weekends to Greenwich Village in New York City where he met Hart Crane and Paul Robeson and heard Allen Tate read Crane's newest poems. He read the journal *Hound and Horn* and began to follow the American literary movement associated with it. He also confessed that the place where he heard the poetry was a basement speak-easy named Squarcialupi's, where he drank alcohol illegally during Prohibition. He sometimes drank on the sly in Princeton as well. He justified these breaches of his oath as a teetotaler with the observation that when he followed the principles of dissent in America and acted against the established order, it meant for him to violate the law on Prohibition. In America he associated his dissent with poetry, drink, and Bohemianism.[39]

College and Napoleon

Butterfield's return to Peterhouse in the Michaelmas term of 1925 coincided with his father's sudden loss of his job in Parker's Mill in Oxenhope, after years of utterly faithful service to the mill owner. Butterfield watched from a distance. He witnessed first his father's anguish and then his exaltation as the owner of the now expanding Merrall's Mill gave him employment at a higher rank and higher pay than before. The new money enabled his father to move up to the finer house at 60 Rosebank Terrace. Butterfield noted how what appeared a disaster transmuted into a victory for his father, and he professed to have learned something about the Providence of God. At the same time, the episode and the effects of the new mill owner's power confirmed his youthful trust in the diffusion of higher civilization from those above to those below. Pleased though he was, the move meant the loss of his childhood home. Butterfield responded by giving himself more completely to Peterhouse.

Butterfield's rooms in Peterhouse were at the top of the stairs in the Burroughs Building, just opposite Temperley's. By this time Vellacott, Senior Tutor of the college and Butterfield's confidant, had fully established himself as the chief administrator of the college, and he gave less time to teaching history students. Temperley was looking for relief as well. Butterfield stepped into the gap, and his schedule quickly filled up. He took Temperley's place as director of studies in history and devoted many extra hours to advising students about their studies. He also succeeded Temperley as librarian of the college, and spent several morning hours a week in the library. Butterfield resumed the supervision of undergraduates with a cohort of ten or so a year, meeting them one-by-one in the customary weekly sessions during term. College meetings, meals, and socializing among the Fellows and others in Cambridge all took time.[40]

The college elected him to more a secure position as a Research Fellow in 1926. in 1927, Ernest Barker became the first incumbent of the professorship in political science at Cambridge, and Peterhouse elected him to a professorial fellowship. Barker construed political science generally as a study of the history of political thought and was listed with the Faculty of History in the university. This restored the college complement of historians to four, but, as professor, Barker had little to do with students, leaving Butterfield as the only historian active with undergraduates.

He added still further to his workload during the year 1927–1928 when he received his first opportunity to be a lecturer, and hence to increase his income. With the help of the college, he set himself up as an independent lecturer, giving lectures in college space to university students who, in the tradition of the most ancient university practices, paid him a fee to hear what he had to say. In the following year, the college made him an acting lecturer on the college staff and for the first time paid him to lecture.

Butterfield continued his involvement in religious activities after his return from America. He attended Wesley Church on Sundays, he participated occasionally in Peterhouse chapel, and resumed his cycle of lay preaching during term around Cambridge and between terms around Oxenhope. He resumed as well his teaching of church history at Wesley House.

More important to him, he continued to cultivate his inner spiritual life. His diary during February and March 1926 reveals a particularly intense moment in his religious life and in the shaping of his career. He recorded a visionary encounter with God: "I saw God round the corner yesterday. It was where the avenue of trees cuts into Trumpington Road and there was a pretty piece of shrubbery, a momentous play of sunshine, a pause in the wind. Then God came without a sound. He was an elf. Quickly he disappeared — and long as I looked at the shrub I could not make it look like that again, I could not recapture the first elusive vision. I could not find where God had gone. So I felt utterly alone, and friendless, and away from home. Yet in my heart was a song, for I had seen a fabulous thing."[41]

He experienced ambivalence about the path on which his career as a historian seemed to take him. He confessed: "I can quite understand the lure of the cloister, the charm of a lonely sheltered life, the attraction of a retreat from the world. . . . Yet to be in the whirl of it, maddeningly engaged in it, and lifted by the floods, is the supreme exhilaration."[42] His ambivalence embraced his love of Peterhouse and the scholarly life, but also his rejection of the social and academic worlds he had entered. It was the same ambivalence he expressed at a more fundamental level about the dualism as well as the unity of the material and the spiritual elements of life and the personality. His diary revealed that he firmly dissented from the expectations imposed upon him by Peterhouse. He would live as the romantic poet if only he could: "I long to let myself loose. I think there is some eagle in my soul that is hungering for the open sky, the free hills. The whole cloak of respectable life is cumbersome to me, the repressions, the conventions, the shams, the humdrum evasions of momentous issues. If it were not for my people I would break away, and throw myself into the whirlpool of adventure, and write poetry in a garret. For wild horses are inside me, leaping down the lanes of my heart."[43] If he were going to be a historian — if he *had* to be a historian — he wanted to be no ordinary historian: "I feel nowadays that life is a very good thing — and yet I know I am doing very little. . . . I would like to do a creative thing to throw out as a challenge to the sky — to put my footprint in the world and to justify my life before the high gods."[44] His diary shows him mingling his Methodist devotion with his concerns about the course of his life. He was not sure that his research on Napoleon would satisfy his aspirations, and he maintained the uneasy separation he had created between his religious world and his world as a historian. His old desire to be a preacher had not slackened.

Butterfield continued working on Napoleon under Temperley's influence. The object was to produce a book which would establish his position as a historian. Under different circumstances — for instance, had he stayed at Princeton — the work would have become his doctoral dissertation. He was admitted to the Cambridge M.A. degree in 1926. At Cambridge the M.A. required no further work and possessed no academic meaning, being a near automatic conversion of the B.A. The M.A. did confer higher social status, however, and in the milieu of Cambridge it ranked higher than the Ph.D. Butterfield could now wear the master's gown whose simplicity he came to enjoy in contrast with the proliferation of doctoral gowns worn by Americans.

Butterfield's research consisted of reading the letters and despatches of diplomats, foreign ministers, and heads of state. He spent most of his time in Cambridge looking at volumes of published letters and despatches. He went to London for additional published materials in the library of the British Museum, and he read in the unpublished papers of the British Foreign Office kept in the Public Record Office. On the continent he visited only Paris, where he worked in the archives of the French Foreign Ministry. He did not go to Vienna, Berlin, Brussels, Turin, or Rome, where he could have found other unpublished materials useful to his topic. He was prevented from research in Russia where the archives were closed to outsiders. Temperley arranged for him to receive hand copies of some material from the Austrian state archives, but, for the most part, for Europe outside France, he depended on the incomplete and selected published documents available at home. This lack of thoroughness reflected the standards in England during the 1920s for research in diplomatic history. Temperley attracted attention at the time for his advice that young historians should not rest content with the printed sources alone, a standard Ranke had articulated generations before, but he did not press the point with Butterfield. Unlike Ranke, Butterfield and Temperley were not innovators in archival research.[45] In spite of his conviction that archival research was the foundation of historical scholarship, Butterfield excused his own relatively meager digging in the archives under Temperley's direction. He stressed instead the careful integration of sources, in this case chiefly printed materials. He later disparaged those historians who by spending their energies "running to a multitude of archives . . . had left themselves no time for the detailed collation of over-lapping sources."[46]

We can tell from Butterfield's papers that he worked hard on his research. He himself hand copied countless documents and made endless notes on $4'' \times 6''$ cards or larger lined sheets of paper. He covered the period from January 1806 to late in 1808. He adhered strictly to the method Temperley taught him, and he fashioned a hard commitment to the field of diplomatic history as "an excellent discipline for the beginner in research."[47] He rigorously followed each series of correspondence between the government and the diplomats, one country at a time, letter by letter, day by day, from the beginning to the end of the events in question. Then he integrated all his notes from each series chronologically and by theme in order to discern interrelationships among the various channels of communication. Before he had finished his research he began to write, using the act of writing as his way of comprehending the larger story. He wrote and rewrote repeatedly, using his lengthy typescript for the Prince Consort Prize as his base. Altogether he seems to have written at least three, perhaps four, versions under at least three titles.[48] One version reached eight hundred typed pages. In the process he narrowed his topic, reduced his time period, and cut the length of the text.[49]

The initial public product of this intensity was a brief article which the local *Cambridge Historical Journal* published for him in 1927, "A French Minister at Vienna, 1806–1807."[50] It was his first publication based on historical research, and again Temperley helped him. Temperley had founded the journal in 1923 and served as permanent editor. Butterfield eventually emerged with a book-length study of Napoleon's diplomacy surrounding Tilsit in 1807. He finished the book by mid-December 1928, and it appeared in December 1929, not long after his thirtieth birthday. It was still a large volume of four hundred published pages, entitled *The Peace Tactics of Napoleon, 1806–8*. It was his second book, the second published by Cambridge University Press, and his first history book. Temperley had a hand in getting it published, and Temperley himself proudly claimed credit for the role he played in promoting Butterfield's career.[51]

Butterfield's hefty book was all about diplomats, prime ministers, military officers, emperors, and kings, and their public and secret diplomacy, the things he felt able to extract from the diplomatic despatches and private letters. He set October 1806 and April 1908 as his boundaries, starting with new Prussian peace overtures after the victory of Napoleon at Jena, and ending with the isolation of England from the continent. He focused on the diplomatic negotiations which the powers of Europe conducted among themselves at the same time as the allies of the Fourth Coalition fought against Napoleon to prevent his further march across central Europe towards St. Petersburg. In all of this, his dealt with the surface life of the political and military elite, the kinds of activities and people which he claimed in *Historical Novel* that historical study was competent to treat.

The theses he offered about his topic let us know, however, that he was struggling to move beyond his definition of historical study and to reach below to surface of the easily documentable high people and high events. His theses can be analyzed according to degrees of generality and specificity. The most general thesis of the book proposes that the diplomacy of the great powers of Europe constituted to the inner, the essential, and the rational aspect of their relationships, while the wars they fought simultaneously among themselves were merely the external, the superficial, and the irrational aspect of things. He writes, "And yet the rationale of all this, the logic of this muddle and misery, lay in the diplomacy that gave meaning to the fighting and explained what each power was fighting for and determined how long men should go on with the fighting. . . . What each side sought to win, out of the clash of battle, was, in the last resort, a diplomatic advantage, a 'pull' in negotiations. And, since in the year 1807 the outbreak of hostilities did not destroy the thread of negotiation, but kept it moving in unbroken sequence, the diplomatic story is the true index of the fluctuation of fortunes, the real barometer of the war; in a way it is the essential history of the European struggle against Napoleon." For Butterfield, diplomacy is to war as the spiritual is to the material. He fixes his attention on what he regards as the inner elements of the events.[52]

Applied to Napoleon's behaviour, Butterfield translates this general point into the more specific thesis that Napoleon used his armies and his diplomacy as two sides of a common strategy to promote the overall aim of achieving ascendency in Europe, with his diplomacy having the priority. Butterfield believes that in the events before and during Tilsit Napoleon was at the height of his power and his genius was at its finest. His diplomacy at that moment was not an extension of his war policy, not warfare conducted by different means, as the classic definition of diplomacy would have it. Rather, his "peace tactics" were his primary instruments for advancing his imperial design, and his resort to war was secondary.[53]

More specifically still, Butterfield argues the thesis that the system created by the Treaty of Tilsit was the crowning achievement of Napoleon's peace tactics. Napoleon found his ally in Russia and not in Prussia as was widely feared, and he and the czar divided the map, without Prussia, so that Napoleon emerged supreme in Europe while Russia won the prospect of major gains from any future dismemberment of the Ottoman Empire. The irony was that Prussia was the one who first suggested to the czar that he seek alliance with Napoleon, the intention being to undercut Napoleon's aggressiveness, and to surface in the end with a three-way agreement between France, Russia, and Prussia for the control of Europe and the partition of the Ottoman Empire.[54]

Butterfield's most specific thesis concerns the way Napoleon accomplished his master move. The feat involved producing subtle and even unconscious transitions in the czar's attitude towards Prussia and his intentions towards France. In a series of conversations between the two emperors, including a visit alone on a raft in the River Niemen, Napoleon faced the czar with his determination and brought the Russian under "the spell of his personality." In the end, Butterfield contends, Napoleon lured the czar "with visions which he never for a moment intended to convert into actualities," and the czar "finally surrendered in a way that he had not intended, to the personality of Napoleon."[55]

Behind these historical theses lie two ideas which influenced the character of Butterfield's interpretations, one about processes and one about human personality. Both ideas continue what he had put forward in previous writings, but the way he thinks of them now is modified. The first concerns how to understand the processes of history. In his unpublished essay on G. K. Chesterton he wrote about the idea he attributed to Chesterton that at any given moment people did not know what was coming next in the course of their lives. Now he notes another aspect of what he is coming to regarded as the complexity of history, and he combats the view that things proceeded from one event to another in the fashion of "a simple ascending ladder." He prefers the counter-idea that history should be seen as conflict and interaction: "in reality the issue is the result of a conflict of forces, and a collision of wills. There is an interplay of personalities who themselves are not always unities, but, repeating the conflict within their own spirits, are torn with irreconcilable moods and purposes, divided against themselves. . . . It is easy to take a short cut with history and see things move evenly towards some great event; in reality life is more complex."[56] He continues to affirm Ranke's notion of the interconnectedness of history, using the metaphor of a cloth or a tapestry in which no threads are left hanging loose.[57]

The second is the idea of personality which had figured so importantly in *Historical Novel*. There he had stressed how historical study could not adequately handle human personality, since historians were prevented by the evidence from reaching the "hearts" of the people they studied. Personality was the forte of historical novelists. Now he urges that it is utterly necessary for historians, and not just novelists, "to bring the story out of the plane of mere incident and event" and "to value events in their relation to an inner experience." He posits his belief that the human personality can be understood as a unity of the outer and the inner, an amalgam of a person's outward acts and happenings and concrete facts and forms, and the person's inner spirituality and inner mind. The inner personality holds the priority in human life, just as diplomacy held the priority over war, and the spiritual over the material. The difficult task for the historian, working from the evidence available, he now asserts, is "to look upon events with an inward eye." The historian needs to move from the outer shell of the individual to the mysterious inner world and back out again in order to produce a valid history. He adds, "the narrative must break into an essay."[58]

After we hear his points about process and personality, we are better able to comprehend the character of the history book that he has made out of *The Peace Tactics of Napoleon*. He tells us in the preface what he has tried to do: "The story has been told with special reference to the personalities engaged in the work of diplomacy, so that it might become apparent how much in these Napoleonic times the course of events could be deflected by the characters and the idiosyncracies of ambassadors and ministers who were far from home. It is intended that the result should be at least a sample picture of the Napoleonic era, and should illustrate the strange tangle, the hidden undercurrents and the clash of personalities, that lay behind a Napoleonic war."[59] At the moment in the book when he is leading up to his thesis about Tilsit, he wants us not to miss his central contention. He understands the history of diplomacy not as the history of institutions and abstractions, but of personalities in action: "At Tilsit one can make no mistake. Here is the play of personalities, palpable and direct. It is not 'Russia' that takes a course of action, like a piece of mechanical adjustment. It is not ministers of departments who balance an impersonal policy. It is not the government that evolves an official logic. Here 'Russia,' the government, is a Czar, a bundle of emotions and prejudices, an accident in human nature, 'and if you prick him he will bleed.' . . . The whole drama is played out on the spot. A revolution is telescoped into a few days. Everything is determined by personalities that act upon one another immediately."[60] Butterfield seems to be using the idea of personality rather flexibly. He appears to mean the individual human being, composed of the spiritual and the material, of the inner and the outer, integrated by what he calls variously the soul, the emotions, and the mind, and expressive of such matters as spirituality, a psychology, character, reason, intentions, and purposes. He deliberately refrains from providing anything like a definition of personality, and prefers simply to portray the personality of each main character in the story and to use the idea of personality as his ultimate explanation of why the events went as they did in the course of the diplomacy, especially at Tilsit.[61] He formally states his claim about personalities as an interpretation that is specific to Napoleon's era and the events of Tilsit. Yet unmistakably we catch a larger message, that the whole of human history is about personalities, about the inner life and individual people, and not simply about abstractions, forces, institutions, and systems.

Butterfield employs two literary modes in order to give us the history of diplomacy: narrative and portraiture. He is telling us a story or, as he sometimes says, presenting a drama. The primal structure of the work is narrative. Then, from time to time, he says, "the narrative must break into an essay." He stops the story long enough to present a picture of a "situation" and the portrait of a personality. He depicts the "situation" after Jena and the "situation" before Tilsit, and paints verbal portraits of Napoleon, Czar Alexander, Baron Hardenberg, and Canning.[62] Story and picture, drama and portrait — these are the instruments he once said belonged to the historical novelist. To this he has added the occasional supplementary essay on historical thinking, halting the story long enough to contemplate his historical method and the psychological approach he is using.[63] He has deliberately turned his treatment of Napoleon's diplomacy into an apologia in favour of history as the story of personalities.

We need only step back a few feet in order to see what has happened between *Historical Novel* and *The Peace Tactics of Napoleon*. In the intervening years he has clarified his thoughts about personality, and we can glimpse this happening in his diary and his sermons. He has not abandoned his convictions about personalities and the need to know whole situations and circumstances, and he has not abolished his purposes of going below the surface of human events in order to penetrate the inner mysteries of life. He has not ceased to use the metaphors of story and picture in conveying to us how we might gain access to the inner reaches of life. But he has achieved a major change in his thinking. He has transposed all these matters from the historical novel to the history book, from the novelist to the historian. He has reversed himself and asserted the primacy of history over literature. In the process he has ceased longing for the life of the poet and the writer, and transmuted his literary desire into the vocation of the historian.

He has not relinquished the hope of composing his history as literature, however. He has considerably tamed his romantic style in the new book and quite noticeably eliminated the most florid features of his writing. But he is still the writer, writing and rewriting his prose countless times in order to perfect his style. Many of his passages, such as some of those already examined above, strike us as compelling and a delight to read. But there are the other passages where, straining to be literary, he says the same thing two or three or four times, each with a different metaphor: "But one thing we know — and this we have good reason to be sure of — that at some point during the interviews at Tilsit, he [Alexander] lost his grip on externalities, some mist over his eyes blurred his vision of the objective world, and before he knew it he was back in the sky, carried on the wings of a dream, so that the flimsiest promises seemed to him for the moment like actualities and his faith fixed itself on things unsubstantial as a cloud."[64]

The book received mixed reviews. As a piece of writing, W. F. Reddaway, a colleague at Cambridge, called the book "distinguished" as literature. Walter Phelps Hall of Princeton University, whom Butterfield would have known from his year there in 1924–1925, commented in the *American Historical Review* that the book was extraordinarily well written. However, not everyone praised his writing. For instance, the notice in the *English Historical Review* complained about the overuse of inaccurate or mixed metaphors and other "blemishes of style."[65] As a work of history, the reviewer in *History* coupled it with Webster's new magisterial study of Castlereagh and suggested that both books deserved a permanent place as histories of nineteenth-century

diplomacy.[66] In the intervening years Webster's volume has achieved that position, but not Butterfield's. The book did come back into print in 1972,[67] and it
still appears in bibliographies. The *English Historical Review* considered the
work skillful, especially in the subtle handling of Napoleon and Alexander at
Tilsit. However, more than one reviewer observed that his portraits of personalities tended to obscure his presentation of the interactions and events.[68] Hall,
in the *American Historical Review,* suggested that the young historian was
himself too much under the hypnotism of Napoleon.

Perhaps the most severe criticism came from Butterfield himself, who felt
put off by the book when he had finished. However, at the end of his life, when
surveying all his writings, he claimed that he regarded *The Peace Tactics of
Napoleon* to be his best book. He would smile proudly when he mentioned
that Savoie Lottinville used the book as a model of historical narrative in the
twentieth century. He especially liked her praise of the dramatic opening of the
story, which she found wonderfully effective.[69]

In doing *Peace Tactics* he owed precise debts to two people among all those
around him in Cambridge — Temperley, of course, but also George Macaulay
Trevelyan. He mentions Temperley by name in the preface, although the reference hardly does justice to the totality of Temperley's influence over him
still. Specifically, he received the topic and the genre from Temperley, and he
learned from Temperley the methods of historical research, or more exactly
stated, he learned the methods of one style of research in one area of history.
Temperley gave him a version of Ranke that prized precise detective work on
diplomatic documents, approached by means of critical questions designed to
ascertain the truth about what actually happened. *Peace Tactics of Napoleon*
disclosed just how completely he had adopted Ranke in his historical thinking.
It showed in the manner and method of the book as well as in his reliance on
Ranke's history of the Prussian states in the Napoleonic period.[70]

Temperley helped Butterfield solidify his attachment to Lord Acton as well.
Given his deference to those above him socially, Butterfield was in any case
inclined towards unbounded admiration for the aristocrat in Acton. In the
context of *Peace Tactics* Acton's stress on documentary research was important, as was his alignment with Ranke, whom Acton had called "my own
master" and "the real originator of the heroic study of records." But perhaps
more important was Acton's emphasis on personality in history, together with
his stress on the soul, morality, and religion, all of which appeared in Acton's
famous inaugural address which Butterfield knew as an undergraduate.[71] The
role of personality in *Peace Tactics,* where personality and history are fully
connected, hints at the subterranean presence of Acton within Butterfield's
historical thought. Indeed, Butterfield moved straight from *Peace Tactics* into

a period of fundamental reflection on Acton's thought. Hereafter Butterfield referred to Ranke or Acton, or both, in every work of substance as well as countless lesser works that he produced throughout the rest of his career.[72]

Butterfield did not mention Trevelyan, although he should have. Trevelyan was the living exemplar of the tradition of history as literature, who had just taken the appointment as Regius Professor of Modern History at Cambridge in 1927. He arrived in time to gave Butterfield extra encouragement to write history in a literary manner. Trevelyan's inaugural address emphasized the importance of story and the desirability of good style in history writing as well as the importance of personality in history and the need for historians to reach the inner life of their subjects.[73] Butterfield's own literary desires were sufficient to motivate his attempts to write history as literature, but Trevelyan's presence provided a boost, and in later writings he acknowledged his attachment to Trevelyan and the literary tradition with its stress on both writing style and personality. Near the end of his life he admitted that he had tried in *Peace Tactics* to produce the kind of literary narrative characteristic of the great nineteenth-century historians, above all Carlyle, whom he had cited in *Historical Novel,* and Thomas Babington Macaulay, Trevelyan's ancestor. Trevelyan became Butterfield's literary mentor and encouraged him to keep the lineage of history-as-literature alive. Butterfield also noted that, of all the historians in Cambridge, he was one people regarded as perhaps the nearest to being Trevelyan's disciple.[74]

The completion of *The Peace Tactics of Napoleon* marked Butterfield's full and proper arrival as a historian. Altogether the project had taken him about seven years. The stress and overwork confirmed him as a chain-smoker of cigarettes, a habit he retained until late in life. He remained a teetotaler in spite of the overwhelming weight of Peterhouse to the contrary. Soon after finishing the book in December 1928, he received his first appointment in the university, a probationary faculty lecturer in history for 1929–1930. Once again Temperley promoted his advancement, this time as a member of the appointments committee which selected him. The new status, fragile as it sounds, offered greater stability and more income than he had known during the previous two years when he worked first as an independent lecturer and then as an acting lecturer for the college.

His new position made possible a major change in his personal life. He had met Edith Joyce Crawshaw when he was twenty-four, before he left for America. The channel was his religious activities, initially a Methodist youth conference at Oxford, where he became acquainted with one of her brothers, Charles, whom everyone called Felix. When their father, a Methodist minister, took the pastorate in Cottenham, a village north of Cambridge, Herbert visited Felix. There he would see his sister, usually known as Pamela or Pam. She was the fourth and last child, and only daughter, of James Edward Crawshaw and Edith Alice Harbord, born on 17 April 1903. Because the father was a minister and, as such, an intellectual and social leader in the congregation, Pam's family would have enjoyed much higher status than Herbert's family, but Pam's family would have looked approvingly upward to Herbert's personal status as a Fellow of a Cambridge college. Pam and Herbert corresponded while he was in Princeton, and their relationship developed into a romance when he returned to Cambridge. She called him Bean. Herbert apparently had known other women before, but none in this way. In spite of his youthful resolution never to marry, he came to feel that he wanted to marry her. He felt, however, that his meagre income at Peterhouse remained a barrier to marriage, which led him to delay. Peterhouse reelected him a Research Fellow in 1929, which led in 1932 to election as Internal Fellow. Peterhouse allowed him to continue as acting lecturer in the college, and then, on top of these, came the appointment to the university probationary lectureship. Each position brought an income, and the combination of the three enabled him to proceed with his plans. He and Pam were married on 29 July 1929. He was twenty-eight and she was twenty-six.

After ten years of residence in Peterhouse, Butterfield moved out of college and the new couple moved into a flat on Fitzwilliam Street. Pam's great interest was drawing, and she became an active member of the Cambridge Drawing Society. She tended not to have any particular interest in Herbert's history work. Nonetheless, she helped him by sometimes correcting his book proofs and, in the 1930s and again in the 1960s and 1970s, she often typed his papers. In general, she tolerated his increasingly excessive working schedule and enjoyed it when his reputation increased. Their marriage led him to develop a new, slightly more detached, relationship with Peterhouse.

Altogether, by 1929, it is astonishing how completely absorbed he had become into the world of Cambridge. He had fulfiled his youthful aim to become a writer, but in a manner which surprised him. He had become a historian, a writer of history, and he was able to live on his income as a historian. Intellectually, he had decided what kind of historian he would be, and he had found the idea which hereafter remained the center of his understanding of history, the all-surpassing value of human personality in history. He had not yet satisfied his aspirations about religion. His play with the idea of personality in history and his attraction to Acton suggested that he was seeking a way to connect his own unmitigated religious motivation with his career as a historian. At the moment, however, what appeared to move Butterfield most tangibly was not his thinking or even his vocation, but the need to prepare his lectures.

3

Reconciler

Reconciling Opposites

With his big book on Napoleon finished in 1929 and no major research project on his agenda, Butterfield devoted himself to his undergraduate supervisions in Peterhouse and his lectures in the Faculty of History. His new position in the university History Faculty set him up for his third year of lectures, and his fourth year on the History Faculty list. A new statute for Cambridge University in 1926 had augmented the academic position of the university vis-à-vis the colleges, creating the Faculty of History and the position of University Lecturer. His name was swept on to the first list of the reorganized History Faculty for 1926–1927, one of forty-one historians attached to the university or one of the colleges. But he had no standing that year as a lecturer in the university or the college, and offered no lectures. Officially the title Research Fellow, which he received in 1926, was a result of the new college statute which, like every other Cambridge college, Peterhouse obtained in conjunction with the new university statute.[1]

Butterfield's career as a lecturer started a year later, 1927–1928, when, still without standing, he began his lectures to undergraduates on a fee-paying basis. From the very beginning he adopted the practice, which he maintained throughout his career, of handwriting his lectures word for word and reading from the manuscript to his undergraduate audience. Even as a lecturer he was a writer. During Lent term 1928 he mounted a course of lectures entitled "History of England in the 18th Century," and during Easter term another called "Foreign Policy of Napoleon." His topics show that his interests had not moved one inch from his examination fields of 1922. During 1928–1929, as acting lecturer in Peterhouse, he again offered the course on eighteenth-century England, but not the Napoleon course.

In 1929–1930, with his university position, Butterfield had to meet the requirements and needs of the History Faculty, which meant new work, and a lot of it. It fell to him to offer the traditional core set of lectures, "General European History." He ran the course at Peterhouse throughout the three terms of the academic year. He made a much wider sweep across history than in any of his previous lectures. He began with the Italian Renaissance, which Cambridge traditionally dated from the foreign invasions of Italy of 1494, and concluded in the eighteenth century, traditionally in 1715 after the Treaty of Utrecht.

The lectures altered his intellectual focus. He encountered for the first time the problems of constructing general history. After seven years of intensive study of documents in diplomatic history covering a brief stretch of eighteen months in the career of one man, he now had to offer generalizations at a very high level of abstraction about the history of many nations over a period of more than two centuries. The problems involved in producing such lectures intrigued him. He turned his mind away from research and mused theoretically about doing general history. He thought about the strategies that historians use to grasp the complexity of history, the structure that they give to their narratives, the metaphors they use to represent the conflicts of history, and other issues. He devoted himself utterly to the work and wrote out his lectures in full. Even prior to this year he had toiled long hours every day in order to complete all his tasks, but now he made it his habit to work late into the night and resume early in the morning. He had to hope that Pam would learn to accommodate his schedule, which she did. His efforts pleased his students and impressed his colleagues, and he won appointment as a full University Lecturer in History for 1930–1931. Temperley once again played his protector and advocate as a member of the appointments committee that nominated him.

In the middle of his initial reflections on the problems of general history, he turned his mind to some of the general historical questions raised by two notable Cambridge historians.[2] He contemplated the differences between the approaches of George Macaulay Trevelyn, the current Regius Professor of Modern History, and J. B. Bury, who had held the Regius chair from 1902 to 1927, between Lord Acton's tenure and Trevelyan's. Bury presided over Cambridge historians during that period. Bury's ideas intrigued Temperley, who put together a book of Bury's essays which he published in 1930.[3] Temperley's promotion of Bury in this manner carried with it added poignancy, as a strike against Trevelyan and the appointment system. The Crown had bypassed Temperley in naming Trevelyan to succeed Bury in the Regius chair, astounding Butterfield and all the others who had assumed that Temperley had earned the appointment. In the English system where professorships were few, the status attached to them was exorbitantly high, and the Regius chair was the highest of the high. The university acted quickly to create a new chair in order to compensate Temperley, and in 1930 he became the first Professor of Modern History. The whole episode stirred Butterfield's interest in Bury, who had held the Regius chair during Butterfield's first eight years in Cambridge.

Bury's essays appeared to assert a position just the opposite of Trevelyan's patronage of history as literature and the story of personalities. Bury's inaugural in 1902 championed history as a science. While not denying the importance of personalities or the value of good narrative, Bury argued that history was best understood as a species of science, not literature. By science he meant something more than the Rankean tradition of precise research and careful criticism of documents. Bury urged that the best way to achieve understanding of human actions was to penetrate the surface of events and reach into the underlying realm of laws in history, the king of which was the law of cause and effect. The method of the historian would be to arrange the data of research in series of events, with the events linked to each other in chains of cause and effect. Each series constituted a process. He believed that by establishing events in relation to the law of cause and effect the historian would achieve scientific explanation within historical study. In later years Bury modified his emphasis and, while not revising his view of laws, showed himself more intrigued by the problem of the intersection, or the conjunction, of the chains of cause and effect. Taken separately, each series of events might appear to exhibit sequences of cause and effect, but when two or more series intersected, cause and effect seemed to vanish, and the consequences would appear haphazard. The conjunction of such series of events Bury attributed to "chance," and he referred to the complexity that surrounded such conjunctions as "conditioning circumstances."[4]

Butterfield felt the pull of something true in what Bury wrote, just as he did with the ideas of Trevelyan, but he also disliked elements of the thought of both historians. He wished to reconcile the two apparently opposing positions. He already had the experience of using what he called his stereoscopic vision on the religious options that he encountered during his undergraduate days when none of the available versions of Christianity satisfied him. He had the same experience with the political options confronting him left and right.

He found it hard to say a straightforward yes or no to the views advocated by others. By now it began to look as if he had elevated the intuitive use of stereoscopic vision into a method. It was a dialectic method, a way of reconciling opposites and creating a higher unity. Rather than choosing simply for one side against another, he would intuitively allow himself to be attracted to each conflicting view in turn, and then to dissent from what he felt were the errors and exaggerations of each in turn. He would then reconcile the residue of truths on all sides and, at the end, dissent from all sides, formulating his own conclusions at a higher level of integration. His reconciling method had affinities with the *via media* of Anglican theology and practice, the deliberate incorporation of the best in opposing positions while creating a higher and more comprehensive way to walk.

At the same time, Butterfield found a method which allowed him to carry on his own new thinking, a way of thinking by writing. He would try to clarify his views of the ideas swirling around him by writing out his thoughts on sheets of paper. He produced what we might call "thought-essays," mostly incomplete, in which he spontaneously wrote out what he was thinking about some matter. These thoughts took the form of coherent prose, some only a few lines long, others extending to several pages. He would often write down his thoughts in this fashion while reading a book or essay, or after a conversation with another scholar. His diary indicates he spent much time during 1928–1930 talking with Alfred Nock, a classicist, and Michael Oakeshott, a philosopher, both young Fellows at the time in Cambridge. He would pile up these little "thought-essays" by the scores. He apparently retained none of those from the late 1920s and 1930s, but hundreds of them remain from 1931 onward.

The engagement with Bury's views about the process of history compelled him to move intellectually. By 1930, using his newly emerging methods, Butterfield came to some conclusions about history that took him beyond the thought underlying his *The Peace Tactics of Napoleon*. He began with the emphasis he shared with Trevelyan on personalities and narrative. Then he adopted elements of Bury's views, appropriately modified, about process, conditioning circumstances, and the conjunction of events. Butterfield could feel that Bury's thought on these themes comported well with things he had been saying since *Historical Novel* about historical conditions and combinations of circumstance. He also felt that Bury's ideas coincided with a trend present in his own thought since around 1925, a trend which already involved him in a criticism of Trevelyan. At about that time, before Trevelyan returned to Cambridge, Butterfield presented a paper at Jesus College, Cambridge, on Charles James Fox and 1792. It was the first time he ventured to give a paper outside Peterhouse. The paper touched on Trevelyan. He accused Trevelyan of distorting the political views of Fox and other figures he discussed in his book *Lord Grey of the Reformed Bill,* published in 1920.[5] He claimed that Trevelyan failed sufficiently to understand the views and politics of Lord Grey in Grey's own context because he interpreted Grey too much in the light of the present.[6]

By 1930 Butterfield was no longer thinking about Trevelyan as such, but about Lord Acton. He had begun to see Acton as the problem and not Trevelyan. Acton, he thought, went far beyond Trevelyan in taking what he approved in the present as the standard for the interpretation of all history. The views which agitated Butterfield were those contained in Acton's inaugural address of 1895, a text Butterfield must by now have known by heart. Acton claimed that the unity of modern history lay in the achievement of liberty. By "liberty" Acton made clear that he meant the political, religious, and economic forms in his own day admired by those who named their creed "liberalism." Acton believed that knowledge of the slow progress of liberty towards this approved present was what he called "a work-day key to history." With this key he could discern the "advance of civilisation" and the "improvement of the world," all of which he attributed to "the action of Christ" and "the wisdom of divine rule." He spoke in particular of "the progress of the world towards self-government." He continued, "And this constancy of progress, of progress in the direction of organised and assured freedom, is the characteristic fact of modern history, and its tribute to the theory of Providence."[7]

Butterfield became perhaps even more exercised over Acton's pronouncements on history and morality. Acton enjoined historians to issue moral judgments against the people and their actions in the past. Both in the inaugural address and in a famous exchange of letters with Mandell Creighton in 1887, when Creighton was Dixie Professor of Ecclesiastical History at Cambridge and editor of the *English Historical Review,* Acton made extravagant statements in favour of the historian as moralist. In the inaugural he spoke memorably and with fervour as he admonished historians to engage in moral judgments against both people and causes: "But the weight of opinion is against me when I exhort you never to debase the moral currency or to lower the standard of rectitude, but to try others by the final maxim that governs your own lives, and to suffer no man and no cause to escape the undying penalty which history has the power to inflict on wrong."[8] In the Creighton letters he warned of the consequences resulting from any compromise by historians of what he called the "inflexible integrity of the moral code." He added, "Then history ceases to be a science, an arbiter of controversy, a guide of the wanderer, the upholder of that moral standard which the powers of earth, and religion itself, tend constantly to depress. It serves where it ought to reign; and it serves the worst better than the purest."[9] Butterfield had been struggling with Acton on moral judgments since at least 1924, as his diary attests. In 1930 he found Acton's proclamations especially troublesome.[10]

Whigs

Butterfield meditated often during 1930 and 1931 on questions raised by his lectures on general history as well as by his encounters with Bury, Trevelyan, and Acton. He put his immediate responses into his thought-essays, some long, some short, and the number of thought-essays added up. He collated some of his thought-essays into a longer essay and allowed Vella-cott to read it and no one else. Vellacott vigorously urged him to published the essay. He rewrote again, expanded it, and finally took what he had to G. Bell and Sons in London, one of Temperley's publishers. Bell liked it. In the fall of 1931, shortly after Butterfield turned thirty-one, his essay appeared as a little book of 132 pages, wearing the curious title *The Whig Interpretation of History*. He dedicated it to Vellacott.[11]

In the essay, Butterfield takes care to characterize his intentions about the genre of the book so that people might understand him rightly. He says it is simply a "study," a study of what he calls the "psychology of historians." He acknowledges that it contains "theses," but he denies that the work has any connection with philosophy of history. He offers no philosophical description or analysis, and his theses, he said, with a gratuitous swat at philosophy, "would be unaffected by anything the philosopher could state to explain them or to explain them away." We might go further to observe that the work belongs to the tradition of the university prize essay, of which he had written a few in his time, except that now he was too far along in his career to submit the product to any competition. It was the first completed essay which he wrote entirely on his own initiative.

There is more to his statement about eschewing philosophical analysis than the historian's traditional distrust, or dislike, of philosophers. We may surmise from his text that he is distancing himself from at least two schools of philosophy broadly familiar to him: the English analytic school, which focused on language and logic, and the tradition associated loosely with Hegel, which looked for the movements of "spirits" in history, spoke in terms of universals, and devised rational deductions from general principles.[12] His protestations against the Hegelian school are not entirely convincing, since he included in the essay an ample share of spirits and ideals and universals and general principles. He does well to draw away from the new analytic philosophy of history, however. That school would trash the essay. When we read *Whig Interpretation* we find little argument and his writing is disconnected, rambling, vague, often confusing. He makes assertions, not arguments, and he makes his assertions indirectly, by prefacing each one with apparently unassertive language. Page after page carries expressions like these: "there is at least a chance that," "it might be true to say that," "it is not a mere coincidence that," "it is difficult to see that," "it is not malicious to suggest that," "we may suspect that," and so on.[13] It is a style that avoids saying things straightforwardly, not because he has inadequate warrant for his assertions, but because he does not want to overstate, or to offend, or to seem to judge. He expresses his points in metaphors. As in his earlier writings, he uses metaphor to be literary, and once again we find him overdoing the effort. He says the same thing two or three times, each with a different metaphor, and sometimes working a metaphor too long and too hard, turning metaphors into agents and explanations. Here is a sample:

> It seems possible to say that if we are seeking to discover how the medieval world was changed into the world that we know, we must go behind Protestantism and the Reformation to a deeper tide in the affairs of men, to a movement which we may indeed discern but can scarcely dogmatise about, and to a prevailing current, which, though we must never discover it too soon, is perhaps the last thing we can learn in our research upon the historical process. It does seem for example that before the Reformation some wind had set itself to play on the side of kings, and in many a country a hundred weather-vanes, on steeple and on mansion, on college and on court, had turned before the current to show that the day of monarchy had come. . . . Further it is possible to say that when there is such a tide in the affairs of men, it may use any channel to take it to its goal — it may give any other movement a turn in its own direction. For some reason Renaissance and Reformation and rising Capitalism were made to work to the glory of kings.[14]

There are close to no normal supports for what he says — no footnotes, almost no quotations or examples, and very few references to historians who were attached to the political alliances that in the late seventeenth, eighteenth, and early nineteenth centuries went by the title Whig, in contrast with those called Tories. Thirty years later E. H. Carr had great fun at Butterfield's expense in making this observation.[15]

The cumulative effect of *Whig Interpretation of History* can be infuriating. Annabel Patterson experienced it as a "tirade." We cannot be sure we know what he means to say and with whom he wants to disagree, and as a consequence we often find his thought difficult to criticize. Nonetheless, the book also comes across as charming, and Butterfield wins his readers over to his side. We can even find the critic who believes that his "analytical terms are very clear, and for a historian, extraordinarily exact." The medium is strictly

Butterfieldian. When we finish reading the essay we are sure that we have experienced a distinctive and compelling personality.[16]

Butterfield may not want to attach *Whig Interpretation* to philosophy of history, but he treats topics that historians, if not analytic philosophers, would associate with philosophy of history, particularly with what we call historiography — studies produced by historians about historical discourse and the character of historical events and processes. The essay is written by a historian, addressed to historians, and designed to discuss things historians routinely deal with. The topics he raises are many — the interpretation of history, the marks of historical study, the structure and conjunctions of history, the relations of past and present, conditioning circumstances and events, personalities in history, the gap between research and the writing of general history, and the problem of making moral judgments. As a genre of writing about history, the essay belongs with *Historical Novel* and the little supplementary essays on historical thinking inserted into *Peace Tactics of Napoleon*.

Whig Interpretation displays Butterfield as the critic of a tradition, a tradition dominant in English historiography and taken for granted. Indeed it was the very historical tradition in which he had been raised from his youth. The book is not a work of detached scholarship, but an attack upon a way of understanding history that he considers untrue. Butterfield is the dissenter. In his characteristically imprecise words, he names his target: " 'the whig interpretation of history' in what I conceive to be the accepted meaning of the phrase." He adds, "At least it covers all that is ordinarily understood by the words, though possibly it gives them also an extended sense." As far as we can see, however, that name was not widely circulated currency at the time. When we crack his language open, we realize that he is telling us candidly that by his assemblage of the components of his target he had invented "the Whig interpretation of history." And when we amass everything that he designates by that name, we understand that he has criticized not any one school of historical thought, but a whole way of constructing history. Here is the closest he comes to a definition of what he wishes to attack: "What is discussed is the tendency of many historians to write on the side of Protestants and Whigs, to praise revolutions provided they have been successful, to emphasize certain principles of progress in the past and to produce a story which is the ratification if not the glorification of the present."[17] A little further along he writes, "It is astonishing to what an extent the historian has been Protestant, progressive, and whig, and the very model of the 19th century gentleman."[18] The essay is unrelenting in its assault on an alliance within historical writing of a particular kind of religion, politics, and social hegemony. The configuration that he labels the Whig interpretation rested on the rendering of the history of En-

gland as the irresistible triumph of civil and religious liberty, a discourse beneficial to the upper classes. Michael Bentley observed that Butterfield's charge
fingered a theme common to a huge mass of English historical writing, and
discounted as secondary any differences and variation to be found there.[19]

There were readers who understood the work as simply anti-Whig, an attack against Whigs by someone who is not a Whig, perhaps a Tory attack in
the tradition of David Hume. This is the reading Annabel Patterson gave the
book. Indeed there is a blatantly anti-Whig sound to the essay. Butterfield
much later would admit that he was in an anti-Whig phase at the time. It is
tempting to think that Butterfield has in mind Ranke's own campaign against
"Whiggism" in English historical writing as instantiated by Thomas Babington Macaulay's *History of England from the Accession of James the Second* in
six volumes (1848–1861). The politically conservative Ranke felt pushed by
what he regarded as Macaulay's "narrow Whiggism" to write his own six-
volume version, *A History of England Principally in the Seventeenth Century*
(1875).[20]

However, the more we read the more we realize that Butterfield is actually
attracted to the very people he attacks. He is ambivalent towards the historians of an earlier time who were political Whigs. His criticisms are there, to be
sure, but they are the criticisms of a line of thought with which he has very
close connections. He is, for instance, a Protestant, he is more progressive than
conservative, he is attached to a college modeled on the life of the nineteenth-
century gentleman. But is he Whig?

When the book appeared, Charles Smyth, a historian in Cambridge, an
Anglican cleric, and, according to Butterfield, "a hard-headed Tory," told
Butterfield that it offered no consolation for conservative proponents of a Tory
interpretation of history. Smyth observed that the proper title for the book
would have been *An Appeal from the Old Whigs to the New.* The allusion is to
the title of a celebrated essay by Edmund Burke, *An Appeal from the New to
the Old Whigs.* Burke was rejecting the New Whigs of his day, notably Charles
James Fox, whom he regarded as too liberal, and appealing from their mistaken views to the original tradition. By reversing the figures in Burke's title,
Smyth signified the young historian's Whig affinities, and suggested that Butterfield had written as the New Whig who sought to improve the old tradition.
Butterfield accepted the point. He commented, "I am complaining — at least —
I am complaining that the Whigs are not liberal enough, you see. They don't
extend to Tories in the past the same techniques of human comprehension that
they are willing to extend to the Whigs in the past." Here we have the clue to
Butterfield's perspective in *The Whig Interpretation of History.* He wrote to
reconstruct the tradition, not to revert to an older stage of the tradition,

and not to defeat it. Fox, not Burke. Butterfield emerges as the twentieth-century New Whig.[21]

Butterfield's affinities with the Whig tradition become even clearer to us when we realize who he had most in mind to criticize when writing the essay. At the time, and until the end of his life, Butterfield would say, when asked, that the aim of his attack was a defect found in the works of a whole body of writers of history, and not any particular person. In *Whig Interpretation,* he referenced the magisterial books by "great patriarchs of history-writing" and the school textbooks by lesser figures that shaped the interpretation of British history conveyed to the young. Of the "great patriarchs," Macaulay would readily come to mind, as Michael Stanford suggested, and we can imagine the histories Butterfield found on his father's shelves at home, the cast-offs from the wealthy mill owner in Oxenhope.[22]

Having thus fueled the gossip, Butterfield would then go on to admit that his special target was Lord Acton. Indeed, we can feel the personality of Acton in passage after passage of the book. But, as if he finally sensed that we would want to be told outright, Butterfield acknowledged the role of Acton near the end of the book in his characteristically indirect fashion: "It might be true to say that in Lord Acton the whig historian reached his highest conscious-ness."[23] By now Butterfield was intellectually bound to Acton, but he felt he still had to deal with the elements in Acton that troubled him, above all the issues of religion and morality in history. For Butterfield personally, *Whig Interpretation* was the public display of his inner struggle with Acton, driven by his compulsion to purify and improve on Acton. The connection between Acton and the discourse Butterfield styled as Whig strikes us as odd only because Acton differed so radically from the historian-type Butterfield pro-fessed to be discussing. Acton was a Roman Catholic through and through, and Roman Catholics are not Protestants; he was a new nineteenth-century Liberal, and not an antiquarian seventeenth- and eighteenth-century political Whig; and he was an aristocrat, much more than a mere nineteenth-century gentleman. Moreover, as Roland Hill noted, Acton himself, while not quib-bling over whether he was a Whig or Liberal, firmly believed that he "had a universal view," and flatly rejected any suggestion that he espoused "narrow Whiggism" on English history.[24] Acton exactly matched Butterfield's defini-tion on one point only: he was a believer in the progress of liberty.

Butterfield found the empirical basis for *Whig Interpretation* in his own experience of detailed historical research and especially in the subject matter of his lectures and teaching. For instance, Napoleon gets a long section near the end of the book.[25] His old favourites, Sir Walter Scott and Thomas Carlyle, are there. From his eighteenth-century studies there are Charles James Fox,

William Pitt the younger, and Edmund Burke, the Magna Carta dear to Whigs, the historian Henry Hallam as the chief Tory interpreter of the British political tradition, and the historian Edward Gibbon as the cynic against Christianity. Nicolò Machiavelli is there from the Italian Renaissance.

But these are not the big references. The running illustrations throughout the work, the themes preoccupying him, are the religious conflicts of the six-teenth century in England and France, the work of Martin Luther and John Calvin, and the question of religious liberty and toleration. His treatment of these themes derives directly from his lectures on general European history and the need to work out his interpretation of the Protestant Reformation. We find him making some reference to early Christianity, coming straight from the teaching he was still doing on the side at Wesley House. He had been teaching Methodist ministerial students in supervisions since 1922.[26] The intensity and persistence which mark his attention to religious and moral questions betray a profound personal involvement. His struggle with Acton entails working out his own interpretation of religion and the moral questions pertinent to histor-ical study. He is wondering whether he can unify his powerful religious moti-vations with his work as historian.

According to Butterfield, the Whig historians committed a fundamental mistake in the way they understood the course of human history. They studied the past "for the sake of the present." What historians ought to do is to study the past "for the sake of the past." The point came straight from Ranke, which Butterfield would have absorbed within Peterhouse from both Adolphus Ward and Harold Temperley. All other difficulties with the Whig view of history derive from this basic defect. In a moment of overstatement which we might excuse as poetic, he writes, "The study of the past with one eye, so to speak, upon the present is the source of all sins and sophistries in history."[27] Butter-field seems unperturbed by the imprecision and ambiguities of the phrase "for the sake of the past." We cannot be certain that he did not mean, for example, things such as that historians should work for the benefit of the past, or for the honour of the past, or on account of the past, or in fulfilment of the wishes of the past, although such meanings would make little sense.[28] At first glance we easily notice the continuities between what he says now and the view he expressed in *Historical Novel*. There he asserted that the historian by profes-sion should be wedded to romanticism and love the past for its own sake, in the sense of trying to live in the past or relive the past. Certainly he remains the romantic, and he easily drops a reference in his text to "the romance of histor-ical research."[29] But he has taken his thinking to another level of analysis in which his interest is not first of all romanticism, but the task of constructing historical study and understanding the workings of historical process. He has left literature almost entirely behind, and he has even let go of research for the moment. He has refocused on the problems of historical thinking and, more exactly, how historians create their discourse. We can gather more of his meaning when we think with him along such lines, keeping in mind that systematic clarity was not his intent.

By charging the anonymous Whig historians with failing to study history for the sake of the past, Butterfield sounds as if he wants to polarize past and present and opt for the one against the other. It would be easy to accuse him of creating a false dilemma between past and present, and in his actual statements he probably does. On closer reading, however, we find that his message is more subtle and complex than that. He can notice several strata. He is partly raising the question of emphasis in relating past and present. He does not complain that Whig historians and their history are influenced by present considerations, and he does not insist that present matters do not or should not impinge upon how historians understand the past. Indeed, he explicitly allows for the legitimate, albeit limited, function of the present in our study of the past. He has in mind especially being fully aware of the impact and implications of our orientation to the present, and of the need to put our accounts of the past into terms which we can understand today.[30] His objection is that Whig historians study the past "with direct and perpetual reference to the present." They overemphasize the present in their historical thinking and they organize their "scheme of history from the point of view of [their] own day." Many years later, still thinking about how English historians read the Magna Carta, he summarized his point: "And nothing is more plausible to the unthinking than a past that has been made to appear like the world that they know in their own lifetime."[31]

Using a term not in Butterfield's vocabulary we might say, with David Hackett Fischer, that Whiggish historians commit the presentistic fallacy. Whiggish history commits the fallacy of presentism. Another term might be anachronism, a term Butterfield does use, although there may be some sense and some settings in which anachronism might be technically unavoidable, as both P. B. M. Blaas and Marshall Poe suggested, in so far as historians must utilize their own language to access the past. Still another term, suggested by J. C. D. Clark and Kevin Sharpe, might be teleology. Whig history is teleological history.[32]

Butterfield means much more than this, however. In the first place, according to Butterfield, the Whig historians "turn our present into an absolute to which all other generations are merely relative." In this manner they construct their history to support the causes and achievements which they approve in English history, such as representative parliaments and what they counted as religious liberty. The effect is simply partisan history which classifies the people of the past into those who furthered the course of progress to the approved state of affairs in the present and those who hindered it. In a balanced view of past and present, studying the past for the sake of the past would mean, rather, seeking simply to understand the past, without a primary agenda in the present. If this is all there were to it, however, the point would sound innocuous and lose the need for all the energy Butterfield puts into it.

There are indeed other strata to Butterfield's complaint against the Whig view of history. By studying the past for the sake of the present the Whig historians stress the likenesses between the past and present, finding "roots" and "anticipations" and "origins" of the present in the past. On first reading Butterfield appears merely to invert the Whigs and to choose for the unlikenesses instead. But when we look more carefully, we find him suggesting that historians ought to be more astute than this.

Although he does not say so bluntly, his words amount to the message that past and present are marked by both likenesses and unlikenesses. Without the likenesses between human beings and situations of any era we could not enter into worlds and lives different from our own. But without careful attention to the unlikenesses we destroy the particularity and validity of the past. As a matter of strategy, Butterfield posits that historians ought to look first of all for unlikenesses between now and then and to see the past as if it were a foreign country. The chief function of historians, he asserts, is to mediate between other generations and our own. The aim is to seek to understand the past, to comprehend the actions and beliefs of the people in the past so well that they begin to seem plausible. Instead of asking "How did religious liberty arise?" and supplying an answer which retraces the path from then to an outcome we now approve, historians should ask "why men in those days were so given to persecution."

By putting things this way, Butterfield unwittingly illustrates the difficulty of satisfying his own criterion. He does not seem to realize that to use the word "persecution" to name certain things people did in the past is to interpret those actions from the standpoint of what he today would call "religious liberty." The authorities of the past whom he calls "persecutors" did not in the least regard their deeds as persecution, as harm done to others because of their religion. Rather, they construed their deeds as salvific acts which preserved the true religion and which might work to save the souls of others from eternal perdition.[33]

Butterfield's problem with the role of the present in the Whig historians goes further, to an understanding of how things change and the causes of the changes, to a knowledge of the transitions of history. Butterfield charges that

Whig historians oversimplify the course of change and causation by drawing straight lines from specific events and people in the past to something or other in the present, like the supposed line "which leads through Martin Luther and a long succession of whigs to modern liberty." He can detect his struggle with Lord Acton's interpretation of the history of liberty as "a work-day key to history."

In reality, says Butterfield, the course of history is crooked and immeasurably complex: "It is not by a line but by a labyrinthine piece of network that one would have to make the diagram of the course by which religious liberty has come down to us, for this liberty comes by devious tracks and is born of strange conjunctures, it represents purposes marred perhaps more than purposes achieved, and it owes more than we can tell to many agencies that had little to do with either religion or liberty."[34]

Looking into the labyrinth just a little, he observes that the process of history divides into levels and runs in currents. His observation is not precise, and he speaks in metaphors. Events and the actions of personalities are visible at the top, while underneath the surface, stirring at numerous gradations of depths, are broader and slower movements in history, all of which operate in ways interrelated with and inseparable from the whole.[35] The process moves by means of the clash of wills and the interplay of countless personalities, but also by the intersection of numberless conditioning circumstances. The process is loosely predictable only in the smallest and most proximate details, but unpredictable in the larger scale of things. Results emerge "that probably no man ever willed" and which turn human purposes "to ends not realized." Butterfield's thinking shows him holding tight to the basic effectiveness of individual personalities in history while also trying to found a place for the apparently impersonal forces and tendencies of history. In a reference to the traditional view that we should use history to teach lessons, a line of thought which we would expect him generally to oppose, he pauses to comment that perhaps the greatest lesson of history would be simply that history as a whole is utterly complex and unpredictable. He might also have added the lesson he seems continually to learn about the primary role of personality in history. We can detect the continuity of his thinking about interaction in history with the way he spoke in *Peace Tactics of Napoleon,* but now he wants to raise the complexity of history to the nth degree and, next to personality, add the element of impersonality in history.[36]

Butterfield's suggestions about past and present and the process of history lead him to think about causation. We can see him picking up Bury, turning Bury's proposals in a different direction. If historians are to speak of causes and effects, he says, they cannot isolate chains of events extending over periods of time which intersect only here and there. Again and again he stresses the complexity of history and repeatedly uses the metaphor of "entanglement." Any particular action of any single person is immediately involved with a vast network of other actions by other people, all of which conditions all of what is to happen next. Historians may be able to trace "the sequence of events from one generation to another," but they should not seek "to draw the incalculably complex diagram of causes and effects forever interlacing down to the third and fourth generations." The reference is against Bury, and he takes over nothing of Bury's talk about "laws" in history.[37]

Butterfield summarizes his alternative view of causation in a striking way: "It is nothing less than the whole of the past, with its complexity of movement, its entanglement of issues, and its intricate interactions, which produced the whole of the complex present; and this, which is itself an assumption and not a conclusion of historical study, is the only safe piece of causation that a historian can put his hand upon, the only thing which he can positively assert about the relationship between past and present."[38]

In the broadest sense, it is hard to dispute Butterfield's assertion — the whole past produces the whole present — and the grandeur of the scale of his vision is awesome. But if what he proposes is merely an assumption and not in some crucial sense also a result of historical study, we wonder why anyone should agree with him. He seems close to being overwhelmed by the massiveness and the complexity of history. He is prepared to abandon "causation" as a worthwhile category for historians. In the face of such a history, all that historians can do effectively is "to unfold the whole story and reveal the complexity by telling it in detail." If historians are to hang on to "explanation" in any sense at all, this would be it. The "last word of the historian" would be to give "a piece of detailed research." He later won support for this point from a surprising source, the analytic philosopher John Passmore. Butterfield would reject causation but hold fast to research and narration, which together would provide all the explanation we need.[39]

Butterfield did not consider the argument that retreating to research and narration does not exempt historians from dealing with the factors and results to which people refer when they speak of "causes and effects." It merely pushes the problem out of consciousness and forces historians to posit causation without thinking about it. Moreover, he did not take up the point that if the problem is the sheer immensity and the complexity of things, then even the most detailed history that historians could construct captures at best a minuscule fraction of the numberless details of what goes on in human existence.

Historians are no better equipped to recount the infinity of details of the transition from "the whole past to the whole present" than to delineate the "causes and effects" involved.

Butterfield takes a step further still in his thinking about the Whig historians who study the past for the sake of the present. He draws a distinction between historical study as researched history and as general history. He observes that the defect of the Whig historians seems most severe when they embark on general history. When operating on the broad scale of general history they tend to do history "for the sake of the present." By contrast, the fallacy seems to disappear, or nearly so, when historians go to their microscopes to conduct detailed historical research, the very thing they are vocationally suited to do. Historical study is properly a strictly limited undertaking which uses sources and weighs evidence in order to give attention to the particular, the tangible, the concrete. Historical study should keep clear of the generalizing domains of religion, morality, politics, and philosophy, and stand impartial among their various claims. Unlike these other domains, historical study should abstain from proffering general truths and general propositions which profess to have universal validity. Historical study, like travel writing, is a form of description whose subject is the events of the external world with all the relevant accidents and conjunctures included. These are the things he is now associating with a loose notion of "science" in historical study. The marvel of it all, he asserts, is that when historians conduct their detailed research and engage in their descriptions they tend willy-nilly to study the past "for the sake of the past."

Butterfield then adds a long passage on the creative use by historians of imagination, what he calls variously "historical imagination" or "imaginative sympathy" or "insight and sympathy and imagination." This imagination brings colour and passion to the study of history and enables historians to achieve understanding of the past. It gives expression to historical study as "a venture of the personality," involving the feelings and giving aesthetic delight, and it permits historians to "recapture the richness of the moments" and "the humanity of men." Butterfield affirms that imagination belongs to historical study, and reaffirms that he has transposed to historians and historical study the basic features which he used to attribute to the novelist and literature. These descriptive and imaginative functions seem, in Butterfield's thought, to correspond to what he was calling the outer and inner aspects of history and human personality.[40]

The problem does not go away in detailed research, however. Butterfield observes that the Whiggish historians always carry their interpretation of the course of the ages and their orientation towards the present around in their heads. They hold their mental presumptions about history when they commence their detailed research. Then they momentarily let go of them as they become absorbed in their detailed research. But as soon as they collect their findings they remember their initial presumptions and simply fit their findings into the preexisting bigger story of the ages. Butterfield is still trying to hold onto a space amid the details for Whig-free historiography. But he overreaches himself. If the power of the historian's presumptions of general history is as great as he admits, we may expect to see them operate, however subtly, even on the microscopic level.

Butterfield's antidote to the affliction of the Whig fallacy is to operate on two fronts simultaneously. On the one hand, historians should always aim to move "from the general to the particular, from the abstract to the concrete." On the other hand, they should construct better general histories and learn the art of the abridgment of history. He does not go so far as to suggest that general history is inherently defective in the Whiggish manner. Rather, he posits that it is possible to achieve good abridgments. Whatever their length, good abridgments would give faithful "impressions" of the complexity of interrelations of all the detail and would eschew "the selection of facts in accordance with some abstract principle." Butterfield takes a lengthy excursus to talk about how to abridge history and in the process adds a new element to his thinking about historical study. Good abridgment would respond to the results of detailed research and would yield a continuous revision of our general interpretation of history.[41]

So far the complaints we have seen Butterfield hurl against the Whig historians are the many parts of his claim that they distort history by studying the past for the sake of the present and not for the sake of the past. When we read Butterfield more closely, however, we notice that he makes another claim. The Whig historical defect rests on a fundamental flaw in religion and morality. With this clue in mind, we begin to notice his discourse about religion and morality everywhere in the book. The opening pages of the introduction and the entire concluding chapter wrap the essay in a discussion of morality and religion. The heart of the concluding chapter features his personal struggle with Lord Acton. And running through the essay from beginning to end are repeated references to religion and morality. On reflection, we understand that he does not offer the passages on religion and morality as mere appendages to his thought about history. We may say that his historical thinking and his religious and moral thought depend on each other, even though we detect a strong and enduring tension between the two. We perceive him to be involved in a new phase in his struggle to integrate his own religion and his vocation as historian.

From the point of view of morality, the fundamental fault of the Whig historians, Butterfield tells us, is that they attempt to act as judges of history and thereby to give to historical study a finality it does not warrant. This, for Butterfield, is the problem of moral judgments in history. On this issue Acton stands in the centre of Butterfield's horizon. But with this theme in mind it is easy to look past Acton to the general tradition that enveloped European historical writing as a whole, including Acton himself.

Ranke identified the tradition: history's task is to judge. In his first book, *The Histories of the Latin and Germanic Nations,* published in 1824, Ranke wrote the most famous statement of his long career. Seeking to break with the tradition, he clarified his design: "The book seeks to comprehend all these and other related events in the history of the Latin and Germanic nations as a unity. History has had assigned to it the office of judging the past and of instructing the present for the benefit of the future ages. To such high offices the present work does not presume: it seeks only to show what actually happened [*wie es eigentlich gewesen*]." We can see Butterfield taking the side of Ranke against Acton, even as Butterfield binds himself to both Acton and Ranke. For Ranke, as for Butterfield after him, the rejection of history as judge is contained in the affirmation of history as an act of self-limitation, which becomes, in Butterfield's idiom, history as science.[42]

It is not easy to understand precisely what Butterfield means by moral judgments in history and what admonition he wants to offer on the subject, for, unlike Ranke, he goes on at great length to complicate the matter. But the gist of his message is unmistakable. The Whig historians distort history by "the dispensing of moral judgments upon people or upon actions in retrospect." Midway through the essay he states his position succinctly: "Behind all the fallacies of the whig historian there lies the passionate desire to come to a judgment of values, to make history answer questions and decide issues and to give the historian the last word in a controversy. He imagines that he is inconclusive unless he can give a verdict; and studying Protestant and Catholic in the 16th century he feels that loose threads are still left hanging unless he can show which party was in the right."[43] In the final chapter, on the theme of moral judgments in history, he adds, "His [the whig historian's] concern with the sphere of morality forms, in fact, the extreme point in his desire to make judgments of value, and to count them as the verdict of history."[44] He then lays out quotations from Acton's inaugural address and the letters to Creighton. The Whig historian, he observes, plays the avenger and the judge of history and surveys the ages from his vantage point in the present. For him "the voice of posterity is the voice of God and the historian is the voice of posterity." It is in the historian's present that the conjunction occurs between the Whig historian's moral position and his interpretation of history. The effect of this interaction is to endow the present with a value greater than that of the past—indeed, Butterfield says, to count the present as final and absolute. From this moral position with respect to the present the Whig historians need take only a small step to the distortion of history by their study of the past for the sake of the present.[45]

Butterfield urges that the most effective way to avoid the errors of the Whig interpretation of history is to stop them at the source. "Above all," he writes, "it is not the role of the historian to come to what might be called judgments of value." Making moral judgments on the past is "the most useless and unproductive of all forms of reflection." He adds, "The sin in historical composition is the organization of the story in such a way that the [historian's moral] bias cannot be recognised." Moreover, historians should not seek to identify what he calls "the place where moral responsibility resides."[46]

It would be important for historians to know what Butterfield wishes to prohibit by using the terms "judgments of value" and "moral judgments in history." The actual words of his definitions seem clear enough. By means of "judgments of value" historians assess who is right in any given controversy and determine the validity of the various religions, philosophies, and ideals that people hold to. They also assess people. In like manner, historians enunciate general truths and teach lessons which they believe they derive from the tangled events of history.[47] "Moral judgments" are the most heightened form of judgments of value. They are absolute judgments that historians pronounce upon people or acts or the results of their acts. With these, historians separate good from evil, avenge wrong-doers and the wrongs they perpetrated, and reward the righteous and their righteous deeds. Like the judgments of God, moral judgments settle the matter ultimately and for eternity. They possess the finality of the voice of "History" itself.

Butterfield draws a stark picture. Ironically he seems to commit the very fault he condemns: he deals in absolutes. First he construes moral judgments as absolute, eternal, and final, the kind that can only belong to God to be delivered at the Last Judgment. Then by means of *Whig Interpretation of History* he appears to issue one long absolute moral judgment against the Whig historians. Surely, by definition, no human being should venture to make the judgments which belong to God. Indeed, no human being can. Butterfield seems not to recognize a distinction between, on one hand, rendering a judgment that is moral and, on the other, inscripturating the judgments of God. He overlooks a whole range of intermediate moral judgments. These are the utterly human and rather ordinary proximate evaluations of people and their actions past and present, assessments of what is good and what is right to do. We disagree among ourselves, across cultures, and over the ages about what these proximate judgments ought to be, but none of us has found a way of living without making them, not even Butterfield.[48]

The more we read, Butterfield's apparent clarity in his initial delineations becomes muddled. We notice that Butterfield allows what he calls "our judgments that are merely relative to time and circumstance," judgments that show, for example, "that one religion is more favourable in its sociological consequences than another" or that tell us "that a thing is good or harmful according to circumstances." On the face of it, such assessments would seem to be judgments of value. We cannot be sure where Butterfield would draw the line. His objective may be simply to drive historians away from making anything like ultimate and eternal judgments — historians ought not to judge what he calls the "ultimate consequences through time" or to weigh "material losses" against "spiritual and eternal gains."[49]

We become more uncertain when, in a separate passage, Butterfield explicitly allows historians to make judgments of value and moral judgments in the histories they produce, provided they make plain they are doing so, provided they offer them as superficial additional comments, and provided they do not organize the structure of their history around them.[50] Judgments of value and moral judgments are the direct expressions of what he regards as the historian's "personal bias," and as such they are not intrinsic to historical study and do not belong in it. The preferred stance is for the historian not to make them. The next best option is for the historian at least to write them in a different colour so the readers may easily find them and deduct them from the rest of the text. Butterfield seems to have in mind the comments historians make that seem the most blatantly editorial, and to underrate the degree to which everything historians write is in some sense structured according to their moral perception of history.[51]

We become even less sure of what Butterfield wants us to avoid when we notice that throughout the essay he himself makes what we would routinely regard as moral judgments about people and their actions. These moral judgments do not take the form of additional comments. They structure his history. For example, he repeatedly refers to the "sins and errors" of certain people in the sixteenth century, and calls their behaviour "religious fanaticism." These are terms of moral judgment dependent on Butterfield's own present valuations. He allows the historian to do the following: "he can give evidence that Napoleon lied, that Alexander VI poisoned people and that Mary Tudor persecuted; and to say that one man was a coward, or another man a fanatic, or a certain person was a habitual drunkard may be as valid as any other historical generalisation." Butterfield calls such language "description of a man's characteristics, the analysis of a mind and a personality," but it would be hard for us not to notice that it is very much the language of moral judgment. Some of his judgments are against acts and some are against people. All of the key words in the passage — lied, poisoned, persecuted, coward, fanatic, habitual drunkard — are morally loaded and presume moral norms in Butterfield's present which Butterfield believes those people violated, whether in their acts or their character. For example, in order to say that Napoleon lied, Butterfield has had to see in Napoleon's words a violation of norms about telling the truth which he regards as applicable to Napoleon. To call a man a fanatic would be to say that he has internalized in his character the violation of norms against absolutizing some human purpose. What Butterfield calls "description" doubles as "moral judgment."[52]

Butterfield finally ruins our ability to discern what his injunctions against moral judgments intend to exclude when we study a lengthy passage detailing his version of the rise of modern liberty.[53] We come to realize that he is just as interested in the history of liberty as Acton and the Whigs. We also notice that he contravenes his own most explicit admonitions about the structure of the narrative. He organizes the whole structure of his account around a fundamental moral judgment in the present and then distils general truths from his version of the story of modern liberty.

Here is how he works. As the dissenter, the nonconformist, he believes that it is right to treat religion as a matter for voluntary, private, and individual expression, and that the best provision for religious liberty in society is to accommodate a plurality of such religious expressions. He also believes that it is wrong for society to establish the religion of the ruler as the only acceptable religion of the land. Accordingly, he believes that British society in his own day comes closer to enabling such free expression of religion than sixteenth-century European societies. Then, by taking his present-day view of religion and religious liberty as the moral norm, he can, against his own stringent advice, tell us how we got from then to now, and how, for example, the Politiques in France "helped the cause of liberty."

Moreover, he is able to derive from his version of the story two general "truths," something he alerted us not to do. These are the truths: first, if one generation plays havoc with religion, the next will devote themselves to securing religious peace; and second, provided the religious destruction in the former generation is not total, the new generation will find ways to turn the old disasters into good things, or as he enunciates the truth, "there is no sin or error or calamity can take place but succeeding generations will make the best of it."[54]

We soon realize that Butterfield has constructed his own version of the history of liberty, and he has done so according to the structure of his own dissenting Methodist moral judgment, which privileges voluntarism, personal belief, and independence from the state and rejects whatever is contrary to these. If there were heroes to be found, they were the Dissenters and Catholics who continued to worship God their own way in the face of domination by the Church of England. *The Whig Interpretation of History* emerges as a dissenting Methodist book.

What does Butterfield think is wrong with making moral judgments in history? We can find his answer in the midst of the long section on Lord Acton in the final chapter.[55] Two of his criteria come directly from, and are peculiar to, his view of historical study which we already know about. In order to find these points compelling, we would have to agree with his version of historical study. First, making moral judgments exceeds the limits of the competence of historical study, a study which deals with the past by finding and weighing evidence, describing particulars, and so forth. If others, like philosophers and religious thinkers, wish to render moral judgments about history they should do so after the historians finish their work, and the moral judgments such people would make should remain external to the history. The historian, Butterfield asserts, "stands impartial between Christian and Mohammedan," and "any history that he writes ought to be as capable of varied philosophical interpretation as life itself seems to be." Historical study should be kept separate from political ideology, religion, and philosophy. In this context it is curious to note that Butterfield is not saying that moral judgments as such are inappropriate or wrong, merely that historians should not make them.[56] Second, making moral judgments undermines historical study by cutting off at least half of the procedures of history, notably the use of historical imagination which leads to historical understanding. When historians dispense moral judgments, historians have failed to show us the people and their acts sufficiently well so that we are enabled to understand them and thus to see that what they did was entirely plausible under the circumstances. This sort of understanding "actually disarms our moral judgment." Butterfield does not take into account in this context whether, after we come to understand the people of the past in this way, we might be able, or still want, to render a moral assessment of them or their actions or the effects of their actions.

Butterfield's remaining criteria do not relate directly to his view of history, but derive from his view of human personality and God. And again, we would have to accept his understanding of personality and his allocation of moral judgments to God in order to agree with him on these points. First, making moral judgments about others intrudes upon "the secret recesses of the personality where a man's final moral responsibility resides." Presumably, Butterfield would not object to any person rendering moral judgments about oneself.

Second, moral judgments, defined in the absolute terms he has laid out, usurp the role of God, who alone could make "ultimate judgments upon the things which are happening in time." These last two criteria would bar anyone, not just historians, but even philosophers and religious thinkers, from making moral judgments about other people and their actions. And if moral judgments belong to God alone, no one would be right to make any such judgments, not even about oneself. Underneath his actual statements against moral judgments — that is, if we can understand Butterfield — we sense there lies one of the primal injunctions of the New Testament. The Gospel of Matthew gives these words as a saying of Jesus in his Sermon in the Mount: "Judge not, that you be not judged. For with the judgment you make you will be judged, and the measure you give will be the measure you get." The Gospel continues: "You hypocrite, first cast out the log from your own eye, and then you shall see clearly to cast out the splinter from your brother's eye." Butterfield accepted the message of Jesus as utterly binding and sought to implement it to the full.[57]

In the midst of his discussions, Butterfield alludes a number of time to "Providence," and we begin to notice the prominence of the term in his discourse. Keith Sewell has argued that the notion of Providence becomes a defining feature of Butterfield's historical understanding.[58] Butterfield quotes the classic sentence in St. Paul's letter to the Romans which Christians traditionally have repeated as the definition of divine Providence: "We know that all things work together for good to them that love God."[59] He applies the sentence to human action and the historical process. He attaches Providence to one of the "truths" he had discovered in history. A new generation, he says, is "for ever playing providence" and making "all things work together for good" when they take even the disasters of the old generation and turn them into something creative. This they do even with calamities as horrific as the Black Death and the Fire of London. Butterfield believes that the very complexity of the historical process may be understood as the instrument of "some providence that guides the destiny of men." The process of history shows us that the ways of Providence are "mysterious" and "how strange [are] its caprices." If we want to be grateful to anything for religious liberty in the modern world then we might "choose to be grateful to that providence which turned so many conjunctions to our ultimate profit." In all the subtle mediations of history, such as, he says, the transition from the medieval world to the modern world, Providence is at work. There is, says Butterfield, "the history-making that is going on over men's heads, at cross-purposes with them, . . . that historical process which so cheats men of their purposes — that providence which deflects their labours to such unpredictable results."[60]

Butterfield's allusions do not add up to a theology of Providence, but they do signal that he has Providence on his mind and that he is prepared to adapt the traditional Christian belief to his understanding of historical process: interactive, complex, nonlinear, unpredictable, supra-individual. This is the first time he has written about Providence, although he did mention Providence as an illustration in *Historical Novel* in 1924.[61] Once again he sings in unison with Acton whose inaugural address contained ample reference to Providence. We remember that he had been thinking about Providence at least since the mid-twenties when his father lost the job he had held for a couple decades, but, surprisingly, soon received a new and better one with another textile mill. It was for Butterfield a case of good emerging out of bad. We may be sure that he heard about Providence from his youth in the Methodist chapel in Oxenhope as well as from his father.

Running through what Butterfield tells us in *Whig Interpretation* we detect a tension between two apparently contradictory beliefs about the world which he holds simultaneously: the world is basically a duality of the material and the spiritual, and the world is ultimately a unity. The world as duality informs his distinction between the realm of morality and the realm of history, a distinction upon which his view of history depends. The one is the "lofty moral realm" and the other is the "realm of historical explanation." If we scan his discourse with this duality in view, we can collect many pairs of terms which suggest the range of the two realms. The realm of history treats things material, relative, temporal, external, public, human. The realm of morality handles things spiritual, absolute, eternal, inner, private, God-like. History belongs to the one realm while philosophy, political ideology, and religion belong to the other. We recall that he has professed this duality for at least as long as we have the sources enabling us to glimpse his thinking. His point against moral judgments by historians amounts to saying that historians should stay in their proper realm.[62]

But at the same time Butterfield also tirelessly reaffirms the contrary belief in the ultimate unity of all things, unity beyond the duality. We sense his stress on unity in what he tells us about the importance of seeing the whole of the past, the role of general history, the centrality of personality, the workings of Providence, and so on. But all that vehemence against the Whiggish fallacy and all that passion against moral judgments in particular make us sense that there must be more to it than meets the eye so far.

When we look deeper, we detect the drive towards unity at precisely the moment when he most emphasizes the duality. It works like this. To head off moral judgments by historians he accentuates the difference between history and morality, between historian and moralist or religious thinker or politician, and he warns against interjecting morality into historical study. However, as soon as he does this, he begins to sound amoral, as if there is a realm in which morality does not apply. He quickly recoils from the possibility, and stresses the ultimate unity of all things. The world is moral through and through, and so is historical study.

Butterfield promotes what can only be described as an explicitly moral program within historical study. We feel his desire to preach animating his delivery of the message about the moral task of the historian. The message comes in two parts. First, "Judge not, that you be not judged." This we have already heard. He implores the historian not to act as the judge and avenger of history, as did Acton. We do wonder whether his intensity on this point might not betray that he is tempted more than he would admit to issue moral judgments in the manner of Acton.

Then he moves on the second part: "Be reconciled to each other." The historian can be the reconciler. Far from excluding morality from history, the historian may choose a better moral program. Butterfield proposes an improvement upon Acton. This is the message with which he opens and closes *Whig Interpretation:* "one can require that he [the historian] shall be still more godlike, and regard himself rather as the reconciler than as the avenger; taking it that his aim is to achieve the understanding of the men and parties and causes of the past, and that in this understanding, if it can be complete, all things will ultimately be reconciled." He continues: "But if history is in this way something like the memory of mankind and represents the spirit of man brooding over man's past, we must imagine it as working not to accentuate antagonisms or to ratify old party-cries but to find the unities that underlie the differences and to see all lives as part of the one web of life." And still further: "It must be remembered that, by merely enquiring and explaining, he is increasing human understanding, extending it to all the ages, and binding the world into one. And in this, rather than in the work of 'perfecting and arming conscience', we must seek the achievement and the function and the defense of history."[63] Butterfield writes as plainly as he can so we will not mistake that he understands historical study to be a moral undertaking. We hear his affirmation of the unity of life and the interconnectedness of all things which he has been expressing all along. He has found the intellectual means to unify his desire to preach and his vocation as historian. The historian is a reconciler. The means is the reconciliation of the opposites at a higher level than first perceived.

But, almost as if he is about to be found out as the Methodist preacher in the fenland, he affixes a codicil to his energetic sponsorship of the historian as reconciler. "History is all things to all men," he writes, and if we are to personify history at all, "it is best to treat her as an old reprobate, whose tricks and juggleries are things to be guarded against." With this he retreats to the safety of his strict construction of historical study as merely an act of description supplemented by imagination. We watch him vacillate.[64]

We sense that he manufactures the problem by interposing a division in the wrong place, between history and moral engagement, as if history were not moral and moral engagement were not historical. He overlooks other ways to make the distinction he is searching for: the difference in genre between the moral essay and the history book, or the vocational difference between the ethicist and the historian, or the difference in modes of discourse between the moral and the historical. In a world that is at once both thoroughly moral and thoroughly historical, the ethicist, the philosopher, and the theologian might focus on moral considerations while drawing upon historical inquiry as a resource, and the historian might focus on the study of history and in so doing engage moral concerns.

In *The Whig Interpretation of History* Butterfield has assembled his own view of history. We may style his discourse religiously as dissenting Methodist and politically as New Whig. In spite of the narrowness of the title of the essay, he has managed to settle his thinking about a wide range of things — individual personality as well as impersonality in history, historical process and historical study, research and general history, duality and unity in history, morality and religious commitment, Providence in history — and he has fastened on religion, politics, personality, and liberty as historical themes. He has found a way to reconcile his opposing vocations as historian and preacher by uniting them at a higher level in a type of historical study with a new moral message. Not least, the book gave him something to say to the world. For him the last two years had been creative, even though he had accomplished no research.

As for the response of others, the volume was not widely reviewed at the time. The reviews he did receive were usually brief and full of criticisms about his writing style, the vagueness of his argument, the lack of examples, or the blundering title.[65] Butterfield later said that he claimed no infallibility for the title of the essay, suggesting that the tendency to interpret history as a success story in favour of one side or another in the present may well be due to a general trick of time perspective which entrapped Whigs and Tories, Protestants and Catholics alike. He had linked the tendency to the Whig historians because he thought that others at the time usually associated Whigs with the views in question.

If attention outside Cambridge was negligible, within Cambridge his little book made him instant food for gossip at college high tables. It seemed obvious in Cambridge that the young Peterhouse don had assailed the great Trevelyan, Regius Professor of Modern History. Butterfield later recalled, however, that even at the time he had insisted that the person he had in mind was Acton, especially in the last chapter on moral judgments. He certainly had not singled out Trevelyan. "I was so much a friend of Trevelyan," and Trevelyan was, he said, "the only man amongst us who was a great man." In any case it is curious to see how much of what Butterfield said in *Whig Interpretation* mirrored a passage written by Trevelyan in his essay "Clio, a Muse" in 1905, even down to the reference to the Whigs, although he went well beyond Trevelyan in his definition of the problem. David Cannadine suggested that Temperley put Butterfield up to writing the book against Trevelyan as revenge for Temperley not getting the Regius chair. But Temperley was not a factor. Vellacott was his confidant, and Temperley was not in on the project. More important, the suggestion misses the historiographical impetus driving Butterfield's thinking at the time. And, as John Fair pointed out, the book could just as easily be turned on Temperley who, along with the rest, converted English history into the story of the inevitable rise of liberty.[66]

Whig Interpretation, in 1931, made him a celebrity in his own house, though not beyond. One by one, people within Cambridge confessed that Butterfield was right about a distilled version of his message: interpreting history too simply in light of the preferences of the present day produces distortions in historical study. The event changed his life, but only in Cambridge. We must be careful not to read the future tale of the book, twenty years later, back into the 1930s. In Cambridge people now knew him as someone to watch, a provocative writer about history, a don who might one day get a professor's chair. But historians ambitious to be professors needed to give themselves to important research projects, not to essays. Both Butterfield and the gossips wondered what his might be.

4

General Horizons

Fox

Butterfield had not yet begun his search for a major project when in early December 1931 he received a resolute offer from an unexpected source. As he recalls the story, the venerable Trevelyan had just read *The Whig Interpretation of History* and found it disturbing. Trevelyan summoned Vellacott to his rooms in Trinity College. "I am the last Whig historian," he declared, pacing the room, and asked if the book was directed against him. Vellacott persuaded him it was not. Vellacott would have known that Acton was the target. But he also would have known of Butterfield's paper on Charles James Fox in which he criticized Trevelyan's handling of Fox in *Lord Grey of the Reformed Bill*. That was the episode that had started him thinking about the problems he eventually discussed in *Whig Interpretation*. Then, too, Trevelyan's *History of England*, published in 1926, was undoubtedly Whig in Butterfield's sense. Butterfield did indeed later explicitly classify Trevelyan as a "Whig historian." Nonetheless, Vellacott's assurances put Trevelyan into a better mood. In the course of the conversation that followed, Vellacott mentioned in passing that Butterfield as an undergraduate, ten years earlier, had referred to a youthful fantasy of writing a biography of Fox. It happened that Trevelyan was intending to write the life of Fox, and, indeed, had in his possession a large body of Fox letters. This cache of letters once belonged to Lord John Russell, who had used them to write his book on Fox published in 1866. The letters then passed to George Otto Trevelyan, Trevelyan's father, who published a book on the early Fox in 1880. Butterfield had known of Trevelyan's plans for some time and had long ago dismissed his fantasy of writing on Fox.[1]

Very soon after Trevelyan and Vellacott talked, two large crates of Fox papers arrived unannounced in Butterfield's rooms in Peterhouse. Trevelyan had sent them, together with the insistence that Butterfield should write the biography. Butterfield was overwhelmed. He confessed years later, "I accepted the new proposal as though it were the voice of God." From this moment onward Trevelyan became his utterly loyal friend and ardent promoter. Butterfield now began to say that he was writing a biography of Fox. That was 1931.[2]

The Fox biography became the second major research project assigned to Butterfield by someone else — Napoleon and Tilsit from Temperley, and now Fox the English Whig from Trevelyan. The Fox project would require Butterfield to continue giving primacy in his historical research to the study of one man, to personality, and to the politics of the few at the top of the affairs of state.

Butterfield claimed that the appeal of Fox was not necessarily his Whig politics. As a youth he had learned to associate Fox with the advent of English freedom, but now, having just finished *Whig Interpretation,* he was ambivalent towards the Whigs and even Fox's Whiggism. It was Fox as a personality whom he found exciting and endearing. He recalled years later, "I had found him such a rich and attractive and lively human problem." Butterfield first did research on Fox as part of his extra work for *Peace Tactics of Napoleon.* In a passage written around 1928 in still florid prose, one of many sections he had expunged from his oversize typescript, he portrayed Fox's personality and behaviour: "A strange patchwork of clashing colours makes up the life and character of Fox. The fashionable youth with the feather in his hat, the spoilt child of aristocracy, the leader of the Marconis parading London streets with red-heeled shoes and blue hair-powder, spent himself in wild endeavors to hurry and anticipate democracy, came to lead a revolt against the eighteenth century pride of dress, waged war on the wig and the cocked hat, and earned a reputation for slovenliness. . . . One might call him the fortunate profligate with a rich erratic genius in him, burning at times through his clay, but coming out in broken and partial lights. . . . He is a standing paradox, and flaunts himself at history, and catches a romantic eye."[3] Butterfield felt the attraction of what he called, around 1935, Fox's "independent spirit."[4] As early as 1922 he intimated in his diary that he felt some attraction to Napoleon as an independent spirit, which must have animated him throughout the long years of

research on Napoleon. In *Peace Tactics,* he portrayed Napoleon in large, heroic, and romantic terms, a man of genius who broke free of the confinements
built by society around him.[5] Fox was an even better subject than Napoleon
because he was more subtle and had no cast of tyranny about him.[6] It may be
that Butterfield became attached to rakes and rogues, as Maurice Cowling
suggested, and perhaps he came under the spell of Fox's charm, as Ved Mehta
heard him say. He certainly liked people who refused conformity with the
expected social and political stereotypes.[7]

We are reminded of the Butterfield of 1926 — the romantic, the dissenter —
who, after returning from America more independent than he had been a year
before, uttered his complaint against the social and academic conventions
around him in Peterhouse and Cambridge: "The whole cloak of respectable
life is cumbersome to me, the repressions, the conventions, the shams, the
humdrum evasion of momentous issues." In the 1930s, even with his intensifying loyalties to Peterhouse, he still found Cambridge socially and academically
stultifying.[8]

This, together no doubt with a certain measure of rising ambition, made
him quite prepared to leave Peterhouse. He was thirty-five when he went for
an interview in January 1936 for appointment to the Woodrow Wilson Chair
of International Politics at University College of Wales in Aberystwyth. He
was one of four candidates interviewed out of forty considered. The professorship went to E. H. Carr, then forty-three, and Butterfield settled in further at
Cambridge.[9]

Butterfield knew from the start that Fox would take him a very long time.
He realized by now that he was a very slow worker who laboured over the
research as well as the writing and rewriting. But he also complicated things
for himself and made things take longer than perhaps they needed to. First, he
chose to make the biography a complete life, covering a span of time and a
range of subjects infinitely greater than the few months and limited themes of
Napoleon's diplomacy that had occupied him for seven years. Second, he
intended to produce a work of archival research, in place of one based on
other people's books and the published letters. Third, he decided to make his
research comprehensive and exhaustive, greatly increasing the sheer bulk of
material he intended to seek. He proposed to consult the archives and papers
of all the important families and government officials touched by Fox's life.
Fourth, he persisted with the microscopic method he learned from Temperley
for use on published diplomatic correspondence. This required him to move
minutely through the sources and correlate his findings by theme and date.

Butterfield was capable of driving himself to all this extravagance by extending his own theory and practice. But the recent example of Lewis Namier's

two new books on British politics in a period during Fox's lifetime must have added enormously to his research expectations. Namier set a far higher standard of thoroughness for research in the papers of members of the English Parliament than anyone before, and it would not be hard for Butterfield to feel that he could scarcely do less.[10]

Butterfield probably started his research on Fox in 1932. He began first in Cambridge University Library, which held all the published papers he needed. Certainly by September 1933 he was working in archival material in the Manuscript Room of the British Museum in London. It was not easy for him to work in London for long stretches of time. He could manage a day-trip to London only now and then during term. Between terms and during the long vacation in the summer he could occasionally put together three days at a time, rarely a week. He researched steadfastly during the 1930s, becoming most intense between 1936 and 1939. His library shows that he acquired a large number of rare books published in the eighteenth century.[11]

Butterfield's papers contain abundant evidence of his research style in the 1930s. He applied to Fox the method he had learned from Temperley for research in diplomatic documents. He had come to think that method was normative for any historical research. During his research forays he would add up note upon note and copy out letter after letter. In the days before photocopies and microfilms, this took much time. He gave up the 4″ × 6″ cards he had used for Napoleon and worked instead with great quantities of 3½″ × 5½″ slips of paper, which he manufactured by folding and tearing larger sheets. On each slip he put a different bit of information. He proceeded collection by collection — the Liverpool Papers, the Egerton Manuscripts, and so on — and gathered notes around periods and episodes. In 1933 he was looking for information about Fox in the 1770s and early 1780s. He focused on the years 1779 and 1780 fairly quickly, probably as soon as 1933. He would go over the letters and newspapers in their day-by-day sequences, make excerpts and notations on the slips, collect his slips from various sources, and bundle them by dates and themes. From the many sources, he was collating all the overlapping evidence inch by inch. Before he had finished collecting information on something, he would compose brief narratives, trying to create a story about whatever episode caught his attention. The narratives would give him a structure within which to place further information. As soon as he gathered more material about an episode he would often write a new narrative. He was thinking by writing and constructing the history piecemeal as he went along.[12]

At the same time he felt compelled to work out the interrelations of the Fox story with the larger political and intellectual story of England. If his use of the slips of paper tended to atomize the information, his narratives forced him continuously to shape and reshape the information into a story, and his connection of the Fox strand with the other strands forced him ever outward to the still larger story of English politics. He was working through the interconnections of incidents to an episode, of small episodes to larger episodes, and of large episodes to whole stories. He tended to think narratively and integratively, even as he gathered countless bits of material. The more microscopic his research, the more interconnections he pursued with the wider affairs of English public life. In *Whig Interpretation* he had praised the quest of the innumerable details of history, but he had also proclaimed the doctrine of the entanglement of all things in history. Now in the course of his historical research he seemed to drive himself to extremities in both directions — details and complexities without end.

Butterfield produced no book on Fox by the end of the decade comparable with *Peace Tactics* at the end of the 1920s. The gossip network and Butterfield's reputation were such that he had two publishers already asking for his Fox book.[13] His historical method yielded one very small publishable result after five years, "Lord North and Mr Robinson, 1779," once again for the local *Cambridge Historical Journal,* which appeared in 1937. The article dealt with a minuscule subject from the very brief period he had selected for his initial investigations, and it was not about Fox. It signalled that he was not getting very far in his research or in his construction of a narrative, and that he could easily be distracted from his primary subject.[14]

One thing led to another as he followed out the entanglements of Fox. He had already produced another very brief article, published in the local *Cambridge Review* in 1933, entitled "Bolingbroke and the 'Patriot King.'" It too was not about Fox but was related to the wider political ideas of Fox's day, starting from 1760. The article was a study of the immediate history of a political idea. The idea, promoted in pamphlets at the beginning of the reign of George III, urged that the king, acting as a patriot on behalf of the realm as a whole, was the best agent to defend the nation's liberty against challenges from any one party within the nation. Butterfield traced the idea to an early eighteenth-century political treatise, *The Patriot King,* by the Tory politician Viscount Henry St. John Bolingbroke, and argued that Bolingbroke's thesis lay behind George III's image of himself. The article shows us that Butterfield, at least as early as 1933, was contemplating the question of the intentions of George III at the commencement of his reign in 1760, and that he was already concluding that the new ruler intended to play the "patriot king."[15]

Butterfield chased the question about George III further. During 1935–1937, he mounted a special course of lectures to undergraduates, "George III and the Constitution, 1769–82," the period of the ministry of Lord North. He took as the centre of his analysis the issue of the political system and the intentions of George III. In keeping with his style he wrote out the lectures in detail and read them to his undergraduate listeners. He included Fox in the lectures, but only as one actor among many. He broached large questions: human personality in history, the structure of government, the emergence of party politics and an opposition, and repairing the damage done by the Whig interpretation of history.[16]

Butterfield's pursuit of Bolingbroke led him on a tangent even farther away from Fox, and brought him, of all places, to Nicolò Machiavelli, the early sixteenth-century Florentine. Machiavelli had been on his mind at least since the time of *Whig Interpretation,* where Machiavelli makes a couple of appearances.[17] Or perhaps it was Napoleon who led him to think about Machiavelli in the later 1920s. He worked references to Machiavelli's influence on Napoleon into a little biography of the French conqueror, entitled *Napoleon,* which he published in 1939 as his fourth book.[18] Or then again it may have been Acton who drew his eye to Machiavelli. Acton had published a succinct and provocative introduction to Machiavelli for the Oxford edition of Machiavelli's *Il Principe* in 1891.[19]

It was George III who drove his interest now. Butterfield presented a paper on Machiavelli in Cambridge in January 1938. He developed the thesis that behind Bolingbroke's *Patriot King* lay the influence of Machiavelli's *Prince.* The suggestion disturbed him. There was a large discrepancy between the malevolent behaviour apparently recommended by Machiavelli for Italian princes and Bolingbroke's espousal of the intervention of a patriotic English king on behalf of the common good of the English nation. Butterfield turned his pursuit of the problem into his fifth book, *The Statecraft of Machiavelli,* a 167-page study issued in 1940 by Bell, the publisher of *Whig Interpretation.*[20] Most of the book discussed Machiavelli as a thinker, but Butterfield eventually wound his way back to Bolingbroke in the final chapter. He concluded that the English thinker had managed to purge the sinister elements from Machiavelli's model for princes and had created in its place the image of a king who imposes limits on himself, chooses against corruption, and acts in favour of the good of the nation.[21]

As if to remind himself of why he had spent all this time on a figure so far removed from Fox, Butterfield closed the book on Machiavelli with what amounted to an appendix on George III's intentions as king at the start of his reign in 1760. He suggested that George III did loosely adopt the idea of the "patriot king" as his model at the start of his regime. As part of the evidence, he took a document brought to light by Lewis Namier, a letter from the king to the Earl of Bute, and gave it an interpretation opposed to Namier's. In this letter, said Butterfield, the king lamented that, although he wanted to restore well-being to the country, he was trapped in a political system controlled by government ministers who achieved their ends by fighting corruption with more corruption. It was a picture of a leading personality who willed to act for the good, but who was constrained from doing so by an entangling system. The image represented a modification of the model of freely interacting personalities in history that he had constructed in his version of Emperor Napoleon and Czar Alexander alone on a raft in the river at Tilsit.[22]

His excursus during the 1930s into Fox's entanglements had taken him far enough away from Fox for us to notice that his work on George III had become a pursuit in its own right. In the process he had reached a conclusion from his immersion in empirical details which stressed the power of political and social systems to impede the free operation of personalities in history.

General History

Butterfield's lack of progress on Fox during the thirties troubled him, since, on his own view, to be a historian and a writer required him to produce history books based on minute research. If his method guaranteed that his work would be slow and if his historical interest was easily diverted, his decisions to involve himself heavily in other things also gave him less time for his research on Fox. He spent much time on his activities in Peterhouse, on his domestic life, and, above all, on his lectures in the History Faculty. In the process his thinking about general history continued to enlarge.

In Peterhouse Butterfield's success with *Peace Tactics of Napoleon* and *Whig Interpretation* added to the college's still growing reputation for history. With the addition of Professor Barker and the promotion of Temperley to the new professorship in modern history, Peterhouse now boasted two professorial Fellows listed in the History Faculty. When Vellacott left Peterhouse to go to Harrow School as headmaster in 1935, Butterfield surfaced as the senior history Fellow, still teaching undergraduates in supervision and still examining in the entrance examinations. He still served actively as librarian, and his voice counted for more in the affairs of the college. To maintain the history complement after Vellacott's departure, the college elected M. M. Postan a Fellow in history in 1935.

The new Master of Peterhouse, Field-Marshall William Riddell Birdwood, elected in 1931, was a military man, the only master in Butterfield's time who was not a scholar. He did, however, support the college reputation in history and, because of his frequent absence, allowed the Fellows to run the place. His military service embraced nearly fifty years in India, and like Lord Chalmers before him, he brought stories of the British Empire and non-Western culture into the senior common room. He enjoyed connections with the royal household and eventually received the title of baron in 1937, a year before his death.[23]

Throughout the 1930s Butterfield's reputation as an undergraduate supervisor soared. College teaching kept him in touch with all the areas of the Cambridge history syllabus. He continued to supervise about ten undergraduates in history per week throughout the academic year. His pupils were all young men. Brian Wormald, his student from 1931 to 1934, described his methods. Butterfield tried to soften the hard style of Temperley, but he offered a different shock of his own. For each weekly supervision the student would write the mandatory essay, which Butterfield would read and discuss, never offering much in the way of praise or blame. He tried to practice his belief that the supervisor should exercise a concern for the whole intellectual development of the person, and not merely mark the student's paper for the week. His approach followed a pattern. After reading the essay, Butterfield would make a plausible point that was exactly the opposite of whatever the student had written. This created a set of opposing positions. He would then move the discussion towards a revision of the student's initial thinking and the reconciliation of the opposites at a higher level of thinking. Wormald testified that he "turned everything upside down, everything was different from what you thought, everything became more complicated." The effect was that the student could not be sure he knew what position Butterfield himself was taking on any question, and the whole approach could seem perverse.

The method adapted one of Acton's strategies. As Butterfield put it, Acton sought to lay out and argue for the views of his opponents better than they did for themselves, much in the way "an actor will try to assume the mentality of Hamlet on one night, and Macbeth on another night." The student might go away thinking that he did not know when to trust that Butterfield meant what he was saying. Wormald recalled that he had come to regard Butterfield "as the arch-liberal and arch-sceptic." Over the longer haul, in the cases where the method worked well, as with Wormald himself, the student would begin to feel Butterfield's impact as "gentle steering." Some students must have felt continually undermined. The aim was bring the young men to make decisions for themselves and to cultivate the drive that took them beyond wherever they were when Butterfield met them.

Wormald also spoke of Butterfield's effectiveness as lecturer. Although he would read his lectures word for word, he sounded as if he were talking personally to each one in his audience. Although his voice was soft and his manner mild, he radiated an energy, an intellectual interest, and a moral intensity that could feel powerful and utterly captivating.[24]

Butterfield had no research students in the 1930s, but he sometimes discussed history with other people's students, whose number was increasing. William O. Aydelotte was Temperley's student, but felt severely bruised by Temperley's behaviour towards him and apparent lack of intellectual support. He went to Butterfield for help and found Butterfield kind and easy to talk with. J. H. Plumb was Trevelyan's doctoral student at the time, but felt severely neglected. He recounted how he gravitated towards Butterfield, eleven years his senior, whom he found willing to talk frequently and for long hours, sometimes into the night. Plumb recalled, "He was brilliant, exasperating, devastating, mischievous, mixing in equal quantities malice and generosity. He dragged his principles before my enraged and bloodshot eyes with the skill of the matador. He forced me to reconsider every idea I had; I got better at defending myself, and through Butterfield I gradually knew that I would never truly belong to the profession of history. I loved yet distrusted Butterfield's impish qualities, his almost electric versatility at times daunted me but his major principles — the deep belief in the role of Providence (Christian of course) in human history — left me, in the end, bored as well as disbelieving." Plumb felt that as a matter of method Butterfield sought deliberately to heighten whatever point he was making "in order to provoke the inevitable outburst, for deep down he loved to shock, to be contrary." Plumb received the Cambridge Ph.D. in history, a member of the early set to do so. In effect the Ph.D. replaced the practice, which Temperley himself had followed in 1925, of submitting published work for the honorary Litt.D. awarded by Cambridge.[25]

At home, Butterfield's life changed completely with the birth of three children, all boys, during the 1930s — Peter in 1931, Giles in 1934, and Robin in 1939. For twelve years he lived with at least one child under the age of five at home. The capitalist economic depression in the thirties scarcely affected him. His income from Peterhouse and the university was secure and rising. In due course Pamela and he decided to send each of their boys to private schools in Cambridge. Peter and Giles attended the Leys School, founded by Methodists in 1875, and Robin went to St. Faith's School, founded for the sons of Cambridge Fellows in 1884. Both were located off Trumpington Road not far from Peterhouse. They affiliated with each other within a joint foundation in 1938. The social style of the two schools was many notches down from that of the grand English "public" schools, such as Eton and Harrow. Methodists with money were not Anglican elite, and Cambridge dons were not wealthy, but the schools still served to set the boys socially apart from the rest of the school population. The Butterfields followed the example of many around them, including Temperley, who had sent his son to St. Faith's. The decision to send their sons to private schools was costly in financial terms, but it had the merit of giving them the presumed social and educational privileges which Butterfield felt he had missed in his own education in Keighley at the nondescript Trade and Grammar School for the sons of capitalists.

Before Peter's birth, the Butterfields moved into a flat owned by the college on Tennis Court Terrace. They moved to Belvoir Terrace in the mid-thirties. By the end of the decade they managed to purchase a comfortable high-Victorian attached house, named Chistlehurst, at 89 Tension Road. They acquired the domestic services of Ethel Wolfe, a former neighbour from a college flat on Tennis Court Terrace, who worked for them as cook and daytime housekeeper. The emblems of Butterfield's modest gentleman's status — or in the changing terms of the 1930s, his upper-middle-class position — were all suitably affixed. All the same, he refused to assume an elevated social manner, but retained a simple life-style that left him accessible to his father and the ordinary folk of Oxenhope. He continued his regular attendance at Wesley Church and gave more time to his piano playing.

Butterfield's "General European History" lectures in the History Faculty stimulated his interest in thinking about the most general horizons of history. The work on the lectures animated his creativity far more than his research on Fox. Even with *Whig Interpretation* behind him, he continued to think about the problems of general history. He handwrote his lectures at home, working into the night, sometimes through the night, for delivery in the morning. Each lecture took an hour, in some years at 11 on Tuesday, Thursday, and Saturday, in other years at 9 on Monday, Wednesday, and Friday. He went on like this for eight weeks per term during all three terms of the Cambridge year. That amounted to seventy-two separate manuscripts on general European history in the course of the year.

When he received his full appointment to the History Faculty for 1930–1931, he was one of twenty-four University Lecturers in history, together with seven Professors, among a total of forty-five names on the History Faculty list. Temperley was lecturing on antecedents of the First World War, and Vellacott on the history of political thought. Trevelyan treated English constitutional history from 1688 to 1832, while George Kitson Clark, who had joined the faculty in 1929, lectured on English constitutional history since 1485. Previté-Orton and G. G. Coulton handled the medieval segments of general European history, and E. A. Benians and W. F. Reddaway each lectured on the modern segment of European history, parallel with Butterfield.

The tradition at Cambridge that Butterfield inherited in the lectures on modern history reflected the curriculum common to universities in Europe, the British Empire, and North America. The dominant model for the study of history meant concentrating on wars, governments, and diplomacy, with the occasional reference to the church in relation to the state. The attention went to the eye-catching man at the top, the extraordinary war, and the exceptional treaty or negotiation. These were the things that the tradition ranked as most important in history.

The list of lecture topics contained standard items — the Renaissance, Martin Luther, the Thirty Years War, the War of Spanish Succession, Frederick the Great, and so forth. The method of study depended chiefly on published documents produced by the foreign ministers, the diplomats, and the heads of the states in question. The tradition understood modern history as the history of Europe, and construed Europe primarily as the network of interactions among the larger states of the continent. Europe did not include England, or Great Britain, except in so far as Britain participated in the interactions among the continental states. General English history belonged to a separate track of lectures and focused on the constitutional history of the British state. The modern period began in 1492 or 1494, with the French invasion of Italy, and ran to a date near the present — the finish line was continually moving and had now reached the end of the Great War. Cambridge broke the lectures into two courses by dividing the modern era around 1715, before and after the Treaty of Utrecht. Preceding modern history thus defined was medieval history, which ran from the coronation of Charlemagne in 800. Such other histories related to Europe as were taught in Cambridge were dispersed elsewhere. For instance, ecclesiastical history as a distinct subject was lodged in the Divinity Faculty, literary history appeared in the literature faculties, and intellectual history primarily surfaced in philosophy or political thought. Economic history became firmly recognized as a subject only with the establishment of a professorship in the field in 1928. Social history was not taught as a field, and neither was the history of science.

At first Butterfield more or less accepted this constricted tradition and even helped to perpetuate it.[26] He agreed to join a publisher's project promoted by Methuen to produce a three-volume set of documents representing the Cambridge version of European history to students in the sixth form, the last year of secondary school before university. He edited the third volume in the series, *Select Documents of European History, 1715–1920,* published in 1931. The other two, also by Cambridge lecturers, were R. G. D. Laffan's on 800–1492 and W. F. Reddaway's on 1492–1715. Butterfield's selection consisted almost entirely of diplomatic and other government documents, and included nothing or next to nothing on industrialization, new social class formations, religion, science, technology, and intellectual trends. The volume seems not to have been reviewed, and we do not know how widely it was used. We do know that Butterfield began to abandon the interpretation of European history that he promulgated in it almost as soon as the volume appeared.[27]

Butterfield's reflections on general history led him gradually to reject, at least in theory, the dominant historiography which featured the great leaders and the great events in diplomacy, war, and national politics. In doing so he blended with a general tendency among historians in Europe and North America during the 1930s. In France the work of Marc Bloch and Lucien Febvre, and the *Annales d'histoire économique et sociale,* the journal they founded in 1929, promoted a widening of the subject matter and methods of history. In Great Britain the work of Arnold Toynbee and the first volumes of his *Study of History,* from 1934 onwards, stimulated more comprehensive thinking about history. In North America the movement was associated with the series of volumes under the title *The Rise of Modern Europe,* edited by William Langer, which, beginning in 1934, discussed all aspects of the history of European society since the Italian Renaissance.

Butterfield's movement towards a wider view of the subject matter of history began after the publication of *Whig Interpretation,* in his early thirties, for there is no hint of such breadth in that essay. He did not launch a program that was well conceived from the start, but he thought about things as they came up when he worked on his lectures. Butterfield eventually formulated an attack during the 1930s on the inheritance of diplomatic and political history. In the 1950s he looked back on this moment with pride, exaggerating how early in his life he had taken action against the dominant model. "From my youth," he wrote, "I made continual protest against the kind of European history which chiefly occupies itself with the external relations of the various states." He attributed the dominance of foreign affairs and war to "an educational routine," and belittled the notion that people truly believed that such things were the most important matters of European history.[28]

His emerging historiography disclosed by his lectures featured four elements, all aiming to reconstruct the general history of modern Europe on a more comprehensive basis. The first three elements were closely related, and they derived from influences very close at hand. He was still receiving his primary inspiration from within the small world of Cambridge.

First, he endeavoured to remove the nation as the basic unit of the general history of Europe and to replace it with a vision of Europe as a whole, an interactive unity which transcended the mere interrelationship of the several individual states. His inspiration came specifically from doctrines propounded by Acton. One was the idea from Acton's inaugural address that modern history should be represented as an organic unity. The other came from Acton's preface to the *Cambridge Modern History,* where he defined general history as the study of the affairs and characteristics held in common throughout Europe.[29]

Second, Butterfield extended the geographical range of Europe beyond the customary emphasis on the western European nations. He aimed to embrace all of Germany, Scandinavia, Poland, the Slavic states, Greece, the Ukraine, and Russia. Here he had for his teacher Temperley, whose first love was central Europe and the Balkans, but he also had his own two years of undergraduate study of medieval history, which, under the influence of Bury, embraced everything eastward to Russia and Byzantium. He had come to believe that if a historian of modern Europe approached the modern period by way of medieval Europe, rather than from his own position in the present, the meaning of Europe would naturally widen geographically and the concept of the unity of Europe would look more plausible.

Third, he proposed to revise the periodization of modern European history by relativizing the importance of 1715. He wrote a paper for the History Faculty, probably in 1935, which argued that the division of the modern era at 1715 was detrimental to an understanding of the whole period. He urged dropping the two-course sequence and installing one course to cover the centuries from 1492 to the Great War in a unified fashion.[30]

Butterfield's fourth point was more radical. He began to construe Europe as a "civilization," or a "society," shifting the focus away from the importance of nations and states. He was not precise about his terms. The strategy was to be inclusive. His notion of a civilization, or a society, now stressed the integration and interaction of the many elements of life — politics, diplomacy, thought, art, religions, economics, society, geography, and science. This broad construal seemed to coexist with the view of civilization he had expressed in the mid-1920s. At that time he had represented civilization as the intellectual and spiritual superstructure which had the power to raise the "economic needs and animal instincts" of the substructure of life to a higher synthesis.[31]

The sources of his thinking on this point were still centered in Cambridge. To some extent he was probably following Acton. He had also heard Temperley argue for the inclusion in history of aspects of life besides international diplomacy, and he was sympathetic with the drift of Trevelyan's ideas about social history.[32] He acknowledged the influence of G. N. Clark's study of seventeenth-century England which constructed English society as a unity and described all together the various facets of the society in that age. His interest in the history of science as part of the totality of civilization may have been stimulated by the successes in science at Cambridge University. He once suggested that it was during the 1930s that he began to notice the colossal scale of the impact of science on society.

He did begin to look a little beyond his parochial environment, to new resources outside Cambridge. We may attribute his absorption of a wider meaning of the term "civilization," in the sense of the totality of human experience and culture, to his reading of Toynbee, *A Study of History,* volumes 1–3, which he discussed in 1934. He praised Toynbee's volumes as "the most remarkable work of the year."[33]

We may suppose that at some moment in the 1930s he heard about the efforts by the French historians associated with the *Annales.* Butterfield's reconception of the general history of Europe looked similar to what Bloch and Febvre propounded in one important respect, notably their aim to construe society, indeed human history, in terms of totality that went well beyond the traditional limits of political history. However, we have no reason to think he was reading the new French histories at that time. He was not at all thinking about the social sciences which the French historians were reconsidering under the aegis of historical study. He commented much later that his own views were entirely in agreement with those of Marc Bloch's *Apologie pour l'histoire, ou Métier d'historien,* and he enthusiastically welcomed the publication of the English translation of the book under the title *The Historian's Craft.* His views in the 1930s on the reconstrual of European history were well ahead of the journal *Past and Present,* founded in 1952 to work in Great Britain within the tradition of Bloch.[34] We can detect the barest hints during the early 1930s that he began to doubt the validity of thinking of the state as a real social unit, drifting instead towards the view that individual personalities are the only real existents. The more he conceived of the state as actually unreal the less he would think of concentrating as such on states as historical units. Because of his studies in the Italian Renaissance, he knew Jacob Burckhardt's *Civilization of the Renaissance in Italy* and the interpretation of the Renaissance which integrated politics, philosophy, literature, society, gender, economics, religion, and many other aspects of life.[35]

The role of Marxism in his reflections became crucial in the 1930s. He acknowledged in general the impact of Marxist discourse on his shift towards a more comprehensive understanding of modern European history. He was already primed by his own sense of the complexity and interconnections of history to accept some tutelage from Marxists about the workings of society. His experience of aggressive capitalism and money-conscious materialism in America in 1924–1925 had left him convinced of the reality of the material conditions of life. Then some of his students at Peterhouse in the early 1930s induced him to think earnestly about Marxism. They were turning towards

Communism as a plausible alternative to both capitalism and Nazism. The defects in capitalism became evident to him during the world economic depression in the 1930s, and the authoritarianism of Nazism became visible with the accession of Adolf Hitler to power in Germany in 1933.[36]

During the academic year 1932–1933 Butterfield received a request from F. R. Leavis, editor of a Cambridge-based literary journal, *Scrutiny,* to comment on the value of Marxism for historical study. He took the invitation as the prod to read Marxist historical writing. Most notably he read the Russian historian and theorist Georgi Plekhanov and the young British economist-historian Maurice Dobb. Plekhanov was known in English at the time for *Fundamental Problems of Marxism,* published in London in 1927. Dobb was Butterfield's exact contemporary in Cambridge, a lecturer in political economy since 1924 and author of *Capitalist Enterprise and Social Progress,* published in 1925. Both writers advanced a materialist view of history while at the same time giving credit to ideas and individuals. We may suppose that Butterfield read some writings by Marx himself, although if he did, he gives no hint of it. The writings of the Marxists impressed him, which seems to have surprised him. He applied to the Marxists his by now habitual reconciling method. He discovered the things he liked about Marxist discourse and noted the things he refused, and he turned whatever he absorbed from the encounter into his own thinking.[37]

In March 1933 Leavis's journal published Butterfield's "History and the Marxian Method."[38] The receptiveness to Marxism which the article displayed further enhanced his position as dissenter within the Cambridge environment. Butterfield posits a division between Marxism as a method for the study of history and Marxism as an interpretation of history. He concludes that the Marxists are more successful with their method than with their interpretation of the course of history. It is remarkable how much of what he praises about the Marxist method he takes to be consistent with the views he expressed in *Whig Interpretation.* By use of their method, he writes, the Marxists are able to show how the work of individuals is forever complicated by historical processes which transcend them. They rightly see how history proceeds by interaction and dialectic, even conflict, and not by straight-lined logical development. They teach us how to take society as the unit of historical study and how to perform "a deeper structural analysis, a closer study of the inter-relations between the various departments of life." They show us that civilization rests on an economic and material base, and that this base, and not the government or ideas, requires recognition as primal within historical interpretation. As a consequence, they remind us of the power of "conditions" in history, the elemental limits operating upon intentional human action.[39]

The defects of Marxist historiography appear, he asserted, when Marxists convert their method into an interpretation of the course of history. The result is exaggeration and oversimplification. They deny the reality of anything other than the material, interpret everything as due to economics, devalue individuals, ignore the power of ideas, reduce history to a story of class struggle. They make their admirable method subservient to a materialist philosophy of life. He signalled that he knew the Marxists themselves would not accept the dualism he created out of their approach to history, since he knew that what he saw as two was for them a unity. Cowling took the essay to be "the outcome of an unconscious compact which Butterfield had made with those of his pupils who were sympathetic to Marxism" to keep them within the bounds of the sort of historical study he himself promoted.[40]

The transformation of Butterfield's discourse about general history and the reconstruction of his lectures did not come swiftly. It took him the decade of the 1930s to work out his new ideas. It is likely that from the very start of his lectures on general European history, in 1929, he began to implement the conception of Europe as embracing both the British Isles and greater Russia. He may have begun to work with the notion of Europe as "organic" at the same time, stressing the features of Europe that he regarded as common to all of its parts. He may have brought the history of science into his lectures as early as 1931 or 1932. His notes show that he was reading the history of science in the mid-1930s, and it looks as if he composed whole lectures on the subject at that time.[41] He may have added something on economic and social history around 1933 and 1934, after he read the Marxist historians. In 1934 we find him for the first time criticizing another historian for neglecting the economic conditions of society. The subject of his criticism was Benedetto Croce's idealist work *The History of Europe in the Nineteenth Century.*[42]

In 1935 he was elected to the board of the Faculty of History, taking the seat vacated by Vellacott. He immediately began to work towards a formal change in the periodization of the general European history course. By 1938 he succeeded in getting the History Faculty to adopt a new regulation along his lines which redefined the conception of the course and the corresponding undergraduate examinations. He wrote the 1938 formula, which emphasized the treatment of modern European as a civilization having within it countless interactions among religious, political, intellectual, social, and economic movements.[43]

Butterfield produced his lectures under various titles which mirrored the migration of his treatment of the subject. From 1929 until 1935 the faculty retained the traditional rubric "General European History." From 1935 to 1937 it was "Modern European History, 1492–1715." Next, for 1937–1938, it became "Modern European History, 1492–1648," with the Peace of West-phalia as the terminus. Then under the 1938 regulation the title changed to "Development of European Civilization, 1492–1789." Butterfield supplied the new title and created a revised course of lectures over three terms befitting his theory. He achieved only some of what he wanted. The new terminal date cut off the entire nineteenth century as well as the Great War. Nonetheless, the designation served him adequately, and he used it until 1944, when he discontinued his lectures after his election as Professor of Modern History. In later years Butterfield made the claim that he was chiefly responsible for transforming the conception of modern European history in the Cambridge curriculum. He was aware that his work was part of a general trend in historical study in the 1930s.[44]

When we look at the topics of his lectures in the 1930s, even after he had implemented all his changes, we are struck by how little he actually changed. The old topics persisted, indicating the remarkable power that the traditional construction of European history had over him: the Renaissance, the cult of Antiquity, the Reformation, Martin Luther, the Thirty Years War, the War of Spanish Succession, Frederick the Great. Even when he consciously sought to transform the subject, and in spite of his own advice in *Whig Interpretation,* he retained the old interpretative structure and merely inserted a few new topics next to the old ones. Notable among the new topics were several lectures a year on the history of science, and a few on historical geography. The lists of his titles as well as the lectures which survive in his papers show no obvious coverage of economic and social history and only the barest reference to economic and social factors, although the record of his lectures is not complete.[45]

Scientific History

The importance that Butterfield began to give to the history of science in his lectures accompanied a new willingness to think about historical study as a science. He had behind him the tradition of Acton and Ranke, who spoke of historical science in the German sense of *wissenschaften,* by which they meant chiefly the methodical gathering and criticism of source documents. He knew well Bury's view that historians could render their histories scientific by employing the concept of the law of cause and effect in their explanations, although he rejected the idea. In *Whig Interpretation* he showed no interest in the notion of history as a science as such. He referred only in passing to the legacy of Ranke with the comment that historians have "placed upon a scientific basis only one aspect of their study — the use of sources and the weighing of evidence."[46]

It was his encounter with Marxism that pushed his thinking further about history as a science. He begins to talk in earnest about scientific history. It is noteworthy that nowhere in the *Scrutiny* essay on Marxism does he mention the Marxist claim that their method is scientific, and he avoids reference to the claim made by some Marxists that what makes their method scientific is their discovery and application of the laws of history. Nonetheless, he broaches the issue of scientific history in the opening lines of the essay and then returns to it in his conclusion. After he has finished absorbing what he can from Marxist historiography, he surprises us by mounting a defense of scientific history. If, as he thinks, he can disconnect the method of studying history from the interpretation of history, the Marxist objection notwithstanding, he goes a step further to disconnect these two together from the notion of scientific history.

To do this he employs the metaphor of a journey in suggesting how scientific history relates to interpretations of history. At the start of the journey are the many interpretations of history populating the world. As samples he mentions Marxist, Roman Catholic, Whig, and Bourgeois interpretations. He agrees with the Marxists in regarding the Bourgeois view as the interpretation governing modern capitalist society. These interpretations differ from one another from the start, in that each privileges a different particular element in life as the key to the whole of history. In the case of the four views, they feature, respectively, the class struggle, the church, English liberty, and property-owning individuals operating in the market. These interpretations each tell a different overall story and make the connections among the details in different ways. Next on the journey come their different historical methods, which provide guidelines about what to do and see in their research. But then, when they engage in the actual historical research, they cease to differ, and they all use precisely the same techniques of research, which are universal for all: document search, criticism, and so on. The work of research becomes a process of multiplying details, overlaying the original thesis with "a thousand complications," and submitting the initial formulae to "drastic re-visualization." Finally, at the end of the journey comes the history produced. He continues: "And at their highest, Marxist and Whig will end by laying out very much the same piece of detailed history on a given subject—though they will speak in different terminology and move in a different order of ideas. It would be wrong to imagine that it is only the bourgeois system that can refine itself into what we call scientific history. For in the end both Marxist and Bourgeois must learn that the interpretation which they regarded as the verdict of history was itself neither more or less than the assumption which they brought to their study of history; they must learn that in our interpretation of history we begin under the tyranny of our own present." We hear the echo of his words in *Whig Interpretation* about how historians explain things by simply adding more and more detail, and about the dangers of reading the past from the perspective of something valued in the present. But he is saying more here. Scientific history enables historians to surpass their differences in interpretation and to achieve a *single* outcome. No matter what their initial interpretations of history, the procedures of research and the details produced will be, in the end, the *same* for all historians.[47]

Once he has said this, the doubts set in. As a matter of observation, it would appear that the actual histories written by Marxists, Roman Catholics, Whigs, and Bourgeois are not at all the same in the end. Adding more detail seems simply to reinforce, rather than transform or eliminate or surpass, the interpretative structures inhabited by Marxist, Roman Catholic, Whig, or Bourgeois historians. Butterfield's notion that his account of scientific history defines the universal method which produces universal results for all historians is simply his notion, one interpretation next to all the others. And his interpretation represents just another value from the present thrust upon the past. Butterfield knows this. He immediately encloses his statements about scientific history in modifying language. Maybe the Marxist is right that "we never really abandon" our interpretations, maybe most historians never really become scientific historians, maybe those who become scientific historians really do so only "within the detail of some restricted field," maybe we never really escape operating out of allegiances in the present. Under the circumstances, he is saying, perhaps the best we can do is to accept the reality of difference among historians, drop the ideal of a common history, and simply welcome the Marxists to the scene. At least the Marxist interpretation might rejuvenate history by starting from a more recent present and comporting better with our modern society than the more antique Catholic, Whig, and Bourgeois interpretations. When we finish reading the final paragraphs of Butterfield's essay, we realize that his list of "maybes" has undermined the force of his assertions about the universality of scientific history.[48]

Butterfield goes on nonetheless to extend the divide he puts in position between the interpretation of history and scientific history. Scientific history should be set off not only from the interpretations of history provided by Marxists, Bourgeois, Roman Catholics, and Whigs, but also from their religious convictions, philosophies of life, and politics. As he sees it, Marxist "materialism" is a philosophy of life which, like religion, provides devoted Marxists with a fundamental orientation to all of life and guides the course of their lives. It is a presupposition about the universe and not an outcome of historical inquiry. As such it ought to be kept rigorously separate from scientific history, which consists of careful research. Scientific history is, in effect, neutral to religion, philosophy of life, and political ideology.

Butterfield's proposal relies on the assumption that it is a simple matter to set philosophical, religious, and political presuppositions to one side when engaging in historical study. Applying the assumption to Marxism, he shows how to do it. The Marxist insistence on being "materialist," he says, can be released from any philosophical statements about the character of the world, and reread to mean nothing more than the urge to be "matter-of-fact" in accessing things material in historical study. As he wrote in *Whig Interpretation,* in contrast with religion, the historical method as such is equipped by definition to treat things material, external, and concrete, and to do so by accumulating more and more details. The term materialist may be understood, says Butterfield, to "signify nothing more than the modern scientific method in historical study." Butterfield has performed a word trick. His reading of Marxist materialism misses the point of the Marxist claim to scientific history, which does not mean at all what he means. It obliterates all that is special to the interpretation, and tries to reduce it to his view of things material and the character of scientific history. He removes the sting of a Marxist interpretation of history.

In *Scrutiny* he co-opts the Marxist notion and calls what he is saying materialist: "And if God is at the back of everything, still the historian cannot say so; and if transcendental ideas are behind the rumblings of nature or the tides of human life, still they do not come within the reach of historical evidence; and though the materialist explanation of the universe may not be a full explanation, or really an explanation at all, still it is the only kind of historical explanation that our apparatus enables us to give. Concerning man himself it may be said that the historian can never reach the essence of him; for the historian can only study him in his external relations, his overt acts, his interplay with the environment." Butterfield is overstating his position when he claims that the historian's apparatus can give us merely a materialist explanation. He declines to mention his deep convictions that a person is a whole personality and that everything is interconnected, and he omits the role of imaginative sympathy, which he said in *Whig Interpretation* enabled historians to go beyond the merely material and gain entry into the interiors of other people. In other words, he keeps quiet about the unity of life. At the moment, while engaging Marxism, he needs to stress the duality of life, the polarity of the material and the spiritual, in order to establish the separateness of scientific history from religion, philosophies of life, and politics. His drive is to take from a Marxist interpretation what he can, even as he rejects the rest. We realized that we are witnessing his reconciling method at work. We also see the dissenter in operation as he tweaks the British establishment by his display of sympathy for Marxism.[49]

During the 1930s, after this encounter with Marxism and while he created his lectures on the history of science within modern European history, Butterfield continued to meditate on scientific history. It was during his study of Machiavelli, quite apart from Bury and even the Marxists, that he faced the question of laws in history, or at least the phenomenon of historical maxims. The bulk of *The Statecraft of Machiavelli* consisted of an analysis of Machiavelli's method and contribution to what Butterfield regarded as the scientific study of politics. His analysis rested on a careful collation of Machiavelli's various writings — *The Prince, The Discourses, The History of Florence,* the letters — and not merely on the much disputed *Prince.* He took the position that saw continuity in thought running across all the writings and counted *The Prince* to be more akin to the other writings than not. He argued that the same maxims and the same "scientific statecraft" recurred throughout the corpus.[50]

Approaching Machiavelli as the historian, Butterfield detects the presence of unintended and even unrecognized consequences. Machiavelli's intentions, he argues, were to bind himself firmly to Greek and Roman antiquity and work entirely in the manner of the ancients, without the slightest inkling of performing something new. Machiavelli wished simply to discuss the "lessons of history" and by deduction to identify the maxims which might prove useful to a prince desiring to achieve or retain power in the state. However, says Butterfield, in the process of doing this, Machiavelli stumbled upon something quite new, what came to be designated as the modern method of inductive thinking and the modern use of history for the scientific study of political action.

When Butterfield speaks of Machiavelli's "science," he has two notions in mind. The first would have been recognizable to the man himself. Using the terms of Pasquale Villari, Machiavelli's early biographer, Butterfield contends that, to Machiavelli, science would have meant "the demonstration of precepts relating to political action." The purpose of this sort of study was to identify specific precepts — or maxims — pertinent to public life, and then to collect them for the benefit of the state. The appropriate use of these maxims would grant to rulers the power to control certain kinds of events previously believed to be products of mere chance.[51]

How were the maxims demonstrated? At this point Butterfield shifts his focus and introduces a second notion, which Machiavelli would not have understood. He contends that Machiavelli goes beyond merely finding maxims in the writings of the ancient authors, and that quite without intending it he engages in a different kind of process, thinking by induction. Machiavelli happens on a method that later became a mark of modern science. Science in this modern sense referred to the methods of inductive analysis and the knowledge derived thereby. Butterfield depicts Machiavelli as a gatherer in the field of history, picking up instances of certain kinds of political happenings and then submitting his findings to comparative analysis. For example, Machiavelli found many cases of conspiracies against rulers, compared them all, and perceived in them causes, sequences, and consequences that happened whenever a conspiracy occurred. Butterfield calls this mode of reasoning induction. The statement produced by Machiavelli at the end of this process of thinking is the "maxim." The maxim is a generalization, put in the form of an implied or explicit conditional clause using "if . . . then." The maxim could serve to guide the ruler when he wished to avoid the conditions which made for a conspiracy.[52]

Butterfield finds examples of the appropriate maxims in *The Discourses*. Machiavelli offered maxims such as the following, found in a famous chapter on conspiracies: "it will be found generally that they [conspiracies] are made either against the country or against the prince. . . . In the first instance we will treat of those that are aimed against the sovereign and examine the causes that provoke them; these are many, though one is more important than all the rest, namely, his being hated by the mass of the people. . . . A prince, then, should avoid incurring such universal hatred; and, as I have spoken elsewhere of the way to do this, I will say no more about it here." The reference to elsewhere, says Butterfield, is to *The Prince*. The generalization is about types of conspiracies and recurrent causes. The form of the statement is an implied conditional, that is, if a prince wishes to prevent a conspiracy, then he should avoid incurring such universal hatred. That is the maxim. The maxim bears the marks of one variety of what in Butterfield's time was often called a "law."[53]

Ostensibly, Butterfield is merely providing a historical description of Machiavelli's thinking. But he is also bringing himself to affirm the validity of the comparative analysis of recurrent events as a method of constructing useful historical knowledge. In modern hands, Butterfield concedes, the method "may lead to the discovery of quasi-technical political maxims, which are valid, humanly speaking, and are of practical use." He recalls his engagement with Marxist historical thought in the early 1930s, and, under the impulse of Machiavelli, now half-acknowledges a major subject which previously he had avoided, namely the Marxist claim that their history is scientific by virtue of their dealing with the laws of history. He writes, "And the Marxists have made an interesting extension of Machiavelli when they have gone to history to learn the science of insurrection, the mechanics of subversive activity, and the wider doctrines of revolutionary strategy." Butterfield is cautiously exploring the themes of lessons and laws in history, but he strains not to mouth the word "lesson" or even "principles," and he is certainly not ready to speak of "laws" in history. So far he is willing to admit nothing more than that the concept of science embraces what both Machiavelli and the Marxists do when they think about history. Does scientific history include working with the idea of historical laws? At this moment he does not say.[54]

The Statecraft of Machiavelli is a history book of sorts, but it is also an exercise in thinking about historical discourse. In particular, it is the first time at length in print that Butterfield has discussed the notion of the scientific study of history. Equally important, he has added a new particle to his understanding of history as a science: the notion of "maxims." He has also made Machiavelli a fixture on his scholarly horizon.[55] By the end of the 1930s, as a product of his engagement with Marxism, Machiavelli, and the history of science, he has securely placed the notion of scientific history in his portfolio of historical language. And he means by the notion more than Ranke and the careful search for and criticism of documents.

Projects

Butterfield's work during the 1930s added substantially to his local reputation. Throughout the decade he filled five or six invitations a year to present papers to the historical societies of various Cambridge colleges. He became a founding member of the university's inter-faculty committee on the history of science in the mid-thirties and helped persuade the university to authorize weekly lectures on the history of science in 1937. He continued a member of the History Faculty board from 1935 onwards and was elected to the degree committee. He became acting editor of the *Cambridge Historical Journal* in 1936, and then in 1938 he succeeded Temperley as the second permanent editor of the journal, greatly increasing his stature.[56] Except for occasional visits to Oxford as an examiner during the mid-thirties, Cambridge continued to absorb his life and interests.

In 1939 Cambridge University Press, aware of his successes, approached Butterfield about writing a book in connection with his lectures on modern European history. At first the Press had in mind a sixth-form textbook. Butterfield showed little interest. After some thought, the Press returned with a different invitation. They asked him to write *The Concise Cambridge Modern History*. The reference to Acton's great idea was inescapable. This time they excited his imagination. He signed a contract on 8 December 1939 to produce 450,000 words, amounting to two huge volumes, due at the Press by 31 December 1942. Butterfield's modern history would parallel a medieval history by Previté-Orton, now the Professor of Medieval History. The work would allow him to go beyond Acton. He could make his own contribution to the reconstruction of general history.[57]

The 1942 deadline was not as unrealistic as it might seem on the face of it. When he agreed to the contract he knew he had other writing projects already on his table, but he had reason to believe that he could resume, indeed was resuming, the productive practices he once followed during the 1920s. Writing at top speed, he had just completed *Napoleon,* his little biography of the French emperor published in 1939. He had in his hands a nearly finished manuscript for *The Statecraft of Machiavelli,* targeted for publication in 1940. Moreover, he already possessed a tall stack of manuscripts for his lectures on general European history, virtually a first draft of the *Concise History.* For the sake of his commitment to general history he convinced himself to put aside his research on Fox in order to "write up" his lectures as a book.

Butterfield's life swiftly became more complicated than he foresaw. When he signed the contract for the *Concise History* in early December 1939, what we came to call the Second World War had already begun. The Germans had already annexed Austria and annihilated the Czech state in 1938. Now, in 1939, they rolled their armies into Poland on 1 September. The French and British responded by declaring war on Germany on 3 September. The Russians invaded Poland on 17 September, then imposed their domination on Estonia, Latvia, and Lithuania, and on 30 November invaded Finland. We can be amazed that Butterfield agreed to the 1942 deadline at such a moment. Neither he nor the Press understood the magnitude and intensity of what was happening. He did complete *Statecraft of Machiavelli* by January 1940. But then in February 1940 the war moved westward, and the Germans soon conquered Norway and Denmark. By May they conquered the Netherlands, Belgium, and Luxemburg, and invaded France. British forces retreated from Dunkirk on the coast of France at the end of May and early June. Italy entered the war against Britain and France. By mid-June the Germans took control of France. In July they conquered the British Channel Islands of Jersey and Guernsey. In August they bombed mainland Britain. Butterfield's little world collapsed. There was no longer time to pick up his manuscripts for the *Concise Cambridge History,* and the war raged on.

Patriotic History

Quietism

The movements leading to the Second World War in the 1930s as well as the war itself directly affected Butterfield's work as historian. Throughout the thirties, while he continued his research on Fox and produced his lectures on general history, he felt the expansion of his world horizon. He began to shift his attention away from his narrow fixation on the notable Cambridge historians who had inspired him. He reflected on world affairs and read a wider range of historians.

He felt most disturbed by the cacophony of voices in England and on the continent of Europe proclaiming their conflicting truths for the world. The voices he heard were many. There were his students advocating Marxism from the early 1930s, and upholding the Soviet Union as their example. There were the Nazis staging their rallies in Cambridge to trumpet Adolf Hitler's rise to power in Germany. Butterfield attended a Nazi rally on Parker's Piece in Cambridge in May 1933 to witness their appeal for himself.[1] There were the advocates of the Spanish Republicans and the advocates of the Spanish Phalangists. There were the capitalists who, in spite of the economic depression after 1929, put their trust in the revival of their markets and businesses and banks, and heralded the good life. There were others devoted to family, and still others committed to fun and drink and sex. There were the political parties in England — Conservative, Liberal, Labour, Communist, and the rest — offering their solutions for the desperate ills of the country and society.[2]

Butterfield responded to this chorus of certainties by trying to articulate what he regarded as basic in life. We find him expressing his convictions in religious terms in two brief statements in his diary from 1932 and 1933. One of these amounted to a profession of faith in which he made affirmations of God, personality, and a spiritual universe, beliefs he had held for a long time: "For if we have a passion it is better that this should be for God than for country or business or family. If we have an obsession it is better that this should be for spiritual things than for sex or liberty or war. If we have an aim it is better that we should desire to rescue personality and open to men's minds a spiritual universe than to promote a political cause or a party programme. If we have a certainty, a pole-star for our minds, much better fix ourselves on God than on anything in this world of endless mutation."[3]

The other statement added affirmations of the necessity of inward piety and outward charity towards others: "To live a life of piety is inwardly to trust God and often to have communion with him and also to place one's treasure in heaven. The fruits of this are contentment and reconciliation within the self, and the acquisition of inner life — the building up of a fund of spiritual resources, and the deepening of personality. The blossom is in charity that overflows to all men, and in a life that is lived humbly in the world. In all this there is something very difficult for sophisticated men. And it is utter foolishness to those who are worldly wise."[4] With these statements Butterfield signalled his ever more resolute attachment to a philosophy of personalism, an ethic centred on personal spirituality and interpersonal morality. His words mirrored his ever more conscious practical abandonment of matters connected with politics, the economy, and society. He found in his personalism the resources for dissent from any political party and program whatsoever. His ethic took the form of a quietism that left the world free for the reign of the status quo and the counter-certainties of others.

He voiced these things in his diary. It was a message consistent, we may suppose, with his preaching on the Methodist circuit since his teenage years. Now, however, he began to doubt whether he should try to preach his piety at all. In his diary for 1933 he admitted to an inhibition against preaching arising deep within him: "A lover who misjudges can be borne; a lover who lapses into infidelity may be forgiven; but one who speaks of his mistress with vulgarity can never be allowed, for his sin is a spiritual one. I think perhaps a Christian should talk little of his religion lest he fall into this sin. It is the part of a spiritual man to be austere with his thoughts and to know what is fitting. . . . I think that the best evidence of Christianity in the heart is quiet assurance, and a flame that burns in silence, and a charity forever expressing itself, forever unexpressed; and with these a serene orderliness and a calm reliance on providence."[5] His reflections passed from sexuality to spirituality and back again. A high doctrine of personality was his central tenet. But now doubts arose in him that he could not suppress. He began to wonder whether the defects in human personality might not outweigh the glory of human beings. The implication was clear. The defects might challenge the doctrine of divine creation itself. In his diary he was frank: "I should like to know whether the universe was created as a magnificent stage on which human beings were to play out their lives, or whether men are but the bye-product, the accident of cosmic processes, perhaps representing or containing in themselves some disease, or implying a derangement in the cosmic processes; perhaps they only signify different ways of looking at the same thing."[6]

His reflections induced less certainty about his warrant to preach. He took fewer engagements for lay preaching on the Methodist circuit in the early thirties. By 1936 he allowed his lay preaching to lapse altogether. His appearance as a Friday evening preacher at Wesley House in June 1936 could well have been his final sermon. He allowed his name to remain on the list of lay preachers on the Cambridge circuit, however, and there it stayed until he died forty-three years later. We should be clear about what happened. Ceasing to preach in public meant no slackening of his religious motivation or his commitment to worship or his quiet loyalty to the Methodist Church. He continued his teaching of ecclesiastical history at Wesley House, continued his support of the Wesley Society for undergraduates in the university, which he had began doing in 1933, and attended Wesley Church as usual. He went home to Oxenhope at least once a year and stayed close to his father and his Methodist roots.[7]

Butterfield meditated on the questions of morality and history which had occupied him in the last chapter of *Whig Interpretation* in 1931. He filled his diary with his thoughts and wrote little "thought-essays" to himself. He read a paper, "History and Ethics," to the Cambridge History Club in February 1936.[8] Acton was still the prod, but now he contemplated public events around him. He particularly disliked the outcry in 1936 against King Edward VIII because of his relationship with Mary Wallis Simpson, a divorced American woman with no aristocratic standing. Butterfield interpreted the episode as a prime case of self-righteousness.[9] He occupied his mind with the problems of making moral judgments against people, with the harm resulting from what he began to name as "self-righteousness," and with the inescapable presence of sin in everyone. He began with himself. He contemplated his own behaviour and thoughts, and had new feelings of his own ability to sin. The issue was not abstract for him, and his feelings affected his historical thinking about moral judgments.[10] His reflections mingled thoughts of sin, sexuality, and understanding. He was frank about himself: "I can see in myself all possibilities of sin except — homosexualism. One may condemn heartlessness; but, if one understands, one will scarcely condemn a man for the mere contravention of the customary code in matters of sex."[11] In another entry, he wrote of sin and charity: "The supreme sin in a Christian is to refuse understanding to sinners. When my own sins come home to me, how can I feel other men so sinful as I know myself to be? And in any case must I not have an eagle's eye to my own sins, and charity towards the sins of others?" His awareness of his own proclivities, and his sweeping condemnation of himself gave impetus to his admonition to understand others and not to play the judge.[12] Butterfield's comments on the universality of sin, starting with oneself, and his emphasis on the sin of self-righteousness appear to date from this period in the mid-1930s. The belief in human sinfulness occupied a secure position in the creeds of the Christian religion, and Butterfield would have known this from his youth, but now he began to place such an emphasis on the doctrine that it became hereafter a characteristic feature of his historical thought.

Without a pause he expanded these reflections on moral judgments and personal behaviour to politics, notably to the Fascists: "I do not defend the Fascists for being violent; but I wish that the enemies of the Fascists could be more gentle. Though we may regard a certain doctrine as working to corrupt and degrade the world, it is our duty to understand that doctrine, and to give sympathy and imagination to those people who have been seduced by it."[13]

His views of spirituality and morality shaped his political behaviour in the 1930s. His self-imposed injunction against promoting "a political cause or a party programme" gave him little motivation for political activity. His desire to "give sympathy and imagination" to those people whose practices and doctrines he might dislike impeded his taking sides for or against a political party. He acknowledged late in life that throughout his entire career he almost never voted in parliamentary or local elections. He recalled voting "only once or twice" at each level. He supplied the explanation that to vote for one party over others implied that he judged one party to be morally and politically superior. And given his general attitude of dissent, he disliked voting for a winner, lest the winner consider the result a license to act superior to the others and proceed to abuse power. In any case, his new quietism discouraged his vote. He relished the memory of one occasion when he voted in a general parliamentary election in the 1930s, most likely the election of 1935. Under the existing laws he had the right to cast three votes. He cast one for a Conservative, one for a Liberal, and one for a Socialist, thinking he had balanced things nicely. To his surprise all three candidates won. He declared that he found the outcome so disconcerting that he "hardly ever entered a polling booth since that date."[14]

Opposing Moralities

A test of his injunctions against the intrusion of moral judgments into historical study came in 1938 in relation to Hitler and the Nazis. Quite against his stated views, the episode drew him unmistakably into politics. A lecturer in the English Seminar at the University of Bonn, who knew of Butterfield's *Whig Interpretation of History*, arranged for the university to invite him to come to Bonn in December 1938 to present a paper on the history of the Whig interpretation. The invitation soon expanded to give the paper at the universities of Cologne, Munster, and Berlin. Butterfield found the topic instantly appealing, replying that, although he had never thought of looking into the question, he would welcome the inquiry intellectually. Because of his appreciation for Ranke and Acton, he had an affinity with German traditions in historical scholarship and recognized immediately that the history of historical thinking and writing had long attracted German intellectuals.

The timing and settings of his appearances in Germany were politically awkward, however, and Butterfield knew this. In March 1938 the Germans had invaded and annexed Austria. Neville Chamberlain, the British prime minister, went to Germany to negotiate with Hitler in mid-September, and again on 29 September at Munich. There he talked with Hitler, as well as Benito Mussolini, and Edouard Daladier of France. The negotiations yielded British approval of Hitler's annexation of the Sudetenland, the German-speaking areas of Czechoslovakia. The next couple of months were particularly tense.

In the face of these events, Butterfield "took advice," as he called it, in Cambridge, from whom we do not know, but surely Vellacott, before deciding whether to go to Germany. Butterfield's record of behaviour towards the Nazis up to this moment was ambiguous. Since at least the mid-thirties he had made clear to his students that he disliked Hitler's "unlimited dictatorship." As the dissenter against state hegemony and establishment, he could scarcely do otherwise.[15] Nonetheless, he did not follow Trevelyan and Gooch, two people close to him, whose practice he could easily have made his own. Since 1933 both Trevelyan and Gooch had publicly opposed Hitler and given direct assistance to anti-Nazi scholars fleeing Germany.[16] Instead, Butterfield adopted a policy consistent with his views of the universality and neutrality of scientific history. His policy called for him to engage in historical discussions and promote cordial relations with any historians who sought his company, without regard to their political views. He knowingly applied his policy to German historians amenable to the Nazis. His attitude was the analogue to the British prime minister's policy of appeasement towards Hitler. He favoured Chamberlain's strategy of negotiation with Hitler as a plausible way to avoid war. At the same time, like Chamberlain, he abhorred the German takeover of German-speaking Czechoslovakia and personally favoured Czech independence.[17] At a more profound level, however, the views he had written in *Whig Interpretation* committed him to separate historical study from politics and to treat historians differently from political figures. His academic connections with German scholars, whether Nazi or not, were, to him, appropriate to scholarly activity, and not a question of politics at all.

After reflection, Butterfield concluded that he would go to Germany. In December 1938 he lectured in Bonn, Munster, Cologne, and Berlin, Hitler's capital. He knew that his hosts supported Hitler and the Nazi government, and that the people in his audiences probably did too.

His policy had led him during the 1930s to get close to Hans K. Galinsky, whom he knew to be a Nazi and whose Nazi views he knew well.[18] Galinsky was a specialist in seventeenth-century English history, and he made frequent trips to England both before and after Hitler came to power in 1933. While in England he sought to recruit English scholars for the Nazi cause, or at least to soften their resistance to the Nazis. He often came to Peterhouse to see Butterfield. Galinsky arranged the invitation for Butterfield to lecture at Berlin in 1938 and served as his host for the occasion. To Galinsky, Butterfield's presence at that precise time in four German universities, especially in Berlin, boosted the Nazi cause. Butterfield's act helped legitimize Nazi rule, even if Butterfield uttered not one explicit word of politics during the visit. Soon afterwards, in March 1939, following the German annexation of Prague and the elimination of the Czech state, Butterfield welcomed Galinsky once more at Peterhouse and took him strolling along the River Cam. This he did even though, he said later, the German assault on Prague angered him intensely, more than any other event in international politics up to that time.[19] Nonetheless, Butterfield was determined against all the pressures as well as against his own feelings to draw a distinction between the acts of the German government, which he might dislike, and the acts of a German scholar, even when his support of the German scholar abetted the acts of the German government.

When the Germans invaded France in 1940, the German government quickly installed Galinsky as professor of English at the University of Strasbourg which, along with everything else, came under German control. After the defeat of the Nazis and the end of the war, the restored French authorities removed Galinsky from the chair in Strasbourg. Butterfield wrote references on his behalf in 1946 and 1948 to help him secure an academic appointment in post-Nazi Germany. About his Nazism Butterfield stated, "Though I disapproved of some of his views in the 1930's, I did not feel it difficult to understand how he had arrived at them, and I always thought that his case was one that could be humanly explained." He added, "I did not think him unreasonable in his love of his own country." And further, "if I thought that he had, perhaps, an excessive love of his country, I don't think he had more of it than many men of other countries, including our own."[20]

The Galinsky story indicated how Butterfield's political quietism, his prohibition against moral judgments, and his doctrine of the separateness of historical study from religion, life-philosophies, and politics had the ironic effect of inducing him to abet Nazi interests. His acts possessed distinctly political meaning at the time. Butterfield's views during the 1930s, and particularly his trip to Germany, stimulated talk around Cambridge that he had fascist tendencies. The talk stung him, and, as he would recall years later, he felt he had been seriously misunderstood. Noel Annan was among those who circulated the story ever after that Butterfield was soft on Nazis.[21]

Butterfield received another invitation in 1938 which carried exactly the opposite political meaning and led him to express precisely the opposite politics. In May 1938, after the German annexation of Austria, he signed a contract with Duckworth, an English publishing house, to write a short life of Napoleon for their series "Great Lives" in history. It was a publisher's project, timed to take advantage of the analogy then commonly drawn between Napoleon and Hitler. With events in Europe moving rapidly, the contract demanded that he write in a rush. The manuscript was due 31 December 1938, immediately after his trip to Germany. He probably saw the book as an opportunity to round off his Napoleon interest, although he could not overlook the political connotations of a work on Napoleon at that very moment.

The writing took longer than planned, and the new timing fulfilled the publisher's wildest fantasies. His little book of 143 pages, entitled *Napoleon*, appeared in the fall of 1939, moments after the German Blitzkrieg against Poland. Hitler's armies, like Napoleon's before him, were rolling across Europe. Butterfield supplied English readers with all the parallels between Napoleon and Hitler that they needed to understand their current despair.

Butterfield's language in the book is clear. Napoleon was a tyrant. Napoleon was intentionally a tyrant. Butterfield filled the book with judgments which looked like the kind he had forbidden in *The Whig Interpretation of History*, judgments against Napoleon, against the man as well as against his actions. He structured the historical narrative around an implicit moral judgment: that dictatorship is wrong, that dictators themselves are wrong, and that individual liberty is right. His primary thesis delineates Napoleon's transition from what Butterfield called "an initial liberalism to a higher distillation of tyranny," from a "war for freedom and self-determination" to a "fabulous career of conquest." He raises Napoleon up on a stick in order to display two lessons of history: "the corrupting effects of unbridled power," and the inevitability of the "downfall of a dictatorship."[22] The echos of Lord Acton reverberate through the book.

Trevelyan's review of the book in January 1940 caught the point. The "chief interest of this little book," wrote Trevelyan, "is the light it throws on the origins of the present disastrous condition of Europe."[23] Butterfield wrote the book with the image of Hitler on his mind, and he contradicted all the admonitions against the presentistic fallacy which he had issued in *Whig Interpretation*. And by means of the analogy between Napoleon and Hitler, he used his historical thought for explicitly political purposes: to support the emerging British position against Nazi tyranny.

History for the Sake of England

Butterfield spent the entire Second World War in Cambridge. Unlike many other historians, he was not asked to do government war service, and he did not volunteer. The contrast with Temperley's and Vellacott's history of war service was stark. He stayed at Peterhouse and helped keep the college and the Faculty of History going. He was one of only four Fellows of the college who remained in Cambridge throughout the war, and no vacant fellowships were filled. The undergraduate enrolment dropped from the average of around 150 during the 1920s and 1930s to about 100 in 1940–1941, and then declined to about 50 in 1944–1945. Butterfield's supervisions actually increased to fifteen per week. He busied himself with general college duties and took instruction in how to extinguish German fire bombs if any landed on Peterhouse.[24] The college hosted for a time the faculty and students of Chichester Theological College. Peterhouse also played host to the London School of Economics during most of the war after its evacuation from London in 1939. R. H. Tawney and Harold Laski became regulars at high table, and a Socialist Club convened in the college.[25] Butterfield rejoined the board of the History Faculty for most of the war, and held the central administrative position of secretary.

Peterhouse had fallen into a crisis of its own at the opening of the war. In 1938 things had looked extremely good for the college. Temperley was elected Master upon the death of Lord Birdwood, returning the college to the headship of a scholar and a historian. Temperley, then fifty-nine, was the Senior

Fellow as well as Professor of Modern History. He lived at the peak of his fame. In the same year Postan married Eileen Power and became Professor of Economic History on the retirement of J. H. Clapham, giving Peterhouse three professorships — Barker, Temperley, Postan — out of the now eight in the History Faculty. One of Butterfield's own students became a Fellow with the election of Brian Wormald, who had come up to Peterhouse in 1931. He filled Temperley's spot as a Fellow after Temperley's assumed the Mastership, permitting Peterhouse to boast five historians out of ten Fellows and a Master. The Peterhouse reputation for historical studies was immense.

Then the crisis unrolled. To the shock of all, Temperley died in less than a year, in July 1939, only sixty years of age. Acting quickly, the college recalled Vellacott from Harrow as the new Master, keeping an academic and a historian at the head of things. On top of this, Barker retired, costing Peterhouse a professorship among the Fellows. Again acting quickly, when Denis Brogan succeeded Barker as Professor of Political Science, retaining the historical emphasis of that chair, the college elected Brogan a Fellow of Peterhouse. With the start of the war, the college lost even Vellacott as Master when he was called up for war duty. The college had to make do with an acting Master, R. Lubbock, an engineering Fellow.

The death of Temperley threw open the professorship of modern history. His obituary in the *Cambridge Historical Journal,* written by Butterfield, praised him as "the epitome of Cambridge History." The tribute by G. P. Gooch for the British Academy gave him highest praise as well.[26] It would require a historian of stature to succeed Temperley. All the signs made it plausible to think of Butterfield himself as the successor. He was Temperley's intellectual heir, and he had followed Temperley as editor of the *Cambridge Historical Journal.* He was already an influential historian, the voice on general modern history to whom others listened. Cambridge University Press thought of him as the match for Previté-Orton, already the Professor of Medieval History, to write the *Concise Cambridge Modern History.* He had already published four books with a fifth on the way. Trevelyan, still the Regius Professor, told him after reading *Napoleon,* "Now, for the first time, I am sure you will be a remarkable historian and do big things, if you will get along and write some larger book."[27] It would be hard not to imagine even Butterfield thinking of himself as the successor in the chair. The rising ambition was palpable.

The war halted the speculations, however, as well as all new appointments, and the chair in modern history went vacant. Three more history professorships soon fell vacant — the Dixie chair in ecclesiastical history, the Regius chair in modern history, and the chair in medieval history.

The war and the events in England surrounding it pulled Butterfield irresistibly into the war effort. His own experience illustrated precisely the model of human action which his recent work on George III had brought him to: social systems could override the free actions of individual personalities in history, and the entanglements of history can overwhelm the will of the single personality.

Butterfield had signed the contract to write *The Concise Cambridge Modern History* in December 1939, during the earliest moments of the war. He may well have perceived his production of so large a work as just the right kind of a service for a historian to render to his nation in time of trouble. Such a purpose might explain why he agreed to do it at that point. He could give the English the general history of Europe they needed to orient their understanding of their current terror and help them look beyond the present by means of a wider knowledge of the past. With such a purpose in view, Butterfield might have felt an urgency to write for the 1942 deadline to which the contract bound him.

Butterfield the historian inserted a war-related point into *The Statecraft of Machiavelli,* which Bell published early in 1940: "The only true portrait of Machiavellianism is a Napoleon Bonaparte. And he is the clearest commentary upon the system." It took merely a breath for the reader to utter the name of Hitler as well. Butterfield's historical studies could continue to help the English understand their present circumstances. Ironically, German bombs blunted the point. The bombs fell on the publisher's warehouse in London and destroyed all but a few hundred copies of *Statecraft of Machiavelli.* The book received very little circulation at the time. It was not until 1955, when Bell issued the second printing, that it drew much attention. The publisher then made much of the destruction of the first printing during the war.[28]

The year 1940 which brought the war to England brought it close to Butterfield. On 24 September, German bombs shattered the glass in his home on Tension Road. Just two weeks later, on 8 October, the day after his fortieth birthday, he was in Broadcast House, London, at the invitation of the BBC, to discuss the analogy of Napoleon and Hitler on national radio. Butterfield had abandoned his remaining inhibitions against speaking directly to the need of the hour. He delivered what the BBC wanted. He told his listeners that Hitler was more terrible than Napoleon, "the incarnation of a more sinister thing." Nevertheless, he gave the assurance that bolsters sagging spirits. Provided Hitler did not invade England, he proclaimed, "we . . . may find our comfort in the Napoleonic analogy," and expect the defeat of this latest dictator in the end. In the style of historical analysis which he had learned from Machiavelli and Marx, Butterfield compared the rise and fall of two dictators. He presumed it to be a maxim of history that dictators eventually collapse under their own tyranny.[29]

Throughout 1940, while the Germans bombed London, Coventry, and Cambridge, Butterfield listened attentively as Winston Churchill, the new aristocratic prime minister, urged the English to rely on the legacy of their history for strength in their darkest hour. This was a message Butterfield the historian could feel directed at him. We do not know exactly when he abandoned his support for negotiation with Hitler. Even after the war began, he disliked the resort to war and still preferred a negotiated settlement with the Nazis. Cambridge gossip long afterwards claimed that Butterfield favoured a separate peace settlement with Germany as late as 1943, when the Allies were pressing for unconditional surrender. The gossip also had Butterfield going to parties in the German consulate in Dublin — Ireland remained officially neutral — in 1943. We may conclude from his diary in 1940 and his broadcast "Napoleon and Hitler" for the BBC in October 1940 that at least by then, if he ever had such thoughts about a separate peace, he no longer had them. *Cambridge Review* published his BBC talk in June 1941. In 1944 he acknowledged that Churchill's war appeal in 1940 was instrumental in the change he made in his own views.

Butterfield joined the fight against Hitler. But this he did on his own terms, as the dissenter and in a way that comported well with his dictates on moral judgments. In his diary for 1940 he wrote firmly yet characteristically: "Fight the Germans — yes, certainly, if we have to. Fight to save human beings from oppression or even to save the homeland from being invaded by foreigners, however virtuous. But do not think of them or treat them as sub-human. . . . Let us say rather: 'What did we do wrong? What could we have done to prevent the Germans from feeling that they must turn to Hitler?' "[30]

Butterfield found other tangible ways to join the war effort against Germany, and to do so as a historian. Both of these came before 1943. First, he agreed to participate in a project directed by J. M. Wordie for the Naval Intelligence Division of the Admiralty. The project was based at a sub-centre established at Cambridge for the purpose. The task was to write a history of France as a large section of a four-volume handbook on France. The handbook, one of many in a series on countries of the world touched by the war, was intended for use by commanding officers and other personnel to help them in their conduct of the fighting. It was designed especially for naval use, but also with the army, air force, and other government departments in mind. The handbook also included sections on French geography, the economy, and government, as well as a final section on French ports and communication systems. The fourth volume contained photos with multiple views of French ports, maps showing access to harbors, diagrams, tables, and lengthy descriptions — the sorts of things helpful as background for invasion, which Naval Intelligence nicely caught by the term "visits to a new country." All four volumes were stamped "restricted," not to be shown or made available to the press or other members of the public. The new volumes replaced the originals first produced for used during the Great War.

The chief writers of the section on French history, entitled "Historical Outline: 1789–1940," were the historical geographer H. C. Darby, who served as general editor, Denis Brogan, and Butterfield, with help from Ernest Barker and I. L. Foster. It was a heavily Peterhouse undertaking. Naval Intelligence issued the volumes between June and October 1942, with volume 2, Butterfield's volume, dated September. Cambridge University Press printed the volumes, and the title page identified the Naval Intelligence Division as the publisher. It was most certainly government-sponsored history.[31]

Butterfield produced his share in a white heat. The war effort needed help. The handbook from the first war was badly out of date, yet still being used. He wrote most of the section covering the period from the French Revolution and Napoleon I to Napoleon III. Nearly half of his text represented a condensed version of his book *Napoleon*. He dwelt on Napoleon, whom he depicted as the military dictator and heir of the revolution, and then skipped rapidly from 1814 to 1870. The analogy with Hitler was obvious in the context, as in his BBC broadcast in 1940 and his article in 1941. His rendering of the history offered the traditional concentration on politics, diplomacy, and war, to the neglect of social, economic, religious, and intellectual themes. As war work it was useful. Naval Intelligence liked it. As history it was not something Butterfield was particularly proud of, and after the war he forgot, or liked to think that he forgot, that he had done it. Nonetheless, well after the war Cambridge University Press turned the history section into a book, *A Short History of France*. Only the title and headings were changed, with new chapters added on the postwar period. It circulated widely.[32]

Another project involved him an extraordinary multinational adventure against the Germans. In 1941, unprompted, he made contacts with various European governments-in-exile in London, including the Czechs, the Free French, and the Poles, and successfully located some exiled historians. He joined with Ernest Barker to organize two conferences of refugee historians at Peterhouse, one in March 1942 and the second a year later. Czechs, Poles, and Hungarians dominated the conferences. He cancelled a third conference scheduled for 1944 because, he said, things had become too busy. It looked, rather, as if Butterfield had lost his spirit for the project.

The conferences had activated conflicting sympathies within him. On one side, he desired to support the war effort in favour of the nations overrun by Hitler. On the other, he wanted to promote what he now began calling the "academic view" among historians of all nations as well as a general and non-nationalistic approach to European history. He came to feel that the historians at his conferences were more interested in simply combatting the Germans. Their weapons were nationalistic and explicitly politicized versions of the history of their own homelands. Butterfield felt caught between his own patriotic politics and his historical theory. He tied himself in knots worrying about fostering what appeared to him to be history as political propaganda.

His initial solution to the problem in the extremities of the moment was, as he wrote to colleagues in Cambridge, "in the present situation [to] depart from the rigidly academic view." He decided to facilitate the "moderate" propaganda of the refugee historians, allied as they were with England, but to reject the push for "passionate propaganda, rising to very heated rhetoric." He was unsure how to draw a straight line between the two. During the second conference, he participated in a discussion of "German perversions of historiography." Butterfield perhaps eased the inner tensions he thus created for himself by simultaneously serving on a national British committee which recommended writing "text-books on the history of European civilization of an objective character."[33]

Butterfield continued to lecture to undergraduates at Cambridge during the war, and he sought to use his history teaching to help the war effort. In 1943, during a particularly awful moment of the war, he conceived a course of lectures which he called "The Historical Background for General Knowledge." He got as far as constructing an outline. The function of the lectures would have been to take the students behind the headlines and provide them with a deeper understanding of why things in Europe had led to war. He believed that history, and especially historical geography, could be particularly useful as an agent of understanding. He never got to give the course, however.[34]

At that same moment in the war, he actually wrote a 330-page draft of a book on historical geography in Europe, which related tangentially to the idea for the course of lectures. His purpose was to explain in historical terms the reasons for the geographical distribution of the peoples and governments of modern Europe. The manuscript covered all the nations caught up in the war, going back into late Roman and medieval times and extending into modern times, but it dealt especially with Germany and eastern Europe. Butterfield was acquainted with a large two-volume work by E. A. Freeman, which J. B. Bury had republished in 1903, entitled *The Historical Geography of Europe*,

suggesting yet another influence of Bury on his thinking. He sent the manuscript for criticism to Z. N. Brooke, a Cambridge medievalist, who responded
enthusiastically and suggested only minor revisions. Butterfield did nothing
further, however, and allowed his big manuscript to go to waste. For the
moment, nothing came of this attempt to help the war effort.[35]

None of Butterfield's projects and designs must have seemed good enough
to him as supports for the English war effort. He recalled the charge of Churchill to rely on England's history for strength in time of war. Butterfield had
already enunciated in his own words a historical thesis that would fulfil exactly Churchill's wish. In *Napoleon,* in 1939, he wrote that the "crime of
Napoleon" was due in part to the sequence of things emerging from the French
Revolution, to "the dialectic of events themselves" in France. By contrast, he
claimed, overlooking Oliver Cromwell, the English have never produced a
dictator comparable to Napoleon. Hitler came to mind too. England, not
France, was the source of modern liberty. He had his doubts about Germany.
Then he wrote, "Liberty comes to the world from English traditions, not from
French theories."[36] There was nothing novel in the thesis, long associated with
Edmund Burke's *Reflections on the French Revolution* of 1791, but for Butterfield it supplied the message he needed to respond personally to Churchill's
war appeal.[37]

With the war at full intensity, he thought about the sources of English liberty
and the differences between English and French and German history. Already
pertinent was his lecture in Germany in 1938 on the history of the Whig
interpretation of history, as well as his reflections on the analogy between
Napoleon and Hitler. Here was a history project for the war, a self-appointed
war work, more timely for the nation than *The Concise Cambridge Modern
History,* more immediate than the lectures on historical geography. He had
allowed the 1942 deadline for the *Concise History* to pass unnoticed, and he
abandoned his lectures and manuscript on historical geography.

The outcome of his reflections on English liberty was an extraordinary little
book of 139 pages, *The Englishman and His History,* written and rewritten as
the war proceeded, and finished in February 1944. The book was published by
Cambridge University Press in June 1944, during the high moment of the
reconquest of Normandy and northern France by the British, Americans, and
Canadians.[38]

We may understand the work as a war essay which amounted to a piece of
historical scholarship in service of English patriotism. It is likely that Butterfield at the time understood his patriotism as his participation in the common
response of the English people to a terrible situation. But he hinted that he
somehow knew that what he wrote was more than that. He could feel his work

to be remarkably similar to the "moderate" political propaganda of the refugee historians that had caused him such unease.

On the first page of *Englishman and His History* he acknowledges what must have felt like a betrayal of his own norms for historical study. "Sometimes we think that our history is the impartial narrative," he wrote, but perhaps even our best work is "only the supreme expression of what is really the English version" of the story.[39] In the opening line of the introduction he also acknowledges the political inspiration that evoked the book. He alludes to Churchill and others, during what he calls "the crisis of 1940," who "continually reminded us of those resources in the past which can be drawn upon to fortify a nation at war." Butterfield aims to identify some of those resources by studying "the relations of Englishmen with their history."[40] Much of the work has the character of a history of historical writing and thinking, and some of it includes a rendition of general European history. However, streaming through even the ostensibly historical sections and then surfacing to full view as the essay reaches the middle and rushes to the conclusion are statements of Butterfield's political ideology, moral convictions, and religious confession of faith. This time he wrote history for the sake of England, for the sake of the present in England, not for the sake of the past. In Cowling's phrase "the past was made to confirm or justify the present."[41]

Butterfield says very little in the book about his views of historical study, but ample clues in the text suggest that he still holds to the distinction he expressed in *Whig Interpretation* between the realm of history and the realm of morality. He may even have become more stringent in his theory of the limits of historical study. Notably, he distinguishes "the technical views" of the functions of historical study from "the moralizings" of the historians. He introduces the term "technique" to refer to the method which properly belongs to historical study, and he depicts his own historical work as dealing with "the mere mechanics" of the rise and operation of his subject. In one section he describes what he calls the "defects in historical technique" before the twentieth century, and we sense that he has in mind a set of proper techniques reached by historical study in his own day, against which he may judge the performance of historians for all time. We get a sense of what he meant by his statement in connection with the refugee historians that he wished to take the "academic view" of his subject.[42]

His still active promotion of the limited function of historical study makes *Englishman and His History* all the more remarkable. He wrote a book which appears diametrically opposed to the foremost teaching of *Whig Interpretation,* his warning against the study of the past for the sake of the present. After he reread the book in 1970, long after the urgencies of war had slipped into the mist, he acknowledged candidly that the excessiveness of his patriotism struck him as "comic."[43] However, in 1964, when Churchill died, he showed that he was not entirely repentant for the surge of patriotism he felt under Churchill's leadership during the war. Cambridge selected Butterfield to pronounce the eulogy of Churchill at a memorial service. To his audience gathered at the University Church of Great St. Mary's he explained that Churchill had established a special relationship with the nation as a whole: "When we remember the year 1940 all differences about politics and policies seem to become irrelevant." For Butterfield, Churchill surpassed politics and embodied the ideals defined in *Englishman and His History*.[44]

To carry out his analysis, Butterfield devised two distinctions in *Englishman and His History*. The first is a distinction between the Whig interpretation of history as created by Whig historians, which was wrong history, and the use made of the Whig interpretation of history by Whig politicians, which facilitated the creation of a liberating mode of political change. He puts the point early in the book: "But in England [as contrasted with France] we made peace with our middle ages by misconstruing them; and, therefore, we may say that 'wrong' history was one of our assets. The whig interpretation of history came at exactly the crucial moment and, whatever it may have done to our history, it had a wonderful effect on English politics. For this reason England did not need a revolution of 1789 to save her from the despotism of the past." And further: "Studying these things, we can hardly help commemorating those whigs of the past who were always so much greater than the whig historians. We shall see how they evolved an attitude to the historical process, a way of co-operating with the forces of history, an alliance with Providence, which the whig historians were much slower to achieve — which they were even perhaps too partisan to discern."[45]

He uses blunt terms, wanting to be sure that people would not miss the difference between historians and politicians. The Whig historians, who were well meaning, produced wrong history, while the Whig politicians, usually not well meaning, generated good politics. The politicians converted Whig history into an "asset" that helped create "a wonderful effect on English politics." He draws the analogy with Churchill's use of English history in 1940: wrong history with beneficial political results. Butterfield even builds the distinction into the two-part structure of the volume, part one, "The History," and part two, "The Political Tradition." So different are the parts from each other in their message, style, and construction that they seem to be almost two separate works.[46]

The second is a distinction between the story told by the Whig interpretation and the methods used to construct that story. He asserts, "It is not necessary or useful to deny that the theme of English political history is the story of our liberty." Alluding to himself, he refers to those "who, perhaps in the misguided austerity of youth wish to drive out that whig interpretation." Now, he says, people should direct their attacks not against the story itself, but merely against the "surviving defects in historical method" that once appeared intrinsic to the Whig interpretation of history.[47]

Reviewers and commentators for years thereafter missed his all-important distinctions. They poked fun at him for surrendering his fiery criticism of the Whig interpretation of history, and they played the early Butterfield off against the mature Butterfield. E. H. Carr, in his hugely influential book *What Is History?*, mocked him and cited Butterfield's supposed reversal as a prime illustration of the subjectivity of historical study. A generation later David Cannadine, in his biographical defense of Trevelyan, chuckled dismissively at how "Butterfield had recanted his youthful polemic." In 2002, Annabel Patterson, as part of her reclamation of a Whig interpretation of history, spoke of Butterfield's repentance of the message he uttered in his previous "short-sighted" work. The claim that Butterfield had abandoned his eye-catching criticism of the Whig interpretation of history became commonplace.[48]

His critics might be excused for missing his points, however, since Butterfield covers the distinctions with a host of qualifying phrases and details. The first part of the book expands the topic of his controversial lecture in Germany in 1938. It is a ponderous reading of the history of the Whig interpretation in which he itemizes what he believes are the false accretions to the tradition of historical thought. He is still unrelentingly frank about the defects of the Whig historical method. But there are a few differences in his treatment of the interpretation which are important to notice. We are struck, for instance, by a shift in his wording which, in effect, relativizes what had been his main point about method. Instead of talking about the study of the past "for the sake of the past," the norm of proper history which he claimed the Whig historians had violated, he now speaks innocuously about "the attempt to see the past with the eyes of the past," a thing which he regards merely as "at least one of the historian's aims."[49] He now explains the emergence of the defects in historical method quite apart from the problems of politics — as the innocent consequence of applying the lawyer's mode of reasoning to historical interpretation. Picking up a suggestion by F. W. Maitland, a Cambridge legal historian contemporary with Acton, he urged that the Whig interpretation of history can be seen as the legacy of the way lawyers interpreted English common law. Unlike historians, who properly ought to seek the meaning of a law for the people who originally enacted it, English lawyers were interested the present use of the law and searched the past for precedents. Decades later G. R. Elton saw this very observation in Maitland and put the notion forward about Butter-field's criticism of the Whig historians as if Elton were the first to think of it.[50]

Most significantly, in the first section of the book, Butterfield elevates the Whig interpretation of history to a higher place. He renames it nothing less than the "English interpretation of history." It had become the English view and not merely the view of anonymous Whig historians and textbook writers. In the terms used by Joseph M. Hernon, Jr., it can even be construed as the consensus of the nation at the time, "the accepted popular consciousness of British history." There are no longer other options, certainly not a Tory view of history which elevated the monarchy or maybe the empire. At best a Tory view offers little more than kindly treatment of George III. The Whig view is an intellectual inheritance which cherishes the history of England as the story of liberty and which has become "the Englishman's" view.[51]

The second and shorter part of the book, lighter and more essay-like in style, more committed to conveying a message, takes the form of an exposition of the English political tradition. Here in part two, together with portions of part one, Butterfield demonstrates how he would read English political history as the story of liberty. As we might expect, he highlights in general the interaction of Whigs, Tories, and Radicals, Catholics and Protestants, and gives priority to no one party in the mix, showing them together creating and responding to the sequence of political events. However, when he gets to the salient events of the revolution of 1688, when the Roman Catholic king, James II, was expelled and the new Protestant rulers, William and Mary, were installed in his place, he abandons his customary interpretation. Instead, he moves the Whigs to centre stage and credits them with acting virtually above the conflict. He describes the way the Whigs listened to the "lessons of history," particularly the "lessons of civil war" in the seventeenth century. He records their maxims of political behaviour drawn from their historical experience of recurrent events. He portrays the ideology of "whiggism" and the "whig method" in politics which he believes emerged between 1660 and 1715. Without wincing, he praises the events of 1688, which he puts to the credit of the Whigs, as "the most masterly episode in English history." We puzzle over his political interpretation of English history which elevates one party and one event above the entanglement of things.[52]

It takes us only a moment to realize why he exalts the Whigs. He is signalling his approval of what he called "whiggism" and even of a properly chastened Whig interpretation of history. He still feels remarkable affinity with these Whigs, and he accepts 1688 as the high revelatory event of Whiggism. What he tells us about Whiggism and the Whig contribution to the art of politics actually corresponds with his own views of politics and religion and, notably, of the best way to perceive and work with the historical process. His views are completely continuous with the views expressed in *Whig Interpretation*. The whole exercise shows Butterfield still to be the "New Whig," trying to handle the subtleties of saying both yes and no to the Whig historical tradition while also trying to reinterpret the interaction of past and present in English political history with an improved historical method.

It took Butterfield until 1961 to respond publically to the near universal judgment that in *Englishman and His History* he had given up his criticism of the Whig interpretation of history. E. H. Carr provoked the reply by repeating the view. Carr was devastatingly clever. He wrote: "To draw attention to these reversals of outlook is not an unfriendly criticism. It is not my purpose to refute the proto-Butterfield with the deutero-Butterfield, or to confront Professor Butterfield drunk with Professor Butterfield sober. . . . My purpose is merely to show how closely the historian mirrors the society in which he works. It is not merely the events that are in flux. The historian himself is in flux." The reference to biblical criticism was suggestive, but the allusion to drink shows how wildly off target Carr was in understanding Butterfield.[53]

The reply came in Butterfield's review of *What Is History?* in the *Cambridge Review*. He vigorously affirmed the continuities between his two works. He had not changed with the times as Carr had supposed. This is the moment when he told the story of Charles Smyth's observation about *The Whig Interpretation of History*. The Cambridge Tory historian, whom he called "the most acute of the critics," realized that Butterfield had actually written in alliance with the Whig historians with the aim of improving upon their practice. Like Smyth, Carr should have seen, quipped Butterfield, that, far from giving up his criticism, he retained his criticism of the Whiggish fallacy precisely because of his abiding deep sympathy with the Protestant Whigs, both historians and politicians. He was, he confessed, "merely anxious to have the Whig historians more liberal-minded," even as he wanted Protestants "to transcend private opinions and topical prejudices when they come to technical history." Butterfield thus admitted the play of his own religion and politics in both books. Oddly enough the admission came couched in an overall reassertion of the independence of historical science from politics and religion. Contrary to his aim of quashing the tendency he saw in Carr's argument "to undermine the status of history as an autonomous science," he inadvertently supported Carr's main point, that historians are themselves the products of their society and history.[54]

The correspondence between the two colleagues that followed was cordial but did not advance their understanding of each other's positions. The two talked past each other. Neither realized that Carr had simply mislocated his criticism. He had concentrated too much on history as flux and hence upon historians who change with the times. When Butterfield told Carr that chapter 1 of *Englishman and His History* reproduced virtually intact his lecture in Germany from 1938, Carr wrote back to quibble over whether Butterfield had changed with the times by 1938 or 1944. He did not realize that Butterfield's attachment to Protestant and New Whig allegiances had roots in convictions derived from his youth in Oxenhope, which Butterfield had iterated in the review. Butterfield's views as historian were surely socially and historically situated, but in a sense different from what Carr imagined. Butterfield reflected history as continuity, in this case his continuity with his youth when he had formed his convictions from within his situation of that day.[55]

The intrusion into their discussion by Ved Mehta, who wrote an article on the pair for the *New Yorker,* was no help. Mehta's journalistic embellishments of his conversation with Butterfield compounded the confusion. Jonathan Haslam, writing his biography of Carr, somehow missed hearing Butterfield's report to Carr that chapter 1 of *Englishman and His History* was virtually the text of the 1938 lecture, and implied that Butterfield was insincere. He also did not catch Butterfield's chief point in reply to Carr — the distinction between Whig history and Whig politics — and chose to perpetuate the claim about Butterfield's presumed change of mind. Meanwhile, Carr's *What Is History?* spread the laugh through a quarter of a million copies sold as of 1999.[56]

In *Englishman and His History* Butterfield likes to think of Whiggism as a "non-doctrinaire view of politics," and the Whigs' method as their way of "co-operating with history," or, as he also styles it, "the whig mode of co-operating with Providence." This Whiggism endorsed a distinctive strategy of change: "There emerges into the clear light of day the type of whiggism which became so familiar to historians — the whiggism that chooses only a moderate pace of reform, a cautious progress to whatever end may be desired; the whiggism which, abhorring revolutionary methods, seems now mildly left-wing, now almost indistinguishable from conservatism itself."

Under the guise of detailing the English tradition in politics, he spells out his credo. Butterfield, Whig, and the English political tradition become interchangeable terms. The English tradition, he asserts, encompasses many things: a tempered faith in the course of history, due humility concerning the limits of political improvement, a feeling for "certain imponderable things" accruing from the continuities of history, a respect for the other "man's" personality, the pursuit of "the highest practicable good," an inclination to moderation and compromise. Butterfield still alludes to the complexity of history. Now, however, instead of accentuating conflict as before, but without denying its importance, he praises the merits, in English history, of "a steady, ordered progress" which takes the place of "desperate conflict leading to revolutionary up-heaval."[57] This is the Englishman's mode of political change.

Butterfield now arrives back at his starting point. He rediscovers the clue he had already found in his own proclamation from 1939, "Liberty comes to the world from English traditions, not from French theories." Appropriate to this New Whig's reconciling view, the point sounds remarkably similar to Burke's critique of Fox. The Englishman's mode of change differed radically from French practice since 1789, with revolution alternating with counterrevolu-tion. More than this, it differed as well from the equally destructive experi-ences of the Germans under Hitler, the Irish of the Irish Republican Army, the Italians under Mussolini, and, by implication, Soviet Russia under Stalin. Twice in the second part of the book he surveys general European history since 1789 in order to proclaim the superiority of the English tradition. "How much richer" the French would be, he comments, and so too all the others, if they had mimicked the English method of joining and rejoining past and present. We marvel as we watch even Butterfield swell with patriotism and throw aside the usual entanglements of qualifying phrases he attaches to his comments on traditions different from his own.[58]

To depict the character of the political change over the centuries, he again pulls out the term "organic," which had served him from time to time since his undergraduate essay "Art Is History Made Organic." If his meaning had been unclear to us before, we can make no mistake now. With this term, he moves onto another level of analysis. English political history converts into the his-tory of the English nation, which is something more inclusive than the history of politics and government. He likens the English nation to "the life of organic creatures," treats it as "a living thing," and contrasts it with the "paper-constructions" and "deliberate manufacture" of France and some other na-tions. The contrast is not in the least novel — biotic development is natural, human construction is artificial — but it is new to his discourse. He offers a bio-organic interpretation of English national history. The Whig politicians used their method to care for the living thing of English history, much like the gardener tending the plants or the nanny nurturing the child. They maintained a national history that is better than that of France, Italy, Germany, Russia, and so many others. The English have not had "the uprooting of things that have been organic to the development of the country." English history has followed "a natural course of development" and has not experienced the jerks and starts common to the rest of the world. The transition to democracy in England was happier than in other countries who were "not ripened by their internal and moral development" to be ready for it. England has enjoyed "the growth of liberty," "the growth of liberal-mindedness," and so on. Butterfield depicts a placid scene of steady growth in English history since 1688 where another historian might find instead the struggles of industrializing classes, the triumph of the middle classes, the impoverishment of the underclasses, the suppression of the Irish, and the imperialism of expansion overseas. Looking back in English history, he treats the conflicts of the Reformation of the sixteenth century and the struggles of the Revolution of the mid-seventeenth century as something like alterations in the growth rings of an ancient tree, suitably contained within the long-term growth of the English nation. Even if we allow that Butterfield intended the organic reference merely as a metaphor, we notice that this metaphor displaces all others in the crucial passages, and he gets himself into difficulties because of it. He still wants to use the idea he attributed to Ranke, and with which he once smashed the Whig historians, that each successive epoch in the past has its own special quality independent of what comes afterwards. Yet his reliance on the imagery of organic development counteracts his intentions on at least two counts. In organic development, if all goes well, things advance on a generally predetermined course, and earlier stages find fulfilment in later ones. In the case of human beings, for example, the infant becomes the child, the youth, the adult, and the old person. Thus infancy of the nation is unfulfiled without childhood, youth, and maturity. Moreover, organic development also ends in decay and death. Hence the metaphor of organic growth serves poorly to praise a nation, since it also says that sooner or later the nation will decay and die.[59] Butterfield is on better terms with his own theory when he applies his method of reconciling opposites, and speaks as he does at the very end of the book, of people reconciling continuity and change, mediating past and present, affirming both tradition and progress, and at the same time refusing to rule out the validity of revolution when the ruling powers become entrenched.[60]

The bio-organic interpretation of the history of the English nation does not come unmixed in Butterfield's treatment, however. He blends into it an interpretation of social class in order to explain the social changes that enabled the Whig political method to work. The influence of Marx is evident, but the version he presents is not Marxist. He replaces the Marxist notion of class struggle with the idea of class harmony, and he is noticeably generous to capitalism. He detects in the capitalists no more greed than in the workers, relieves them of any special responsibility for oppression, and pronounces the "capitalistic system" to be the work of Providence. The effect of his generosity is to legitimize the capitalist status quo. Butterfield had already made the same points about capitalism in his 1942 review of Archbishop William Temple's *Christianity and the Social Order,* where he insisted on withholding a moral judgment against capitalism only to end up by justifying capitalism as a mighty product of history and Providence.[61] Nonetheless, in *Englishman and His History,* his sympathies are not with the capitalists, but with those both higher and lower on the ladder of social class. If Marx sided with the workers, and capitalists with the bourgeoisie, Butterfield identifies simultaneously with the aristocracy at the top and the nameless masses at the bottom. His appreciation of the Whigs as aristocrats is everywhere, and he designates the lower classes as "the solid body of Englishmen," the quiet mass of the population who admire and follow the people at the top in any time period.

The class interpretation commences with 1660–1715, the period he believes to be "the crucial stage in what proved to be the most significant transition in a thousand years of history." This stage included a whole series of interrelated movements — intellectual and religious changes, technological progress, discontinuities in social class, financial developments, commercial enterprise, and the "scientific revolution."[62] Under the restored monarchy, the ruling class was then the aristocracy, whether Whig or Tory. Their politics was "a struggle between members of a governing class," members of the same class, who behaved with relative urbanity towards each other and who took care not to threaten their own position. In the French case, there emerged a protracted struggle between nobility, church, and tradition on one side, and bourgeoisie, rationalism, and revolution on the other. The history of England, by contrast, proceeded through harmonious adaptation, "due partly to the traditions of an aristocracy which have expanded into the heritage of the people." The aristocrats at the top reached down to the bourgeois below them before bourgeois complaints became too loud. They agreed to enough bourgeois demands to secure bourgeois silence, and shared with the bourgeois a portion of the privileges of the aristocracy. In time the process moved further down the social scale to incorporate elements of the working classes into the benefits initially reserved to the aristocracy. The process functioned flawlessly except in relation to the people Butterfield called "those classes that are without political traditions — without that brake which the actual responsibility for government imposes." Such people, he said, "tend naturally to be impatient, overestimating the amount which can in any case be achieved by political action." Nonetheless, the process successfully enveloped all three great modern political parties — Liberal, Conservative, Labour — as well as the labour union movement since the nineteenth century, turning them all into inheritors of the Whig aristocratic traditions. He continued,

> Some have laughed at the English for aping the gentry, and some prefer that extremism of the Right or the Left which seeks to proletarianize everybody, reducing politics to naked hatreds. Our latter-day whigs (who at least had the

merit of striving for the growth of liberal-mindedness) were more amiable in that they held at the back of their minds the notion that all should be turned into gentlemen. They were wool-gathering when they threw out the idea of "an Eton for everybody" into the bargain, but their dream — the "nationalization" of the best in an aristocratic tradition — has not, in English politics at least, proved quite the joke that it might have appeared to be at first sight. It is thoroughly whig in its conception of a progress that makes capital out of the very continuity of history.[63]

On the first page of the book, long before we have read far enough to make the observation ourselves, Butterfield acknowledges that the transportation of aristocratic traditions down the social ladder benefits the ruling class above all. He admits with candor, "We can scarcely help it if this kind of history is at the same time the one most adapted to the preservation of the existing regime." He depicts the process as a transfer of ideas, attitudes, habits, and values, and he offers no discussion of the social and economic factors, the class conflicts, and the political power and oppressions involved in promoting the hegemony and the survival of the ruling class. This is not the kind of interpretation of English history we would expect a dissenter to endorse.[64]

There is more to his class interpretation. Undergirding England and persisting throughout all the changes are "the solid body of Englishmen." These are the humble people who live without class consciousness and political awareness and who recognize the virtues of the traditions descending from on high. In the conclusion of the book, where Butterfield issues his final praise of English history and the Whigs, he reserves the place of highest honour for these nameless Englishmen. In the closing line of the book he commends their patience in their relations with their superiors and lionizes their way of "waiting to steal for the whole nation what they could appropriate in the traditions of monarchy, aristocracy, bourgeoisie and church." Their merit consists in aping their superiors and absorbing the traditions sent down from above. He seems unaware of any independent contributions these ordinary Englishmen might have made to English history and equally ignorant of any opposition they have mounted against the upper classes. And he remains oblivious to the presence of the very poor.[65]

Meditating on Butterfield's final words, we recognize the model of social change he assimilated from his father in his youth. There is his father standing respectfully before the mill owner of Oxenhope, passing from mill floor to mill owner's office, taking the mill owner's domestic for his wife, receiving the mill owner's surplus books and music, buying the piano the mill owner discarded, and leading the younger mill workers to adopt the mill owner's dress and social manners and Methodism. Then we notice that Butterfield dedicated *The*

Englishman and His History to his father. Suddenly we realize that "the Englishman" is his father.

We recall two days in his father's life—the day the mill owner deprived his father of the position he had occupied so faithfully for so many years and gave it to the mill owner's relative, and the day not long after when the mill owner discharged his father altogether. We perceive the patience, the quietism, and the humiliation demanded of "the Englishmen" in order to maintain and operate a system calculated to entrench the ruling class.

There is yet another major element to Butterfield's interpretation of the history of the English nation. He began with a rendering of English political ideas and political method since especially 1688, transformed it into a bio-organic vision of the English nation, then added a class analysis of the English people which extols the absorption of aristocratic values by the lower orders. To these at last he adds a religious interpretation of English history which features the role of Christianity in the working of the English system. In so doing he gives no evidence of having interacted with any particular thinkers, whether theologians or historians. He is offering an appreciation of England as a Christian nation voiced by countless others at the time—bishops, politicians, clergy, authors, scholars. They all appealed to the Christian traditions of the nation for strength during the war against the Nazis and Fascists. His contribution to this joint appeal was his practice as a historian who reflects directly and at length on the interpretation of English history. What he says about religion are the sorts of things he used to write in his diary and preach in his sermons, naive thoughts arising from his meditations on his own religious convictions and experience.

His interpretation goes like this. The Whig aristocrats in his story were all Christians, and the traditions they embodied were those of the Church of England. Whiggism and the Whig method were permeated with and expressions of Christian morality. The Nonconformists and Dissenters who revolted against the Whig aristocrats and their established church directed their objections against certain details about establishment, worship, and doctrine, and not against the Christian religion. They remained within the Christian tradition, and they too were motivated by Christian morality. In social terms these Nonconformists eschewed revolution and actually allied themselves with the upper ranks of society and the established church to nurture steady political and social growth at every level of English life. By thus participating in the long and unbroken continuity of Christianity in England they facilitated the transmission of Whiggism and the Whig method from the ruling class to the nation as a whole. In a sense, too, they helped transmute the Anglican method of the *via media* to the nation as a whole. That method absorbed the best from opposing sides, discarded the negative elements found on any side, and created a new, more comprehensive, and more variegated way through life.

At this religious level, in Butterfield's hands, the English case contrasted radically with the French. In France as well as some other places on the continent of Europe secular liberalism in politics and the "philosophic movement" of the Enlightenment created a "breach with tradition." The result was a fundamental movement away from Christianity which he called "a great secularization of life and thought." He observes that, ironically, secularization on the continent produced not greater freedom as the secularists promised, but totalitarianism and the pagan state. He had in mind Napoleon and Hitler.[66]

Butterfield's treatment discloses several perduring Christian beliefs which he thinks animate English political life to the benefit of the nation. He enumerates four beliefs from which he draws implications for understanding history generally. We quickly sense that he is actually representing his own confession of faith and allowing us to see the contours of his own religious beliefs as of this moment. The items he identifies were, arguably, common to the several forms of Christianity in England, but he also gives his selection a distinctly Nonconformist cast. For example, he includes no mention of doctrines which were specifically important to the Church of England, such as the centrality of the church and the sacraments in the life of the nation, and he states at least one of his items in a way that would be most congenial to a Nonconformist like himself.

First, Butterfield continues to stress that God is the One above all, the only judge of the ultimate merit of human action in history. In the context of the politics and war of the time, he translates this belief into the admonition that people ought to refrain from "making gods out of things of the world." Thus, he rejects what he calls "naked individualism," by which he means an idolatrous emphasis on individual persons, probably referring to uncontrolled capitalism. At the same time, he opposes all political movements which "deify the state," all attempts to make "gods . . . out of their abstract nouns." He has in mind Nazism, Fascism, and Soviet Communism. He throws one caveat towards the English. The Christian impact on the nation is so immense, he says, that the English have become used to thinking of themselves as God's Chosen People, "saddling us with too great a burden of self-righteousness." His statement about "abstract nouns" gives us the first unambiguous indication that his social views have hardened into social nominalism and that he considers what we call "the state" to be simply a phenomenon of our vocabularies, not a real social existent.[67]

Second, he is very free with the expression of his faith in Providence in history, more so than in his previous works, where he merely dropped the term into the text from time to time. He still does little to help us know precisely what he means by Providence, however. The belief appears most often in the phrase "co-operation with Providence," a locution he seems to interchange with "co-operation with History." He nowhere refers to Providence as the "Providence of God," although he does want to associate what he says with the long Christian tradition of belief in divine Providence. He appears to use the term Providence to refer entirely to human action, either directly or indirectly. He may well be attempting to examine the human processes and vehicles he believes have been used by divine Providence in the course of human history. For example, in the manner of his earlier writings, he speaks of "man's reconciling mind" repeatedly "playing Providence" on past mistakes and disasters and bringing good things out of bad. He writes of "an overruling Providence" which he attributes to "the work of History herself." It is difficult to know how to understand him when he personifies history and speaks of "History herself" or "itself" as something that stands up and acts: "Not man's sovereign action alone governs the pattern which things are taking; but man working on material which itself rebels against him, and working in co-operation with factors that are just not calculable. However well we may strive to play our part in the orchestra, we must not imagine that we are quite the composers of the piece. History herself puts limits to our actions and volitions, or at least deflects their consequences; if only by compounding our wills with those of others, or overriding them by forces that are beyond our control; if only by revenging itself on our wilfulness and releasing the fury of the ungovernable storm." We might suppose that "man's sovereign action" refers to the acts of an individual person, rather than to collective human sovereignty as contrasted with divine sovereignty. "History herself" would then refer to the totality of the interactions of all individual human actions, an utterly vast complexity that surpasses our capacity to trace connections back to our own individual acts. On this reading, we recognize in Butterfield's fresh formulations the legacy of notions he has been expressing for a long time about the process of history, especially about the limits placed on individual personalities by the entanglement of things in history, and the unintended consequences of our actions. The difference is that now he calls this Providence.[68]

Third, he reiterates his long-running belief in the all-importance of human personality in history. In the past he had written in his diary and preached in his sermons that the idea of human personality was essential to Christianity, but he had not yet stated this belief in his public writings. Now, in this work of historical study, he tells us explicitly that his view of personality has a religious base. He claims in particular that it was the Nonconformists in England who especially emphasized the value of human personality. He expresses the belief in a way that comports better with Methodist sensibilities at the time than with the Church of England. He refers to the belief in personality as a doctrine of the church: "Human beings, though fallen from the state of innocence, move as gods and bear the image of God; they are not part of the litter of the earth, to be left uncounted like the sands of the sea. Each is a precious jewel, each a separate well of life, each we may say a separate poem: so that, without taking them in the mass, every single one of them has a value incommensurate with anything else in the created universe. In the light of this doctrine, the riches of human personality, the possibilities that lie in human nature and the fullness of humanity itself, were fostered and treasured by the teaching of the church." We notice two things in particular about this statement. He asserts that human beings possess the highest value of anything in the universe, and that they are to be taken above all as individuals. He offers a theological reason for the first point — they bear the image of God — but he offers none for the second. With this statement he is confirming his belief in the primacy of individual human beings in history, even though he acknowledges that their primacy is constrained by innumerable limits. He is prepared to use the term "individualism" to identify his views on the matter. The individualism of Englishmen — Butterfield's individualism — is a special kind, one that is "rooted in tradition and sentiment." He distinguishes this individualism from both the "secular" individualism of the French tradition, which has cut loose from Christianity, and the "naked" individualism found in some forms of capitalism, which glorifies the pursuit of self-interest.[69]

Fourth, he confesses his belief that human beings are sinners, and that all human action in history is marked by sin. Here too he elaborates on a point he has mentioned often before. He refers to the traditional Christian doctrine of the Fall, and speaks of human "cupidity" as synonymous with sinfulness. His use of the word "cupidity" soon becomes one of his trademarks, and it strikes the ear as quaint. He commented years later that he especially liked the way the word "cupidity" came off the tongue when you say it emphatically. His point is to note the universality and the equality of sin among human beings. All people are characterized by "original sin." He draws from this belief the implications that no one person is morally better than anyone else, that no political program will eradicate evil in history, and that any political program designed to eliminate the ultimate evil from history is either useless or harmful. He thinks that the Whig method of working with history respects the reality of human sin by aiming for moderation and compromise. By contrast, the methods which derive from the French revolutionary tradition, he says, place unbearable weight on the effectiveness of politics and rely on the power of the state to single out and exterminate some "enemy" who is held responsible for causing all the trouble.[70]

Englishman and His History received adequate recognition in reviews in England at the time, even apart from the misunderstandings of Butterfield's treatment of Whig history and Whig politics. His thesis affirming the role of an interpretation of history in politics was widely accepted in general by historians after the war.[71] Surprisingly, however, in spite of his wishes, the book made virtually no contribution to the public perception of English history during the war. Perhaps the book was too unclear and maybe the connections between the two parts were too difficult to follow. Maybe the long first part was too specialized. Perhaps the book added nothing substantial to what had already been said often enough by others during the war. In any case, the book probably came too late to help fortify the English national will, as Churchill had wanted. It might have served the national need three or four years earlier when catastrophe fell upon England, but now, in 1944, with the Allied reconquests of France and Italy underway, that need had vanished. In 1944 people in England were thinking of what might happen after the war was over, not about the crisis of 1940. If Butterfield wanted his reflections on English history to be heard in 1944, his book needed to do more than "consecrate the Churchillian consensus," as Cowling put it. Cast in different terms, the book might have had more effect if he had looked to the future and contributed his version of English history to the reconstruction of the nation after the war.[72]

Yet while *Englishman and His History* may have had little impact at large, its role in Butterfield's own development as a historian was vital. Whether we agree with his analysis of English history is not important. What matters for historical thinking is that he has succeeded in defining, albeit incompletely, a type of approach to history which does two things at once. First, his historical approach honours the multiplicity of factors operative in any given historical process. He has proposed a multiple-level interpretation of history of the English nation that gives preeminence to no single factor, but combines organic, political, intellectual, social, and religious interpretations into a general historical interpretation. Second, his historical approach rejects a self-contained treatment of English history and entails instead a comparative interpretation which correlates English history with the history of several nations of the continent. Butterfield proposes implicitly that multifactoral and comparative history are two very useful and remarkable features of an approach to historical interpretation that would respect the complexity of historical processes and enlighten the study of any historical topic. On top of this he has identified the interpretation of relations between past and present as a fit subject for historical study. The book is a worthy offspring of the rethinking of general history and historical thought which he conducted during the 1930s.

The book also signalled Butterfield's arrival at his own unambiguous political position and his willingness to make his political views known in public. Under the pressure of the war crisis, and in spite of his apparent desire in theory to segregate politics and history, he explicitly revealed that his politics informed his historical approach. *The Whig Interpretation of History* had already shown his New Whig sympathies, as Smyth observed at the time. However, until Butterfield devised the distinction between Whig history and Whig politics, he had lived with ambivalence towards the Whig tradition. His ambivalence may even have diluted his enthusiasm for writing the life of Fox. Now, after *Englishman*, he could call himself a "New Whig" with no reservations. The baffling label sounded curiously antiquarian. But it makes sense: he was the loyal critic working for the reform of a tradition to which he still belonged. It was a political position that required him to make no choices in contemporary political affairs and left him standing completely outside of twentieth-century politics. It had the merit of allowing him to dissent from all then current political options — fascist, conservative, liberal, Christian democrat, labour, socialist, communist — and to fasten his attention upon the profoundest principles that underlay the conduct of public life. Late in life he described his politics from the war years onward: "My Whiggism is different from liberalism in the continental or the American sense in that it is not utopian. Apart from hoping that human beings will be virtuous it does not operate by assuming they are virtuous. My politics would operate by assuming that there is a great deal of egotism and cupidity in human beings, especially in those you say haven't got any cupidity."[73]

Englishman marked as well another stage in his handling of religion and historical study in his life. What strikes us as important is not the statement of his beliefs — he has indicated his belief in these things often enough before — but the explicit subsumption of his ideas about history under the language of religious discourse, and the disclosure of his religion to the public. The exigencies of war evoked his first major statement in a professional medium indicating explicitly that he approached history as a Christian. The book represented a Christian interpretation of history. He had moved his Christian testimony from the semi-public pulpit of the lay preacher before the Methodist congregation to the fully public stage of the history book. As with his politics, he had once again gone against his previously stated theory, in this case, to keep history separate from religion. Instead, he had candidly acknowledged in public the unification of his vocations as historian and preacher. In both his politics and his religion he revealed himself publicly in terms that resembled the views of his father. It seemed all the more appropriate that he should dedicate the book to the person whom he believed best instantiated the archetypical Englishman.

The years just before and during the long war were an extremely important time for Butterfield as historian. His responses to the political and social movements of the day and especially to the war upset the apparent simplicities of his historical thinking. His theory seemed to call for the demarcation of history from life, but his practice displaced any attempts to keep academic history so unspotted from the world.

Overall during the war years he was extremely productive in his work. He did nothing on Fox, and he did not meet the 1942 deadline for the *Concise History,* and he did not give all the lectures he planned, but he served Peterhouse and the Cambridge History Faculty well, he published three more little books, *Napoleon, Machiavelli,* and *Englishman,* raising the number of his books to six, and he greatly increased his reputation for historical thinking.

In 1944, all England, Cambridge, and Butterfield, too, began to think of reconstruction after the war. There would be vacant professorships to fill, most notably the professorship of modern history. Butterfield did not allow himself to dwell on speculations about his future in Cambridge. Instead, after twenty-five years at Peterhouse, he turned his ambitious mind once again to thoughts of leaving Cambridge to take a professorship elsewhere.

Herbert Butterfield (c1903), age 3, with his sister Edith, in Oxenhope, West Yorkshire, England. Courtesy of Lady Butterfield.

Butterfield (c1910), age 10, with his sister Edith and younger brother Arthur, in Oxenhope. Courtesy of Lady Butterfield.

Butterfield (c1922), age 22, about the time of his admission to the B.A. degree, Peterhouse, Cambridge University. Courtesy of Lady Butterfield.

Butterfield (c1949), age 49, around the time of the publication of *George III, Lord North, and the People, Origins of Modern Science*, and *Christianity and History*. Courtesy of Lady Butterfield.

Butterfield (c1955), age 55, around the time of his election as Master of Peterhouse. Photo by Edward Leigh, courtesy of Lady Butterfield.

Butterfield (c1963), age 63, around the time of his election as Regius Professor of Modern History, Cambridge University. Photo by Edward Leigh, courtesy of Lady Butterfield.

Butterfield (1977), age 77, in retirement at his Tudor house, Sawston, Cambridgeshire. Photo by C. T. McIntire.

Butterfield's birthplace (in 1900), Worker's Cottages, Upper Town, Oxenhope, West Yorkshire. Photo by C. T. McIntire.

Butterfield's home (during 1955–1968) as Master of Peterhouse, the Master's Lodge, Peterhouse, Cambridge. Photo by C. T. McIntire.

6

Professor

Whirlwind

By the spring of 1944 the British and their allies could believe that the war in Europe had turned in their favour. The Italian Fascist government had collapsed in July 1943, and about the same time the Soviet army took the initiative against the Germans on the eastern front. The Allied armies of Britain, the United States, and Canada had been working their way through Sicily since July 1943 and up the Italian peninsula since September 1943. By June 1944 the Germans were routed from Rome and Allied forces landed at Normandy to begin the reconquest of France.

In March 1944, far from the Allied assault on the Germans at the ancient monastery of Monte Cassino, the electors for the chair in modern history convened in Cambridge and selected Butterfield to succeed Temperley as Professor of Modern History, effective 1 April 1944. The act was an affirmation of patriotic hope, since the end of the war was not in sight, and return to normalcy was not at all possible. Butterfield, now forty-four, had waited patiently for nearly five years during the war, since the death of Temperley, for this recognition. The appointment was his, even though he had not presented an application as was customary. The Cambridge members of the committee of electors for the chair included the history elite in the university: Trevelyan, the former Regius Professor; G. N. Clark, the new Regius Professor; Clapham, the recent Professor of Economic History; E. A. Walker, the Professor of Imperial and Naval History; and J. R. M. Butler, later appointed Regius Professor to succeed Clark. Among those they passed over was E. H. Carr, nine years Butterfield's senior, reversing the outcome at Aberystwyth in 1936 when Carr got the professorship.[1] Butterfield once again abandoned his thoughts of leaving Cambridge for another university, and accepted the appointment.

The choice was widely applauded in the university. Trevelyan, now Master of Trinity College, expressed to Butterfield the hopes that he had for the new professor: "If after the war you can use the relative leisure for writing that the Professorship ought to mean (as you rightly think) to put the same high intellectual qualities into some *big* book, you will take the place that you ought to earn among English historians." But there were also detractors, and his elevation to professor elicited feelings of resentment or jealousy among a few, feelings which could issue in denigrating comments about him personally from the occasional historian. Such comments about Butterfield became a strand of oral tradition and even years later a few people were still voicing them.[2]

Dorothy Temperley, Temperley's widow, expressed her hope that Butterfield might prepare a memoir of her husband's life as historian. She had started her own memoir after he died and written three chapters. Butterfield responded in July 1946 with a pledge to write a small book-length memoir of Temperley. In 1948 she gave Butterfield the bronze bust of the young Napoleon that had been her husband's prize trophy, and acknowledged him to be Temperley's successor. In 1949 he was actively thinking about the project. He placed a notice in the *Times Literary Supplement* asking for Temperley letters. Dorothy Temperley arranged to deliver to him a sizeable chunk of the Temperley papers to facilitate the task. During the early 1950s he devoted considerable time to the project.[3]

The new position changed Butterfield's life. Trevelyan had offered him advice: "cultivate the power of saying No." Butterfield ignored the warning and threw himself into a whirlwind of activity which absorbed absolutely all his time. As professor he no longer held supervisions of undergraduates at Peterhouse, but in place of this he added an astonishing number of new commitments, many of them recorded in his *Cambridge Pocket Diary*. He said yes to one invitation after another to join a committee or give a lecture or write an article.[4] He was astonishingly diligent in his committee work and continued to compose every lecture word for word. He laboured long hours day and night, and became busier than ever before. By the beginning of 1945, he was telling people that he felt overwhelmed by all the duties he had taken on.[5]

It was important to him that the professorship meant a rise in salary and that from this moment onward in his career he no longer experienced serious financial stress. The professorship also awarded him still higher social status, lifting him into the ranks of the upper bourgeoisie. The Butterfields remained in their ample nineteenth-century attached house on Tenison Road, and Ethel Wolfe continued to come to the house each day as housekeeper and cook. He persisted in his simple lifestyle and still refused to behave in a more elevated social manner. When Ethel gave him a pre-tied bow tie, a thing any proper gentlemen would disdain, he wore it out of respect for her, even though the Fellows poked fun at this un-Cambridge behaviour.

The professorship in Cambridge also crowned him with national status. He began to receive invitations from across Great Britain and Ireland, most of which he accepted. This led to special lectures at other universities, in local chapters of the national Historical Association, for the Royal Historical Society, and on national radio with the BBC. Over the next few years the number of these lectures outside Cambridge increased by two or three each year, going from none to perhaps fifteen in 1948–1949. For topics he drew on a cycle of five or six titles which reflected his current interests: "History and Ethics," "The Dangers of History," "Fox and the French Revolution," "The Marxian Interpretation of History," "The Seven Years' War." Even when he repeated a topic, however, he would rework what he had delivered before. During the same years he began to accept requests from elsewhere to examine doctoral theses and to recommend people to history professorships and lectureships. By 1948 he joined the editorial board of *History,* the national journal of the Historical Association.[6]

In Cambridge, Butterfield's election maintained the Peterhouse reputation for history, with three Professorial Fellows in history: Postan, Brogan, and now Butterfield. Vellacott's return from war service restored a historian to the head of the college. At the same time, in 1944, the college replaced Temperley, or in a sense replaced Butterfield as an ordinary Fellow, by giving a fellowship to David Knowles, a medievalist, a Roman Catholic priest, and a monk. The appointment raised the number of historians to six out of the nine Fellows and Master. Butterfield was the prime mover in bringing Knowles to Peterhouse, and that success gave him the greatest pleasure. The two became close friends. Butterfield always sought the advice of Knowles, who was four years his senior, and came to regard him as someone who, like his father and Carey Francis, embodied a saintly Christianity.[7] The college added a seventh historian in 1947 when Denis Mack Smith, Butterfield's student during 1944–1946, received a fellowship, and soon became Tutor of the college. Butterfield thought of himself as the one who had urged Mack Smith to go into historical scholarship. Simultaneously, however, the college enlarged the number of Fellows to fifteen and diversified its fields, thereby reducing the proportion of historians. In the same year, 1947, Knowles became Professor of Medieval History, and Butterfield persuaded the college to retain him as a Professorial Fellow, in spite of the animosity displayed against Knowles by the Master, Vellacott. The total of Professorial Fellows in history at Peterhouse now numbered a record four out of the nine professors listed with the History Faculty.[8] On top of all this, in 1946, the college gave an honourary fellowship to R. H. Tawney, noted historian from the London School of Economics who had resettled at Peterhouse during the war when the LSE fled London, and, in 1948, made Henry Steele Commager, professor of history from Columbia University, a Fellow Commoner after he completed a year in Cambridge as the Professor of American History and Institutions. Peterhouse may have been a little community by comparison with other Cambridge colleges, but it was unsurpassed in the world per capita for historians. The Peterhouse reputation for history rose still higher. Butterfield thrived amid such colleagues.[9]

Meanwhile, after the war ended the undergraduate population of Peterhouse rose slowly, returning by 1948–1949 to the prewar average of about 150. In place of supervising undergraduates, Butterfield began to supervise Ph.D. dissertations, adding a new dimension to his workload, his influence, and his college. He took on an average of two new research students a year, including among his first, from 1945 to 1949, Duncan Forbes, Peter Hardy, W. E. Mosse, H. G. Koenigsberger, and T. G. A. Pocock. He met his students often and read their work thoroughly. In 1947 he ceased being college librarian, an office he had held for twenty-two years, but he added a lengthy number of other involvements. He became secretary of the Peterhouse Society, the association of the alumni of the college, served on the High Table committee, joined the committee of the college history club, participated in the meetings on the admission of scholars, and attended countless other college meetings. When the relationship between the university and the colleges became a controversial issue after the war, he stepped forward as an articulate promoter of the teaching role of the colleges. He candidly admitted that college membership could steal time from research and writing by mounting up the distractions. On one occasion he listed them all: "the meetings of the governing body, the committees, the negotiations, the exacting nature of the supervisor's work, the hours spent informally with undergraduates, the unspecified demands on time, the threat of unwanted administrative work, the chilly bedrooms and whistling chimneys, and the incessant knockings on the door."[10]

In the History Faculty, his professorship meant a modicum of specialization. He no longer tutored undergraduates on a broad range of historical topics, and he gave no further lectures on general European history. He thus lost contact with the medium which facilitated his work on the *Concise Cambridge Modern History*. In place of this, however, he offered three courses of lectures lasting one term each: "History of England, 1688–1792," "European History, 1493–1559," and "Factors in German History." He automatically held a seat on the History Faculty board and he met often with Clark, the Regius Professor, to discuss the needs of the faculty in modern history. He worked on a general reform of the History Tripos, and joined the degree committee and the film committee. Around Cambridge he remained active on the history of science committee, soon became a member of the university's new Board of Research Studies, continued as chief editor of the *Cambridge Historical Journal,* and participated in the Cambridge History Club, the Cambridge Historical Society, the History of Science Society, and the Cambridge Historical Association. He discontinued teaching at Wesley House, and he no longer served as lay preacher — although his name remained on the circuit list of lay preachers — but he joined the Wesley House Oversight Committee and entertained the Wesley Society at Peterhouse. All this activity added up to a phenomenal amount of administrative work, and it did not help him concentrate on research and writing.

The professorship required him to deliver an inaugural lecture, which he did on 14 November 1944. It soon appeared as a booklet, *The Study of Modern History.*[11] The war was not at all over, but, in the wake of the Allied reconquest of Normandy in June, Butterfield as well as the rest of England began acting as if the Allies would eventually triumph over the Germans. The Allied military victory which made the final defeat of the Nazis look possible — the Battle of the Bulge in northern France, in December 1944 and January 1945 — did not come until after Butterfield's lecture.

In the middle of just this timing, Butterfield speaks freely against Nazi and Fascist totalitarianism, but warns against perpetuating anti-German attitudes. He draws out his old doctrine of imaginative sympathy which he asks his audience to apply to the Germans, their historians, their government, and those who "for some reason have fallen in love with a foreign power." As in the case of Galinsky, his Nazi academic friend from Germany, he likens Nazi loyalty to Germany to English patriotism, a sentiment which he himself had experienced during the war.[12] At the same time, he speaks a word for the independence of all historians from subservience to any government, from anything that might count as government-favoured history.[13]

In the tradition of inaugural lectures, Butterfield meditates on the needs of his field of study. He declares his attachment to the outlook and technique that Temperley taught him and affirms his dedication in particular to the method of diplomatic history, praising its value for the training of new historians in any subject. On this occasion, after a decade and a half of lectures on the modern history of Europe, he wishes to state his views on what he called the "other history," one reaching well beyond the history he had learned from Temperley. He projects two kinds of history. One is dependent on original research and takes the form of narrative. The other is based on history books and exhibits a character that is hard to specify. He gives no names to these histories, although he seems to think of the one as narrative history and the other as having to do with general history.[14]

He is most at ease when he characterizes narrative history, the form he knew as diplomatic history and had championed for many years. He had written about it in *The Whig Interpretation of History,* and he adds nothing new to what he had already said. In his view, narrative history employs a technique of research, concentrates on resurrecting details about events from day to day, deals with the individual personality "as a fountain of activity," and results in the historian telling a story. This is the history that is close to his religious convictions about the primacy of individual personality.

He finds it more difficult to speak of the "other history" and its association with general history. We sense that he is still searching for the language to describe it, still unsure about what he means by it, still trying to convince even himself of its validity. He specifically abandons the things he said in *Whig Interpretation* about general history being a kind of abridgment of history. Now he believes that a special kind of exercise of the mind is required in order to think that certain sequences of events over long periods of time may be perceived as, for instance, the development of Europe or the fall of Rome or the transition from the medieval to the modern world. Such locutions are the typical stuff of general history and they are "misunderstood," he now says, if we think of them as "the abridgment of narrative."

When he tries to characterize this "other history" and to identify the mental operations historians go through to produce it, he becomes very imprecise. He offers six or seven suggestions about what he means by the other history, and they come to us scattered throughout the second and third sections of the lecture. First, the other history may be the search for meaning and patterns in history. Second, it may be analysis, whether the analysis of structures lying deep below the surface, such as the social systems and thought structures of a period, or the analysis of slow-moving processes that take centuries, such as social movements and trends of thought. Third, it may be exposition, taking account of differences as, for example, between the centuries or stages of development. Fourth, it may be explanation, by which he here means putting things in context. Fifth, it may be the disclosure of connections and wider interactions among economic, social, political, religious, and intellectual affairs. Sixth, it may be the identification of the "system of necessity" and the conditioning circumstances which operate beyond the control of individuals to shape particular events. Seventh, it may be depiction, portraiture, of the "social fabric of an age."[15]

We know not to expect a systematic statement from Butterfield, but here he outdoes himself in the apparent randomness of his thought and vocabulary. The characteristics he suggests do not all amount to the same thing. For instance, the search for meaning is not the same as the analysis of deep structures, and putting things in context is not the same as either of these, nor is it the same as disclosing the connections among things, and so on. Moreover, most of these characteristics are not absent from good narrative history. For instance, narrative rests on analysis, always puts things in context, and discloses connections among things. Conversely, general histories have taken the form of narrative and featured individual personalities. In other words, most, perhaps even all, of the characteristics he mentions refer to features involved in almost any form of historical thinking — search for meaning, analysis, exposition, explanation, and so on. He mislocates the difference between the two histories when he distinguishes narrative from analysis, exposition, explanation, and the like. Butterfield seems to notice the problem when he acknowledges that a very good narrative history of the Reformation, for example, would be steadily improved and the story line transformed by the impact of more and more analysis.

Yet, we get the drift of Butterfield's suggestions. There is a difference between individuals and wider movements, between surface and depth, between some particular topic and all the interactions of that topic on a great scale, between short-term happenings and longer-term trends, between small problems and grand problems. He wants to urge historians to move beyond narration, beyond individual happenings, beyond the actions of individual personalities, beyond the obvious. He is calling for the conscious incorporation within historical thinking of wider and deeper and larger and longer-lasting matters of human existence. In sum, he wants historical study to acknowledge and account for the sheer complexity of human activity over the ages.

He performs his customary obeisance to Acton in the lecture, but he ventures a major criticism of his exemplar which convinces us that we are indeed catching his drift. Acton's version of general history, we are told, was too simple. Acton privileged role of ideas in history, especially one idea, the idea of liberty. Now, Butterfield suggests, we are obliged to reach much farther than this, to "the realm where economic, social, political, and intellectual or religious movements intertwine."[16] We hear on the near horizon the many voices that helped him enlarge his discourse about general history during the 1930s, and we watch him project an approach analogous to those of contemporary Marxists, Toynbee, and the French historians of the Annales variety in the lineage of Bloch and Febvre. He is not abandoning his favourite history, and he makes sure in a footnote that we know he still believes that narrative history about individual personalities is the essential starting point for historical study. However, he is saying that shifting one's attention to general history is not a matter of telling the story in shorter form. On any scale, "mere narrative" is insufficient. Historians "must" move onward to the "other history." We may infer from what he says that doing so entails bringing to consciousness all the mental operations involved in any historical investigation and working with them in relation to greater and greater complexity over greater and greater ranges of time. He imagines such historical thinking extending to the whole of modern European history. He did not yet — but he could — project the problem onto the scale of global history from the beginning to the end of time. And he did not raise the question of law in history, although his thinking during the 1930s and early 1940s did broach the subject.

Near the end of the inaugural lecture Butterfield uttered what we may take to be his primary message. Whatever historians may do with their histories, they must above all evince "elasticity" of mind. "There is no wisdom to be gained from history that may not be reduced to devastation by a heavy and rigid mind," he declared. And farther on, "But for us the great crime is to be deficient in elasticity." Still later, "There is a half-way house, a home of half-baked history, where everything is dogmatic and all the lines of the picture are hard." He means that he wants historians to be open to seeing history in ever new ways. He lets us know that he is willing to change his own thinking, even while maintaining a deeper continuity. More than this, he hopes to use historical thinking to upset the reigning doctrines of his day and to undermine our tendency to hear only what we already want to believe. His primary instrument for encouraging the mental elasticity he deemed appropriate would be to teach and write that "other history." This is the dissenter speaking to us again.[17]

Fox Diverted Again

With the inaugural lecture out of the way, Butterfield turned again to his research and writing, the work expected of him as professor. He received especially strong support to this end from an unexpected source — Eve Bogle — a talented secretary and administrator whom he had met in 1942. He was forty-two and she was a few years older. She had taken a house with her children in Cambridge, near the Butterfields, while her husband remained in London in government service during the war. Her son James attended the same school as Butterfield's son Giles, and the two boys soon became close friends. Butterfield and she became good friends as well. For her war service she contributed secretarial work through the Women's Volunteer Service, and, she recalls, in that capacity she eventually typed her first letter for Butterfield in 1945.

After the war Bogle decided to work for Butterfield. She became devoted to him, typing his letters and writings, and generally serving as his personal secretary and research assistant. From this moment on, thanks to her, Butterfield's papers are voluminous. She generated and preserved the hard copy and created his archives. She agreed to work for a nominal stipend, well below the standard rate. Butterfield paid her out of his personal income. She explains that she accepted the pay inequity because she wanted to help him and she knew he could afford nothing higher. She had to work hard to keep up with the constant race of writing that he ran in the postwar period. Her working days with him were long. In his intensity he would smoke forty cigarettes a day, always passing the pack along to her. She often helped him with his research, going, for instance, to Cambridge University Library to copy things for him from the Acton papers. She went on research trips with him, and together they hand-copied documents in the Royal Archives in Windsor Castle, the British Museum manuscript room, and many other archives. Like Pamela, she called him Bean. Unlike Pamela, she loved to hear about and involve herself in his historical scholarship, which gave Herbert and her a special bond. She worked with him for twenty-five years, until she had to stop in 1970 because of her ill health. "He was the most exciting man to work with," she remembered, "he would always surprise you." She added, "He introduced me to the historical Jesus."[18]

Butterfield had to struggle very hard to make time to write. He wrote after hours and into the night, on weekends and between terms, and during the summer vacation. He committed himself to following several parallel, yet connected, lines of writing at once. Above all, he resumed his work on the life of Charles James Fox, professing to those around him that he counted the book on Fox as his primary duty after the war. He set to work in earnest on his Fox biography, but gradually his research and writing on Fox were transformed into something else. For the second time in his life he found himself pursuing a tangential question of general history arising out of the Fox materials, leading him far away from Fox. The previous occasion came during the 1930s when he had asked a question about George III, moved on to Bolingbroke, and ended up writing a book on Machiavelli. The pull of writing biography was not as strong as other questions.

In October 1945, he wrote the British Museum to say that he was ready to continue his research on Fox after a lapse of six years. He got himself restarted before the end of 1945. In November 1945 Eve Bogle began typing manuscripts he had drafted before the war on the years 1779 and 1780. By October 1946 she had typed at least twelve or thirteen papers short-titled Fox, or George III, or North.[19] In December 1945 he told the librarian of the York City Library that he was preparing a life of Fox and that "incidental" to this he had decided to produce a paper on the Yorkshire Association during 1779 and 1780, and wished to arrange research time in York later in the month. In January 1946 he corresponded with several county and private archives, mentioning his life of Fox and asking for access to materials for a short "by-product" on county meetings and associations in 1780.[20] In March 1946 he presented a paper to the Royal Historical Society, "The Yorkshire Association and the Crisis of 1779–1780," which he revised and published in 1947, his second article on these years.[21] During 1946 and 1947 he carried on research in the British Museum and other archives.[22] The effects of the methodology that Butterfield had adopted for his Fox research were evident in the materials he used to construct this new study. The effects were overwhelming. In the 1930s he had imposed on himself the mandate to make his research microscopic, comprehensive, and exhaustive, and he reaffirmed that mandate now. Namier's example of thoroughness must have impacted him daily.[23] Butterfield added enormously to the pile of notes he had been accumulating since at least 1933 on the years 1779 and 1780. By 1947, he had amassed hundreds upon hundreds of little slips of paper, each slip containing one bit of information or one extract from a letter, a speech, a memoir, a newspaper. He arranged the slips first by topic and then by date within each topic, day by day, and tied them in little bundles. He began to admit that he had lost his focus on the "purely" biographical matters about Fox and was really working on general problems related to the reign of George III. He realized slowly that his work on an incidental theme had ballooned far beyond one paper or even several papers. He later justified this obsessive diversion of his energies with the claim that he simply could not resist being attracted by "the teasing nature of some of the problems involved" in the events of 1779 and 1780. He began to reconceive the miscellaneous topics scattered in front of him as intersecting lines of subject matter which might be handled together as a book. By the fall of 1947, he had reworked his materials into what he was now calling chapters. Altogether he produced several handwritten drafts and Bogle produced several typescripts.

Then, early in January 1948, he collected merely a portion of all he had written, created a table of contents, added a title, and sent a very large typescript to the publisher.[24] He selected Bell of London, publishers of *Whig Inter-*

pretation, Machiavelli, and his inaugural lecture, rather than Cambridge University Press, publishers of *Historical Novel, Peace Tactics of Napoleon,* and *Englishman.* He seemed to blame Cambridge University Press for the lack of notice which *Englishman* attracted. He thought that Bell, as a commercial house, would give his new book wide circulation and generate public discussion.[25] In July 1948 Butterfield explained to Trevelyan the complicated and unpremeditated process that led to this book, and asked for approval to dedicate it to him, and Trevelyan agreed. He also acknowledged for the first time how dependent he had become on Eve Bogle to accomplish his work.[26]

While in the white heat of productivity Butterfield also finished an article, "Charles James Fox and the Whig Opposition in 1792," which he placed in the *Cambridge Historical Journal,* the journal he himself edited. This piece, on a topic falling outside 1779–1780, included themes he had raised in the first paper he had given outside Peterhouse in the mid-1920s. It reminds us how long he had thought about Fox.[27]

The typescript of the book sat at the publisher for a year and a half before finally appearing early in October 1949 under the title *George III, Lord North, and the People, 1779–1780.* The article on Fox and 1792 came out at the same time. The book was Butterfield's seventh, his second based on serious research. It satisfied Trevelyan's fixation on size. It was a big book of 419 pages, surpassing the 400 pages of *Peace Tactics of Napoleon,* and Trevelyan was delighted.[28] In keeping with Butterfield's theory, the writing is chiefly narrative, telling stories about the activities of individual personalities. The book on every page shows the results of his minute research methodology, and as a research achievement it far surpasses *Peace Tactics.* At the same time, like *Peace Tactics,* the text gives evidence of virtually no interaction with the pertinent scholarship on his subjects. This is a curious omission for someone by now normally so taken up with the history of the treatment of historical themes. We can tell from his notes that, nonetheless, he may well have read the relevant historical studies.

The book is by and large a narrative history of various topics during a period of about eight months, from the fall of 1779 to April 1780, a stretch of time even shorter than the little period he encompassed in *Peace Tactics.* As he moves through the text he seems to have in mind the plot of some general story about well-known events involving the king, Parliament, and the government which he wants to refashion. He is rejecting the inherited Whig interpretation which, he charges, sees in the events a case of Whigs against the Crown, and the righteous against the wicked. He believes that he is offering a reconception of the whole story, although it is not easy to follow anything like a general story throughout the book.

When we analyze the contents, the book appears to be a miscellany without an integrative structure, indicative of the makeshift process of afterthought by which he compiled the book. Three topics predominate: the ministry of Lord North, the prime minister of the day; the activities of the Yorkshire Association and its leader the Rev. Christopher Wyvill; and the parliamentary operations of Edmund Burke and Fox. Three other topics surface from the text, however: the efforts by a few politicians to promote greater Irish parliamentary independence, the conduct of the war against the American colonies, and the Gordon Riots in London as expressions of Protestant anti-Catholic feeling. Still other topics, more general in character, emerge from time to time: the intentions of George III, his political system, and the question of political parties during his reign. We notice that his research is most intense when he touches George III, Fox, and the Yorkshire Association, and most sketchy on the North ministry and Ireland. He gives his greatest attention to a few London-Windsor based individuals at the top of the political structures: the king, the prime minister, and some members of Parliament. But he also attempts to look seriously at extra-parliamentary political activity outside London, notably in Yorkshire. This accounts for the allusion to "the people" in his title. He occasionally mentions the agricultural and industrial economy, social ranks, population figures, and religion, and his mention of these things exceed anything he has put in his historical writing before. None of this is enough to turn the work into a social history, however, and it remains chiefly a narrative about some individuals in national politics.

Butterfield's handling of the "other history," that general history which he contrasted with narrative history and applauded in his inaugural lecture, is difficult to detect. What he does say makes us suppose that he regards the entire book as a blending of both modes of historical writing. The clearest statement about the two histories comes early in the introduction. During the reign of George III, he suggests, there are two levels of drama occurring simultaneously, and they are properly the subject of two levels of history. The "surface-drama" — the narrative history — is a battle between the king and the aristocracy in which neither side defeats the other. The deeper drama — the general history — is "a movement long, slow, and deep," representing a "tide" which brings "wider classes of Englishmen to intellectual awareness and a realization of the part they might play in politics." In the long run, these wider classes of Englishmen triumph over both the Crown and the aristocracy, bringing effects that he believes benefit English liberty. Butterfield interprets the actions of George III and the Lord North ministry as belonging to the "surface-drama." He sees evidence of the deeper drama of the emergence of "the people" in the activities of several movements and their leaders: Christopher Wyvill's York-

shire Association, John Wesley's Methodism, and John Wilkes's radical political activity in the London-Middlesex region in 1769–1770.[29]

We find a number of passages in unpredictable places where he makes the
"other history" explicit. They allow us to observe his method of correlating the
two histories. In the middle of a long section on the Yorkshire Association, for
instance, Butterfield offers this statement of the general connections he observes between the work of Wyvill and aspects of wider, later history: "He and
his collaborators launched upon the country, and set fairly and squarely on its
course, the most important of the movements that have made the modern
world. The Yorkshire Association bridges the gulf between Middlesex radicalism — Wilkesite, undiscriminating, and half-disreputable — and the national
movement of parliamentary reform. It assists the transition from eighteenth-
century parties based on 'connection' to the modern kind of party which is a
matter of issues and principles." Butterfield's method, judging from this case,
demands that the historian look at the plethora of detail generated by the first
history — the narrative history — and perceive within the mass a historical form
of longer duration and wider connection. It is an act of intuition, not of
analysis, and it requires no actual further research. Butterfield "sees" something more than what the evidence directly reveals. He places his specific events
of 1779–1780 on a trajectory running into a future history which could not
have been known by Wyvill and would have meant nothing to him, but which
is known to Butterfield and important to him. Wyvill himself was not designing
a future national movement of parliamentary reform or a future political party
system based on ideology, but Butterfield interprets his program as contributing to the creation of such things. The selection of both the Wyvill movement
and the later outcomes, and intuition of a connection between them, depends
on Butterfield's own political ideology. In keeping with what we learned about
Butterfield's preferences in *Englishman and His History,* he likes the respectability and the nonrevolutionary character of the Yorkshire Association. He
also delights in the moderate reforms of Parliament which occurred subse-
quently during the nineteenth century and which he ranks extravagantly high
as a factor making the modern world.[30] In other words, Butterfield reads a later
present, which he approves, back into the past, and relates the events under
study to a version of general history which he imports from that later present. It
is an act which violates his injunctions in *Whig Interpretation of History* not to
study the past for the sake of the present, but it comports well with his approach in *Englishman and His History,* where he freely mixed and mingled
past and present in his portrayal of the English as the bearers of a moderate
Christian heritage in politics which produced modern liberty.

When we look closely at the way Butterfield conveys to us that "other history," it seems that he does not heed very well his own admonition to integrate the detailed story and "the other history" or to blend general analysis into the narrative. Aside from his remarks in the introduction on the two histories, what he does is to break into his story every once in a while to refer to a long-term trend or state a maxim or launch himself on an excursus about historical study. The strategy is the same as *Peace Tactics,* and he really has gained very little ground on how to do what he is advocating in his statements about two histories. The result is not the mingling of two histories, but merely the peppering of the dominating narrative medium with miscellaneous insertions and ad hoc comments. Perhaps the most significant consequence at the level of his discourse is simply that he remains intent on dealing with historical study as a matter of two histories, whatever this means, and not merely with history as narratives about individuals engaged in politics, diplomacy, and war.

The comments about historical study that he inserts now and then into the text reveal nothing new in his thinking. For instance, early in the book we find an excursus in which he restates his customary convictions about the process of history. Here he stresses how the intentions of a single individual, such as George III, constantly intermingle with "countless other wills" to produce results unlike what any one of them expected. He refers to the "predicament" or the "situation" or the "entanglements" which restrict a leader's action and force him to decide for things he really does not want. In the preface he repeats his oft-told complaint about historians and moral judgments. Consistent with *Whig Interpretation of History* he objects to a construction of the narrative which casts one side of a conflict as pushing in a direction we approve, here once again the favoured Whigs, and the others as their obstacles, especially the king and the Tories: "It is not a clear case of the righteous fighting the wicked — and even the Rockinghamites (though we may love their cause) have their egoisms, their vested interests, their pettinesses and their wilful ways. At the same time even George III will be seen to have had his impressive qualities." As a matter of method, he wants to look at the principal figures and their interactions with each other from the perspective of each in turn, and to look at the stated ideals as well as the actual behaviour of each. He wishes to achieve thereby what he describes as "something like the stereoscopic picture." His words recall the reconciling method he advocated in *Whig Interpretation.* Although he does not say so, we may assume that he has Lewis Namier on his mind, and is offering an alternative to what he would take to be Namier's overemphasis on the "vested interests" of politicians to the neglect of the recognition of their "higher purposes."[31]

His maxims number in the scores and are scattered throughout the book, making him sound more and more like the Machiavelli whose methods he discussed several years before. The maxims represent matters that he believes hold true in a general way over long periods of time. He gives the maxims an explanatory role in his text. He still does not call them "laws," but he states them in a general form, using the enduring present tense which makes them sound as if they are laws in history. For example, he alludes to a coincidence between actual advancement in the condition of Ireland and the emergence of Irish disquiet, and then writes, "The same features would appear to confirm the accepted view that a revolutionary spirit arises when things are beginning generally to improve; the view also that the discontented find their opportunity at the moment when a government is trying to be kind." A moment later he adduces another maxim: "Men in any case are prone to see grievances — and to make much of them — and it requires an effort to induce them to be still for a moment and to count their blessings." By making general statements such as these about human behaviour and applying them to certain events in Ireland he provides an explanation of why things happened as they did there. As maxims, they are the final link in the explanatory chain, so to speak, and require no argument or justification. His maxims sound as if they should be the results of his analysis of a number of cases of the same kind of activity — political discontent, for instance — but we find no evidence that he has conducted such analysis. Machiavelli was more explicitly empirical than he is. Butterfield's maxims are intuitions linked to his own political and moral preferences. He would like governments and the discontented to meet in the moderate middle, and he would like people to "count their blessings" rather than complain.[32]

Butterfield sought to bind the book into a unity by presenting a large and daring thesis, stated in the opening two pages. Between the fall of 1779 and the spring of 1780, there was, he proposes, an extraordinary "heightening of political conflict" which created a "quasi-revolutionary" threat to the government of Lord North. The crisis was created by three movements which were sufficiently simultaneous and "so curiously inter-connected" that they need to be seen together. The three were activities in Ireland promoting Irish parliamentary independence, the extra-parliamentary campaigns of the Yorkshire Association, and the passage of Dunning's resolution in the House of Commons calling for a decrease in the influence of the Crown in government. Butterfield claims that because Lord North overcame these movements, all of which challenged the very structure of British government as well as the ruling position of North and his ministry, the world has forgotten the seriousness of the crisis. According to Butterfield these events during the months in question possess a historical importance of the highest rank: "It would even be perhaps not too far-fetched if we were to say that the real 'revolutionary moment' in this whole period of English history is the moment at which catastrophe loomed threatening, but was circumvented — was escaped by a fairly narrow margin. Our 'French Revolution' is in fact that of 1780 — the revolution that we escaped."[33] He spends little time in the book supporting so grandiose and comprehensive a thesis. He looks instead at the details of each of the elements that he says created the crisis. His approach is not systematic, and while he devotes enough time to the Yorkshire Association to convince us of the seriousness of its activity, he tells us relatively little about the movement in Ireland, and even his treatment of the passage of Dunning's resolution is meagre. As evidence of actual protorevolutionary eruption, he points briefly to the anti-Catholic Gordon Riots in London in what amounts to an appendix at the end of the book. The Gordon Riots did produce something like fear of political disorder among members of the government and the ruling classes at the time. However, the convoluted lead into his thesis about the revolution manqué in England ("It would even be perhaps not too far-fetched it we were to say that . . .") as well as the summary of his conclusions in the final pages of the book both hint that even he knows he is overstating the case. What mighty contortions the historian would need to perform to elevate the fear produced by the Gordon Riots into the possibility of a national crisis on the scale of the French Revolution.[34]

The themes that particularly hold Butterfield's interest in the book are not really those belonging to his grand thesis about the English near-revolution. He is captivated instead by the constitutional issues raised by his notions that George III had a "system" and that "party" and "opposition" are emerging in English politics. He interprets one document — a brief, unfinished reflection in George III's hand from about 1772 — as the key to the king's behaviour from the moment of his ascent to the throne in 1760. He argues that the king began his reign with the purpose of uniting the nation around the House of Hanover and the royal settlement of 1688–1689, ridding society of the contentiousness created by unnecessary party division, regaining for the Crown the superintending role enjoyed by his predecessors before the Whig aristocrats had usurped royal authority, and bringing to an end corruption in government. He would be the "Patriot King," the benevolent father of his country portrayed by Bolingbroke. What the king got instead, Butterfield argues, is a system which manifested the corruption he sought to eradicate, a network of royal influence and patronage which went beyond the proper moral bounds of the day and traded loyalty to the Crown for social favour, government office, and financial benefit. It perpetuated the existence of party connections based on vested interests and personal profit, not on principles and political ideals. The king bound even Lord North to him by such methods. Butterfield lays against the king's system the moral judgment that it represented a "whole vast edifice of influence or corruption." The structure of his story about 1779 and 1780 depends on his claim that there is a ruling system such as he describes, and that it is corrupt. He counts the Yorkshire Association and the extra-parliamentary pressures in Ireland and London as movements against corruption. They are promoters of political principle, agents of reform, and their actions produce consequences whose effects ranged far into the future, far beyond their known horizon. What matters most to Butterfield in his narrative is his insistence that George III did have intentions, political intentions of high moral worth, as did many of the figures on all sides of the conflict, and that government corruption and crass material self-interest were not the only factors in human affairs, although they were certainly operative as powerful forces.[35]

In other words, Butterfield's historical account turns on his moral assessment of human behavior as ambiguously both righteous and wicked. It rests on his moral judgment of what constituted corruption, as well as on his appreciation of the moral mission of the historian as the reconciler. He constructs his narrative to favour his own "New Whig" politics of moderation and accommodation, and at the same time to demonstrate the futility of disruptive radicalism. George III, the Whig aristocrats, and the respectable Yorkshire Association all win his praise, while the Gordon rioters, the unruly Irish, and the disruptive Wilkesites do not. Butterfield wants to convince us that moderation triumphed in 1779–1780 and that the English successfully avoided the disorder he associates with the French Revolution. *George III, Lord North, and the People* is a very long footnote to *The Englishman and His History*.

The book did not get good reviews. Almost no one at the time accepted his thesis about the English "French Revolution" that did not happen. Nearly every review referred to that thesis as extreme or overstated. His lesser thesis about the "people" found no support either, and no one picked up his thesis about the intentions of George III as compared with the corrupt system that emerged in reality. R. R. Sedgwick, one of his examiners from his undergraduate years, recognized Butterfield's allusions to Lewis Namier's work on the early years of George III, but charged him with failing to grasp Namier's point. One review after another deplored the number of details and quotations from letters, calling them excessive. Reviewers noted the absence of reference to secondary literature. In spite of his attempts to suggest relationships between all the details and general history, more than one reviewer wanted to know what the significance of it all was. One man estimated that his topic was worth no more that an article. All in all, he received very little praise. The reviewer in the *Listener* called his treatment of the Yorkshire Association valuable, the

Times Literary Supplement writer thought his view of the king was "balanced," Irish reviewers liked the attention he gave to Ireland in a book mainly about England, but that was about it. Even his writing style was criticized — too many metaphors, too much repetition, too abrupt an ending. The one piece of unlimited approval came from G. Scott Bremner in the *Yorkshire Post*, who, in a burst of regional enthusiasm, thought the book written by this man from Yorkshire was clearly destined to become required reading for the student of English constitutional history and would arouse the lively interest of every Yorkshireman. The picture evoked the question of whether Butterfield might have allowed his Yorkshire sympathies to run away with the material.[36]

In later years the book fared better among historians. His younger colleague at Cambridge, J. H. Plumb, adopted his main thesis completely, and said so in a volume that became the much reprinted standard introduction to eighteenth-century England. Plumb praised the book for showing "how constitutional, political, and social history can be combined to achieve the reconstruction of a great crisis in our history." Harold Parker noted how Butterfield's historical writing exactly matched the recommendations he offered in his historiographical writing, and how any defects in the book were due to his not following his own recommendations fully enough. Some years later John Derry suggested that the book "can now be seen as possessing something of a pioneering character" in its move to connect high politics with broader currents in the country. Geoffrey Elton agreed, and ranked the book very high as technical history. He too saw it as pioneering in the way it demonstrated the significance of looking beyond London when analyzing the growth of radical politics. Butterfield's moves became commonplace in English historical writing. J. C. D. Clark regarded Butterfield's thesis about the revolution that did not happen as important for the analysis of the problem of revolutions and rebellions generally, whether in English history or elsewhere.[37]

At the time, however, Butterfield admitted that the reviews discouraged him. By his own standards *George III, Lord North, and the People* was not an important book. It was merely a diversion from his real task of producing the biography of Charles James Fox. The Fox book could hardly seem farther away than it did to him now.

Modern History

Next to the intense activity which produced *George III, Lord North, and the People*, Butterfield resumed a second line of writing after becoming Professor and after the war ended. He returned with diligence to his work on the *Concise Cambridge Modern History*, neglected during the war. The lectures he had composed during the 1930s and early 1940s were his base. He criticized his own work severely and forced himself to rewrite everything he had done. By 1949 he had redone, and Eve Bogle had retyped, perhaps fifty lectures. Of these about one-third were on politics and war, a quarter on religion, one-fifth on intellectual themes including science, the same number on historical geography, and one or two lectures on economic or social themes. Cambridge University Press spoke with him about the book in January 1949, and he convinced them that the work was going well. He now envisioned a large one-volume book in place of a two-volume set. He would make no promise of a deadline for the finished product.[38]

Butterfield's inaugural address in November 1944 was his first major statement on how to approach the subject of general modern history. He made a second statement in April 1945 when he presented a paper, "Tendencies in Historical Study in England," to the Conference of Irish Historians in Dublin. It was the first of what became a long list of visits and connections with Ireland throughout the rest of his life. He speaks in the paper as if there were a revival of interest in Acton's thought, and uses Acton as both guide and opponent. Ostensibly it is a review of current trends, but it amounts to a concise summary of what he felt he himself was achieving at Cambridge in the study of general history and in defining the moral content of historical study. It is a surprisingly immoderate identification of his own views as the wave of the future in historical study. One has the feeling that Butterfield has begun to delight in issuing the pronouncements on history which his role as Professor entitles him to issue. Gone for now is the painful shyness that marked his career in the twenties and thirties.[39]

The dominant trend in historical study in England, he suggests, is to treat modern history as the growth of western civilization and to reduce the concentration on diplomatic history and ideas in history. This change is in sympathy with Acton's idea of history as organic process, but away from his concentration on ideas and politics. The new tendency means demoting the state and international relations from their positions of centrality and replacing them with "society" and "civilization." It then entails analyzing what Butterfield called "the inter-relation between various factors: the interactions of economic, social, political, religious, and intellectual movements." It minimizes the notion of a break between medieval and modern, and features instead the idea of a gradual transition over many centuries. The scientific revolution of the seventeenth century becomes more important and the Italian Renaissance becomes less so. Eastern Europe and Russia get included and western Europe is relativized.

All this we recognize as a summary of Butterfield's own stated program. We recall, however, that his practice — in his lectures or in his drafts for the *Concise Cambridge Modern History* — failed to match his professed intention. Moreover, while he might speak in favour of widening the geographical scope of general modern history to embrace eastern Europe, he explicitly rejects the attempt to include any of the rest of the world. He bluntly opposes the teaching of more Asian, African, and Latin American history in the university. As he puts it, "we are in danger of running as fast as we can after superficiality," and he fears that even English history will be taught inadequately. He sounds firmly Anglocentric in his approach to modern history.[40]

After the war, Butterfield continued to find, or receive, opportunities to promote his vision of general history as the organic growth of civilization. One of these was a new course of lectures entitled "History of England, 1688–1792" in which he applied the approach to the study of his own nation. He explained his intentions to his students on the first day: "we shall not be merely economic or social or political or constitutional or ecclesiastical historians — because these are only artificial divisions which we make to help us in certain kinds of analysis. We must take a glimpse of England as a whole, and envisage English history as a single web of growth." The texts of his lectures indicate that he still devotes most of his attention to politics, but he makes an ardent attempt to incorporate material on nonpolitical themes.[41]

Another opportunity came from Cambridge University Press in February and March 1945. The Press invited G. N. Clark and Butterfield, the holders of the two Cambridge chairs in modern history, to give advice concerning the revision of the *Cambridge Modern History*, the monumental collaborative venture which Acton had spawned. The Press had in mind simply bringing the volumes up to date with recent scholarship. Both historians did their homework before responding with a report. Butterfield read the notes and correspondence in which Acton set down his original plan. Here was a chance for Butterfield to practice his ideas of general history on a grand scale.[42] Their conclusion, given to the Press in April 1945, determined the course of what happened next: "After considering how far the *History* fulfils the requirements of the present time, we have come to the conclusion that no mere revision would be satisfactory, and that a new work is needed." Since Acton's day, they wrote, "the accepted idea of general history has changed." Clark and Butterfield agreed on the proposals that followed, which mirrored Butterfield's ideas on general history.[43]

Within a month the Press adopted their concept of an entirely new modern history and asked Clark and Butterfield to serve as the general editors. Butterfield exhibited particular enthusiasm for the role. He immediately projected a plan for a giantesque *New Cambridge Modern History*, expanded from the original dozen volumes to twenty-four. Volume 1 would begin with 1494, the final volume would close with 1918, and 1715 and 1815 would mark the principal divisions within the period. He designated the first three volumes for the Renaissance, the Reformation, and the Counter-Reformation, and named all the remaining volumes, except one, for some political or military event or figure. The exception was a volume he called "The Heritage of the Scientific Revolution, 1679–1714." Butterfield's plan was extremely conservative. Here was the extraordinary opportunity to reconstruct the history of modern Europe as the development of European civilization and society, and in his hands he had the concepts enabling him to do so. In practice he kept the traditional Cambridge chronology and retained the traditional emphasis on European history as politics, diplomacy, and war, with a smattering of other things.[44]

Butterfield was ready to accept the editorship with Clark, and he had Vellacott encouraging him to do it. To Butterfield's surprise, Clark declined the invitation, giving as his reason that he wanted to spend his time as a historian and not as an editor. In the face of Clark's refusal, Butterfield withdrew as well, adding that he would not want to accept sole editorship or even a joint editorship with someone other than Clark. He, too, now professed that he did not want to be an editor, estimating that the enterprise would take fifteen years to complete, not ten as the Press predicted. He did volunteer his services as a contributor. It must have been wrenching for him to refuse the chance to succeed Acton at the head of the new Cambridge modern history.[45]

As things turned out, the Press put pressure on both Clark and Butterfield to relent. This time Butterfield gave the refusal, while Clark consented to devise a plan for the project and draft instructions for contributors. There would be an advisory committee with Clark as a member, but no general editor. Eventually Butterfield received invitations to contribute to the volumes on the Renaissance and the eighteenth century, but he refused again and again, and the project went forward without any support from him. He told himself and others that he had come to believe that a large cooperative history was unsatisfactory in itself. But he was no doubt upset with how things had gone and with Clark for carrying on without him, and he became simply stubborn. When the thirteen volumes of the *New Cambridge Modern History* were completed twenty-four years later, it was shorter and took longer than even Butterfield had expected, and it contained nothing by the person who had thought more about the problems of modern history than any one else in Cambridge.[46]

Soon after backing out of the *New Cambridge Modern History* Butterfield received three more invitations to join collaborative projects, two on general history, and one on Edmund Burke. At the time he was not drawn thematically to either project on general history, and, after his experience with the *New Cambridge Modern History,* he found all three easier to decline. The first was an invitation from the Society Pro Helvetia, via the Swiss legation in London, to edit a one-volume history of Switzerland. He suggested the names of historians who might each contribute a part of the history and eventually recommended that G. R. Potter write the entire work. Potter agreed to write the book with two others, and by 1952 produced the *Short History of Switzerland.*[47]

The second invitation came from Norman Sykes, the Dixie Professor of Ecclesiastical History at Cambridge, and Bishop Stephen Neill, then a Fellow of Trinity College, Cambridge, to collaborate with them in planning a proposed *Cambridge History of the Christian Church.* Butterfield consulted Vellacott, who urged him to stay out of the project. He then declined, and the project failed. Eventually Oxford University Press picked up the idea and began to publish the *Oxford History of the Christian Church,* with Henry Chadwick and Owen Chadwick as general editors.[48]

The third was an invitation from Alfred Cobban in 1947 to edit a volume belonging to a new series on the correspondence of Burke. Butterfield's volume would be the letters on English politics, Ireland, and America. He had a longstanding attraction to Burke, much as he did to Fox, but in his present mood he refused even this.[49]

Modern Science

The curious volume on the scientific revolution which Butterfield projected for the *New Cambridge Modern History* revealed a clue to his thinking on a theme that had appealed to him for years, the importance of science in modern history. His interest derived from his treatment of general history. He had attached a lecture or two on science to his general European history course back in 1929 or 1930. It is not clear what initially induced him to do so, but his experience as a youth in Keighley School, which promoted science and mathematics above all else, must have been a factor. Perhaps his awareness of the former renown of Peterhouse in the sciences was a factor. Perhaps the important thing was merely his reading of European history. He once observed that even when the tradition stressed diplomatic, military, and constitutional history, it was hard not to refer to art in the Renaissance, religion in the Reformation, and science in the period from Copernicus to Newton. Once he got the idea that general history should be constructed with more than the history of war, politics, and ideas, it was easy to move science onto the stage. He had joined the Inter-Faculty Committee on the History of Science at Cambridge from its beginning, and by the end of the 1930s he was giving five or six lectures a year on science in his course.

Sometime near the end of the war his ideas about the role of science in the history of Europe showed evidence of changing. He used to say, simply, that science should be treated as part of the development of civilization. In 1946 he was still publishing in this fashion.[50] He highlighted science in his outline for the *New Cambridge Modern History* and even referred to what he called the scientific revolution of the seventeenth century, without suggesting anything beyond the point that science was important in modern European history.

Prime indication of major change in his views appeared in his lecture "Tendencies in Historical Study in England" in 1945. There he advocated using the term "scientific revolution" to name the scientific thought of the seventeenth century and proposed that historians give science "a more central place in our general history." He meant not merely to urge the importance of science, but also to demote the Italian Renaissance of the fifteenth century from its position as "the great dividing-line" between medieval and modern times and to place greater emphasis on the scientific revolution instead.[51] In an article shortly thereafter, his first on the history of science, he described the "scientific revolution" as "pivotal" in Western civilization, and charged that our whole picture of human intellectual development is "warped" unless we conceded the point.[52]

Butterfield became a public advocate for the history of science in the fall of 1945 when he proposed to the BBC a series of sixteen talks on the subject to be presented by a team of scientists and historians that he would assemble. His explicit aim was to persuade schools to introduce the history of science into their curriculum. The project went nowhere at the time, except that the BBC asked him to gave one broadcast himself.[53] Even though he included scientists in his plan, he bluntly accused scientists generally of being "not quite satisfactory as historians" because they tended to think ahistorically. He both applauded and lamented the drift of some scientists towards Marxist interpretations of history which allotted room for science in the history of civilization. He had on his mind especially Joseph Needham, Cambridge biochemist and historian of science in China who had sympathies with both Christian and Marxist approaches to history. This experience, along with the events of international affairs after the Second World War, drove Butterfield to meditate further on Marxism. He gave a paper in several Cambridge colleges on the issues that Marxism raised in relation to historical interpretation.[54]

With the university returning to full operation after the war, the Committee on the History of Science, now chaired by Butterfield, won approval to run a special course of lectures, although still detached from the Tripos examinations. Butterfield recalls being pressed by several people, including at least one university administrator, to stay active in the history of science in order to diminish the influence of Marxists in the field. Joseph Needham, as an Anglo-Catholic, a communist, and a biochemist, was a key figure in the 1930s and again when he returned to Cambridge in 1948. Butterfield and he generally found themselves in agreement. The committee decided to heed Butterfield's advice to secure a historian, not a scientist, for the lectures. Anna-K. Mayer showed that the matter at issue was part of a bigger agenda within Cambridge to move the study of the history of science into the humanities away from the control of the scientists themselves. The committee surprised Butterfield by looking to him as the candidate. He testified later that, in an attempt to avoid the invitation, he stayed away from the meeting on the day the committee planned to come to a decision. The committee invited him anyway. Butterfield declined, but the committee persisted. After negotiations, he agreed to present a course of lectures on the history of science during 1947–1948, provided that he offered no other courses during the year, and that he not be asked to do it again. As it turned out, Butterfield's lectures contributed significantly to the establishment of the history of science as a study in its own right.[55]

In preparation for the lectures, Butterfield started with the typescripts of the several lectures on science contained in his course on modern European civilization. To these he added new reading on the history of science, squeezed into his incredibly busy life during 1947. His notebook shows him studying George Sarton's *Introduction to the History of Science* and available reference works on the lives and work of scientists. He seems to have read one or two articles or books on each scientist he discussed. A high portion of this reading apparently occurred during the early 1930s when he first worked up lectures on science. He must have read or reread the primary writings of Copernicus, Bacon, Descartes, Boyle, Newton, Fontenelle, and other scientists of the period, and he interpreted their writings for himself, without the benefit of careful reading of the scholarly literature.[56]

Butterfield presented twelve lectures on Saturdays at noon during the Lent and Easter terms in 1948, starting in January. The series title was "Origins of Modern Science, 1400–1800." He had no time to prepare the lectures until after he had sent *George III, Lord North, and the People* to the publisher early that same January. He appears to have written each lecture in full just before giving it, working late into the night. He rewrote his lectures during the summer vacation and put them into the hands of Bell in August. It was a stunning accomplishment. He was hoping for quick publication and was disturbed when Bell took until October 1949 to issue the volume. The title was slightly revised, *The Origins of Modern Science, 1300–1800*. The term "origins" in the title for the lectures might have been provided either by the original sponsor, the Committee on the History of Science, or by Butterfield. In any case, we have to assume that he was satisfied with the term, since he surely had ample opportunity to insist on a different title for the book if he had wished one.[57]

The book retains the character of lectures, with all the repetitions, the sweeping generalizations, and the imprecision one expects in such a medium. He adds an introduction which prepares the reader well for what follows, but he finds no way to conclude. He simply stops when he reaches the end of lecture 12. He calls the work a narrative, a story, but it is not a continuous story surveying the history of science during the years indicated, and he disparages thinking of it as an abridgment. Rather he traces what he believes are "the lines of strategic change" and emphasizes "those moments that seem pivotal."[58] He does not tell us the rationale behind the selection of these twelve topics rather than others, and leaves us with the same impression we have received before from his published work: the book is a miscellany. The title suggests wide coverage, chronologically and thematically, but the book delivers much less. Butterfield concentrated on the years from around 1550 to the 1680s, and he fixed on the physical sciences to the neglect of the biological sciences and mathematics.

It helps us understand Butterfield's achievement if we treat the book as a series of reflections about a problem in the history of science and general history. The problem is the character of the changes in science from Copernicus to Newton and the relationship of the changes to the general history of Western civilization. He proposes the thesis which in 1948 and 1949 was still novel, that the scientific attainments of those years amounted to a "scientific revolution" producing a thing he called "modern science." He was aware that others before him, especially Alexandre Koyré in France, had written about the work of scientists in the seventeenth century as amounting to a veritable revolution in thinking. But by employing the term "scientific revolution" and tying it to the creation of "modern science" he creates a meaning which went well beyond anything said before.[59] He interprets "modern science" as a new phenomenon achieved in the 1680s by Isaac Newton. It succeeded the Christian religion as the presiding force in the ongoing construction of Western civilization. The magnitude of his claims for the scientific revolution and modern science would be difficult to surpass:

> Since that revolution overturned the authority in science not only of the middle ages but of the ancient world — since it ended not only in the eclipse of scholastic philosophy but in the destruction of Aristotelian physics — it outshines

everything since the rise of Christianity and reduces the Renaissance and the Reformation to the rank of mere episodes, mere internal displacements, within the system of medieval Christendom. Since it changed the character of men's habitual mental operations even in the conduct of the non-material sciences, while transforming the whole diagram of the physical universe and the very texture of human life itself, it looms so large as the real origin both of the modern world and of the modern mentality that our customary periodisation of European history has become an anachronism and an encumbrance.[60]

His words ring out as hyperbole and echo his rhetoric in *George III, Lord North, and the People* when he suggested that the unremembered, local events of 1779–1780 were really England's French Revolution narrowly escaped. Later on, in the mid-1950s, he became even more insistent on the point. "For my own part," he wrote, "I should like to cry from the housetops that the publication of Newton's *Principia* in 1687 is a turning-point in history for peoples to whom the Renaissance and Reformation can hardly mean anything at all." He would prefer to periodize European history around the ascendency of Christianity, rather than the fall of Rome, and the scientific revolution, rather than the Renaissance and Reformation. The extravagance of his statement caught the eye and thereafter historians referred to it routinely.[61]

Butterfield considers his subject on two distinct levels. On one level, the first eight lectures plus 11 and much of lecture 12 depict the scientific revolution as a narrowly intellectual event, and approach the science of which he spoke as a topic in the history of ideas. Most of the text is a diagnosis of ideas — ideas of impetus, motion, matter, gravitation, phlogiston, and so on — and the scientists appear before us as minds. He maintains an introverted focus. He passes lightly over or neglects their technology, their experiments, their discovery of evidence, their social communities, their economics, their politics, their techniques, their moods and emotions, and mentions little about the impact on their work of their life circumstances, war, the universities, industry, public power, and social class. He explains the scientific revolution as the product of interior mental operations occurring in the minds of a relatively few men who were spending their time contemplating specifically intellectual questions. The ideas, mentalities, and religious beliefs of the scientist are foremost in the sequence of things. A dozen times or more he has the scientists "picking up the other end of the stick" and thinking about the very same things from another perspective. It is astonishing, for instance, how much of the new science is due to Christian belief and the tangible search for the ways of God and the order of creation. The essential changes in science come not from new data, new instrumentation, new social or economic demands, new relations of power, or new material conditions, but from new thinking, "a different kind of thinking-cap" put on by the scientist himself. In one sense the ideas march in a continuous and accumulating series, the next scientist building on and working from the ideas of his predecessor. In another sense, however, the ideas emerge as discontinuous innovations, the results of a scientist surmounting some giant intellectual hurdle, some obstruction, and reaching an entirely new mental ground. In the end, the discontinuities count for more. The really big changes upon which all else depends, he declares, are not the results of accumulated knowledge, but of distinctly new ideas of motion, matter, and the movement of the earth. Everything culminates in Isaac Newton's new synthesis published in 1687, which integrates all the new individual ideas into one big intellectual system.[62]

On the second level, Butterfield throws the subject onto a very broad plain in lectures 9 and 10 and some of lecture 12. Here he discusses the scientific revolution as a phenomenon within the general history of modern Western civilization. Most of the time he speaks of civilization in the all-inclusive sense which he has propounded for so many years, as the expression of the totality of the human experience, from economics to religion, from geography to politics. He sometimes still uses the notion of civilization to mean the refinement of humanity and the opposite of "barbarian." Other times he thinks of the term in the plural and speaks of Western civilization as one of many such congeries of refinements that coexist or succeed one another in world history.[63]

A fundamental ambiguity appears in his presentation. He is sure that the modern world, and not merely modern science, emerges by the end of the seventeenth century. He displays uncertainty, however, about the role of the scientific revolution, conceived as a mental transformation, in producing the modern world. In one mood he sees the new science as the great factor which initiates the modern period and propels modernizing changes in all aspects of life. In another mood he says science is only one big factor among many in a remarkable convergence of big factors which move the Western world into the modern era: the formation of the bourgeoisie, the ascendency of the nation-state, overseas discoveries, new economic activity, the eclipse of Christianity among intellectuals, a new secular worldview, and so on. The ambiguity mirrors his interpretation of the scientific revolution as a narrowly intellectual matter which nonetheless generates utterly universal implications.[64]

It was this ambiguity in Butterfield's argument that Arnold Toynbee probed in *A Study of History.* Toynbee insisted that the question of the emergence of modern science and the modern world could not be understood without analysis of the wider factors, especially religion. Butterfield, he thought, had misstated the novelty in the career of science in the sixteenth and seventeenth centuries. The genuinely new thing was the reversal of roles of science and religion. Science was elevated from the position subordinate to religion in previous centuries to the dominant position, from which religion was then ejected.[65]

It is noteworthy how Butterfield's interpretation of the science in this period displays his own mental operations. He is the model of his own historical interpretation. His lectures looked at no new evidence, employed no new techniques, announced no new discoveries. His preparatory reading was slight and even perhaps a little out of date, and his concept of science was narrowly intellectual. What dominates the book is Butterfield's historical thinking. The book reveals Butterfield as above all the historiographer. *Origins of Modern Science* can be understood as a book about historical thinking, one which takes its place next to his more obviously historiographical writings, especially *Whig Interpretation of History*. In *Origins of Modern Science* Butterfield applies his historical thought to a specific topic within general history, in this case, well-known ideas and figures in the history of science. He shows his audience an extended example of how one might approach an ordinary topic by "picking up the other end of the stick" or putting on "a different kind of thinking-cap." If the invitation had come from a different sponsor about a different subject, he could just as easily have applied his historical thinking to any other important theme in general history, such as the history of religion, or historical geography, or perhaps even material life.

In the introduction to the lectures he itemizes the principles of historiography which he follows. He reiterates them in different guises throughout the book. They amount to a summation of his message for historians at this moment in his career. Look closely at the moments when the dominant mentality changes, he advises, rather than strive for encyclopaedic coverage. Study the lesser and forgotten figures in interaction with the famous names, rather than mount up the biographies of the greats. Look at the mistakes and the dead ends, in addition to the successes. Concentrate on the process of investigation, rather than on the results alone. Put the scientists in their own times to disclose what they sought to attack or overcome or solve, rather than compare them to modern times. Move from the earlier to the later, with the future indeterminate, rather than taking the later as the goal to which the earlier tends. Butterfield articulates an approach to the history of scientific change that differs dramatically from the accumulationist and presentistic style of a Whig interpretation of the subject.[66]

He follows his own advice rigorously, except for one thing: his handling of the relationship of his scientists and their ideas to things "modern." This issue is central to his argument. His intention is to speak only of "transitions" in science, and not to act as if "modern science" were the destination to which earlier science tended. According to his stated view, "there is just the unbroken web of history, the unceasing march of generations which themselves overlap with one another and interpenetrate, so that the history of science is part of a continuous story of mankind going back far beyond the ancient Greeks themselves."[67] Nevertheless, we find him repeatedly going against his own counsel. We are struck by his language about earlier science that betrays the priority of the "modern" in his analysis. He writes of "foreshadowings," "anticipations," "stunted development," "hints of a more modern kind of mechanics," "a remarkable approach to the modern view of gravitation," "the intellectual obstruction which . . . is checking the progress of thought." We wonder at statements like this one where he is discussing medieval scholastic philosophy: "Perhaps the lack of mathematics, or the failure to think of mathematical ways of formulating things, was partly responsible for what appeared to be verbal subtleties and an excessive straining of language in these men who were almost yearning to find the way to the modern science of mechanics." On Butterfield's own terms, it would be impossible for medieval thinkers to "yearn" for something that did not appear until centuries later and that issued from entirely unknowable processes lasting hundreds of years. It would impossible for them to meet the standard of Newton's science three or four hundred years in the future, and it would not make sense to accuse them of a "lack" or a "failure" or "excessive straining" as judged by that standard. Indeed, even the title of the book characterizes a relationship between earlier and later science that, on Butterfield's terms, is impossible, because it treats something which appears later ("modern science") as a fixture and purports to find features of it ("origins") before it existed. We then realize that he has structured his history so that "modern science," from the 1680s onwards, serves as both the destination of, and the universal standard for, all the science that precedes it. For Butterfield, modern science is the real science, and all other science is inferior, marred by incompleteness, mistakes, half-truths, and falsehoods. And in this he joined the best of the scholars of the history of science in his day. For instance, his Cambridge colleague Joseph Needham, in his studies of China, found anticipations of modern science here and there over the ages amidst all the other traditional gropings after nature. In this respect, paradoxically, Butterfield had produced a classic volume of the very thing he had sought to demolish, a Whig interpretation of history.[68]

The immediate responses to Butterfield's *Origins of Modern Science* were overwhelmingly favourable. He had every reason to feel elated. The reviewer in the *Times Educational Supplement* welcomed it as "a brilliant piece of historical writing." The reviewer in the *Times Literary Supplement* described the book as full of "genuine and profound historical thinking" which "has given scale and proportion, hitherto lacking, to one of most important periods in the history of science." Just about everyone accepted his major thesis that there was a scientific revolution as he depicted. Most also accepted his explanation of the revolution as chiefly the product of new mental operations, rather than new discoveries. And almost everyone praised his placement of science within the general matrix of modern civilization. Even the scientists who reviewed the book liked it, despite his barely hidden complaint about scientists who write ahistorical history of science.

There were a few hesitations. Henry Dale felt that he downgraded Newton by filling in too much detail. His colleague A. C. Crombie, in the *Cambridge Review*, downplayed his originality by calling the idea of a scientific revolution already conventional, deriving from Koyré. Crombie argued that it would be more innovative to find the start of the revolution in the thirteenth century. He also commented on the neglect of biology, as did A. R. Hall in the *Cambridge Journal*. J. Bronowski complained that the book was studded with too many "historical truths." But even these voices praised the book.[69]

All in all, Butterfield had written an important book which won immediate and near unanimous admiration among both historians and scientists. Very quickly it became the standard work in the history of science for undergraduates, both in Great Britain and North America. When Butterfield published a revised edition in 1957, William Stahlman noted, "perhaps no single volume has been so widely used in introductory courses dealing with one or another aspect of the scientific revolution." Examples taken from the book resurfaced in general discussions of historical knowledge and historical thinking, as in Carl Gustavson's *Preface to History* in 1955. Reviewing the book after another printing a decade later, Stephen and June Toulmin gave this assessment of the enduring value of his achievement: "As a starter, it is still hard to improve on Butterfield's *Origins of Modern Science*." They called it "a triumph, locating within a context of general history the sensitive points of intellectual debate from Copernicus up to Darwin." Thomas Kuhn's *Structure of Scientific Revolutions*, published in 1962, promoted a thesis about the character of deep change in science that seemed to echo Butterfield. Gerd Buchdahl noted the similarity in a review and connected Kuhn's notion of paradigm shifts with Butterfield's metaphor of the scientist putting on "a different kind of thinking-cap." Kuhn later acknowledged the impact of Butterfield on his thinking, and with Butterfield, of Koyré. Provided readers looked past the issue of the anticipations of the modern, Butterfield's mode of explanation of the scientific revolution, now reenforced by Kuhn, continued to offer an alternative to Whig-style interpretation of the history of science.[70]

More than this, people soon began to realize that a new field of study was emerging in university curricula, the history of science. Scholars included But- terfield's name in the short list of the founders of the academic discipline. The very term "scientific revolution" people linked to Butterfield. People knew that he was not the first to use it, but they suggested that he was probably the one who converted the term into the common currency of the academic lexicon.[71]

Whenever possible in the coming years Butterfield continued to give pub- licity to his notions of the centrality of the history of science in historical study, the pivotal character of the scientific revolution, and the seventeenth century as the dividing moment between the old and the new Europe. He summarized his views of general European history for two multivolume encyclopaedias in the next few years.[72] He also promoted the history of science as "a bridge between the arts and sciences," a thing suggested in the opening sentence of *Origins of Modern Science*. He had tried since 1945 to talk the BBC into arranging a series on the history of science. They finally gave him one oppor- tunity in 1948 to broadcast his ideas on national radio. Soon afterwards, they gave up their resistance to his proposal for a series and, following a plan arranged by Butterfield with the Cambridge Committee on the History of Science, presented a number of talks by scientists and historians throughout the academic year 1949–1950. The talks, including two by Butterfield, ap- peared as a book in 1951 with the title *The History of Science: Origins and Results of the Scientific Revolution*. Butterfield, behaving like the missionary, was doing what he could to persuade people to work the history of science into the school curriculum as well as the university lecture list.[73] Many years later Karl Schweizer, one of his former doctoral students, collected some of his subsequent writings on the history of science into a book.[74]

Butterfield was in full stride by 1948 and 1949 as Professor of Modern History. What had started out as Fox and general history transmuted into unexpected things. He had a big book to his credit and another little book, and he had gained himself a reputation that matched even the most exalted expec- tations of his professorship.

Religion

Morality, History, and the State

Fox and general modern history were only two of the parallel, yet connected themes that Butterfield pursued after the Second World War, both with unintended results. Simultaneously he pursued another set of themes on history, religion, and morality which had also occupied his mind for many years. The outcomes were extraordinarily surprising.

Embedded within his important lecture in Dublin in April 1945, "Tendencies in Historical Study in England," were a few brief passages about moral judgments in history which summarized where his thought on the subject had come. His message echoes *Whig Interpretation of History* of fifteen years earlier, but there are new elements in what he says. Once again he is brash to identify changes in his own discourse as the dominant trend in English historiography. He represents the trend in the form of "counter-theses" to Acton's famous dicta on moral judgments. He cannot keep himself from continuing the combat with Acton which he began long ago.

In place of what he takes to be Acton's vision of history as a moral conflict between good and evil, with the historian declaring who is on which side, he recommends construing history according to a more ambiguous morality. We can now see, says Butterfield, that history may be characterized more appropriately as a theatre of both cooperation and tragic conflict. The development of modern science, for instance, is a cooperative achievement of many people, and is not easily explained as a conflict between good and evil. For this purpose, the better metaphor is the leaven that leavens the whole lump, a new metaphor to which he returns often hereafter. The tragic character of things is created by the reality that sin is distributed on all sides of any human event and that all people are sinners and act more harmfully than they ought. All are embroiled in predicaments that constrain or foster their behaviour for good or ill, and no side is merely righteous and the other simply unrighteous. The troubles of the world are due not to the struggles of the righteous on one side and the wicked on the other, but to a general "perversity in human affairs not yet subject to human control." More true to history, he says, are two notions that become symbols of his thinking for the rest of his life: that "very little sins sometimes have disastrously disproportionate consequences," and that perpetual struggles occur "between one half-right that is too wilful and another half-right that is too proud."[1]

We can hear his words as self-chastisement for what, on his own terms, was a lapse into moral judgment and patriotism during the war, and for his own surprising behaviour which found him one moment cooperating with interests helpful to the Nazis and the next joining with efforts to defeat them. As the war carried on, he had increasingly used his role as a historian for political purposes, above all for the victory of the Allies over Germany.

Butterfield's lecture reveals a preoccupation with what he regards as the perversion of historical study under the impact of war and contemporary international affairs. His case in point is the question of the origins of the First World War, a topic that had occupied his mentor Temperley. In particular he is alarmed by reinterpretations of the war's origins. He argues that since the rise of Hitler in 1933 and the catastrophe of the Second World War itself English historians have tended to give the subject a mistakenly anti-German ring, making the Germans more responsible for the origins of the First World War than they were previously said to be.

The great antidote which Butterfield prescribes against the poison of such politicized and moralizing history is scientific history. Not surprisingly, his model scientific historian is a German, Friedrich Meinecke. Butterfield noted that German historians, like so many others, had routinely forsaken the rigours of scientific history in order to write history for political purposes: in support of German nation-building in the nineteenth century, for the German war effort during both world wars, on behalf of the Weimar Republic in the twenties, for or against Naziism. Against this overwhelming flood in the very land that Butterfield believed produced the ideal of scientific history stood Meinecke. Butterfield admires an essay Meinecke wrote in 1916, in the midst of the Great War. He represents, and approves, Meinecke in such circumstances as "vindicating the role of that academic history which refuses to be shaken from its lofty seat — refuses to step into the arena to take part in the game which is being played." The view amounts to an exaggeration of anything Leopold von Ranke, the putative father of scientific history, might have said, since the history Ranke himself had written emitted strong Germano-political sounds. Butterfield imagines a scientific history which transcends all conflict, thrives beyond the reach of politics and war, isolates itself from contemporary affairs, and operates unimpacted by the present. The notion is an extension of things he has been saying since *Whig Interpretation,* but now with a special emphasis on the transcendence of scientific history.[2]

Butterfield continued to strike hard against the histories which blamed the First World War on Germany. He went to the BBC with a proposal for a broadcast on "this whole German question," but the BBC declined it. In other writings he elaborated his point. Anti-Hitler scholars reinterpreted the pre-Hitler period to show Hitler-like tendencies in German history long before the dictator appeared on the scene. This anti-German reading of history, said Butterfield, actually reversed long-standing English admiration of things German before the First World War. We recall the shock to his teenage sensibilities caused by that war at the time and especially the English attacks on his heroic Germany. Butterfield's efforts won him the reputation of being pro-German. He was aware of this, and did not mind. He acted as if his own pro-German view were not politically motivated. He was adamant that the anti-German view of the origins of the First World War depended on politics, and not on the sober findings of scientific history.[3]

The irony of Butterfield's heightened emphasis on the transcendence of scientific history is that he did not adhere to his own prescriptions about morally and politically clean history. His own moral sense was acute, and his estimation of the crisis of the times called for large-scale moral thinking. He actually continued his wartime tendency to implicate his historical study in the very matters whose impact he warned against. The Second World War, the First World War, contemporary international politics — these were the experiences which drove his thinking on history from 1945 onwards, not his mental reflections on historical research or his reading of other historians or his contemplation of specifically intellectual questions. Unlike the scientists whom he presented in *Origins of Modern Science* as so many minds processing ideas, he himself generated his thinking by feeling and responding to the impact of war, politics, and international crisis. Indeed this he had done for a long time, and now he continued to do so. Butterfield was evidencing a disjunction between his actual practice and what he earnestly advocated about scientific history.

The ending of the Second World War itself reinforced Butterfield's reflex to link international politics, morality, and his historical views. He was certain, he wrote in June 1945, "that we are living in one of the great ages of history," and he could only hope "that it was not equivalent to the age of the barbarian invasions."[4] When the Americans dropped their nuclear bombs on Hiroshima and Nagasaki in August 1945, Butterfield exclaimed in his diary, "The atomic bomb — the ultimate prostitution of human endeavor — the judgment of God on our civilisation."[5]

As the Allied and Soviet armies were sweeping towards Berlin from opposite directions and crushing German military power, Butterfield chose to give a course of lectures to undergraduates in Cambridge during the Lent term 1945 entitled "Factors in German History." Consonant with British foreign policy and the Allies generally, he was already thinking about the reconstruction of Europe after the war. He offered the course two further years, 1946 and 1947, firmly into the postwar period of reconstruction. The lectures resounded with moral and political notes on contemporary international affairs. The most important matter of the day, in his judgment, was the handling of Germany, and the course was his contribution as a historian to the proper treatment of Germany. The course grew out of his attempts in 1943 to do something for the war effort with his history teaching and writing. Although he never mounted a course at that time, and his book-length manuscript on the historical geography of Europe died on his table, his labours served him now. He worried that England would support punitive measures against Germany. The best opposition he could raise against such a prospect was the clamour for historical understanding, the sort of thing that he insisted historical study should provide.

His lectures deployed historical geography and swept across large political, social, and religious themes. He assembled a host of big issues to consider, such as how the divisions of Germany came about, and what the effects of the Protestant Reformation have been in German history. His intention was to render Germany's resort to war more understandable. He wanted to make German action and even Nazi behaviour seem less a matter of sheer evil and more the product of the historical predicament of Germany. He hoped to blunt English impulses to blame the Germans. It is possible that he believed, or believed the self-deception, that his words in favour of understanding were apolitical and detached from the impact of international events. He could picture himself as the dissenter against the dominant trend. In the highly charged postwar era, however, they functioned as starkly political statements in favour of leniency for Germany.[6]

Very quickly he made tangible his postwar politics of understanding towards Germany. He sought to work independently of governments and to promote unofficial exchanges with German historians. But he was soon accepting entangling alliances with the British government. His first connections were with the British Council, an agency fully funded by the state. In 1945, in keeping with British postwar foreign policy, the Council offered him a way to establish cultural contact with German historians. He agreed immediately to work with the Council in spite of its semi-governmental status. At the Council's request, he gave them advice, suggested names of German scholars who might visit Britain, and discussed going to Germany himself. He continued to work with the British Council off and on until his retirement in 1968.[7]

The British Foreign Office intervened to ask him to go to Germany under their auspices. He hesitated initially, not wanting to be perceived as an agent of the government or a supporter of British policy to "re-educate" the Germans in the ways of democracy. But then he agreed to compromise himself and make the trip in 1948 under Foreign Office sponsorship when the University of Göttingen came forward with an invitation addressed to him directly, rather than via the Foreign Office. It turned out that he never went. The trip was at first postponed by the organizers and then cancelled.[8]

He eventually travelled to Germany for the first time after the war in July 1950, sponsored by the British Council. In Cologne he read a new version of one of his standard papers, "The Dangers of History," which was then published in a German academic journal. The paper attributed great power to historians who are able to determine the historical framework used by countless people in their interpretation of their relationship to the past. But these frameworks soon become rigid, and block the way to human understanding. Historians must then help people unlearn their old history, and learn new history that corrects the distortions of the old. And so on, again and again. The process demands considerable "elasticity of mind." Spoken in postwar Germany, Butterfield's message comforted his German audience, who were eager for the occupying foreign powers to "unlearn" the history which uncovered the deep roots of Nazi totalitarianism and German militarism in the German past.[9]

He faced the problem of history and the state from another angle. During the war he had actually written history intended entirely for use by the state — his collaboration on the history of France published by British Naval Intelligence for the benefit of naval intelligence officers. With such government service on his record, he was quite naturally approached by Grahame Clark, using the letterhead of the British Air Ministry, about giving his support to the official history of the role of aircraft in the war. The specific question was whether the Cambridge History Faculty would permit research undertaken by young scholars within government departments to be presented for graduate degrees or fellowship competitions. Butterfield held a number of conversations about the question with colleagues in Cambridge, and came out firmly opposed to the proposal. He gave as his reason that historical work for official government purposes invariably involved restraint on the independence of historical scholarship, no matter how clear the safeguards or how well intentioned the people involved.[10]

The episode triggered Butterfield's worries about various government-sponsored history projects that went forward during the next few years. He took special interest in the sequels to the volumes on British foreign policy and the origins of the first war edited in the 1920s by Temperley and Gooch. The original volumes had appeared under Foreign Office patronage. Volume 1 of the new series, *Documents on British Foreign Policy, 1919–39,* edited by E. L. Woodward and R. Butler, came out in 1947. Simultaneously W. N. Medlicott and Woodward were working on the history of British foreign policy from 1939 to 1945, and Medlicott was handling the history of British economic warfare during the same period. These and other projects had turned the British government into a monumental patron of historical scholarship, employing some of England's best historians and most promising young researchers.[11]

The issue touched Butterfield directly in 1948. One of his own students at Peterhouse, Desmond Williams, who came from Ireland, whom he would liked to have made a young Fellow of Peterhouse, took employment on the government payroll. Williams became a researcher in the archives at Whaddon Hall in Bletchley, Buckinghamshire, repository of the German documents captured by British forces. The aim was to publish large amounts of these documents along side of whatever the Americans released from their vast holdings of captured German papers. Williams wrote letters to Butterfield and visited him at Peterhouse to report on the project from the inside.[12]

Butterfield disliked what he heard, and his scepticism about government-paid historians turned aggressive. He hurriedly wrote a paper warning against what he labelled "official history." He arranged with his Irish historian friends to read the piece in Dublin in December 1948, and exacted their promise of immediate publication in an Irish journal. The principle he defended was the free expression of thought, which he believed "official history" put in jeopardy. The corollary of intellectual freedom is, he wrote, "an independent science of history" which presents "the cause of historical truth," and operates "over against" the state. He built a very high wall around what he now sometimes called "academic history" and sometimes "technical history" to segregate such history from the work produced under government sponsorship. He appealed once again to Meinecke's statement uttered amid the exigencies of the First World War in favour of the entire detachment of "academic history" from life.[13] Privately to A. J. P. Taylor he pronounced himself the consummate dissenter, the ideologue of a politics of anarchism and distrust of the state: "I am as an historian against all governments, or rather I believe that something oblique is going on behind all governments, giving them a seamy side."[14]

Desmond Williams aggravated Butterfield's alarm with the report that the Foreign Office might withhold certain documents from researchers. Butterfield rebounded with an instruction to Williams that it was his "duty to resign and in a signal manner." His article denouncing "official history" appeared in June 1949, and immediately he mailed copies to a list of highly placed historians around Britain. His campaigned utterly failed. Nothing changed. Medlicott and Woodward, the chief "official historians" in question, did not resign. They proclaimed their complete agreement with everything he said on the subject, and then carried on producing official history. Even Williams did not resign. Government patronage flourished. Butterfield abruptly dropped his one-man crusade. As an important by-product of the episode he developed a lasting relationship with Williams. Williams took a history position at University College, Dublin, in 1949, and thereafter occasionally brought Butterfield to Dublin and saw him at Peterhouse. Williams became Butterfield's partner in high-class gossip. Even Bogle thought that Butterfield enjoyed Williams's company more than that of any of his other friends.[15]

The episode about "official history" hardened Butterfield's dissenter attitudes towards the state. He now adopted ever more severe demands for the cleansing of academic history from political and ideological contact. In one case, not long after these events, he received an invitation to participate in a project on world history sponsored by UNESCO. He refused without a second thought, saying that the involvement of a United Nations agency in the venture transformed it into "quasi-official" history, and academic historians ought to stay clear of it.[16]

The figure behind Butterfield's agony over the relations of history, politics, and morality was once again Acton. Indeed, Butterfield's political and moral attachment to Germany in particular was due very much to his allegiance to the German tradition of historical method that had nourished Acton, notably the work of Ranke.

Butterfield re-encountered Acton on a number of occasions from 1944 onwards, leading him to think intensely about Acton once again. His preparations for his inaugural address as Professor of Modern History in 1944 readily took him back to Acton. The invitation from Cambridge University Press in 1945 to collaborate on what became the *New Cambridge Modern History* induced him to study Acton's letters about the first *Cambridge Modern History*. He had Trevelyan comparing him to Acton in 1946 after Trevelyan read

Butterfield's "Tendencies in Historical Study" and offered the opinion that his philosophy of history was closer to reality than Acton's.[17] He meditated on Acton's life in 1946 when the *English Historical Review* invited him to review David Mathew's book on Acton, a book he decided was too hagiographic.[18] Working on the review persuaded him, during June 1946, to look for the first time into the Acton papers stored in Cambridge University Library. He had David Knowles and G. P. Gooch encouraging him in 1947 to write on Acton.[19]

During 1946 and 1947 he went to the library frequently to read in the Acton papers, especially looking in the drawers of Acton's notes, the endless and undated enigmatic jottings of quotations, sayings, lists, and records of his readings. He began to feel he had crossed to the other side of the public facade of the man, and the experience captivated him. This is the moment when he first asked Eve Bogle to go to the archives to transcribe papers for him. He was ecstatic when he discovered the journal that Acton kept during his first visit to Rome in 1857, when he was twenty-three. Here, to his astonishment, he encountered Acton warning historians against issuing moral judgments. He could hardly believe it was Acton admonishing historians to limit themselves to questions of causes and effects in a person's life, and to leave any moral judgments to God. Butterfield seized upon this young Acton as his ally against the older Acton who marched about with moral judgments in his hand. Butterfield uncovered a series of such diaries and journals, and proposed to edit a small book of Acton's diaries from 1852 to 1859. He managed to publish an article on the Roman journal of 1857, but the book never appeared.[20]

He did produce a small booklet on Acton for the Historical Association, written quickly in 1947 for their pamphlet series. His primary theme in *Lord Acton*, published in 1948, was the big split he believed he discovered between a flexible and liberal-minded early Acton and rigid later Acton. As Butterfield drew the portrait, early Acton professed with Ranke that every epoch of human existence is valid in its own right, whereas later Acton treated the past as a odious epoch of tyranny to be overcome by the march of liberty. Early Acton handled persecution and tolerance with balance and asked historians not to play the moral judge, while the later Acton called persecution a crime and urged historians to issue moral judgments. Early Acton was more Christian than Whig, while later Acton was more liberal than Catholic. Butterfield now said it was the later Acton who personified the Whig interpretation of history, and who was obsessed with interpreting history as the story of liberty.

Butterfield was not prepared to apply the understanding to Acton that he wanted everyone else to apply to the Germans. He did not consider, for instance, that Acton may have changed his mind for worthy intellectual or religious reasons. Instead, he denounced Acton with a moral judgment. And quite out of keeping with his preference for intellectual explanations, he attributed the perceived change in Acton to psychological factors. He speculated there might be a defect in Acton's personal relationships which caused "some small spring of emotion" to become "frozen up inside him."[21] He thought of editing a volume of Acton's essays and lectures which would demonstrate the change, and proposed the book to Bell publishers. Like the edition of Acton's diaries, this volume never appeared.[22]

Butterfield threw other criticisms at Acton in his booklet, making it seem as if he were taking distance from his perennial hero. Acton's approach to general European history was too narrow, he charged. Acton restricted himself too much to intellectual and political history and neglected economics, geography, science, and the rest of civilization. He created too sharp a break between modern history and what preceded it, and neglected the medieval and ancient worlds. He dwelt too much on western Europe and neglected eastern Europe and Russia.

Nonetheless, in the same booklet, and perhaps without realizing it, Butterfield revealed deep continuities running between the two Actons. In so doing, he disclosed once again his own fundamental identity with Acton. At this deeper stratum, Butterfield shared with the Acton the allegiance to German historical scholarship, particularly to Ranke. Like Acton, he too wanted history to be "organic," and he too sought to trace the interconnectedness of all things through the sweep of general history. He believed with Acton in the centrality of individual personalities in history, and he feared the all-powerful state. With Acton he gave priority to Christian commitment in his life and to the action of Providence in history. Like the Acton who withstood the authorities of the Roman Catholic Church, he dissented from any church authoritarianism and church establishment. And like Acton he understood the historian's task to be a moral vocation. Compared with his affinities with this deeper Acton, Butterfield's criticisms, even on moral judgments, appear as minor adjustments by a faithful disciple. Butterfield felt so strongly about Acton's doctrine of moral judgments in history because he himself held equally intense moral convictions. We can imagine Butterfield, in spite of his stated theory, struggling daily to restrain himself from making the moral judgments that would rise up willy nilly within him. It is not difficult to think of Butterfield as becoming obsessed with Acton.[23]

Butterfield's dealings with Acton materials took a sharp turn in July 1948. Aelred Watkin, a Roman Catholic Benedictine monk from Downside Abbey, wrote him with the revelation that Abbott Gasquet, also of Downside Abbey, and later made a cardinal, had tampered with Acton's language before publishing in 1906 an edition of Acton's letters, entitled *Lord Acton and His*

Circle. Butterfield was electrified. Watkin documented for Butterfield the discrepancies between Gasquet's version of Acton's correspondence and the actual letters in the Downside archives. Gasquet had omitted or changed words and phrases he regarded as unsuitable for public knowledge about Acton. Butterfield was hungry for more information and more Acton letters, and took the findings out of Watkin's hands. He persuaded Watkin to get him access to the abbey archives. He then threw out the draft of an article Watkin had prepared and wrote a new article under his own name. Father Watkin deferred to Butterfield's eminence, but the monk requested that his name appear on the article too. He wanted the world to know that Downside itself had cooperated in revealing and rectifying Cardinal Gasquet's transgressions. The new version appeared under their joint authorship in 1950, but without any indication that it was the monk and not the professor who made the discovery. Butterfield got the credit. His Cambridge colleague Kitson Clark held the article up high in his book *The Critical Historian* as a model of critical scholarship.[24]

Butterfield took every opportunity to speak out on the public issues circulating during the postwar years. The problem of the handling of Germany was the most immediate and most poignant to his sensibilities, but he moved outwards to a host of other issues. He felt acutely the problems of the devastation of human life and culture caused by the war, the expansion of the Soviet Union and the heightening of American power, and the uncertainties created by the atomic bomb. Like so many other thinkers at the time, he worried deeply about the future of Western civilization.

To Butterfield's perception, problems of such magnitude were best understood as matters of morality and religion in history. The moral opinions he had briefly articulated in "Tendencies in Historical Study" in the spring of 1945 became a message for him to proclaim in various media during the postwar period. He expounded his views in his papers on the lecture circuit: "History and Ethics," "Marxian Interpretation of History," "The Dangers of History." He contributed an "opinion" article against dogmatic history to *Time and Tide* for January 1946. He went on the BBC in the spring of 1947 to talk on the "Limits of Historical Understanding." He published "Reflections on the Predicament of Our Time," a major statement on religion, history, and civilization, in the inaugural issue of the *Cambridge Journal* in the fall of 1947.[25]

The common feature of all these statements was the interconnection he perceived among history, morality, religion, and the monumental problems of the day. His message was continuous with *Whig Interpretation of History*, but much expanded, with new emphases and new concerns. He stressed the power of "predicament" to circumscribe human good and human evil, the reality of what he often called the "cupidity" of every person, the urgency of treating the problems of the world as primordially matters of "human personality" and "human relations," the need to discern "the ways of Providence" and to learn from the "judgment of God" upon the civilization, the importance of "elasticity" of mind. Indeed, the very terms he repeated — predicament, cupidity, human personality, human relations, Providence, elasticity — became marks of the Butterfield approach, and he gained a reputation as a moral thinker and religious historian. He was searching to identify what he called "the things to which we can still hold fast" when the civilization appears to revert to the "Dark Ages."

Christianity and History

Butterfield's public excursions between 1945 and 1947 into the themes of religion and morality in history attracted the attention of the Faculty of Divinity in the university. The Cambridge Divinity Faculty was sponsoring a series of extra lectures for undergraduates on Saturday mornings, and had already decided that the lectures for Michaelmas term in 1948 would be on Christianity and history. The topic was proposed by undergraduates who had attended the series during the previous year on Christianity and philosophy. Professor H. A. Hodges had lectured effectively on "The Logic of Christian Belief." The series was designed for the large number of postwar students who, like many in the older generation, felt moved towards Christianity by the crisis of the times. Many of them were veterans of war service who had experienced the trauma of death and devastation. They were particularly responsive to broad representations of their chosen fields of study.

The Divinity sponsors approached Butterfield with the request that he find them a historian to handle the subject of Christianity and history.[26] To enhance the appeal of the lectures to students outside Divinity, they wanted a historian who was not a cleric and not a specialist in ecclesiastical history. When Butterfield could suggest no names that satisfied them, they came to the point they had had in mind all the time and invited *him* to give the lectures. Butterfield resisted vigorously, citing the extra load of lectures on the history of science that he was carrying in the first half of 1948. He trembled, he later recalled, at the thought of proclaiming before a university audience what he considered to be the "intimacies" of religion, things he had only uttered previously in the seclusion of Methodist chapels. He was terribly conscious of the strongly antireligious element within the Cambridge historical world. Yet he gave way in the end, and accepted the invitation, he said, as if it were a call from God to preach the Gospel. He once again became the Methodist lay preacher, but this time with the university lecture hall as his chapel and the community of historians and students as his congregation. And not a few of these historians would be derisive of his linkage of history and religion. He went ahead nonetheless and united his religious and professional worlds, which he had worked so assiduously to keep apart.

The subject was not at all new to Butterfield, because, as a Christian and a historian, he had thought about the associated questions for a long time. In *Whig Interpretation of History* he had already dealt energetically with at least one of the issues, moral judgments. Until *Englishman and His History*, however, he had kept his explicit confession of Christianity separate from his professional work as a historian. Since then, the combination of new opportunities and his moral impulses had been pushing him to make ever more overt statements of his Christian orientation. The lectures he now contemplated required him to put his thoughts in order on a wide range of matters pertaining to Christianity and history. The assignment asked him to frame his reflections with the non-Christian student chiefly in mind.

There was very little time at hand to prepare the lectures, only the spring and summer of 1948, when he also had to revise the lectures on modern science for publication. He realized immediately that he was completely out of touch with critical scholarship in theology, biblical studies, and religious history, and that he would have no possibility of reading in these fields. He decided to do what he knew best. He read the Bible with the eyes of the historian as well as the eyes of the lay preacher, took notes, and meditated on what he read. He filled notebooks with quotations and extracts from the Old Testament, mostly from the prophets, the Psalms, Ecclesiastes, and the Wisdom of Solomon. His notebooks contain nothing from the first four books of the Pentateuch and nothing from the New Testament.

At the same time, he carefully reread St. Augustine's *City of God*, and looked up information on the history of Israel and the geography of Palestine. A little before this time, he read William Blake and T. S. Eliot. The list of books in contemporary theology that he appears to have read was very short. It included Reinhold Niebuhr's *Nature and Destiny of Man*, Anders Nygren's *Agape and Eros*, R. H. Charles's *Eschatology*, and C. C. J. Webb's *The Historical Element in Religion*.[27] He would tell anyone who asked about his lectures that he had no intention of setting himself up as a theologian or biblical scholar. He had no feeling of being part of a wider movement for the renewal of Christian views of history. He remarked candidly some time later, "No, I just thought of myself as picked on to do this job."[28]

Butterfield presented seven consecutive lectures on Saturdays at noon during October and November 1948, the very same time-slot as his lectures on the history of modern science during the first half of 1948. He turned forty-nine as the series began. Simultaneously he kept a regular course going on Mondays and Wednesdays on the Renaissance and Reformation. As with his series on science, he wrote the lectures on Christianity and history week by week in time for the Saturday deadline, but with even less time for preparation. They must have come easily out of his pen. Several hundred students and dons crowded the university lecture hall on Mill Lane to listen to this slight professor speak in his soft, but emphatic voice. Christopher Wright recounted how the lectures had "the 'feel' of an intellectual Event." Many decades later Kingsley Joblin talked excitedly about the lectures as if he had heard them yesterday. They were exhilarating, he said, and stimulated animated discussion among the students.[29]

Butterfield talked on weighty topics: Christianity as a historical religion, the limits of historical scholarship, the primacy of human personality, the tragedy of history, the harmfulness of moral judgments, the reality of Providence, the historicity of Jesus. He seemed to be meditating aloud on the Bible, with little awareness of recent critical scholarship. To most of his audience his words and message were thrillingly novel and timely. The lectures were Butterfield popularizing Butterfield, and his listeners found them enormously stimulating. The series produced in many people an experience of intellectual and spiritual awakening that they would remember vividly years later.

The specifics of his message startled his audience by seeming to reverse the commonplaces of the day. Butterfield surfaced as the perpetual dissenter in what he said and how he said it. He refused to grant that Hitler was worse than Napoleon. "I can imagine myself a Stalin," he said, driven to do certain things because of the predicaments he was in. He assigned responsibility for the catastrophes of the age to every ordinary person, claiming that their little cupidities, when multiplied by millions of people, produced greater havoc than the biggest wars waged by the Hitlers of the world. He chided the English for making things worse by blaming Germany for both world wars. He praised the Marxist interpretation of history at a time when people lived in dread of the Soviet Union. He trumpeted the merits of academic history, which he regarded as most useful to society when least in touch with society and current problems. He derided the ecclesiastical interpretation of history in lectures intended to draw the non-Christian to the faith. Paradox reigned.[30]

It was a stunning performance. The lectures were a wild success. The BBC immediately asked Butterfield to repeat them on national radio.[31] He shortened the first two lectures into one, touched up the others, and for six consecutive Saturday evenings around Easter 1949 he broadcast his lectures to the whole of Great Britain. Peter Laslett, in the *Radio Times,* estimated that the series must be "the longest sustained effort of broadcasting ever attempted by an individual speaker." Martin Wight figured that they were "the only university course of lectures ever repeated over the wireless." Butterfield spoke from a lighted reading stand in the Council Chamber of Broadcast House, London, to an audience of 120 in the darkened room. The listeners at home were calculated to number 100,000, probably a record at the time for the broadcast of an intellectual event. He felt exceedingly self-conscious about the traces of his Yorkshireman accent when he heard his voice played back over the radio.[32] The daily and the religious press reported his lectures as they happened, while the *Listener*, published by the BBC, printed the complete text week by week a few days after each broadcast.[33]

The broadcasts turned Butterfield into a national celebrity. He was certain that he was ruining himself for life among his professional colleagues by speaking so publicly about religion, and achieving such popularity outside historical writing. And these were not feelings of simple paranoia on his part, since there were around Cambridge, as elsewhere in Britain, many historians who exhibited general animosity to religion and to any connections made between religion and historical study, especially in public.

Butterfield signed a contract with Bell to publish the lectures as a book, although he very nearly accepted an offer from Collins instead.[34] He restored the lectures to the original seven, added an introduction, and made minor revisions here and there, retaining the wording and tone of texts intended to be read aloud. He claims that for the book version he came very close to adding a lecture from another occasion entitled "Christianity and Human Relationships," perhaps also slipping it into the German edition, but he left it out in both instances. That lecture emphasized the theme of Christian love, or as he called it, Christian "charity," and derived from his thinking on the Gospels and the writings of Paul. He had in mind to complement what he felt was the very Old Testament tone of the Cambridge lectures with their stress on the reality of sin and the tragic character of human history.[35] Bell published *Christianity and History*, a volume of 150 pages, in October 1949.

The book was Butterfield's most substantial statement yet about history and historical thinking. The finished product can in no way be regarded as a systematic account of his ideas about religion or even as a venture in the philosophy of history. Maybe it has enough of an academic character to warrant taking it as a theology of history. It is perhaps best understood as sermonic, as the presentation of a historian's faith with the aim of eliciting faith in others. He uses all of his signature words: personality, predicament, Providence, cupidity, elasticity, human relations. He cites his customary range of male leaders and events from political, military, and church history, and none from social and economic history. He acknowledges his usual brief list of historians — Acton, Ranke, Temperley, Trevelyan, Bury, adding Toynbee. He attempts neither to persuade nor mount up evidence. Instead he exhorts. Both Malcolm Thorp and Keith Sewell make a study of *Christianity and History* central to their analysis of his thought about religion.[36]

It is surprising that in a book devoted to a discussion of Christianity and history Butterfield does not devote the first chapter to religion, or even religion and history. Instead, he begins with a characterization of the nature of historical study. It is not a statement which tingles with excitement. Such a start must have disappointed or at best confused eager listeners who came to the series expecting something declaratory about the deeper meaning of life. The beginning fits Butterfield perfectly, however. He wants to disturb his listeners and deflate their expectations. He wants people to know for certain that he does not pose before them as a theologian or philosopher, a poet or a prophet. He refuses to serve them an interpretation of life and the whole human drama. He comes to them as a historian, and he wants them to know that historians deal not with grand questions of meaning, but with mundane historical study. Moreover, he wants them to realize that they look in the wrong place if they ask historical study, or any academic study, or any academic figure, to provide them with the big answers they desire in life or the overall look at the course of the ages which they seek. For these they must look to religion, and not historical study, for only religion fulfils such grand expectations.

Paradoxically, Butterfield does give them a big answer by starting in this way. The dominant message of the whole book, repeated again and again in various guises, urges people to look to God for the key to the meaning of life, not to anything in nature or made by human hands. Nothing in this world may substitute for God — not our human systems, not the democratic state, not the capitalist economy, not human reason, not human prowess, not even human beings themselves, and certainly not academic study and scientific learning. His message stresses the importance of each person's ultimate trust in God whom Christians know supremely in Christ, accompanied by acceptance of the real but delimited value of anything human and natural. He symbolizes the balance he preaches in the extraordinarily compelling final sentence of the book: "We can do worse than remember a principle which both gives us a firm Rock and leaves us the maximum elasticity for our minds: the principle: Hold to Christ, and for the rest be totally uncommitted." In a moment when civilization might appear to be collapsing all around, he has satisfied his own quest for "the things to which we can still hold fast." It is a statement of certainty about what matters to him, and a declaration of dissent from whatever others might press upon him as certainties.[37]

The road Butterfield takes to this austere conclusion starts with discourse that seems to pull in the opposite direction. He pronounces in favour of the separation of historical study and religion. He acknowledges that historical study possesses genuine merit so long as it remains within its proper sphere, but warns that it becomes a danger when historians attempt to seize wider power. He means by the limits of historical study not its inadequacy, as he did in *Historical Novel,* but its range of legitimate competence, as he did in *Whig Interpretation of History.* The sort of history he commends goes by several names which we take as interchangeable: academic history, technical history, historical scholarship, scientific history, historical science. As in *Historical Novel,* he distinguishes historical scholarship from other valid ways of gaining access to the past, such as songs, stories, piety, nostalgia, traditions, literature, and religion.

The continuity of his thinking on the subject is unmistakable, but now he elaborates. Of Butterfield's several attempts to summarize his view in the first chapter, perhaps his best statement is this one: "Historians, limited by the kind of apparatus they use and the concrete evidence on which they must rely, restrict their realm to what we might almost call the mechanism of historical processes: the tangible factors involved in an episode, the displacements produced in human affairs by an observed event or specific influence, even the kind of movements that can be recorded in statistics. All this tends to give historical narrative and historical scholarship a mundane and matter-of-fact appearance."[38] His adjectives are familiar, ones we have heard since *Whig Interpretation.* They suggest the domain he has in mind—concrete, tangible, observed, specific, mundane, matter-of-fact. Scientific history is bound to externals, outer things. In the surrounding passage he contrasts and pairs these words with other adjectives common to his rhetorical vocabulary—theoretical, intangible, intuited, general, ethereal, philosophical. Scientific history does not give historians sure access to internals, inner things. Historians do not deal with the whole of anything, not with whole institutions or whole events, not even with whole people. They engage in abstractions from wholes and, so to speak, "decide that for purposes of analysis they will only take notice of things that can be weighed and measured." Their critical apparatus involves the manipulation of documents which remain from the past, mere bits and pieces of past events and people. Historians handle the shell of human activity and not the whole of human affairs. They deal with mechanisms, and not spirits. Butterfield speaks of this penchant for concrete particulars as the first step in historical study during which a historian establishes "specific facts" about which we can be reasonably certain. He offers a few examples of such "facts": the date of his grandfather's birth, what exactly the Venetian ambassadors wrote, and the "mechanical operation of a constitutional device." The minimalism of these "facts" contrasts starkly with the expansiveness of the claim that accompanies them.[39]

Securing the specific facts in the manner described is only the first step in scientific history. The second step is the search for the possible relations among the many specific facts. In pursuit of the wider interconnections of the facts, the historians may strive to reclaim the wholes from which he abstracted the particulars in the first step. By means of careful and clever detective work, the historian eventually moves on to reconstruct a complicated episode, and then other episodes, until finally he creates a larger story containing the many episodes he has gathered in. Butterfield says little more here about this phase of the historian's labors.[40]

Butterfield shows here that these two elements — establishing the facts, and reconstructing their interconnections — constitute what he calls the "peculiar structure" of history as a science. The structure seems clear enough to him, but he feels he must add a few "comments" about the way the historian works with this structure, about the attitude of the historian when applying these techniques. On one side, historians should beware of too much scepticism, lest they close off too much or come to ludicrous conclusions in the face of the evidence, and thereby block themselves from reaching good and proper achievements. On the other side, historians need to add a healthy dose of insight, sympathy, and imagination in dealing with persons and their situations, lest they fail to see even a little bit beyond the mere externals that the method is fitted to work with. Imaginative sympathy should be involved in both the establishment of the specific facts and the reconstruction of episodes. It permits the historian to approximate something of what lies inside people, to estimate their motivations, their feelings, their true thoughts, their deepest commitments and values, their actual character. In *Whig Interpretation* Butterfield thought imaginative sympathy was useful merely to add colour and humanity to the picture drawn from the documents. Now he depends on it to gain any entry at all to the world behind the externals which the apparatus displays. But, even as he calls for imaginative sympathy, he expects few genuine results from it, because, he believes, human interiors lie fundamentally closed to historical science. The historian "cannot reach the seat of the personality." Butterfield has granted imaginative sympathy very little actual power.[41]

As if to finalize his vision of scientific history in our heads, he returns to one of his "facts": "if I demonstrate that my grandfather was born, shall we say, on January 1st, 1850, then that thesis must be equally valid whether I present it to Christian or atheist, whig or tory, Swede or Dane. In respect of points which are established by the evidence, or accepted by the judgment of common sense, history has a certain validity of its own, a certain minimum significance that is independent of philosophy, race or creed."[42] Butterfield did not insert the passage into the BBC version of his lectures. The facts stand on their own, no matter what the religion or politics or nationality or race or philosophy of the historian or the reader. Paradoxically, the thesis came straight from Acton's inaugural lecture, that *locus classicus* of Acton's exhortations on moral judgments which Butterfield so thoroughly dismissed.[43] Technical history stands apart, it seems, from the rest of life. Technical history has limited competence. It can tell us that certain specific things happened and happened in a certain order. Then people of all beliefs — "the liberal and the Jesuit, the Marxist and the Fascist, the Protestant and the Catholic, the rebel and the patriot" — may add "their varied commentaries" upon these facts and sequences, and surround them with an interpretation of the whole human drama. Religion and ideology cannot unseat the facts gathered by technical history, but people of all kinds and causes can use the facts differently to fill out their commentaries on life as a whole. When the religions and ideologies do battle against each other, academic history comes forward with its talent for achieving reasonable assurance about particulars and their interconnections, and offers a place of calm outside the battles of life. This is *the* scientific method: one method, the same for all historians, valid for all kinds of history.[44]

Butterfield's emphasis is so strong on the independence of the "facts" and the "sameness" of the methods and results of technical history for all historians, quite apart from their basic philosophies, politics, and religious beliefs, that a brief comment he makes to the contrary almost escapes us. The comment is about the importance of "our ordinary doctrine concerning man," and the context is his affirmation of the universality of sin in human nature. He claims that his view on the subject is supported by Christian as well as non-Christian thought, and that everyone, Christian or not, holds some "doctrine of man," whether they admit it or not. He writes, "It means that we ought to consider very carefully our doctrine on the subject of human beings as such in the first place; and it is a mistake for writers of history and other teachers to imagine that if they are not Christian they are refraining from committing themselves, or working without any doctrine at all, discussing history without any presuppositions. Amongst historians, as in other fields, the blindest of all the blind are those who are unable to examine their own presuppositions, and blithely imagine therefore that they do not possess any."[45]

Butterfield lets this comment about presuppositions stand without apparently realizing the implications for his account of the methods and products of technical history. For instance, it would not be surprising if historians with different presuppositions about human nature would see humans and their actions in history differently from each other. It would be plausible for the difference to touch each point in the study and writing of history where the historians had to make decisions about what they are seeing concerning their human subjects. The difference might extend from the search for the evidence to the examination of what they find as well as to the production of the historical account. And there might be presuppositions about other fundamental issues, such as the nature of power, the impact of social relations, the role of material factors, the perceptions of gender, and what counts as true or what serves as a satisfying explanation. Indeed, Butterfield's statement about presuppositions could simply wash away his discourse on scientific history. But Butterfield has an answer to his own observation about presuppositions. The doctrine of human beings that he espoused, although derived from the Christian tradition, had become the scientific view and ceased to be a presupposition. It was simply the common property of scientific history as such. If historians hold a different doctrine, they need to become aware of it and get rid of it, or at least keep it to the side as their private view and away from historical study. Presuppositions are things that historians need to overcome in the presence of scientific history, which then continues to operate independently of historians' religions, politics, gender, and philosophies.[46]

Arnold Toynbee spotted the passage on presuppositions and transmuted the point into a searing analysis of "the unconscious credulity of professed agnostics." The historians who believe themselves most liberated, said Toynbee, carry around an even greater portfolio of assumptions about a greater range of matters than those who acknowledge their presuppositions and work with them creatively. Toynbee's list of presuppositions ran well beyond Butterfield's example of the doctrine of "man." He included notions of "Europe" held by Western historians, pictures of an "Unchanging East" in the minds of Orientalists, and archaeologists' images of "primitive peoples that have no history." Presuppositions such as these are not readily cast aside, but belong to the network of deep convictions that historians rely upon, for good or for ill, to construct their histories at all.[47]

Butterfield says very little about historical explanation in his discourse on scientific history. He merely lets us know in passing that explanation, for him, is not an extra step, but an ingredient within the makeup of the scientific method as he has already constructed it for us. His words amount to a variation on his earlier view that historians explain by laying out more researched detail. Historians explain by telling "how" things happened as they did, not "why" they happened. He counts the question "why" as the more fundamental, and places it outside the competence of the historian to answer with the methods of technical history.[48]

We quickly realize that Butterfield has not weakened his aboriginal commitment to historical study as a study of individual personalities. He writes, "History deals with the drama of human life as the affair of individual personalities, possessing self-consciousness, intellect and freedom." He continues two paragraphs later, "History, as we have seen, envisages a world of human relations standing over against nature, and this means that it puts the story in a different universe — a universe in which every human being is a separate well of life, a separate source of action, and every human being, so far as mundane things are concerned, has his aspect as an end in himself." He is making two points — human beings are individuals and human beings are personalities.[49]

For Butterfield, human beings exist as individuals. Individual human beings are the only thing real in the world. Individuals are the basic units of history. Individuals are the movers of history, the creative origins of events, and the composers of social structures and collectivities. Individuals are souls of eternal value as well as sinners prone to self-righteousness and cupidity. Individuals are, under God, the purpose of history. Christians, he maintains, are particularly committed to this view of people as individuals.

The things we call society or the state or the species are not real existents, but simply what he now bluntly labels "collective nouns" covering interconnections among innumerable individual people. It is possible to write history as if these collective nouns act and create and do things, and we can schematize their structures and diagram their development, but we falsify history when we do, and we make collective nouns into persons, which they are not. Butterfield agrees with the Christian tradition which regards governments as valid in appropriate circumstances, but he places a specific meaning on the tradition. He grants that governments may be useful organizers of collective action and restraints on the practice of sin, but he concedes them no life apart from the individuals which make them up. Butterfield's social theory is unashamedly individualist and nominalist.[50]

Butterfield understands each human being to be a person. Each human being comes in two parts, an inside and an outside. These correspond with soul and body, the spiritual and the material. It is the inside that makes a human being a person, that constitutes personality. From the inside arises everything fundamental in human life — thinking, feeling, loving, believing, valuing, sinning, doing good, and so on. Indeed all action and creativity come from the inside, and his triad of basic human attributes — self-consciousness, intellect, and freedom — dwells in the human interior. Starkly put, it would seem that nothing derives from the outside of individual human beings. The outside is inert, unviable, static, mechanical, mere surface. The inside is what primarily matters and is interesting. The outside is like a dwelling for the inside, and the outside matters only derivatively because of its relationship with the inside. The inside is what matters, for there is the person. His theory of human nature is, as William Speck has noted, personalist.[51]

We link onto a long-extending element of Butterfield's view of history in general, one previously made most explicit in *Whig Interpretation*. Now he has elaborated his idea considerably. Butterfield commonly uses the word "history" to refer to historical study and the writings that historians produce, but beyond that he understands "history" to mean two very distinct things. In the first and most comprehensive sense, history is the world divided from nature, indeed history stands "over against" nature. History is the drama, while nature is the stage. History in this sense refers to the realm of human beings with their individuality and personality, while nature is the realm of the nonhuman, characterized by impersonal processes, the absence of moral decision, and the development of the species instead of the individual. He writes, "[The historian] picks up the other end of the stick and envisages a world of human relations, so to speak, over against nature — he studies that new kind of life which man has superimposed on the jungle, the forest and the waste. Since this world of human relations is the historian's universe, we may say that history is a human drama, a drama of personalities, taking place as it were, on the stage of nature, and amid its imposing scenery." It is a stark separation he demands between history and nature, and an unflattering perception of nature. Only after distancing history so severely from nature does he allow that we can go on "to discover how deeply man himself is rooted in earthiness." Hitler's great error was to start the other way around and to think of human beings as belonging to nature, not history. The idea seems to be that the things of nature might be manipulated for human purpose, but that humans must not be manipulated. Butterfield complements the dualism of history and nature with God, giving him ultimately a three-tiered vision of all things: God, history, nature. At the end, he comes to the affirmation that God is God of nature as well as history.[52]

There is a second meaning of history for Butterfield. Within the realm of history, hence human beings, understood as divided from nature, there is a further divide, the dualism created by the division of human beings into an outside and an inside. In this sense, history is the world as it is on the outsides of human beings, while religion and morality refer to the world as it is on the insides of human beings. This dualism structures his mental horizon as he discusses historical study and religion. He embeds the dualism in the title of the book, *Christianity and History.* Historians study merely the external world of human beings, while religion penetrates to the deep recesses of the personality on the inside of each human being.

We now better understand the awkward tension he creates for himself by his definition of historical study. His two meanings of history are in conflict. On one hand, he insists that the historian must bring the insides of human beings into the discussion, since history is a matter of personalities. This is history in the first sense, as over against nature. On the other hand, he warns that the apparatus and evidence with which historical study works permit the historian to reach only the externals of human behaviour. This is history in sense two, as over against religion and morality. He repeatedly urges in one voice that historical study deals with personalities which he warns in another voice, even with imaginative sympathy, is virtually impossible to do.

As in *Whig Interpretation*, Butterfield supplements his view of history as a matter of individual personalities with an understanding of history as process, what he calls "the historical process." This is a further dualism, personality and process. He adds little to what he said eighteen years earlier, and occasionally since then. The language he associates with historical process — conditioning circumstances, predicament, conditions — is familiar. However, he allows us to glimpse an aspect of his understanding of process which we have not previously met. His chief concern now is not about the historical process as a relationship between past and present, as before, but about the historical process as a consequence of the actions of many individual personalities. He talks about the historical process as a work of history-making: "by our actions and by all the interplay that goes on between us we are engaged in a work of history-making — engaged in weaving that fabric of events upon which the historians of the future will have to write and speculate. It is necessary, however, to remember that the pattern of the history-making which we will carry out will not be the product of my will or of yours or indeed of anybody else's, but will represent in one sense rather what might almost seem to be a compounding of these wills or at least of their effects — something that no single person will either have intended or anticipated." Millions of individuals go about doing their own business and pursuing their own cupidities. The results are the systems and large-scale events of the world, the things we call society, the nation-state, the economy, international diplomacy, the industrial revolution, capitalism, civilization. It is a feature of process that the tiny sins of millions of individuals get transformed over the long term into catastrophes. These systems and long-term consequences become the framework of organization within which the millions of individual personalities continue to live their lives. These are the conditioning circumstances of life. The systems and conditions are externals and belong to the outsides of individual human beings. The conditions regulate what individuals may do and the range of action available to them at any given moment. If internal personality represents freedom, the external conditions of life represent constraint, necessity, and determinism.[53]

None of the conditioning circumstances was intended or predictable or controllable. They are merely derivatives of numberless individual actions. At the end of the day, however, we may look back on these results and see patterns — dialectics, renaissances, cycles, spirals, and lines. Even the image of history as cooperation and tragic conflict, which Butterfield prefers and discusses at length, is something we see only in retrospect. He is willing to talk about progress in history, but only in a loose way with a backward glance, and only with regard to the externals of life and not in connection with human beings as personality. We are permitted to talk about patterns in history so long as we remember that the patterns lie in our own eyes, and do not really exist in history. Butterfield holds tightly to his conviction that only individual personalities really exist. All the rest, even the systems and processes, in a fundamental sense lack reality. Such are Butterfield's individualism, personalism, and nominalism.[54]

Butterfield's view of process adds another layer of awkward tension to his understanding of history and historical study. On one hand, Butterfield asserts that individual personalities are the important thing in history. He believes that processes and systems are merely the interactions of individual wills, and he demands that historical study treat history as a matter of individual personalities. On the other, he is prepared to attribute less and less to individuals in history and more and more to processes and conditioning circumstances, and to describe historical study as competent only with respect to these external conditions. He speaks of himself as still in the middle of changing his mind about the relationship between individuals and the processes of conditioning circumstances. Now he is inclined to think that he and many other thinkers "in practice ascribe too little rather than too much to conditioning circumstances in our estimates of human beings." His drift is towards a higher estimate of the importance of processes and structures, but only as constraints upon or conflations of individual action. He does not give himself firm support for the study of social history or even institutional history. He is inclined towards scepticism about the validity of such studies, yet he concedes that such histories need to be undertaken.[55]

Butterfield's understanding of the question of moral judgments in history turns entirely on his views of the character of historical study, human personality, and conditioning circumstances. He remains as adamant as ever in his insistence that historians should not make moral judgments upon the people who are their subjects, but he also opposes moral judgments upon the course of events such that human actions turn into a war between good and evil, right versus wrong. On one level, his meaning appears much clearer now than it did in *Whig Interpretation.* Technical history does not enable historians to see inside people or to know "what allowance has to be made for conditions." People and history are too complex, and too much is beyond or hidden from the reach of the historical method. Our historical apparatus does not enable us to assemble enough details and factors to complete the analysis of external conditions, and our imaginative sympathy is inadequate to disclose much within the human interior. Historians are not qualified to issue what he calls a "final" moral judgment on the personalities of particular human beings, or to decide who is worse or better "in the eyes of eternity," and they should "leave it till the Judgment Day." Moreover, they cannot, as historians, sort out right and wrong within the admixture of good and evil on all sides and in all persons in the human drama. The ban on moral judgments holds whether the historian speaks of Hitler, whose deeds we may think are awful, or St. Francis of Assisi, whose works we admire. The historian as historian, and by means of historical study, cannot determine in either case how much was due to wilful evil or pristine holiness on the inside, and how much was due to the particular combinations of external conditions enveloping each figure. Even with someone as apparently easy to judge as Hitler, Butterfield remains unrelenting in his opposition to making a moral judgment against him. We cannot say that any of us under similar external conditions would not use the opportunity to do great harm. And we cannot boast that we are fundamentally different from Hitler and that inside each of us there is no perversity mingled with our higher motives. Butterfield comes once again to his long-standing confession that everyone is a sinner.[56]

For Butterfield, the dualism between external conditions and internal personality in history is so nearly absolute, and the limitations of historical study are so extremely great, that he leaves the historian entirely without competence to make a moral statement about anyone or the course of events. Although he never explicitly takes the next step, there seems to be nothing in his logic prohibiting the historian from making moral judgments that would not also bar all other human beings from doing so. Indeed, the objections he raises are sufficiently general to apply to everyone without exception. He at least has every reason to keep himself from ever making moral judgments about anyone, past or present. Butterfield operates with a very short list of options — no moral judgments about others or about events, self-judgments, and divine judgments at the end of history. He appears still to leave no room in his prescription for what we might call ordinary and proximate, rather than ultimate, moral assessments of people and their deeds or the accumulation of human interactions in what we call events and situations.

The ostensible clarity of Butterfield's view at this level of analysis is lost when we examine another level on which he speaks of moral judgments in history. He affirms his belief that there are "moral judgments that lie in the very nature of history." He calls this type of moral judgment by various names: "the operation of the moral factor in history," "judgment . . . embedded in the very constitution of the universe," "the moral element in the structure of history," "moral retribution which seems to be worked out in the very processes of time," or simply "nemesis." His prime example is the case of Germany: "I do not think that we are interpolating anything fanciful into the structure of history, however, if we say that, whether in 1918 or in 1933 or in 1945, or in all these together, a judgment has been passed on the militarism of Prussia — a judgment which we have no reason to believe that she would have had reason to suffer if she had avoided an actual excess. And it was a judgment both on the Hohenzollerns as a dynasty and on the Germans as a people — it was not a judgment that fell on Frederick the Great and Bismarck personally, for these men were permitted more than the ordinarily-expected span of power." As if to soften the aggression of this comment about Germany and even the German people, he adds remarks about some such moral judgment falling on the Allied powers as well. Moral judgment of this type occurs within the ordinary course of history, and links together events from widely different times, usually over a very long time. Like everything in the historical process, the later events which execute the judgment are entirely the unintended results of the combination of millions of individual actions. The original moral defects which eventually come under judgment did not generally appear to be defects to the people alive at the time.[57]

He is consistent with his previous statements when he insists that a moral judgment of this type is not made against individual personalities, for he has always objected to a moral judgment in history against persons. It is surprising that he speaks of this as a moral judgment against social systems, nations, and collectivities. Such social things do not belong to the inner world of persons, the realm where moral judgment is relevant, but to the external world, the world of conditions, frameworks, and technique, which is the realm of history. It is also surprising that he regards this type of moral judgment as an act of the Divine. Heretofore he has spoken of divine judgment in absolute and final terms, the sort of thing that happens beyond history, at the Judgment Day. The moral judgments he is now calling divine are relative and proximate, and appear during the course of history.[58]

It is most surprising that he allows for the category at all, given his abhorrence of historians making moral judgments. He does not seem to notice — as we cannot fail to do — that it is Butterfield who applies the name "militarism" to Prussian military activity and counts it as a moral fault, and who regards the catastrophic effects on Germany of the two world wars and the rise of Hitler to be divinely executed moral judgments against the German people. He does talk as if the type of moral judgment he identifies occurs in history independently of whatever the historian might believe or think about the events. Nonetheless, by seeing the events as he does, it is Butterfield who renders the moral judgment, and he does so as a historian. The moral judgment he makes is not against one individual person, but against Germany and the German people, which, in his terms, means against millions of individual persons widely spread over time. He calls the judgment an interim one, which would seem to moderate its meaning and impact. But by locating the judgment within so utterly complex a network of events extending over centuries, by associating the judgment with colossal human carnage and hate, and by regarding the judgment as in reality divine, he actually renders a moral judgment that exceeds our human ability to comprehend. Butterfield has rendered a moral judgment against the German people that seems infinitely more heinous than deciding — along with just about every English woman and man — that Hitler was worse than Napoleon. Simultaneously he interprets the long course of German history in a manner apparently antithetical to his warnings about the dangers of history. His judgment would feed the most obvious anti-German accusation then available.

When we read further in *Christianity and History,* we realize that Butterfield's idea of moral judgments in the very nature of history is really an aspect of his idea of Providence. And like his understanding of moral judgments in history, his idea of Providence is dependent on his views of individual personalities and historical process. He defined historical process as the ongoing interplay among millions of individuals all going about their own business and producing unintended results from the combination of countless wills. It is, he says, "that kind of history-making which goes on so to speak over our heads, now deflecting the results of our actions, now taking our purposes out of our hands, and now turning our endeavors to ends not realised." When we look more closely, we notice that he calls this process of history-making "the providential order." In one sense, historical process and providential order are synonyms.[59]

However, Butterfield seems to add considerable embroidery to his meaning when he represents the process of history as the providential order. The initial meaning refers simply to the interplay of millions of individuals yielding unintended results over time. The supplemental meaning includes an assessment of whether the interplay and the results are good or harmful. When he focuses on the harmful effects of human action in history, he leads to the discussion of the type of moral judgments he finds embedded in the very course of history. When he considers chiefly the beneficial effects of human events he begins to refer to "a providence, in fact, which moves over history with the function of creating good out of evil." He designates this as "another kind of Providence which it may be permissible to call human," and it is the fruit of "something like the collective wisdom of the human race." As an example, he mentions the Fire of London in 1666 which wrecked the city and caused immense human suffering, but which, after a suitable time of mourning, the survivors reinterpreted as the cleansing of an unkempt fabric. Londoners and the Crown responded to the devastation by rebuilding the city on a superior plan.[60]

Almost by a sleight of hand he shifts his language from "providential order" to "Providence" with a capital P. He begins to insert statements about "the reflecting activity of an ordaining and reconciling mind" and "the direction of a superintending intellect." He introduces these phrases tentatively with prefaces like "it is as though . . ." and "we picture the course of things as if. . . ." He now has before us a being, or at least a mind, who acts and produces consequences. This being is "Providence" who in the form of "History herself," he says, "has risen up and determined to have a hand in the game." This being is an "it" with clear and substantial limits. Butterfield writes, "And so Providence produces a world in which men can live and gradually improve their external conditions, in spite of sin — in other words it does the best that human beings have left possible for it at any time. The industrial revolution and the rise of the capitalist system are the best that Providence can do with human cupidity at certain stages of the story." Providence has great power, but it is a power merely to react to the acts of human beings. Providence superintends the course of events, but it does so by using no other materials than what human beings provide for it. Providence cannot simply do anything it wants, but only the best it can under the circumstances set up for it by human action.[61]

Butterfield depicts the relationship between Providence and human action by means of a metaphor to which he returns several times. History is like a performance in which we humans, as members of an orchestra, are playing a piece of music that the composer is composing only one note ahead of us as we play. Depending on how we play each note, the composer makes up his mind about the next bar of the composition. Butterfield writes, "Indeed the composer of the piece leaves himself room for great elasticity, until we ourselves have shown what we are going to do next." The metaphor adds some depth-of-field to the previous picture we have of numberless human beings carrying on their own affairs and Providence turning them into unintended results.

We can now understand that Butterfield envisions history as an interaction between Providence and the multitude of human beings, with each side exercising a decisive role in the creation of the outcome. Human beings and Providence are both the creators of history. Neither one is sovereign. Each one needs the other in order to create. The big difference between Providence and us is that we make mistakes and do harm, while Providence does only good, sometimes renders moral judgments in the course of history, and often brings good out of evil.[62]

Once we know about the work of Providence, Butterfield recommends a course of action. Human beings do best when, he says, "we conceive ourselves not as sovereign makers of history but as born to co-operate with Providence." He brings us full circle to *Englishman and His History.* We recognize his familiar message about political change. He used to call this "the whig mode of co-operating with Providence," and he had argued that the Whig method became the English political tradition. Now he has universalized the message. Cooperating with Providence is the best thing anyone anywhere can do in life. Whig insight and English practice are simply wisdom.

The sin he abhors is presumption. We commit the sin of presumption when we act on the conviction that we can calculate all the variables and all the contingencies at a given moment, and make everything occur on schedule. We thereby act as if we can control the course of history and force Providence to turn in our favour. Butterfield is uncharacteristically free with his moral judgments against people for their presumption. The peace-makers of 1919 were guilty of presumption when they entirely redrew the map of Europe, and their failure was terrible. The Germans committed the fault of presumption in both world wars, and they enlarged the disaster for themselves. Political activists who use government legislation to force their will on the nation are presumptuous and merely compound the troubles. By contrast, the English cooperate with Providence when they "muddle through" and are sufficiently flexible to adapt themselves to each change in the weather. The diplomats in the eighteenth-century system of Europe cooperated with Providence by never taking too much power away from a defeated state. We all cooperate with Providence when we forsake the intervention of the government and follow the policy "that each of us should rather do the good that is straight under our noses." The people in life who cooperate with Providence are the ones who, like himself, stay away from politics and government, and instead, he says, "seek to achieve good in their own small corner of the world and then leave the leaven to leaven the whole lump." He adds the comment that the time to work for good is now. No person and no generation should postpone doing the good thing now at hand for the sake of the promise of a better arrangement in the future. When Butterfield makes these points, he hands us the key to his own political quietism.[63]

So far in his presentation Butterfield has refrained from making any claims for God in history. Now, at the end of his discussion about historical process and Providence, he reveals his belief that everything he has been telling us has to do with God. Providence is not an "it" after all. Providence is God in history: "To a religious mind all these providential dispositions which I have attempted to describe must appear as Divine, as the orderings of God Himself; and in the workings of history there must be felt the movement of a living God." Christians may trust in Providence, regard Providence as living and active, both in themselves and in general history, even take Providence as a "special Providence" for the religious mind and within the history of Christianity. Christians may know history as purposeful and model their understanding of Providence upon the Old Testament. Analysis of the historical process lets us know the ways of Providence, and our study of history gives us the details of how God deals with the course of history.[64]

We finally realize that his discourse about historical process has amounted to a long, complicated, and intrinsic argument for God in history. In a circuitous way Butterfield was actually seeking to do what the philosopher Sidney Hook later chided him for not doing, provide a proof of God's existence before asking us to leave moral judgments to God. His mode of argument is not systematic, but metaphorical, and he lets his metaphors float around together. When we sort everything out, we notice that his presentation has advanced in five stages. The first stage is his description of the historical process, what he called "the very nature of history." At the second stage he gives to the historical process the name "the providential order," a term unmistakably hinting at the religious meaning he does not yet reveal. He believes that what he has told us in these two stages derives from his competence as a technical historian and from the domain of technical history, hence upon mere observation of externals. He warns that "we are liable to serious technical errors" if we do not regard the process of history as constituted in the way he describes, hence as "a providential order" in which events always pass beyond our intentions. He explicitly adds that looking upon the historical process in this manner does not depend upon anything like a religious belief.[65]

The third stage is to introduce the image of "a superintending intellect" who directs the course of history, reacts to human decisions in the manner of the composer with the players of the music, and brings good out of evil. The fourth stage is to name the intellect "Providence" with a capital P, a traditional religious designation for the activity of God in history. We cannot keep ourselves from thinking of God. Yet, Butterfield insists that even seeing history in relationship to a superintending intellect known as Providence does not depend upon religious belief. It derives from, he says, "merely a secular analysis of the way in which history happens," that is, from mere external observation by a person "who puts on the thinking-cap of the ordinary historical student." The European diplomats of the eighteenth century were successful because, even though they were "losing the religious idea of Providence, they clung very tightly to that purely secular conception of a providential order which I have already mentioned." At the fifth stage he explicitly acknowledges Providence as the living God in history, as did the ancient Hebrew scriptures. To see God in this way takes more than the historical mind or method. It takes "a religious mind" to whom these things "must appear as Divine."[66]

When we get to the climax of his presentation, it strikes us that Butterfield has had his destination in view all the time. When he describes the historical process as a "providential order," asserts the presence of a superintending intellect, and calls this intellect Providence, he is applying the version of the Christian idea of Providence which he believes to be true. Technical historical analysis has not led him to see history in this way. He has been guided by his prior knowledge of God in history. Concomitantly, secular intellectual analysis since the eighteenth century has led others to project not Providence, but a host of images of history that bear no resemblance to what the Christian tradition proposes: images of impersonal process, the survival of the fittest, inevitable growth, or randomness, for example.

We have now come face to face with the theme which Butterfield sets into the title of the book, Christianity and history. We notice immediately his tendency to treat the subject as a question of two matters — religion and history. This pair reflects the essential dualism which we have always detected in his perception of the universe. The dualism consists of his distinguishing and pairing the spiritual and the material, the religious and the secular. The spiritual and the material relate to each other as higher relates to lower. He operates with this dualism in his thought, inducing him to present his ideas via the medium of pairs of contrasting items. Each pair forms a two-member hierarchy of opposites. When we review the many things he advocates, we recognize this dualism in different guises. In the list that follows the first member of each pair manifests the religious and the second the material: religion and technical history, imaginative sympathy and documentary criticism, whole and abstract, ethereal and mundane, insight and observation, reconstruction of episodes and specific facts, history and nature, freedom and necessity, active and mechanical, individual and collectivities, soul and body, mind and matter, inner and outer, internals and externals, personality and process, intentions and conditioning circumstances, morality and history, Providence and historical process. The pairs go on and on in Butterfield's discourse.

Butterfield's method of treating Christianity and history is to begin by stressing the opposing character of the two. We see this insistence at each point in his discourse as he multiplies the contrasting pairs. He defines technical history as starkly separate from and independent of religion. He emphasizes the solidity of the findings of technical history, apart from the influence of religion and anything the devotees of the religions want to debate among themselves. Technical history establishes specific facts, while religion adds commentary upon the facts. Historical study enjoys ready access to the outsides of people, but not their insides, for which we need religion and poetry and, he might have added, psychology. Historians can deal easily with the mechanisms of historical process and the externals of human organization, but only religion can reach the interior seat of the personality. Historians can tell us details and certain things about the connections between the details, but for the wholeness of knowledge of the human drama of the ages we need prophets and poets and theologians. Historians must not make moral judgments about people, since only God can see us as we really are. Historical study can show us the complications of the process of history, but only religious people can see history as the domain of Divine Providence. The separation between Christianity and history seems complete. We can easily still read Butterfield as the strict positivist who believes in the neutrality of the "facts" and seeks to isolate historical study from the contaminating impact of religion and morality, indeed from life.

Butterfield's method goes further, however. While starting with the opposition between Christianity and history, he strains to keep both members of the pair together. This he does with every manifestation of the dualism he perceives in the universe. He stands, as it were, on one side of the dualism and reaches out to include the other side as well. His dominant metaphor is "combination," starting with one side of the dualism and then combining it with the other. And so Butterfield tells us that technical history establishes the specific external facts, but historians must also employ imaginative sympathy in order to see as far as possible into the interior of other people. Historical study abstracts, but we need the commentary religion provides in order to see things whole again. History is not nature, but history plays on the stage provided by nature. Human beings are individuals, but we need the constraints supplied by society. Individuals are souls, but they are rooted in earthiness too. Historians should not make moral judgments, but moral judgments are made anyway by the course of history itself. History is a process, but it is also a providential order. And so on. The polarities each include two elements, and both are required to complete the picture.

When we look more closely at his discussion, we notice that Butterfield's method goes even further still. We sense that he is striving to transcend the dualisms he perceives in the universe, transcend even the metaphor of combination, and discern a unity that is somehow more basic than the opposition. As we examine his sayings about religion, particularly about Christianity, we detect his drive for transcendent unity. The understanding we gather is that he desires the reconciliation of the opposites he perceives in the dualisms of the universe. He wants to achieve this reconciliation by means of religion, and in particular by means of Christianity. It is the same drive towards reconciliation in his thought that we witnessed in *Whig Interpretation of History*.

We take notice of certain passages where his drive towards unity is vivid. After summarizing his view of technical history, Butterfield writes: "But for the fullness of our commentary on the drama of human life in time, we have to break through this technique — have to stand back and see the landscape as a whole — and for the sum of our ideas and beliefs about the march of the ages we need the poet and the prophet, the philosopher and the theologian. Indeed we decide our total attitude to the whole of human history when we make our decision about our religion — and it is the combination of the history with a religion, or with something equivalent to a religion, which generates power and fills the story with significances." He continues later on: "Our final interpretation of history is the most sovereign decision we can take, and it is clear that every one of us, as standing alone in the universe, has to take it for himself. It is our decision about religion, about our total attitude to things, and about the way we will appropriate life. And it is inseparable from our decision about the role we are going to play ourselves in that very drama of history." And much later: "One of the most fundamental of the differences between people must be the question whether they believe in God or not; for on that depends their whole interpretation of the universe and of history." The drift of such passages is towards the ultimate unity of religion and history. Religion encompasses all, including even the entire history of the ages. Religion gives us our interpretation of history, indeed our interpretation of life as a whole, and informs us of how we fit in.[67]

His inclination towards the ultimate unity of religion and history becomes especially evident when we review his thought about Christianity in connection with particular points concerning history. At each point we discern a religious understanding behind his characterization of the "material" and "secular" member of any pair. For instance, underlying his insistence on the limited competence of historical study is a religious message not to absolutize scientific method and scientific knowledge, not to make a god out of science. He warns against treating "abstract nouns," like "the State" and "Society," as real since he wants to protect the individual as the bearer of the soul. He allows room for social structures in keeping with the tradition of Christian thought that governments and society exercise an appropriate role in ordering human behaviour. Human personality derives from the inner soul, but envelops our material life as well. God turns out to be the God of history as well as the God of nature, the God of our soul as well as of our earthiness. Historians should not make moral judgments against persons since persons are sacred and are known profoundly only by God. The melding of countless individual wills into unintended consequences indicates Providence working in the historical process. The complexity of the process of history discloses the way that God deals with the universe. And so on.

The culminating expression of his belief in the transcending unity of religion and history appears in his characterization of Christianity. He depicts Christianity as a historical religion in a sense that goes beyond the observation that Christianity, like every religion, has a history. Christianity, Butterfield tells us, is bound to the life of Jesus, the people of ancient Israel, and the communities of the early Christians. The Christian teachings of the incarnation, the crucifixion, and the resurrection all interpret events in the life of Jesus. The Bible, in both the Old and New Testaments, he notes, "unfolds the religion to such a considerable degree by telling its history, and conveys a message to men by the narration and exposition of historical events in general." In an allusion counteracting the thought of Rudolf Bultmann, the German New Testament scholar, Butterfield concludes, "And it would be a dangerous error to imagine that the characteristics of an historical religion would be maintained if the Christ of the theologians were divorced from the Jesus of history." In Butterfield's thought the unity between history and Christianity as a religion could not be more secure.[68]

Butterfield completes his emphasis on the unity of history and Christianity with the definition of a recognizably religious vocation for the technical historian. The very thing he most vociferously distanced from religion turns out to be religious. His message reaffirms the mission he assigned historians in *Whig Interpretation*. When devotees of all the competing religions and ideologies are, he writes, "howling at one another across the interstellar spaces, all claiming that theirs is the absolute version," academic history serves humbly in their presence as a "bridge" for peace and communication among them. The historian has a task that parallels, and in a profound way expresses, the reconciling power of religion: "once battles are over the human race becomes in a certain sense one again; and just as Christianity tries to bind it together in love, so the role of the technical historian is that of a reconciling mind that seeks to comprehend. Taking things retrospectively and recollecting in tranquillity, the historian works over the past to cover the conflicts with understanding, and explains the unlikenesses between men and makes us sensible of their terrible predicaments: until at the finish — when all is remote as the tale of Troy — we are able at last perhaps to be a little sorry for everyone." In Butterfield's vision, the technical historian is the reconciling mind at work amid the opposites of the universe. In this way the historian mirrors and cooperates with Providence, that supreme "ordaining and reconciling mind" who brings good out of evil.[69]

All in all, the tendency towards affirming the unity of history and religion is strong in Butterfield's discourse at this moment. It is possible that he is not entirely aware how strongly he pushes in this direction, and he provides us with no single statement of the point. On the contrary, his most obvious statements, the statements which most impress us, accentuate the opposition between Christianity and history and the incompatibility of academic history and religion. He insists time and again that historians must not overlay their history with their religious beliefs, must not make moral judgments, must not use their religion to influence their history. Yet, Butterfield himself provides the religious justifications that we have noted for his understanding of technical history, the study of human personality, moral judgments, and process, and it is he who formulates the religious vocation of the technical historian as the reconciling mind. The contradiction between the two sides of Butterfield's thought on this matter seems palpable.

Butterfield backs away from claiming that his view of history and historical study is a Christian view. Yet, when we search we have no difficulty detecting just how fundamental the religious basis of his thought really is. The assumptions are there. He is assuming, without saying so, that not only his view of the religious and the spiritual, but even his view of the material, the mundane, and the technical is a Christian view. And more than that, he is assuming that his view of the universe as a dualism of the spiritual and the material represents a Christian view. In this manner, he reconciles the dualism of opposites in the universe within the transcending unity of religion.

Our examination of Butterfield's views as expressed in *Christianity and History* allows us to notice one other general feature of his historical thought. It occurs to us that he builds his universe of history and historical study out of "individuals" in several senses. Most important is his belief that human beings exist as individuals. The basic unit of history is the individual person. He regards every social structure — state, church, family, nation, university, and so on — as merely a collection of individual persons covered by a name applied by conventional usage. The social structures are not themselves units. We also see that he understands a process to be a collection of individual actions in time sequence, or more accurately, a collection of individual actions by individual people in time sequence. A historian gathers individual actions into a collection which is named as an individual event, and then collects many individual events to form and name an individual episode. Many episodes become an individual process. However, the real unit remains the individual action by the individual person. The process, the episode, or the event does not become a unit. Those are merely names for collections of individual actions, which over time add up to millions of actions by millions of individuals. Going further, we note that he assigns to historical study the task of defining the individual fact. Eventually the individual facts number in the millions times multiple millions. The reconstruction of an episode is a historian's way of putting the individual facts together. Historical evidence comes in the form of individual documents containing combinations of individual words, and the meaning of a document commonly hinges on an individual word in the document. His historical method emphasizes the gathering and collation of countless individual items. The unit is the fact, the document, the word. Further still, we understand that, for him, religion is a matter of individual souls, and Christianity is merely a collective name for the beliefs and actions of countless individual persons. The unit is not the religion, but the individual Christian. And finally, how does Butterfield know that things go on inside other people, that the wills of many people are molded into a process of unintended consequences, that all people are sinners, that everybody's motives are mixed, that Providence acts in history? He knows by analogy with his own individual experience, and he cautiously projects his individual experience onto the course of history.

Thus, Butterfield's individualism is radical and blends easily with his personalism and nominalism. It extends across his understanding of social structure, historical process, historical method, religion, morality, and politics. For him the problematic questions concern the supra-individual coherences of life. It is a problem for him to grasp a state or a capitalist corporation or a church as a community that transcends the powers and activity of its members, or to comprehend events or actions or episodes as manifesting an integrity of their own that surpasses the details, or to perceive information in the documentation that incorporates more than what the words say. The remarkable thing is that Butterfield's programmatic statements on these issues as found in *Christianity and History* comport well with the sort of history he actually wrote in *George III, Lord North, and the People* and *Origins of Modern Science*. Butterfield may have tied himself in knots by admonishing historians to keep history separate from politics, moral judgment, and religion, and then not doing so himself. But in connection with his individualism, personalism, and nominalism he was entirely consistent with himself.

Christianity and History received more reviews than any other book he had written to date, and, as it turned out, by far the greatest number of reviews of any book in his whole career. And, in contrast with the discouraging reviews of *George III, Lord North, and the People,* the reception was overwhelmingly positive. The reviews appeared in the daily press immediately, then in the weeklies, the religious press, and academic and religious journals, in Great Britain and throughout the English-speaking world, including India. The reviewer often paired him with Reinhold Niebuhr, Emil Brunner, Arnold Toynbee, Marc Bloch, or, in India, Swami Akhilananda, each of whom published a book on historical thinking about the same time. Many newspapers published his photograph, as if he were a celebrity. The photo in the *Montreal Gazette* and the *Church Times* offered the image of the unconventional intellectual and the poet with a cigarette hanging from lips. In religious circles both the BBC lectures and the book received virtually unanimous acclamation. The reviews came from across the spectrum of Christian traditions, at national levels and in local newsletters: Methodist, Anglican, Roman Catholic, Lutheran, Congregational, Baptist, Presbyterian, evangelical, liberal, and so on. These reviews appreciated his linkage of Christianity and history, had no problem understanding him, admired his literary style, and remarked on how important it was that he spoke and wrote as a professional historian and not as a theologian. There were those who hesitated over this or that point but then rallied to resounding support for what he had to say. The Anglican Bishop of Lichfield exclaimed in the *Church of England Newspaper* that it was the most outstanding religious book of the year. Roger Lloyd in the *Church Times* observed that the book became a standard work for clergy study circles. The public press reviews around the world were overwhelmingly appreciative as well. The *New York Times,* comparing him with Toynbee, said Butterfield exhibited "a more authentic feeling for history and a deeper understanding of religion."[70]

The academic reviews were also chiefly positive, and he stimulated debate. His views on "technical history" in relation to religion set off a discussion that went on for years. Keith Sewell's exegesis of his text was the most notable. Martin Wight published, in 1950, the first academic article on Butterfield's thought, on technical history and moral judgments, in contrast with Reinhold Niebuhr. But many academic reviews were not positive. In general, but not always, it seemed that the factor evoking negative comment, whatever the genre, was a feeling of discomfort with Butterfield's self-exposure as a Christian in the historical profession. Butterfield had known that he was taking a risk in doing the lectures. Sydney W. Jackman, in *ISIS*, applauded his bravery in the face of religious sceptics and devotees of science. As the reviews unrolled, those sympathetic to his views seemed to find his language clear, his style scintillating, his religious discourse inspiring, and his imagery poetic. And indeed, by contrast, the uncomfortable reviewers tended to find the book muddled. For instance, the review in *Mind* slapped him until it hurt because of the way he stated his big notions about religion and history. Patrick Gardiner, then a young Fellow of Magdalene College, Oxford, said the worst things an Oxford analytic philosopher could say about another scholar: his notions were odd, were marked by vagueness, were riddled with obscurities, left the reader at a loss, had doubtful logical status, were not open to falsification, and abounded in unresolved problems. A few in Cambridge at the time raised similar complaints, and among a certain sort of critic the charge of muddledness passed from mouth to mouth over the decades until Noel Annan codified it in *Our Age* in 1990. Butterfield's writings on Christianity and history, said Annan, "at times reached a point of such Delphic ambiguity that attentive readers were baffled."[71]

Enough readers understood his message, however. As a book, *Christianity and History* contributed to the creation of a body of work which instantiated the rhetorical separation of religious discourse from historical writing. Until at least the end of the nineteenth century, and in many cases right up to the mid-twentieth century, the writings of historians in Christian traditions, as well as Islamic, Jewish, Hindu, and Buddhist traditions, freely mingled language about divine presence and spiritual realities with the language of human actions and natural things. For instance, the histories published by so significant a symbol of scientific writing as Ranke contained explicit religious language within the histories themselves. Indeed, in the very passage where Ranke articulated the standard ever after associated with strictly scientific history ["wie es eigentlich gewesen"/"how it really was"] he speaks of "how we deal with humanity as it is . . . and, at times, with the hand of God above them." The passage introduced his *Histories of the Latin and Germanic Nations, 1494–1535* of 1824.[72] The new discourse filtered out such religious language and placed it into a new genre of literature written by historians for the purpose of producing explicit statements about religion and history, especially statements about their own religious commitments. This new genre ran parallel to the new genre of religion-silent history-writing thereby created. But that they wrote religion-silent histories did not mean that authors, when writing their histories, stopped holding onto the commitments they uttered in their religion-and-history writings, that, for instance, they stopped believing that God acted within human history. It became possible to use the genre of religion-and-history as a medium of access into the historical writings themselves. The explicit writings revealed some of the things the historians presumed or rendered implicit in their writing of history. The number of writings in the new genre of religion and history was increasing. Butterfield's *Christianity and History* participated in, indeed helped stimulate, what became a wider movement of the renewal of Christian views of history in the mid-twentieth century.[73]

October 1949

By looking so closely at Butterfield's discourse, we might easily overlook what he had just accomplished. He had just published three books in one month. Bell in London issued all three in October 1949: *George III, Lord North, and the People, Origins of Modern Science,* and *Christianity and History.* He now had published ten books altogether. As a result of amazing conjunctions over a period of at least two decades, the simultaneous appearance of three books in three seemingly unrelated fields made an enormous impact. J. R. M. Butler, the Regius Professor of History, wrote him, "I can't tell you how much I admire and envy your productivity and the original ideas you produce. It is a great gift." Butterfield gave all three books to Trevelyan, and Trevelyan honoured him: "It gives me the warmest pleasure to see how productive of important works you have made your professorship. Your range is extraordinary and so now is your performance." The *Times Educational Supplement* observed that he had now become "a real force in the world beyond the circles in which academic scholarship, for which he has the highest reputation, provides the major topics of interest." People began to speak often of Butterfield and Lord Acton in the same breath. The *Times Literary Supplement,* in a leading article, gave Butterfield the highest compliment he could wish for. His lectures on Christianity and history were "the most outstanding pronouncement on the meaning of history made by a professional historian in England since Acton's Inaugural."[74]

The overall effect of so much research and publication, given so much attention in academic and religious circles as well as among the general public, and met by so much praise, even when mixed with criticism, was to transform Butterfield into the star historian of Great Britain. He was in the midst of what Cowling called "one of the most remarkable public performances in twentieth-century England." Butterfield, barely turned fifty, now lived at the top of his career.

Public Figure

Creative Distractions

Butterfield did not wait around for his achievement of October 1949. He left Cambridge for the United States, and when his three books appeared, he was far across the Atlantic visiting the Institute for Advanced Study at Princeton, next to the university that had treated him well in 1924–1925.[1] He went by himself for the fall term, without Pamela, or the three children, who by now ranged in age from seventeen to ten. While he was crossing the ocean aboard ship, his thoughts wandered to his encounter with Bohemianism and Prohibition in Greenwich Village twenty-five years earlier, and the encouragement the experience gave to his dissenting attitudes.[2] He told everyone that his purpose at Princeton was to resume work on the life of Fox. He also had the *Concise Cambridge Modern History* on his mind. He did some work on Fox while in America, chiefly reading recent scholarship on the eighteenth century and working on drafts from his notes. The time was too brief, however, and the pace of his method too slow to allow much progress on the book that was gradually becoming his life work, his magnum opus. He did nothing on the *Concise History,* a project that was also beginning to feel like a life work. He made some arrangements which helped establish the chair for a visiting professorship in American history at Cambridge.[3]

His time in America coincided with a period of extreme hostility between the United States and the Soviet Union. The American politics of anticommunism repelled him, and, consistent with his dissenting ethos, he responded at first by seeing the good in communism. Then he began to apply his understanding of historical process to an analysis of the structure of the relations between the two great powers. He had already suggested a little of this applied thinking in the final lecture of his series on Christianity and history, which he first presented in December 1948.[4]

In January 1949 he had addressed a conference at the London School of Economics on the merits of including international relations as a subject in the university history curriculum. His interest in international relations was a direct offshoot of his primal appreciation of diplomatic history. The events of world history continued to stimulate and focus his meditations on morality, historical thinking, and the problems of teaching. Everything was coinciding to push him ever so gently into offering comments on contemporary world politics. All he needed was the invitation.[5]

The opportunity came in the United States. He produced a lecture, "The Tragic Element in Modern International Conflict" which he presented at Harvard University, Bryn Mawr College, and the University of Notre Dame. His theme was the predicaments faced by people in history, by now one of his long-standing motifs. He applied the idea directly to the heightening conflict between the Soviet Union and the United States. He pictured the existence of two great powers facing each other across the world. Each faced a predicament, he said. Each felt self-righteous in the face of the "enemy," and because neither one knew the other's intentions and calculations, both were unsure and fearful. This situation posed the riddle of the Hobbesian fear. The situation presented a highly volatile predicament which could induce either or both powers to go to war, unconnected with the ideologies of either. Any diplomacy on either side that treated the crisis as primarily ideological seriously mistook the situation and merely exacerbated the problems involved. His view made the Soviet Union appear less simply evil, and represented anticommunism as destructive. It was a risky argument to make at that moment in America, and it sparked interest from the left in American politics.[6]

Butterfield returned to Cambridge at Christmas to resume the hectic rhythm of his life as Professor of Modern History and Fellow of Peterhouse. He continued to be inundated by his involvements in the university and the college during the next few years, and he added to his overwork by taking on new outside activities.[7] He became more active in the Carlyle Club, an elite circle of British intellectuals who elected him to membership in 1947,[8] and he accepted election to the Council of the Royal Historical Society and regularly attended its monthly meetings in London until his term expired in 1953. He served on the manse committee of his local Methodist church and became faithful in his participation in a Methodist Class Meeting, like his father.

Until 1953 he continued his university lecture course, "Renaissance and Reformation." During one year, 1950–1951, he gave a new course, "Diplomacy and the Diplomatic Revolution of the Eighteenth Century." Then, contrary to his pledge, he agreed to help establish the history of science as a regular examination subject. In 1951–1952 and 1952–1953 he offered a new course of lectures called "History of Science" which he created with Rupert Hall, a young Cambridge historian whom Butterfield considered in some sense his student. Hall had been lecturing on the history of science since Butterfield's lectures in 1948, and he continued to do so after 1953 when Butterfield discontinued his participation.[9] For each new lecture, each new course, Butterfield wrote out his text in full, as he had always done. He continued to accept new research students, including, between 1950 and 1954, J. Roselli, Hedra Ben-Israel, Peter Hennock, and J. H. Elliott. He maintained his reputation as readily available to his students and a surprising, yet supportive critic. In October 1950 his oldest son, Peter, now graduated from Leys School, entered Peterhouse as an undergraduate in history.

The big new thing in Butterfield's life from 1949 onward was his status as a public celebrity. He turned into a very public historian. He received an avalanche of invitations to review books, publish articles, write essays, give lectures, preach sermons, and present talks throughout Great Britain and Ireland as well as Germany and North America. Some of these invitations brought him extra income, some did not. The quantity of his correspondence multiplied, and historians from outside Cambridge, especially Germans and Americans, made the journey to Peterhouse to see him. He often took his visitors to lunch in Peterhouse.[10]

To help him cope with the deluge Eve Bogle worked longer hours, still for a modest fee paid from his own pocket, offset by his fees for lectures and newspaper reviews. She kept his engagements organized, produced his typescripts, and managed his mountainous correspondence, which by now he had learned to compose by dictation. He secured a literary agent, A. D. Peters of Buckingham Street, London, to help him with his publications. He took subscriptions to not one, but two international press clipping services, Durrant's and U.P.C.A., both of London, in order to collect the public discussion about himself and his work. He eventually filled eight scrapbooks with clippings from newspapers. Pamela and he hired the first of a series of au pair girls from the continent to help them at home, something people of his social status in Cambridge were beginning to do to replace the old-style domestic service worker.

Butterfield's publisher took advantage of the moment, in October 1950, to reissue *The Whig Interpretation of History*, the book that secured his local reputation in Cambridge almost twenty years earlier. Publishers in North America joined in. Scribner in New York released the American edition of *Christianity and History* 1950, followed by the American edition of *Whig Interpretation* in 1951. Simultaneously Macmillan in New York produced the American edition of *Origins of Modern Science*. Translations of *Christianity and History* appeared in German, French, Italian, Spanish, Norwegian, Swedish, and Finnish as well as Chinese in the 1950s, followed by *Origins of Modern Science* in Italian, Spanish, Danish, and Polish in the late 1950s and early 1960s. Collins issued *Christianity and History* as a popular and cheap Fontana Paperback in 1957, and the sales of the book rose into the thousands annually until at least 1962.

Butterfield's fame mushroomed, as did his income from books. It was all quite heady. *Whig Interpretation* received reviews extolling its brilliance and appropriateness, usually without the negative references made at the time of the book's initial appearance. The extraordinary impact and international reach of *Whig Interpretation* dates from the early 1950s, not from the early 1930s. It circulated to whole new audiences, including universities, schools and the general public, in Great Britain as well as throughout the whole English-speaking world. *Whig Interpretation* gained new life, especially in the United States. Butterfield commented that the histories written by Americans about the United States were probably more profoundly shaped by the Whig interpretation than histories of England. Donald Creighton admitted that Canadian historical writing was Whiggish through and through. Then J. W. Burrow turned Butterfield's lens on mid-Victorian England in his study of the uses made of the English past by a quartet of Whiggish historians: Thomas Babington Macaulay, William Stubbs, Edward Augustus Freeman, and James Anthony Froude, not all of whom were politically Whig.[11]

People began to locate and deal with Whiggish history in field after field. David Watkin showed just how Whiggish the history of architecture had been, and applied Butterfield's ideas toward a reconstruction of the field. Donald Kelley noted the Whiggish tendency of the history of political thought. The history of science was riddled with Whiggish history. Peter Slee came close to suggesting that the history of the study of history in higher education is inherently Whiggish. J. C. D. Clark objected that Butterfield had failed to notice that Marxist history was at least as culpable of Whiggishness as Whig history. He suggested that the new Marxist historians, such as Eric Hobsbawm and E. P. Thompson, were the real heirs of Whiggism in history. He then observed that the treatment of economic history in general, especially what historians called the Industrial Revolution, was routinely and heavily Whig-gish. Bonnie G. Smith eventually suggested that the Whig interpretation of history was a male interpretation of history, in addition to its presentism and progressivistic streaks, making it appear that dominance by men was the natu-ral course of history. She thought that the new women's history might pry historians free from Whiggish history. Handbooks on how to study history adopted Butterfield's criticism and used Whiggish history as a prime example of the pitfalls to avoid. J. H. Plumb agreed that *Whig Interpretation* marked the beginning of the defeat of self-serving presentism in English historical interpretation, but then suggested that no matter how valid Butterfield's rhe-torical attack on the persistence of Whiggish history might be, the view was collapsing anyway. The political oligarchy that had found the Whig inter-pretation useful for the perpetuation of its power was in radical decline in any case, and the worldwide British Empire with its conceit of the superiority of English liberty and civilization was then beginning to dissolve. Butterfield had toppled a historical edifice whose social and imperial foundations were al-ready undermined. With a flourish, Geoffrey Elton skewered Butterfield with his own stick by labelling his *Origins of Modern Science* supremely Whiggish history. From the 1950s onwards Butterfield's point was so taken for granted by historians and history students that it was enough simply to call a piece of historical writing "Whiggish history" in order to defeat it.[12]

In the face of so formidable an assault on "Whiggish history" it took an act of heroic self-assertion for Christopher Hill, in support of his progressive reading of history, to affirm in 1967 that the Whig interpretation was "the only possible historical attitude." It was with a mixture of trepidation and bravado that Annabel Patterson, in 2002, sought to "reinstate" a Whig view, what she called her "New Whig interpretation of history."[13]

F. L. Woodcock, of Richmond Surrey, could not resist asking Butterfield to name some important historians who did *not* succumb to the Whig error. Butterfield responded with a surprising list: Harold Temperley in "his more important works of research"; "in general . . . [Samuel] Gardiner, [F. W.] Maitland, [C. H.] Firth, [Maurice] Powicke, [Arnold] Toynbee and [Lewis] Namier were as little subject to the 'Whig' fallacy as I should expect historians to be as a rule"; and even Lord Acton "in much of his history is less Whig than most people." Four of these were nineteenth-century historians, and four twentieth-century. Michael Bentley guessed that among English nineteenth-century historians Butterfield would have found only Thomas Carlyle to be free of the Whig fallacy. Frank Eyck was keen to argue that G. P. Gooch belonged on the list of those who were not Whiggish at all.[14]

Reviewing books became a major part of Butterfield's life. In 1950 he published reviews of eight books, including works by Reinhold Niebuhr, Alan Richardson, Ernst Cassirer, and George Kitson Clark, as well as books on eighteenth-century England. He became a regular reviewer for the *Times Literary Supplement* from 1950 onwards. Beginning in the mid-1950s, he published an average of five book reviews a year for the rest of his career. In belated response to a plea from Kathleen Bliss after his lectures on Christianity and history, he wrote a series of four essays for the final issues of the *Christian News-Letter,* a British ecumenical publication of some influence. He extended his discourse on Christianity and history by considering the merits and effects of contrasting interpretations of history — academic, Old Testament, Marxian, and ecclesiastical.[15] He gave *Time and Tide* two essays on the problem of "predicaments" in current history.[16] And there were other essays in other media.

His schedule of special public lectures between February 1950 and the end of summer 1951 was gruelling. During the first six months he presented perhaps twenty special lectures, including his trip to Cologne, Germany, in July. During the next twelve months he gave another forty-five lectures, including another trip to Germany in May and a lecture trip to the United States in July. Among these last forty-five lectures, three distinct audiences emerged. About 40 percent of his appearances were for academic audiences, about 20 percent for local units of the Historical Association which combined scholars, schoolteachers, and the general public interested in history, and the remaining 40 percent for a new audience, churches and church-related organizations covering the full range of denominations in the United Kingdom, Roman Catholic, Anglican, and Protestant. Besides these lectures there were a couple of talks on the BBC. His pace could have been worse: he declined at least twenty other lectures during the same eighteen-month period. Butterfield wrote out each lecture, and even when he repated a paper under the same title he could not keep himself from revising the text every time.[17]

Most of his topics were extensions of the theme of Christianity and history. He behaved like the historian as itinerant lay preacher. His thinking fanned out in numerous directions at once: "The Role of Christianity in European History," "How Christianity Affects the Teaching of History," "History, Religion, and Ethics," "The Scientific versus the Moralistic Approaches in International Affairs," "Providence," "God in History," "The Christian Idea of God." A few of his lectures continued his propaganda for the history of science, reiterating things he had said many times before: "Leonardo da Vinci," "The History of Science." He repeated some lectures he had constructed before 1949: "The Dangers of History," "Fox and the French Revolution," "The Marxian Interpretation of History," and "The History of the Enquiry into the

Seven Years War." There were miscellaneous other lectures about topics perpetually on his mind: "History as a Branch of Literature," "The Teaching of History," "The Renaissance." It was an extensive list of topics on which he pronounced his views.

A new stage in Butterfield's career as a publishing scholar was taking shape. He began to publish books derived from special lectures. The trend began with his triumph of October 1949 when he published *Origins of Modern Science* and *Christianity and History*. The BBC series which he created on the history of science, with lectures by him and others, turned into *The History of Science: Origins and Results of the Scientific Revolution*, a book published in 1951 in Great Britain and North America, with him as de facto editor. Certain of the new invitations included publication as a part of the arrangement, notably the Riddell Lectures at the University of Durham, and the Murray Lecture at the University of Glasgow. *Christianity in European History*, a little book of sixty pages, published by Oxford University Press in 1951, came from the Durham lectures and drew upon his extra teaching over the years at Wesley House on the history of Christianity.[18] *The Reconstruction of an Historical Episode*, a booklet of forty-three pages about the Seven Years' War, also published in 1951, was the result of the Glasgow lectures. This little work had distant roots in his course on modern European history and related to his comments in *Christianity and History* about how historians connect individual facts into episodes. It was another study in a field that was attracting his attention more and more, the history of historical scholarship.[19]

It occurred to Butterfield that he had found a direct and fertile route to publication. The occasion of a lecture fastened down a deadline, and the genre of the published lecture, even with the marks of the spoken text left in, enjoyed respectability and could attract wide public notice. His habits of thinking by writing and writing out every lecture for his courses had trained him to write in lecture-length units. He became extremely productive of published lectures, and he ceased to predict when he would complete the life of Fox.

Butterfield had read the suggestion in a review of his work by Martin Wight that he collect his special lectures and essays on theoretical themes. Others, now or later, expressed the same interest, including Trevelyan. He began to scribble possible tables of contents of a book in his diary and notes.[20] He had certainly heard the criticisms of his proposals on moral judgments in history and the relations between religion and history, complaints which initially arose after his lectures on Christianity and history, and which the republication of *Whig Interpretation* stimulated. Some critics had disliked his views about moral judgments and commented that he sounded as if he wished to divorce his moral sense from his work as a historian, and create a phalanx of mere technicians. A few pointed to the irony that the Butterfield who had spoken so loudly about Christianity and history seemed to segregate his Christianity from his history. Butterfield was stung by what he regarded as grave misunderstanding of his positions, and he revised his lectures as essays with the criticisms on his mind.[21]

He began to think about a publisher. By now he had several firms asking to become his publisher, including Cambridge University Press, headed by a new and more aggressive Secretary, R. J. L. Kingsford. Butterfield reaffirmed his commitment to write the *Concise History,* but he turned Cambridge down flat for anything new, telling Kingsford that he felt CUP was "rather sticky" with authors in history and did not "push books hard," and that he disliked their assumption of the role of arbiter of what counted as "Cambridge History." He intimated that he still carried resentment against CUP for not publishing his inaugural lecture in 1944 or his *Statecraft of Machiavelli* as far back as 1940.[22]

His literary agent convinced him that Collins of London would generate wider sales than Cambridge, and made the arrangements for Collins to produce his new work in 1951. The book bore the title *History and Human Relations,* 250 pages containing eight of Butterfield's essays.[23] This brought the total to three books published in 1951, his eleventh, twelfth, and thirteenth. Three of the essays had been published before. At least six, probably seven, and possibly all eight, originated as lectures between 1945 and 1950, while the print versions had appeared in journals between 1948 and 1951.[24]

The volume stimulated even more vociferous criticism of some of his proposals, especially on the question of moral judgments. The opponents of his views were a formidable lot, and the list was growing: Arnold J. Toynbee, Martin Wight, Pieter Geyl, A. J. P. Taylor, Geoffrey Barraclough, Isaiah Berlin, and many, many others.[25] Some of the critics liked the book anyway. For instance, Taylor went on to describe the book as "his most effective," and he applauded Butterfield's success in creating links between the professional historian and the general public. Barraclough liked his criticism of "the ordinary arguments of causality" because of their inability to explain sufficiently "the next turn of events." Others reviewers were simply effusive in their praise. Arthur Bryant opened his review in the *Sunday Times,* "This is a very wise book: I think the wisest Professor Butterfield has yet written, and one of the wisest of our time." The *Times Literary Supplement* devoted a leading editorial article to the book and noted the reemergence of "the historian as moralist," linking Butterfield with Toynbee and Niebuhr. The editorial remarked that Butterfield was "a thinker of exceptionally candid and open mind, anxious to the extreme limit of conscience not to load the dice in favour of his own side." Trevelyan praised him, "I think it is your strongest book of essays so far. . . . I am glad you have got the influence you have, for your thought is most sound, both on history and on other subjects."[26]

Butterfield now had seven of his books in current circulation, six new and one republished, all released during the years 1949–1951 and all being reviewed at the same time. His reputation rose still higher. Five of the six new books came from special lectures which he presented in their latest form between 1948 and 1950. His writing in these volumes retained the attributes of the lecture meant to be spoken. If his publications from 1949 onwards may be called essays, they were essays derived from lectures, and not pieces created as literary works. In a manner imperceptible even to himself, he had transformed from a writer who used history as his medium into a speaker, a lecturer, who published what he had written for purposes of oral presentation. Of his two youthful ambitions, the preacher had absorbed the writer in style and medium.[27]

The preacher prevailed in his message as well, the preacher with the training and mentality of the historian. Butterfield carried his thinking forward during these years within the context of his meditations on religion and history. Starting from the base he created in his lectures on Christianity and history, he had expanded his discourse considerably, while the ingredients of his thought remained remarkably constant. He thought as a historian, not as a theologian, a philosopher, or a political scientist, and he used the methods and the knowledge of the historian who was driven to pursue themes in religion.

Butterfield attached a theological explanation to his decision to accept all the invitations he was receiving. He was aware that he was following a route for his life sketched out by others, taking him far away from his major work on Fox and *The Concise Cambridge Modern History*. He confessed, "I often allowed myself to be side-tracked on a theory that if I do what I seemed called to do Providence will make everything come out right in the end."[28] He had applied the very same interpretation to his receipt of the Fox papers from Trevelyan in 1931, and he liked the results. Since *Englishman and His History* he had been publicly urging the view that the genius of English political history was the willingness to refrain from overmuch resistance to the course of events, aiming instead to cooperate with Providence in the out-working of history. It made sense to him to cooperate with Providence in his own life and not try to impress his will on events too hard. The continuing good results from *Origins of Modern Science* and *Christianity and History* were perpetually a surprise to him and to others, and he was willing to think that he was doing the right thing for his life.

Love and Technical History

Butterfield's essays collected in *History and Human Relations* show new thinking about a number of themes, all connected with his discourse on religion. The most notable are human personality, the methods of technical history, Marxism, his injunction against moral judgments, and the relations between his convictions as a Christian and his work as a historian.

After all the emphasis on sin, cupidity, judgment, and conflict in *Christianity and History,* his new comments on what he calls human personality come as something of a shock, and a relief. The essay entitled "Christianity and Human Relationships" is about love and spirituality, and people as capable of loving others. This piece, although not part of either the Cambridge or the BBC series, is the one he later said that he had wanted to include in the published version as a counterbalance to the dark talk that dominates the book. He later claimed that he felt misunderstood on this point. He was really more interested, he said, in the essentials of Christianity, such as love and spirituality, "though these are not the things that I write about." He left these essentials out of *Christianity and History* by design. He said, "As a matter of fact it was understood from the first that when I wrote or talked about Christianity I should not deal with its essentials but only with certain mundane aspects that are of interest to the general historian." He put this explanation into the preface of the German edition of the book.[29]

The explanation leaves one wondering, however, since Butterfield surely believed that human personality and human cupidity are "essentials of Christianity." These apparently "non-mundane" matters pervade *Christianity and History* from start to finish and are basic to his discussion of "academic history" in that work. It is instructive about his outlook that he did not readily situate the theme of love foremost in his vision of human personality and historical study, and that even in this essay about love he quickly lapses into a discussion of sin and judgment.

Nevertheless, it would be hard for him give more importance to love than he now does: "For those who follow the New Testament the ultimate principle in question is that law of Christian love which comprises amongst other things all that we know of charity or of charitable-mindedness. For the Christian this is not only the first of laws but it is a unique one — it stands through time as the source of all others that might be prescribed. And it is absolute." This one ultimate law, the law of love, or, as he sometimes says, the law of charity, "regulates the conduct of life and applies to all circumstances and stands as the final measure of all action." It is definite and clear, but at the same time, it is "in a certain sense almost a definition of elasticity itself." Given the centrality of the term "elasticity" in Butterfield's discourse, we know we must surely be in the presence of something of the highest possible significance.[30]

His text elaborates on two lines in the New Testament: "Love God and love your neighbour as yourself," and "God is love." He plays with various emblems which exemplify the role he envisages for Christian love in life: love your enemy, fight evil with love, love all people even though they are sinners, love nothing in this world too much, love is the spiritual realm installed right here and now, love is ever inventing and discovering, love creates true liberty. He voices the classic Christian denigration of Judaism when he pronounces New Testament love as the fulfilment of the law of Moses, and as a development in righteousness beyond "mere obedience to sets of commandments" and beyond a "gravely confused" righteousness "governed by the demands of what we should regard as ritual and ceremonial."[31] We can see how the law of love connects with his insistence on the exclusive reality of personality and individual human beings. Love is something individual people do, and the appropriate recipients of love are other individual people. Love your neighbour does not mean to love the "state" or "mankind" or "society" or any other such "abstract noun," but actual individual people. Our neighbour is any person as soon as that person "actually comes into our orbit" or "within the range of our thinking in any way." Such love then becomes a source of human history as "the very dynamic behind right conduct" and "the actual mainspring of virtuous action." We experience the effects most completely in the lives of the saints, whose lives embody love and whose deep influence on history far surpasses our imagination.[32]

These indeed are major things for a historian to notice about love in human life, but Butterfield virtually leaves the theme alone except for this one statement. Only rarely does a reference to "Christian charity" appear in his writings before and after this moment. When it does, we can tell that he ranks the notion at the highest level in his appreciation of history. For instance, it serves his occasionally as a tool enabling him to explain in extremely general terms the presence of the features of European civilization which he finds most desirable. A case of this appears briefly later in *History and Human Relations*. In contrast with the effects of "modern barbarism" which he believes so marked the first half of the twentieth century on all sides, he points to intangibles such as "modern liberty," respect for human personality, and certain movements of social reform. These were due to the influence of Christian charity in the lives of ordinary people over many centuries, people without political ends who were simply living their lives within the spiritual environment created by the message to love God and their neighbours. We can as a result, he says, perceive and cherish "the leavening effect" of Christian love in the very make-up of our civilization.[33] In *Christianity in European History* he briefly elaborates the same reading of history, and with the same meaphor.[34] There are similar brief references in later writings when he is generalizing about European history over the long term.[35] But nowhere does he give the theme of love the attention he lavishes on other themes, especially those he is most developing in the wake of *Christianity and History.*

The theme of "technical history" takes first place in importance, a subject very close to his heart. The actual space he assigns to this theme is meagre, but the function of his new discourse on the subject is colossal. He begins essay after essay with a disquisition on technical history. His purpose in discussing technical history is actually not to clarify his understanding of historical study, although he does this to his satisfaction. He discusses technical history chiefly as a preface to advocating particular causes about which he feels very passionate. His understanding of technical history serves as the medium for the construction of his discourse on Marxism, moral judgments, religion, God in history, and, later on, the history of historical study and international affairs.

The use of the term "technical history" is crucial. He had used the term before, but now it virtually replaces "academic history" and even "scientific history," the terms he favored in *Christianity and History.* His aim is to delimit very precisely the range of competence of historical study, but in so doing to elevate its possible achievements to a high level of reasonable certainty. He tries to accommodate the opposing poles of the dualisms in his thinking and the tensions within his discourse become palpable.

He pushes in one direction to identify the precise boundaries of technical history. He uses familiar vocabulary: concrete, tangible, observable, matter-of-fact, details, facts, mundane, outside, material, the historical realm. This is history as mere technique, an apparatus, reduced to describing mere external things. This technical history operates quite separately from religion, politics, and ordinary ethical judgments. Indeed, says Butterfield, the technical historian, whatever his religion, "is willing to jettison for the time being his private views and personal valuations" in order to accomplish the work of technical history. Butterfield uses the metaphor "self-emptying," an image taken from St. Paul in the New Testament with reference to Jesus, to accentuate just how thoroughly he expects technical historians to divest themselves of their deepest religious convictions when engaged in technical history.[36]

But then he realizes that he has pushed too far in one direction and bound historical study to what he professes are not the most important matters. So, he recalls his emphasis on "imaginative sympathy" and pushes strongly in the other direction: outlook, feelings, insight, insides, personality, spiritual, the spiritual realm. This is history as an art, he says. The term is new for him in this context. It is not enough to report as the outside observer about those things the scientist can measure, he says. The historian must feel and think "as though he were that man," and "see the personalities from the inside." He continues, "Without this art not only is it impossible to tell the story correctly but it is impossible to interpret the very documents on which the reconstruction depends." But what does this do to "technical history"? Does the necessity of this art vitiate the value of "technical history"? He responds by stretching his category: "We may even say that this is part of the science of history." The art belongs to technical history.[37]

The reason he gives for expanding his category is new to his argument on the subject. He wants to say more than he did in *Christianity and History*, where he noted how much history as a science depends on imaginative sympathy. Now he claims that the art of imaginative sympathy can be assessed in the same way as can the "facts" and the "documents." The art of seeing past personalities from the inside "produces communicable results," and even the insight of one historian "may be ratified by scholars in general." In other words, the art yields virtually universal results. With this, he has added a layer to his earlier insistence that historians all share the same techniques, the same evidence, the same facts. They even produce the same "insight" into the personalities of the past. The claim surprises, for it is hard to see what is "technical" about getting and having "insights." "Insights" would appear to be, in his language, nonconcrete, intangible, nonfactual looks inside other personalities which historians take not by means of their detailed research, but via their very personal and private imaginative sympathy. Hence, insights would exemplify features directly opposite to those he admires in technical history. In adding historians' insights to the list, however, he does not in the least relax his stringent requirement of virtual universality for technical history. Just to be sure we understand, he repeats what he has told us before, that technical history "proves" its findings "for all men," it "attests" its results "to all men (whatever their philosophy)," and "its argument is valid for Catholic or atheist, for Marxist or Mohammedan." The word "all" covers a lot of historians. Indeed, he seeks to strengthen the claim by going still further: the tangible evidence actually "forces" the historian, no matter what his religion or philosophy, to believe particular things "whether we like them or not." In Butterfield's hands, technical history is a wonderful and powerful producer of reasonable certainty within its proper domain. Now he tells us that even historians' "insights" belong to "the same limited realm." And he even declares the point with seeming certainty.[38]

But Butterfield has his doubts. We find them displayed in his new essays on Marxism where his characterization of technical history orients his assessment of Marxist history. Given the role of Britain as ally of the United States during the early years of Soviet-American polarization, the sympathy he presents for Marxism and Marxist historians at this moment is remarkable. Again he plays the dissenter, but perhaps in doing so he neutralizes the punch of the Marxists. Sidney Hook was convinced that Butterfield and other non-Marxists like him sympathetic to Marxism denatured Marx's views "to a point where anything distinctively Marxist about these views disappears." In both "The Christian and the Marxian Interpretation of History" for the *Christian News-Letter* in 1949 and "Marxist History" in *History and Human Relations,* Butterfield itemizes the defects of Marxism as a philosophy of life, but praises the benefits of Marxism as history. The difference between the two seems clear enough until he speaks of the impact of the Marxist philosophy of life on the Marxist history. We look for examples of Marxist historians, but he provides no names except for Plekhanov, one of the few names he mentioned in his essay on Marxism in the 1930s, and we wonder whether he has been reading anybody new. Butterfield objects categorically to what he regards as the intrusion of Marxist philosophy, or ideology, into the domain of technical history. As in the 1930s, he tries to draw a dividing line where the Marxists refuse to draw one.[39] Even in the hands of "flexible" Marxists, such as Plekhanov, Marxism impacts the historical study too much, he says. He generalizes his complaint: "I wonder if I am merely being foolish when I say it is better for the ordinary technical student not to philosophise but to do history, just historically to enquire. But I suppose it is true that mere evidence is useless to a person who is reading history altogether in the wrong way of approaching history; there is a right feeling to have for historical events; there is a sensitiveness that one may have, a proper awareness of the character of the historical process." The rebuff of philosophy echoes the gratuitous insult in the preface of *Whig Interpretation of History,* where he said that his theses "would be unaffected by anything the philosopher could state to explain them or to explain them away," and suggests how little he has changed his attitude. He wants to stand firm in his confidence that "just doing history" is its own corrective against the imposition of philosophy and religion on historical study. Technical history is self-cleaning. And with the evidence itself able to "force" things on the historian no matter what the historian's outlook or resistance, the "facts" are self-revelatory and self-empowering.

But here he is not so sure. There is a "wrong" way and a "right" way to approach history, he says. The "wrong" approach nullifies the evidence. Without the "right" approach the evidence is impotent. Technical history may not be virtually universal after all. The historian's philosophy, or approach, makes a crucial difference, and in some quite basic way takes precedence even over the evidence. The historian must use the right approach and thereby enable the power of the evidence to function correctly. The right approach is, of course, Butterfield's. We may presume in this context that he believes his approach to be philosophy-free, ideology-free. In other words, his approach is the universal, the same for all historians no matter what their religion or philosophy. Approaches which differ from his are sullied by philosophy or religion, and wrong. The challenge from Marxist history messes up the picture he has drawn of technical history, and has unsettled his certainty, even if just for a moment. His image of technical history is shaken by the brief vision of its impotence, and thus the inadequacy of his rendition of technical history. He later admits that technical history "may never exist in its absolute purity." Maybe it is merely an ideal, he says.

For now, however, Butterfield catches hold of himself and issues a resounding call to anyone who will listen: "Let us study history and see where the facts take us and find even delight in facts as such. And, when quarrels occur, let us go back again to our history — go back again and study it in still further detail."[40] This episode reminds us of his brief comment in *Christianity and History* about historians' presuppositions concerning human beings, a point that threatened to undo his construction of the universality of technical history. In that context he simply let the comment sit without making connections with the other parts of his discourse, and moved on.[41]

If his latest encounter with Marxism failed in the end to change his mind or weaken his stated belief in the universality of "technical history," it did induce him to modify his view of "technical history" in another way, one that touched something more fundamental: his commitment to individuals and personality. In *Christianity and History*, in a passage that sounded as if he were thinking out loud, he signalled that he was in the middle of changing his mind about the relationship between individual personalities and processes.[42] Until now he has declared repeatedly that only individual personalities really exist, and has remained unswerving in his loyalty to the treatment of history chiefly as narrative about individual personalities. He continues completely unchanged about the first commitment, the exclusive reality of individuals, and, contrasting himself with Marxist history, he rejects unequivocally the view that things such as economic factors, financial situations, wars, and political crises "cause" anything or that they even "exist," he says, "except as abstract terms and convenient pieces of shorthand." His credo remains, "It is men who make history — who really do things." By this he means individual personalities "regarded as so many separate wells of life." This he reiterates clearly at the outset of his essay "Marxist History."[43]

But vis-à-vis the second commitment, the absolute priority of individuals over processes, he presents himself as a changed historian. By means of curi-ously impersonal discourse — he uses "we" throughout — he volunteers the admission that he "imputes too much to individuals," and that he is no longer "satisfied to observe the surface-drama of events," or content with "mere literary narrative of personalities in conflict."[44] For this new attitude he gives credit to the Marxists: "The chief contribution of the Marxists has been that they, more than anybody else, have taught us to make our history a structural piece of analysis — something which is capable of becoming more profound than a piece of ordinary political narrative. Instead of stopping with a drama of personalities, Charles I fighting Cromwell for example, we move further to a kind of geological survey, we try to see what was happening below the surface, we envisage the stresses and strains that take place in the structure of the whole country. Even ordinary political narrative is bound to be altered as a result of this kind of structural analysis; and a further range of territory is brought under tribute for the purpose of assisting us in the elucidation of the story." Butterfield's words amount to a serious criticism of his own work, above all *Peace Tactics of Napoleon*, but also *George III, Lord North, and the People*. And the implications of his criticism for his own biography of Fox would be considerable, perhaps serious enough to discourage him from fur-ther work on the enormous project.[45]

The structural analysis he has in mind discloses a domain he has long recog-nized and counted as important, the realm of process, conditions, and condi-tioning circumstances. But now he means something different by this realm. He no longer speaks of it simply in relation to individual action, as the unin-tended consequences of the interactions of millions of individuals over cen-turies. His discourse does not say how the processes and conditions got there, but takes them as given, as there, with the implication that more is involved than simply conflating individual actions. The examples he offers of structural analysis — putting a person in his age, viewing a person in context, and exam-ining a person's environment — show that he remains a world away from the Marxists or the French historians of the Annales variety or even Namier. He treats structural analysis as a matter of studying the conditions affecting hu-man actions. Some conditions are of a special kind, what he calls hard and inescapable conditions, such as that people must eat in order to live, and that social structures must have reached a certain level of complication for people to engage in experimental science. All this adds up to "a system of necessity" which envelops and conditions individual persons, but without completely determining their actions. With structural analysis, the historian no longer regards people as sovereign shapes of their own lives, but perceives them as shaped by the system of necessity.[46]

Butterfield has found a new way to explain history, and a new position for explanation in his picture. He used to say, in *Whig Interpretation of History* in 1931, that the only explanation historians needed to offer was to give more detail, "to unfold the whole story and reveal the complexity by telling it in detail." In *Christianity and History* he passed lightly over the problem of explanation by calling it the answer not to the question "why," but to the question "how" things happened, with the answer appearing in the way the historian lays out the "facts" and their interconnections in episodes.[47] Now he provides a new definition of what it means to explain something historically. He places explanation in a privileged position, paired with description, as one of the two tasks of the technical historian. To explain historically is to situate people within the system of necessity and to display the conditioning circumstances which enveloped and shaped them, delimiting and in some sense even necessitating their actions, without completely absorbing their freedom as individuals.[48] The technical historian may no longer rest on the surface of history, content with describing people and their actions and narrating the appropriate story about them. The technical historian descends below the surface to analyze the structures operative within the system of necessity surrounding people and their actions, and then supplies the appropriate explanation.[49] Butterfield has written about "conditions" continuously since the 1920s, and he has alluded to the "system of necessity" now and then, as in his inaugural lecture as professor in 1944 and *Christianity and History,* but without attaching any explanatory significance to the term.[50] Now he has gathered in his own legacy of discourse, refocused it, and found the key to "historical explanation," which he consigns to the technical historian.

Butterfield has thus stretched "technical history" still further, but without abandoning the hard and austere requirements he has placed on the discipline. He speaks about "explanation" in exactly the same language as he once reserved for the simple gathering of "facts," such as the date of his grandfather's birth. He writes, "the technical study of the past is in any case concerned with a limited and concrete explanation of the human drama, since it looks for the earthly or mundane things, it looks for the things which can be discovered by its peculiar kind of apparatus and attested to all men (whatever their philosophy) by the tangible evidence."[51] He has left us to assume that the explanations arrived at by the historian when engaged in technical history are also marked by universality, that they too are the same for all historians regardless of their religion, philosophy, politics, race, or nationality. We can only marvel at the way "technical history" has ballooned to enormous dimensions without Butterfield reconsidering whether the characteristics of "technical history" which he initially designated as belonging to the task of simply collecting the "facts" might still apply.

Moral Judgments and Christianity

Butterfield's disquisitions on technical history are the springboard for his arguments about moral judgments in history. His essay entitled "Moral Judgments in History" in *History and Human Relations* gives a longer and more concentrated look at the theme than *Christianity and History*, where his treatment was brief and sparsely scattered throughout the book. With this essay Butterfield marks the fiftieth anniversary of the death of Lord Acton in 1901, and, as so often before, takes Acton as his partner in dialogue throughout. His understanding of moral judgments connects directly with *Whig Interpretation*, where he featured the theme twenty years before. Gordon Wright suggested that *History and Human Relations* initiated a new phase of debate on the theme of moral judgments. In any case, we can say that the attachment of Butterfield's name to the assertion that historians should not make moral judgments dates from the discussion of *History and Human Relations* in the 1950s and not *Christianity and History*, not even *Whig Interpretation of History*. The ubiquity of the attachment of Butterfield's name to the no-moral-judgments position dates from 1959 and the publication of the large-circulation paperback *The Philosophy of History in Our Time*, edited by Hans Meyerhoff, which reprinted and discussed Butterfield's essay "Moral Judgments in History" from *History and Human Relations*. Hereafter Butterfield's views routinely appeared in writings by historians, such as Gordon Leff and Howard Zinn, as well as philosophers, such as Behan McCullagh, on the question of moral judgments in history.[52]

Much has transpired in the world since 1931 that might be expected to affect Butterfield's handling of the question of moral judgments. The surprise comes, however, when we discover that Butterfield says little about moral judgments beyond what he has already said. He words it better and more clearly that he did in *Whig Interpretation*, and, perhaps because of his new celebrity, he presents himself with fewer qualifying phrases and inverted sentences and with greater sheer assurance that what he says is right. His repeats his long-standing objections to historians making moral judgments. They include variations on the argument that the medium of technical history does not equip or authorize the historian, as historian, to render moral judgments. He updates his argument with the additions of imaginative sympathy and explanation to the strictly technical domain of technical history, all of which he separates from the world of moral judgments. His objections also represent his conviction that the inner life of individual personalities, where piety and moral responsibility reside, is not finally open to the technical historian, not even through the exercise of the art of imaginative sympathy.

This is the moment when we realize that the point of his new discourse on moral judgments, indeed of the whole of *History and Human Relations,* is not to provide disquisitions on technical history or moral judgments or anything else for that matter. He wishes to clarify himself to his critics, perhaps even to defend himself against their criticisms. Among his chief worries were the critics who understood him to be promoting historical study as an amoral or extra-moral endeavour, or, conversely, those who felt that he himself was issuing morally indefensible statements, especially his comments about Hitler and Stalin in *Christianity and History.*

Privately he began to claim that he had always opposed Nazism and communism. He explained this to Max Beloff: "I don't at all believe that ideology is unimportant, and I used to say that Nazi-ism and Communism were the Anti-Christ, though now, as you would find in the last of the three Riddell lectures, I would state that case rather differently."[53] Later he wrote another correspondent in stronger terms: "I am probably more enthusiastic than you about the matter as I think that communism incorporates the anti-Christ of our time, and I also think that communism is the prior evil that provoked Nazism and Fascism."[54]

But he said none of this publicly, and the researcher is hard put to find where he had previously called Nazism and communism the Anti-Christ. His public self-defense in *History and Human Relations* is pure Butterfield. He says just the things that fuel the criticisms. He writes this intentionally provocative sentence near the top of his presentation: "And in view of the situation that has been described, it may be possible to reduce the shock sometimes produced by the thesis which denies any ethical character (in the usual sense of the words) to the technical historian's universe."[55] And another: "The principles imply that the biography of the worst of murderers could conceivably be written in such a way that he would be what in a technical sense we call the 'hero' of the story, so that our pity and sympathy would be around him as we followed him up from childhood. By the same argument what we should desire even in the case of a man like Hitler is not a mere angry denunciation. What would prove of incomparable value, if it were possible, would be an intimate account of him by a person who did not hate him too much — an account which would enable us to see how a lump of human nature (how a boy playing in a field) could ever have come to be *like that.*"[56] His dissenter's method drives him to say just the opposite of what he knows his critics want to hear, and he seems to delight in doing so.

Having voiced the first statement, he follows with assertions about moral judgments and technical history belonging to different realms and about how mixing the two hinders historical inquiry. After the statement about Hitler, he goes on to emphasize the enormous power of conditioning circumstances in the shaping of personality and the technical historian's inability to fathom the depths of another person's interior motivations and personal responsibility. This sounds like amoral history. Then, from the bottom of the pit, he leads his critics out along his own pathway. In the first case, he declares that he does not deny "morality in life" and points in the distance to an understanding of historical study that is fully moral "in a higher sense altogether." In the second, he reaffirms his primal conviction that individual persons always possess ultimate responsibility for themselves and remain the sources of morality in the world, no matter what the conditioning circumstances.[57] Then he reaches his self-liberating destination, the higher morality: the law of charity and the primary duty of historians to extend charity to all. We may presume that, with this vision, he does not deny the moral role of the historian as reconciler, as he used to say. Reconciling and extending charity appear to be, for him, two ways of saying the same thing. Instead of historians acting as moral judges, let them act in charity towards the people of history. In the end, in other words, and in spite of his provocative rhetoric, he registers technical history not as amoral, but as differently moral. His treatment of Hitler affords an opportunity to assess the application of what he believes is a higher morality. We wonder whether his nonjudgmental extension of charity to Hitler would not have the effect of exonerating Hitler, or, at the least, leave historians without the resources to expose the inhumanity of Hitler's ways, and thus render historians and their histories actually harmful and not merely irrelevant.[58]

If historians are going to listen to Butterfield when he pronounces against moral judgments, they need to know what he asks them to eschew. The question is not so much why historians should not make moral judgments, which he has made clear enough, but what exactly is it that he so vociferously prohibits historians from doing. In the past, especially in *Whig Interpretation of History,* where he launched his attack on moral judgments, he spoke against making moral judgments upon individual people, their actions, whole groups, causes, and the results of actions. He especially objected to moral judgments built into the organization of the narrative. In *Christianity and History* he specifically opposed moral judgments by historians upon the people who are their subjects, and the moral judgments involved in constructing the actions and events of human history as a war between good and evil, right versus wrong. All in all, Butterfield appears to leave very little room for historians to come to moral judgments of any kind.

In "Moral Judgments in History" he offers clarification. He repeats numerous times that he opposes moral judgments of a quite specific kind, namely moral judgments against *persons,* and that he does not object to those made against acts or behaviour or events. After his provocative statement denying "any ethical character" to technical history, he sought to qualify his meaning: "The thesis may be asserted in so far as it means that moral judgments on human beings are by their nature irrelevant to the enquiry and alien to the intellectual realm of scientific history." A little later: "In fact it is questionable whether any retrospective ethical judgment—I mean the kind of judgment which is directed against a personality—is worth anything, except in the form of the judgment that all men are, and men always have been, sinners." And again: "It follows from this that moral judgments of actual people cannot defensibly or usefully exist in concrete cases except in the form of self-judgments."[59] To be sure his readers get the point, he explicitly declares that he permits moral judgments against what people do, against their acts: "For my own part I am willing to say that religious persecution is always wrong. It is wrong even when it is committed by people who are unaware that it is wrong." And again: "From the same standpoint it is easy to say that an action is wrong therefore—the action is itself wrong even if the man who performs it is unaware that it is wrong."[60] Indeed he becomes very free with the language of moral judgment about people's actions. He talks about a person's "follies," "crimes," and "wilfulnesses," and he speaks of "atrocities . . . committed against the weak or the poor," the "barbarity" of "killing and torturing of human beings," "the criminality of religious persecution or wholesale massacre or the modern concentration camp or the repression of dissident opinions," and the historian's "exposure of the wickedness of the action itself."[61] We have already seen him use some of this sort of language in *Whig Interpretation, Napoleon, Englishman and His History,* and *Christianity and History,* but in those settings he did not acknowledge that he was using the language of moral judgment nor did he grant that moral judgments upon people's actions were acceptable for historians to make. Now he has given himself permission, in his role as historian, to denounce certain human actions as morally wrong and to utter terms of moral judgment against them. This is new, different from the way he handled the same problem in *Whig Interpretation of History,* in that he now admits that historians—that he—may morally judge human actions. To be sure, he trips over doing so. We find him still naming what he is doing as "description," that is, he writes, "merely describing, say, the massacre or the persecution, laying it out in concrete detail, and giving the specification of what it means in actuality." Such terms are familiar parts of his characterization of the apparatus of technical history. It would appear that he has now added the moral judgment of people's actions to the list of competencies of the technical historian. The move represents a new flexibility on the question of moral judgments, even as he seeks to contain the implications of what he has allowed by placing moral judgments of actions under the rubric "purely descriptive." He has, yet again, expanded the category "technical history," and, once again, done so without modifying his universalist expectations. Presumably his moral judgments of actions, posing as descriptions, may be expected to be the same for all historians. But he halts his flexibility here, and he will move no further. His clarification is complete. What he now asks historians to abjure is moral judgments specifically directed against persons.[62]

Yet in spite of Butterfield's proffered clarification on moral judgments in history, certain contradictions appear to remain within his treatment of the subject. He has now accepted the view that historians may display their moral judgments upon actions by means of the language they employ to describe what the people of the past were doing. At the same time, however, he reaffirms his abiding objection to building moral judgments into the organization of the narrative, especially by mounting the story as a war of right versus wrong, not merely as right people against wrong people. If we extrapolate from what he has told us, we can see how this "yes and no" works. Butterfield says that the modern concentration camp was wrong, and he permits the historian to describe the camps and the use of the camps in so detailed and vivid a manner that the reader will see that they are wrong. For instance, if we apply his point to a specific case, we may suppose that the historian is permitted to provide a description of the camps for Jews in Nazi-controlled Poland which enables the reader to see that they are wrong. But, at the same time, the historian is barred from constructing the history with respect to the camps and the Jews as a matter of right versus wrong. The apparent contradiction arises between what Butterfield has allowed and what he has disallowed. To "describe" in the manner he accepts is to "organize" the narrative in a way he opposes. If we go a step further, we may presume that he regards the conquest of the concentration camps as right, and that the historian may describe the campaign against the camps in such a way that the reader will see that it is right, while the camps are wrong. Thus, to present the history as, in part, the campaign against the concentration camps is to construct the narrative with respect to this point as a matter of right versus wrong, which Butterfield opposes.

The contradictions seem to increase when we go further. The concentration camps did not just happen and neither did their destruction. People were responsible for the camps and people were responsible for their destruction. Historians engage in historical analysis, which includes figuring out which people were responsible for what, and their histories tell who they are. Thus, with respect to the concentration camps, even if the interior lives of people on all sides of this point were morally mixed, and even if the circumstances were drastically different on all sides, and even though all people are sinners, and even though the judgment cannot serve as the Final Judgment for all eternity, some people, even on Butterfield's terms, were, on this point, morally wrong and other people were morally right. The indication of morally wrong action entails ipso facto the indication of people who were morally wrong to engage in that action. Or to switch to another of Butterfield's prime examples, if the historian calls the action "religious persecution," which he believes is wrong, then the people whom the historian finds were responsible for the action become the "persecutors," and they were morally wrong to persecute. In other words, by making moral judgments against certain actions Butterfield also engages in moral judgments against certain people with respect to certain actions. Moreover, for Butterfield to choose the term "persecution" or "massacre" or "atrocity" to "describe" certain actions in history is choose terms that contain a moral judgment against wrong action, and hence to take sides for the "right" against "wrong." For instance, we know that the people on the other side did not call their own actions "persecution" and set themselves up as "persecutors." They claimed that they were right, that they were engaged in preserving the peace and unity of the realm and taking decisive action against the would-be destroyers of the realm. It was even crucial to act decisively against such people for the sake of God and eternity. And the German authorities responsible for the concentration camps for Jews did not call their actions "atrocities," or name themselves as "murderers." They said that they were right to take effective measures to secure the purity of the German people and to defend the integrity of the German Reich, and the operators and attendants of the camps claimed that they were following orders and doing their patriotic duty. For Butterfield to "describe" the one case as "persecution" and the other as "atrocities" is for him to take sides and to construe the history in each case as a conflict of right against wrong. As if to compound the contradictions, he bolts right past all his arguments and calls one person an "irreligious scoundrel" and another person "the worst of murderers," and all through the book he repeatedly calls still other persons "saints." He may regard these words as terms of "description," but they contain within them moral judgment for and against people. The contradictions in Butterfield's discourse on moral judgments seem to multiply.[63]

If we return to Butterfield's desires about how to write the history of Hitler, his most provocative example of the workings of technical history, we hear echoes of the same apparent contradictions. Butterfield called for a history "even in the case of Hitler" that forsakes the moral judgment against him and provides an "intimate account" that "would enable us to see how a lump of human nature (how a boy playing in a field) could ever have come to be *like that*." In the light of Butterfield's ethics-free depiction of technical history, it is easy to hear his words as prescribing amoral history, or perhaps immoral history that cleanses Hitler from the awfulness of his politics. But on second hearing, we notice that Butterfield actually structured into his statement the moral judgment against Hitler as a person: "even" Hitler, the person who "could ever have come to be *like that*." A soft moral judgment, to be sure, but there it is nonetheless, the very same kind of moral judgment, against a person, that he wished above all to eliminate with the help of his clarification. Unclarity triumphs over clarity in the theme of moral judgments in history, and historians are left still to wonder what Butterfield wants them to do.[64]

Butterfield's delineation of the limits of technical history served also as the preface to his discourse on the relation of religion to historical study. Time and again his rhetoric has headed ostentatiously in one direction. In *Christianity and History* he posited the separation of the historian's religion, politics, nationality, race, ethical evaluations, philosophy — a person's deepest convictions and identities — from technical history. He trumpeted the power of technical historians to produce results that are valid for "Christian or atheist, whig or tory, Swede or Dane." He relished how "the liberal and the Jesuit, the Marxist and the Fascist, the Protestant and the Catholic" might all abhor academic history as "a bloodless pedestrian thing." He reiterated the point in his essay "The Christian and Academic History" in *Christian News Letter* in 1949.[65] In "Moral Judgments in History" he absolutely approved the technical historian who "is willing to jettison for the time being his private views and personal valuations" in order to accomplish the work of technical history. His most arresting and memorable statements have accentuated the incompatibility of historical study and the historian's religion, along with the alienation of ethical valuations from historical study.

But now, from the very same preface about technical history, Butterfield propels himself in the opposite direction. In his essay "The Christian and Historical Study," included in *History and Human Relations,* he tells us that his approach to historical study is actually founded on religion, on his own Christian convictions, to be precise.[66] We perceive that here too he rises to his self-defense against his critics, those who bemoaned his apparent divorce of historians' deepest commitments from their work. As soon as we hear about the religious basis of his proposals, we recall that he had also placed the message of the ultimate unity of religion and historical study in *Christianity and History*. Indeed he uttered boundless affirmation of such unity as the transcendence of opposites in the universe. It was possible, in that book, to detect the religious, even Christian, basis of his discourse, as for instance when he presented the vocation of the historian as reconciler. However, he most certainly refrained from claiming that his views of historical study were actually Christian, and we wondered whether he realized the implications of what he was proposing. We get a sharp impression of contradiction between the two directions of his discourse, towards the separateness and towards the unity of religion and historical study.

Butterfield now wishes to recognize, even confess, that behind the major points of his characterization of historical study are impulses that are congenial to Christians or even specifically Christian. Given that he has stressed the opposite for so long and so loudly, we are not surprised that, to tell us this, he reverts to his older style of seeming to wrap his assertions in qualifying words and to hand them out while walking backwards.

To start with, the scientific method itself, as he depicted it, is connected with Christianity. His approach gives scientific history a very precise, humble, and beneficial role which makes no claims to explain the whole of life or to replace God, and instead provides the vehicle for historians to operate with maximum "elasticity" and to examine at close range "the ways of Providence and the structure of the providential order." The method does this by enabling historians to search out ever more details, to disclose "secondary causes" rather than ultimate causes, and to find "rationality in the universe" manifested through the processes and necessities of history and expressed perhaps in the form of historical laws. The method was originally devised by natural scientists and historians who, as Christians, were not denying God but simply putting away their religious squabbles. Together they "found a better means for studying the ways of Providence." How, then, is the scientific method related to Christianity? He answers with a variety of phrases which take some care to decipher. He writes, "there are reasons for suggesting that this approach to any science is a specifically Christian one." And, "this, too, is not to be regarded as uncongenial to the Christian outlook." Later, "if it is not a specifically Christian thing, it did at any rate develop in the heart of a Christian civilisation." And then, "it is in itself a neutral instrument" which can work to the advantage of "worldly-minded men," but so too "it gives great leverage to the spirituality of spiritual men."[67]

Along with the scientific method per se, the central roles given to personality and imaginative sympathy in historical study, as he describes it, are also connected with Christianity. Accentuating personality makes room for individuals, freedom, moral responsibility, art, spirituality, and the unpredictable in history, while the emphasis on imaginative sympathy permits at least a little more "correct" treatment of history from the insides of personalities. How do these connect with Christianity? He writes, "this attitude to the study of the past, if it is not to some degree the effect of our traditions — our Christian civilisation, with its high view of personality — is particularly congenial to those traditions and particularly appropriate for the Christian." Further, the application of imaginative sympathy to others "ought to commend itself to the Christian." He adds, "In this sense the whole range of history is a boundless field for the constant exercise of Christian charity."[68]

Beyond the scientific method and personality is the question of the interpretation of the whole human drama from a Christian point of view. According to Butterfield, Christianity itself contains an outlook on history which touches the activity of Providence, the meaning and purpose of life, the story of sin and salvation, and so on. This interpretation gives the Christian something extra with respect to history: "If in life a man has accepted the Christian view of things, he will run these values throughout the whole of the past, and, taking the very basis of the narrative which historical scholarship has provided, he may see every event with an added dimension. He will have used historical science in order to become a closer and better student of the ways of Providence. He will see the vividness and appropriateness of the Biblical interpretation for the study of any country in any age of its history." The connection with Christianity is direct — the interpretation is part of Christianity — but there are things the Christian may not do with the interpretation with respect to historical study. For instance, it is illicit to give a Christian organization to the history, or employ history to vindicate and justify the church, or turn the study into a Protestant or Catholic version of history, or use history as polemical argument for or against Christianity. Rather, the Christian interpretation of history remains an outlook which the Christian "brings to history in the first place" and which "as a Christian he puts upon human events."[69]

When we sort through the rhetoric, we hear Butterfield admitting in his distinctive fashion that his approach to historical study is driven by his Christian convictions. The perennial tensions between his tendencies both to unify and to separate his religion and his history are once again visible, however. The theme of separation appears when he speaks of the neutrality of the scientific attitude, and of the Christian adding the Christian view to the history provided independently by the universal voice of historical scholarship. But then he asserts the theme of unity when, albeit by means of inverted wordings, he identifies cardinal points of his historical approach as Christian or Christian products: the features and limits of technical history, the high view of personality, insistence on human freedom and responsibility, imaginative sympathy and the exercise of charity, perceptions of rationality in the universe and the mitigating effects of processes, elasticity of mind. Hence, scientific history is not neutral, but specifically Christian, and Christianity is not an addition, but present in the very stuff of his approach to historical study. Butterfield is struggling to transcend the opposites at a higher level of unity provided by his Christian religion.[70]

We also note that the view he presents is not held by all Christians, let alone by Muslims and atheists, but is itself one particular version of a Christian understanding of historical study. His view, ironically, is merely one particular Protestant view that privileges individuals, personalism, voluntary choice, interior spirituality, and dissent. His view also specifically, and strongly, objects to the emphases on the church, liturgy, society, and corporate spirituality which are central to understandings of history held by so many among Roman Catholics, Anglicans, Orthodox, Lutherans, and Reformed, who make up the vast majority of Christians in the world.

Furthermore, against his own urging that Christians not build their religion into the organization of the narrative, he proceeds to recommend an outline of a narrative which structures his religion into the history of Western civilization. He justifies doing this, he says, in order "to illustrate the importance of Christianity in that mundane history which is under discussion." He builds his narrative around Christian charity, the autonomy of spirituality, and the spiritual character of individual personality, and he privileges the theme of "modern liberty," fostered, he says, by his own Nonconformists in opposition to the alliance of the dominant Church of England with the English state.[71]

Butterfield's parallel book, *Christianity in European History,* went on to elaborate. With sweeping generalizations, he made clear enough his sheer opposition to the establishment of the Christian Church as the state religion after Constantine. He likened medieval Christianity to Soviet communism. As he explained to Charles Van Doren, the church, analogous to communism, achieved dominance "by monarchial command or by military conquest or wholesale conversion," and then in order to maintain dominance "set up an authoritarian system, controlled education, insisted on obedience to Rome, emphasized orthodoxy, and so forth." His dissenting ethos left little room for subtle analysis of the institutional church in either the Roman Empire or medieval Europe. By contrast, in his most characteristic thesis, he argued that the most impressive of all the mundane results of Christianity was the "real christianization of Europe," due not to the work of the institutions of church and state, or to the effects of the economy, social status, and conquest, but to the preaching of the Gospel among the common people, the spreading of "New Testament Love," and the pious influence of the saints. He drew a sharp line between these spiritual means and consequences, on one side, and the work of the institutional church and Christian rulerships, on the other. Kenneth Scott Latourette, the notable Baptist historian, was effusive in the *American Historical Review*: "The importance of this little book is out of all proportion to its modest size."[72]

Not long after, in another set of special lectures, this time at Queen's University in Canada, in January 1952, he carried the theme of liberty still further. The result was a small volume of fifty-nine pages, *Liberty in the Modern World*, his fourteenth book, on the theme which had preoccupied Acton and which also preoccupied Butterfield. The volume was not published in Great Britain and was not known there. William McGill rightly singled out the book as the best place to look for a statement of Butterfield's understanding of liberty. The terms of the lectureship at Queen's fit his personal convictions exactly. The lectureship assigned the duty to promote understanding of "the individual person in society." His lectures represented a strong statement about the individual person as the only real existent in human history, and represented all social relationships and institutions, particularly the state, as nothing other than names for collections of individuals. Out of all societies of the world, he situated England at the centre of the movement of history towards "modern liberty," and, out of all the things one might say about England, he claimed that "the basic theme of English history" was the story of liberty. He could hardly render history more in Acton's terms than this. Given all his research in Acton's notes and given his continuing suggestions that he get involved in publishing Acton material, it would be easy to think of him editing Acton's notes for the history of liberty. But this project he left for someone else, and George Watson eventually did just that.[73]

These two little books, taken together, surpassed even *Whig Interpretation* and *Englishman and His History* as constructions of history that built Butterfield's religious and political convictions into the very organization of the narrative, contrary to his own warnings. Thus, with *History and Human Relations*, supported by *Christianity in European History* and *Liberty in the Modern World*, Butterfield mounted his self-defense against the charges that his version of history was amoral and a-religious. His history was, after all, undoubtedly both moral and religiously driven. Referring to his own Christian religious commitment, he described himself to Max Beloff as "the holder of what is in a sense an ideology myself." It would be hard to find a tag more completely opposite to the sound of his claims for technical history than this label self-imposed, Butterfield the ideologue.[74]

A System After All

Butterfield had put forward many sweeping ideas in his special lectures between 1948 and 1951, and, while they appeared to manifest a unity derived from his beliefs about religion and history, they represented a scattering of thoughts expressed to suit each occasion. He was not a systematic thinker, and he habitually resisted any pressures to reduce his discourse to logical order or to transmute it into theory.[75] However, he appeared to feel the need to achieve some integration, and this impulse, too, came in response to a specific occasion.

He had long played with the dualist polarities of freedom and necessity, personality and processes, spiritual and material. During the 1930s and early 1940s he had shown fascination with the theme of historical laws as a way to render the experience of necessity in history, but without allowing the language of laws to settle into his discourse. Now, in the context of his reengagement with Marxism and his still continuing interest in the history of science, he was entertaining talk of historical laws as analogous to the laws dealt with by natural scientists. However, the notion of laws seemed, on the face of it, to conflict with his earnest assertions of the freedom of individuals in history. He apparently wanted to give room to both emphases, but he had no comfortable way to do so. Depending on the occasion and the subject, his discourse swung from one of the poles to the other.

For instance, as part of his reflections on his own Christian commitments and historical study, in his essay on that theme published in 1951, he suggested that discourse on historical laws "is not to be regarded as uncongenial to the Christian outlook." He was sceptical, to say the least, about whether the universe operated according to laws. In keeping with his traditionally nominalist outlook, he was willing to treat laws simply as the verbal products of the scientists and historians who described them. The question of laws was back on his table, and he reacted once again by asserting the priority of human personality and freedom.[76] At the same time, June 1951, in a lecture in London to the Royal Institute of International Affairs, Arnold Toynbee's abode, he juxtaposed what he called a "scientific" approach to international affairs and a "moralistic" approach. In this context he swung to the necessity pole. He urged placing the analysis of international politics, especially in relation to Soviet-American conflict, on a "scientific" basis. This would mean emphasizing the overriding effects of predicaments and structures in history instead of focusing on the role of free, moral decisions taken by individual persons. He referred merely in passing to the relation between the two poles of human freedom and necessity in history as a problem.[77]

Two months later, at Bangor, Wales, in August, Butterfield addressed an ecumenical assembly of youth from various church traditions, and at the request of the ecclesiastical sponsors spoke about belief in God in the modern age. In his audience were perhaps a thousand students from Great Britain and overseas. It must have been a thrilling moment for the diminuative professor of modern history. The echoes of his days as Methodist lay preacher must have been strong. The Church of England Youth Council published his address in its newsletter and later as a pamphlet under the title "God in History."[78]

True to himself, Butterfield remained the historian, and cast so explicitly a theological topic as a problem of history, rather than as a piece of straight theology. He discussed the role of God in history and sought to counteract notions of an absentee, irrelevant, or nonexistent God. With such an aim he was bound not to polarize God and history, and he did not speak of "adding" God to the "common" history devised independently of religion by technical history. Instead he directly connected the theme about God with the poles of freedom and necessity and the concomitant issues which he had raised countless times, namely personality and processes. The result raised his general historical thinking to a higher degree of integration and represented the closest he had ever come to a systematic exposition of his discourse about history. We get the impression that he is becoming more amenable to questions of theory in relation to historical study.

Butterfield told the students that there were three ways of looking at the events of history and nature, and, accordingly, that there were three different kinds of analysis to be carried out at three different levels. The three were neither opposed to each other nor contradictory. Rather, all three were true at the same time about the same events. The first is the "biographical" way, in which we see human beings making history. We study individual persons as free to decide and act, as morally responsibility for their actions, and as liable for "blame." The second is the "historical" or "scientific" way, in which we see history as a realm of law necessitating what goes on, and we see processes and not people making history. We examine the deep forces and long-term tendencies of history, and uncover the conditioning circumstances which surround and restrict human action and render people less "blamable" than we first thought. The third, which he leaves unnamed, is the "theological" way, in which we see God at work in history, operative in both the lives of individual personalities and the processes. We confront the choice between Providence or Chance as the source of history, and if, we are Christian, we learn to recognize the presence of God as the One, in the words of St. Paul, "in Whom we live and move and have our being."[79]

The formula of the three ways suggests the makings of a historical theory, but the rough spots and inconsistencies in his presentation are considerable, for he is not engaging in genuinely systematic thinking. For instance, he polarizes human beings and processes, whereas even the processes are really people acting and interacting over time. He refers to the history which "men themselves do not make," and speaks instead of the processes and even the laws as making history, whereas the notion of "making" in human history requires, by definition, humans to do the making. He treats the realm of laws as the only "historical" way, whereas his point is to show that all ways are historical, all three are ways of looking at history. By understanding the first way as "biographical" he swings excessively towards "biography" as the privileged mode of history and appears to construe the study of human history as the compilation of so many individual biographies, such as his own intended biographies of Fox or Temperley or the young Acton. He lumps together under the second way the notions of "processes," "laws," "conditions," and "necessity," which are not the same things or even intrinsically related. The slippage of the designation "scientific" to the second way is confusing, since he used to apply the notion to the whole of his "technical history," both the detailed search of the documentary evidence about individual persons and their interactions as well as the pursuit of explanations via recovery of conditioning circumstances. He appears ambivalent in his understanding of laws in history. In one sentence he characterizes laws as convenient ways we rationally explain history after, and not before, the events have happened. In others he speaks of laws and regularities as belonging to the makeup of the world, entertains the use of the laws for prediction in human affairs, and posits the need for people to live in harmony with the laws in order to enjoy a wholesome life. In one line he denies that God created the world according to law, but in another he refers to "a God who ordered things in that particular way." After spending his career opposing moral judgments by historians, and especially after only recently attempting to focus his objection simply against moral judgments of people, we are completely unprepared for his suggestion that historians may "blame" people in the "biographical" way, even if the "historical" way makes them less "blamable." And so on.

These are rough spots, to be sure, and there are moments when it sounds as if Butterfield is making up his theory as he goes along. Nevertheless, in spite of the inconsistencies and the incompletes, the general relaxation of the tensions in his discourse feels very tangible. The overriding message we hear is reconciliation. He strives to achieve intellectual reconciliation via the image of the noncontradictory coexistence of three kinds of perceptions of the same history. He used to deal in what we might call a double dualism: he transmuted his basic polarity of freedom versus necessity into the historical pole of a second and more inclusive polarity, the historical realm versus religion. And then further along in the discourse he sought to transcend the double dualism via the higher unity of religion alone. At least in "God in History" he has eliminated the dualistic polarities, and refrained from constructing his historical understanding out of opposites. He has instead articulated his vision in terms of "both . . . and . . . ," and even "both . . . and . . . as well as . . . ," rather than the usual "either . . . or . . . " and "this versus that." It is a comprehensive vision which enables him to hold together the ideas he has been propounding without the loss of anything that matters to him. The stimulus, appropriately, was the religious need of the historian-preacher to affirm before a thousand students the presence of God in history, not as an addition, not as something inserted from the outside, not as an extra, but as intrinsic to the very same stuff of history that historians study.

Death in the Family

Butterfield was ready to go to America for part of 1952 as a visiting professor at the University of Chicago, but he withdrew because of the poor health of his father, Albert Butterfield. He kept one appointment to travel briefly to Canada, to Montreal and Kingston, for lectures at Queen's University in January 1952. He wrote the three lectures, later published as *Liberty in the Modern World,* under the strain of his father's illness.

Butterfield returned from Canada just days before his father died on 24 January 1952. His father was almost eighty, and he had lived long enough to witness his son's triumph. More important for both the father and the son, he lived to see Herbert convert his career as a historian into a means of preaching the Gospel, beginning with the lectures on Christianity and history. Herbert had remained close to "Dad" over the years, returning to Oxenhope at least once every year, sometimes as the featured attraction at a local event in his home village or in Keighley. Herbert felt that his father in later years admired him almost too much and discounted his own achievements as inadequate. Herbert, in return, idolized his father as a gentle man and spiritual figure, and ranked his father as the greatest influence on his life. He recalled, "There never was a moment when I did not put him at the top of the list.

Herbert, the oldest child, planned the funeral, functioned as executor of the will, and worried about his mother's well-being. Long ago he had mellowed towards his mother and noticed that she and his father enjoyed happiness in the later years of their life together. He wrote the date of his parents' wedding in his daily book. They were married nearly fifty-four years. With his father gone, he meditated on the new relationship with his mother, and his mind wandered to Acton and his mother. He wrote the date of Acton's mother's death in his daily book. He was contemplating his own mother's death. He was not close to his sister, Edith, known as Edie, who never married and was a public health nurse in London, or to his brother, Arthur, who had been dying of cancer in a hospital in Bradford, but he felt dutiful towards them and towards Arthur's wife, Hannah, when she moved to Belfast after Arthur died not long after their father.[80]

9

On War and Historiography

Acton and Modern History

When things settled down after his father's death in January 1952, Butterfield felt uncertain about his major projects. A few months earlier, and now again, he surveyed his recent life, and each time he confided in Paul Vellacott, the Master of Peterhouse. He admitted that he had spent too much time "in outside lectures and in forms of propaganda," and acknowledged that he had done so by deliberate decision. He was pleased that publications resulted, but confessed that he regarded them as incidental. He catalogued what he counted as his real work, the historical writing which seemed to proceed only slowly, if at all: Fox, the *Concise Cambridge Modern History,* the Temperley biography, the Acton diaries. He continued to affirm that the Fox biography was his main task, and admitted to severe anxiety over the difficulites attached to completing the minute research that both his theory and his temperament imposed upon him.[1]

He tried to clear out some of the bramble from his activities, especially his outside lecturing. For 1951–1952 he reduced his special commitments to about ten occasions, and to perhaps seven or eight occasions for each of the next three years. In a surprising move to gain time, he resigned as editor of the *Cambridge Historical Journal,* a post he had held for fourteen years. He remained on the editorial board and continued to express strong opinions about the direction of the journal.[2] He had attempted to resume his research in the fall of 1951, and again arranged to take Eve Bogle as a copyist with him to the royal archives, but he managed to work only sporadically.[3] His research style was upset in 1951 when he had to give up the Fox papers which he had on loan from Trevelyan. He had kept them in his house for twenty years. He had not read much in the papers all those years, but had merely dipped into them from time to time when he wished to see how these Fox materials fit with information he was finding elsewhere. In October 1949, after *George III, Lord North, and the People* appeared, Trevelyan had first raised the matter of his intention to give the papers to the British Museum. Butterfield asked to keep them longer, and Trevelyan consented. Now, however, Trevelyan was insistent. The time had come to deposit the papers permanently where they could be cared for and made accessible for research. Butterfield acquiesced, and in May 1951 personally escorted two crates of Fox papers to London. Fox suddenly seemed even further away.[4]

A new project unexpectedly pressed in on him, threatening to keep him away from Fox for a long time. It was a case of the clash of deep loyalties within him. The project concerned Acton, by now his alter ego and almost the only thinker he considered when taking new steps. Douglas Woodruff, a devout Roman Catholic, and husband of a granddaughter of Lord Acton who was the custodian of the Acton papers, approached Butterfield in 1951 for help in publishing an ample collection of Acton writings. Woodruff had read Aelred Watkin's article written with Butterfield in 1950 exposing Cardinal Gasquet's tampering with Acton's wording in his edition of Acton letters. Woodruff imagined an edition of perhaps twelve volumes of Acton essays and letters. He invited Butterfield to co-edit some volumes of letters selected from the immense Acton correspondence. Butterfield recoiled. "Selected letters" violated the norms for scientific history, which required complete runs of extant letters instead of pieces and fragments. He had to save Acton from mistreatment. He declined the invitation, saying he was too busy and, as before, that he did not want to be an editor, especially not a co-editor. But then he urged Woodruff to stop the project if it meant publishing merely a selection of letters. Woodruff replied that he would carry on with the plan anyway, and hoped that Butterfield would nonetheless be willing to provide occasional help. He put the Acton correspondence with Ignatz Döllinger, his teacher, at the top of the list for publication.[5]

Butterfield's alarm increased. He had to protect Lord Acton and defend scientific history. He acknowledged privately that he intended to block Woodruff from publishing a sloppy or incomplete series of Acton correspondence. During January 1952 he devised a fourteen-page plan for the publication of the complete Acton correspondence. With support from both Vellacott and David Knowles, he sent it to Cambridge University Press, overlooking for the moment his fairly recent negative comments about CUP. He talked lavishly about current interest in Acton as if there were a major revival of Acton scholarship. So great was his anxiety that he offered to serve as editor himself if need be, in spite of his repeated refusals to become an editor.[6]

The project was huge, and he realized that it would "wipe out" his work on Fox for the foreseeable future.[7] He would give up another project as well, a small book on Edmund Burke, the figure whom Acton described as "the most intelligent of our instructors." In the fall of 1951 he had discussed with Collins a volume on Burke for their "brief lives" series. The proposal strongly appealed to him since, after Fox, Burke ranked extremely high in his approval list as both a politician and a historian. He even suggested eliminating some other work so he could complete the book during 1952. Some drafts of the beginning of a life of Burke remain in Butterfield's papers, suggesting that he made a start on the book.[8]

Cambridge University Press accepted the proposal for the Acton correspondence in May 1952, with the proviso that Butterfield would be editor.[9] For the scheme to work, Butterfield needed Woodruff's cooperation, since Woodruff's wife controlled the rights to Acton's letters. Amazingly Woodruff was conciliatory in the face of Butterfield's firm insistence, even though it would mean trashing his own plan. Woodruff had gone ahead as he promised, and at that very moment was bringing out his first volume, Acton's essays on church and state.[10]

Butterfield received a tip from Maurice Cowling, then a young Cambridge scholar contemplating writing a life of Acton, that the first Woodruff volume altered portions of Acton's text. Butterfield was certain he could smell a new case of tampering with documents because of religious ideology. The possibility fired his motivation to defend Acton and scientific history. He wrote letters to the editors of two historical journals, *History* and *English Historical Review*, urging that they ask Cowling to review the Woodruff volume, but he had to rest content with communicating his complaints to Duncan Forbes, who had already been assigned the review for the *EHR*.[11] He confronted Woodruff directly with the charge that the volume contained textual changes, hinting that he suspected some of the changes were due to ideological manipulation. He declared that the project would set back Acton scholarship by fifty years and asked Woodruff to abandon the entire undertaking. Vellacott felt that his approach to Woodruff was severe, and remarked, "I would have gone out and hanged myself." Butterfield had actually drafted a much stronger letter directly uttering the charge that Woodruff's volume contained ideological tampering, but on Velacott's urging he sent what, by comparison, was a softer letter.[12] Woodruff was hurt. He explained that omissions were deliberate since the volume was intended to be no more than extracts, and attributed any other changes to mistakes by the copyist. To establish his innocence of ideological wrong-doing, his wife granted full approval to Butterfield and Cambridge University Press to publish complete sets of the Acton correspondence under her control. Woodruff agreed to abandon his own project and offered to let Butterfield start the Cambridge Press project with the much prized Acton-Döllinger letters.[13]

Butterfield had succeeded, but now he was stuck with the enormous Acton project, something he really did not want to be doing himself. He consulted with David Knowles and suggested to CUP that the first series for publication should be the correspondence with Döllinger, Richard Simpson (Acton's collaborator in the journal *The Rambler*), and Cardinal John Henry Newman. He also thought of the correspondence with Mary Drew, daughter of William Gladstone, the Liberal prime minister. Butterfield settled into the Acton papers in the Cambridge University Library during 1952. Since 1946, when he found the young Acton's diaries, he had squeezed in time now and then, both in Cambridge and London, to read Acton notes and letters. He and Eve Bogle hand-copied Acton material onto hundreds of pages. They arranged many of these sheets by topics, and quotations and references to persons are listed in an alphabetical catalogue. Butterfield was fascinated by Acton as letter-writer. He regarded the letters as more than merely personal communications. They were almost like essays in which Acton presented historical reflections in addition to revealing traits of personality. In keeping with Butterfield's minutely detailed method of research, he had already begun constructing a day-by-day chronology of Acton's early working life. The aim had been to prepare a "Portrait of Acton as a Young Man" to accompany his projected edition of the young Acton's diaries. This was the research that lay behind his willingness to edit the Acton correspondence.[14]

Butterfield's interest in Acton caught the eye of the BBC, probably through the person of T. S. Gregory, a friend of Woodruff, and he received an invitation give a broadcast on Acton in June 1952 to mark the fiftieth anniversary of Acton's death. He published the text in the *Cambridge Journal* as "Lord Acton," in 1953. Butterfield's approach was biographical. He emphasized the difference between the young Acton and the old, and cast the older Acton as obsessive and rigid on the question of moral judgments. He extolled Acton, nonetheless, as a historical thinker, a daring and paradoxical thinker, who could enter the "higher reaches" of reflection upon history, religion, and political life.[15]

Making his interest tangible, he had given notice in the BBC broadcast that he wished to dissect Acton's historical treatment of the massacre of French Protestants which began on St. Bartholomew's Day in 1572. He followed through with an article "Acton and the Massacre of St. Bartholomew," published in the other local journal, *Cambridge Historical Journal,* in 1953. It was a further study in a field he was making more his own, the history of historical study.[16] He claimed in "Lord Acton" that Acton was "by far the greatest historical thinker that England has ever had," more important for his historical thought than for his writings, which were relatively few, or even for his learning, which was vast. Butterfield's assessment matched the self-description, and perhaps self-justification, that Acton offered in his inaugural address in 1895. By what he praised in Acton, Butterfield gave a clue to his understanding of himself and his own emerging aspirations. To promote historical thought, Butterfield would be willing to postpone even his own research on Fox and cancel Burke.[17]

To his dismay, Butterfield learned in January 1953 that Woodruff had reversed himself and, in spite of Butterfield, had decided to proceed with the publication of the Acton material, including the correspondence. Butterfield's efforts to thwart the project collapsed, and he abruptly withdrew from his counterproject for the Acton correspondence with Cambridge University Press. He expressed relief about not having to spend years as an editor, but proclaimed loudly that he was not through with Acton. He might want to write a "very detailed" biography and analytical study of Acton, or at least to complete the Acton diaries. He confessed that he might still be tempted by a smaller plan to edit the Acton letters for the early years, say 1858–1870, or maybe the Acton-Döllinger correspondence. For now, however, he did nothing more.[18]

It was three years later, in January 1956, that Butterfield learned to his astonishment that Woodruff was again giving up the Acton publishing project. It did not occur to Butterfield in the new circumstances of that moment to reconsider doing the Acton correspondence himself. A few months later, Victor Conzemius, a Roman Catholic scholar from Luxembourg, appeared at his door wanting to read the Acton papers for a biography of Döllinger, and Butterfield recounted the story of the Acton letters. By December 1956 Conzemius had the agreement of the Académie Bavaroise to publish the complete Acton-Döllenger correspondence at their expense. Butterfield gave his blessing. The letters began appearing in the 1960s.[19]

In due course, Butterfield's wishes were fulfilled for the rest of the main units of the Acton correspondence. Butterfield learned in the 1960s that the edition of the letters and diaries of John Henry Newman being published by Oxford

University Press would include Newman's correspondence with Acton.[20] In 1965, two American historians, Damian McElrath and Joseph Altholz, came to him about an edition of the Acton letters with Richard Simpson. McElrath soon discovered five trunks of Acton letters at Aldenham, the Acton family estate. Butterfield and David Knowles persuaded Cambridge University Press to publish the Acton-Simpson material, and three volumes were eventually published in the 1970s.[21]

Butterfield's home life, meanwhile, was entering a new stage. His second son, Giles, finished the Leys School in the summer of 1952 and entered Peterhouse in October to study engineering. With Peter in third year, he now had two sons in Peterhouse at once. Giles was still a close friend of Eve Bogle's son James, and by all reports was a very likable person. He occasionally had shown symptoms of emotional disturbance, and hopes were high that the change would be good for him.[22] Butterfield's third son, Robin, remained at home for one more year at St. Faith's preparatory school before going away, at age thirteen, to Clifton College, a private boarding school near Bristol. From the fall of 1953 onwards, Butterfield had no children at home, and his schedule became more flexible.

With the Acton plan behind him and the new arrangements at home, Butterfield felt free to return to his long-standing projects. Fox, the biggest project, was the easiest to neglect, and he managed only once in a while to pick away at the research. For instance, in September 1953, he made arrangements to go to Aylesbury with Eve Bogle to read the papers of the second Earl of Buckinghamshire on Ireland, 1776–1780.[23] Against this, Vellacott had been urging him since at least October 1952 to give up everything in favour of the *Concise History*. Cambridge University Press was just then publishing Previté-Orton's *Shorter Cambridge Medieval History*, a two-volume companion to Butterfield's modern history, making him feel very far behind in his work.[24] The Press had not lost interest in his modern history, or in him, but there were hints that their priorities might be changing. When Butterfield was trying to attract the Press to his Acton scheme, Kingsford in response explored whether Butterfield could be persuaded to write a new *History of Europe in the Nineteenth and Twentieth Centuries* to replace a volume by Grant and Temperley from the 1920s. He gave Kingsford no encouragement, but the inquiry reminded him that he was not tending to the *Concise History*.[25] Now he debated whether to aim for a single volume covering the four hundred years since 1494, or a two-volume set with the sixteenth and seventeenth centuries put into a first volume which could appear when ready. He told Vellacott that such a first volume "would not take me very long" and would have the advantage of reinforcing his view that the scientific revolution at the end of the seventeenth century marked the end of a period which he would call "early modern."[26]

Before the end of 1952 Butterfield arranged with the History Faculty once again to take over the general modern history course, now called simply "European History from 1494." When he became Professor of Modern History in 1944, he had relinquished the course which then carried the title he had worked so hard to attain, "Development of European Civilization." Starting in Michaelmas term of 1953, he returned to the arduous and self-imposed task of three lectures per week for three terms a year, with each lecture written out in full. He kept up that pace until 1957. The peculiar appeal of the lectures to him at this moment was the routine and the timetable they afforded within which he could revise his chapters for the *Concise History*.[27]

He pulled out all his earlier typescripts for his lectures as well as the book. His work so far fell into at least two layers, one from the 1930s, one from the early 1940s. During this revision he managed to produce at least forty typed lectures, with seven or eight numbered as chapters — the Renaissance, the maritime discoveries, invasions of Italy, church and reformation, Luther and the problem of Germany, Charles V, Swiss reformation, and so on. Over half of the pieces focused on politics, diplomacy, or war, nearly half on general themes, religion, and ideas, including science, a couple on historical geography, and none on economic, material, or social themes. The typescripts covered topics from 1494 through the 1870s and the period of Bismarck. His actual topics show that he continued to feature the traditional version of modern European history, even though his theoretical statements continued to construe Europe as a civilization manifesting a multiplicity of interacting factors. Butterfield proceeded very far in his revisions for the *Concise History*, but new commitments intervened which stole his attention from this and Fox before he had finished even the pre-1700 period which he said would require little time.[28]

Diplomacy and War

Butterfield's new preoccupation was a major outside lectureship for July 1953, and he soon accepted a second such invitation for November 1954. The first occasion was a national Methodist Church lectureship on the connections between Christian principles and social themes. He took the opportunity to run headlong into questions of international relations and war. The second was the inaugural lectures for a new foundation, the Wiles Trust, to take place at the Queen's University, Belfast, Northern Ireland. He used them to go farther than he ever had into the history of historiography. Both engagements took him into fields that were emerging as new interests, and kept him away from his primary projects of historical research. Both led to books, adding to his string of works connected to special lectures. The first lectureship yielded his fifteenth book, a small volume of 125 pages published in December 1953 by the Epworth Press, the Methodist publishing house, under the title *Christianity, Diplomacy and War.*[29] The second produced *Man on His Past: The Study of the History of Historical Scholarship,* a book of 238 pages, his sixteenth, published by Cambridge University Press in 1955.

The burden of Butterfield's new discourse on international relations was to convince people of the horror of what he was calling "wars for righteousness." His campaign was in every way a moral one, impelled by his Christian religious convictions. The subject evoked his commentary on the contemporary global situation created by the Soviet-American crisis and the nuclear bomb, and sent him on a survey of the twentieth century since 1914 and, in particular, eighteenth-century Europe. He had raised the problem of "wars of righteousness" at the close of his lectures on Christianity and history in 1948 as a sample of how to apply his religious understanding of history to contemporary events.[30] As the world crisis became ever worse, we can see him churning over his thinking on the subject in some of his special lectures thereafter. Notable among these were "The Tragic Element in Modern International Conflict" at the University of Notre Dame in 1949, "Scientific Diplomacy" over the BBC in 1951, "The Scientific versus the Moralistic Approach in International Affairs" at the Royal Institute of International Affairs in 1951, and "Reflections on Diplomatic History" to the Cambridge History Club in October 1952.[31]

The lectures in 1953 which became *Christianity, Diplomacy and War* concentrate on the defeat of the outlook that promoted "wars for righteousness," what Butterfield regards as the modern form of war. Once again, as in the case of his Canadian lectures on liberty and the individual, the demands of his forum shape his thought, or better, he shows that his thought is elastic enough to stretch precisely as far as the polar opposite of his emphasis on the individual, namely, the needs of the state and international relations. Butterfield uses the book to put forward provocative comments on a wide range of issues in international politics and diplomacy, in both current affairs and past history.

A bulky section of *Christianity, Diplomacy and War* denounces the practice of war since 1914. He condemns especially the warfare of the anti-German powers in both the First and Second World Wars. Instead of fighting for the limited goal of defeating presumed aggression and the disruption of the balance of power, the Western governments, he charges, had gone over to a modern "heresy" which justified unlimited warfare provided the aim was "to root out a great evil." By their actions during and after the war of 1914–1918, they reintroduced an extreme mode of war, and brought down upon their own heads, in due course, the emergence of Soviet Communism, two generations of German resentments, the reign of Fascism and Nazism, the Second World War, the continental predominance of Russia, and the permanent threat of total war under the canopy of the nuclear bomb.[32]

In Butterfield's view, "wars for righteousness" are really wars of religion, even when the combatants are not calling them that. They are total wars, wars without limits, the purpose of which is to eliminate the evil that exists on the other side of the conflict. They are driven by ideology in which both sides construct the conflict as a clash of beliefs and morality, a battle of right versus wrong. The "heresy" driving them is the denial of universal sin. They trust in the promise that human evil can be eradicated by means of that one final war. The combatants are focused on blaming the other for the origin of the war, and they permit no compromise of the correct outcome, the total defeat of the enemy. The ultimate medium of righteous war, the instrument of total destructiveness of the enemy, is, he warns, the nuclear weapon.[33]

Butterfield believes that the Soviet-American struggle ranked as the nearly perfect example of the "war for righteousness." The Western powers present themselves as the agents of world freedom and democracy against the tyranny of Communism, while the Soviet Union comes forward as the liberator of the world from the oppressive yoke of capitalism and Western imperialism. The war between the Nazi-Fascist powers on one side and the Western-Soviet alliance on the other possessed the same structure — a "war for righteousness" — even though the issues and the combatants were different. The First World War projected the new democratic order against the traditional order under the banners "make the world safe for democracy" and "the war to end all wars." The structure of all of these conflicts mimics the wars between the Catholic and Protestant powers in the sixteenth and early seventeenth centuries as well as the war for and against the French Revolution and Napoleon, and the American Civil War.[34]

The antidote to the mentality which generates "wars for righteousness," proposes Butterfield, is a "scientific" rather than a "moralistic" approach to international affairs. The strategy employs the techniques of both scientific history and what he calls variously "scientific diplomacy" or "technical diplomacy." The continuity between Butterfield's analysis of the past and his analysis of the present is evident both in his language and his mode of thinking. His study of diplomatic history has blended into his study of contemporary diplomatic relations, and technical history, whose structure he derived from his style of diplomatic history, transmutes into "scientific diplomacy" as against "ideological diplomacy." He manages to leave his message of "no moral judgments" in his argument as a component of his attack on "ideological diplomacy." For Butterfield, at this point, the keystone of the scientific approach, whether in past history or contemporary history, is the analysis of the "predicament" created by the structure of human situations. The scientific treatment of international power and war analyzes "predicaments" rather than persons and ideologies, structure rather than the moral responsibility of the principal leaders or the meaning of the ideologies articulated by either side. Predicaments, he thinks, function almost according to a mathematical formula.[35]

In the example of Soviet-Western relations, he lays out the predicament as follows. The Soviet Union and the Western powers, as allies in the Second World War, successfully combined to achieve the total defeat of Germany, leaving a huge power-hole in the centre of Europe. The Western powers and the Soviet Union quite naturally flow into the hole from either direction, and suddenly find themselves face to face. New sides form. Neither side can allow Germany, or east central Europe, to fall into the orbit of the other, each side is sure it is in the right, and neither side can be sure of the intentions of the other. Each side is gripped by an absolutely opposite fear of the other, and neither can perceive that the other has that fear too. Each side feels compelled to arm against the other just in case, and up looms the possibility of new war. There, says Butterfield, is the predicament and the potential for enormous conflict, produced by the relations of power entirely apart from differences in ideology or morality. It functions like geometry, and the consequences are tragic. Threatening to wage a "war for righteousness" against the Communist Soviet Union misses the point.[36]

Butterfield's reading of history since 1914 once again amounts to a defense of Germany, and even shifts the fundamental blame for both world wars, and considerable blame for the achievements of Hitler, to the Western powers themselves.[37] At the same time, his line of thought leads him to take positions vis-à-vis the Communists that seemed highly provocative in the context of the international crisis of the late 1940s and early 1950s. Once again he fully enjoys playing the dissenter. For instance, he asserts that the predicament involved in the contemporary crisis would be the same whether the government of Russia were in the hands of the Christian czars or the atheistic Communists. He levels the differences between the two giant powers: "but the greatest menace to our civilization today is the conflict between giant organized systems of self-righteousness — each system only too delighted to find that the other is wicked — each only too glad that the sins give it the pretext for still deeper hatred and animosity." Because of the predicament the Western powers acquiesced in the Soviet domination of east central Europe after the victory over Germany, even though the magnitude of the territorial consequences was far greater than the Nazi invasions of Czechoslovakia and Poland, which led to war. The horrors and dictatorship which the West associates with Soviet Communism are better understood as "organic to the phenomenon of revolution as such" or as connected with situations where society has "broken down" due to war and economic collapse. As he put it to Max Beloff two years earlier, "I can't help thinking that the fact of a state revolutionary is more significant for diplomatic purposes than the character of the revolutionary creed." In any case, Christians themselves perpetrated similar horrors and tyrannies throughout the history of the church, a record that brings no end of complaint against Christianity, and it could easily happen again. The charges of materialism and atheism which the West throws at Communist societies can be thrown with at least equal force at Western societies. Given their public policies of health, education, and welfare, Western European societies are moving closer to Communist ideals than the Western powers wish to admit. The appeal of Communism to many peoples of Africa and Asia, together with the play of the West against the Soviet bloc, has encouraged some subject peoples to throw off Western colonial power sooner rather than later. And so on. Butterfield adds one statement after another to his list of surprising comments, all connected with his analysis of predicament.[38]

When we review these and other such statements they appear remarkably unlike findings of "science," and rather noticeably like moral and political positions, indeed religious positions, with respect to contemporary international politics. He is representing his own moral views as "scientific" and neglecting to notice that the alternative to "moralism" which he advocates is not "science" but a different morality in international affairs. This is a case of one political morality versus another. His views about American-Soviet relations places him as the dissenter in the context of those times, in the liberal-left range of the political and religious spectrum. He opposes not merely the stringent anti-Communism of the era, but also the official policies of all the Western powers with respect to the form of their opposition to the Soviet Union. He could even sound at times like an apologist for the Soviets. For instance, he seeks to explain the horrors in the Soviet Union as derivative of a special situation, namely revolution itself and the dictatorship which occurs where the social order has already broken down. With this he overlooks the persecutions, massacres, and politics of starvation which extended, and recurred, well beyond the early period of the regime. By emphasizing so greatly the structure of the "predicament," and understating the moral choices available to the leaders at the time, he appears to offer excuses for Stalin akin to those he seemed to provide earlier for Hitler. In place of the embrace of "both . . . and . . . as well as" which he achieved in "God in History" in 1951, he resumes his dualistic swings between opposites: from freedom to necessity, from personality to structures, from "morality" to "science."

But Butterfield also evidences a strongly conservative tendency in his political morality for international affairs. He builds his argument against "wars of righteousness" upon a decidedly archaic appreciation of eighteenth-century European diplomacy and aristocracy. Central to his purpose in *Christianity, Diplomacy and War* is to illuminate the structure of international affairs by learning from the experience of the past, and using historical study to access that experience. His work joins the lengthy tradition of those who seek to benefit from "the lessons of history." The past he has in mind, in general, is the Christian experience of human nature over the ages and the teachings of the Christian tradition about "just war." More particularly, he wishes to learn from the experience of international relations gained by the diplomats and rulers of Europe in the eighteenth century. Butterfield was convinced that the states-system they constructed, beginning with the Treaty of Utrecht of 1713, and reaffirmed by the Treaties of Vienna in 1815, represents a uniquely successful achievement in international order and the control of power. In spite of important challenges, the system lasted until the prosecutors of the war of 1914–1918 and the authors of the Treaties of Versailles destroyed it. At that moment, the "new diplomacy" with its "wars for righteousness" replaced the traditional diplomacy of controlled power and limited war.[39]

It is remarkable that Butterfield, with his lifelong hold on individual personality as the moral absolute and the sole human reality, should care so earnestly about the European states-system. Contrary to his usual practice, he seems to treat the system and the states that comprise its membership as supra-individual social realities, and not simply as abstract nouns. The states-system was, he says, an international club. All those diplomats and rulers were Christian and, however messy might be their personal piety or morality, they moved within a system coloured by the traditional teachings of Christianity about "just war" as well as by the legacy of Christian humanism of the Renaissance. They were also aristocrats and royalty who shared a common life, culture, and social style, and often enough they were even related by family. The states-system, he says, embodied "a hundred imponderables" and "the subtler virtues" which modulated the behaviour of its members: tolerance, moderation, the practice of reasonableness, self-discipline, urbaneness, civilities, the "feeling for quality," the attributes of a "civilized world." The members operated according to the principle of the balance of power, and directed all their activity towards the limitation of war and the preservation and extension of the international order itself.[40] Following Ranke, Butterfield summarizes their project: "They had achieved a superiority in civilization and a supremacy in technique which secured them against any overwhelming attack from the rest of the continents of the earth and were moving towards the unification of the entire globe. Given time, and proper realization of the required conditions, it was not inconceivable that the international order itself should be extended until it came to cover all the branches of the human race."[41]

The statements which appear within his rendition of the eighteenth-century world of diplomacy are as politically provocative as his statements about the Soviets, but this time on the conservative side. He pronounces a view of the stages of civilization which privileges aristocracy, elevates Western civilization over the cultures of the rest of the world, and justifies world domination by the empires of the great powers of Europe. He establishes an implicit ranking of the peoples of the world on a scale running from "barbarian" to "civilized," and the "civilized" peoples on a scale running from "lower" to "advanced." In particular, he berates eastern Europe and Russia for their "backward state," and singles out the Balkans for their "barbarism." He especially bemoans the "barbarism" of those unnamed countries who have "assimilated the science and technology" and "copied democratic institutions" of civilization without absorbing the "imponderables" that supported them in the civilization of Europe. The subtext points to the countries of Africa, Asia, and Latin America.[42] A different set of hints points repeatedly to England and the British Empire, in spite of their sins, as exemplars of civilized peoples living according to the "imponderables," and as societies manifesting "the growth of reasonableness" as well as the transposition of aristocratic values to the lower social ranks.[43] If for Hegel and Ranke world history moved towards the model of Prussia, for Butterfield it is England. His idealization of England echoes *Englishman and His History* and the praise he there lavished on the tradition of passing aristocratic virtues down to the ordinary Englishman, as modelled by his father.

The instrument Butterfield employs to access the experience of the past is the "maxim." We feel immediately that we are back with Machiavelli and Butterfield's *Statecraft of Machiavelli* in 1940. There he depicted the Renaissance thinker as the producer of maxims derived from reflection on history, and as such as the progenitor of "political science." Now, throughout *Christianity, Diplomacy and War,* he himself generates maxims, dozens of maxims. It is surprising to find that his claims on behalf of science, with Machiavelli and here, do not pivot on a view of "law," and although he deals in general statements, he does not represent his views as theory. He professes merely to be interested in fundamental principles. The term "law" appears only occasionally in the book. He could well have used the notion of "law" as a way of indicating what science is about. Only recently, in "God in History," he had stressed the importance of law as one of the three ways of understanding history, and again in "The Scientific versus the Moralistic Approach in International Affairs" he had bound a scientific approach to the consideration of "laws" in history. As a sample "law" he cited Acton's postulation "power tends to corrupt and absolute power corrupts absolutely," or, in his own paraphrase, "the possession of unchecked power has a corrupting effect on a man."[44]

In Butterfield's vocabulary the maxim would appear to be more commonplace, less rigorous, less precise, than the law. He represents the maxim as a piece of "accumulated wisdom" about human conduct that would "embody the results of man's long-term experience on the earth." The Christian tradition generates maxims, expressions of "worldly wisdom which condense the experience of centuries." Especially important to him are those which he deems relevant to the affairs of the nation and the European order as well as to the whole "civilized" world.[45]

Two kinds of maxims appear in Butterfield's discourse at this moment. The first are those he articulates within his own account of what he is for and against, most notably as part of his endorsement of limited wars of self-defense, his opposition to aggression, his condemnation of wars for righteousness, and his interest in the control of armed power. These maxims serve as units of historical explanation: they come as generalized assertions which purport to sum up undeniable, universal experiences, appeal to which closes the need for further explanation. We may look at one example. In a long section on the creation of an international order after the Second World War via the agency of the United Nations, he cites the reference made by certain powers to the model of the British Commonwealth of Nations. He argues from history against the relevance of using that model, and to clinch his case he states, or implies, several maxims in rapid succession. By inserting numbers into his text we can identify the maxims as follows:

> We all know that we should demonstrate to these powers [1] how such a thing is not made, but must grow — [2] how a paper organization and the mere copying of our institutions represent the least important aspect of the matter; since [3] it is only much profounder historical processes which can release the imponderable factors that it is part of our purpose to study — [4] imponderable factors which we know are an essential part of the working of our Commonwealth. [5] A purely formal international system — a mere skeleton of institutions — shares the weaknesses of a revolutionary regime, precisely because it lacks the assistance of these imponderables. In other words, [6] an international system is precarious [6.a] if its only sanction is force, and [6.b] if it depends on the combined power of a temporary or permanent majority — [7] it is weak, for example, if it can operate only by threatening the offender with the nuclear weapon.[46]

In the context of this passage Butterfield provides no supporting examples or historical narrative. Rather he offers these assertions as his own best distillation of things he has learned from the study of the relevant history. They represent, presumably, his own wisdom on the matter.

The second kind of maxims are those Butterfield represents as the wisdom of the eighteenth-century aristocrats and royalty who created and preserved the European states-system that he admires. Although he cites no eighteenth-century sources of the maxims, he suggests that we might find them in writings on international law, works by publicists, diplomatic memoranda, and parliamentary debates. He quotes no maxims taken readymade from the texts of the day, but rather seems to derive them himself by inference and implication from the practice of eighteenth-century diplomats and rulers.[47]

The maxims that excite him most pertain to the international order, especially to the limitation of war and the security of small member states. He introduces each maxim with a generalizing attribution, such as "it was long ago realized that," or "our predecessors . . . were familiar with the maxim that," or "it was realized even in the eighteenth century that." The keystone maxim is this:

> if there is to be an international order, all the members of it must have a real interest in its preservation.

The second is this:

> no power ought ever to be allowed to become so desperate . . . that . . . it would pay any price for revenge, even if this meant pulling the whole house down and destroying itself along with the rest.

And the third:

> an international order can never be allowed to remain static . . . , but is subject to violent upheaval if its machinery merely serves to freeze the status quo.

The fourth:

> a victor should not provoke undue resentment in the vanquished party.

And the fifth:

> reformers should move prudently, so as not to be responsible for goading the vested interests to desperate action.

Butterfield goes on in this manner, maxim after maxim, creating a system which he nowhere finds in the eighteenth century, but which he attributes to eighteenth-century diplomats and politically minded people. He calls their reliance on maxims "the science of the preservation of a civilized order," and "what was really a scientific kind of diplomacy."[48]

The system of maxims that Butterfield lays out, disconnected from the historical analysis of eighteenth-century texts and practice, seems tangibly unhistorical when placed next to historical studies of the period. As science, the scheme of maxims, which he wishes the powers-that-be to apply in his own day, sounds remarkably idiosyncratic when compared with twentieth-century social scientific renditions of international politics. We come to realize that we are witnessing the elaboration of Butterfield's own international politics. He situates himself in an idealized bygone era, and once again takes as his model the England of the Whig politicians whom he lauded in *Englishman and His History.* In doing so he underestimates, overlooks, or removes from this context the events which are contrary to his model. Most notably, he makes an exception out of the Seven Years' War of 1756–1763 in which certain powers sought to eliminate Prussia, he blames the twenty-five years of near continuous war surrounding the French Revolution and Napoleon on the work of "revolution itself," and he does not mention the dismemberment of the small state of Poland and the distribution of the parts among the neighbouring great powers.

Consistent with one side of his political morality, Butterfield emerges noticeably conservative in his general approach to international affairs. In this vein he directs all his social criticism against what he calls "international revolution." He dislikes any movement whatsoever in the modern period which upsets stable society, foregoes moderation, and prevents the slow ripening of the "imponderable" attributes of "civilized" life.[49] At the same time, however, the way he applies his model bespeaks the politics of the liberal-left of his day. His prescription for ending the conflict between the Western powers and the Soviet bloc is to abolish "ideological diplomacy," abandon the diplomacy of moral judgments, abjure the goal of the destruction of Communism as such, and construct instead an "international order" analogous to the European states-system after 1713 and 1815. He takes for granted that the Communist states are here to stay, and urges that so long as they exist they should be members of the new international order. They and all the other states of Europe as well as the states elsewhere derived from European sources, such as the United States, Canada, and Australia, would operate together within a "mechanically self-adjusting and self-rectifying" system. One wonders where he places, for instance, Argentina, Mexico, and Brazil, since they too are Europeanized states. The system would depend upon the shared commitment to preserve the international order and refrain from acts which provoked "wars for righteousness." Membership in the international order would move the Communist states past their revolutionary stage. They too would contribute to "the slow growth of reasonableness." He could imagine the order becoming worldwide as other states eventually absorbed European influence.[50]

Butterfield's ideas about international affairs alarmed some critics and sent thrills of new discovery down the spines of others. He drew attention from scholars, politicians, and news magazines. On one side, Stuart Hampshire, H. G. Wood, and Maurice Reckitt, among others, asserted contra Butterfield the notion of "a scale of relative evil," on which the sins of Hitler or Stalin and other militaristic dictators would rank worse than the mistakes of Chamberlain, the idealistic British prime minister, or the foolishness of the Americans. Martin Wight accused him of creating a false image of eighteenth-century diplomacy, given, for instance, what the system did to Poland. Apparently Butterfield roused little support for his version of diplomacy as sheer mechanics and technique. Before the book was published, C. A. Coulson, Professor of Theoretical Physics at the University of London, urged him to drop the idea of "scientific diplomacy" as being an inappropriate use of the term "science."[51] In the United States, *Life* magazine featured the book as a prescription for "amoral diplomacy" that committed the disqualifying error of assuming that Soviet Russia was already a potential member of the renewed international order.[52] *Time* magazine had photographed him a year earlier for an article on the same theme that in the end never appeared.[53]

On the other side, Butterfield received ample applause. The *Times Literary Supplement* published a featured article that praised his warning against "wars of righteousness." Charles Webster took comfort that the British government under Churchill was following the precepts Butterfield preached. A. R. Burns congratulated him for puncturing the complacency of his public.[54]

However, none of his critics, for or against, followed his apparent separation of moral judgments from considerations of international affairs. He chafed at the repeated comment that his views represented "moral relativism" or "ethical indifference," and said so in a vigorous thought-essay. Reckitt suggested that his outlook on morality in international affairs was "becoming more and more idiosyncratic and even perverse." Reckitt's comments stung Butterfield, provoking him to break his rule that he would never respond to negative comments by a reviewer of one of his books. In a letter to Reckitt he protested that he was simply enunciating the main tradition in European diplomacy, not a view peculiar to him, and that he had no special sympathies for the eighteenth century, save their recognition of the maxims of international order and limited warfare. Butterfield felt gravely misunderstood.[55]

Isaiah Berlin, then a Fellow of All Souls' College, Oxford, was willing to debate Butterfield in Oxford on the question of moral judgments, but Butterfield resisted. Berlin sent Butterfield the text of a lecture he gave at the London School of Economics in which he expressed his dislike of Butterfield's views. This evoked a cordial but pointed correspondence between them, illustrating, if nothing else, the difficulty people had in deciphering exactly what Butterfield's views were. In response, Butterfield sent him *Christianity, Diplomacy and War,* with the warning that, because of the religious content of the argument, "parts of it must be nauseating to you and you will need to transpose as you read." Butterfield suggested that their disagreement might derive from "some deeper and more structural difference over a wider area of our thinking." Trying to name the difference he posed polarities: perhaps it was his own "extremely moralizing Old Testament basis," or, on the opposite side, maybe it was his willingness to set aside "my Old Testament views, my Protestant principles, my moral judgments" when engaged in "technical history," or, in opposition to all that, maybe it was his "New Testament view" that individuals "are more highly conditioned," and hence less morally culpable, than the making of moral judgments would allow for. Berlin phrased it this way: "But regarding the main issues I think that you are right—that we do start from positions which are not in the end reconcilable at all. You do believe that it is arrogant and ignorant and dangerous to condemn, denounce and fight campaigns on moral issues. I, on the whole, do not." He put himself squarely on the side of individual moral responsibility and human free will against what he saw as the suggestion of determinism and the absence of moral judgment in Butterfield's view. Butterfield chafed again, and in a seven-page, single-spaced reply expressed feelings of hurt about some of what Berlin attributed to him. He asked Berlin to change some wordings in his lecture, and sought to show by an elaborate argument how they really did agree on the basics after all. Berlin agreed to change the text, and affirmed his highest admiration for Butterfield, but said that he sensed that they were farther apart than Butterfield might now see them to be.[56]

Butterfield had presented himself in his writings as the detached technical historian, but it is not difficult to see him as politically engagé in favour of a particular line in foreign policy and even in domestic affairs. Sir Richard Acland, a Christian socialist member of Parliament, invited him to join the campaign called "Let's Start Waging Peace," a proposal to reduce the threat of war by rendering society more just and humane, especially towards the poor. Butterfield declined, describing himself as apolitical, a "mere historian" concerned chiefly with the past, and interested in the present only at the level of being "clear about certain principles." He took no thought that anything he might say would have any effect at all on contemporary life. He continued, "I sympathize with all you have to say even on social questions, but I would not feel able to call myself a socialist, though I should feel still less able to call myself a conservative." In foreign policy, he acknowledged that he feared both Russian and American imperialism and that he would like England to pursue a policy similar to India's: between, and sometimes in opposition to, both the great powers. Acland went away disappointed.[57]

Butterfield received another letter more to his liking a few months later. His little book attracted Reinhold Niebuhr of Union Theological Seminary and Hans Morgenthau of Columbia University, who interpreted his approach to international affairs as compatible with their own. They were then calling their approach "realist" in the sense that they regarded sheer power as basic to relations among states and the analysis of power as the starting point for worthwhile thinking on international affairs. The Rockefeller Foundation had begun to fund meetings of a small group in New York animated by Niebuhr and Morgenthau, whose purpose was to discuss theoretical approaches to international politics.

The letter to Butterfield came from Kenneth Thompson, an administrator of the Rockefeller Foundation. It was an invitation to become something like an overseas associate of the group. Butterfield showed interest. If he did not call his work theory, these others did, and it made him think that his discourse about maxims might be compatible with their work on the theory of international politics. In agreeing to participate, he acknowledged his conviction that "the frontiers of thought itself can be enlarged by this genuinely fundamental approach." He began to receive the papers of the New York group and soon met Thompson in Cambridge, but he saw no immediate prospect of visiting America, and nothing substantial came from the contact at the time. The episode indicated nonetheless that he was quite prepared to move deeper into international affairs and that his series of references to power, diplomacy, and war, capped by his book, revealed a genuine trend in his intellectual development.[58]

History of History

The second set of lectures distracting him from Fox and the *Concise Modern History* was the series on the history of historiography for the Wiles Trust in Belfast. The invitation to do the lectures came in May 1953, but his involvement with the Wiles Trust ran back at least to October 1952. He had largely drafted their statement of purpose: "to promote the study of the history of civilisation and to encourage the extension of historical thinking into the realm of general ideas." The lectures were to be both research-based and connected with more general historical reflection. Faced with the invitation, he objected at first that he had nothing more to say befitting the lectures' purpose as he had helped define it, but he later agreed when he thought of giving his "interim conclusions" on the history of historiography.[59]

A lengthy synopsis of his topic, which he drafted in January 1954, read like a manifesto. Vellacott was cheering him on. He proposed to play the missionary whose aim was to convert people to the study of the history of historiography as a subject. Coincidentally, the BBC was asking him to prepare a series on themes similar to his "Acton and the Massacre of St. Bartholomew." He jumped at the idea of adapting the lectures for broadcast after the event, to be followed by publication as a book. He would speak with Kingsford, with whom he now said he felt "on very intimate terms," and try to persuade Cambridge University Press to take on the book. The whole sequence deliberately replicated the process he fell into with his lectures on Christianity and history.[60]

Butterfield's scheme unrolled as he hoped. He presented four lectures in Belfast over a four-day period in November 1954, under the nondescript academic title "The Study of the History of Historical Scholarship." Butterfield had proposed those words as the subtitle. During four subsequent weeks in late November and December, he broadcast a condensed version over the BBC, with the bland title "Man and His Past."[61]

The Wiles Trust quickly made him a trustee, and he served the fund for twenty years. The university at Belfast awarded him an honourary doctorate in 1955, his third. Kingsford did get the Press to publish the four Belfast lectures as a book, released in October 1955. At the request of the Press's marketing interests, the title again changed, this time to something more aggressive, *Man on His Past,* with the academic title from Belfast attached as the subtitle. The subtitle referred to "historical scholarship" instead of the less recognizable "historiography," the term Butterfield used consistently in the lectures. Butterfield convinced CUP to add two previously published pieces as chapters five and six. These were his studies of the origins of the Seven Years' War and the massacre of St. Bartholomew. The book was studded with footnotes, making it his first book published from lectures to carry the visible signs of research. He managed also to append six sets of extraneous excerpts from Acton's notes in the Cambridge library. Much of this scholarship was due to all that work in the archives with Eve Bogle. The additions expanded the material from 140 pages to about 240 and gave the book the appearance of a miscellany.[62]

Looking for unity in retrospect, Butterfield suggested that all but one of the chapters related to Acton. In reality the Acton thread is longer than he admits, since Acton appears in every chapter, as does Ranke. We are not surprised. He actually bolstered the Ranke presence at the last minute when he substituted "Ranke and the Conception of 'General History' " for a lecture he intended to give on the underlying ideas of modern historiography.[63] In Butterfield's vision, both Ranke and Acton, along with the historians of the University of Göttingen, whom he also studies, belong to what he calls the German historical school. His emphasis on this tradition gives unity to the book, even as it also creates the impression that German historians, to the neglect of many other historical traditions and sources, are the real progenitors of historical study in "its modern form."[64]

The preliminary sketch of his topics, as well as the preface to the book, gave the appearance that he would plunge deep into the waters of the philosophy of history. His primary purpose was, he said, "to describe and illustrate the rise, the scope, the methods and the objectives of the history of historiography." From the very first, however, he made it clear that he remained the historian, even when he considered general questions about the nature of the field of study whose merit he applauded.[65] In the actual lectures, at each stage in his text, he would raise a general point he wished to make by saying how some historian, and frequently several, had talked about it before him. He would let his audience know what he favoured or promoted by the way he put his points and by the commentary he added on the margins of the history as he went along. He was offering the history of historiography as a subject of study as well as a method of discourse. His approach was bound to irritate philosophers, but it could speak well to historians.

Butterfield had already worked for a long time on the history of historiography, both as subject and as method. He himself dated his interest to the invitation to tour German universities in 1938 with a lecture on the history of the Whig interpretation of history. *Englishman and His History* of 1944 contained a greatly expanded version of that lecture. His foraging in Acton's notes since 1946 ensured his continuing interest when he saw how completely Acton relied on the history of historiography.[66] But we can trace his interest back much farther, at least to his undergraduate days at Peterhouse, between 1919 and 1922, when he learned to talk about "historical-mindedness" and "interpretations of history." His first book, *The Historical Novel* of 1924, and *Whig Interpretation of History* of 1931 were both historiographical and included elements of what he was now calling the history of historiography.

The origins of the Seven Years' War and the massacre of St. Bartholomew displayed his new attention to the history of historiography as a method. The theme of the Bartholomew massacre connected with his new research on his master, Acton, and his unflagging obsession with Acton on moral judgments. The theme of the Seven Years' War, the war George III inherited when he ascended the throne, belonged to his eighteenth-century studies and his classic dependence on diplomatic history, and we are not surprised when we remember that his other master, Ranke, made the Seven Years' War the subject of a book in 1871.[67] By November 1945, for a lecture in Dublin, he had probably converted his approach from straightforward diplomatic history to the analysis of the history of the historiography of the subject.[68] The theme assumed a new look. In his hands, the Seven Years' War appeared particularly analogous to the war of 1914–1918 and blended into his resistance against "blaming" the Germans for the origins of the two world wars in his lifetime. He returned to the topic several times thereafter, culminating in his Durham lecture in 1951 and chapter 5 *Man on His Past* in 1955.

The Seven Years' War served as something like a laboratory for developing his own approach to the history of historiography. He quickly went on record with a strong pronouncement against mere histories of historians or histories of history books, and in favour of progression to a higher stage of historical analysis of historical science as the only truly acceptable version of the history of historiography. By *Man on His Past* he was casting his studies of the Seven Years' War and the Bartholomew massacre as models of the right approach.[69] He had long advocated narrative history as normative, and he had urged historians, as practitioners of historical science, to engage in detailed documentary research, coupled with analysis, collating the findings from overlapping series of documents. In *Christianity and History,* from 1948 and 1949, he had added a distinct layer to the duties of historical science, namely "the work of historical reconstruction" whereby historians connected the detailed "facts" together into "episodes" in order to create the continuous narrative. Over time, he said, new "facts" usually forced the rebuilding of the "episodes." He presumed that, however long it took, however tortuous the route, and given enough time, hard detective work, and debate, the process would issue in renditions of particular episodes which received near-universal agreement by good historians, no matter what their religion or politics.[70]

The two new studies demonstrated how he saw the history of historiography working. He retraced the process by which historians had built and rebuilt each episode. He covered centuries of historical study of each topic by successive historians as he analyzed the shapes and counter-shapes which historians gave to particular historical episodes. He showed how they connected and reconnected multitudes of individual details, uncovered new details, and relinquished old details found wanting. In each case he held to his presumption that the historians would eventually get it right, exactly reconstructing the events as they had happened. He would, as he put it, "show how the enquiry developed, how the facts were established and how the story came to be assembled."[71] The concept of the "reconstruction" of episodes became the centrepiece of a proposed distinctive method for the history of historiography.

Butterfield sets up his history of the treatment of the Seven Years' War by historians as an answer to a single question. He means to test the validity of an accusation made by one party to the events, Frederick the Great, king of Prussia: did a serious conspiracy against Prussia exist in 1756, as Frederick claimed, and hence was Prussia provoked to invade Saxony that August by a genuine threat to his monarchy? Posing a question like this permits Butterfield to test the traditional version of the origins of the war which blamed the onslaught on the Prussians. Butterfield ends by shifting the attention to Russia and Austria, and claiming that there was actually a conspiracy by these two powers against Prussia, that, of the two, Russia was the real culprit, not Austria, and that Prussia faced a genuine threat. He relieves Prussia of "war guilt," and mirrors his handling of Germany and the First World War. It is easy to recognize his own politics at work in support of better political attitudes towards Germany and German scholarship.[72]

The analysis turns on repeated references to the established "facts," what "we now know," what is "now clear," and "the truth," contrary to what earlier historians thought was the case. He constructs his history of the subject on the analogy of the three-stage model of his history of science: the pre-Copernican stage, the Copernican stage of transition, and the scientific era as the world's "adult stage." He prepared his readers in the preface and on the very first two pages of Man on His Past for the scientific analogy, where he acknowledged that he regarded the history of historiography as really "a sub-section of the history of science." He apparently considered his Wiles lectures as the complement of his lectures on the origins of modern science. And like his Origins of Modern Science, where he set up "modern science" as the destination of all previous attempts at "science," here he places historical study "in its modern form" at the end, with the final reconstruction of the episode—what "we now know"—as the undoubted terminus of historical inquiry into the origins of the Seven Years' War.[73]

The differences between the model and his statements of the method are striking, however. As important as his single question may be, it touches only a few salient details out of thousands upon thousands of important details that comprise the episode, and even if he is sure about these few items of diplomatic relations and war, there remain all the other diplomatic and military details, and all of their interrelationships, not to mention all the nondiplomatic and nonmilitary factors involved. His version of the tale emerges one-sidedly Prussian, and relies excessively on the work of German historians to the neglect of wider and more diverse scholarship. In his eagerness to relieve Prussia of guilt he settles too quickly on one culprit, neglecting even Austria as the co-conspirator with Russia, and omitting his usual emphasis on the complicatedness of things and the general sharing of responsibility for common events.

The three-stage vision of progress towards finality appears inadequate when we learn that there are repeated "relapses" and "regressions" and that the most recent period, the twentieth century, displays one long regression, and when at the end he withholds clear support for the reconstruction he has argued is the destination of by then two hundred years of historical study. Against his own teachings, he reads history backwards and turns earlier historians into "precursors" of later ones and thanks certain earlier modes of historical study for bringing us "to the very brink of modern world." We may doubt the "scientific" character of the whole process when he awards highest praise to Ranke's version of the events which he says Ranke achieved by his "genius," "hunches," and "sheer insight," not by careful research, examination, and reconsideration of all the documentation.[74]

Butterfield's study of the Bartholomew massacre sets Acton's as well as Ranke's analysis of the mass killing of French Protestants in August 1572 within the history of the treatment of the topic. Butterfield uses this highly controverted episode to demonstrate the value of the history of historiography as a method. His choice of the massacre as his case demonstrates once again how much his moral and religious sensibilities connect with those of Acton and Ranke. Perhaps more important for him personally, the massacre becomes a test case for assessing the interplay of Acton's science and Acton's ethic of moral judgment. Butterfield recapitulates Acton's own method. He examines how historians had answered the question of whether the Catholic queen of France, Catherine de Medici, had premeditated the massacre or decided upon it suddenly, and whether the Catholic Church and even the papacy were implicated. Butterfield is determined to practice the microscopic research technique he was applying to Fox, and to retrace Acton's research and thinking on the subject "inch by inch." He mimicked Acton himself and recorded all of Acton's relevant notes and writings, arranged them by historians and themes in chronological order, constructed lists of Acton's arguments and the counterarguments, and read the principal historians and documents Acton had seen, in French, German, Italian, and English.[75]

In his study Butterfield lays out no less than five conflicting versions of the episode during the first two hundred years: Protestant, Catholic, Politique, Enlightenment, and French Revolutionary. Then came the struggle in the nineteenth century for the "scientific" version which would transcend the politics and religion he saw steering the previous reconstructions. He notes the appearance of still more versions, driven, he says, by ideology and religion. Eventually he signals the achievement of "the final story," which gives the true reconstruction of the episode.[76] The "final story" that emerges is simple: there was no premeditation and there was no Catholic or papal conspiracy. Butterfield then mounts the accusation that Acton allowed his religious and political opposition to authoritarian Catholics and his penchant for moral judgments to skew his scientific scholarship. Acton managed, overlooked, and underestimated evidence and steered towards the false conclusion that the massacre was premeditated. And in this Acton fell below the standard of Ranke, who had taken a more nuanced view of the material. He casts Acton, the early champion of scientific history in England, in the role of the polemicist undermining the scientific message. Even with his fixation on Acton, Butterfield is able to be the critic as well as the admirer. Roland Hill, in his biography of Lord Acton, remarked how Butterfield's handling of Acton took some of the edge off Acton's reputation as a historian. Happily for Butterfield, however, Acton eventually fell into step with the modern scientific movement, and late in life even converted to the "scientific" view of the Bartholomew events and accepted the "final story."[77]

As with his study of the Seven Years' War, Butterfield leaves behind a trail of doubts about his picture of the triumph of the "scientific" version. Once again, in spite of his rhetoric about progress through the stages to the "final story," his account actually draws no straight line rising into the scientific era, but rather presents what we might call a motion picture of alternative views over time. Butterfield's preferred "scientific" view turns out to be merely one view amid the plethora of views, religiously and politically coloured in his own particular way. His view favours inclusivity and charity, opposes intolerance and extremism, admits the treacheries and atrocities committed on all sides, and scatters the blame around a situation that looks like one of his "predicaments." His view is closest to that of the Politiques in the sixteenth century who wished to transcend the polarization between Catholics and Protestants, end the religious wars, and secure the peace of the realm. The finality of the "scientific" view withers away when he acknowledges that there is no positive evidence that shows there was no premeditation, and that competent historians are able to give the same evidence alternative readings. He ends the study with the admission that there are "loose ends" in the tapestry, "pieces left over" even after the jigsaw puzzle is completed. He tries to minimize the discrepancies, but he realizes they can render his version of the story invalid. In any case, as with the Seven Years' War, the question he investigates is only one out of countless interrelated problems that affect the histories historians write about the events of St. Bartholomew's Day in 1572, and the historical enterprise goes on.[78]

Yet in spite of the difficulties with Butterfield's accounts, his two studies showed what the history of historiography might accomplish. The examination of how historians over the ages handle and rehandle the same particular events can illuminate things people took for granted and open vistas never before seen. He does not limit the history of historiography to the reconstruction of episodes, however, even though the prominence he gives to his studies as models might appear to do so. We may observe, for example, that he did not categorically reject the value of histories of historians or histories of books, although he surely belittled them as disconnected chronologies, "mere ropes of sand," belonging to a "primitive stage."[79] After all, his protestations notwithstanding, his own pieces on the reconstruction of episodes were actually simultaneously histories of historians and books, or in the case of his handling of Acton, who published no history books, a history of scribbled notes and articles. Over many years, he spent an inordinate amount of time thinking and writing about the history of one historian, Acton, and even *Man on His Past* was largely the history of two historians, Acton and Ranke, who dominate the book. Even his own accounts of the rise of the field of the history of historiography as a whole and the rise in particular of the German historical school at the University of Göttingen followed the structure of tracing the books of one historian after another.[80] Butterfield, perhaps unwittingly, demonstrated the enduring attraction of the history of historians and their writings, even as he opened new avenues for study.

He promotes many other tasks for the history of historiography as he delineates the scope and utility of the field.[81] He catalogues a lengthy list in the opening lecture of the series. One could, for instance, examine the history of historical method, or the history of the concepts historians use, or the history of a particular theme, or the history of the influence of historical study on human history, or the history of the previous treatment of a subject one wishes to study. The strikingly new element on Butterfield's horizon at this moment is his notice that it is possible to study something as vague as the history of "historical-mindedness." He deliberately picks up the term from the student discussions in Peterhouse Historical Society thirty years earlier. Now he repeatedly stresses that the transformation in historical consciousness from the end of the eighteenth century to the end of the nineteenth century — to Acton — constituted a historical revolution in humane studies that paralleled the scientific revolution in the natural sciences in the seventeenth century, or, as he put it, "the Scientific Revolution in historical study."[82]

In his most missionary mode, Butterfield argues strongly that the history of historiography can help historians in multiple ways. For instance, he endorses the mandate he found in Acton's notes: "Teach to look behind historians, especially famous historians." He prescribes it as the antidote to the effects of a historian's unrecognized assumptions. He especially urges the benefits of investigating the history of any theme the student undertakes for study. It could unpack the content and display the problems of even seemingly routine areas of history.[83] Perhaps his most startling historical contribution, one rooted in research, pursues this very lead. He applies a procedure he advocated in *Origins of Modern Science,* examining the antecedents and milieux of the big names in a field. He argues that the little-known historians of the University of Göttingen between the 1760s and the 1820s were the real founders of the German school of historical scholarship, a full generation and more before Ranke and Barthold Niebuhr, the famous names commonly deemed the originators.[84] The range of Butterfield's suggestions about the history of historiography pointed to far wider applicability than even he named. As with everything human, one can examine historically any aspect whatsoever of historical study and historical discourse, and the effects can extend to everything the historian does as historian.

Man on His Past surely does feature the history of historiography, but there is another agenda on Butterfield's table which he seems to take for granted and does not specifically acknowledge as central to the purposes of the book. He continues to campaign on behalf of his characterization of historical study as a science. He uses the term "scientific history" often enough, but the term he puts into service in passage after passage is "technical history." He touts "a precise piece of straight diplomatic history" as the preferred training for research students instead of "vague and indefinite subjects" found in the "marshy fields of intellectual and social history." We detect his will to play the dissenter, even — or perhaps especially — in the face of his explicit awareness that he enjoys almost no support among historians for his emphasis on historical study as a matter of technique and "precision-work."[85]

He both opens and closes the published version of the four Wiles lectures with assertions about history as a science in the special sense of "technical history." In between, the language of "technical history" dominates his discourse about historical study. At the very start of his exposition of the history of historiography Butterfield sets "technical history" at the centre. He asserts, "Indeed it would appear that in this field the primary object of study has always been the development of a more technical form of scholarship, the rise of a more scientific history, and the progress in the critical treatment of sources." This he says even though his argument about the scope and utility of the field indicated the presence of very many objects and purposes, none obviously more primary than all the others.[86]

The very first page of the book twists Acton in his direction, and has Acton sounding like Butterfield on history as technique. He quotes Acton from an undated note in the Acton papers: "Each science has to be learned by a method of its own. But also by one and the same method, applicable to all, which is the historical method." In Butterfield's paraphrase this becomes: "In this connection he [Acton] pointed out more than once that there were now two ways in which every branch of science was to be studied: first by its own forms of technical procedure, and secondly by an examination of its history."[87] Eventually, he chides Acton for not really accepting "technical history" in the sense that Butterfield means it.[88]

Then the fourth lecture, a substitute lecture inserted at the last minute, closes with a rousing affirmation of "technical history." Keith Sewell has analyzed the concept at length. In remarkably blunt statements, contained in one paragraph, Butterfield makes it unmistakably clear, in virtually the same language he has used for years, that, on one side of his being, he remains the positivist who has deviated not one millimetre from his convictions about historical study as "technical history": "The truth is that technical history is a limited and mundane realm of description and explanation in which local and concrete things are achieved by a disciplined use of tangible evidence. I should not regard a thing as 'historically' established unless the proof were valid for the Catholic as well as the Protestant, for the Liberal as well as the Marxist." And it is not only the individual "facts" collected by historians, but also the interconnections among the facts within the "events" they construct that are covered by the same strict division: "When the events have been laid out by the technical historian, they can be taken over by the Catholic or Protestant or atheist — they are equally available for Whig or Tory. Each of these can add his judgments and make his evaluations; and they can at least begin by having some common ground for the great debate that still lies open to them." The technical historian thus has "eliminated in advance" the deepest issues of religion and politics, indeed of life, without implying that they are thereby "in fact eliminated from life."[89] Butterfield gives the impression that this was Ranke's view, but on closer reading we notice that the association with Ranke comes via Acton who, while not holding to the view himself, "imputes" the view to Ranke. We may be sure the view is Butterfield's, who would like very much for it to be Ranke's as well. But as Butterfield also notes, Ranke's histories did not blank out his politics, religion, and moral sensibilities.[90]

Instead, we recognize in Butterfield's statements a view distinctively his own, marked by the same dualistic polarization of technical history over against religion as well as politics — indeed the historian's life — which his discourse continuously exhibits. He still overlooks the way his own religion and politics have shaped his own historical writing. The paragraph in which these statements appear seems almost gratuitous, a rude intrusion into a passage on Providence. We would wonder why he felt compelled to put the statements in at all if we were not grateful that he finally made explicit the assumptions about historical study that colour everything he has told us throughout the book. Because of the wide distribution of the book, new readers encountered Butterfield on technical history for the first time, and, for many, these statements became the authoritative exposition of his views about the nature of historical study. Pieter Geyl for one was shocked at Butterfield's neutered version of technical history which "eliminated in advance" the issues over which Catholics and Protestants, Whigs and Tories, Liberals and Marxists might disagree. On the contrary, Geyl argued, the historian does not come to the research only as a technical historian, but as a human being who eliminates nothing in advance. The shock Butterfield gave him confirmed, he said, "my own belief that history cuts down to the deepest issues of life."[91]

As if to mitigate the starkness of his apparent elimination of the historian's deepest being from the historian's study of history, Butterfield quickly adds a second paragraph to his representation of historical study. It is a succinct statement of his notion that people can think about the same historical events on three levels. The passage gave wide circulation to the suggestion he had published in "God in History" in 1952 in an obscure newsletter of the Church of England Youth Council. Michael Hobart realized the importance of the suggestion and constructed his analysis of Butterfield on history and religion around the notion of three levels. Geyl felt the power of Butterfield's perennial dualist drive, and missed a level of his discourse, reducing the scheme to "thinking at two levels." The idea is that people can view an event on one level as an act of human responsibility and free will, in which people make their own history. They can also regard the same event on another level as subject to historical laws, conditions, and necessity, in which people find their actions remarkably circumscribed and predictable. They can then see the same event on a third level as a work of Providence, in which they themselves serve as participants in a divine drama. For Butterfield, all three levels are true at the same time about the very same events. The notion is highly unitive and non-polarizing, reconciliatory and inclusive, giving impressions precisely opposite to that of his language about technical history. As apparently different as the two paragraphs are, they both come from the same person at the very same moment, and they both recall tendencies present in his discourse for decades.[92]

The passage trails off into a rhapsody about the poet, the prophet, the novelist, and the playwright, who, he insists, "command sublimer realms than those of technical history because they reconstitute life in its wholeness." And we feel his dualism at work again. He recurs to the outlook about the superiority of the literary and the religious over the historical which we first saw in his *Historical Novel* forty years before, and which he reiterated in *Christianity and History*.[93] He also elevates the project of general history which he lionizes throughout the book, polarized over against technical history. Juxtaposing the two, his language about technical history turns pejorative: "we will lock ourselves in some local topic, or burrow in a special field, or isolate a single aspect of history." General history arises as the liberator from this myopia: general history "must preside over the works of multiple specialists," and "carry historical thinking to a higher power."[94] He urges the necessity of general history in order to honour the utter interconnectedness of events, a notion which long ago he picked up from Ranke, and which again he credits to Ranke's genius. In the case of Ranke, as with Butterfield, the thinking that leads to general history continues onwards to religion, notably the Christian religion, and we can detect the Christian impulses driving the work of both historians.[95] Butterfield chides the exemplars of the tradition of history teaching at Cambridge and the *Cambridge Modern History* inspired by Acton for the narrowness of their vision of general history, which limited the focus to Europe, above all western Europe. He notes with approval that the aim of both the Göttingen historians and Ranke was "universal history," which in some sense meant world history, but at this moment he holds back from adopting the desire for world history as his own.[96]

Now we come full circle. Butterfield's project of the history of historiography is at the same time a project of general history. In his eyes, the history of historiography is a mode of general history. In his account of the field, in *Man on His Past*, the historians who most called for the history of historiography — the Göttingen historians, Ranke, Acton — acted out of their desire for general history and gave themselves to historical thinking. Butterfield joked about the end of historians whose work was out of date: "The death which the outmoded historian has to suffer is more complete and pitiful than ordinary death." But we can be sure he had on his mind what it takes for a historian to last. In revealing moment he wrote, "The historian who survives seems to be the one who in some way or other has managed to break through into the realm of enduring ideas or gives hint of a deeper tide in the affairs of men." Historians do not last because of the merits of their "technical history." They last because of their historical ideas and their contribution to general history.[97]

Although he might hesitate to admit it, his account of the history of historiography as general history seems to undermine his own claims for what "technical history" delivers. There would seem to be no lasting "final story," and no lasting "technical historians," but only further historical study and the generation of different historical ideas.

Butterfield won the respect of most, but not all, reviewers for the value of the history of historiography, and his rediscovery of the Göttingen school of historians evoked loud praise, especially for the way he demonstrated the usefulness of Acton's dictum to look behind the famous historians. But there were voices, including Eric John, Duncan Forbes, and Arnold Toynbee, raised against his apparent award of first place in historical scholarship to the Germans, to the neglect of the French and English and Italians and the rest of the world, and against his infatuation with the German historical school's obsession with minutiae in the manner of German state bureaucrats. There were objections, from the *Economist*, the *Tablet*, and others, to the exaggerated place he was giving to Acton. Some commentators, including the *Times Educational Supplement* and G. M. Young, complained that his style of writing was tortuous, and Ernest Nagel spoke as a philosopher against the unclarity of his statements of his own views, making it difficult to be sure of exactly what he meant to say. It seemed that just about everyone, however, bowed to Butterfield's learning and to the vitality of his historical thinking. Some took inspiration from his call to view wider vistas and sought to approach their fields with broader perspectives. Eric Sharpe, for instance, evoked Butterfield's appeal for breadth as a counterpoise to severe specialization and as support for a more ambitious rendering of comparative religion.[98]

Given his argument in *Man on His Past,* we can picture where Butterfield might wish to head in his own future work. In a curious way he had undermined the importance of "technical history," at least the sort executed as he defined it. His comprehensive and highly detailed technical history of the life of Fox could seem distinctly unappealing and unpromising. Perhaps *The Concise Cambridge Modern History* held the promise of general history that endures. Perhaps more writing about historical thinking would be worthwhile and lasting. His general historical thinking had already produced significant results, including *The Whig Interpretation of History* and *Christianity and History. Origins of Modern Science* had helped define the history of science as a field of study, and *Man on His Past* seemed well on the road to defining the history of historical study as an academic field. Why not further thought about history?

Time of Trial

Very few people at the time realized the unthinkable magnitude of the personal trauma that Butterfield passed through in 1954 as he prepared for his lectures on the history of historiography. The sequence of events during that year rolled one shattering experience on top of another. Butterfield's style of handling wrenching emotional events seemed to be to wall off the personal turmoil from his work as historian. The style could make his actions and words about the crises seem crass. He seemed actually to live out in his daily existence the dualism of his own thought about the clean detachment of "technical history" from life.

The first crisis Butterfield seemed to find unspeakably awful. His son, Giles, committed suicide on 15 April 1954.[99] By the spring of 1954 Giles had spent nearly two years at Peterhouse. He had begun with the intention of doing engineering, and may well have felt considerable need to find his own direction in an environment in which his famous father and older brother were both in history. His studies at Peterhouse did not succeed. The college Tutor, Denis Mack Smith, became aware from talking with Giles that the young man was distraught, and took the liberty of letting Butterfield know about it. There was a history behind his emotional condition. While at Leys School he was known to run away sometimes and be brought back by the police, and the headmaster recommended consultations with a psychiatrist in order to deal with other recurring symptoms of instability.[100] By March 1954 he had dropped out of Peterhouse, expressing the desire to work as a technician behind the scenes in the theatre. He went away to Perth Repertory Theatre in Scotland, but was expecting a call-up from the Royal Air Force.[101] On April 3 he received the notice of his call-up, the next day he wrote a note describing his gifts, he returned home on the 10th, and on the 15th he died. Giles used the gas stove in the kitchen of the Butterfield home on Tenison Road to kill himself. The funeral at Wesley Church was the 20th. The family went away to the sea to begin recuperation.[102]

On 26 April Butterfield was back at work answering his correspondence and trying to feel as if things were normal after having, as he calmly worded it, "suffered the loss of our second son in rather tragic circumstances." On the 28th Butterfield found Giles's note about his gifts, and then began the reconstruction of the episode of his son's death. It seemed as though he were dealing with another problem of technical history. Two months later he was talking about still dealing with "a period of considerable anxiety" and perhaps "getting the whole family nicely on its feet now." Such descriptions masked any signs of disturbance. Butterfield's language at the time was the very image of cramped emotions. He showed the same unwillingness in his historical writings to say a hard message straight. He let no one publicly see his pain. Unlike Toynbee after his own son's suicide, he left no clue to his agony in his writings. Eve Bogle was the one who conveyed the news of Giles's death to Vellacott, the Master, and Mack Smith, the Tutor, because, she said, "he couldn't face the college." Bogle said that she was not surprised that Giles committed suicide. Butterfield found it possible to confide in Brian Wormald, and Wormald felt that Butterfield was perhaps more humane after the tragedy. Butterfield's sister, Edie, came from London for the funeral, and the two became closer thereafter. Vellacott and the Fellows apparently were helpful, and certainly not judgmental, taking it as one of those tragedies that happens in the best of families. Butterfield, looking back on the event twenty-five years later, acknowledged that Giles's death was the most difficult moment of his life. This he uttered in a voice hardly audible. Trying to keep life and technical history apart had been costly.[103]

The second trying episode touched his professional life directly. David Knowles, not Butterfield, received the Crown appointment to the prestigious Regius professorship of modern history. The Regius chair fell vacant with the retirement of J. R. M. Butler. It was widely believed in Cambridge that Butterfield would be the choice. He was the senior modern historian, already the holder of the professorship in modern history, and probably possessed the widest and most substantial reputation of any historian in Cambridge. He had just recently been elected president of the Historical Association, the largest historical society in Great Britain, with his term of office to commence in 1955. He was already receiving honourary doctorates, the first from Aberdeen University in 1952 and the second was coming very shortly from University College, Dublin. But to everyone's shock, including his own, the Regius professorship went to his friend and colleague at Peterhouse. Knowles was not at all a historian of modern history, but a medievalist and current occupant of the chair in medieval history. The Crown passed over Butterfield. His friends commiserated with him and commented about the indiscretion of the *Manchester Guardian* in noting Butterfield's defeat. Butterfield, probably truthfully in some naive way, said he was very happy that Knowles received the honour and that he did not understand the reference in the *Guardian*. Nonetheless, Butterfield now had to wait a second time for the promotion that appeared to be his due. For years to come people commonly addressed him by the title of Regius Professor, so sure they were that the chair belonged to him. It was a sign of the character of the two men that no estrangement occurred between them. Others noted that Butterfield seemed to exhibit no signs of resentment or jealousy. For nine years, from 1954 to 1963, the two members of Peterhouse and spiritual confreres presided together over modern history in Cambridge, the one as Regius Professor and a Roman Catholic, the other as Professor of Modern History and a Methodist Dissenter. The combination would have dumbfounded Action.[104]

The third difficult experience involved his oldest son, Peter. Peter was pursuing a course of action that Butterfield could genuinely approve, but that could not fail to add to the stress of the year. Peter had completed Peterhouse in 1953 and was fulfiling his national military service in 1954. He had undertaken preparations with the intention of conversion from the Methodist Church of his upbringing to the Roman Catholic Church. Part of the context was Brian Wormald's simultaneous move towards the Roman Catholic Church. Wormald, a Tractarian Anglican and former chaplain of the college, was Butterfield's protége and intimate friend. Peter's conversion was expected before the end of the year.

Of course, Butterfield could not have foreseen that his third son, Robin, still a teenager, would in due course emerge from his undergraduate years at Oxford University as a convinced non-Christian. All three sons chose paths unlike his own.

There is profound sense in which, after the suicide of his second son, the loss of the Regius chair, and the expectation of his first son's pending conversion, Butterfield made a new start during the summer by throwing himself into the writing of his Wiles lectures for Belfast on the history of historiography, the series that became *Man on His Past*. It was a new lectureship, and a new field, primed for new thought on history. He gave the lectures on 4–9 November, the product of trauma and tragedy, and readers of *Man on His Past* do well to remember that. He returned to Cambridge on the 10th.

Then a further traumatic event intervened. Paul Vellacott died prematurely. For thirty-five years, from the time Butterfield came up to Peterhouse at age nineteen to encounter the awesome Temperley, Vellacott had been his confidant, his protector, his father away from home. Now Vellacott too was gone. Butterfield wrote the obituary for the *Times,* which appeared on the 16th. The funeral was the 25th.[105]

On the 17th Knowles presented his inaugural lecture as Regius Professor, which Butterfield attended without the slightest hint of chagrin or stress. Exactly one month later, on 17 December, Peter was received into the Roman Catholic Church by baptism.[106] David Knowles wrote Butterfield a moving note about the conversion: "I hope and pray this is a wise decision—that is, that it comes from a real desire to know and serve our Lord, for in that case he will be happy, and I cannot but feel happy for his sake. But it must be something of a suffering for you and his mother, in a year which has not been without times of testing for you." So much loss in so short a time.[107]

On top of all this, Butterfield received the shock of his life from the Fellows of Peterhouse. After a meeting of the Governing Body on 6 December, the Fellows approached him informally with the proposal that they elect him Master in succession to Vellacott. The plan was for him to serve as an academic Master, and leave the running of the college to the Fellows, devoting less time than Vellacott to the duties of the office. The idea was for him to use the time to write. Everything in Butterfield's system braced him against any plan to make him Master. Not long before this offer the Governors of Birkbeck College, University of London, had approached him about allowing his name to stand as Master. He replied with one of the least obscure letters he ever wrote. All his aptitude, he said, was confined to teaching, writing, and research, and that was how he had concentrated his time. He concluded, "I am not suitable for the post." The Peterhouse Fellows prevailed, however. Perhaps he saw it as an alternative to the Regius chair, for had he not failed to received that honour, they would not have thought of him as head of a Cambridge college. By a notable turn of events, David Knowles, who got the Regius chair, was instrumental in shaping the process which brought him to the top of his college. The result was swift. Before December was out, he accepted the plan of the Fellows to make him Master of Peterhouse.[108]

Master and Aggression

Management, not Scholarship

In January 1955, Butterfield became the forty-fourth Master of Peterhouse, the latest in a line that ran back 670 years. He remained simultaneously Professor of Modern History. He was the fourth historian among the six Masters in the twentieth century, the fitting successor to Temperley his teacher, Vellacott his protector, and Ward his personal link with Acton. He was the first Methodist head of the college and possibly the first Peterhouse Master with working-class origins. He accomplished his striking rise into the upper reaches of the gentlemanly class entirely by means of academic merit, scholarship money, and success as historian. He was a prime example of "the scholarship-boy," what Maurice Cowling, speaking of Raymond Williams, called "one of the most important cultural categories in England" in the twentieth century. The local newspaper in Keighley took proud note of the feat.[1]

On 19 March Pamela and he moved from their home on Tenison Road where they had lived since the late 1930s into the architecturally splendid early eighteenth-century house on Trumpington Street that served as Master's Lodge. His status and income increased appropriately. He had ascended far above the worker's stone cottage of his birth. The long front room upstairs became his office and study. The walls were oak panels. The fireplace was large. The furniture was solid. The windows looked onto the attractive college scene across the street: the gates, the porter's lodge, the chapel, the courtyards, the Fellows and students coming and going. The college provided the house-keeping and arranged the cooking at a level of quality suitable for the Master's entertaining. Ethel Wolfe left the Butterfield's service and ran a bed and break-fast in her flat near the college to which Butterfield would send visiting scholars. Eve Bogle continued as his private secretary and research assistant, still paid out of his own purse, and worked with him in the Master's Lodge. Pamela and he retained ownership of their house on Tenison Road, which they rented out for income.

Butterfield loved Peterhouse and took delight in his new position. Sitting in his new study he remarked to Eve Bogle, "If I die tonight, I shall have been Master of my college." Butterfield was fifty-four, but his youthful face, his slight frame, and his approachable manner made him seem, disconcertingly, forty.

The contrast between the social status of the position and the personality of the man was notable. He was quiet and unassuming, simple in his tastes, and a leveller in his social manners who treated Fellows and college servants as equals. People around him remarked that he did not become the least bit snobbish and never presented himself as anything other than what he was. They did notice, however, that he tidied up his dress and put away his bright red shirts upon becoming Master. He was seen wearing a bow tie in place of the more ordinarily bourgeois long necktie. In his approach towards food he was virtually ascetic, and towards drink still a teetotaler and reluctant social consumer of ginger beer, which some people in ignorance mistook for ginger ale. The only obvious deviation from the abstemious life, and the one thing people commented on repeatedly, was the cigarette that still hung perpetually from the lips of this relentless chain-smoker. Ved Mehta, a journalist for the *New Yorker,* who was blind, depicted Butterfield with the cigarette so vividly that Butterfield asked him with astonishment how he did that. Mehta recounted the episode, "I didn't say that he talked as if he had a cigarette there—that would be cumbersome. I converted a sound impression into a visual image." Butterfield continued to have no inclination towards sports, which put him at some disadvantage when relating to those undergraduates for whom intercollegiate sports were nourishment. He worked even longer hours. Bogle recalls that he deliberately trained himself to do with little sleep. He admitted to her that before going to bed he would relax in a very hot bath, reading a detective thriller. The librarian in the local public library would put new detective novels aside for him. By now he had acquired a baby grand piano, which he played frequently for relaxation, often after lunch or after mid-morning coffee. Bogle, one of the few people who heard him play often, observed that he "was a very fine amateur pianist and sight-read extremely well."[2]

By statute he ceased to be a college Fellow. As Master he held considerable power over the college, but he proposed to act as the dissenter in the heart of the establishment. He strove immediately to make his exercise of power informal, and to bridge the chasm that opened between the Master's Lodge and the rest of the college. Nonetheless, Pamela and he very quickly experienced living in the Lodge, for all its loveliness, as isolating, a house without neighbours whose imposing character seemed to oblige those who entered to behave according to the rules of proper manners. His sense of the loneliness of the position mounted when he began to notice that people tended not to speak freely with him. He complained of losing touch with the real situation. Ironically, however, as Master he again became involved with the life of undergraduates, perhaps more so than when he held supervisions in the years before his professorship.

The college over which Butterfield presided still favoured history among the senior members. There were eighteen Fellows plus the Master. Seven of this number were professors, a greater proportion of professors than any other Cambridge college at the time. Four of these professors were historians — Postan, Brogan, Knowles, Butterfield — and they numbered four out of the ten professors then listed with the Faculty of History.[3] With Wormald, Mack Smith, and R. W. K. Hinton also on hand, the total number of historians in Peterhouse added up to seven. Hinton had become a Fellow in 1952 and, like Wormald and Mack Smith, was in some sense a former pupil of Butterfield. Barker, Tawney, and Commager remained as Honourary Fellows. Such an array induced Trevelyan, looking on from Trinity College, to pay tribute to "the remarkable group of historians at Peterhouse."[4] The number rose to eight historians in 1958 when E. A. Wrigley was elected a Fellow to handle geography and history.

It was at least open to question whether such a formidable academic presence, especially concentrated in one area, worked entirely to the advantage of the students. Tim Voelcker, a Peterhouse undergraduate, charged publicly that the preeminence accorded the Fellows in the affairs of the college established an "oligarchy of dons." Their interests came first, their rooms occupied too much of the college space, and their world was too segregated from the undergraduates.[5]

Butterfield's college remained among the smallest of the nineteen attached to the university, with 150 three-year undergraduates, 25 fourth-year undergraduates, and 20 research students, for a total of less than 200 students.

Butterfield, as professor, still held no supervisions with undergraduates, but even as Master he accepted additional research students, both from Peterhouse and from other colleges, including between 1955 and 1959 H. A. Mac-Dougall and John Derry. The new undergraduates for the year 1954–1955 amounted to 2.4 percent of the new matriculants in the whole university. Among the three-year undergraduates, history had the largest enrolment of any field in the college, comprising about 20 percent, but the students in math, natural sciences, mechanical sciences, and medicine formed a majority of about 55 percent.[6]

A statistical survey of the three-year undergraduates taken not long before Butterfield became Master filled in other aspects of the college profile. In religious terms, about 35 percent of the students identified themselves as practicing members of the Church of England, about 12 percent were distributed among various Nonconformist churches, about 8 percent were Roman Catholics, one was Jewish, with most of the rest at least nominally linked with one of these groups. About half of the students said they attended the college chapel regularly or occasionally. In politics, 41 percent called themselves Conservatives, 14 percent Labour, 6 percent Liberal, and 30 percent not identified with any party, although probably tending Conservative, in addition to three students who claimed to be Communists and one a Fascist, with the remainder not responding. Economically, about 30 percent had their university expenses paid fully by their parents, and most of the rest had their expenses paid nearly in full by their parents with the remainder paid by a small grant. In social terms, most dressed in corduroy trousers with college jacket and tie, most belonged to college societies, most played some sport, and most drank beer. The picture presented an all-male student population skewed towards the natural sciences, the Conservative party, the Church of England, the well-enough-to-do, drink, and sport. Butterfield matched precisely none of these dominant tendencies in the student population over which he presided. Nonetheless, such had been the changes in himself and Peterhouse over the years that it was easier for him to be Master in 1955 than it had been to be a new student in the Peterhouse of thirty-five years earlier.[7]

The new Master entered into his duties with greater enthusiasm than he was at first willing to admit. Perhaps the position touched some deep affinity within him for authority and political manoeuvre, contrary to his dissenter and would-be apolitical self-image. It quickly became evident that the plan for him to act as an uninvolved scholar-master would fail. His research on Fox stopped entirely, and he ceased to work on his general history, the *Concise Cambridge Modern History*. He discovered that he could not hold himself back from the daily administration of the college, and that he actually liked

274 Master and Aggression

committees. He constantly consulted with the people involved, took advice on what seemed to be every decision, wrote letters late into the night to clarify a point with someone or correct a fault he committed during the day. He found himself a member of more committees than ever, and chairing more of them than before, both in Peterhouse and in the wider university. He chaired the Governing Body of the college, met regularly with the heads of the other colleges, joined the Council of the Senate of the university, and represented the university on the Board of Governors of Wesley House, a position he held from 1955 to 1961. He quickly earned a reputation as a forceful chair, a fighter at one moment for what he thought right, and a mediator or umpire at the next, hoping to draw out of people what they thought.

His social life became intense, as an endless stream of scholars, distinguished visitors, research students, and undergraduates paraded through the Lodge, whether for lunch or tea or dinner or dessert. He accepted countless invitations to visit other colleges. In 1955–1956, for instance, he attended the annual sumptuous feasts in St. John's, Sidney Sussex, Trinity Hall, Jesus, and Trinity, and the annual dinner at Wesley House, in addition to the Cosin and Perne feasts in Peterhouse. On each occasion he ate virtually nothing and drank nothing but ginger beer and water. He participated in numberless ceremonies, and when the queen came to Cambridge he attended the lunch for her at Trinity College. In order to overcome the estrangement between senior members and students in the college he frequented innumerable events in student societies, from the Boat Club breakfast to the meeting of the Wine Society, though he cared about neither rowing nor drinking.

He regularly participated in college chapel worship, which, while no longer the proper centre of the corporate life, involved more students than any other single activity in the college. His participation included receiving Holy Communion according to the Church of England liturgy. Even so he also attended the same Methodist Church and, as was his long-standing custom, sat quietly in a pew near the back.

He displayed evident sympathy for the students, and his attentions were well received. In spite of his stated desire, however, he seldom appeared for lunch in the Combination Room, traditionally the preserve of the Fellows in any case, and not the Master's domain. Besides lacking time for scholarship, he only barely kept up with his professorial lectures on European history from 1494, three times weekly in all three terms. For the first time in his career, he repeated his lectures from old manuscripts.[8]

Already ardent for the college system, he became ever more passionate, and profusely attributed his own achievements as a historian to the vitality of the collegiate tradition. He began to write about Peterhouse. Soon after becoming

Master, he started a memoir of the college and produced a lengthy manuscript, "Peterhouse in Temperley's Time." He never finished the memoir.[9] He did complete a brief history of Peterhouse for the Victoria county history of England, for which he conducted an extraordinary amount of detailed research in the college records. It was a critical history, not hagiography, referring to many facets of the college — economic, administrative, religious, geographical, academic — much as he once recommended for the history of Europe.[10] Before his election as Master, he had served for ten years as secretary of the Peterhouse Society, the organization of graduates of the college. He wrote four consecutive booklets reporting to the alumni on the current history of the college. These publications reflected the same well-roundedness he advocated for historical writing — statistics about students and Fellows, portraits of what he called college "personalities," and a record of college activities large and small. The series ended when he stopped being secretary, but as Master he addressed the members of the society annually on the progress of the college. Later, when he was about to step down as Master, he wrote another booklet summarizing the affairs of the college during his period as head. And, from what he reported, his readers could tell that he felt they had been good years.[11]

If being Master of the college as well as Professor of Modern History were not enough, he soon began his three-year term as president of the Historical Association, 1955–1958, which he entered into with almost as much zeal as the mastership. He was an authentic believer in the activities of the association. He strongly endorsed the practice of bringing together university lecturers and professors with schoolteachers and general readers in order to improve the quality of history teaching, the history curriculum, and general historical knowledge.[12] He had long participated loyally in the Cambridge Historical Association, and since his election as professor in 1944, and especially between 1950 and 1952, he had filled invitations to lecture in local association meetings all over Great Britain. Now as president he felt duty-bound to accept more invitations. During 1955–1956 he fulfiled some forty engagements, and during the next two academic years a further twenty-five each year, in places such as Norwich, Wolverhampton, Coventry, Bournemouth, Welwyn Garden City, Ealing, Southampton, and Croyden. In addition he lectured in universities around Great Britain and in the three foreign countries he most frequented, Ireland, Germany, and the United States.[13]

His new round of special lectures seemed to evoke no new historical thought. He pulled out old papers on the history of science, another on Leonardo da Vinci, and recycled bits of one paper he had already published.[14] He collected his old thoughts on method for a new lecture, "The Historian and His Evidence," which he repeated in several local branches of the association. The paper offered a neat survey of the rules he would like to follow when handling evidence as a historian. All of his advice pertained to diplomatic and political history and to the documents generated by government figures and diplomats. He urged the use of critical judgment in handling the differences between, for example, memoirs and the direct acts of government. He entirely omitted any references to social, economic, intellectual, demographic, or geographical materials. He exhibited none of the awareness of other aspects of life that he practiced in his histories of Peterhouse past and present. It was as if he had reverted to the problems he confronted thirty years before when working on *Napoleon's Peace Tactics* under Temperley, or as if the documents about George III's intentions which he dealt with during the 1940s, leading to *George III, Lord North, and the People,* represented the whole range of sources involved in historical research.[15] His presidential address to the Historical Association in 1955, "The Role of the Individual in History," reiterated points he had made many times over about the validity of approaches to history which stressed the influence of individual people as well as approaches that noted laws and conditions in history. He even projected his points onto the works of his two masters. He concluded, "In the richest kind of historical writing, like that of Ranke and Acton, both of the two types of history which have been described will be found to be combined, so that there is interaction between them." It was his old polarization of individual free will and impersonal necessity, and, although he spoke of their combination, he gave priority to individuals and the modes of history, particularly diplomatic history, which he believed were able to focus on individual people.[16]

Immediately upon taking office as president he faced preparations for the fiftieth anniversary of the Historical Association, founded in 1906. The association had asked Grace Stretton, a research assistant for history projects in the British Foreign Office, to write a pamphlet about the history of the organization. Her draft was revised by her supervisor, W. N. Medlicott, the same Medlicott with whom Butterfield had tangled over "official history" a few years earlier. When Butterfield saw the draft he thought it inadequate and intervened. He rewrote the text along lines compatible with his own historical thinking. The kinds of changes he introduced provided almost a checklist for the approach to general historical writing, as distinct from diplomatic history, that he had been advocating for some time. He transformed it into a critical history of the association as a whole, instead of a hagiographic chronicle of official acts, names, and local branches. He included portraits of the important people, added more quotations to show what people were thinking, integrated happenings inside the association with trends in the general history of historical thinking and history teaching, and constructed a chronological narrative of events, putting special emphasis on the beginning of the association. He had, he explained, a "prejudice" for "no end of detail about the minute origins of things." Stretton politely agreed to the changes. The work appeared anonymously as *The Historical Association, 1906–1956,* with a foreword by Butterfield as president.[17]

Simultaneously, and at his instigation, the *Times Literary Supplement* invited him to act as adviser for a special issue timed to coincide with the jubilee of the Historical Association. He was the de facto editor of an oversized special insert in the *TLS* for 6 January 1956, entitled *Historical Writing.* Seventeen historians discussed the historiography of their fields during the last fifty years in England. Butterfield supplied the integrative opening essay, and wrote "Clio in Council" as the leading article for that issue. At the jubilee event itself in January 1956, Butterfield, as president, addressed the meeting at the University of London.[18]

Looking over the previous fifty years of historiography in England, he identifies two significant trends. On one hand there are new types of special history and new historical problems. He has in mind especially the buildup of studies in economic history and the history of science, and the debates about the origins of modern capitalism and the deeper structures of a period or society or institution. These he welcomes in themselves. On the other hand he acknowledges the tendency to diminish the role of political and diplomatic history in the construction of general history. Here he responds with a yes and no to the trend. Yes, the relations between states are not adequately captured by the materials located in Foreign Office archives, and yes, the conventional kind of political narrative "seems less fitted to serve as a condensation of 'general history' than ever before." But no, we cannot allow the economic historian "to take charge of general history in its entirety, presiding over the whole and turning his particular subject into the Queen of the Sciences," and no, the accounts of underlying structures cannot be made to do more than set the stage for an epoch. He continues: "When French Revolutions and Napoleons rear themselves up, the personal and political narrative must indeed provide ribs for any reconstruction that we make. The two kinds of history must be married. There is a chronological story, but it turns out to have deeper layers than we previously realized, and it has to be thickened with a heavier load of expository material."[19]

The discrepancy was great between, on one hand, the range and diversity of his *TLS* material, his jubilee presidential address, and his treatment of the association's history, and, on the other, the restricted range of topics, documentation, and examples discussed in his lecture "The Historian and His Evidence" and his presidential address "The Role of the Individual in History." It was apparent in his utterances from the end of 1954 to early 1956 that, talk as he might about viewing history as a multifaceted study of societies and civilization, his actual orientation remained fastened on the narrative and research styles of diplomatic history and the centrality of individuals even in general history. He felt, he said, that he must be "the last person in the world to go on believing" such things. At the very moment when he stood as president of Great Britain's Historical Association he was terribly conscious of the isolation of his attachment to the field into which he was socialized as a historian under Temperley. Butterfield's historical thought seemed to be stalled along with Fox and the *Concise Cambridge Modern History*.

Aggressive Historiography

Butterfield's work on Fox was dormant, and he only barely seemed aware that a shift was occurring in his scholarship on the eighteenth century. From his commitment to the full-scale biography of Fox, he had moved into the general questions about the reign of George III, and from there he was moving onwards to the historiography of George III. The trend led from detailed historical research to general thinking about history. After his Wiles lectures and *Man on His Past*, he was taking practical action to win acceptance for the history of historiography. He was calling for scholars to produce histories of the historiography of their special subjects, as a prod to new thinking and an instrument for disentangling historical investigation from partisanship.[20] He succeeded in persuading the Cambridge Faculty of History to erect an exam subject on "the history of historical science," construed as a branch of the history of science, and secured Brian Wormald's agreement to do the necessary lectures.[21] He also guided some of his research students into doctoral dissertations on historiography, practicing what he preached in *Man on His Past* about using that field, along with diplomatic history, as a suitable teacher of "precision-work" in historical technique.[22] All of his efforts surrounding the jubilee celebrations of the Historical Association featured the importance of the history of historical writing. Nothing was more significant to his cause than the special insert *Historical Writing* in the *Times Literary Supplement* which he had stimulated and arranged, discussing the last fifty years of historiography in England.

Butterfield's work initiated what became a chorus of historians over the coming years who wrote the history of historiography in Butterfield's key. Three exemplars among these stand out. Felix Raab acknowledged Butterfield's inspiration as well as his place in the history of the interpretation of Machiavelli in England in *The English Face of Machiavelli: A Changing Inter-*

pretation, 1500–1700. Donald Kelley thanked Butterfield for stimulating the thinking that led to his book *Foundations of Modern Historical Scholarship: Language, Law, and History in the French Renaissance.* Joseph Levine credited Butterfield with identifying the topic of his work *Humanism and History: Origins of Modern English Historiography.*[23]

Butterfield had already taken his own advice and begun as early as 1946 to apply his historiographical method to the material about George III. He sought to learn how historians had worked over the evidence, the events, and the personalities having to do especially with the early years of the reign. The issue as Butterfield defined it concerned the apparent increase of royal power soon after George III become king in 1760. The question was whether the new king had intentionally pursued policies that enlarged the power of the throne against the aristocracy on one hand and the House of Commons on the other, and thereby pushed the British constitution off balance and subverted British liberties. Just about everybody accepted such a formulation of the problem.

Butterfield accumulated over the years hundreds of pages of notes on large-size paper on the history of the historiography of George III. He wrote several long drafts on his findings, most of the work being done by 1952. This study paralleled his review of the historiography of the Seven Years' War as well as his inquiry into Acton's historiography in the Acton papers. He had come to realize that he differed greatly from the general approach to history taken by Lewis Namier, Professor of Modern History at Manchester University and the paramount figure in the field. Namier had established his reputation in 1929 with his landmark book, *The Structure of Politics at the Accession of George III,* and was since 1951 the director of a monumental cooperative project on the history of Parliament in the eighteenth century, housed at the Institute for Historical Research in London. Butterfield considered using his Wiles lectures to examine the theme of royal power and Parliament during the first years after the accession of George III, but hesitated because, he admitted, he was not ready to take on what he came to call "the whole Namier school." G. R. Elton later observed that after 1945 Namier's views became generally accepted, indeed, he quipped, "became embalmed in a general adulation from which few dissented."[24]

It is plausible to think that Namier's apparent domination of the interpretation of the English eighteenth century may have felt to Butterfield like the effects of a "Namier school." Indeed, J. H. Plumb, who talked with Namier from time to time, thought the notion was not silly. Said Plumb, "Namier hated Butterfield, a hatred that deepened year after year and became a kind of obsessional rage. He spoke of him with sneering bitterness, arranged for his books to be savaged by anonymous reviewers and wrecked his reputation whenever opportunity offered." Even so, Butterfield might have responded once again simply as the dissenter, and rested content to challenge Namier's historical interpretation. But his treatment of Namier's ideas took a surprising turn. At least since receiving so many bad reviews for *George III, Lord North, and the People,* reviews which he blamed on people friendly to Namier, he carried around uncommonly ill will toward the man. By 1955 he was privately imputing bad motives to Namier and accusing him of "being unfair whenever possible," ready to "pounce on the slightest slip."[25] He claimed that, by means of the massive project he directed on the history of the British Parliament in the eighteenth century, Namier was attempting the "trick" of "merely trying to establish a monopoly . . . where he could even confine the use of papers to his own disciples." In Butterfield's eyes, Namier was committing an offense against a cardinal norm of scholarship, open access to the archives. In a crescendo of hyperbole that ran back to the 1930s, he declared, "I have assumed for twenty years that I would never get any concessions from Namier."[26] Namier was, he said, "an old enemy of mine in the academic field." The vehemence of the accusations and the sheer bad tone of his words directed against Namier sound in sharp contrast with his repeated injunctions against moral judgments against persons and his general admonition to show charity to all people. What he came to say of someone else might be said of his own approach to Namier: "It is almost as though [Namier] were a personal enemy."[27]

It is perhaps from this period in the mid-fifties onwards that we encounter from Butterfield more than just the occasional expression of animosity towards others, more than we have heard him say in the 1930s and 1940s. We begin to notice about this time similar bad tone and strong words about certain people in letters of evaluation he was asked to write in connection with their applications for professorships, lectureships, and fellowships. A few years later, in a lengthy unpublished essay on the achievements of historians close to him, he worded his criticisms in gratuitously unkind ways. About Trevelyan, who was in some sense a mentor to him: "some of his books seem to me to be rather weak." About Tawney, with whom he had become associated in Peterhouse during the war: "Tawney could not help turning his studies into propaganda for the Labour cause." About George Clark, who also had helped him much: "I do not regard him as a powerful mind." Perhaps these were no more than the sort of cutting remarks lightly thrown at each other by academics in Cambridge. Perhaps they reflected a changing style of criticism, a new kind of candour, a stark reflection of his admission that "I, too, seem to relish the game." Such remarks became common in Butterfield's rhetoric, and other people noticed the change and began to wonder.[28]

By March 1956 he had another long draft ready on the historiography of

George III, possibly intended initially as an article for the *Cambridge Histori-cal Journal,* and then by July a new short draft for delivery to the Anglo-American Historians Conference in London.[29] Soon afterwards, however, Butterfield's plans took a sharp turn. The *Cambridge Review* invited him to review a new book on Lord Chatham's administration of 1766–1768 by John Brooke, a young historian who worked closely with Namier on the history of Parliament project. The book annoyed him. He attributed the praise it was receiving to the presence of a preface — he labelled it an "imprimatur" — by Namier. While noting positively the massive research that supported the book, he charged that by concentrating on the underlying structures of political behaviour and on the baser motives of the politicians, Brooke's method "at-omized" the material, missed "the very things that governments and parlia-ments exist to do," and excluded the ideas and nobler purposes of the people involved. Butterfield issued his by now familiar call for the creative combina-tion of structural analysis and chronological narrative about individual per-sons. Ironically, he himself had long downgraded even the existence of states and governments, which he considered little more than abstract nouns cover-ing the work of countless individuals in and out of office.[30] The *Cambridge Review* soon asked him to follow with a review of *The Rise of the Pelhams* by John B. Owen, another historian particularly sympathetic to Namier. This book he praised lavishly for achieving the integration of structural analysis in the style of Namier with political narrative, but then he criticized Owen for neglecting the writings of previous historians and presuming originality in his findings where earlier historians, working from hunches and insight, had al-ready anticipated him. Again ironically, Butterfield's own *George III, Lord North, and the People* had received sustained criticism that the book lacked references to other history books and other historians.[31]

It is not clear what precisely drove Butterfield to take the next step. The conjunction of the superabundance of his research notes, the gargantuan scale of his written drafts, his vigour to promote the merits of the history of histo-riography, the undertone of his hostility to Namier, the praise heaped upon the Brooke volume which he considered substandard, the feeling that he needed to rise to the defense of historical scholarship, his need during a dry spell in his productivity to publish another book — all these factors would have inclined him to write something long. Perhaps at the end, the pressure from Collins, his publisher, to give them a new book pushed him onwards. Collins had been pressing since January 1952 for Butterfield to give them some manuscript as "a by-product of the great *Fox* opus."[32]

Early in 1957 he sent an aggressive article to *Encounter* entitled "George III and the Namier School," published in April, "as a sort of kite to see whether it will draw any fire, all of which is a preliminary to a full dress attack, which possibly he [Namier] may even be aware of by now."[33] Then on 1 April he sent Collins his typescript of the book. By the end of summer he sent a synopsis of the book to *History,* the journal of the Historical Association, whose editor had requested an article from him on some theme of his choosing. In the middle of this sequence Cambridge University awarded Namier an honourary doctorate, and Butterfield declined to have him at Peterhouse.[34]

The text he sent to Collins was not a continuous and integrated work, but, like *George III, Lord North, and the People,* a patchwork of writings, and he was still writing the final section intended for the volume. The first part was the lecture "The Historian and His Evidence," which he had taken to so many branches of the Historical Association during the last two years. The second part was a long and detailed review of the treatment of George III by historians until the 1920s, focusing entirely on the question of the intentions and consequent actions of the new king upon ascending the throne in 1760. Butterfield probably had put this piece together by 1952. The third part was a miscellany about historical method and Namier, shorter than the other parts, rambling, repetitive, evidently hurriedly written, even dishevelled, containing passages expanded from his book reviews of Brooke and Owen, and other comments on R. R. Sedgwick. These, together with Namier, were the only names Butterfield listed as members of "the Namier school," the phalanx he feared marching through the historical profession. The fourth section was to be a long study of one of his old topics, "England and the French Revolution, 1792," which he thought he would complete by the end of April. This piece seemed to have no organic connection with the others, and was left over from his George III studies from the 1930s and 1940s. The publisher took Butterfield's suggestion to go ahead with the first three parts, and showed interest in using the remainder for another book. The text of the book as published simply stopped after the last sentence of part three, leaving no ending, no conclusion.

Collins raced the material through production. *George III and the Historians,* a 300-page volume, was ready by late October 1957, in time for the new book season. It was his seventeenth book. There was, said Collins in triumph, "a paucity of serious historical writing this year, and *George III and the Historians* should have the field almost to itself."[35]

When Butterfield saw the book, he was mortified. The advertising cast him as an "authority" on George III, the very thing he disclaimed in the preface, where he warned against the increasing tendency to defer to "authorities" instead of cultivating independent, critical judgment. He protested to Collins that he preferred to appear as "a poor David" before "this colossal Goliath who has such a squadron behind him."[36]

Worse, he seriously misquoted Namier, and he committed, or failed to catch, scores of other mistakes in the text. He tried to explain to his publisher that the errors were due to his rush to finish the writing and get the book into print.[37] He later admitted privately that he had not carefully looked over the last third of the book, the controversial section on Namier.[38] His great error was to drop a section out of a quotation from Namier, making it appear as if Namier were trying to inflict a strict discipline on a "school," when what Namier actually wrote said the exact opposite. The quotation was taken from a sentence in Namier's foreword to Brooke's *Chatham Administration,* part of the series edited by Namier for Macmillan Publishers under the general title *England in the Age of the American Revolution.* Namier wrote:

> And while the *History of Parliament* is a cooperative undertaking in which the individuality of the collaborators merges into that of the team, every volume of *England in the Age of the American Revolution* will be individual work, the author's garden plot on which he labours.

When Butterfield took hold of the sentence, he reversed Namier's meaning:

> One of the more recent works of the Namier school is the volume by Mr. John Brooke on *The Chatham Administration, 1766–68.* It is part of the series which is being produced under the title "England in the Age of the American Revolution," and which, according to Sir Lewis Namier, is, in one respect at least, "a co-operative undertaking" so that "the individuality of the collaborators merges into that of the team."[39]

Butterfield's misquotation created a proof-text for "the Namier school," the derogatory label he tried to sew on Namier, Brooke, Owen, and Sedgwick.

Butterfield wanted *George III and the Historians* to demonstrate at length the merits of working out the history of historiography of a major theme. His analysis of the historiography of George III, especially the early years, is thorough, researched based, and intriguing, and he demonstrates the profusion and succession of interpretations, beginning contemporaneously with the events. As in his other historiographical forays, he presumes that the emerging medium was "technical history" and the goal was the emergence of what he would call the "final story." More pointedly, he wishes for the book to initiate a public debate among historians focused entirely on the "higher regions" of the questions of historical approach and method that he believes separated Namier's history from his own.[40] To accomplish this aim, he inserts passages on historical method here and there into the midst of longer passages of exposition of Namier's work. He insists that he in no way wishes to deny that Namier's work was original, in both its methods and its findings. He expresses a certain admiration for Namier's *Structure of Politics at the Accession of*

George III. He also claims to appreciate aspects of Namier's project on the history of Parliament. It was a gigantic undertaking involving a team of researchers who were engaged in the orderly collection of information on every single member of the eighteenth-century body, drawn from every conceivable source, with the goal of compiling systematic and compact biographies on each one. Consistent with his long-standing modus vivendi, Butterfield wants to see the truth in Namier's work and incorporate the best of Namier into his own thinking. His chief complaint against Namier is the appearance of one-sidedness in the interpretation of political history. Butterfield charges that Namier concentrated too narrowly on the underlying structures and hidden forces involved in the political events and not sufficiently on the individual personalities as agents. Namier overrated the operation of baser motives in politics, such as the pursuit of social status, personal gain, family connection, and career advancement, and tended to overlook or obscure the functioning of higher motives, such as commitment to political principle, defense of liberty, and devotion to public responsibility. The slant in Namier's results, he thinks, was due partly to the sheer detail of the investigation, which could obscure the larger picture, and partly to his preference for a certain type of information calculated to disclosed the workings of the baser factors, to the neglect of the evidence which might indicate the higher intentions. Butterfield concludes that Namier constructed a version of the eighteenth-century world that stressed the irrationality of political processes, or, at best, the sheer self-interest of political leadership. On Butterfield's pivotal question about the intentions of George III in the early years of his reign, the effect of Namier's method, he says, was to accentuate the king's opposition to encroachments upon the constitution by Whig oligarchs, and hence to paint the king in more or less Tory colours.

Butterfield's antidote to Namier is the approach he had already advocated many times. He urges the combination of both narrative and structure, freedom and necessity, analysis of the deep processes and conditions as well as the story of individual actions, ideas, and purposes. The effect would be to produce a picture wholly different from Namier's of George III and the political world of the mid-eighteenth century. If the parliamentary debates and the letters of George III were taken seriously, he says, we would discover that the king and the politicans had, besides their selfishness, both rational purposes and noble ideals. The king in particular would emerge less partisan, less self-ish, and more devoted to the ideal of the "patriot king" who stood above the play of parties and acted according to what he took to be the well-being of the nation as a whole. Butterfield echoes a point he had been making since at least 1933 when he published a brief article "Bolingbroke and the 'Patriot King' " in the *Cambridge Review.* He then appends the complaints he had made against Brooke and Owen in his reviews of their recent books.[41]

The book certainly aroused discussion and generated controversy, but not about the "higher regions" of the questions of historical approach. The discussion focused instead on Butterfield's inadequacies. John Cannon called it "one of the most curious books of our time." By uncanny coincidence, Macmillan issued Namier's magisterial *Structure of Politics* in a second edition at the very same moment that Butterfield's volume appeared. Collins had failed to take notice of the pending event and seriously miscalculated the publishing season. There, under new books, sat Butterfield and Namier, juxtaposed. Reviewers compared Namier with the critique.[42] One reviewer after another expressed shock at Butterfield's misquotation of Namier. They cited his many inaccuracies, accused him of overdramatization, lamented the disconnectedness of the book, and complained about the unclarity of his writing, which made them unsure about exactly what the offenses were that he opposed.[43]

Just about everyone noted the inappropriateness of the label "the Namier school." Upon seeing the book, Professor Alfred Cobban objected to Butterfield's use of the term "Namier school" in a parallel article, "George III and the Constitution," scheduled to be published in *History,* the journal of the Historical Association which Cobban edited. Butterfield defended the term as an attempt not to appear as if he were attacking individuals. In the *Times Literary Supplement* he tied the notion of a school to those who followed the lead of a "giant" and who identified with a "system." But he quietly agreed to delete the offending label from the article. When the article appeared in February 1958, "Namier school" occurred only once, in contrast with its repeated usage in the book, and he substituted other, more respectful wordings, such as "Sir Lewis Namier and his followers," "Sir Lewis Namier and those who accept his interpretation," and "Sir Lewis Namier and Mr. Rodney Sedgwick," none of which are in the book. But the label stuck. Even thirty years later Ian Christie, who had sided with Namier at the time, felt obliged to defend the independence of the writers Butterfield may have had in mind.[44]

There were reviewers who expressed agreement with Butterfield's point that Namier was one-sided, or at least agreed that Namier could be understood as one-sided if taken to extremes, but none of these adopted Butterfield's case straight. Derek Beales, then a research student in Cambridge, gave Butterfield the most solid support he received in print at the time. Beales believed that Butterfield was right in the end on two of his primary points, that Namier undercut ideas in history and produced in effect a Tory interpretation of George III.[45]

Both Sedgwick and Owen reviewed the book. Sedgwick, who, ironically, had been Butterfield's examiner for the final undergraduate Tripos at Cambridge in 1922, itemized Butterfield's errors, and in a second review presented a plausible restatement of Namier's and his own intentions. In so doing, he demonstrated in practice that he and Namier did actually believe there were such things as intentions. Their chief aim was not to discuss intentions, however, but to submit some of the commonplaces about the eighteenth century to the scrutiny of exhaustive research and new methods. Hence, their work was not designed to present the whole picture. He challenged Butterfield to give his own version of the early years of George III, in distinction from the two views he had attacked, the Whig interpretation and now Namier's "Tory" interpretation.[46]

Owen also listed the errors, and then, after allowing that he may not have understood Butterfield correctly because of Butterfield's verbally "indirect approach," stated his feeling that only one criticism in the book might apply to him, namely the neglect of previous historians and, hence, his unawareness of when another historian had already made his points. He did not see the problem, however, since his interest lay with the evidence and what could be constructed from the evidence, and not with the second-hand thoughts and undocumented hints of historians. By way of counterattack, he expressed his belief that Butterfield's method of the history of historiography took historians on an unnecessary detour away from an understanding of the eighteenth century.[47]

Namier decided to reply. He sent a letter to the *Times Literary Supplement.* Under the circumstances, Namier could play the role of the senior scholar, and chide Butterfield for the misquotation of his words. He called on Butterfield to admit the error. Butterfield did so, but only after Namier's prodding.[48] Namier than magnanimously invited Butterfield to visit the "History of Parliament" project at the Institute of Historical Research in London. Butterfield accepted the offer at first, then wrote to postpone, and eventually set a new date a year later, but in the end never actually went to see Namier. Namier died in August 1960 at age seventy-two.[49]

George III and the Historians enabled Butterfield once again to show the scholarly benefits of the history of historiography. But, instead of demonstrating, as he thought, the twists and turns leading to the triumph of "the final story," he documented something else he did not notice, that the history of historiography recounts the ongoing career of diversity in historical interpretation without coming to an outcome that is good once and for all. Butterfield's version of the intentions of George III became just another account, and joined the two-hundred-year-long queue. His version remained consistent with the story he initiated in *Whig Interpretation of History,* "Bolingbroke and the 'Patriot King,' " and *Englishman and His History.* As Sedgwick let him know, he had discussed the Whig interpretation and now Namier's Tory interpretation, and the path was clear for him to lay out his alternative. He may not have gone as far as Sedgwick wished, but he had made enough of a start for us to tell where he was going. Within the history of the subject, Butterfield's interpretation could not long pose as the neutral offering of "scientific history." The effects of his politics and moral sensibility on his history were strong enough to mark his rudimentary version of the early years of George III as New Whig.

The mistakes as well as the animus against Namier guaranteed that Butterfield stimulated no authentic discussion of historical approaches to the eighteenth century. He realized that he had undermined his own case for critical scholarship. In what may have been the understatement of the year, he admitted privately that he had "made more howlers than I knew about." He had acknowledged publicly in the *Times Literary Supplement* that he misquoted Namier. After Owen's review, he decided to write a letter to the *Cambridge Review* against some of Owen's criticisms, and then let the world know in a rousing fashion that he had not "given away on the main point."[50]

Butterfield impeded historiographical discussion in another way as well. Besides the misquotation, he misstated the differences between Namier and himself. His persistent dualism and individualism misled him. It was not a question of individuals versus structures, ideals versus necessity, higher versus baser, with Namier dealing in structures, necessity, and baser things, and Butterfield championing the intentions, beliefs, and higher motives of individuals. Namier's method actually depended on dealing with individuals, and he operated by gathering certain kinds of detailed information on individuals who were members of Parliament. Butterfield's counter-complaint centered on individuals as well, and accentuated the need for other kinds of information about the very same individuals whom Namier placed on his list. Both knew about intentions and both also knew about nonintentional factors. In any case, both historians dealt with self-interest as well as with actions for the good of the realm. And neither historian noticed that the pursuit of family interests or advancement of career or increase of wealth may or may not be morally base, depending on how these things related to the totality of human relations and political action at the time. Moreover, neither historian possessed a strong concept of the state or Parliament. If Namier omitted the workings of political institutions and public office in his search for the impact of other factors, Butterfield's reduction of the state to an abstract noun induced him to treat the workings of the state merely by-the-way as he analyzed the lives of political individuals, most notably George III and, we might add, Charles James Fox.

Their difference might better be construed as a clash of historical methods and the aims of their projects, in addition to differences in their politics, not to mention personal factors and baser motives. Butterfield aimed to understand the ideas and intentions of certain political figures, while Namier specifically sought to understand the operation of factors other than those consciously known and intended. In the history of Parliament and in his *Structure of Politics,* Namier employed social and collective biography to understand certain political figures, while Butterfield favoured the study of their political activities and written statements. Namier favoured information related to each figure's wealth, status, family, career tractk, patronage, and so on, anything that allowed him to draw connecting lines from figure to figure on such social things. This in turn enabled Namier to disclose broader trends and unexpected connections among social factors and political consequences, relationships not perhaps consciously known to the people involved at the time. He and his co-workers looked everywhere to find the information they wanted, including the literary evidence. By contrast Butterfield privileged certain kinds of literary materials, especially parliamentary debates, royal correspondence, personal letters, political pamphlets, and, lately, historical writings. In these materials he looked for what the very same people said they intended, believed, and regarded as right.

Such differences in historiography were crucial, but they would not explain why Butterfield turned their differences into something sounding so personal. Their differences in politics may have been a factor. Butterfield named Namier's historical outlook as Tory, which according to Butterfield's concept of scientific history would be a damning intrusion. It would also clash with Butterfield's own, usually unadmitted, New Whig political outlook. Of possible baser motives, no hint of anti-Semitism rose to the surface, and in any case Namier had long ago converted to Christianity. Perhaps Butterfield felt Namier to be his competitor for control of the interpretation of the history of eighteenth-century England. Perhaps he felt jealousy of Namier's successes. Maybe he had merely locked into the trait Elton had suggested Namier exhibited, that he was "rather good at making enemies." Butterfield did not appear to follow his own advice, to look inside himself and ask why he threw such darts at another historian.[51]

The episode achieved the status of a historical controversy of great importance. In retrospect three decades later, however, Christie challenged the assumption on which the controversy turned. The problem was a mistaken construal of the power of two kings. There was no increase of royal power in the early years of George III since it now appeared to be the case that royal power had not declined during the reign of George II. George III merely continued to operate on the same level of power as his grandfather. The questions about George III's intentions or his hypocrisy, his long-term political policy or his arbitrariness, thus become quite secondary. It was all a tempest in a teapot. J. H. Plumb had already pointed out in 1969 that Namier had arrived at the same conclusion from a different starting point and using a different method. In *The Structure of Politics* Namier had shown that there was no royal resumption of prerogatives by George III, no Tory attempt to seize power from Whigs, and no Whig counterattack in defense of English liberties. Paradoxically, Butterfield and Namier jointly, by different historical methods, with different assumptions about human behaviour, and at about the same moment, had demolished the Whig interpretation of English history, and Butterfield had not noticed.[52]

In spite of the missteps towards Namier, Butterfield surfaced intact from the turmoil. Linda Colley, in her biography of Namier, conceded that Butterfield was "one of his shrewdest critics." *George III and the Historians* took on service as the most extensive analysis of the historiography of the subject. In the long term he won general acceptance for his main criticism of Namier. One historian after another agreed with his observation that Namier's approach belittled the stated beliefs and purposes of the politicians in eighteenth-century England, or, as Ian Christie put it, that "Namier was over-inclined to attribute statements of political attitudes to hypocrisy." G. R. Elton entered the point into his general disquisition on how to do political history properly.[53]

Butterfield generated the public perception that he was the chief commentator on Namier. Twice after Namier's death, in 1961 and 1964, the BBC turned to him for broadcasts on Namier from their national platform. Ved Mehta of the *New Yorker* called Butterfield's first broadcast on Namier "his funeral oration." Butterfield again praised Namier, as in the book, but then relaxed his accusation not even a little that Namier was constricted by his own technique, so that he left "high politics" and statesmanship out of history. He still allowed just a little of his hostility to Namier and Namier's method to show when he suggested that Namier's career after 1930 was misspent, and expressed the wished that, instead of directing team research on the history of Parliament, Namier had written "rather on great statesmen" or produced "a narrative of higher politics" in the reign of George III. Butterfield reviewed the biographies of the members of Parliament from 1754 to 1790, edited by Namier, when they were published posthumously in 1964 with the assistance of Brooke. With one hand he distributed praise for the work as "a magnificent piece of reference," but with the other hand he offered the damning judgment that the biographies were not history. While the teamwork that lay behind them was admirable, he said, the volumes lacked genuine insight. Insight issues from the individual historian working alone, not from a team of semi-official personnel. Then he quipped that, with these volumes now available, historians no longer need to fear that "a whipper-snapper" on the Namier team might catch them making mistakes about some member of Parliament. Brooke wrote the BBC to object to Butterfield's name-calling against the historians and research assistants on the team at the Institute of Historical Research, but Butterfield did not reply, and did not withdraw the comment.[54]

Butterfield summarized his attitude in 1962 in response to a request from the executive secretary of the American Historical Association to identify "the most exciting historical study (or studies) now going on in Britain." He placed foremost the work of Namier and those associated with him: "You will realize that though I recognise the new insight that comes from this kind of thing, I think it liable to be dangerous on the one hand and infertile on the other hand, unless conducted by people capable of the same kind of intuitions as were necessary for distinguished historical writing in the days when, shall we say, the school of Ranke prevailed." Curiously it sounded as if Butterfield was conceding Namier the victory, and signalling his awareness that his own kind of history in the spirit of Ranke was not going to be taken for granted in the future.[55]

Also curiously, as their controversy faded into the past, people began to view the two as if they were on the same side. Both came to be seen as critics of the Whig interpretation of history. Butterfield's criticism had long been obvious. Namier's, on the other hand, was less obvious. It could be argued that his focus on the seemingly aimless shifts in alliances due to the operation of self-interest, patronage, and place, and his denigration of purpose, intention, ideology, and policy in the politics of the eighteenth century rendered the Whig interpretation meaningless. For example, both J. C. D. Clark and Annabel Patterson, for different reasons and with different effects, classed the two together as responsible for the presumed defeat of the Whig interpretation of history.[56]

By 1957 Butterfield held in his hand a typescript for what might have been part four of *George III and the Historians*. Perhaps in the heat of the action of April 1957 he began to expand his text, and, by the time the first book appeared in the fall, he had in hand 250 pages towards another book, this one on *England and the French Revolution, 1792*. He was telling Collins to expect the completed volume within eighteen months. Five years later he was still saying that he intended to finish a book on 1792 which would give equal weight to

Fox, Burke, and William Pitt the younger. The typescript continued to sit in the pile of projects that he had on his desk.[57]

The Namier episode was a disaster. Besides the turmoil, it evoked no new thoughts about history. Butterfield's analysis of the treatment of George III by a long succession of historians represented older work, rooted in his interests during the 1930s. His chief point against Namier amounted to a repetition of his old message to mingle structure and narrative in order to produce balanced history.

Several ways to take his scholarship were opening before him in 1958. He could work more carefully on themes of historical thought and historiography, a road he had by now walked a long time. There was still his interest in Christianity and history. Perhaps he might take up Sedgwick's challenge to construct his own version of eighteenth-century events, his alternative to the Whig historians and the Tory Namier. This was also a road he had walked a long time, and it would lead him back to the biography of Fox, or perhaps to work in earnest on the early reign of George III. And there was also his recent involvement in topics in international relations, the sort of things he broached in *Christianity, Diplomacy and War*. Meanwhile, he remained the Master of Peterhouse.

World Ideas, World Politics

Ideas of History

In the wake of the Namier debacle, Butterfield followed his by now normal course and accepted what other people put before him. He confounded those near to him who observed how adept he was at engaging several themes all at once.

Paramount among these themes was further study of historical thought and historiography, which he followed at the invitation of other people. Quite apart from the excitement surrounding Namier that occupied what little time he had for scholarly work during his mastership, his discourse on historiography took a startling new turn in the work he threw together on the side. The initial medium of his new thought was a pair of lectures at the Hebrew University in Jerusalem in December 1957. Following these he presented an abbreviated version of the Jerusalem lectures at the London School of Oriental and African Studies in January 1958. This was the very moment when the Namier turmoil was exploding all around him.[1]

Prior to this moment, his chief interests in historiography pertained to questions about historical scholarship, particularly history as technique, the criticism of documents, the reconstruction of episodes, and the handling of themes by successive historians. His new discourse pursued the broad road of ideas of history and world history. These were the sorts of things suggested by the notion of "historical-mindedness" which he mentioned in *Man on His Past,* or by the passages in *Christianity and History* about "the whole human drama." There were indications that he was becoming more aware of the importance of cultures and peoples outside Europe. The connections were strong between his thinking about religion and the new thoughts he entertained about world history. Perhaps without being precisely conscious of it, he began to explore the vague and misty area of questions about what would lead historians to differ profoundly. One historian, such as Namier, decides to stress chiefly the details of vested interests and ulterior motives, while another, such as himself, insists on adding a person's ideas to the picture and drawing in all the lines of connection with general history.

The first hints of new thinking about ideas of history surfaced in an incidental lecture in December 1955 to the London School of Economics, "History as the Emancipation from the Past," a lecture Butterfield scarcely had time to write. He discusses there what it means to possess an idea of the past which enables people to free themselves from domination by the past. He brings into the open an assumption he had carried with him at least since the 1920s, the idea that there are "stages" in general history as people made "progress" in the course of the ages from the "barbarian" and "primitive" stage of society to the "civilized" and "adult" stage we call civilization. In the lecture he articulates the notion that people in the "primitive" state lived within tightly knit societies characterized by "herd spirit," deference to authority, and subservience to the past. They could easily believe that the customs and rituals they honoured were an inheritance from a Golden Age in the remote past when their all-powerful ancestors lived in harmonious communication with the sacred and invented the practices they perpetuated. People would "advance" towards civilization when they generated the spirit of individuality, adopted the critical outlook, and developed a sense of history, particularly when they gained the knowledge that they themselves could change the common inheritance and create novel culture. In the lecture Butterfield focuses on the issue of the appearance within a culture of an idea of history which enabled people to reconstruct the past and aim to transform the future. His notions are rudimentary and amount to little more than side comments about a stupendous vista, rather than serious reflections on the history of world civilization. They represent highly conventional expressions of self-satisfaction with modern European culture and prejudice against cultures in other times and places. But they signal a desire to enter a wider realm of world history and historical sensibilities.[2]

Soon afterwards, during January and February 1956, in a series of lectures on his basic religious beliefs, he included a couple of sentences suggesting that a new awareness of the world outside Christendom was dawning on him. The first ties his thought to past history: "One of the reasons why I think that history is valuable is that it helps us to grasp something of the totally different experiences of life which other men and other ages have had, and which complement our own." The second indicates a sense of the multiplicity of cultures and religious experiences in contemporary history and the future: "We do not know how much the traditions of Christianity may not still be enriched by the many things that we have to learn from the mysticism of Asia and from the other religious of the world. . . . It will be interesting to see what our religion will mean when worked out in the terms of a culture far removed from the Graeco-Roman." Butterfield had not talked like this before, and his comments reveal how uninformed he was about, among other things, the ancient history of Christianity in regions such as India or Ethiopia or Armenia.[3]

In Jerusalem his theme was the influence of the Hebrew scriptures on the idea of history active in what he was calling "Western civilization." In the lecture he is careful in Israel not to pose as an expert on Hebraica. He refers to a kind of influence that would be detected almost by intuition, rather than through precise documentation. It concerns what he identifies as "man's general attitude to the whole panorama of world history, the whole drama of human life throughout historical epochs, the general course of events in time." The reference to "the whole drama of human life" came directly from *Christianity and History,* where he sharply distinguished history in such a comprehensive sense, which belonged to the function of religion to disclose, from the history which academic history was competent to reconstruct. It was, he says, "the region almost of what I might call unconscious assumptions," the ideas people scarcely know they hold. He knows he is talking far removed from the "technical history" he lauded as the scientific model. This is not the terrain of his admonitions about the difference between memoirs and government documents which he issued in "The Historian and His Evidence." He moves his thinking onto the most expansive horizon he knew, far more comprehensive than the treatment of general history he had hitherto contemplated in his exposition of the modern history of Europe.

Before his Israeli listeners he plays with the notion he had raised in *Christianity and History* that the ancient Jewish scriptures left to the Christians the legacy of knowing God as the God of history and not merely as the God of nature. He embraces the suggestion commonly made by others that the Jewish scriptures, via Christianity, may have provided the wherewithal to break with a perception of history as endless cycles, and given to "Western civilization" the idea that history moves towards a goal. He makes no comment on the cyclic themes central to Christian religion, themes such as renewal, revival, and resurrection. He suggests that the beliefs that history is meaningful and that every moment and every person count may have come from the Jews. He also credits the ancient Jews with originating the concept of universal history, the history of the world seen as a whole. He gives no hint that he is acquainted with Hindu or Buddhist or Chinese renderings of universal history. He suggests that the ancient Jews may have contributed to the modern idea of progress, but only via a secular transmutation that denuded a Jewish idea of history of its spiritual character and excluded the elements that perceived history as cataclysmic and tragic. He agrees with the commonly held notion that the modern idea of progress was a recent and secular invention. He places the conception date after the scientific revolution of the seventeenth century, the events which he has long insisted mark the dawn of the modern period. As his discussion proceeds he considers four ideas of history in something like historical sequence: ancient Jewish, Greek, Christian, and the modern Western secular idea of progress. He specifically notes the rise of a Christian interpretation of history via the Gospels, Augustine, and Eusebius.

These were new thoughts for Butterfield, but he was far from a pioneer among thinkers. All of the ideas he put forward were conventional, and he adopted them uncritically. What is interesting is that he began to reflect on the character of an "idea of history" as such, and that he brought to the enterprise the mentality and priorities of the historian and not the theologian. Butterfield was being tempted to join the trend towards comparative world history stimulated politically by the successful pressures for decolonization in India and Africa.

Butterfield's intellectual interests and his concerns about international politics coincided. At the time of the Egyptian nationalization of the Suez Canal in 1956, Butterfield went on record, in a letter to the *Times* of London, with what was for him a rare political statement. He favoured a new internationalism which featured the voluntary abandonment of imperialism by the British and French and welcomed the rise of the peoples of the Middle East, Asia, and Africa "to read equality and independence."[4] In intellectual terms, he readily acknowledged the role of the London School of Oriental and African Studies in expanding the horizons of British scholars, including his own. He mentioned Christopher Dawson as an antecedent, and he might have added Reinhold Niebuhr, whose *Faith and History*, with its theological sweep of comparative history, he had reviewed with favour some years earlier.[5] He had recently acted as a referee for Philip Bagby's *Culture and History*, whose global perspective he found stimulating, and it was his report that persuaded the publisher to bring out the book.[6]

Above all, he deferred to the work of Arnold Toynbee whose final volumes of *A Study of History* were published in 1954, amid wide public acclaim.[7] Toynbee published *An Historian's Approach to Religion* in 1956, derived from his well-known Gifford Lectures in Edinburgh in 1952 and 1953, which incorporated the religions of the world in a wide-ranging analysis of the historian's mode of study.[8] Butterfield's attraction to Toynbee dated from at least 1934, when he applauded the first three volumes of *A Study of History*. He had made a point to keep in touch with Toynbee since at least 1950 by sending Toynbee copies of some of his publications. Toynbee used some Butterfield references approvingly in the final volumes of his magnum opus. He also reviewed *Man on His Past* favourably, albeit chiding Butterfield for his universalization of so called scientific history. Toynbee reminded him that the historical thought he was talking about was merely one type of history among all the varieties of history available throughout the ages. Butterfield's "scientific history" was really the style of history created within the culture of late modern German universities. Toynbee invited Butterfield to the dinner of distinguished scholars feted by Oxford University Press when the final volumes were published. When Toynbee's extraordinary volume *Reconsiderations* appeared in 1961, Butterfield in turn reviewed it and announced his fundamental sympathy for what he considered to be Toynbee's colossal achievement. Toynbee was, said Butterfield, the one man in a generation who "instead of burrowing into some microscopic period, brings an analytic mind to the whole panorama of the historical civilisations."[9]

In his lecture at the London School of Oriental and African Studies (SOAS), in January 1958, Butterfield admitted his ignorance of the historiography produced in cultures outside Europe. The inner force of the comparative method would compel him to enlarge his reading. He was already listening to an Islamic research student at Oxford who was urging him to begin a study of Islamic historiography, and in the London lecture he offered his first, albeit brief, comparative reference to Hinduism and Buddhism.[10] It would appear from his notes that he began reading, or at least collecting bibliography about, some non-European historiography during 1958 or 1959, immediately after his lecture at SOAS. It was a case of the venue influencing the speaker more than the speaker influencing the venue. He apparently showed interest from the start in Chinese, Mesopotamian, and Egyptian historical writing, and, in comparative religion, the works by Mircea Eliade. He postponed his reading about Islamic themes.[11]

In 1958 he accepted an assignment to review the study of the history of historical writing for the International Congress of Historical Sciences in Stockholm, scheduled for August 1960, and, in a departure from his traditional practice, decided not to limit the scope of his survey to European or merely English history. His attention did remain centred on Europe, but he turned his own preparatory reading to non-European work, notably China, and sought the assistance of scholars in non-European fields. He had Eve Bogle taking notes for him on British historiography.[12]

In the aftermath of his visit to Israel, he received an invitation to write the article on the history of historiography for the *Encyclopedia Hebraica*. He agreed, and produced a summary, running to 150 pages of typescript, of historical writing linked to "Western civilization," but also, and pointedly, included references to non-European-centred traditions of historical writing.[13] Butterfield had found a new line of inquiry for himself and he was eager to follow it.

His enthusiasm had limits, however. When Geoffrey Barraclough, then Stevenson Professor of International History at the University of London and Chatham House, Toynbee's former chair, proposed that Cambridge create a chair or lectureship in world history, Butterfield resisted. Global history, he objected, was too vast ever to become a proper teaching subject, and he hardened in defense of the preeminence of European history. Nonetheless, he admitted that the history of science and the history of historiography are defective unless they are treated in a manner that situates them within a world milieu.[14]

"Insurgent" Christianity

Butterfield kept getting invitations to talk about religion and history, and he would respond unfailingly that he had "nothing more left in the bag." Then he would accept the invitation anyway and proceed to repeat things he had said before.[15] The Jerusalem and London lectures served as a spur to break with this pattern and to renew his engagement with religious themes and particularly with the way he treated the Bible. The more he considered the problems of historiography in general, and the more he contemplated ideas of history within the global horizon, the more he felt the inadequacies of his knowledge of biblical criticism.

His commentary on the Bible in the 1948 lectures on Christianity and history had come straight out of his own meditation on biblical texts over the years. His approach to the Bible was spiritual and experiential, and amounted virtually to a pre-critical reading of scripture. He had realized for some time that he possessed debilitating weaknesses in the area of biblical studies. His studies in the history of historiography had stressed the impact of critical studies of the scriptures on the rise of modern historical studies. But he was too busy, and too interested in other subjects of study, to take the time to enter into critical biblical studies himself.

The *Times Literary Supplement* provided what may have been the initial occasion for him to engage biblical criticism as an element in theological scholarship. The *TLS* persuaded him to review Rudolf Bultmann's Gifford Lectures, *History and Eschatology*, published in 1957, in which the German theologian and New Testament scholar commented favourably on Butterfield's *Christianity and History*. He took the decision to immerse himself in critical biblical scholarship and biblical theology.

He set to work, and began by reading five or six of Bultmann's other books, plus Friedrich Gogarten, and worked out his response in "thought-essays." He liked Bultmann, especially the notions that the present moment is always open for decision and that Jesus Christ is repeatedly present for the Christian. He also accepted Bultmann's interpretation of the New Testament as the expression of the faith of the first Christian communities, a point he counted as essential to good historical criticism. But he objected to what he considered Bultmann's one-sidedness. The existential accent is valid when not erected into exclusive existentialism, and the claim that the Gospels were the believers' confession about Christ which believers today can experience now for themselves is true if the historical Jesus is not "reasoned away" and Christianity does not "lose its roots in actual history."[16]

Butterfield determined to retain biblical scholarship in his schedule of readings, and he seems to have kept up his readings during and after 1958. He made it clear that, although he would not pretend to have expertise in biblical criticism or theology or just about any area of comparative scholarship, he would proceed with a mind of his own. His special mark would be to bring the historian's outlook to the study. He was entering the stage of critical thinking about scriptures, religion, and ideas of history, and he showed that he could do his homework.

Nonetheless, he also retained the belief that religious commitment and the religious life are not the products of scholarship. When people invited him speak on Christianity he continued to give his confession of faith, and even felt duty-bound to do so. The most recent occasion, and the most notable since 1948, was a memorable series of lectures in Bristol in January and February 1956. These were published in 1979, shortly before his death. The title assigned by the sponsor was open-ended, "Christianity in the Twentieth Century." He decided simply "to make confession" of what he believed, and "to testify to the faith." It appears that he restudied the Old Testament and the New Testament for the occasion, approaching the scriptures in ways that evidenced his rising consciousness of biblical criticism, and then wrote out what was in his mind. The result amounted to an extended personal witness to his religion.[17]

The Bristol lectures offer an enchanting revelation of his deepest convictions, together with his advice for the future of Christianity, filtered through the perspective of the historian. They tell us the beliefs and assumptions he carried with him into his new studies. They also reveal the astounding continuity in his religious convictions with those expressed in the earliest of his writings extant. The will to preach still burns in his heart. He remains the dedicated Methodist and the consummate dissenter, and continues to emphasize the absolute centrality of individuals and human personality in history. Butterfield made similar statements in another lecture in 1956, this time on the theme of the historical development of the principle of toleration in British life, sponsored by the British Council of Christians and Jews.[18]

The summary of his religion in the Bristol lectures is concise. Christianity, he insists, is a religion that addresses itself "to what is most sovereign in human personality" and that "assumed and demanded the voluntary act of the individual." He considers it deadly to Christianity to cater to the interests of merely conventional Christians or to submit simply to the authority of the church or the Bible or to grant the church as an institution too much place in the Christian life. What matters is the relationship between the individual person and God, a connection that comes revealed to us most fully in the personal and solitary act of contemplation. There needs to be a convergence between the Bible and the inner self: "the authority which the Bible has for us in so many of his parts is not a matter of superstition or authoritarianism but a sort of self-ratification that it carries — a feeling that this teaching speaks to me, cutting into my deepest experience of myself and expressing my highest aspirations."

He depicts Jesus Christ as the encapsulation of three notable transitions he sees recorded in the Hebrew scriptures, three transformations in religion to which, he says, the Jewish people testified out of their experience of exile in Babylon. First, their religion changed from a national religion to a religion of contact between God and the inner life of each separate individual. Second, tendencies towards righteousness centred on themselves fell to the side, while themes of forgiveness and mercy moved to the centre as all individuals might come to recognize their own sin. Third, God appeared less the judge and more the God of love. Butterfield embraces each of these outcomes as his own.

The implications of these beliefs lead him to project as the model form of Christianity those small aggregates of early Christians who were surrounded and besieged by an antagonistic world that followed other gods. He excoriates the abandonment of this pristine Christianity and the establishment of the Christian religion as the religion of the Constantinian state. With the accomplishment of what he regards as the secularization of the society of his own day, Christians might once again enjoy their freedom from entanglement with the state and society. The important task for Christians now, he urges, would be to guide people towards contact with the living Christ, rather that to build up the organization of the church, or promote social and political programs, or even foster moral improvement. In no case should Christians seek a new alliance with the powers of the world. They should live as the emblem of dissent and the critical presence within the world. If there were to be social change, it would have to start with the transformation of the individual from the inside, not with social movements. All the individuals, thus remade, and living in spiritual contact with God, would act as leaven in the world, and produce unintended side effects of their spirituality.

He attaches his views to the Nonconformist lineage of dissent from established religion within British history and, while gently admonishing the Nonconformists for their recent "conformity" with society, he calls for a renewed Nonconformity. He expects the Nonconformist impulse to emerge everywhere, including in contemporary Methodist but also in Roman Catholicism and the Church of England. He urges his hearers to distinguish themselves from all that surrounds them, and to renew their spirit by fresh experience of the Gospels. He calls for people to stop playing the role of the "conventional Christian." Nowhere in his entire life of believing in and practicing dissent does he put as succinctly as in these Bristol lectures what he intends: "The twentieth-century situation seems to me to require what I have called the 'insurgent' type of Christianity — not the kind which binds up its fortunes with the defence of the status quo. By 'insurgent' Christianity . . . I mean the kind of Christianity which . . . is constantly ready to return to first principles, to make a fresh dip into the Gospels and the New Testament revelation."[19]

Religion and International Relations

Themes of international relations also moved onto Butterfield's table during 1958. He pursued topics he had raised in *Christianity, Diplomacy and War*, published in 1953. Once again the initiative for his involvement in the field came from others. This time it was the Rockefeller Foundation, renewing a proposal first made to him in 1954. Butterfield agreed to convene a small group at the Master's Lodge at Peterhouse in September 1958 to begin discussion of the theory of international relations. Given that he had usually denied that he was doing anything that could be called theory, his involvement is surprising.

Butterfield's participation issued from a series of events which unrolled in the aftermath of *Christianity, Diplomacy and War.* Kenneth Thompson, then assistant director for the social sciences on the staff of the Rockefeller Foundation, himself a theorist of international relations, liked the book, and so did Reinhold Niebuhr and Hans Morgenthau, both of whom had written on the subject. The Rockefeller Foundation was already funding the American Committee on the Theory of International Relations, based in New York and chaired by Niebuhr and Morgenthau. The pair invited Butterfield to meet with them if ever he came to New York.

The opportunity eventually came in June 1956 when Columbia University and Harvard University brought Butterfield to the United States to award him honourary doctorates. Niebuhr asked him to state his views on morality and international politics. He produced a paper for the purpose under the title "Morality and Historical Process in International Affairs." His audience was a group of seven men gathered at Columbia University.[20] The paper expanded some things he said in *Christianity Diplomacy and War,* and added a brief opening section drawn from a talk he made to the Peterhouse Chapel Fellowship in April.[21]

The New York paper provided vital clues to the direction Butterfield was taking his discourse on international relations. In the Bristol lectures, Butterfield's message was all about individuals and personality and the inner life. He made no more than fleeting references to law, process, and conditioning circumstances in history, and he virtually discounted the state in the face of his vehemently dissenter attitudes against affinities between religious bodies and institutions of public power. In New York he sound like a man speaking out of the other side of his mouth. Now he emphasized law in history and dealt exclusively with the international behaviour of states. The separation between the two poles of his persistent dualism seemed stark. For someone who did not know the tentative synthesis he had articulated in "God in History" — his notion of three ways to understand the same events — it would be easy to think that Butterfield was simply contradicting himself. He aroused animated discussion.

In his paper, Butterfield states abruptly at the start, and in very few words, that his views rest on the assumption that only individuals exist, and that he understands the term "state" to be a shorthand way of referring to a large number of individuals. He aligns himself with what he calls the "doctrine of individualism," but he appears defensive in doing so. He acknowledges, perhaps for the first time, the objections of those Christians "who seem to despise the doctrine," among whom he suspects would be the very people in his audience. Even in so sympathetic a group he would be the dissenter.

He quickly moves on. For the rest of the paper he speaks readily about what he variously calls "the state," "the social order," and "political society." He even assigns an "object" to political society and the state: "The object of political society is to establish an area of peace and order in which men can develop the life of reason and the world can grow in reasonableness. And I think that the state, without removing human sinfulness, in the means of establishing a tolerable mode of life, establishing a field for the play of reason, in spite of sin." These are purposes which go well beyond the mere interplay of large numbers of individuals, and presume the reality of social institutions and relationships that enjoy a basic existence of some kind. Contra Niebuhr's famous thesis about the difference between the "moral man" and "immoral society." Butterfield wants to insist that there is no separate realm for politics, no variation in moral responsibility between the person in politics and the same person out of politics. Only individual people exist, some of whom are statesmen and politicians, while others are professors or poets or something else. Whatever the activity, each person would encounter problems of human relations, and "constantly be confronted by the alternative between an act which is more moral and another which is less moral." He does not expect the person who, for instance, is a Christian and also a statesman to suspend in politics the Christian virtues of humility, charity, self-judgment, and cooperation with Providence.[22]

The bulk of his message comes in two parts. The first half reiterates his usual objections to moral judgments, but he puts the point in perhaps the clearest phrase he ever wrote on the subject: "withholding of the absolute condemnation of human beings themselves even where the actions as such call for condemnation." The phrase showed precisely how he is moving his position in response to the endless criticisms that his "no moral judgments" rhetoric kept receiving. He explicitly sanctions moral judgments against acts that warrant condemnation, and, by inserting the word "absolute," opens the door for a range of limited moral judgments against people.[23] He continues with the familiar point that those making moral assessments of human conduct must mitigate their judgments in recognition of the conditioning circumstances surrounding acts and events. He tries to explain more than he had in previous writings what he means by "law" in history. His writing is frustratingly inexact, precisely the thing that theory cannot be. Numerous terms or phrases seem to function interchangeably: maxim, reflection on history as process, generalization, historical law, the formula that provides what might be called a norm, the connection of acts to circumstances. It is difficult to find the element common within the lot of terms, but we might suppose that he is referring to recurrence. Whatever the term, he seems to be talking about the products of a human thinking when people are trying to make sense of actions that seem to recur. His language is not entirely translucent when he explains that the statement of laws by a thinker would need to exhibit great flexibility: "The laws that are produced are perhaps true in a conditional sense only — true sometimes only 'other things being equal,' or valid only as representing a tendency or bias in events that we must take account of. Or they stand as formulas that provide what might be called a norm; and it does not necessarily matter if in every actual historical case there may some different kind of departure from the norm." As an example of a possible law, he cites the thesis that revolutions "tend to move ever further to the left, or to greater extremes." He argues that once people know this law they can respond to revolutionary situations in ways that overcome the tendency.[24]

The rest of his message applies his view of law and revolution to international politics. He restates the prescription for the conflict between Communism and liberal democracy that he had proposed in *Christianity, Diplomacy and War*. In so doing, he discusses the international order in terms analogous to his treatment of political society and the state, and designates the purpose of the international order: "the real object of foreign policy is the establishment of a *modus vivendi*." And, "In the international world it is peace that is the primary object; and this means the development of an international order in which the issue can be decided by reason and the world can grow in reasonableness." Thus, foreign policy should aim not to destroy Communism, but to create a modus vivendi within a new international order embracing both the Soviet Union and "the West," and directed towards peace.[25] His recommendations rest on his assessment that Communism contains beneficial elements attributable to Christian antecedents, and that the defects in the practice of Communism by the Soviet Union, and even the faults of Stalin, are due to the revolutionary situation itself. He expects the awful deeds attributed to the Soviet Union to fall away as "the work of civilising and humanising" progresses. For his scheme to work, he says, the world would have to rely on "the healing effects of time." He derives his model from the example of the transformation of the relations between Protestants and Roman Catholics since the Reformation of the sixteenth century. He suggests that the strategy which produced the change was "the gradual separation of the doctrinal conflict from the operation of diplomacy as such."[26]

The report of the discussion of his paper within the New York group shows that the exchange was friendly, but that the disagreements expressed were substantial, particularly those by Reinhold Niebuhr. Niebuhr considered it wrong to say that only individuals exist and to suggest that states are unreal. He doubted the validity of the thesis about revolutions, and objected to the method of generalizing about historical events widely separated in time and culture. He disputed the disconnection of the ideology of Communism from the political situation of Communism, and rejected the analogy between Catholic-Protestant relations and the relations of the democratic states with Communist states. Niebuhr countered that Soviet Communism is worse than Butterfield admits, and represents an alien political religion. Nevertheless, it is also apparent from the report of the discussion that Niebuhr and the group as a whole welcomed Butterfield's excursion into theory. They appreciated his historical arguments for a move towards detente and away from simple antagonism between the two great powers. Butterfield much later charmingly described the experience as a time when he was "heckled by them over one of my papers."[27]

The meeting between Butterfield and Niebuhr's committee issued in two very tangible results, and both signalled an important turn in Butterfield's intentions towards international politics and towards theory. The first was an invitation from Niebuhr and John C. Bennett to become a contributing editor of *Christianity and Crisis,* the bi-weekly journal of liberal-left Christian opinion which they edited. Butterfield gladly accepted, but attached the caveat that he was "not a proper student of current affairs," and that his interest extended only to "the questions of principle involved." He received several requests from the journal to write on foreign policy, an area which he acknowledged "represents one of my primary interests and I find myself constantly wanting to read and write about this subject."[28]

About the same time, the new conservative journal in New York, *National Review,* edited by William F. Buckley, asked him to write for them. The Buckley group would have found his doctrine of the individual and his aversion to the state congenial to both the individualist and the libertarian strands of the emerging American conservative movement, but not to the Catholic traditionalist strand present within the same movement. His friend Adam Watson, then a member of the staff of the British Embassy in Washington, urged him not to get caught writing for what he called that "right-wing" magazine. Butterfield politely refused the invitation, claiming the tightness of his schedule. That his views appealed to journals from opposite ends of the political spectrum exemplified the difficulty of neatly classifying Butterfield's politics.[29]

The association with *Christianity and Crisis* lasted until 1965, but yielded only two articles, one in 1957 on new internationalism and another in 1958 on the end of colonialism. In both pieces he reissued the call for a new international order which he had sent to the *Times* on the occasion of the Suez crisis. He advocated an international order which included the peoples of Africa and Asia on equal terms with Europeans and North Americans, and urged the British and French in particular to relinquish their empires peacefully. He accentuated the need for nonviolent methods of changing the status quo in the world. His historical argument contrasted the merits of his own proposal with the futility of the system of Count Metternich after the Napoleonic wars. Metternich's system failed, he said, because it sought to reestablish and then preserve an international order which entrenched the aristocratic past and blocked the rise of the democratic tendencies of the day. The new internationalism, said Butterfield, would require continuous flexibility in international relations. The great powers, especially Britain and France, but also the United States, would need to perform repeated acts of self-restraint while at the same time they accepted the worthy demands of the newly emerging peoples.

He recommended his favourite case of social change, the model provided by the English over the centuries who adhered to "a method which prevented crises from reaching the desperation point, ensured the gradual development of liberty, and provided a model of the kind of change which is just in time to anticipate the resort to violence." Above all others, England provided light for the road through large-scale change. Although he did not give his model a name, it was the same Whig practice of politics which he had praised so lavishly in *Englishman and His History* during the Second World War. Butterfield's New Whig patriotism was still alive, and though it seemed in some ways quaintly antiquarian, it proved attractive to the liberal-left policy of *Christianity and Crisis*.

In the new situation, before decolonization, his views on the harmfulness of even the allegedly most benign empires appeared radically subversive. The French and British empires had to give up their self-serving policy of world stabilization. They had to withdraw from Africa and Asia, and soon, with the goal of equality among the peoples of the globe. Butterfield's 1957 article "Internationalism and the Defense of the Existing Status Quo" was later selected as one of the most significant writings published in the journal between its founding in 1941 and 1966, and the editor asked him to write the preface for the book in which they were collected.[30]

The second outcome of Butterfield's meeting with Niebuhr's Rockefeller group was his agreement to form the twin Rockefeller committee in Britain, leading to the meeting at Peterhouse in 1958. He had stressed in his opening remarks to the Americans that he did not pretend to think as a philosopher or theorist, and he even confessed that he had long harboured aversion to theory, indeed to any approach to humane scholarship except historical thinking. He admitted, however, that he was beginning to look more approvingly at theory. The motives behind his change of mind, he suggested, were his ethical concerns and his interest in the generalizations which historians make in their writings. The Americans noted during the conversation with Butterfield that he was "more of a theoretician than his opening remarks would lead one to believe." The observation was apt.[31]

The interest in what other people might recognize as theory was not new, however. Butterfield had long shown a penchant for thinking about the problem of generalizations about historical events and processes. He usually said he was interested in the question of "maxims" derived from historical reflection. His encounter during the 1930s with Marxism, Machiavelli, and the history of science contributed to his play with questions of "law" in the human affairs. His repeated insistence upon a "scientific" approach to understanding history, war, and international relations drove him in the direction of theory. In tacit criticism of his former self, he confessed that he now doubted the value of overly rigorous attachment to minute historical research and excessive allegiance to mere narrative history, both of which led to the neglect of wider dimensions of history and broader questions about historical processes.

The force that moved him across the conventional line by which he separated history and theory was the offer of Rockefeller money and the example of Niebuhr's New York group. The Rockefeller Foundation, in the person of Kenneth Thompson, had been suggesting to Butterfield for some time that money could be made available for a British committee. Thompson had simultaneously pursued E. H. Carr of Trinity College, Cambridge, with the proposal, but Carr had turned the offer down. After Butterfield's adventure in New York, he eventually signalled to Thompson that he was ready to move forward with the project, and Thompson granted him the guarantees he needed. The theory Butterfield had in mind was not historical theory as such, but the theory of international relations. But even this theory, in Butterfield's hands, became a species of general historical thinking about human affairs. Butterfield remained the historian.[32]

The meeting Butterfield convened at Peterhouse in September 1958 included only four people: Desmond Williams, his former student and friend at University College, Dublin; Martin Wight, his friend and critic at the London School of Economics; Donald MacKinnon, professor of philosophy at Aberdeen University, suggested by Wight; and himself as chair. The four agreed to the Rockefeller design, and called the group the British Committee for the Theory of International Politics. It was the start of a program of semi-regular meetings invariably chaired by Butterfield. The project kept his attention until the mid-1960s, when he left the committee. The group would meet for a long weekend two or three times a year at Peterhouse to discuss their papers circulated in advance. Rockefeller supplied the funding and Peterhouse provided the accommodations and board.

Their task, in Butterfield's words, would be "the study of the principles, etc., underlying the conduct of international affairs and the methods by which that field can be more scientifically studied." The approach would be austerely historical, construed as analytical reflection on the recurrent historical processes of relations among states. He insisted that the group meet in Cambridge, independent of the university, rather than in London, to keep it from drifting under the influence of the department of international relations at the London School of Economics. The group would have the structure of an intellectual club, requiring a unanimous vote for the election of a new member. Whatever others might want, he made it clear that he would exclude social scientists, purely diplomatic historians, and those having only contemporary politics as their focus.[33]

The early additions to the membership included Michael Howard, a military historian at London, G. F. Hudson from Oxford, William Armstrong from the Treasury Department, Adam Watson from the British Foreign Office, and Hedley Bull from LSE. Butterfield managed to block an invitation to E. H. Carr with whom, he said, he had differences in approach to international affairs. Carr, meanwhile, harboured resentment against Butterfield even though he himself had previously declined the Rockefeller invitation. Butterfield, as chair, remained very much in charge and even kept the record of the discussions. He believed that the work of the committee was urgent in the present state of the world, and he devoted much time to it.[34]

The first formal meeting of the new British committee eventually took place in January 1959 at Peterhouse. Butterfield, Martin Wight, and Donald MacKinnon prepared papers. Butterfield's contribution had affinities with his New York paper over two years before, but now he stressed the opposite point. He still attributed most of the abhorrent conduct of the Communists in the world to revolutionary situations, and not to their ideology, and he continued to refer to the "law" that revolutions tend to move to greater extremes. However, he now talked about a real conflict of ideology between the two big power blocs that dominated world politics. His focus had shifted to the uncommitted peoples of Africa and Asia, a change attributable especially to his reaction to the Suez crisis. It is just possible that Niebuhr's disagreement with him about the effect of ideological difference on "East-West" relations pushed him to contemplate anew the conflict of ideologies in the world. More likely, as was his habit, he was holding in tension two apparently contrary viewpoints, one of which he expressed in one situation, the other in a different situation.

In his paper his sympathies run towards the peoples under colonial rule, and he endorses their aspirations for radical social reform and self-determination. He articulates a maxim to this effect: when dominant powers do not anticipate or heed the just demands of those under their control, acts of rebellion will occur; when the dominant powers still do nothing, more ruthless and unscrupulous leaders will replace moderate ones and the violence will increase. Once again he has in mind, he says, the Whig historians who charged that tyranny would respond not to reasonable entreaties, but only to desperate resorts to violence. He reiterates his recommendation that the European powers abdicate their domination.

Then he proposes the surprising analysis that seems to reverse his former denial of the signficance of ideological difference in the current world crisis. With respect to the uncommitted nations, he suggests, the conflict between the two blocs is not essentially structural, but assuredly ideological: "The stage is now act set for a conflict of ideals in the world at large — a more clear-cut issue of ideals, perhaps, than existed in either the First or the Second World Wars. We may be unfitting ourselves for what is really the main issue in the middle of twentieth century history, if we are too preoccupied even with questions of power, and with the requirements of a hypothetical major war between the Eastern and Western blocs." If the history of his Germanophile attitudes were not known, it would be difficult to comprehend his characterization of the war against Nazi Germany as ideologically less clear-cut than the world situation at the end of the 1950s. His message now addresses entirely the question of the approach to the African and Asian peoples. He recommends that the European powers, the United States, Canada, and their partners unroll a massive ideological campaign to propagate liberal, democratic, and humane ideals around the world. They should seek to convince the uncommitted nations that, in addition to offering tangible and material benefits similar or superior to those the Soviets promised, they also offered the liberating effects of their ideals. The proof of those ideals, he says, would be for the colonial powers to withdraw voluntarily from their positions of control and facilitate the independence of the subjugated peoples, and to accomplish the step before the rebellions forced them out.[35] The paper elicited little response in the committee, and the discussion moved on to other themes not directly related to Butterfield's presentation. By the second meeting, in April 1959, Butterfield himself was dealing with a different issue, the notion of the balance of power in international affairs.[36]

But there was more to come on the new international order, Communism, and the peoples of African and Asia. In October 1958, Butterfield had lectured in Washington, D.C. at American University and Wesley Theological Seminary, both Methodist institutions, on themes closely related to his New York paper for the American Rockefeller committee. He also had a request from Ruth Nanda Anshen to send her something for one of her new book series with Harper and Brothers in the United States. In response he sent her a book-length typescript which intertwined things he had said on different occasions. He took material from his lectures in Washington, his paper in New York, and his first paper for the British Rockefeller group at Peterhouse, as well as from his Bristol lectures and his lecture to the British Council of Christians and Jews in London on toleration.

Harper issued a volume of 120 pages in 1960, under the title *International Conflict in the Twentieth Century: A Christian View,* his eighteenth book. Butterfield's was the second in the series "Religious Perspectives," following Christopher Dawson's *Historic Reality of Christian Culture.* He expressed his disappointment to Anshen that his volume appeared in "Religious Perspectives" instead of her parallel series "World Perspectives," which he said he had expected and preferred.[37]

This book, like his other books from lectures, was a miscellany. Most of it recapitulated themes he had repeated often enough over the years, and one marvels that he could keep doing so: the priority of individual personality, recognition of the effects of conditioning circumstances, the operation of predicaments, the use of the "scientific method" in international affairs and politics, the sin of self-righteousness, and so on. He resumed his explanatory style which employed maxims to make the point he expected would clinch his argument.

He seems not to have modified his positions on "individualism" and "the state" or towards "historical laws" in the face of the criticisms he received from Reinhold Niebuhr and the American Rockefeller committee. If anything, he reenforces his statements on these subjects and pronounces them even louder, while simultaneously increasing the confusion about what exactly he means. For instance, he expands the provocative opening passages from the New York paper, where he claimed adherence to the "doctrine of individualism" and the unreality of the "state," and converts them into the "Introduction" to the book. Whereas in front of Niebuhr and company the first line of his paper had read "It is possibly a mistake to discuss politics in a separate intellectual realm," for the first line of the book he changed the sentence to read "It is dangerous to discuss politics in a separate intellectual realm." At the same time, he appears to assert just the opposite point by erecting a separate realm of politics where scientific method applies. He discusses it in chapter 2 of the book under the title "The Scientific Method in the Realm of Politics." We may assume that, in keeping with his usual dualism he also retains the realm of morality which he has spoken of over and over. Moreover he strengthens his statements about "individuals" as the sole reality. For instance, he adds the sweeping line "The word morality is applicable only to individual people," and instead of saying merely that he did not understand the notion of "political morality," he now dismisses the notion as belonging to "a world of trick mirrors and optical illusions." In a concession to Niebuhr, however, he inserts a line recognizing that the modern doctrine of individualism "does not seem to please all Christians." He also enhances his assertions against the existence of the "state" and "society" by inserting here and there throughout the text phrases calling them merely "great aggregates of men" or "great agglomerations of humanity." Nonetheless, and contrary to his stated belief, he continues to speak of the "state" as an organization or structure, or as an agent that did things.[38]

Likewise he extends his passages about "laws" and a "scientific" approach. He follows his custom of placing notion on top of notion as if each new term were in some sense synonymous with what preceded, and would help us know what he means. For instance, in the space of the brief chapter "The Scientific Method in the Realm of Politics," he included references to the following: analogy, recurrence, methodical thinking, systematic thinking, correlations, long-term tendencies, processes, relationship between events, conditioning circumstances, predicaments, constants, predictability, maxims, generalizations, structural analysis, laws, and background. The implication seems to be that they all have to do with the same thing. Speaking loosely at his dualistic best, he located them all in the realm of necessity instead of the realm of freedom, which were in turn, he said, "two aspects of the historical realm," as contrasted with the spiritual realm. It is not clear where the separate realm of politics fits in the picture.[39]

Butterfield's style is to take a long running start through the familiar material, and then leap to the new points he was going to discuss in public for the first time, which in this case are his comments on how to deal with Communism and the threat of the atomic bomb. His words are cast in generalities and peppered with universal maxims, but his focus on Communism and the bomb is sharp. These were the items he elaborated upon in 1958 in Washington, D.C., the capital of the United States. He added force to his words by publishing his message with a major American publishing house. That was early in 1960. Then he raised the matter to a higher power still by going to the Soviet Union in September 1960 at a time when the United States government looked upon such visits as politically explosive. Consistent with Nikita Khrushchev's new policy of peaceful coexistence, the Institute of History of the Soviet Academy of Sciences invited a team of British scholars to Moscow and Leningrad. Butterfield made the journey with E. H. Carr, Charles Webster, Hugh Seton-Watson, and George Bolshover. Both the Americans and the Soviets looked upon such visits as political acts.[40]

In the charged atmosphere of the Cold War, when American fear of the Soviet Union and global fear of nuclear war were intense, Butterfield's comments on Communism and the bomb in *International Conflict* could hardly sound more provocative or self-contradictory. The United States and Europe need to stop thinking of Soviet Communism as an alien ideology, he says. The events connected with Soviet Communism since 1917 should be treated as a function of the operation of the historical "law" of revolution, not as the natural expressions of an evil ideology and evil people.

At the same time, however, the United States and Europe should indeed see Communism as an ideology within the conflict of ideologies in the world at large, and one worthy of engagement by ideological means. Moreover, if there have been crimes associated with Soviet Communism, these belong first of all to the effects of revolutionary process as such, and not to Communist ideology. At the same time, from the standpoint of ideology, it would be crucial to appreciate the egalitarian ideals of Communism and to admit the good services that Communism has provided in various parts of the world. It would be better to envision Communism perhaps as "a benevolent thing gone wrong" and not as "mere unredeemed and diabolical evil." In response to Niebuhr's scepticism about Butterfield's "law" that revolutions tend to move further to the extreme on the left, he added a passage about the exceptions to the general trend, namely, the revolutions of 1688 in England, which Butterfield approved, and 1830 in France, which was hardly extreme. The exceptions only reinforce the "law," he says, since by knowing what revolutions tend to do if left unchecked, people can take the steps that divert events to a different plane, and achieve different outcomes. Thus, "scientific" knowledge of a law of revolution can offer controls over events otherwise felt to be beyond control. He also adds the caveat that all his comments on the defects of revolution itself perhaps apply only to the societies of Europe and North America. By contrast, revolution may well be the best option for the peoples oppressed by European empires in Asia and Africa, even if the outcomes predicted by the "law" still happen. In these ways, against Niebuhr's objections, he reasserts the validity of making comparisons of events widely separated by times and cultures.[41]

Détente is the immediate goal to seek in the conflict with Communism, Butterfield insists. As an extended example of the way "scientific" analysis works to illuminate contemporary international affairs, he reasserts the analogy between the current conflict with Soviet Communism and Protestant-Catholic conflicts in the sixteenth century. This he does in spite of Niebuhr's earlier objections, perhaps drawing the lines of similarity more sharply than before. To this he adds the analogy of the conflicts between democratic movements and the aristocratic order throughout the nineteenth century. He draws arresting parallels. In each of the previous cases, he says, the new people on the scene — the Protestants, the democrats and republicans — committed atrocities, behaved as tyrants, supported dictatorship, promulgated absolutist ideologies, as did the old order in each case. And each side reckoned the other as false and evil. Yet, over time, all sides moderated their beliefs and their behaviour, achieved détente, learned toleration, and practiced cohabitation within the same overall system. While the aristocratic order eventually all but disappeared, Protestants and Catholics both carried on, appropriately chastened and renewed, and very often even embraced each other as partners. This same détente, he suggests, can happen between the European-generated democracies and the Communist societies, provided both seek the necessary modus vivendi in the short term within the new international system.[42]

The remarkably new message in the book is a startling revelation of his politics towards the bomb. The utter destructiveness of the bomb, he says, outweighs any possible reason for its use, except by a Hitler-like dictator in the final moments before a desperate defeat. His proposal indicates that, unlike members of the New York Rockefeller committee, he does not consider himself to be a straight "realist" who calculates the weights and measures of power politics and regards the appeal to moral idealism in international politics as illicit. In a rare counter-dualist mood, he rejects the notion that idealism and realism were antithetical. He called his position a "Christian-Grotian synthesis" that, he said, "combined the merits of both." He places his position in the context of his idea of the predicament of mutual fear, the same Hobbesian fear he had delineated in *History and Human Relations*. The predicament of mutual fear could impede either side from taking the first step towards détente. The fear increases astronomically in the face of the atomic bomb held by both sides, creating a world under what he called the "dominion of fear."[43]

Butterfield dressed his statements about the bomb in multiple negatives and indirect assertions, and compelled his readers, and previously his lecture audience, to give very close attention in order to get his message:

> There is so great a risk in having the hydrogen bomb that there can hardly be greater risk if we unplug the whole system, and if our governments refuse to have anything to do with the weapon. Even if there were, the radical differ-

ence in the quality of these risks would cancel it; for with modern weapons we could easily put civilization back a thousand years, while the course of a single century can produce a colossal transition from despotic regimes to a system of liberty. I am giving a personal view; but I am not sure that the greatest gift that the West could bring to the world would not be the resolution neither to use the hydrogen bomb nor to manufacture it any further. Certainly the East would hardly believe us (at least for some time) if we said we were not going to resort to this weapon for any conceivable end. We should have to take the line, therefore, that our determination was not dependent on anything that other people believed. Even if the East refused to join us in the assertion, we can declare that the hydrogen bomb is an unspeakable atrocity, not to be used in any war, and not even to be the basis of any form of threat.

He concludes: "In any case, we cannot say that we will not receive the bomb — we can only say that we will not be responsible for the sin and the crime of delivering it. Supposing we do have to receive it, the one thing we can do is to choose the cause on behalf of which we will consent to be sacrificed."[44]

Through the opaque wording the message emerged. Butterfield is suggesting that the United States undertake unilateral nuclear disarmament. He is uttering out loud the same cry he made more simply in his diary in 1945 upon learning that the Americans had dropped the nuclear weapon on Hiroshima and Nagasaki: "The atomic bomb — the ultimate prostitution of human endeavor — the judgment of God on our civilisation."[45]

The proposal is far from "realist," and certainly not "scientific," and, in his own language, it may even be "moralistic." This is a radical proposal by a dissenter, a proposal which perhaps would "tip the balance slightly in favour of humanity and faith at such a point as this." The act of the denial of nuclear weapons would be a voluntary human choice, taken, paradoxically, not by individuals but by the state, the American state, in order to break through the structure of the current situation. This, he urges, would dash the predicament of mutual distrust that freezes the Soviet Union and the United States in a relationship of mutual fear and generates the situation of extreme instability in international affairs. The proposal does not assume the good will of the opponent or the eradication of sin. He believes the act is so important as an expression of basic humanity that he recommends it even if it does not "work," even if the consequence would be death from the bomb launched by the other party. The act would express the doctrine of love at a time "when the world is in extremities." With this proposal, Butterfield shoots right past anything like a "scientific" approach, and preaches the message of love which he derives from his Christian resources. We can now understand the subtitle of this book about international conflict: A Christian View.[46]

It would appear that he took the decision for absolute opposition to nuclear weapons by 1958 at the latest, before his Washington lectures and well in advance of the public campaigns for nuclear disarmament of the 1960s. In 1958, quite against his usual practice, he agreed to join the World Council of Churches' Commission on Christians and the Prevention of War in an Atomic Age. In 1959 he spoke against the bomb to the Christian Action Group, an activist group in Cambridge against nuclear weapons. It was almost unique for him to join a church commission at all, given his general dislike of the institutions of established religion, and he was almost equally averse to activism. As a member of the WCC's commission he dissented spontaneously from the dominant view that weapons, especially nuclear weapons, served as deterrents against war. The atomic bomb seemed to him to be a weapon in a class by itself, too completely a terror to be covered by the historical arguments for just war. He wrote a minority statement describing the atomic bomb as an atrocity and asking Christians to work for "the uni-lateral abandonment" of the weapon. Christians, he said, should mount the campaign against the bomb not by creating pressure groups directed at the state, but by testifying to the power of the Spirit and the basic value of human personality, enabling Christians thereby to become a leavening influence in society against the bomb. True to his own political style, he did not care in the least that the commission moved ahead without him.[47]

The final chapter of *International Conflict* entitled "Christianity and Global Revolution," contains his most explicit statement so far of the global perspective he had come to adopt. In just a few pages he sweeps across thousands of years and vast regions of the world from western, central, and eastern Europe to the Middle East, India, and China, from Africa to North and South America, encompassing politics, world religions, agrarian revolution, decolonialization, and the economy. He makes one stunning connection after another as he sketches out what amounted to a view of universal history and the future of Christianity. He utterly relativizes the Soviet-American conflict, the subject occupying most of the book, with remarks that show just how temporary and how localized that conflict is in the context of the staggeringly long histories of cultural preeminence, power, and conflict in China, India, Africa, and the Mediterranean region. He throws his support to the colonized peoples of the world and their movements for independence, as he lambasts the European empires for holding on to their illicit gains too long. The Europeans themselves, by their illicit imposition of themselves on the rest of the world, engendered the expansion of world Communism as the liberating answer for so many subjected peoples.

He also unequivocally endorses any action that stripped Christian churches of their garments of political power, worn ostentatiously since Constantine. He speaks heavy words against any churches allied with the state, chastising equally Anglicans, Lutherans, and Roman Catholics. He admonishes his own Methodists. He writes, "It is perhaps even the case that a subtle secret sympathy with the *status quo* now almost robs nonconformity of its historic role in England, making it no longer a body predisposed to opposition (and in this sense perhaps inclined to uncharitableness) — no longer so intent upon measuring the existing order of things by a standard outside that order itself." The words may be difficult to track, but they are the words of the dissenter at his best. They lead straight into his repetition of the call from his Bristol lectures for Christians to take the pristine religion of the New Testament as the motor for a Christianity of "the insurgent type." He would expect such Christianity to appeal massively to the newly liberated peoples of Africa and Asia, and, as people got used to the disconnection of religion from established power, perhaps even to the people of Europe.[48]

General History

Amidst all his engagements, writings, and provocations, Butterfield continued as Master of Peterhouse. He also continued his service as the university's representative on the governing body of Wesley House. Most important to him, he kept his lectures on modern history going. He sought likewise to fulfil at least some of the administrative responsibilities of his professorship. All was not smooth for him. For one thing, because of his busy life, and to his great dismay, he continued to repeat his old lectures in his course. And worse, he did not, as he hoped, use the lectures as a prod to rewrite his materials for the *Concise Cambridge Modern History*. Barely a year after becoming Master he notified David Knowles, the Regius Professor, that he wanted "to cut out my big course of Modern History Lectures, which is a pretty heavy affair." He liked the course and the students, he assured Knowles, but he wanted to free some time for the *Concise History*. He thought he would revert to his smaller and shorter one-term course on the Renaissance and Reformation which he had discontinued after the academic year 1952–1953. He did not take the step, however, and carried on with the modern course as before.[49]

At the same time, disagreements within the History Faculty over policy and curriculum became troublesome, even painfully awful. Differences between Butterfield and George Kitson Clark, historian of modern English history, turned into open warfare between 1955 and 1958, and led to a collapse in their personal relations. Noel Annan felt it was a remarkable case of the war of dons as administrators. J. H. Plumb, as a member of the board of the History

Faculty at the time, was witness to the play of their personal antipathy, which dated from the 1930s. Butterfield confessed privately to David Knowles that, had he been able, he would have denied Kitson Clark the new readership in constitutional history created for him in 1955. As Plumb saw it, they differed in their visions for the history curriculum. Kitson Clark campaigned for wider options, more subjects focused on themes, and more subjects connected with the specializations of the lecturers. Butterfield, by contrast, wished to maintain the focus on English and European history, with only a limited range of special subjects, continuing the emphasis on the general education of nonspecialists. In due course Butterfield lost out to Kitson Clark, and the Historical Tripos entered a period of near continuous revision. But before too long even Kitson Clark became disillusioned by the trend, which he felt by the 1960s resulted in fragmentation and lack of purpose as well as a loss of students. Kitson Clark's centenary lecture in 1973 on history at Cambridge evidenced a mellowed attitude towards Butterfield personally, and he sounded for all the world the same as Butterfield in his statement of the general educational mission of the Historical Tripos.[50]

They also differed over the handling of research students. During the same month in which Butterfield became Master, Kitson Clark proposed to organize a society of research students on the American model, enabling the students to see each other regularly and read papers on their research. Butterfield objected that the plan would undermine the Cambridge Historical Society, whose design united senior historians and research students on an equal footing for public discussion of their current work. In any case, he argued, a society for research students would fill no need, since research students were by occupation bound to spend endless hours in isolation, and disinclined to congregate together. Kitson Clark then thought of mounting his own seminar for research students in English history, in which the students would talk about their own thesis topics. This, too, Butterfield considered wrong-headed, since the students would not know the documents behind someone else's paper. Butterfield's model for a research seminar was a very small number of students in the same specialized field analyzing documents together with a professor. Kitson Clark next suggested a course for research students in English history lead by four instructors, Geoffrey Elton, J. H. Plumb, Butterfield, and himself, on the sources of English history and historiography since 1500. Butterfield opposed it as too diffuse and dominated by the professors, and he had the support of Knowles against it. Kitson Clark dropped the issue.[51] Kitson Clark eventually convened a very popular general colloquium in which senior historians, visiting scholars, and research students alike read papers on English history. Later, in the 1960s, Butterfield actually agreed to participate in two courses much like Kitson Clark had suggested, with several professors talking on the documents and methods in their special fields, but Butterfield made sure that the courses were not mandatory for research students.[52]

Butterfield had to face a palace rebellion against his own course in modern European history. He had not dropped the course as he hoped, chiefly because he felt strongly that a general history of the whole modern period since 1494 should form the framework for all study of modern history. His approach, as before the war, still featured an analysis of long-range trends encompassing the whole of Europe, structured around the close examination of pivotal historical moments. He also still understood Europe not as a relationship of states, but as a civilization having many aspects. He attracted about 100 students out of the 230 doing the History Tripos, and met them three times a week for the whole year.

The opposition to his course had been simmering for a while among the teaching staff in the History Faculty. It finally boiled over in February 1957 when eight lecturers in modern European history, out of the thirty university lectures in history, met with him in the Master's Lodge at Peterhouse. The meeting spilled over into a correspondence which included a circular letter from Butterfield to the lecturers and some exchanges of letters. It fell to Betty Behrens to voice the criticisms apparently shared by others in the group. They objected to his course on several grounds, she explained. It covered too many centuries, provided nothing intellectual beyond what a good history book surveying the period could give, allowed students to run away with generalizations which were too detached from real historical study, led to excessive memorization for the examinations, and took too much time for too many students, undercutting the attendance in the other courses. The lecturers wanted his course either discontinued or drastically shortened, and they favoured a wider selection of specialized courses instead. Paradoxically, most of the points were ones Butterfield himself might have made, but he perceived the objections as an attack on him and was plainly upset. He at once offered to give up his course, but then withdrew the offer and proceeded to defend the course vigorously. Ironically, less than a year after telling Knowles he wanted out of the course, he now found himself strongly asserting his intention to remain in, come what might. He repulsed all of the objections, except for the point about the students' time, as not germane to what went on in his course. He then expounded his idea of the nature of a general course in history. His course, he said, was in no sense an outline survey of information. It was an intellectual analysis of the structures of European society conceived as a general unit over several centuries. That kind of analysis could not simply be shortened. He offered as an example the need to know the relations between

French and Germanic societies over a long period in order to comprehend the problem of Alsace-Lorraine at the moment of German unification in 1870–1871. His argument depended on his concept of the importance of historical thinking as such and on his habitual distinction between underlying structures and the day-to-day events amenable to narrative. In the wider faculty, David Knowles and J. H. Plumb urged him to go ahead as he thought best, while Kitson Clark took the side of the lecturers. Butterfield chose to carry on with his course, thinking that it was right for the professor in the field to try to influence the teaching in the subject by his example. For the next two years, 1957–1959, he took J. H. Elliott into the course as joint lecturer. His intention was to groom Elliott, one of his former research students and a new addition to the History Faculty, to succeed him in the course.[53]

A streak of lightning intervened at just that moment from entirely outside the History Faculty to bring Butterfield's course problems to an end. He was approached about accepting the position of vice-chancellor, the highest administrative office of the University of Cambridge in a structure where the chancellorship was merely symbolic. The office traditionally was filled by one of the college heads. The term was two years, starting in the fall of 1959, preceded by a transitional year as deputy vice-chancellor, to begin in October 1958. If he accepted, he would have to delegate most of his ordinary duties as Master to others in Peterhouse, and he would offer no courses. His problems with the modern history course would wither away.

Butterfield needed little time to decide. The opportunity to be the dissenter at the head of the whole university appealed to his feeling for politics, in spite of his ideology against institutions. It also appealed to his missionary impulses on behalf of the educational ideals he had promoted for so many years. He accepted the position, knowing very well that his work as historian would suffer. Once again he altered his career as historian by agreeing to what other people wanted him to do.

Just before Butterfield commenced his term as vice-chancellor, Peterhouse arranged for his official portrait as Master to be painted by Ruskin Spear, the same artist who had done a view of Vellacott, the previous Master, that created so much stir that it was still not hung. Indeed, in an effort to place a suitable image of Vellacott in the Master's Lodge, Simba Vellacott, his widow, offered to donate a copy of the portrait done for Harrow School to replace Spear's work. Spear's portrait of Butterfield rendered him almost clown-like, and although Butterfield did not think it resembled him particularly well, he had it mounted in the Lodge anyway. He was, he said, not one to interfere with an artist.[54]

I 2

The Top and After the Top

High Administration

Butterfield became vice-chancellor of Cambridge University on 1 October 1959, a few days before turning fifty-nine.[1] The year as deputy vice-chancellor had brought no particular difficulties, and had the merit of warning him of the mound of duties that would be heaped upon him for two years. When he was elected Master, his aim was to carry on with research and writing. He became instead virtually a full-time head of the college. Now he became the chief executive officer of the whole university as well.

In outlook, sympathies, and approach, Butterfield very much remained the historian, the historian at the top. We can regard his activity as vice-chancellor as Butterfield putting his historical thought to work. He behaved like the devotee who was granted just a few moments to promote his cause, and threw himself fully into his new duties. The cause was his vision of the individual, the university, academic research, and education, and he seemed to enjoy thoroughly the politics that provided the medium. Cambridge University, a fairly large institution, became an arena something like a "state" in which he could actually exercise power in keeping with his own maxims for politics and international affairs. He tried to fulfil the role of the wise leader concerned with broad policy, not the administrator of detail or the wielder of power. He would aim to consult widely, seek advice from everyone in question, and consider the history of the issue, just as he often did as Master. He could appear maddeningly indecisive and unsure of himself.[2] "I am," he complained, "working hard throughout the day and well into the morning hours, both harder and more unremitting than ever before in my life and cannot keep pace with the administrative problems of College and University." He wryly observed, "I seem to be receding from history altogether."[3] He was quite conscious of the importance of the office and the brevity of his time at the top. He kept a journal that eventually became "the very big Diary which covered the two years of my Vice-Chancellorship."[4]

He was an ardent believer in the practice of having an amateur vice-chancellor at the head of the university, a scholar only temporarily in office whose primary commitment remained with scholarship. The strategy tended to disperse power at the top, reminding the university of the academic purpose of the enterprise. Since the vice-chancellor was also the head of a college, it allowed the colleges to keep an exalted position within the university ensemble. Though small in number, the permanent members of staff in the central offices of the university exercised considerable de facto power because of their sheer continuity. Policy making remained in the hands of an array of committees composed of academic members, with the Council of the Senate as supreme. The hovering omnipresence of the British government, the supplier of university finances, could be felt at numerous pressure points. The colleges were, to a large degree, financially independent.

The meetings were endless — the Council of the Senate, the General Board, the Financial Board, the Registry, the committees for particular purposes, the building committees, special meetings to discuss reports, meetings with professors, meetings with heads of colleges, meetings with the government officials, meetings with the vice-chancellors of other universities as well as the many ceremonies. He entertained distinguished visitors. In his time, Queen Elizabeth, Princess Alexandra, President John F. Kennedy, the archbishop of Canterbury, the king and queen of Siam, and a string of lesser lights shone in the Cambridge sky, with Butterfield at the centre. He gave speech after speech, all written out word for word, at the lunches or dinners of university societies and local groups, from the Cambridgeshire Air Squadron to the Cambridge Branch of the Trustee Savings Bank. He dined at more than half of the colleges, and hosted numberless guests at the Master's Lodge of Peterhouse. The usual format for guests at Peterhouse was the formal dinner for fourteen on Saturday nights in the Lodge. He worried about the quality of the wine and the food to be served, not because he had turned gourmand, but to build a counterimage of himself, lest his guests expect the austere meals and ginger beer they heard were his diet in the Lodge. Butterfield, the teetotaler, ordered better wine for the college wine cellar.

His moment as vice-chancellor occurred precisely at the dawn of a period of extraordinary change in the university. Undergraduate enrolment had begun to rise. From 1949 to 1959 the number of new students entering had fluctuated around 2,800 per year. From 1959 to 1969 it rose steadily, from 2,800 to over 3,500 per year, an increase of 25 percent. The old colleges were just starting to expand their memberships, and new colleges were being built or planned. During Butterfield's term of office Churchill College received recognition as the first new undergraduate college since Selwyn College in 1883, and Fitzwilliam House made plans to become a college. Sociology finally became a regular teaching subject, and new accommodations for the social sciences were nearly finished on Sidgwick Avenue. The science and engineering faculties were expanding, and new buildings were under construction around town to house them. Butterfield presided over a long debate and enquiry about salaries in the medical school, which were rising considerably higher than those in other fields. He argued strongly for the financial equality of the arts faculties with medicine and the sciences. Before the matter was settled, he put the government on the defensive by reminding them that the autonomy of the university from external domination of any kind was necessary for the well-being of the kingdom. The needs of research students pressed for attention. As the numbers of research students began to rise, it became more unreal to treat them as mere appendages to the undergraduate population, the traditional focus of the colleges and the university. Butterfield discarded the view he had argued against Kitson Clark that research students were by occupation meant to be isolated, and came out in favour of new facilities to serve their common needs. Most important to him, when the government created a commission, chaired by Lord Bridges, to enquire whether to maintain the traditional double teaching system in Cambridge and Oxford as represented by university lectures and college supervisions, he defended the academic validity of the colleges, even though the system could look redundant, costly, and inefficient. Undergraduate teaching was, he said, "the most momentous of all the problems of the academic world." The colleges had the particular duty, he argued, "to keep watch over the development of individual students and elicit the originality that may be latent in them, and in any case not simply stoke them up for examinations." His rhythm had two beats — the centrality of teaching in the colleges and the autonomy of the university and advanced research.[5]

Like the lay preacher on the circuit, Butterfield tended to repeat his message at every forum available to him, inside the university as well as outside it, from the conference of the chief education officers of Great Britain to the meeting of the chief executives of Shell Oil International. What he said in his speeches perfectly coalesced with what he published in his books. He had no doubt that his belief in the all-importance of individuals in history, which he had preached all his adult life, applied to the world of the growing university. The New Whig model of social change which he praised in his historical and political writings would serve Cambridge University in its period of great and rapid change. He reiterated this model in his final address upon stepping down as vice-chancellor. He liked the Cambridge he had known since the 1920s, but, he said, it was urgent for the university not simply to defend the existing order. The university must discover flexibility within itself and respond in good time to the notices of genuine needs before the boiler burst into revolution and destroyed the whole lot. Turning his sense of the recent past towards the future, he predicted that the decade of the 1960s could be "the most momentous in the history of universities." "Momentous" was his word as vice-chancellor.[6]

Years later when assessing Butterfield's achievement, Owen Chadwick summarized a widely shared opinion about his tenure in office: "Controversial or not, he has been declared by a qualified judge, who disagreed with him over the medical question, to be an outstanding vice-chancellor of that epoch. Butterfield's defence of the university, against the most formidable onslaught yet directed against its entire system of teaching, has become celebrated." He embodied his own doctrine of individualism, as well as his ethos of dissent, this time, dissent at the top. At such a moment as this, if a person with opposite views had occupied the office of vice-chancellor, the outcome might well have been different, and the system of colleges as centres of academic vitality might have dissolved.[7]

Shortly before becoming vice-chancellor, Butterfield travelled to the United States at the invitation of Wabash College in Hanover, Indiana. He came away with many good things to say about the small self-standing liberal arts college in the United States, even claiming to see redeeming qualities in college fraternities. He suggested, however, that "the very friendliness" of the place may be a disadvantage "if it helps to produce low pressure or prevents the elastic from being kept at a stretch." His experience in middle America warmed him up for his defense of the Cambridge system. Cambridge, he said, combined the educational relationship between one teacher and one student in the small college with the scholarly resources and energy of a multitude of scholars "keeping one another on their toes" in the large university.[8]

Soon after his term at the head of Cambridge ended, the Lindsay Lectures at the University College of North Staffordshire, later named the University of Keele, gave him the opportunity to summarize his views on education in the light of his recent experience. The small book of 110 pages that resulted, *The Universities and Education Today,* his nineteenth, revealed how little he had strayed from his convictions of the 1920s and 1930s. In the book he centres his thought on the relationship between the individual teacher and the individual student, which he calls "the most important aspect of all education": "Now the first point I want to put to you about universities is that they ought primarily to be regarded as the arena in which there is to occur the electric contact between teacher and pupil. The generation of the electricity that would turn cold wires into live wires . . . is the central requirement of any teaching system, the supreme object of all our educational arrangements." His second point is the obligation of universities to promote originality in "the development of science, scholarship and thought," a task they accomplish by enabling autonomous individual scholars to devote themselves to research. His vision features collections of individuals driven by the creative impulse to know, to understand, and to go beyond their teachers: "We have to avoid and to counteract the illusion which the examination system so often tends to foster — the notion that knowledge just exists in a fixed state — when, in reality, the whole point of the exercise is to capture it while it is fluid. . . . In the realm of ideas the best kind of organization is the one that is most conducive to elasticity of mind." Butterfield's words give evidence that he possessed no idea of the university as a whole, no sense of the university as a community that transcends the mere sum of the individuals attached to it. Yet, at the same time, he upholds the example of Cambridge University as a whole, including the Peterhouse he had always known, as the norm for the universities in general.[9]

Butterfield became an activist for his vision of the individual, teaching, and research. In 1960 he was elected to the Executive Committee of the Association of Universities of the British Commonwealth, to the Commission of Higher Education of Ireland, and to the Administrative Board of the International Association of Universities. In 1961 he joined the Court of Governors of the London School of Economics, and, after the death of Namier, the Committee of the Institute of Historical Research in London, and in 1962 the Advisory Council on Public Records. He faithfully attended the meetings of all these boards. The University of Hong Kong gave him his sixth honourary doctorate when he visited there in 1961 for the Commonwealth group. In the International Association of Universities, from his first meeting in Mexico City in September 1960 through five more annual meetings, in Paris, New Delhi, Peterhouse, Moscow, and Tokyo, he advanced his version of the Cambridge model and promoted the autonomy of universities from governments, industry, and the church. When Manchester University proposed to award him an honourary doctorate in 1966, the vice-chancellor asked him to make the autonomy of the university the theme of his acceptance address, and he gladly obliged by delivering a vigorous statement against government intrusion.

Butterfield seemed to be more insistent than usual in preaching the message of the individual. In one sense, his accent on individuals came merely as the next turn in the cycle of his perennial thinking which would stress at one moment the individual personality and at the next the processes and structures of history. He was also likely at any moment to play the dissenter and raise the opposite point from the one currently voiced. This time he spoke out of his experiences as the head of a large and still growing institution, the University of Cambridge, and his live encounters with the British state and Shell Oil executives. In such contexts he could feel that it was particularly important to repeat as often as possible that individuals are the real units of human society. However, he would signal that his stress on the individual was not simply topical. He seemed to want people to know that he was a Methodist. He made a number of statements around the time of his vice-chancellorship to say that his belief in the individual was an extension of his religion. On such occasions he would omit the qualifying words that usually hedged his assertions and became much more direct in his language. He told the head of the Methodist publishing house in Britain: "I am essentially an individualist, and I believe that religion is a matter between the soul and God. I don't believe in the state as a corporate person at all, and I don't like the idea of the state as being solid and corporate in a single religion. I know it is a very nice thing if all individuals believe the same thing, especially if they believe the right thing, but I don't think that the state has a soul."[10]

He presented a public lecture in Cambridge in 1959, just before rising to the vice-chancellorship, titled "Why I Am a Non-Conformist," explaining to the crowded assembly of students the intellectual factors that kept him securely within the faith of his youth. His reasons were many, but chief among them was his historical judgment that modern individualism "develops out of non-conformity": "It springs in the last resort from the Christian view that it is the single human being — not the state or the corporate society — which has the soul, has the connection with eternity. In fact the challenge of Christ is addressed to the individual soul." His custom had been that whenever he said it is the individual who has the soul, he would attach the authority of Acton's name to the statement, but now he dropped the reference to Acton and took responsibility for the assertion himself. He made it clear that, in reality, he had long ago made Acton's formulation his own. It had always been ironic for Butterfield to cite Action, the Roman Catholic, in support of the doctrine he attributed to Protestant Nonconformity, especially since Acton held such a strong doctrine of the Catholic Church. Lest he be misunderstood about what he meant by "individualism," Butterfield would tell people that his individualism was not the thing associated with self-interest or the self-centredness of much of contemporary society, but the Christian version which insisted on the supreme value of each human personality.[11] He reiterated this message in various formats, including his address on religion and individualism at the first conference, convened at Peterhouse, of the International Society for the History of Ideas, and at a Methodist conference also held in Cambridge.[12] For years to come he would continue to call himself an "individualist," quickly adding that he meant the term in the spiritual sense, and not as used in politics or economics.[13]

The Afterlife

When Butterfield stepped down as vice-chancellor in October 1961, he complained that he felt distinctly older and physically ill for the first time in his career. He now joked about his image in the mirror each morning looking more and more like Ruskin Spear's clown-like portrait of him.[14] He had no respite from administration, however, since he still had his duties as Master of Peterhouse.

Butterfield's college, like the other colleges, experienced in miniature aggrandizing trends similar to those in the university as a whole.[15] Under his guidance, the college allowed the number of its three-year undergraduates to drift upwards from about 150 to around 200, but, unlike the university, placed a ceiling on further increase. He continued his about-face in favour of research students, and led the college to be among the first in Cambridge to emphasize meeting their needs. Their number doubled to around 40, which, with the fourth-year students, put the total student figure at about 260, keeping Peterhouse still among the smallest in Cambridge. Butterfield was able to direct part of the large bequest from William Stone, a wealthy alumnus of the college, towards the assistance of research students, including, from 1961 to 1963, nine new nonvoting research fellowships. New common facilities for research students were established in an old part of the college near the Hall, but they were not used much. The college took over the building vacated by Fitzwilliam House next to the Master's Lodge, and soon converted it into a residence for research students, called The Hostel. Butterfield himself continued to take on research students, who during the 1960s included C. B. McCullough, Frank O'Gorman, and Patrick Cosgrave. However, with the swelling in the overall number of research students in Cambridge, he supervised many fewer in this period than Kitson Clark and the very active younger historians Owen Chadwick, Geoffrey Elton, and J. H. Plumb.

The college also increased the number of Fellows, bringing the total to twenty-six by 1962–1963, and expanding the fields covered by the college, particularly in the sciences. To accommodate the Fellows, some of the Stone money paid for an new eight-storey building in the college gardens, a modern structure that easily elicited jokes about putting "the solemn and sober Master on the top floor." When Denis Mack Smith left the college in 1962 for All Souls College, Oxford, and David Knowles retired as Regius Professor in 1963, the elections of Roger Lovatt and Maurice Cowling as Fellows kept the history-related contingent at eight. The temporary addition of J. R. Vincent raised the number briefly to nine until M. M. Postan retired in 1965. The departure of Knowles and Postan reduced the professors in the college who were listed with the History Faculty to Brogan and Butterfield. Brogan's retirement in 1967 left Butterfield as the lone Professor of History, within a cohort of seven remaining historians. The retirements of the professors, which could not be helped, and the increase of the number of Fellows and the diversification of fields, both pursued according to sound educational policy, had the unintended effect of reducing the relative importance of history within the college. Ironically, it was the historian Butterfield who promoted and presided over the end of the dominance of historical studies in Peterhouse.

At the end of his vice-chancellorship, Butterfield freely admitted that his historical work was suffering severely. He appeared particularly contemplative about his own contribution as a historian thus far in his career. Near the end of 1961 or early in 1962, he wrote out a lengthy memoir commenting on the achievements of several historians active during his time. The subtext was his unspoken reflections on his own place within twentieth-century English historiography.[16] The collage of comments revealed his own desires about himself as a historian. To his arch-opponent Namier, who had just died, he accorded less than a sentence, set within his remarks about someone else. But what a sentence it was: "No one could say for a moment that he [John Neale] had the brilliance and the imaginative vision of Namier, or the extraordinary insights and originality — all those things which in Namier went beyond mere technique." Perhaps only Trevelyan received the higher praise. On Butterfield's reckoning, Trevelyan was the one English historian who "most definitely bears the marks of greatness." He was not a great technical historian, he made no discoveries through research, and he was a poor lecturer, but he made the past live again and expressed "a deep human wisdom which is his commentary on the story he narrates." Trevelyan had been Butterfield's constant admirer since 1931, when he gave the young historian the Fox papers and opened the road for him to pursue the biography of Fox. Trevelyan died not long after Butterfield drafted this private memoir, the Fox work still unfinished. Butterfield accorded Toynbee high praise, calling him the doyen of those historians still at work. In spite of Toynbee's inaccuracies and apparent egotism, and although the form of his project was archaic even when he began, "what he has done has real significance and importance, because it has been so stimulating and has provoked so much discussion." Butterfield liked R. H. Tawney, who had just died, admired his compassion for the poor and the cause of the working class, and praised his powers in technical research which produced the things that made students "change their structural ideas," but he objected to Tawney's slant, which made so much of his work propaganda for Labour, just as Trevelyan could not help being the Whig historian. G. N. Clark, he thought, "has altered our view of the nature of general history, since he sees the importance of studying all the various facets of an age," and he regarded him a the principal editor of history of his day, but, he continued, "I do not regard him as a powerful mind." T. H. Ashton was "the most genuinely unassuming of all the historians," a patient collector of data without wide horizons, but a real master about industrialization, the "limited world" he had chosen to examine. Of the Oxford historians, both A. J. P. Taylor and Hugh Trevor-Roper were brilliant historians, Butterfield said, as well as "exceptionally clever and prolific journalists," but not trustworthy guides to history. They slapped down their work too fast, especially Taylor, who "reviewed one of my books without having read it," and became impatient when his book on the origins of the First World War took more than six months of his time.

Butterfield left ample clues in other places about his emerging self-assessment. In November 1961 Temperley's son, Neville Temperley, now a scientist, revived the question of the biography that Butterfield had promised twenty years before to write about his teacher and protector, reminding him that Temperley's papers were still in Butterfield's basement. Butterfield confessed that he was quite aware, as he put it, "that all my long-term writing projects are held up — including my main researches, commitments which go back earlier than the memoir, and earlier even than 1939." In 1958 he had already made the painful admission to his teacher's widow, Dorothy Temperley, that he had damaged his productivity as an academic historian by allowing himself to undertake so many lectures and papers over the years: "If I hadn't adopted the policy of publishing these and digging out for publication things largely written many years ago, I'm afraid I should have produced nothing." In any case, he confessed, the Temperley memoir had gotten out of hand and turned into a much larger project than he initially thought. "I rather dreamed of making it something of a model of its kind," he told her.[17] Neville Temperley's inquiry led Butterfield to meditate on his mentor's life as well as his own. He sat down and in short order wrote out a 173-page memoir of

Temperley as well as another 67 pages of autobiography covering his relationship with Temperley, Vellacott, his father, and his teachers in his youth. The hoped-for little book on Temperley remained on his unfinished list, however. The Temperley family asked him to return the papers they had loaned him. Some of the Temperley material did make it into introductions Butterfield wrote for reprints of two of Temperley's books, one in 1966 and the other in 1968.[18]

Butterfield amplified his self-assessment in the draft of a letter suggesting that he resign from the British Rockefeller committee on international theory which he had founded and still chaired. The vice-chancellorship was over, he said, but he was still Master of his college and immersed in university affairs. He admitted that the plan for him to fill the role of the scholar-Master had failed, and he had no proper time for his own research and writing. He then identified the areas in which he believed he had made real achievements: history of science, history of historiography, history and religion, what he called "the various kinds of history that I have tried to promote. His remarkably candid commentary on himself displayed insight about where to look when evaluating his accomplishments, but he worded the statement as if his work in those three fields impeded the fulfilment of his real calling, which, he said, was to be a research historian.[19] Repeatedly during the 1960s he would belittle the more reflective and theoretical sides of his own work, and tell people, "I am merely a technical historian, essentially a secular historian."[20]

The act which assuaged Butterfield's despondency was his long delayed selection, announced in April 1963, as Regius Professor of Modern History. With the retirement of Knowles, he at last received the Crown's appointment to the most prestigious history chair in Cambridge. He ranked the honour as the capstone of his achievements within the university, worth more to him than the vice-chancellorship. He became the sixteenth occupant since the Crown established the chair in 1724. He could relish the thought that he now was truly a successor to Acton. So much of his life had revolved around certain of the figures who held the chair before him in the twentieth century — Acton, Bury, Trevelyan, Clark, Knowles.[21] He was in their company. The History Faculty now listed ten professors and thirty-one university lecturers, within a total of about a hundred historians altogether. C. H. Wilson succeeded him in the chair of modern history, C. R. Cheney had held the medieval chair since 1955, and Owen Chadwick had been Dixie Professor of Ecclesiastical History since 1958. George Kitson Clark still had his readership, J. H. Plumb had just received one, and F. H. Hinsley received one shortly thereafter. As if he needed more administrative duties, Butterfield became chair of the board of the History Faculty in 1964, and helped superintend the expansion of the university history staff and the next phase of reforms in the curriculum.[22]

The other usual symbols of recognition in England came to him late as well. After six honourary doctorates outside England, English universities finally began to celebrate his achievements — Sheffield (1962), Hull (1963), Manchester (1966), Warwick (1967), London (1968). He was finally elected a Fellow of the British Academy in 1965, nearly twenty years after his friend Knowles. With the Regius appointment in hand, he received, and accepted, the invitation from the Scottish authorities to deliver the prestigious Gifford Lectures in religion for 1965 and 1966, to be held at Glasgow University, joining a list which included Reinhold Niebuhr, Rudolph Bultmann, Karl Barth, and Arnold Toynbee.

At the same time, Butterfield's fame extended still further outside Britain, particularly in the United States, Canada, and Germany. The media were new and reissued editions of his most influential books, especially in North America, and translations of his work into other languages. Scribner reissued the American edition of *Christianity and History* in 1961, and by 1966 the book had been translated into nine foreign languages: German, Norwegian, Chinese, Swedish, French, Spanish, Finnish, Italian, and Dutch. The revised edition of *Origins of Modern Science,* which appeared from Bell in London in 1957, was published by Macmillan in New York as well, and still more reissues came from Collier in New York in 1962, the Free Press in New York in 1965, and Clarke in Toronto in 1968. The book was translated into Spanish, Italian, Swedish, Greek, and Japanese. No translation of *Whig Interpretation of History* appeared, except for the unauthorized publication of two chapters in a French political newspaper. The book remained in active circulation in the English and American editions of the early fifties, and new publishers brought out editions: Norton in New York in 1965, followed by a mass circulation Penguin edition in 1973. *Man on His Past* reached an American edition for the first time in 1960, published by Beacon Press in Boston.[23]

The new life granted Butterfield's books overseas stimulated a constant line of overseas historians, especially Americans and Germans, to come for a visit to Peterhouse, and American and German universities issued invitations to him in abundance. Throughout the 1960s, American institutions issued invitations for him to deliver special lectures or occupy a visiting professorship, many reporting that he would follow Toynbee or Paul Tillich or Karl Popper or some other notable: Harvard, Massachusetts Institute of Technology, Union Theological Seminary in New York, American University, Johns Hopkins, Rice, Colgate Rochester Divinity School, Pittsburgh, Stanford, University of

California at Berkeley, Yale, Dartmouth, Wesleyan, St. Louis, Oberlin, the Smithsonian Institute, Duke, North Carolina, Denver, New York University, Cornell, and many more. In his new mood of self-assessment, he determined to decline all of them, that is, nearly all, protesting that he was too busy or spreading himself too thin.[24] German universities took him to Germany three times in the 1960s. The last was in 1968 when the University of Bonn awarded him an honourary doctorate, his twelfth, for his accomplishments beneficial to German scholarship. In 1967, the American Historical Association, the American Academy of Arts and Sciences, and the Royal Irish Society each made him an honourary member. He was especially gratified when the American Historical Association proudly recalled that Ranke had been the first foreign historian accorded that status. Paradoxically, the grander his reputation became in the sixties, the more despondent he felt about the inadequacies of his achievement as a technical historian.

After 1961 Butterfield had fully intended to settle back into the long-range projects he counted as his real work. These were the life of Fox, "for which I have a lot of material not yet written up," and the *Concise Cambridge Modern History*, "a large volume hardly half finished," which he began to call *The Shorter Cambridge Modern History*. He wrote the administrator at the Rockefeller Foundation, Kenneth Thompson, that he felt both the university and the college "would approve and assist the project of my drawing a hard line across my administrative career, regarding my return to history as the primary object."[25] He was fishing for an invitation to Villa Serbelloni, owned by the Rockefeller Foundation at Bellagio on Lake Como in northern Italy. He had fallen in love with the villa in the spring of 1960 when, as promotional advertising for their newly acquired retreat, the foundation treated him to a couple weeks there between terms. Butterfield caught his fish, and he got the Lent term 1962 at the villa, his first little sabbatical leave since 1949 when he went for one term to Princeton.[26]

He used the time to advantage, but not to further the Fox biography or the *Shorter History*. He wrote up instead the material for two outside lectureships, the very thing he wanted to get away from. These were his Lindsay Lectures from November 1961, for publication as *The Universities and Education Today*, and his Creighton Lecture in History at the University of London from October 1961, which London published as *Charles James Fox: The Peace Negotiations of 1806*.[27] The London lecture did, of course, take him back to Fox in a sense, but not in the way Butterfield wished. He rummaged through his old research notes for *Napoleon's Peace Tactics* from the 1920s, as if neither he nor historiography had moved on in the intervening thirty-some years. At the lecture itself he confessed, "I am appalled to find myself offering for the occasion the useless narrative of one of the craziest negotiations that I have ever studied." He removed the line from the printed version of the lecture.[28]

In the coming months he did pull out his drafts of "England and the French Revolution of 1792," material that nearly became the final section of *George III and the Historians* five years earlier. He added a little more to the manuscript, but did not complete it. He produced a fascinating paper entitled "Reminiscences of an Enquiry into the Crisis of 1792," read to audiences at Peterhouse and Trinity College in 1963, in which he submitted himself to a kind of historiographical reconstruction, analyzing the steps that he had taken since the 1920s in deciding that 1792 was the third "great crisis" of George III's period. The other two crises were the case of John Wilkes and Middlesex in 1769–1770, and the episodes of 1779–1780 which he included in *George III, Lord North, and the People.*[29]

Butterfield was beginning to realize that Fox was slipping too far out of his reach. He told F. M. H. Markham of Oxford, then planning his own book on Fox, that he still had the biography in mind and that "though I am sure that the world will never believe me, I personally think that it will appear some day but not yet."[30] His notes show that he scratched a little further in some Fox materials, perhaps as late as 1967, but not much. At this point in his life he seemed to have genuinely lost interest in Fox, although he kept on telling himself and others that Fox was his real work.

Even the *Concise Cambridge Modern History* was slipping away as well. As vice-chancellor he had given no courses, and now he was entirely free to offer whatever he wished. He could have resumed his lectures on the general history of modern Europe, and used them as he once hoped, to generate work on the book. Instead his big course on modern Europe died quietly and his career as a lecturer on general history simply faded away. His student J. H. Elliott carried on alone with a different course covering a briefer period, 1494–1715. Butterfield took the big decision to devote his university lectures to the eighteenth century. He first devised a one-term course, "Diplomatic History in the 18th Century," related to his interest in the states-system and international affairs. Then, upon becoming Regius Professor in 1963, he switched to "George III and the Politicians, 1760 to 1765," on the political controversies during the first five years of the new king's rule. It appeared under "Special Subjects" leading to the Tripos examinations, and entailed lectures twice a week for two terms. His lectures engaged in the minute dissection of documents in connection with topics that historians had controverted since the 1760s. The subjects seemed genuinely to intrigue him. He raised the same sorts of issues that took him off Fox in the 1930s to begin with and that later channeled his antagonism towards Namier in the 1950s. He told the editors of the *Historical*

Journal, speaking of the early George III, "I don't like the way the interpretation of this period is going; and fundamentally, I think my way of treating the
controversy is the proper one." The immediate question he had in mind concerned the foreign policy of George III, but his remark applied equally to home
politics.[31]

The course was to be the finale of his lecturing career. In a mysterious way it
also took him back to the very beginning, to 1921–1922 when he himself
prepared "George III and the Whigs, 1760–71" for his Tripos. His approach
stressed historical criticism of the documents, although he did not eschew
controversy. He liked the debate about documents that kept things fluid and
questioned the prevailing orthodoxies. It was as if he were seeking to revive the
technical historian within him, the technician who deals precisely with documents. By the time he retired in 1968 he had accumulated at least twenty
lectures running to about three hundred pages of text. Some of the lectures
came in several versions or stages of revision, adding up to many more pages.[32]
His lectures analyzed the reversionary interest, the accession of George III, the
resignation of Pitt, the fall of Newcastle, Bute and Frederick the Great, and the
victory of Fox and Bute. He raised the same questions that had stayed with
him for years: did George III intend to increase royal power? was a two-party
system in operation in 1760? was there a genuine opposition? what were the
relations of the king with his ministers? what was the English role in the
diplomatic revolution around 1763?

In the process, he seemed to give up his acrimonious debate with Namier,
even to undermine his own stringent comments against Namier on the BBC in
1961 and 1964 and in his review of *The History of Parliament* early in 1965.
Namier appeared in the first lecture in the course, the introductory lecture,
where Butterfield set up the historiographical problem. He re-found his reconciling method and, with little fanfare, simply absorbed Namier into his spongy
notion of different "levels" on which to see the same thing. He construed
Namier's work as belonging to the level of the underlying structures and
conditions, while his own work belonged to the level of the reconstruction of
the narrative of the actions of important political individuals: "Here is the
ultimate issue: Given the character and structure of the country as described in
Namier's *Structure of Politics,* looking down on the whole from the top, how
were you to govern a country in that particular state, that particular predicament?"[33] With this as his intellectual resolution of the Namier controversy, he
sought to heal his human relations with John Brooke. He did with Namier's
successor what he failed to do with Namier. He met with Brooke in November
1965 at Peterhouse, where they talked amicably at length about the compati-
bility of their approaches to history. It was an act of virtual self-renunciation.[34]

Butterfield managed to publish a couple of articles and give some special lectures on George III and related themes.[35] He very nearly produced a small book on the king. He signed a contract in 1967 for *George III: Great Lives Observed* in a series for Prentice-Hall which combined a biography with selected documents. But he broke the agreement over what he claimed was the publisher's unfair treatment of authors and alleged deception about the finances of the series. The complaint was convenient, since on second thought, he had found himself unhappy with the format of the series, and felt that if he were going to publish a book on George III or the eighteenth century, he wanted to define the character of the work for himself. After consultation with Butterfield, Denis Mack Smith chose to go ahead with his volume on Garibaldi in the series.[36]

He received other invitations to publish. Geoffrey Barraclough brought him an attractive proposal to write a volume on the eighteenth century, or maybe the scientific revolution, for a new, fully illustrated Thames and Hudson series on European history. Butterfield paused only briefly before turning it down.[37] Later, Robert Blake asked him to contribute the volume on 1760–1865 for the Granada series on British history. He declined this request as well.[38] He nearly became entangled as general editor of a twenty-volume "World History Library" to be published by Paul Hamlyn, who thought Butterfield had agreed to sign on, but he got himself out of the thicket by excusing himself for not being clear when he was trying to say no. He explained, "I am afraid I am a victim of my temperament, and, if I have taken anything on, I often find that through some inner compulsion of my own it gives me a lot of work though nobody intends this to happen."[39]

He occasionally found new general history projects still springing up in his mind. He revived his old love for historical geography from the 1940s, and in 1964 proposed to R. W. David, the new secretary of Cambridge University Press, that he do a *Historical Geography of Europe*. Citing the support of G. R. Potter, he added the suggestion of an entire Cambridge series on historical geography, written and edited by historians. David loved the idea, but the immediate proposal collapsed. The Press eventually carried Butterfield's suggestion forward on a different scale and in another format, but with Butterfield's title.[40] In the meantime, David gently reminded Butterfield that "we still have you cast as the author of the *Concise Modern History*," and during the next few years continued to put light pressure on him to complete the work. Butterfield may have done some reworking of a few chapters in the 1960s, but he seemed not to be able to keep his mind on the project.[41]

All the same, he still found both time and motivation to publish yet another study or two on Lord Acton, almost as affirmation of the unflagging continuity of his historical vocation.[42]

13

Going Global

Global Historiography

The thing that most nourished Butterfield's imagination after his vice-chancellorship was his love for historical thought. Thinking in general about history could go in his head while he was doing something else, even university administration. Subtly, without explicit resolve, he occupied himself more and more with the history of historiography. His thinking became comparative, and expanded to cover the whole globe. In spite of his exaltation of "technical history," he had neither the time nor, apparently, the interest to resume the minutely detailed and seemingly unending research that his method demanded. He had already demonstrated that general historical thinking could produce far-reaching effects, with the promise of long-lasting results. In the history of historiography, he found new purpose, new inspiration, and when he finally gave himself again to the subject, new excitement in his work.

The lecture he delivered by invitation at the International Congress of Historical Sciences in Stockholm, August 1960, while vice-chancellor, laid out a direction consistent with the wide view of ideas of history he had begun to adopt.[1] He issued something like an appeal for the historical profession to pursue "an all-embracing history of History," fully global and fully comparative. As usual he called for an approach that travelled well beyond the mere history of books or the history of historians, but now he also wished to move beyond what he had advocated so earnestly and so recently about technical history as a branch of science in *Man on His Past,* as well as beyond the appreciation of history as a branch of literature which he had promised in the earliest years of his career. The "history of History" would be a species of general history, and bear some of the features of "universal history." He had in mind the notion of the "idea of history," something he had raised before, which he also called an "attitude to the past." He urged the study of the "multiple forms of the whole attitude of human beings to the past — the attitude of the men of any period to the course of events in time." Butterfield's Stockholm address had a missionary ring to it, like his Wiles lectures in Belfast six years previously when he first preached the merits of the history of historiography. Now he embraced the whole globe, many cultures, and many more aspects of the topic.[2]

The breadth and inclusivity of his proposal for the "history of History" appeared very clearly in a plan he was pursuing quietly on the side. In anticipation of Stockholm, he sent an exploratory letter about a possible conference on the history of historiography to Arnold Momigliano of Turin and London, C. H. Phillips of the London School of Oriental and African Studies, and Theodore Schieder of Cologne. His thought was to invite a select number of scholars with a major interest in the subject to Villa Serbelloni, the Rockefeller Foundation's site in northern Italy. He wrote out a sheet of names of possible German scholars, and at Stockholm talked with Stuart Hughes of Harvard, Franco Venturi of Turin, and Giorgio Spini of Florence. When the conference of the International Society for the History of Ideas met at Peterhouse just after Stockholm, he discussed his idea with Karl Löwith, Pietro Rossi, and J. Romein. All encouraged him to carry on. The director of the villa advised him to develop a plan.[3]

Butterfield drafted a lengthy memorandum on the scope and objects of the conference, producing a programmatic statement of his still expanding idea for the study of the history of historiography. Three points mattered most to him, all three comprehensive in their import. The study needed to treat the subject as a whole, reaching into all fields that dealt with historical writings — theology, history, philosophy, classics, biblical studies, Oriental and African studies, literature, law, education, anthropology, and so on. The study had to be comparative, placing culture after culture next to each other. The study also should cover all aspects of the subject — historical writing, ideas of the past, the use of the past, notions of time-process, philosophy of history, historians, historical method, precedent, attitudes to the past, historical education, memory, and more. Perhaps without realizing it, he was playing with a strategy of team scholarship, a collective enterprise closer, ironically, to Namier's model than to his own of the individual scholar working in isolation. The questions raised by such a study would require wide collaboration among scholars in order to arrive at answers. For instance, why did Indian culture seem to lack, as he presumed, the historical sense? Why did Chinese historiography develop so differently from European versions? What has been the relation between historiography and religion in various cultures? What impact have Europe and America had on Chinese and Indian historiography in recent times? He could, of course, multiply questions like these endlessly. Indeed, no sooner did Butterfield write his memo than he realized that no conference could cover what he had in mind. In any case, he was too overwhelmed with his affairs to organize such a complicated conference far from home. He never sent the memo. The proposal for a conference collapsed. Nonetheless, he gained from the experience a clearer picture in his own mind of a field of study which he found wonderful.[4]

While he was spinning all these threads with no result, he received independent support for his leadership in historiography from the United States. George Nadel, an editor of the newly founded journal *History and Theory,* honoured him as the source of inspiration for the wider approach to the history of historiography that motivated the journal: "The fog . . . has been dispelled by you, some of the ground rules adumbrated — in short, we are once more indebted to you for a new avenue of historical study."[5]

Butterfield was also source of renewed inspiration for another journal founded in the United States some years earlier, *Journal of the History of Ideas.* When the International Society for the History of Ideas began in New York in 1959, Butterfield and Gilbert Chinard of Princeton wrote the statement of the objectives of the organization. It was shortly after Stockholm that he hosted the first conference of the new body at Peterhouse. He continued to be active in the society in one way or another into the 1970s.[6]

After Stockholm, Butterfield returned to the London School of Oriental and African Studies in the fall of 1960 to sketch the history of "attitudes to the past." In September 1961 he went on the BBC with a smaller version of the same thing. The theme that attracted him above all was the question of "the emergence of what we call 'the sense for the past.'" This was the same question of "origins" that had concerned him about modern science. Why and how did people come to have attitudes to the past and to convert their attitudes into the drive to create historical thinking and historical writing? He offered no answer in the lecture, and merely suggested what might be needed to answer so comprehensive a question. To find an answer would require, he said, a "deep cut" into many civilizations and a look at human actions as seemingly far apart as astronomy, calendar making, business accounting, religion, law, and philosophy.[7]

China was beginning to stand out as Butterfield's "other" culture, and Chinese historical writing was moving to the top of his agenda as the important non-European tradition to study for comparative purposes. He followed in this choice the example of Joseph Needham, his long-time colleague in the history of science in Cambridge, and the director of a monumental series of volumes on the history of science in China.[8]

China, he decided, was the one society outside "Western civilization" that had developed historical writing and historical thinking on a large scale. Without looking closely at the matter, he accepted the conventional judgment about the insignificance of the historical thought and writing of India, and at this moment in his calculations he overlooked Islamic societies and underrated the oral traditions of Africa and elsewhere. Even his choice of China belittled Chinese achievements. The European and American student, he concluded, "ought to look to China if only in order to learn how historical scholarship may go wrong." This he said over the BBC. He went on to downgrade the historiography of Mesopotamia, Egypt, Greece, Rome, and Latin and Byzantine Christendom. The historical interest, he declared, "emerges as a mixed and mongrel thing, not anything so pure as is often imagined." At first "history" came "entangled" with other things, such as king lists, scriptures, law codes, business records, myth-making, war heroics, the legitimation of power, and much more. Only late in the day, in western Europe, did the world effect the historical revolution in the nineteenth century comparable to the scientific revolution in the seventeenth, and thus achieve the genuine article.[9]

He revealed once again, even when thinking globally, that he celebrated post-Göttingen historiography, the tradition he discussed in *Man on His Past*, as the "real history," and that European "scientific history" served as the norm by which he judged all other historiography. He continued as well to structure the analysis around his habitual separation of "real history" from all the other activities and features of life.

A clear direction opened in front of him, one he himself might wish to pursue. He possessed a compelling interest in the work and held the sketch of a program in his hand, even if negative evaluations of other cultures generated much of the inspiration. In its generality and vast range, this project was the extreme opposite of the model of scientific history he had upheld since the 1920s: the minutely detailed search into the documents, the day-by-day collation of the evidence, and the piecemeal reconstruction of the narrative. The project also shot him straight past Europe as the stuff of general history. If he adopted even a portion of the new program for himself, he would embark on a course of action quite different from the ordinary.

Arnold Toynbee's new work gave Butterfield the opportunity to declare himself. The London *Sunday Telegraph* asked him to review Toynbee's *Reconsiderations,* the extraordinary twelfth volume of *A Study of History,* published in 1961. He pointedly took sides against the specialized technical historians who picked away at Toynbee's work. In *Reconsiderations* Toynbee painstakingly reviewed the mountain of criticism hurled by specialists against his comparative world history, and rethought the entirety of his general theory. Butterfield reviewed the volume and once again publicly announced his fundamental sympathy for Toynbee's monumental achievement. He endorsed the project of global historical analysis. At a moment when Toynbee was out favour with the specialists in both Europe and North America, Butterfield, the arch-exponent of minute "technical history," praised him: "In any case, is it not a good thing if one man in a generation, instead of burrowing into some microscopic period, brings an analytical mind to the whole panorama of the historical civilisations? Where work is of this pioneering character and the area is of such colossal magnitude, to judge a Toynbee by the number of his mistakes, rather than by his contribution to science and human understanding, is to cry for the victory of the second-rate."[10]

Without making a big decision about the matter, Butterfield began to follow his new interest. We can watch as the global "history of History" pushes aside both Fox and the *Concise Cambridge Modern History.* He took three steps. First, he decided to try to read every piece of historical writing emanating from classical China that was available to him in translation. He announced his intentions in his lectures on university education at Keele in the fall of 1961. His references to China over the BBC in September 1961 got him stung by China specialists because of his negative reading of Chinese historiography, but he carried on undaunted, modifying his approach only slightly in their direction.[11] He reviewed very positively, and no doubt learned from, the first three volumes of *Historical Writing on the Peoples of Asia,* produced under the leadership of C. H. Phillips at the London School of Oriental and African Studies and published in 1961. This included a volume on historiography in India and South Asia. He persisted nonetheless in regarding Indian attitudes as ahistorical and continued to assess non-European traditions against the norm of modern European historiography.[12]

Secondly, he studied the rise of historical criticism in western Europe, a theme that drove him to read Greek, Roman, and medieval Christian historical writing in detail. He had made a start on this theme around 1957. He produced his initial paper on the subject for presentation in Oxford in 1962, and then a much expanded version in 1965 as visiting professor at Wesleyan University in Connecticut, the center that housed the journal *History and Theory*. In Cambridge, his share of a lecture course, "Introduction to the Materials of Modern History," which ran from 1962 to 1966, included a lecture on this theme.[13]

Thirdly, and branching off from the second, he sought to understand the rise of Christian historiography. This study brought him back to Augustine, who, he believed, marked "the effective transition" towards the positive appreciation of the mundane course of events that he felt became characteristic of Christianity. Years later he commented, "Augustine is the most interesting person I've studied." In a lecture presented at Rice University in Texas in 1963 he confirmed his judgment that the primary thing affecting the way a Christian historian would interpret history was the interest that Christianity took in mundane history.[14] He returned also to the critical study of the biblical writings, acquainting himself at this time with the work of Gerhard von Rad, H. H. Rowley, John Bright, Martin Noth, and W. F. Albright on the Old Testament, and Ernst Fuchs, James Robinson, B. H. Throckmorton, and more Bultmann on the New Testament. He was struck by what he saw as the emphasis on history in the Hebrew Bible, which he called the Old Testament. Without much comparative reading, and certainly none in the ancient historical writings of India known as the *Puranas,* he appropriated the sharp contrast conventionally drawn by European and American scholars between the "historical" religion of Israel and the "mystical ahistorical" religions and philosophies of Asia.[15]

The invitation to offer the famous Gifford Lectures in Scotland arrived at his door in 1963 as an exceedingly timely gift. He had just been elevated to the Regius professorship of modern history. He had already entered deeply into his comparative studies with no destination in view. He was undertaking global travels for the International Association of Universities — Mexico City, Hong Kong, Kuala Lumpur, Delhi, Madras, and would soon go to Warsaw, Moscow, and Tokyo. Without a pause, he proposed to devote his Gifford Lectures to the theme of the emergence of the historical sense as an element of global history. From this moment on, the prospect of the lectures, scheduled for the fall terms of 1965 and 1966, provided the incentive for him to concentrate his scholarly attention on the world history of historiography.

His decision made, Butterfield mounted a campaign to read across a very wide range of the history of historical writing. He dug into his files and folders over the years and collected all the notes he could find on his readings in historiography. It was already a formidable, if haphazard, agglomeration: cards, notebooks, large sheets, and the familiar $3\frac{1}{2}" \times 5\frac{1}{2}"$ slips of paper that he manufactured himself by folding and tearing A2 size sheets. He arranged his notes by cultures and periods: Egypt, Hittites, Old Testament, Latin historiography, early Christian historiography, medieval, and so on. During the two-year interval between the invitation and the first round of lectures, he read voluminously in historical writings and critical studies, wrote thought-essays and lecture-length drafts. He felt overwhelmed by the gaps in his reading. Probably at this time he began to collect his notes in medium-sized, loose-leaf, two-ring blue notebooks, marked "China," "Hittites," or what-not, which were easy for him to carry from place to place.

To write the lectures, he tried, but failed, to get time in 1964 and again in 1965 at the Rockefeller Villa Serbelloni. He went instead in March 1965 to Wesleyan University, where he wrote part of the first set of lectures. He had started the practice around the time of his vice-chancellorship of taking a room for a week or ten days in a hotel by the sea or in a Suffolk town, and going away with his notes and drafts to write. Pamela would sometimes come and use the time to draw. This he did again to write the Gifford Lectures. The Rockefeller Foundation did give him time at the villa in 1966 to prepare a portion of the second set. Referring to his difficulties with getting time for research and writing, he told the foundation, "Please understand that I have found that, in order to be a scholar, I must always conduct a desperate fight." The closer he got to the lectures the less sure he became about whether he had enough to say.[16]

The lectures in Glasgow were ten in all, five on consecutive Fridays during November and early December 1965 and the remaining five a year later. They bore the general title "History of Historiography." For all the fame of the lectureship and its great importance in the history of ideas, his audience numbered only about fifty people. Butterfield recalled the excitement generated by the hundreds who attended his lectures on Christianity and history in 1948, and decided that times had changed.

In his opening remarks, Butterfield poses his central question: "How did men come to have an idea of their existence in time, a notion of what the past had been like, a conception of that human drama which takes place under the sun?" He adds the specific comparative question that motivated his study: "how (did) the West came to be so historically-minded"?[17]

He constructs his search for answers around the question of origins and what he takes to be the origins of successive phases in the history of historical consciousness. He follows a trail that began in Sumer and Babylon and leads to the customary roster of Germans and Germanophile historians in the nineteenth century. He believes from the outset that the connection between history and religion would provide his focus, and, appropriately, he winds in and out of religious topics. The destination is clear: the achievement of scientific narrative history in nineteenth-century western Europe, especially in Germany. He seeks to trace the origins of modern scientific history as a branch of his study of the origins of modern science. And as he did in *Origins of Modern Science,* so with the origins of scientific history. He maintains an anachronistic focus on the modern fixture at the end of the story.

In the first set of lectures, he treated historical writing in Mesopotamia, the pre-classical empires, the Old Testament, Greece and Rome, and China. In the second set a year later, he discussed the New Testament, early Christian historiography with Eusebius and Augustine, historical criticism, the "Great Secularisation," and the nineteenth-century "historical revolution."[18]

The route he follows through the terrain is the conventional history of "Western civilization" as traced in continental Europe or North America. It is important to him that he begins in Mesopotamia, rather than Greece, the usual starting point for someone in Britain. The choice of Greece registers the impact of scholars trained in classics, but since he had escaped classics by resisting his headmaster at Keighley, he remained free to take the milieu of the Old Testament as the decisive beginning. In a thought-essay written while composing the lectures, he commented: "Even today there are people who are willing to say that Herodotus is 'the Father of History'; and the *Encyclopedia Britannica* begins with ancient Greece, without showing any awareness of the fact that it is starting the story almost exactly in the middle."[19]

The story, as Butterfield unfolds it, travelled from Sumer to Ranke by a process of the progressive revelation of the features of modern historical consciousness and modern scientific history. He retraces the route of the story by looking for the appearance of "firsts." The "firsts" are those aspects of the historiographical legacy of each of the peoples he encounters that are similar to his model. While the destination might be far off, he believes he can gain frequent glimpses of the final product.

The beginnings are the king lists found in profusion in ancient Mesopotamia. The construction of these lists of the succession of kings and things in time required orderly and detailed work and provided, as he thinks, the first inklings of "historical science." Then come the annals of the Egyptians, the Hittites, the Assyrians, and the Babylonians, which contained the first, albeit rudimentary, historical narratives.

The firsts he associates with the scriptures of the ancient Hebrews amounted to a quantum leap forward beyond their neighbours. His handling of these writings evidences that he had absorbed some of the strategies of critical biblical scholarship. He poses the thesis that these writings, for the first time in human history, displayed an interest in the actual events of the past, and differentiated a sense of the past from the need to record contemporary affairs or to transmit the record to the next generation. The pivotal episode which elicited this new sense of the past was the escape from Egypt of a part of the people who became the Hebrews. The memory of this exodus converted it into an act of divine deliverance and transmuted it into the experience of all the Hebrews. Jewish historical writing began in order to preserve the memory of the exodus, and the historical memory helped to constitute the people of Israel. The Jews produced the first historian as such, the figure we know as J, the writer of the Jahwehist document that critical biblical theory projects behind some of the text of the Pentateuch. Butterfield regards the discovery of J as a near matchless feat of modern historical criticism. In Butterfield's story, J replaces Herodotus as "the Father of History." Butterfield observes, speaking of J, "His work confronts us for the first time with something that we can really call history, something that is based on an interest in what happened in the past. . . . And here is the first attempt at anything you can really call a history of mankind [as well as] the first attempt ever known to produce the history of a nation." In addition to the J document, he is willing to name Samuel and the first book of Maccabees as the exceptional pieces of "real history" in ancient historical writing.

The series continued with Butterfield indicating the traits of modern historical consciousness and scientific history as they came to the surface. The Greeks were the first to examine the human factors involved in actual happenings and to put forward rational explanations for events, contributing thereby to "the development of a scientific way of treating the historical data that had been established." Eusebius, an early Christian historian, brought to expression a higher order of genuine historical consciousness and created ecclesiastical history as a genre. Augustine produced the first comprehensive interpretation of world history. Lorenzo Valla brought historical criticism to a higher realm. The Benedictine monk Mabillon established the rules for the scientific criticism of charters. And so on. Butterfield passes through the secularization of historical study to the veritable revolution in nineteenth-century western Europe, personified by Ranke, that established what Butterfield regards as modern historical consciousness and the scientific historical method.

The lectures deviate only once from the traditional route from Sumer to Ranke: the Chinese. Butterfield enumerates their accomplishments. The Chinese, very early, produced actual historians whose names we know, these historians wrote complicated histories, their histories offered rational and human explanations for the happenings discussed, and, from a crucial moment in the second century B.C., their historical explanations turned on remarkably refined exercises of historical criticism. Butterfield had done his homework after his initial excursion into China when the specialists assaulted his handling of Chinese achievements. In response, he discards his merely negative assessment of Chinese historiography. Yet he scarcely takes the Chinese historians in their own right, and he neglects to consider their histories in themselves or the integrity of their histories within Chinese cultures. He places little emphasis on what was different about the understandings of history revealed by Chinese writings and the social relationships and practices associated with them. Instead, he scans the histories for what might seem similar to modern European historiography. The Chinese play the role in his argument of the outsiders who, amazingly, manage to approximate certain of the feats of the main actors in the story in Europe.

After we see what Butterfield does with China, we are able to realize that he has done the same with every culture he encounters in his story, except for post-Göttingen European historiography. Strictly speaking, Butterfield's study of China discloses not "Chinese historiography," but aspects of "real history" in China. Likewise, he examines Mesopotamia, Egypt, Israel, Greece, early Christianity, and medieval and early modern Europe only in so far as they display features similar to, or appear as precursors of, historiography in modern western Europe. J, if not D, the Deuteronomist, was the first historian because he seemed to achieve "real history" that approximated later German historiography. Butterfield scarcely treats any writings of the other historiographies in their own integrity and on their own merits.

His Gifford Lectures deliver much less than the expectations raised by his Stockholm address in 1960. In Stockholm he called for the study of the "multiple forms of the whole attitude of human beings to the past — the attitude of the men of any period to the course of events in time." In Glasgow he delivers merely the ways he thinks certain peoples anticipated post-Göttingen historiography. We now understand better the character of the project to which at Stockholm he gave the name "an all-embracing history of History." The capital H on "History" indicates the one historical method and the final history that are valid for all and belong to all, whatever their politics or religion, and, we may add, whatever their culture or time.

There is, however, an opposite tendency pulsing through his lectures, even if it is weaker than the dominant one. To be sure, Butterfield has not yet found a way to handle the diversity and indigeneity of the historical writings and the historical sense of the astounding variety of the peoples of the globe, all of whom have their own historical traditions. However, he does signal his awareness of the complexity of the experiences of historiography throughout global history. In his introductory statement at the start of his second year of lectures in Glasgow, in the lecture on the New Testament, he writes: "There is a sense, therefore, in which our story has to go back to the beginning again, as it already had to do in a number of cases—the Egyptians, the Assyrians, the ancient Hebrews and the ancient Greeks, for example. That is to say, we have to trace the actual genesis of an interest in the past, a concern for history, in a people initially without it." Even if the sub-story of "firsts" is simple, Butterfield's whole story is not. When he tells us about the historiography of each of these peoples, including the Chinese, he engages, at the very least, the things that encompass the "firsts." The strategy that propels him past Herodotus as "the Father of History" also induces him to enlarge the range of what he calls historical writing. He brings forward as historiography a great variety of writings not normally included by the term, such as king lists, scriptures, law codes, business records, astronomical charts, and more. He suggests the makings of an approach that, further pursued, could honour the sheer variety of modes of historical expression of each people. The global history of historiography to which he points would encompass the special character of each people's sense of history, and the multiplicity of ways the peoples of the world have expressed their historical understandings of themselves and the world. It might not be too large a step, even for him, to pass beyond things written to a global history of historical consciousness, and to embrace, for example, the oral traditions of aboriginal peoples and the peoples of Africa as their ways of giving account of the course of things in time. Butterfield's lectures showed no signs, however, that he would accept the point Toynbee raised previously with him concerning *Man on His Past,* when Toynbee chided him for universalizing modern German historiography.[20] Not even for a moment would he entertain the excision of post-Göttingen historiography as the goal and the guiding light of the "history of History." To do so would require a different history altogether.

Butterfield had barely finished presenting the Gifford Lectures when he announced that it would be a while before the lectures were ready to publish. He was aware that the tradition of the Gifford Lectures involved their publication, but he was determined not simply to reproduce the lectures as a book. Perhaps he knew enough to talk to his audience in Glasgow, he said, but he did not know enough to publish a book on so vast a range of topics. He had only begun his reading on the topics of his lectures, he said, and there were other topics to add.

Without a break in his stride, he moved from the platform to Glasgow to the library in Cambridge. He commenced the ambitious project of trying to read all the relevant historical writing available in translation in English, German, French, and Italian. He read materials from ancient Egypt, Mesopotamia, the Hittite empire, ancient Israel, early Christianity, and China, in addition to a sizeable new block of historical writing from medieval Latin Christianity and early modern Europe. To this he added his already vast reading in European historiography from the seventeenth to the nineteenth century.[21] He filled notebook after notebook and sheet after sheet with extracts and notes from his reading. Before he had completed his reading on one topic he would begin to redraft his material, and then read some more and redraft again. Twice he published references to his work in progress.[22]

For two years after 1966, he battled sporadically with Cambridge University Press over his desire to see a reprint of *Man on His Past* and to secure control over the rights to the book. He repeated to friends privately what he had said long ago, that CUP did not promote books well and that he wanted to move the book to a commercial house. He explained to CUP that he "expects the book to revive when his Gifford Lectures appear in print." He behaved as if that day were imminent, and turned to Peters, his agent, to find a commercial publisher to release both books. CUP quashed the scheme, however, by asserting its control over *Man on His Past* and forcing Butterfield to back down. The episode did drive CUP to issue the reprint edition of *Man on His Past* in 1969.[23]

Butterfield seemed not entirely aware of the scale of the project he had taken on. His pace was slow and his scope was huge, and after only a couple years of work he began to realize that he was nowhere near the end of the plan he had set for himself. It was beginning to appear that he was doing with the Gifford Lectures what he had done with Fox. He defined a project too large and adopted a method too minute ever to finish.

International Politics

The new campaign for the history of historiography did not crush all of Butterfield's other academic activity during the 1960s. He kept alive his course on the early reign of George III, and published a couple of pieces on related topics. These included an article, "Some Reflections on the Early Years of George III's Reign," in the *Journal of British Studies,* and a chapter of general history, "England in the Eighteenth Century," for a volume on the history of Methodism.[24]

He ostentatiously maintained his position as chair of the British Rockefeller Committee in the Theory of International Politics, which had the side effect of creating new initiatives in diplomatic history. While his interest in historiography shifted to ideas of history and the history of historical writings within global history, his attention in international politics turned to the idea of the balance of power and the idea of the states-system. There, too, he came to appreciate the value of a global perspective. He seemed more and more to become the historian of ideas, but one socialized in the methods and outlook of the diplomatic historian. He would tell people, as he always had, that he was not seriously interested in current politics, and ranked the reading of the daily newspaper as his most boring duty. He continued nonetheless to take serious notice of world politics and, in spite of himself, readily allowed his political interpretation of contemporary international affairs to guide and inform his historical scholarship. His historical studies for the Rockefeller committee did not match his model of neutral scientific history.[25]

In his book *International Conflict in the Twentieth Century,* published in 1960, with material dating from 1958, he had already spoken against the bomb and breathed the possibility of unilateral nuclear disarmament, but he had passed this message through a screen of double negatives. It was possible to miss his message entirely. Leonard Liggio, for instance, allowed his own anti-Communist politics, coupled with his overall attraction to Butterfield, actually to reverse Butterfield's meaning. Liggio put him in the camp of those who staunchly opposed unilateral disarmament. Butterfield's abhorrence of the bomb was not a slip of the tongue or a casual feeling of the moment, however. It derived straight from his root-belief in the centrality of human personality and his rejection of self-righteousness in politics and war. The bomb, he figured, surpassed all previous devices of human ingenuity in its power to destroy human beings and civilization, and the use the bomb would constitute a supreme act of self-righteousness. As the nuclear fear worsened in the world at large, he began to remove the qualifying words. He bluntly called himself a "near pacifist" and a "nuclear pacifist." To make himself very clear, he was telling the Rockefeller committee in 1961, "Ultimately I would prefer to see the world Communist or Russian rather than fighting with these weapons."[26]

The explicitness of his discourse against the bomb has the surprising effect of illuminating the strength of his convictions as a Nonconformist in ecclesiastical matters. The creation of the bomb and its role in human affairs, he tells us, present the world with an unspeakable calamity, but not a calamity without parallel in human history. He identified the awful twin of the nuclear bomb before an audience in 1967. It was the establishment of Christianity as the religion of the state in the fourth century, in the wake of the conversion of the Roman emperor Constantine to Christianity. This is no hyperbole. The pair matched one of his fundamental dualisms. If the bomb can materially destroy human personality and civilization, religious establishment destroys human spirituality. This amounted to a maxim of history, and his reading of the history of Christianity demonstrated how the maxim works.[27]

Going public against the bomb had satisfied his sense of moral witness, but he strictly refused to join any religious or political group that sought to pressure governments. He was in earnest about his priorities when he said that public demonstrations and big petitions seek change through force and not through conversion of the heart, and they entangle the peace movement with "undesirable connections." He declined invitations, for instance, to support the Church Peace Commission in New York or the Cambridge University Campaign for Nuclear Disarmament or the petition for The Hague Peace Rally.[28] He certainly considered his position apolitical. His strategy rested on his handling of the biblical metaphor about "the leaven that leavens the whole lump." He told the Methodist Peace Fellowship, when invited to join the group, that the Christian gift to the peace movement ought to be directed not at governments, but at persons: "If it is desired to carry the argument further, then, at the present moment, I believe that the best thing that can be done is to clarify the Christian attitude to the fundamental problem of foreign relations, including the Christian attitude to the Communist system. I regard this as the point where Christians might have something to contribute to the problem of peace." He held firmly to the paradoxical view, expressed most fully in *Christianity in European History,* that Christians have exercised the greatest influence on society for good when they did not try directly to influence society, but went about simply being spiritual and ethical and preaching the Gospel. He walked a fine line. He eventually agreed to join the Methodist Peace Fellowship in 1963, but only after the leaders assured him that they would limit themselves to public testimony for peace and would not try to influence the government.[29] He agreed to let the leading British organization in the peace movement, the Christian Group of the Campaign for Nuclear Disarmament (CND), publish the fourth essay in his book *International Conflict,* where he spoke against the bomb, but he declined their invitation to join the organization. CND published the essay in 1964 as a pamphlet in their educational series, under the title *Human Nature and the Dominion of Fear.* He regarded it simply as his personal testimony, nothing more. The group, however, and the reading public, no doubt took his statement as a useful political instrument wielded by a famous historian.[30] He had earlier permitted the same essay to be included in a notable collection of writings, introduced by Thomas Merton, aimed at peace activism in the United States in 1962. His stand against the bomb appeared even more ostentatiously an act of dissent in the American ambience of the Cold War.[31]

The election of John F. Kennedy as president of the United States in 1960 pleased him, but he became furious when Kennedy sent American "advisers" into Vietnam in 1962, and even more furious when President Lyndon Johnson authorized American military involvement in Vietnam in 1964. American intrusion in Vietnam made him really angry about politics for what he claimed was the second time in his life. The first, he said, was the Nazi invasion of Prague. In 1968, in the privacy of his journal, he condemned the American experience in the Vietnam war as "the most miserable humiliation ever suffered by a great power."[32]

As the sixties proceeded, he displayed fundamental favour towards the movements of protest against the bomb and the war, and felt sympathetic with the stirrings among university students that challenged the assumptions and practices of the educational system. But in his talks and writings during the sixties he frequently remarked that the world in general was disturbed, and he worried whether such ceaseless turmoil might threatened the well-being of universities and historical studies.[33]

Amid all these troubles of the world, new clarity of purpose emerged in his vision for the British Rockefeller committee. The committee itself might be like "leaven" in the world. The strategy assumed that ideas influence action. The key to changing action was not to pit one force against another in a struggle for political power, but to help people to think differently, and so to act differently. The committee would generate ideas about international politics, and these ideas would become available to other people. Butterfield would contribute to the work by means of his own ideas, ideas he achieved by conjoining his historical thinking, his religious and moral commitment, and his interest in global political affairs. In the process he took distinct positions on some of the most important issues of the day, and, through the committee, sought to use the power of ideas to affect the way other people acted in international politics. He continued to claim that his work was not political. While his work with the committee surely did not entail party politics, it bore the marks of politics in a more profound sense.

The undisputed leader of the Rockefeller committee was Butterfield, but he exercised his leadership through an informal inner committee. At first he worked with Martin Wight and Desmond Williams, and later with Martin Wight and Hedley Bull.[34] When the larger group convened for the weekend discussions he kept thick notes, and after each such occasion wrote out a thorough record. The record shows that the committee at the start possessed no overall plan, but allowed the discussions to move where the members decided to go from session to session. The topics of future papers emerged from the discussions, usually determined by common consent, often at the suggestion of one of the members. The committee followed a primary rule which Butterfield considered vital for genuine research: to pursue the hunches and thoughts that come to mind without regard for the consequences. The second rule he felt to be almost equally important: to proceed without the intention to publish. Butterfield was resisting the notion of collective scholarship and the creation of a band of scholars. He figured that the effects of the committee's work would appear in subtle ways within the writings of the members as individuals.[35]

In spite of Butterfield's best efforts, the committee actually fostered team research and created a team mentality, and pulled even him into the act. He began to sing a different tune. By 1962 he was lamenting the lack of results after three years, and suggesting that the committee ought to publish a book of papers. By the end of 1963 he was saying it was time to do some "stock-taking" about the direction of their discussions so that their work together would become slightly less miscellaneous, and in January 1964 he began the process. By 1966 he teamed with Martin Wight as co-editor to publish a collection of twelve papers from the committee, including two of his own. The volume, entitled *Diplomatic Investigations: Essays in the Theory of International Politics*, appeared in 1966, his twentieth book. Butterfield selected the papers, on topics loosely related to international diplomacy, and wrote the preface. At the same time, in 1966, he was calling for the committee to design an actual programme of work. He also confessed that "my present concerns seem so remote from this sort of thing." By 1968, after ten years on the job, he decided to resign as chair, admitting that his interest had waned. Altogether Butterfield wrote eight papers for the Rockefeller committee out of the total of some seventy papers produced by all members during the ten years of his leadership. Participation in the work of the committee, he said, was one of the "really impressive experiences of our lives."[36]

The name of the committee as well as the subtitle of *Diplomatic Investigations* emphasized theory, and indeed, as the discussions moved on, the talk in the committee as a whole seemed to become more theoretical. Members discussed issues of international theory, natural law, foreign policy, war, and disarmament. But it is hard to characterize any of Butterfield's contributions — except his last — as theoretical or anything other than historical studies. He said that he wanted to see what benefit could be gained from the examination of the ideas germane to international politics in the past and from the study of long-term history. After his first paper, in 1959, on his ethical misgivings about contemporary European and North American attitudes towards Communism and the colonial peoples, he undertook several fairly straightforward excursion into the history of ideas and the history of diplomacy: the idea of the balance of power, contrasts between old and new ideas of diplomacy, the ideas of Hugo Grotius, the debate over pro-German and anti-German attitudes in foreign policy before 1914. Little of this work explored the uses of long-term history for the development of theory.

Butterfield surfaced from his studies with renewed, but perhaps slightly chastened, attraction to the diplomacy of the eighteenth century. He had drawn pointed criticism for his one-sided enthusiasm in *Christianity, Diplomacy and War* for the achievements of the aristocratic diplomats without acknowledging their self-righteousness and extravagant uses of power. He still liked what he saw as their emphasis on the preservation of the international order itself, and their attempts to relativize the separate interests of any state, or ideology, or regime. He offered the striking observation that, since the advent of the nuclear bomb, a weapon which rendered resort to total war truly unthinkable, a qualitative change had occurred in international relations. He thought that factors other than sheer power had moved to first position in the calculations of foreign policy, factors such as ideology, propaganda, morality, diplomacy, anger, and simply nasty behaviour. This interpretation of international diplomacy since 1945 brought back onto the table the very factors he had sought to eliminate when he wrote at the end of the 1940s and in the early 1950s against "moralistic" diplomacy and in favour of "scientific" diplomacy. Butterfield's horror of the bomb effected a reversal in his thought. He handled the change by drawing a line between an "old" diplomacy before the bomb and a "new" diplomacy after the bomb. This was a different rendering of old and new diplomacy from his previous version, when "old" meant the beneficial eighteenth-century variety and "new" meant the harmful moralistic jockeying since 1914 over "wars for righteousness." In Butterfield's new analysis, moral arguments and ideology now mattered, and systematic thinking or his own consistency was not for him the issue. He said these things in two essays, "The Balance of Power," from April 1959, and "The New Diplomacy and Historical Diplomacy," from September 1960, both of which he put into *Diplomatic Investigations.*

At some point, possibly around the time when he was putting together *Diplomatic Investigations,* he began to say in the committee that there was no adequate history of diplomacy. He meant a study that dealt with diplomacy as technique over the centuries. The observation paralleled the remark he usually made about the history of historical criticism. He thought a worthwhile question to explore would be "whether the sheer technique of diplomacy really adds anything to the life of the world." As a sideline he began to read and collect notes for a study on "the history of diplomacy as technique," although he seemed not to be clear about whether the scale of treatment would be brief or perhaps book-length.[37]

When Butterfield assessed the work of the committee, he felt that the members were forming a common mind, and, although he did not say it, the characteristics he noticed bore his personal stamp. Such a result occurred partly because he ensured that people congenial to his approach were added to the committee, and partly because he exercised such a presiding hand. He defined the common mind as the concern above all with both history and morality in the affairs of actual international systems of states. He named the approach the "British Classical method." This he contrasted sharply with projects to construct a general theory, or with social scientific approaches dealing primarily with contemporary affairs, or even with the American Rockefeller committee, which he understood to be less interested in historical questions and more absorbed by questions of morality and foreign policy. The "British Classical method," he said, favours the study of continuities in international relations and gives priority to the practical wisdom of the ages over modern abstract concepts. It canonizes the "classical" writers, such as Grotius and Burke, ignores recent sociology and psychology, and inclines towards the study of "the corpus of diplomatic and military experience in order to reformulate its lessons in relation to contemporary needs." The results produced by this approach were what Butterfield meant by theory. He stayed very close to the discourse on maxims he began with his study of Machiavelli in the late 1930s, and continued in *Christianity, Diplomacy and War*. He displayed remarkable hostility towards other approaches to theory, which he called simply mistaken or wrong. His attitude towards them mirrored his enduring hostility towards Namier. He saw no truth in the other approaches and withheld his habitually inclusive and reconciling method.[38]

In his contribution to the committee's stock-taking in January 1964, Butterfield took a new turn in his discourse about the application of historical method to the task of international theory. He proposed that the committee examine the idea and the practice of the "states-system" itself. Almost as an appendix, he attached a paragraph which suggested extending the analysis to "the internal relations of systems existing entirely outside our own." He mentioned ancient Greece and China as possibilities, raising the prospect of a historical and comparative study of "states-systems" or similar political relations throughout world history. The idea of global analysis spilled over from his study of ideas of history that he was simultaneously preparing for the Gifford Lectures.[39]

The committee took the recommendation and commenced a study of "the states-system." Most of the papers Butterfield had previously written for the committee had looked directly at the history of certain ideas. At first it seemed he had in mind merely more of the same when his initial paper on the new topic, in July 1964, discussed the historical meaning of "Great Power." He argued that the term did not refer simply to the magnitude of a particular state's power, but represented a technical designation of the status of a state in the system, and that the actual power of those states called "Great Powers" varied considerably.[40] Both he and the other members began to chase the implications of the reference to global history. It became evident to the members that what they had so far been discussing was not "the states-system," but the modern European states-system, only one of many arguably similar configurations of political jurisdictions throughout world history. Within one year committee members gave papers that looked at the ancient Greek city-states, traditional China, traditional Islam, and medieval Europe. Butterfield's paper in January 1965, entitled "The Historic 'States-Systems,'" probably his last full paper to the group, added other systems to the list of candidates for study — the modern Arab system, the Communist states, Renaissance Italy, the states after the breakup of Alexander the Great's empire, Sumer, the Hittite system, systems on the African continent. The list went well beyond the committee's capacity.[41]

The exploration of "the states-system" that Butterfield launched differed categorically from the way he handled "modern science" and what he called "History," that is, "modern scientific history." Whereas in the latter two cases he took the modern European instances as the normative destination of the tendency of previous history, he did not promote the European states-system as the analogous goal of global political relations. Instead he reflected at a higher altitude on the many cases he cited, from ancient to modern times, and produced a tentative analysis of the factors that might generally operate in favour of creating unified systems of states, even though the particular circumstances and colouration differed in each case. He ventured the theoretical explanation that antecedent common culture as well as common political hegemony seems to be necessary, as well as geographical proximity, perhaps common religion or other shared deep values, and the need to combine against a common outside enemy. He did not ponder the effect of economic factors, or language, or other considerations, but his list of possible requisites was already multifactoral. He had set foot upon the territory of Arnold Toynbee. He was collecting known cases of systems of states, or state-like relations of power, asking a typically historical question about the factors at work in their origins, and coming up with the rudiments of a historical theory about how it is that "states-systems" come into existence. Butterfield had usually quietly harboured the criticism that Toynbee spent his time justifying a theory formulated in advance, rather than the other way around, but after his favourable review of *Reconsiderations* in 1961, he seemed more friendly to the theoretical carriage of Toynbee's enterprise. He saw afresh how Toynbee reconstructed his theory to make it respond more flexibly to the sheer variety of civilizations in world history. Perhaps he did not fully apprehend the implications of such discourse. By stepping onto such terrain, Butterfield went about as far away from his traditional model of the "technical historian" as he could get and still have the nerve, within his own terms, to call his studies historical.[42]

The discussions continued in the committee, and Butterfield meditated on the topic of the "historic states-systems." By April 1967, he was talking about the committee publishing a second volume of essays, one with greater preliminary design, and with members writing made-to-order papers to fill the gaps. He outlined a possible table of contents for a book of essays on states-systems. He would write a chapter on prerequisites of international systems, working out his historical theory about the origins of states-systems. He would write a straight historical chapter, "The Origins of the European International System," a draft of which he had already put on paper. Maybe he would write a chapter on the Ancient World. The plan faltered at once. He himself was too engrossed in his new monumental project on the comparative history of historiography. He admitted to Martin Wight, "We are not properly organized to carry out a serious project like e.g., States-Systems, but we could produce another miscellany like *Diplomatic Investigation*."[43]

Butterfield left the Rockefeller committee in September 1968, and the volume died. *Diplomatic Investigations* remained the only book produced by the committee under his leadership. Martin Wight took over as chair, and the committee went on to other things. There was soon talk of a volume of essays on ethical questions about international politics, with an abundance of candidates available to supply essays for the book. Butterfield continued to receive the papers of the committee after his retirement and occasionally sat in on a meeting, but he took no active part.

Thinking about international theory reenlivened Butterfield's devotion to diplomatic history. Amid the confusing and conflicting voices preaching the values of this or that new type of social and cultural history, he sang the merits of the type of history into which Temperley had initiated him in the 1920s. By the early 1960s he was freely uttering lament for the loss of dominance by political history as written by what he called "the school of Ranke."[44] A paper he read to the Cambridge History Club in 1963 bearing the title "In Defence of Diplomatic History" spoke fervently on behalf of a discipline he knew was out of favour.[45] In the paper he uses the metaphor of the seesaw to indicate why he now emphasizes a seemingly archaic mode of history. After one side of the seesaw gets the weight, then must come the other. Shifting the metaphor to the shopkeeper's scale, he adds, "and one has always to be looking out for the proper balance." His dissenting ethos goes to work against the newly dominant styles of history. He goes further than merely keeping two things in balance, however. He once again proclaims his most basic commitments. To be sure, he does not wish to abandon his commitment to study the history of societies and civilization in their multifaceted arrangements that he had argued for in his lectures on the modern history of Europe, but he feels the need of the day now required him to stress "the importance in history of the decisions men make — the enormous leverage that the historical process can give even to a single man's will."

Diplomatic history is a branch of political history and, as a discipline, studies individuals, he writes. The individuals in question are the wielders of government power operating on the international level. Their decisions affect war and peace, international stability, order and revolution, liberty and tyranny. These include the Hitlers, the Stalins, and the Sir Edward Greys whose decisions produced massive consequences and affected everyone. As an example of the primary role played by diplomatic history, he points to the effects of war and dynasty on society, and argues for the necessity of understanding diplomatic history as a prerequisite for comprehending social and cultural history. War touches virtually everything, he says, including the state, the economy, education, the natural sciences, the arts, ideas, even religion. And dynasty provides the key to understanding the modern map of the nations of Europe. The interactions of the ruling families of the continent hundreds of years ago underlay the division of Europe into separate states, and antedated the power of language, popular national sentiment, culture, and other factors.

The individualist conception of the operation of international relations that Butterfield expounded in his discourse contained no notion of states as institutions of political and military power interacting on a vast scale, and no reference to the operation of states as organizations of monumental economic power within international banking, monetary exchange, trade, and industrial production. At the same time, however, he also overlooked the immense impact of individual people in many other aspects of society, such as finance, multinational corporations, labour unions, religion, social movements, popular music, and Hollywood movies. Even as he explicitly took credit for broadening the Cambridge treatment of general history, he promoted the primacy of diplomatic history, and neglected his argument which stressed the interrelationship of many factors and regarded as vain the conventional search for the "key" factor. Setting to one side his belief in the absolute power of individual spirituality, his case for diplomatic history presumed that international politics dealt with what mattered most in the course of what he called "mundane" history: rulers, political power, war, governments, diplomacy. At least in the way he put the case, he underplayed the significance of culture, the economy, social relations, migration, religion, and even ideas, which he had come to emphasize in his current work. He now admitted, for probably the first time, that the modern study of history, which he called variously "academic history" or "scientific history" or "technical history," grew up under the tutelage of diplomatic history. The rules characteristic of a certain type of diplomatic history transmuted into the rules of "scientific history" as a whole. In other words, the vision of "scientific history" he had so long expounded privileged and promoted the hegemony of not only one branch of history, but one particular way of practicing within that branch, notably the approach generated among nineteenth-century German historians and inculcated by Temperley forty years previously. Butterfield did not allow that academic history might be seen as comprehending many methods, even apparently conflicting methods, each befitting the purposes and subjects of the study. Nor did he entertain the option of developing entirely new approaches to the historical study of international affairs which were attentive to the intertwinement of international politics, international economy, international culture, international religious movements, international charity, and much more. Instead, he perpetuated his assumption that the nineteenth-century and early twentieth-century methods of diplomatic history properly defined the very character of historical study itself. He uttered the most extreme claim he had yet put forward for the importance of Ranke, the exemplar of diplomatic history in the nineteenth century. Ranke was, he said, "the greatest man who ever addressed himself to the work of historical research, and the only mind of anything like Shakespearian quality that ever engaged itself in academic history."[46]

The inaugural lecture that Butterfield delivered on 10 November 1964 as Regius Professor of Modern History carried the impressive title *The Present State of Historical Scholarship*. Of all the things he might have said on so august an occasion, and instead of indicating the way ahead towards creative and innovative historiography, instead of, for instance, urging the global vision he was then developing, he decided to reiterate his support for one particular style of doing diplomatic and political history. He hurls a few menacing words in the direction of economic and social history, the areas enjoying the greatest favour at the time, and then devotes the greater part of the lecture to the importance of his chosen fields. He describes these fields as dealing with "an intermediate realm" lying between society taken as a whole and the submicroscopic world of the millions of social particles treated statistically by certain of the new types of history. Political and diplomatic history, he says, remind the world that individual human wills matter, and that "there is a whole universe of countless possible futures." Diplomatic and political history militate against determinism. Once again he identifies his deepest concern, that individual persons are the only reality in the world. His individualist vision of diplomatic and political history again polarizes individuals over against social relationships and institutions, and blocks his view of the corporate and multifactoral character of the subject matter of those fields. His vision also tricks him into believing that there are no tendencies on politics and diplomacy that inundate individual people. As an aside, he then urges a change in governmental policy concerning "the fifty-year rule," the British regulation that closed the documents of state to research for fifty years after the events. He recommends lowering the limit to thirty years, which, he says, in a world moving swiftly, would allow documentary materials crucial for public understanding to surface more quickly. It is an argument that reveals a political hope that diplomatic history might impact contemporary attitudes in international affairs. Ironically when his own papers reached the manuscript room of Cambridge University Library after his death, the keepers automatically clamped on the fifty-year rule on about 20 percent of his materials, not knowing about his proposal for archival time restrictions.[47]

In 1964, the fiftieth anniversary of the beginning of the First World War gave him the opportunity to reengage in some actual diplomatic history while resuming his old cause on behalf of fair treatment for Germany in the history books. He asked the BBC to let him go on national radio, claiming that the problem "seems to me to be almost a national matter," but he failed to get the time.[48] He made connections with the semi-official British Council and several German universities, including those who had hosted him during the high days of Hitler in 1938. They arranged for him to tour Germany in July 1964, visiting the universities of Cologne, Bonn, Munich, Berlin, Göttingen, and later Mainz, with a lecture on Sir Edward Grey and the crisis of July 1914.[49] He discussed the British tradition of blaming Germany for the outbreak of the war, and what he said sounded good to German ears. He knew that critics could discount him as "pro-German." The whole episode took him back emotionally to his youth in Oxenhope and the shock to his consciousness of the wider world when the British went to war against Germany, the land he had learned growing up was the primeval source of Teutonic liberty. For him personally, the tour renewed his direct contact with German historians and German scholarship.[50]

The research he conducted for the lecture went no farther than the official British volumes of documents edited by his friend Gooch and mentor, Temperley, and the counterpart volumes from other nations, but he managed afterwards to double the size of the lecture and turn it into an article, "Sir Edward Grey in July 1914." It was the first piece of footnoted history he had published since part two of *George III and the Historians* in 1958, work which was much older still. He apparently no longer worried that such volumes of selected documents published by governments functioned as "official history." His elaborate argument wound around to the thesis that, while it is true that Germany was a threat to peace in 1914, so was Russia. Grey trapped himself in "moralistic" attitudes against the Germans, and failed to take the "scientific" view that recognized the double threat embedded within the complexity of the European states-system. Along the way, Butterfield uttered several maxims, which he took to be lessons of history, applicable to situations similar to that of Germany and Russia in 1914. Chief among the maxims were these:

> When there are two of these monsters, however, the threat to liberty is not doubled; it is likely to be greatly reduced.

And,

> A flexible diplomacy is able to address itself to a dual problem of this kind: for it is not a rare thing to have a menace urgently impending from one side, while a remoter threat, not less terrible, looms up from the opposite quarter.[51]

Travelling to Germany again in 1968 to receive his honourary doctorate at Bonn, thirty years after his first visit to the country, he put the case for political history in stronger terms than he had used before, terms according undoubted priority among all the types of history to the historical study of politics. It was a polemic against the domination of history by social and economic history. These fields of history, he said, leave students with a conception of general history with no inner structure. The proper way to provide structure was "to emphasize the leading part played by states and governments in the history of human affairs." At the same time, such an approach would better do justice to individuals and free will in history, and would introduce students to the wisdom of the ages: "Politics still forms the main core of historical study. It provides the strongest ribs in the structure of general history. Without it, the student of history feels men too much at the mercy of conditions — he does not realize the importance of the human will in history. In my view, therefore, it is still true that what our young people need is an education in statesmanship and that the teacher of history should always keep this in mind." He gave no reasons why general history could not just as well be structured around economic activity or daily social life or cultural practices or religion, since any of those human engagements display both comprehensiveness and specificity as well as sequences in time, and all involve individual decision and human will. At the same time, he failed to recognize that politics can seem vague, remote, and deterministic to all but the small elite who exercise power at the moment. In his own mind, there in Germany, he was back in Göttingen at the end of the eighteenth century when, as he had argued, the professors of history were creating the modern form of the study of history and instructing the young men of the German nobility in the wisdom of the ages and the ways of statesmanship. The young aristocrats would then move into the leadership of public life throughout the German states. There was something of old Cambridge in the model as well. Göttingen and old Cambridge were worth emulating.[52]

During the sixties, as the student movement within the universities gained ground, he continued to express sympathy with students' complaints, but hardened his position against their proposals and methods, both of which he felt politicized the university. In the Lindsay lectures at Keele in 1961 he had spoken against the tendencies in universities which he perceived were "proletarianizing everybody." He urged the universities, one might say, to "aristocratize" the students instead. Universities should equip individual students to "seize on the fine things that were the privileges of aristocracies (the enjoyment of a free voice in government being only one of these) and set out to extend them to everybody." He echoed the thesis of *Englishman and His History*, where he claimed that all England had successfully avoided the terrors of revolution by passing the benefits of the aristocracy down to ordinary people. Recalling Göttingen, he began to talk about the role of the university in "the production of an elite," something he insisted was different from creating "elite universities." He agreed with Lord Snow who, reportedly, "implored Englishmen not to go too far in their egalitarianism." With such talk, Butterfield could begin to sound like the historian with working-class roots who embraced and defended the culture and privileges of the ruling elites of the world.[53]

Championing a classical approach to international theory and the priority of diplomatic and political history derived from his moral and religious convictions, and his decision to go against the tide was a direct expression of his dissenter ethos. Throughout the sixties he once again became vocal about his Methodist identity. The events that elicited his renewed public Methodism were the conversations between the Methodism Church and the Church of England aimed at achieving the reunification of the two traditions. What troubled him was not Anglican liturgy or spirituality or even Anglicanism, all of which he had not found unattractive over the years at Peterhouse. Both in his role as Master and out of personal sympathy he participated actively in the life of Peterhouse chapel. He aimed his objection against the official alliance of the Church of England with the state. He developed a talk on Methodism and the role of Nonconformity which he delivered several times to Methodist groups. He emphasized certain ideas which he believed belonged to the very character of Methodism, and which he did not want lost in any conversations with the established church. He contemplated what might be Methodist distinctives, and reread John Wesley, especially the sermons. He noted Wesley's words in the sermon "A Caution against Bigotry," where he said, "Nor are any animosities so deep and irreconcilable as those that spring from disagreements in religion," and in the sermon "Catholic Spirit," where Wesley said, "Love me with the love that covereth all things." The primary distinctive of Methodism, Butterfield thought, lay in its emphasis on experience: "Throughout life Wesley never ceased to be comparatively indifferent to orthodoxy so long as a man had the witness of the Spirit, proving itself in works of faith." Methodists, Butterfield said, had a way of going behind the ecclesiastical traditions in order to meet directly with the experience of the early Christians. The fresh encounter with the New Testament encouraged "radical thinking," "fundamental re-thinking" of the first principles of Christianity in relation to the affairs of today. The emphasis on the laity militated against a clerical church, and the tendency to use the small group, the cell, the Class meeting, weighed against reliance on vast organization and mere activism. At a conference on higher education convened by Marjorie Reeves in 1963, he gave an example of how he dealt in the line of Wesley with religious orthodoxy and intellectual vitality. The Christian doctrine that the truth has been revealed, which he affirmed that he accepted in some sense, poses an intellectual danger when overstressed, as, for example, "when the truth is encased in a few hard formulas, as though here were the end rather than the beginning of questing — a closing-in of thought instead of the opening-out of a mystery."[54]

In 1964 the report of the Methodist-Anglican commission published the proposed steps leading to church union. The document caused Butterfield such alarm that he reacted in a manner entirely unprecedented in his career. He issued a public statement of his misgivings, and persuaded his Methodist friend R. Y. Jennings, Whewell Professor of International Law at Cambridge, to co-sign, both using their professional titles. He did not oppose church unity, he said, but he categorically rejected the plan to make Methodism part of the religious establishment. That status, he charged, was bound to constrict religious development and radical thought. He knew full well that Methodists had divided from the Church of England in clear violation of the teachings of John Wesley, who died a cleric in the established church. But against this he raised the historical argument that, because of the dynamic of passing out of the church establishment, Methodists had gravitated over the years towards the older ecclesial communities of Dissent — the Nonconformists — which originated in the divisions of the seventeenth century. Methodists had already formed especially useful alliances with Presbyterians, Baptists, and Congregationalists. In so doing they had helped save those traditions from unravelling on the fringe of English society, and had developed for themselves a dissenting role against state religion. Instead of a movement towards reunion with the Church of England, he favoured the spontaneous union of Methodists with other Protestant traditions outside the establishment. A united movement of Methodists and the older Nonconformists would serve, he said, "to give spiritual meaning and purpose to the new generation's general attitude of protest."[55]

In another unprecedented act, quite out of line with his usual quietist self, he joined the campaign mounted by the National Liaison Committee of Methodists to pressure the Methodist Church to defeat the proposed reunion with the Church of England. He was not unhappy with the failure of the plans for reunion not long after, and he might be justified in thinking that he had a hand in the collapse.[56]

When Basil Willey, his friend and Peterhouse colleague, retired in 1964 from a professorship in English at Cambridge, Butterfield wrote a tribute which summarized Willey's Methodism: "He has been a Methodist too, still in the tradition of liberal nonconformity — ready as a thinker to take his stand on the validity of religious experience, but determined, in spite of the depths of the feelings involved, to confront with relentless honesty the intellectual problems that Christianity presents." These were the very terms that Butterfield might wish to use about himself.[57]

Surprise

Peterhouse had given Butterfield many shocks in his life, by electing him to a fellowship, electing him Master, and other things. Now it was his turn to give Peterhouse a shock. The date of his retirement from the Regius professorship was set, according to the regulation, for 1968, but the college statues would allow him to continue as Master until 1970, the year in which he became seventy years of age. He testified that he was very happy as Master, but he had been unable to adhere to the plan for him to be the scholar-Master. He confessed to one inquirer, "Perhaps I have been in danger of loving too much the administrative side of the work." He added to another, "I found that I loved it all and to my great surprise I got a tremendous enjoyment out of committees."[58] He felt, however, that his historical scholarship was in shambles. Just after he finished the Gifford Lectures, in December 1966, he carefully reconsidered his prospects for productive scholarship. He was exceedingly hopeful of bringing his new comparative work on the history of historiography to a worthwhile finish. He was content to continue to let go of Fox and George III in order to work on a book from the Gifford Lecture. He was beginning to experience his role on the Rockefeller committee as a distraction.

To the surprise of everybody, Butterfield made his decision and, early in 1967, announced that he would resign as Master two years early, to take effect on 30 September 1968. That same day he would step down from the Regius professorship as well as from the chair of the Rockefeller committee. He explained the extraordinary move as a desperate attempt to write. "I seem to have spent such a lot of time on the business side of university and college life that I would like to make up a bit on the academic side." With a twinkle, he explained, "I decided that at age 68 one has a right to do what one likes — assuming one still has a decent object in life." He recalled the aspirations of his youth, and explained the decision as due to "the stronger pull of my initial boyhood desire to write something good if possible."[59] Looking back over his career, he ranked *The Peace Tactics of Napoleon* of 1929 as still his best book, precisely because of its literary style. When he wrote a new draft of a paper or a chapter or a lecture, his goal was more likely to be better style than better thought. He might wonder if the writer in him had more to come.[60]

His explanation seemed too naive and too sincere in a world where simple reasons sometimes masked intrigue. The gossip suggested that his stated intent to retire was a threat to get his way in college politics, and it took a while for the Fellows realize that he really meant to retire early in order to write. He was well liked and perceived as a devoted and conservative Master. The Fellows came to believe him and accept his wishes.[61] At the end, however, they gave him a jolt in return by electing a still older man as Master, even taking the extreme step of revising the college statutes to permit the later retiring age. Charles Burkill, mathematician, college bursar, and long-time Fellow of the college, succeeded Butterfield as Master of Peterhouse in October 1968, the first non-historian at the head of the college since the 1930s.

Butterfield became an Honourary Fellow of the college, joining his colleagues Postan, Brogan, and Knowles. With his retirement there was no longer any Fellow of Peterhouse holding a professorship in history. It was certainly the end of a long era for history in Peterhouse. In the university, he became Emeritus Regius Professor of Modern History, and his younger friend Owen Chadwick replaced him in the Regius chair.

Queen Elizabeth summoned Butterfield to come to Buckingham Palace on 9 July 1968 and conferred a knighthood upon him for his services to the college, the university, and the historical profession. Hereafter Pamela and he were Lady Butterfield and Sir Herbert. The man born in the worker's cottage in Oxenhope delighted in the knighthood probably more than any other of the honours he ever received.

After nearly fourteen years as Master, and after almost fifty years with accommodation in the college, Butterfield moved out of the Master's Lodge, and out of the college, in July 1968, giving the college time to redecorate for the next Master. Pamela and he retired to Sawston, a village on the bus line a few miles south of Cambridge. He took with him all his papers and all his books, and looked forward to life doing nothing but thinking about history and religion.

14

Nothing but History and Religion

Meditations

The new Sir Herbert and Lady Butterfield found their life in Sawston a
delightful improvement over the Master's Lodge. Sawston was removed far
enough from Cambridge to allow them to make a fresh start, but, being right
on the bus line, close enough for them to go into Cambridge whenever they
liked. The Butterfields had neighbours again and made new friends, took
walks in the village, and, for the first time in decades, did their own shopping
and cooking.

The village differed from Oxenhope. Sawston was smaller and, instead of
hills, was surrounded by flat, fertile land, with new housing developments
rising to the north, and it possessed no industrial legacy. The village had a few
Methodists, a dominant Anglican parish, and a significant Roman Catholic
presence. Sawston Hall, a fine Elizabethan stately home, had remained in the
hands of Roman Catholic nobility through the centuries. Many of the inhabitants of the village and the adjacent housing estates oriented themselves towards Cambridge.

The Butterfields loved their new home, a handsome half-timbered house
from the sixteenth century, near the centre of the village, at 26 High Street. The
sale of the house on Tenison Road made the purchase possible. Butterfield
settled in quickly. Anticipating a busy correspondence, or at least spotting a

bargain, he had 2,000 sheets of new letterhead printed, with the address reading 28 High Street. He thought it wasteful to throw the sheets away, so on every letter he crossed out the number and wrote 26. The supply outlasted him. With the house paid for, they lived adequately on his pension, supplemented by a small income from royalties from his books and from special lectures.

In his large study at one end of the ground floor Butterfield had ample space for his files, his books, and his piano. He had kept his piano playing alive since his youth, and now he had the time to give to it. He rested Temperley's bust of the young Napoleon on a stand near the centre of the room.

Butterfield became a local celebrity in Sawston. He gave talks to Sawston Village College, the Sawston Men's Guild, the Sawston Methodist Women's Meeting, and other village groups. He accepted the chairmanship of the Cambridge Area Methodist Circuit Festival. He became a regular participant in a Methodist Class Meeting for the Sawston area. On Sunday mornings he went faithfully into Cambridge to Wesley Methodist Church. Sunday evenings he attended evening prayer regularly in the local Church of England parish, and sometimes he had lunch with the vicar.

He went into Peterhouse now and then. When he received a visiting scholar, he used a college room shared by retired Fellows or a lounge in the new University Centre on Laundress Green for research students and university teaching staff. Invariably he would focus the conversation on what the visiting scholar was doing, and he gave the impression that he was genuinely interested what his visitor had to say.

Early and repeatedly, he declared that he would devote himself to what he called "my real work at the moment," the task of converting his Gifford Lectures into a book on the history of historiography. He seemed to have in mind the production of a magnum opus. He spoke of the work as his "retirement project," and planned to subordinate everything else to it. He had already put administration behind him, and he fully intended to reduce the number of invited lectures as well.[1]

Butterfield did not stick to his intentions, however. First, his mind kept going on a wide expanse of themes other than the Gifford Lectures, and he brought his new thinking to the public in lecture after lecture in Great Britain and the United States. He spoke often on BBC radio, and made his second appearance on television, this time on the topic "Evil in History," the first having been in 1965 with a talk on the Reformation. His understated personality and utter dependence on reading his lectures may have suited radio superbly, but those traits, together with his slight appearance and lack of animation, scarcely matched the new visual medium. The contrast with the extroverted A. J. P. Taylor, who flourished on TV, could hardly have been more extreme.

Second, he continued to feel the weight of his long-standing projects, and he kept inventing new projects. The Gifford Lectures did receive his attention, but not the exclusive devotion he expected to give them. He became very busy and delighted to tell people, "I'm really engaged in studies — the one thing that a university in these days doesn't allow one to do."[2]

Publishers scrambled to republish his books, and Butterfield's reputation continued to spread. Cambridge reprinted *Man on His Past* (1969), Bell issued a corrected reprint of *Origins of Modern Science* (1970), Penguin Books republished *Whig Interpretation of History* (1973, 1978), after Bell reprinted the book (1968), and various American publishers reprinted *George III, Lord North, and the People* (1968), *Englishman and His History* (1970), *Historical Novel* (1971, 1975, 1977), *Peace Tactics of Napoleon* (1972), and *International Conflict in the Twentieth Century* (1974). Only *Christianity and History* of his most influential books remained out of print. Distinctions continued to come his way. The Royal Historical Society elected him an honourary vice-president in 1968. In October 1970, J. H. Elliott brought him a book of eleven essays by colleagues, scholar-friends, and former students published in his honour, a festschrift entitled *The Diversity of History*.[3] Two more English universities granted him honourary degrees, Bradford in 1973 and Cambridge in 1974, his thirteenth and fourteenth honourary doctorates. David Knowles congratulated him on the Cambridge award, noting wryly that both Butterfield and he had opposed the university giving such degrees to its own members, but that both meekly accepted them when the honour arrived at their door. Oxford did not give Butterfield an honourary degree, although they gave one to Knowles.[4]

Around the moment of his retirement, Butterfield meditated often about the course of his own life and the affairs of the world. His thinking about history went hand in hand with world events, and world events stimulated his historical thinking more than reading books. He attempted several times to write more memoirs. In his speeches, lectures, and correspondence he recalled episodes in his life, sometimes turning his talks into autobiography. A notable example was his address upon receiving the honourary doctorate at Bonn in 1968. He read great quantities of books and articles for his projects, and wrote incessantly to himself. He refused to imitate those scholars, whether in old age or middle age, who stop reading and even thinking, and just churn out the publications. He started a "commonplace" book of his thoughts on world affairs. He began once again to write something of a journal, what we might call "journal-sheets," hundreds of sheets of paper and pages of notebooks, many of them bearing a date, containing his thoughts as they came to him. These new efforts at a journal were not at all systematic or regular, and turn up in widely scattered files in his papers, reflecting the variety of settings in which his comments came to him. Much of what he wrote took the form of "thought-essays," a loose sheet or two, or a few loose sheets, in which he worked out his thoughts by writing. It was a format he had used since the 1920s. Some of his thoughts came out in the form of brief sentences, almost as if they were sayings or maxims, and one can imagine he had in mind the model of Acton and Acton's notes in the Cambridge Library.[5] He used his habits as a historian to formulate his thoughts about history, education, politics, and religion. His meditations surfaced in unexpected places in his writings and public lectures, time and again eliciting the query, "Why did he say that there?" Both in scale and content, his unpublished journal-sheets and thought-essays constitute a major body of meditations on his life and human history.

The passage of the generations and his moment in time occupied his thoughts more than usual. People close to him were dying or becoming ill. During the first month of his retirement, his sister, Edie, was hit by a Green Line bus on a London street, and she died soon after from the injuries. Hannah, the widow of his brother Arthur, died the following year. On the eve of his retirement, his friend G. P. Gooch died, at the high age of ninety-four, a link with Temperley and even Acton. Gooch was an Anglican, but from his earliest years had shown sympathy towards Methodists, which Butterfield sensed. Butterfield accepted invitations from both the British Academy and the American Philosophical Society to write a brief biography of Gooch, and he contemplated in detail a historian's life with interests not unlike his own.[6] Eve Bogle took ill in 1970, and he lost the aid of his secretary, research assistant, and friend of twenty-five years. He was made certain of his own fragility when he became ill with heart disease during most of 1971, and had to begin regular visits to the chest clinic at Addenbrooke's Hospital. He noticed the trouble while he was preparing the Raleigh Lecture for the British Academy. He felt weak even as he delivered the lecture in May, not sure that he would be able to finish. Butterfield, the chain smoker, broke the chain and never smoked again.[7]

At the opposite end of time, Pamela and he kept close touch with their sons and grandchildren. Peter had become a lecturer in history at University College, Dublin, after periods lecturing in Birmingham and Southern Rhodesia. Robin was an English teacher in a school in York. Butterfield liked seeing his grandchildren when he visited Peter or lectured in Dublin. He had often referred to the role of "the tales of a grandfather" in arousing interest in the young about the past, and now he was the grandfather. He commenced a lecture at Southampton, soon after his retirement, with the suggestion that "the tales of a grandfather" may serve as the first source of a historical sense in the ancient peoples of the world as well as in the life of the young throughout much of the world today. It is likely that he himself never heard his own grandfathers' tales.[8]

The student protest movements which reached crescendo in 1968, especially on American university campuses and in Paris and Rome, interested him intensely. By now the American presence in Vietnam had transmuted into the American war in Vietnam, and this too captured his attention. The voices of Blacks and women in many places had become unmistakable in their appeal for justice and equality. Now retired, Butterfield was something of the outsider, but his ardour for apolitical scholarship and the politically removed university diminished not at all. All the same, his method of reacting to the events of the day, especially those that most seriously impacted him personally, evidenced exactly the opposite relationship between politics, religion, the university, and academic scholarship to what his theory delineated. He detested the American war in Vietnam, and he completely sympathized with the student antiwar protests.[9] His sympathies for student protests stopped short at a crucial point, however. He turned adamantly against student activism in universities that aimed to increase the role of students in university government, and that opposed what the students regarded as racism in university hiring, admissions, and campus affairs, and he resisted the emerging aspirations of women in university life. His objections fit exactly with his own oft-expressed views about the role of the historian and historical scholarship, and placed the political character of his vigorous apoliticality in sharp relief. He was prepared to admire the protesters' moral concern, and, had they been content merely to testify of their morality, he would have been happy. When they turned to political action, however, they posed force against force in order to gain power within the university system, and that he opposed. He detected straightforward self-righteousness in their protests. They were too certain of their own cause, too ready to cast blame on others, and perhaps too intoxicated with their newfound power. He wanted the students to direct their energies elsewhere. He wrote in his journal, "I might have been more able to think the young were idealists, trying to better the world, if they had set up their strikes, demonstrations, etc. in protest against the nuclear weapon."[10] He accepted the view that only a "handful of radicals" made all the noise, and he praised the "vast majority" of students, whom he found more compassionate and less self-oriented than students of some other periods.[11]

Cornell University invited him to take up a distinguished research fellowship for one term in 1969–1970. He accepted, but then became alarmed by reports of student sit-ins and Black Power at Cornell. He sought advice about whether still to go. He explained his hesitations to Max Black, professor of philosophy, and chair of the research centre that would host him: "But I should be rather a handful for you in Cornell, for I can never see why undergraduates should have the kind of license they now claim while I, at nearly 69, must take care of every word I say for fear of displeasing them. And I really can't go back to university life under the conditions which the young are now producing in various places." Stuart Brown, a Cornell vice-president, replied that academic life went on unabated, and tried to help Butterfield understand the point of view of the protesters: "There will, I am sure, be student unrest everywhere in the USA so long as the Vietnam war continues and so long as we fail to make major gains towards solving the problems of Black people and the cities in which most of them dwell." Butterfield was not persuaded, and he hardened his position against what he felt was the "politicization" of the university. Academic study and the university ought to stand outside the noisy clamour of ideology and politics, he said. His language echoed his traditional polarization of "technical history" and politics, with the effect that he fought for the existing distribution of power within the system and resisted the movements of protest. He cut his ideal for apolitical historical scholarship and his anti-student politics from the same seamless cloth. His model was Ranke himself. He represented Ranke as taking the position "that the historian should be primarily a scholar, aloof from the movements of his time." He wrote this sentence on Ranke in a significant article on historiography in the *Dictionary of the History of Ideas* which he drafted in February 1969, very shortly before he had to put his beliefs to the test in June in the Cornell episode. In any case, he said, he wanted to carry on his scholarship in peace. He withdrew from the fellowship, even though he would lose much-needed extra income.[12]

The solution Butterfield had in mind for student discontent in universities might allow Cambridge and Oxford, with their traditions of college teaching, to escape the onslaught: "I am sure it is an excellent thing to regard universities as a society of scholars who stimulate one another and advance thought itself — but I think that undergraduates should be regarded as part of that society, treated as part of that society — not just treated as 'students.' " Student participation in the society of scholars, supported by an almost intangible, but no less real, transformation of attitude, would befit the nature of universities better than the political changes now sought by the student protesters. Even more than usual, he exalted the model of Peterhouse, which, he said, "almost provided the intimacies (without the exasperations) of family life." He took no notice of how odd his metaphor seemed amid the rising voices of women for equality in Cambridge colleges. If Peterhouse was a "family," it was a "family" of fathers and sons only, served by other men as college porters, with no mothers and daughters in sight. In the face of increasing political pressures from women, he spoke out strongly against the admission of women to Peterhouse. He declared himself willing to preserve his college to the end, if need be, as the last all-male bastion in Cambridge. In such a volatile context, his expressions of appreciation towards the college porters had the sound of *noblesse oblige*. He congratulated the undergraduates who refused to join any of the protests, stuck to their studies, and felt "that they are lucky to be in Cambridge."[13]

The contact with all that disturbing protest stimulated Butterfield to contemplate change through time, and meditate on the wisdom of the ages. By now his thought ran easily to global comparisons. As his discourse unfolded after 1968, into the 1970s, the sheer continuity of his moral consciousness and historical analysis radiated through his every word, and his long-term memory seemed to grow stronger with every passing day as he leapt over thirty, forty, fifty years of his life. His discourse bore affinities with book after book and article after article that he had already written. Butterfield had settled on the language of "maxims of history" and "wisdom," rather than "laws of history," even though "laws" sounded more like something "scientific." Maxims crowded into his consciousness and became the primary way for him to express his historical thought.

The model of Machiavelli, whom he discussed in *The Statecraft of Machiavelli* in 1940, rushed to the fore. Machiavelli studied the known cases of conspiracies against rulers in order to understand how they worked, and how a ruler might avoid one. So, too, into Butterfield's mind came the methods of the Marxists, whom he first discussed in 1933, who studied revolutions in history in order to find out how they operated and how to make one happen. These approaches, he said, whether we agree with the politics of their progenitors or not, enable historians and theorists to derive maxims from a study of many cases of similar kinds of events. Butterfield ran through possible analogies to the student protests of the day, and came up with examples of other youth movements in history whose aim was political power and whose nourishment was served by some political ideology—the Hitler youth, the young Turks, Mazzini's young Italy, and so on, back at least to the young Jews of the year 66 who pushed for war against the Roman imperium. He sensed that, had he been around, he would have objected to all these youth movements, and so, too, the ones of his own day.[14]

Reflection on revolutions in history intrigued him, as in *Christianity, Diplomacy and War* in 1953, and dominated his thinking. He wrote a major paper entitled "Revolution," delivered at Corpus Christi College in Cambridge in 1972, which he never published. He showed himself to be remarkably flexible and surprising in the observations he made about revolutions as recurring historical phenomena. He was still convinced that revolution would effect no improvement for "Western" society as a whole, and, all the more so, that revolution was no solution for the universities of the "Western" world. He willingly acknowledged the deformities of industrial capitalist society, as in his vividly anticapitalist remarks on America when he studied there in the 1920s. He understood why the young might wish to overthrow capitalism: "We look at the entire order of things under which we live, and we are shocked to see how much it answers to the cupidities of human beings, catering to those cupidities, encouraging the competitive spirit, and leaving the weak so often at the mercy of the strong."[15] Time and again throughout his career he professed that human cupidities never flagged, and he did so once more. He liked the word "cupidities," which seemed more expressive and less sinister than "sins," and he returned to it. If capitalist society were overthrown, the new social order that took its place, whatever the form, would still service human cupidities. The new system would merely alter the pattern of their operation. The source of cupidities lies deep within the human personality, he said, and the best that a social order can do is not to block up the source, but merely to restrain them, and make people behave better than they really are. After fifty years of historical study since the Liverpool police strike of 1919 first shook his naivete about human goodness, Butterfield still drew upon the religious message he then learned by experience: all people are sinners.

The antidote to revolution was the same patriotic prescription he offered in *Englishman and His History* in 1944. In place of revolution, he said, the youth in "Western" society should listen to the maxim of the Whig politicians, that gradual reform worked best, with the conservatives giving way in time and the progressives not pressing too hard, enveloping all within "the slow growth of reasonableness" which transformed the whole. By obeying this maxim, England led the way to moral progress in the "West." England, more than any other nation, internalized the "imponderables," notably "a mood of tolerance, a respect for the other man's personality, a willingness to rely on persuasion and discussion."[16]

Maybe each society needed one revolution, he thought, or at least one revolution somewhere to point to, before the gradual mode of social change took hold. England had its revolution and beheaded a king, and then pursued the gradual path. Russia had its revolution in 1917, and perhaps had settled down. He acknowledged that he felt "less strongly about Communism" than he did after the Second World War, and that he had revised his assessment of the revolution. Occurring as it did in the midst of the awful havoc caused by the First World War, that revolution, after all, may have been "perhaps the most justifiable of any in history," and maybe Communism "has been better in reality for Russia." Now China had its revolution, and, like many regions of Asia, he thought, "the situation is more desperate — so desperate that it is difficult to see how anything except agrarian revolution can be of any use." The Maoists were probably good for China, he said.[17] Ireland had one revolution which was still incomplete. In a letter to the London *Times* he argued that Northern Ireland could not expect the end of revolutionary violence until there was "a complete junction with the Irish Republic." He agreed that resort to revolution in Northern Ireland by Roman Catholics seemed justified so long as their genuine grievances remained untended to.[18]

A clear message was emerging from his contemplation of history and his direct experience of the protests of students, Blacks, and women. It restated a long-present motif in his historical thought, although he registered the message as new: "In contradiction to the views that I held earlier in my life, I think that there is something to be said for the thesis that basic patterns do recur, however much circumstances may have changed in the course of two or three thousand years. . . . The fundamental patterns often repeat themselves in a curious way."[19]

No sooner did he speak of patterns, analogies, and similarities in diverse events over the ages, than he felt compelled to state the opposite. If his discourse about maxims, protest movements, and revolution stressed the recurrences and continuities of history, he wondered about the discontinuities in history. When it came time to prepare the prestigious Rede Lecture at Cambridge for 1971, he decided to consider the effects of discontinuities over time, and, as the new retiree, especially one battling with heart disease, he focused on the differences due to generational change. He gave the lecture the title "The Discontinuities between the Generations." The theme transported him to the early years of his career, when, forty years before, in *Whig Interpretation of History*, he underlined the need to assume that bygone ages were *not* like our own. He showed signs of physical frailty as he delivered the lecture in the Senate House.[20]

Noting the subtleties and paradoxes of historical change was his aim, and Butterfield said things he had never said before. His thought was more complicated now than in 1931, but it was no more systematic. His ideas came as flashes and seemed almost random. The lecture resembled a collage more than a sequenced ordering of meaning. For instance, he noted that each generation, each person, starts over and has difficulty understanding the experiences of previous people, even the experiences of one's parents. Debates are often won and new ideas adopted not because of their merit or the force of argument, but simply because the old generation passes away and the new generation comes along. The influence of the parents can seem mysterious and inexplicable within the same family: "in the case of two brothers brought up in very much the same way, we have the one who becomes a nonconformist minister because his father was a nonconformist minister, while his brother becomes a militant atheist because his father was a nonconformist minister." People blame their parents for the mess that the world is in when they are born into history, but then the parents can blame their parents, who in turn can blame theirs, until no one takes responsibility for what is wrong. It is not the young who should turn apocalyptic, but the very old. The young must be careful to preserve a world to live in, while the aged no longer need the comforts of the status quo and are free to project new visions of better futures. Such discourse sounds like epigrams, and a listener requires time to catch the meaning. The glimpse of Butterfield's own family was inescapable: he the Methodist historian/preacher, and one son the historian/Roman Catholic, one deceased, and one the English teacher/convinced non-Christian.[21]

Suddenly his thoughts stopped in mid-lecture. His glance at the discontinuities felt like an excursus, or maybe an exercise to satisfy his need for balance. He quickly uttered his central message. The discontinuities were secondary. Political experience accumulates over many generations, political wisdom develops in history, if only people maintain sufficient "peace, stability and *détente.*"[22] The accumulation of wisdom ran contrary to the abstractions generated by the forms of political science that careened towards "scientism," the political science that seemed to remove the human element from history and absolutized science. At the same time, Butterfield gave signals that he was softening in his earlier strict opposition to American social-scientific approaches, the view he expressed in *Diplomatic Investigations*. In April 1968 he had participated in a discussion at the Rockefeller Foundation's Villa Serbelloni on the confrontation between approaches based on history and philosophy and those using the techniques of the social sciences. Before going he read American international theory, including works by Morton A. Kaplan and Charles C. McClelland. Afterwards he thought about the matter in his journal: "I might be regarded as holding an intermediate position between those who believe in 'wisdom-literature' and those who prefer 'science'; but I believe so intensely in both that the term 'intermediate' will hardly meet the case. In any case, the important thing is to secure the right relationship between the two ways of envisaging the problem." The solution that he played with was to relate the two methods sequentially. First use the social-scientific methods, and then afterwards work over the material with the wisdom gathered from the historical analysis of continuous long-term human experience and common sense. He was trying to see the good in approaches he formerly dismissed. For the first time in a long time, he was moving his reconciling method into action, the mode of thinking which he had developed in the 1920s and 1930s to handle the opposing options presented him by others.[23]

It seemed like a long step for Butterfield, the historian who consistently presented himself as unconcerned with party politics, to convert his experience of the student protests into reflections on the political parties of England. The connection was probably the reminder that he liked what he knew in England, and that, indeed, he considered English political society since the seventeenth century to be the prime model of moral progress in modern history. He poured out a long thought-essay on contemporary party politics, his most explicit writing ever on the subject.[24] He felt attracted to and repulsed by both the Labour party and the Conservative party, and the Liberal party favoured by his father in his youth had become inconsequential. He felt Labour was too materialistic in outlook, too devoted to the interests of the better-off workers, too ready to "proletarianize everybody." The Conservatives were too prone "to the dictatorship of industrial interests," too much merely anti-socialist, too unthinkingly traditional. He estimated that the majority of the country was really Liberal at heart and rather like him. He would not side with the Conservatives, but he also distrusted Socialism, he disliked the materialism of capitalism, but he also disliked the "grimmer dangers of Socialism." The situation called for the revival of the Liberals, he thought, provided they became "a progressive non-socialist party," and focused their political thought on fundamental principles and long-term horizons for the improvement of the quality of life. He sounded for just a moment as if he could be moved into alignment with a political party if the right one were there. Nonetheless, his meditations on politics brought him no closer than before to getting out to vote.

These were the sounds of the centrist, Butterfield merely measuring his distance from the fences on either side of the political highway. As in the 1920s, he depicted his views as "stereoscopic," taking in both left and right at once and creating his own vision that went beyond the existing alternatives. It was like his search for an "intermediate position" that would reconcile both science and wisdom in political theory. There were echoes of the via media of the Anglican politicians and divines.[25]

He wrote often in his journal. The important question for him, as it had been for decades, was the role of the individual in relation to society, but now his thinking seemed to reach a new resolution of the tensions involved. He continued to say that the individual, not society, has the soul, and he continued to reject the notion of serving society or the state, in favour of simply serving other individuals. On a relative scale, he could regard the Socialists, with their focus on equality, society, and the state, as grimmer than the Conservatives who, in the interests of capitalism, tended at least to promote some individuals, albeit those most privileged by the system. But now he felt that both sides erred in their emphasis. The assertion that the individual matters most, he said in his journal, is made with the divine point of view in mind, but there is another perspective: "I am not sure that anything better has ever been thought of than that both the individual and society exist for the glory of God. . . . From a mundane point of view (but only from a mundane point of view) both are to be treated as ends in themselves and never as mere instruments — never as the one existing for the sake of the other — though it is true that they cannot exist without one another. . . . Their glory is their existence. They are the highest manifestations of creation. But they are created things — not gods." The distinction between the mundane and the divine points of view gave him the pivot he needed to turn towards this more positive appreciation of society. Both individuals and society are creatures, and both live before God in the world. The significance of the rhetorical shift within Butterfield's discourse is huge. He has taken the language he formerly had always reserved exclusively for individual people and applied it for the first time to society as a whole. The implications for his social thought would be equally great.[26]

For years Butterfield had murmured both against "mere individualism" and against "proletarianizing everybody." Now, in his journal, the search was on for a political view of equality, suffering, and the poor that was stereoscopic, beyond both the Conservatives and the Socialists. Characteristically, his political discourse took the form of reflection on historical process. He still did not get very far, but he reached a position consonant with the rest of his discourse that satisfied him for the moment. Nothing in life is ever really equal to anything else, he began, and, in general, the experience of social inequality may have the value sometimes of driving people to improve their condition. But the poor might be a special case, requiring special attention. Their condition of inequality is usually not due to any fault of their own, but to a combination of the inheritance of suffering from the past and the creation of new suffering today by our own systems and acts of social injustice. His consciousness of the tenuousness of life for most of the population of the world was acute: "If it is a question of viewing life on the earth (or life in time) as *cataclysmic* we must distinguish between [the few] and the great masses of people for whom ordinary life was an astonishingly cataclysmic thing *throughout the ages* — how near to death you always were until almost the 20th century — families being numerous but taking death in their stride."[27] If there were to be equality in some sense in society, Butterfield thought, it should come about by bringing the people at the bottom of the social ladder into the good already achieved by the people at the top. The way to the goal would be this: "a gradual process of lifting all men up and heightening the quality of their lives — a thing which the vast majority of Englishmen over 45 must have realised to have gone on in their own case during the last 30 years." He wanted a society of inclusion, rather than conflict or polarization, one which brought everyone to the top, rather than eliminating the top or merely stopping at the middle. The strategy of social gradualism paralleled the New Whig political method he had advocated for decades. The metaphor of "uplift" mirrored his image of England successfully bringing the ordinary Englishman into the world of the "imponderables" enjoyed by the aristocracy. The road to equality was social elevation. Butterfield's strategy was autobiographical, recapitulating the process of social uplift enjoyed by his father, as well as the experience of his own life, moving from the worker's cottage in Oxenhope's Upper Town to the Master's Lodge in Peterhouse.[28]

At every conjuncture, Butterfield's meditations in the period surrounding his retirement brought him to religion. He filled more journal-sheets on religion than on any other subject.[29] The pursuit of the stereoscopic vision, the intermediate position, also affected his attitudes in religion. He felt both yes and no towards the variety of traditions presented to him within Christianity, including his own. He reaffirmed his deep commitment to dissent when he wrote, "The Christian ought to be a nonconformist. Christianity ought to be a sort of opposition." But there were signs that he was tiring of some of the features of his Methodist tradition. In one journal entry, after reading Shakespeare, he remarked that Falstaff "reminds me of the way I have misspent my life, and, having had a little dietary trouble in the course of the day, my whole being now revolts against lemonade, coca-cola, ginger beer, soda-water, grenadine, appelsaft, and tea."[30] At the Villa Serbelloni, after an absence of several years, he observed in his journal, "The wine is certainly as good as ever — the Machiavelli, white and red, giving great pleasure." His rebellion could turn even against his teetotaling.[31] In another entry, he wrote, "I am not happy about our existing (Methodist) 'cult', and . . . I prefer the Church of England prayer-book to the current practices of nonconformity."[32] His practice of worshiping in the college chapel during his time as Master prepared him for his decision to attend evening prayer in the Sawston parish church during his retirement. A few years before retirement he had acknowledged that he liked the historic episcopate and would hope that an ultimately unified Christian church might accept the episcopal system.[33] His attitude of tolerance and flexibility in matters of doctrine and orthodoxy befitted the historical Methodist emphasis on experience, but it also suited the comprehension of the Anglican tradition. Indeed, there is a sense in which he knew that his reconciling method, the stereoscopic vision, replicated the Anglican via media in thought and churchmanship, and Anglican inconclusiveness with respect to doctrinal authority. But one feature of the Church of England repelled him almost more than he had the ability to express: the connection with the state as the Established Church. Comment after comment in his journal railed against Establishment: it associated religion with power, with officialdom, with the hint of compulsion in belief, with the status quo, with rule by priests. Even Nonconformity, he thought, had begun to act like Establishment. His mind swung to the Quakers. He found the Quakers to be the best model of how Christians should act in the world—quietly, with conviction, simply bearing witness without regard for the consequences. He often referred with favour to the Roman Catholic tradition of monasticism. The monks knew how to meditate, how to contemplate, and, although they retreated from the world, their spirituality gave them better balance towards the world, so that in the end they served the world in creative and unpredictable ways. The world needed such contemplation, he said, and even a political party would benefit if it were to send someone into a monastery for a year or two to meditate on things over a longer range and on a deeper level. He looked around at the condition of things in the world and the evidences he saw of religion. In 1968, he ventured a prediction which included a worry. He wrote, "If things go on as they are doing there will be a revival of religion—even a danger of the wrong sort of religion." He had in mind conservative forms of religion, which fostered certainty in belief and practice, and obedience to authority in religion.[34] Like his prediction as vice-chancellor that the decade of the 1960s could be "the most momentous in the history of universities," his estimate of the immediate future of religion during the 1970s and 1980s proved particularly apt.

Clarity on what was utterly essential in religion concerned him. In his journal-sheets he wrote epigrams and repeatedly made lists of the essential things. They tended to relate to Christian spirituality and the "Christian doctrine of man." He looked more and more like the Acton, whose lists and sayings he admired in Cambridge University Library. He was searching to find the things that he might call "timeless." Some items reappeared on his lists:

—hating the sin and not the sinner
—being governed not by one's hatred but by one's love
—regard for personality
—getting rid of self-righteousness
— ...

and

—The one thing that matters is the existence of the spiritual realm

And so on.

The meditations recorded on his journal-sheets frequently showed up in his public statements, usually in a closing statement or a pithy summation of what he thought was essential to say to each audience. The Cambridge History Faculty celebrated his career at a dinner in his honour in November 1968. His speech to the historians with whom he had spent his life was disarmingly autobiographical. Then he came to his parting message: "I think I ought to declare my belief that the future of history depends on its being treated as a Humanistic subject, with great respect for human personality — and great respect for the depth and mystery of it, even though people may exist in great masses and some parts of their activity may be amenable to science."[35] In the Rede Lecture in 1971: "If I were trying to push my comments on human history of the point of greatest generality, I believe I would say that men in the course of their lives, and readers of history in their studies, tend easily to leave certain things out of account. They do not sufficiently understand or try to bring into operation the healing effects of time; the great progress that comes from the gradual growth of reasonableness among men; and the benefits that accrue from long periods of peace and stability."[36] At the University of Southampton in November 1968: "The essential thing is to keep human feeling still warm in a competitive world, keep the personal touch in spite of the machine age. There should be some people working to raise the quality of life, to deepen human personality itself and to promote the slow growth of reasonableness among men. Those who want that gentler kind of world should consider the Christian thesis that it is important to hate the sin without hating the sinner. . . . And if a technological civilisation tends to drain the humanity out of [the] social world or dry up the hearts of men, one ought to ask whether anything less than a deeply-grounded feeling for the spiritual dimension will be sufficient for the most crucial conflict of all: the war against sheer materialism."[37] He continued his tradition of looking for the compelling sentence to end a piece of exposition. Feeling into the role of the old man, he concluded the Rede Lecture to all his Cambridge colleagues with these words: "These latter [the very aged] had better move quietly in the haunts of men, not screaming at all, but bleating and moaning — and, when they meet the odd person in the highway, just murmuring incessantly 'Brethern, love one another.' "[38] At the close of a sermon-address in St. Giles Cathedral, Edinburgh, in April 1970, he put these words: "If I desired to say perhaps one thing that might be remembered for a while, I would say that sometimes I wonder at the dead of night whether, during the next fifty years, Protestantism may not be at a disadvantage because a few centuries ago, it decided to get rid of monks. Since it followed that policy, a greater responsibility falls on us to give something of ourselves to contemplation and silence, and listening to the still small voice."[39]

Remarkably, in virtually all of his statements of the essentials in religion, whether in his journals or in his public talks, he repeated convictions he had uttered at least since the early 1920s, and probably earlier still. The continuity of the basic convictions was unmistakable, but now he said things directly, with a greater tone of finality.

Many Other Claims

Butterfield had always appeared humble about his own achievements, always understated things about himself, but around the time of his retirement he repeatedly used language about the course of his life that went further. His discourse could best be described as self-deprecating. The trait was most prominent in his talks to academic audiences, especially in his humour, his self-deprecating humour.[40] At a dinner, for instance, where he replaced another speaker at the last minute, he began, "It's what I've really been doing all my life — just catching by a fluke honours and pleasures that really belonged to somebody else." He would say, referring to *Whig Interpretation*, that he got a name for himself much too early in his career and he had never been able to live up to it thereafter. In a speech to the students of a well-to-do private school, he joked, "Even after today, I shan't be able to say that I came out of the top drawer." At the dinner in his honour in the Cambridge History Faculty, he opened his reminiscences with the quip that in his own past he could remember only "a succession of gaffes." He closed his speech with the parting message about history as a humanistic subject, and then added the final words, "I apologise for a hundred inadequacies."

Something more than convention lay behind his remarks. Butterfield seemed particularly to have in mind the research he had not finished, the books not written, the plans unfulfiled, the distractions too often followed. "I am drivellingly slow as a scholar and a writer," he said.[41] Upon retirement he solemnly promised to subordinate everything to his "retirement project," the revision and publication of his Gifford Lectures on the history of historiography. But alongside this, he faced a formidable quantity of other unfinished work, and he kept loading on still more projects. He still kept himself working, or intending to work, on all his many writing projects at once. Each of his long-standing projects could claim his promise to complete it, and many insistent appellants came to his door to remind him of his undertakings. On top of all this, he accepted a very large number of new invitations to present special lectures. During the first year of his retirement, 1968–1969, he delivered at least fifteen invited lectures, more than any other year in his career except for 1950–1951 and 1955–1956. He delivered at least nine more during each of the next two years. As usual he wrote out each lecture fresh and in full. It seemed to take his trouble with heart disease from 1971 onwards for him to reduce his outside lecture load.

It became very clear how wide were his interests and how diverse were his projects. On the brief standard form sent him by the American Academy of Arts and Sciences after his election as a Foreign Honorary Member in 1967, he presented the following self-description when he filled in the blanks:

Professional Field
A. *General:* History
B. *Special Area(s):*
Diplomatic History; Political Theory (crossed out); History of Thought; Eighteenth Century
C. *Special Topical Interests:*
Napoleon; History of Science; History of Historiography; the Reign of George III
Avocational Specialties
The relation between religion and history. Music. University Education[42]

The "retirement project" appeared as merely one of his "Special Topical Interests." His many other projects spanned the entire range of his specializations. In the 1970s, he made lists of the projects still on his agenda.

Above all, there was Fox. Butterfield's decision to undertake the Fox biography dated from 1931, nearly forty years before. For some time he had offered people an unconvincing explanation for his delay with Fox: "I personally always like to wait till other people have published their books first — people always condemn me for not having produced my proposed life of Fox ten or twenty years ago, but I always think what a fool I should have been if I had done that."[43] His former publisher, Bell, came after him for the book at least twice after he announced his intention to retire as Master. Bell reminded him that they had talked together before the Second World War about publishing the book. Butterfield replied that he had some other things to tend to first, but that "of course, [I] would still like to do a life of Fox."[44]

In a sense, throughout the forty years, he had never really worked seriously on the *biography* of Fox as such. From the start in the early 1930s he had adopted the strategy of gathering material around specific episodes that caught his attention — 1779–1780, 1792, 1806 — and then letting his mind wander off into the general issues of the reign of George III. So far, after all his research, he had published only two pieces directly on Fox. Both came from very old research, and both studied themes that had interested him since the 1920s, before the biography became his project. "Fox and the Whig

Opposition in 1792," published in 1949, went back to a paper probably presented in 1925 in which he tangled with Trevelyan, and "Charles James Fox and Napoleon: The Peace Negotiations of 1806," of 1962, stemmed from his Napoleon research in the 1920s.

He took the opportunity offered by the important Raleigh Lecture for the British Academy in 1971 to produce his first strictly biographical study of Fox. In twenty-four published pages he compressed forty years of research into his answer to the question whether Fox was sincere as a politician.[45] To write the lecture he gathered the entirety of his collection of notes on Fox, read the notes with his question in mind, and wrote out thought-essays in notebooks. Then he handwrote the paper through multiple drafts. He did all this while feeling weak from heart disease.

The published lecture included references to much of Fox's life, but concentrated on two of Butterfield's favourite years, 1792 and 1806. The results displayed Butterfield working over the life of one man, a politician, trying to figure out a subtle matter of personality and ethics, and, in keeping with his theory about freedom and necessity, estimating what might be the balance between Fox's moral responsibility and the interaction of circumstances beyond his control. When he came to write up what he had to say, he found that two of his long-standing theoretical recommendations conflicted. On one hand, he had repeatedly urged that individuals and political history were best understood through narrative. On the other, he had advocated writing history by focusing on problems, following advice taken from Acton's notes. He had to choose one approach over the other, and produced a lecture about a problem, with very little story. The process shows Butterfield practicing a very intimate relationship between his own theory and his own writing, listening to the messages he had broadcast for the benefit of others.

The lecture opens with the revelation that he has found that single piece of documentary evidence that clinched the argument about whether or not Fox was sincere about parliamentary reform in 1792. It is a letter by Fox to Earl Fitzwilliam in which Fox admitted to Fitzwilliam that he was not. Here, for Butterfield, is a clean classroom case illustrating the point he repeated so often from Acton about the importance of the one hard document that can transform the whole account. But then Butterfield dirties his own example. Fox's admission, he acknowledges, is open to more than one interpretation, depending in part upon what the historian thinks "sincerity really is." The further he goes in the lecture the more complicated his answer to the question of Fox's sincerity becomes. It gets tangled up with changes in Fox's position in politics over many years, and with the unpredictable, often moody, ways in which Fox arrived at his political decisions. Much of Butterfield's exposition amounts to saying that sometimes Fox was probably sincere and sometimes he was probably not. He concludes that, on at least one matter, the historian could be sure of Fox's sincerity, that is, sure that Fox really possessed a political and ethical conviction that would operate with constancy within his politics: "It would generally be recognized that the key to this entire situation — as indeed to Fox's career — lies in his passionate hatred for the king and his extravagant fear of the monarchy. . . . Here, as no doubt everybody would agree, the student of Fox can feel that he has reached bedrock."[46] Butterfield has his illustration of an "actual fact" that the labours of generations of historians working on Fox had firmly established. To enhance his case, in the final sentence of the lecture he throws in the evidence of the overall portrait of Fox, presented in his signature convoluted style: "It is difficult to imagine that a career devoted to the support of government and order would have suited and sustained the libertarian character or conformed with the prevailing impression — the prevailing picture — of his personality."[47]

The lecture finished, Butterfield experienced positive terror when preparing the text for publication. Perhaps because he had grown accustomed to publishing so much without footnotes, perhaps simply because he was ill, he made numerous technical errors in the typescript of his footnotes, and had to send an embarrassing letter to the British Academy correcting them all.[48] When the publication appeared he held in his hands the only detailed piece of biographical writing he had ever produced on Fox. But he knew that he could do no more than this on Fox, at least, not for now, not if he were serious about the Gifford Lectures. So he let go of Fox once again.

Other projects about eighteenth-century England still ranked high in his plans. On the table before him lay three hundred pages of manuscript towards a book on the early years of George III. The present state of the text derived from his course of lectures "George III and the Politicians, 1760–65," which he developed between 1963 and 1968, with roots in his lectures and research during the 1930s. He was telling people that he intended to spend some of his retirement producing a book on the subject.[49] He began vigorously in his usual manner by taking a lecture entitled "The Early Years of George III" to Canterbury, Durham, and York in 1968 and 1969.[50] However, aside from repeating a lecture now and then on "George III and Bute" or some other such topic, he never returned to the theme. On top of this, he still had in his files his 250-page manuscript for a book on England and the French Revolution, 1792, the unfinished final section for *George III and the Historians,* dating from 1957. It is possible he worked on this volume a little in the early 1960s, but in his retirement, although he glanced at it, he did nothing further. The work remained unfinished.

The lecture "The Early Years of George III" signalled that he was shifting around in his views of academic history. By 1968 and 1969, clashes over politics and ideology in historical study had increased rather than diminished among historians. The very same movements that Butterfield felt made things difficult for universities — Vietnam, racism, women's issues — had begun to challenge the reigning assumptions of the historical profession itself. By a surprising twist of events, critics and protesters within the profession provoked historians who had been opponents of each other to unite in a common front against them. Economic and social historians joined traditional political historians in a vigorous defense of "just doing history" against what they called the "politicization" of the profession and historical study. At the same time, Butterfield had made his peace with the work of Namier and reconciled with his supporters. Nonetheless, within the special world of the historians of eighteenth-century England, controversy had not at all ceased. Butterfield's views about the solidity of "facts" and the triumph of the "final story," put him securely on the side of the apolitical model of historical study that dominated the profession. He suddenly found himself in the overwhelmingly majority against the critics, rather than occupying the position of dissent he had intended for himself. The situation was bound to make him feel uncomfortable.

In Butterfield's terms, the issue, in part, was the relationship between "accepted fact" and "political and ideological conflict" in historical study. The treatment of George III by historians, he said, was an excellent case to consider. On one hand, after many generations of working over a subject, historians tend to achieve hard results: "They gradually establish one point after another, building up a solid core of scholarship on which people of all parties can be agreed — demonstrating by the evidence that Luther did actually *do* this or *say* that or proving that a situation was such-and-such — until after a succession of centuries there is a great body of accepted fact — Protestants and Catholic historians can agree in the twentieth century over a remarkable area of the field." On the other hand, ideological differences remain and controversy continues over a broad field. Faced with such an experience, he started to shift his position. He now wanted to accept such ideological controversy as *part* of academic history, actually a valid component of the process of coming to agreement, and not to be excluded because it was ideological:

> Still they will always tell the story differently because they approach it with
> different sets of values. . . . We ought not to deplore controversy in history — it
> seems that problems are properly threshed out, and often in the past it has
> driven scholars to more profound enquiries — new ranges of discovery. It has
> even improved historical technique. . . . A richer, though perhaps more com-
> plicated kind of truth comes to be established at the finish if both sides to

the controversy have fully presented their case and fully criticised the other party's case. But this seems to take centuries — you have to wait until all the evidence has properly shaken down and you have emerged completely from the atmosphere of controversy. Till that stage is reached it is better not to have very hard and very rigid views about the issues that history presents.

He persisted in his faith that ideological conflict would eventually wither away, as academic historians "established" the story at "the finish." At the end, the results of historical science would stand above the wind and the weather. But, for now, that destination seemed indefinitely postponed. A future apolitical history seemed little more than an eschatological hope. In the meantime, academic history carried on, marked by seemingly endless controversy, leaving behind few solid remains. In the case of George III, he said, perhaps the controversies had ceased about the structure of politics, the subjects of Namier's histories. But the controversies still swirled round questions of "our judgment of the policy, the statesmanship, of the leading people during that reign." In other words, Namier may have succeeded in making *his* case, apparently without taking centuries, or was it, perhaps, that Butterfield had ceased raising controversy against Namier? It remained for Butterfield to make his case against his critics about the issues he found compelling. "There is a sense in which I personally would like to keep it controversial," he said.[51] It appears, however, that he gave no more time to the issues as such after 1969.

The *Concise Cambridge Modern History* made exceedingly strong claims upon Butterfield. He not worked on this major project for at least twelve years, probably longer. He was sitting on at least a thousand pages of typescript in various stages of revision. R. W. David at Cambridge University Press still wanted the book, thirty years after the initial contract of 1939, and was still reminding him of his agreement and repeated promises to do it. Almost as a prod, David asked him to review Lord Acton's big project, the original *Cambridge Modern History*, with a reprint in view. Butterfield did his homework and prepared a lengthy report, recommending only a few selected chapters for a special volume. He appended comments on the merits of each recommended chapter. Temperley's chapter "England, 1687–1702" he felt was "beautifully written," and Temperley's chapter "The Age of Walpole and the Pelhams" was "brilliant both in its general political account and in its treatment of Wesley." Gooch's "Growth of Historical Science" was "a remarkable piece of work and led later to the production of his most important work."[52] The review of Acton's offspring pushed him no closer to work on the *Concise Modern History,* but it did remind him that, in 1945, he had wanted to write something on Acton's role in the *Cambridge Modern History.* He uncovered his twenty-five-year-old notes and drafts about the origins of the *Cambridge Modern History,* and in September 1971 made a fresh start on an essay he variously entitled "Lord Acton and the Original CMH," or "The Original CMH — Comedy or Tragedy."[53] Deep down there were also his three hundred pages of *The Historical Background of General Knowledge,* from 1943, the basis of his proposal to Cambridge University Press in 1964 for a book on the historical geography of Europe. He worked no further on the historical geography, and the Acton study still remained unfinished, as did his *Concise Modern History.*

Acton still called, however. Butterfield nurtured remote hopes for the volume of Acton's early journals with commentary, maybe even a biography, which he had planned since the late 1940s. He was still trying to get someone interested in editing the complete Acton letters, adding to the letters with Döllinger, Newman, and Simpson already published or being prepared for publication. He still adamantly opposed publishing any mere selection of letters. David Knowles was suggesting to him an Acton *Opera Omnia.*[54] In 1972, Knowles, Butterfield, and Owen Chadwick, three successive Regius Professors of Modern History, joined together and arranged for Cambridge University Library to purchase from Douglas Woodruff and his wife over five thousand letters by Lord Acton, Regius Professor from another era.[55] Nothing more came of Butterfield's own plans for work on Acton, although he continued his practice of referring to Acton in virtually everything he wrote.

Stepping off the British Rockefeller Committee on the Theory of International Politics when he retired had formally ended his activity concerning international relations, but not his interest. He felt no obligation to work further on the volume of essays he had proposed on states-systems, and allowed it to die at his retirement. But he did play a little further with a possible study of the history of diplomacy, a project he had mentioned while still chairing the committee. It would have been an examination of diplomacy as technique over the centuries. He may have added to his reading on the history of diplomacy at this time. He did put down on paper his observations on the study of international relations at the London School of Economics, which he felt neglected historical study in favour of an emphasis on contemporary affairs. He also produced a long essay, "The Development of Diplomacy." But he went no further. He included a history of diplomacy on his lists of unfinished projects, although he left vague whether he intended a book.[56]

People kept coming to Butterfield with invitations for articles and lectures on international politics which he did not decline. In February 1969, he finished a long article, "Balance of Power," for the *Dictionary of the History of Ideas,* published in 1973. He accepted the assignment in 1967, thinking he would write the article after his retirement. The article was a historical treatment of the idea of the balance of power, an expanded version of his essay on the subject in *Diplomatic Investigations*. His history took the eighteenth-century version of the idea as the norm, calling it "the final synthesis" and "a mature theory of balance of power," and he discussed earlier and later international relations as tending towards the eighteenth-century idea or away from it. He inserted many sentences here and there about the value of maxims derived from reflection on long-term history. He was not as sure as he once seemed to be, notably in *Diplomatic Investigations,* that the threat of the nuclear weapon rendered the idea of balance of power out of date by elevating the importance of factors other than sheer power in international politics, factors like persuasion and morality.[57]

Later in 1969 Butterfield discussed the moral framework of international relations at a conference at Aberystwyth in Wales. He reminded the audience that he was no theorist of *realpolitik,* but a historian contemplating ethical principles. His message reaffirmed his perennial claim that the ethical principles for life in general apply equally to international politics and to any other aspect of life. He named the principles: love, charity, self-sacrifice, respect for human personality, and "doing to others as we should expect them to do to us." He knew very well that he had stated what he regarded as the core Christian principles.[58]

Another foray in the history of ideas in international politics came in 1975, with a rambling lecture on the history of the idea of *raison d'état*. The occasion, at the University of Sussex, was a commemoration of Martin Wight, his friend and successor as head of the Rockefeller committee, who died suddenly in 1972. Unlike his treatment of the idea of the balance of power, Butterfield's approach did not fix the classic version of this idea as the norm and did not make Cardinal Richelieu his hero. He offered no maxims drawn from the study, no considerations of theory at all, merely a few observations on the evolution of the modern idea of the state, with Cardinal Richelieu at the centre of the picture. His approach was a reminder to himself, and his hearers and eventual readers, that he ventured into international theory not as a theorist, but as the historian who occasionally found it interesting to reflect on the long-term course of history. This lecture turned out to be his last excursion in the territory of the Rockefeller committee.[59]

Perhaps first in personal duty came the Temperley biography, the memoir about his master teacher he had been intending to write since Temperley's sudden death in 1939. He possessed a manuscript on Temperley of some 170 pages, dating from perhaps 1963. When it came time for Butterfield to move out of the Master's Lodge, a dozen cases of Temperley papers still sat in the basement, and a smaller lot waited in his study. He faced a repetition of his handling of the Fox papers he had borrowed from Trevelyan for twenty years without reading them. He approached Temperley's son with the request to keep the papers still longer. "I would like to do, not a big book," he said, "but an adequate biography of Harold and a picture of his world, chiefly with the object of getting a Portrait of a Historian — i.e. as much as I can do of his rather vivid external personality and his amazingly human interior." He added the caveat that "this biography isn't the first job I have to do." He got permission from the son to keep the papers, but he apparently never worked on the project again.[60]

On the eve of his retirement, unable to stop himself, Butterfield dreamed of new publishing projects. It occurred to him that he might publish a collection of his essays, putting more of his work into book form. He discussed the idea with A. D. Peters, his agent now for twenty years, who thought that a commercial house might consider a package that included the collected essays. Butterfield played with several possible tables of contents and by 1970 had at least two volumes in view, with third on his mind. His lists covered some thirty-five lectures, articles, and reviews, published and unpublished, running back to his first inaugural lecture in 1944. All of his pieces on Acton went on the lists, and he was, he said, "very attached to grouping the articles on Namier together." In addition to these, he envisaged "possibly a volume also connected with Christianity." Yet in spite of his hopes, he took none of the ideas for collected essays any further.[61]

Historiography and Religion

This left the history of historiography. With all the special lectures and writings, and all the other claims on his attention during his retirement, he allowed himself little time for what he advertised as his "retirement project." When people came to him with invitations related to historiography, in some cases he touched up some of his very old work, and in others agreed to take on several new projects branching off from the Gifford Lectures. Before long he was thinking deeply again about religion and history. The revision of the Gifford Lectures took second place in his schedule even within the area of the history of historiography.

The assignment Butterfield set for himself in revising the Gifford Lectures was clear, but time-consuming. His homework was to keep reading the historical writing produced in the cultures he had selected, notably Mesopotamia, ancient Egypt, the Hittite empire, ancient Israel, classical China, and the early Christian community. On top of the histories, he was also to read modern critical literature produced about the histories, especially criticism about the Old and New Testament. He continued the approach he took in the lectures themselves, and gave structure to his readings and analysis by looking at a problem, rather than telling a story. He also decided to stay with the problem he had chosen for the lectures, the problem of origins, but now perhaps somewhat more precisely defined. For the ancient societies, he examined how historical thinking and writing began within each one. He concentrated on what he described as "civilisations in their early stages where their divergencies can be tracked down." At the moment of his retirement, he summarized the primary questions in his mind: "how historical writing and the historical sense and the impulse to historical research really originated, . . . what factors set the historical enterprise going in the first place, what elements of human nature it catered for, why some cultures never developed history study as recording."[62] For modern European civilization, he would retain his examination of the problem of origins in a different sense, focusing on the beginnings of modern historical criticism and modern secular approaches to historical study.

In the early years of his retirement he apparently gave very little time to the actual study of these questions, but he did produce a number of writings that showed how his thinking about the history of historiography was going. Two quite opposite tendencies seemed evident. The first tendency was to fix his attention ever more narrowly on diplomatic and political history. The second was to swing out ever more widely into universal and global history.

With the first tendency, he continued to constrict his vision for academic history as he did in his inaugural lecture in 1964 as Regius Professor of Modern History and his paper "In Defence of Diplomatic History" in 1963 to the Cambridge History Club. He claimed the priority of political and diplomatic history, understood very particularly as the narrative rendering of individuals in power. In this context, his meditations on the political parties of England formed a component of his increasing stress on politics as the paramount factor in history. In December 1968, in a centenary address to the Royal Historical Society, of which he was now an honourary vice-president, he surveyed the last century of important developments in scholarship on modern history. He constructed the story as if the greatest achievements in historical study since 1868 belonged to the fields of diplomatic and political history, and centred especially on German scholarship and the techniques of archival research and criticism associated with Ranke. His account included merely passing reference to economic history and cultural history, and nothing about social history, religious history, quantitative history, demographic history, women's history, family history, global history, comparative history, or the many other histories then coming into vogue. He made relatively few references to historical study in

Great Britain, and none at all to historical study in the United States, France, or elsewhere, no acknowledgment of, for instance, the French Annales historians, or American social science history. The names he cited repeatedly in the survey were none other than Ranke, Acton, and Temperley. The survey was Butterfield at his most narrow.[63]

In the same vein, he published an article on the evolution of British historiography since the sixteenth century, ostensibly a review of J. R. Hale's anthology on the subject, in which he interpreted the great complexity of British historical scholarship as pivoting on political history, and especially on matters of research technique and narrative exposition. Once again he issued his call for the study of the history of research techniques and criticism, by which he meant history as science. To this he added an explicit appeal for the study of "the development of the art or the technique of historical narrating as such," which he called the study of history as literature. This echoed his interest in writing style and sheer narration dating from the 1920s. Almost by the way he cast a dart or two at historians who indulged in quantification and complicated analysis.[64]

Likewise, for the Stenton Lecture at the University of Reading, in November 1968, he signalled his allegiance to a strictly traditional mode of English political history. He applied his celebrated historiographical method, demonstrated in *Man on His Past* in 1955, to the changing treatments of the Magna Carta by historians in the sixteenth and seventeenth centuries. He rummaged through his old notes on Whig historiography, going back to his materials for *Englishman and His History* of 1944 and even *Whig Interpretation of History* of 1931. The lecture was another classroom illustration of the benefits of historiographical study, this time seeking to demonstrate the role of political history in the development of historical thinking and writing. The case of the Magna Carta, he thought, would clinch his point that political history was central to the whole life of a nation. However, he neglected to consider the relative importance of other factors when making his point.[65]

The epitome of his increasing acclamation of political history, construed as the narrative of the powerful, was a significant paper, "The Nature of Political History," probably written about the same time as his paper "Revolution" of 1972. Like "Revolution," this remained unpublished.[66] He explicitly admitted that his new views on the centrality of political history meant that he now abandoned his earlier commitment from the 1930s to the multifaceted historical study of "civilization" or "society." He denigrated his previous writings which approved such an inclusive approach to historical study, calling them "hymns of praise glorifying this great tendency in historical scholarship." As a result of his study of the history of historiography, he was drawing the conclusion that political history was the most creative generator of historical study in world history, beginning with the empires of ancient Mesopotamia. In his enthusiasm, he now asserted that political history ought to continue, now and into the future, to occupy the central role in historical study.

The supports he offered to bolster his claims for the centrality of political history were really a gathering together of things he had been saying for some time. First, political history provides a clear and precise framework for general historical study. Second, the political centre of a country shapes the affairs of the whole nation, as, for instance, through the decisions about war and the effects of dynasty or other ruling authority. Third, political events reveal human beings as individuals who are free to act upon their choices, actions particularly suited to treatment by narrative methods. Fourth, political affairs over the long term were conducive to maxims and the accumulation of wisdom worth teaching to successive generations. His points were really assertions. He seemed not to worry about the things left out of his way of constructing political history or the things left unconsidered by his assumptions about other areas of historical study. For instance, political history can be vague, the political centre can be inconsequential and remote, political events can overwhelm individual persons, and political affairs in the long term can display confusion or difference or discontinuity. Each of the four points he advances for political history can be said with equal force about economic history or women's history or the history of religion, and so too each of the considerations he left out.

Butterfield's withdrawal into a reductionist view of political history, coming as it did at just the moment when the variety of histories and approaches to history was burgeoning, left him completely out of touch with the new trends in historiography. His new position could appear simply reactionary were it not for the realization that three of his four points represented his enduring beliefs and practice. Only the first point marked a reversal, a retreat from his broadly conceived general history in the 1930s. He seemed to be squirming when he excused his extravagance in favour of political history as a response to exaggerated claims for social history put to him by an undergraduate, not due to the examination of the very best writings in social and economic history. He apparently did not take the time to read the other modes of history. He gave himself no opportunity to apply his reconciling method to women's history, Black history, serial history, and all the other new forms and methods that were then becoming commonplace in historical study.

The second tendency evident in his occasional writings in historiography after 1968 was the opposite of the first. Even as he continued to limit his vision to a particular style of narrative political history, he also continued to elaborate his historical understanding on the widest horizon of universal history. This, too, continued a trend which antedated his retirement, commenced in Jerusalem in December 1957 and at the London School of Oriental and African Studies in January 1958, and leading to his choice of theme for the Gifford Lectures. In 1970 he travelled to Hong Kong as an adviser on curriculum for the Chinese University of Hong Kong. With his interest in Chinese historical writing intensifying, he promoted a vision of historical study that embraced both Chinese and "Western" civilizations. The coming need, he said, was the study of universal history. It was not enough, he said, to picture universal history as the diffusion of "Western civilization," or as the sum of the particular histories of each nation of the world, or as "Western civilization" plus another major sample civilization or two. Historians needed to step entirely out of their culture of origin and adopt a genuinely global conception of world history: "They [global events] ought to be studied on a global scale, and from the point of view of mankind as a whole. It would be wrong even to say that we will study global history from the "Western" point of view or the Chinese point of view — I think it is necessary that we should strive as much as we can for a global point of view, having in mind the overall development of one single world civilization."[67] This was new discourse for Butterfield. It took him into a realm where talk of religion easily floated to the surface. The conception of universal history he recommended directly transposed the European-wide perspective in the study of European history that he had adopted for his Cambridge lectures since the 1930s to the new reality of global experience. The effect would be to deemphasize nations and even civilizations in favour of generating a worldwide perspective for the history of the whole world. With such thinking he was pushing beyond even Arnold Toynbee, who at that very moment was wondering whether his life-long project of constructing world history out of the blocks he named "civilizations" might not be missing the point, the emergence of a worldwide civilization that comprehended humanity as a whole.[68] Butterfield's new understanding of universal history did not come unalloyed, however. He accompanied his advice about a truly worldwide perspective with other, more traditional recommendations. Students should study their own civilization first, he said, and then look at one other. And they should feature political history, and bring the experience of the ages home to themselves via the study of political history over the long term.[69]

In his retirement Butterfield had no opportunity to put his curricular suggestions into practice, and he left no notes about how he might transform his old course on the history of European civilization since 1494. What the Cambridge tradition, and he, had always called "modern history" seemed even more narrow than previously thought when held next to his new statement of the scope of universal history. His new conception of universal history, together with his new assertion of the primacy of narrative political history, could only serve to mount still further impediments to his progress on the *Concise Cambridge Modern History*. The thousand pages of writing he had accumulated on that project stood frozen at the stage reached by his thinking in the 1930s and 1940s. And, in the animated world of historical study in 1970s, that could feel like ages ago.

The two opposing tendencies in his discourse posed no problem for Butterfield. He unabashedly paired the two, and formulated a major thesis to which his massive studies of the history of historiography were bringing him. His thesis surfaced as a generalization which he used to structure a major summary of the history of historiography. The piece was a massive article, entitled "Historiography: History of Historiography," which he finished in March 1969 for the *Dictionary of the History of Ideas* (1973). It ran to 186 pages of typescript. It combined what began as two articles assigned him by the dictionary editors, one on historical criticism and the other on the history of historiography. The outcome he described as "an essay of the *genesis* of ideas and developments in Historiography." It covered all the ground traversed by his projected revision of the Gifford Lectures and represented a masterful condensation by his own hand of his whole retirement project.[70]

The overarching thesis of "Historiography" claims that the multitude of historical writings from the earliest Mesopotamian inscriptions to the histories produced in nineteenth-century western Europe can be "divided in a fairly clear-cut manner into two big classes, one which was always described as universal history, while the other we today at least would call political history." Political history arose out of the mundane need to celebrate or record the contemporary history of one's own state. Universal history emerged as religious history in response to the spiritual need to understand the destiny, purpose, and meaning of human existence in the world. If religious history took the story back to the creation, political history brought the story up to the very present, usually the present of one's own state. Butterfield embraces both types of history with élan. Both are valid and necessary. His perception of the pair neatly expresses the abiding dualism that structures his understanding of life: the spiritual/religious and the mundane/material.

The use of the phrase "the other we today at least would call political history" allows him to obscure a vast complexity. The term "political history" does not mean the same thing over time, and neither does the term "state," as he moves from ancient Mesopotamia through many other ancient societies to eighteenth-century England, and finally on to his contemporary England. The terms mask important differences. He ignores incomparable differences in the organization of life and the deployment of power that obtained in each of those situations. His term "political history" might well apply to one specialized form of historical study produced in his own day, one branch of history positioned next to countless other branches. But when he applies the term across thousands of years, he imposes a modern definition of relationships on dissimilar situations. He misses the range and variety of previous histories that went by a changing list of names from culture to culture. Some of those histories appeared far more skeletal than his modern "political history." Other varieties routinely surpassed the ordinary range of the modern norm, and mingled elements of what we now would call geography and demography, social and economic history, political and intellectual history, and religious history. A trick of the simplification of language enables him to reduce the complicated historiographical field to merely his dualistic pair.[71]

The emphasis on universal history led Butterfield straight into renewed thinking about religion and history. The theme immediately before him was the problem of the origins of a Christian historiography, the subject of two of the original lectures in Glasgow. He demonstrated yet another time that his historical thinking easily transmuted into religious thinking. After 1968 he composed several writings and lectures on religion and history that incorporated or branched out from his Gifford material.

By far the longest was a 200-page typescript for the *Dictionary of the History of Ideas,* completed in May 1970, entitled "Christianity in History." This was his third significant study for that major work of reference. "Balance of Power" was the first, and now these two, "Christianity in History" and "Historiography," both of which are longer than *Whig Interpretation of History* and at least three of his other books.[72]

"Christianity in History" is a piece of historical writing that surveys the course of that religion from its beginning. His treatment might be expected to meet his standards for academic history and present a study that eliminates the historian's religion and politics from the exposition of the history. In actuality it well illustrates exactly the opposite of his theory. It is as much a vehicle for the expression of his own religion as it is a history. The basic categories, the general structure, and the explanatory devices all rest directly on his own convictions about Christianity. The history presents a highly conventional tale centred on western Europe and the outreach of European missions. He divides it into the four conventional periods: early, medieval, Reformation and Counterreformation, and modern. A brief fifth section, virtually an appendix, tells about Christianity in the Orthodox world of Russia, eastern Europe, and Greece. In this way he at least gives some evidence that his emerging global perspective has started to take effect, allowing him at least to notice the existence of a few of the vast and varied forms of Christianity outside western Europe and North America, even if as yet he had no idea how to integrate or expand this knowledge into his history.

The history is structured as a story, but it is sprinkled with Butterfield-created maxims about history and religion. The maxims function in an explanatory manner to move his story along. Here is a sample: "So long as a religious revival retains its character, it is not in its nature to encourage mammonism, a point which even the Puritans of seventeenth-century England illustrate."[73] The maxims as well as the actual structure of the story disclose once again his lifelong belief that Christianity is truly a spiritual experience occurring within the souls of individuals. In keeping with this belief, he arranges his story to show that the well-being of the religion revived when Christians gave their attention to spiritual things, and declined when they entangled themselves with mundane concerns, and that the institutional church was most healthy and the effects of Christianity on society most beneficial when Christians acted as if both the church and their social influence were mere by-products of, and not channels or substitutes for, communion with God. His religious beliefs shape his historical account about the religion, and his history reveals his religious beliefs.

Two journeys to the United States, where his fame ranked higher now than in England, gave him new audiences for his thoughts on Christianity in history. He used his visits to Jewish Theological Seminary in New York, Duke University, and the University of North Carolina, Chapel Hill, in 1969, and to Northwestern University in 1974 to try out a combination of the Gifford material on the origins of Christian historiography and his reflections on religion and history. The ease with which he moves between the historical questions and the theological questions weakens any case he might want to make for the erection of a high wall between history and the historian's religion. In this case, however, the lectures belong to a different genre from historical writing. It is the same genre as *Christianity and History* of 1948 and 1949, wherein he made no claim to be writing academic history, but rather, as a historian, he openly advocated his own Christian perspective on history and historical study. Except for the Gifford material, he adds little that is new to the things he had been saying on these themes for decades.[74]

The message of the lectures did fall on new ears, however, and produced new excitement as another wave of Americans heard Butterfield's paradoxical words for the first time. His thought on the struggle between good and evil appealed to James Reston and Harrison Salisbury, both writers for the *New York Times,* who arranged to place two articles' worth of what he had to say in a prominent spot in the newspaper during January 1973. One article carried the catchy title "The Moderate Cupidity of Everyman." He reiterates his old, but still disconcerting message, that the world needs no monsters or devils to create the evils of history. The little cupidities of each person, when multiplied by millions in one society after another, are enough to cause all the wars, tragedies, and sufferings of humanity.[75] The same material had served him for an appearance on BBC television in 1970 when he gave his talk entitled "Evil in History."[76]

Of all these lectures, Butterfield took special delight in one entitled "Does Belief in Christianity Validly Affect the Modern Historian?" He presented an early version of it at Rice University in 1963, a revised version at Chapel Hill in 1969, another revision at Northwestern in 1974, and in 1977 he was still making revisions to his text. The title mutated into "Can Belief in Christianity Validly Affect the Work of the Modern Technical Historian?" The theme was the same he had treated in "The Christian and Historical Study," published in *History and Human Relations* in 1951. His question forced him to bring face to face two equally strong components of his thought. He still had not adequately elaborated on paper the relationship between his firm commitment to the independence of academic history from religion, politics, and ideology, on one hand, and his unyielding commitment to the involvement of his Christianity in his vocation as a historian. He seemed to want to find a way to formulate their coexistence.[77]

By the early 1970s the world of historical study had changed so greatly that it was becoming less and less plausible to talk about such a thing as neutral history at all. The achievements in the areas of Black history, women's history, and postcolonial history since the 1960s were having an effect on the debates about history in the profession as a whole. The charge that so-called scientific history was utterly political and ideological was getting harder to defeat.

Butterfield is raising questions about the moral and religious character of what passes as scientific history. The new points in his thinking in this lecture are two. First, he filters into his discussion the knowledge he gained in his Gifford researches about the origins and effects of a Christian interpretation of history, giving his reflections on the theme greater historical depth. Second, he frankly concedes, more explicitly and more definitely than ever before, that "perhaps indeed only a comparative few" of the things that historians assert in their publications are, or even can be, "historically established" in so coercive a manner that they hold as true for "any student of the past — Protestant or Catholic, Christian or non-Christian, Frenchman or Englishman, and Whig or Tory." His language shows him clinging to his norm for "technical history" in the midst of the highly politicized environment of the historical profession. But now he is coming to admit that his criterion would apply to very little of what historians actually wrote, "perhaps less than ten per cent." And this, he adds, was not likely to be the most important 10 percent.[78]

That left the other 90 percent of what historians put in their histories. He mentions a point which he might have pursued in the lecture, possibly a third new point: "Historians do not remain mere technicians, therefore, and they must bring all that they know about life and themselves, all their personal experience and their accumulated knowledge of the centuries behind them, all that they have ever felt in the deepest parts of themselves, to enrich their understanding of human events and even their interpretation of pieces of evidence." In the case of Christian historians, he continues, there were things that Christians know about life and themselves that arise directly from their Christianity which validly ought to affect their study of history. So certain is he that he has tapped straight into the source of the truth of the universe that he represents this knowledge as if it were, or ought to be, the common knowledge of the historical profession itself. The things he identifies corresponded with his recent meditations, as well as with what he had reiterated throughout his whole career. Christian historians, he says, ought to have the highest regard for individual personality, to be cognizant of the inner life of people, to try to understand the people of the past and not to blame them, to be conscious of human will and responsibility, to count mundane events as significant, and to value the recovery of the past for the sake of the truth. Christian historians, in other words, ought to write "a humanist kind of history." These are the sorts of things that saturate Butterfield's historical study. They cannot be discussed adequately in terms of the "quantity" or "percentage" of text to which they applied. They inform everything he writes as a historian. Butterfield goes no further. He makes no attempt to give an explanation of the relationship between the study of history and the historian's commitments in religion, politics, or ideology. He does not follow his own lead, that the "historians do not remain mere technicians" when engaged in historical study. At the end of the day, he clings in principle to the neutrality of technical, scientific history, even in the face of profound considerations to the contrary which he readily acknowledges.

All of Butterfield's lectures and writings since 1968 on themes arising from his Gifford Lectures no doubt helped him think about what he wanted to do to turn the lectures into a magnum opus. Nonetheless, he still needed actually to work on the revisions. He seemed to find it hard to concentrate on the project now that he had no deadline. He did not begin solid reading with an eye on his revisions until 1973, seven years after he finished the lectures. By then he had completed the shorter writings he had accepted at the start of his retirement, and he felt physically recovered from his rounds with heart disease.

The notes he took in 1973 show him reading extensively on Egyptian historical writing and copying out the texts of inscriptions and hymns: Thutmosis III, Ramesses II, Menes, Papyrus Harris No. 1, Poem on the Victory of Merneptah, and so on. He was reading studies about the Hittites and filling out his understanding of Old Testament criticism.[79] In his journal for 5 April 1973 he complained that he experienced "tremendous difficulty" in keeping himself from collecting more material and forcing himself to write. "So," he wrote, "perhaps the solution is just to write, without waiting for the inspiration. Perhaps one creates the inspiration for oneself, manufactures it in the very fever of writing."[80] He managed to get more time at Villa Serbelloni as the guest of the Rockefeller Foundation in July 1973, and he carried his materials with him to write. As it turned out, this was his last stay at the villa, a place which gave him some of the best moments of his life.[81]

He seems to have worked intermittently between 1973 and 1976 on further reading and further writing. Some of this reading included histories produced by classical Islamic historians. The work Butterfield completed on the first five lectures, the set from 1965, enabled him to start calling them chapters for the book. The chapters covered Sumer, Akkad, Egypt, the Hittites, Assyria, Babylon, Israel, Greece, and the Chinese. He started revisions on the second group of five, from 1966, but he did not finish them and they remained fragments. This was the set running from the earliest Christian writings to the rise of modern European historical study in the nineteenth century. He wrote out an entirely new and quite tentative passage on Islam which took him beyond the range of the Gifford Lectures.[82]

In comparison with the originals, the revised texts are much longer, contain many more quotations from sources, refer to a wider range of issues, and engage more critical scholarship. The basic structure of the story remains the same. Butterfield still interprets historical writing as moving from ancient Mesopotamia to modern western Europe, and he still travels a route formed by a sequence of "firsts" which he believes anticipated modern western European historical thought and writing. The exception is still China, which serves paradoxically to underline the Eurocentric character of his tale. The main story is about "Western civilization," which he calls "my quarter of the globe." In contrast with Toynbee, who places the beginning of "Western civilization" after the disintegration of Greco-Roman civilization, he begins his "Western civilization" with Sumer and Akkad, reenforcing, indeed exaggerating, the long linear movement of his story towards modern German historical scholarship.

He does not achieve the "global point of view" that he had hoped for. But because he is aware that there might be a "global point of view" to strive for, he does appear, in his revisions, to want to undermine the strong impression of linear movement from Sumer to Ranke produced by the shorter scale of his original lectures. He now singles out China and the "West" as "the two main civilizations of world history," giving him, in principle, two "centres" to his story. He still belittles India and other civilizations for "failing to develop their writing or their scholarship in this field in the way that China and the West developed theirs." But he appears slightly uncomfortable in making the remark. By now he knows better than to handle whole cultures in so dismissive a manner, as he indicated a few years earlier. In a review of J. H. Plumb's new book, *The Death of the Past,* he criticized those historians, philosophers, and scientists who measure everything by its conformity with the modern period, and who see in the past a legion of "wrong" views. He has perhaps become aware of his own guilt in the matter, two or three times over, and is earnestly trying to change.[83]

In the revised text, the linear movement still inherent in the general structure of his story now jostles with a modified cyclic interpretation of the origins of historical consciousness. He certainly believes that there was a line of influence running from the historiography of the earliest cultures of Mesopotamia and Egypt through Israel, Greece, and Rome, and thence to modern Europe. But at the same time, he pictures that, in each of the cultures in his story, "the interest in the past has emerged fairly spontaneously, coming on each occasion in its own way, appearing as a native thing." In a revised fragment of his sixth lecture, on the early Christians and the New Testament, he interprets the first Christians as a people initially without an interest in the past who went through an "actual genesis" of the historical sense. These Christians experienced their own "genesis," different from the "genesis" experienced by the Sumerians, Egyptians, and Jews, and not derived by diffusion from their predecessors. The dominating question in his study concerns the origins of the historical sense. To his surprise, the answer he begins to construct recognizes more than one centre of historical genesis, and displays many origins, indeed a sequence of origins reappearing in cycles, as he moves from culture to culture.[84]

In an essay on the history of encyclopedias for the *Times Literary Supplement* written during this moment we find him trying out his new perspective. He moves freely between China and Europe as he seeks a nonlinear way of construing what he understands as the tendency of human beings to copy, accumulate, and classify what they know.[85]

During 1974, while Butterfield pushed his revisions forward at full stride, two of the people closest to him at Peterhouse died, Dennis Brogan in January and David Knowles in November. He wrote compelling memoirs of each of them.[86]

From at least January 1975, he begun to contemplate death, death in general and his own death. He put many of his reflections into thought-essays. He did not fail to realize the importance of the theme for understanding of historical processes. Under the title "What can we do about death?," he composed an emotionally charged list, almost a checklist, of attitudes that would help a person cope with the end of his personal earthly history. He expressed lament that terror of the nuclear weapon and domination of individuals by mass culture might be contributing to the loss of a sense of personal or group "posterity." He jotted down sayings about death and heaven, such as these:

> The fact of death necessarily raises in a stark manner the question of the meaning of life.

> . . . the bliss of heaven is really the contemplation of God, the undying happiness of eternally experiencing his spiritual presence.[87]

Butterfield became ill in 1976, experiencing some paralysis on the left side. After most of his movement returned he resumed his work, writing a few lectures and reviews, but gave very little time to his history of historiography. Often he felt weak, however, and he came to believe that he might be approaching the end of his work as a historian.

It turned out that his intuition was in touch with events. He became acutely ill and went suddenly into hospital in early June 1979. His body declined very slowly, especially the lungs and kidneys, and he occasionally lost consciousness. He died at home in Sawston on 20 July 1979, at age seventy-eight, just nine days before his fiftieth wedding anniversary, and nearly sixty years after he entered Peterhouse. The small funeral occurred in the Anglican chapel at Peterhouse on the 26th, with a Methodist cremation afterwards, and his ashes were buried in the college chapel. A simple stone remembering his life was placed in the centre of the chapel floor.[88]

In the years from 1975 onwards, after Butterfield began his reflections on death, he would talk about his unfinished work with those around him. He mentioned his big book on historiography several times to Adam Watson, his long-standing friend, whom he called John, and who was, among many appointments in British external affairs, former British ambassador to Cuba. On one occasion, in January 1979, he told Watson, that the first five chapters were ready but that the second half of the book still needed revision. He added the remark that "someone like you would probably have to take a look at it."[89]

In June 1975 Butterfield gave some of his unpublished writings on Christianity and history to me to read, and he later responded with enthusiasm to my proposal to edit a volume of his essays on religion and history. I was unaware that Butterfield had expressed his desire for such a collection to his literary agent around the time of his retirement seven years earlier. In January 1979, before his final illness, a 330-page volume of his essays on religion, together with my introductory essay, appeared in New York under the title *Writings on Christianity and History*.[90] The collection of seventeen essays, which I had chosen, contained all the important short pieces on the theme that Butterfield had written since 1948, and formed a sequel to his famous book *Christianity and History*. The volume was his twenty-first book, and, since all but five of the writings were lectures, added to his list of publications based on lectures. The nine previously unpublished pieces consisted of three of the four Bristol lectures from 1956, the original version of the seventh Gifford Lecture, "The Establishment of a Christian Interpretation of World History" from 1966, his address on the future of Christianity given in St. Giles Cathedral, Edinburgh, in 1970, and all four of the Northwestern lectures of 1974, including the 1977 revision of "Does Belief in Christianity Validly Affect the Modern Historian?" The remaining eight pieces were previously published fugitive works. They consisted of the four short pieces on rival interpretations of history from *The Christian News-Letter* (1949), his most important synoptic statement, entitled "God in History" (1951), his fullest statement on individual personality, under the title "The Role of the Individual in History" (1955), his earliest attempt to identify how Christian convictions affected the historian's writings, the essay "The Christian and Historical Study" (1951), and a major statement on Christianity and politics (1967) written during the intensity of the Vietnam war and student protests. Many other short writings on religion and history remained in Butterfield's papers, but none appeared to add anything important to the writings now published.

No mention of moral judgments occurs in the volume. When I questioned him in 1977 about how his views had changed on the subject, Butterfield responded with an eleven-page essay, bearing the title "Moral Judgments," which he wrote overnight and handed me the next morning. He insisted that he had not changed on the important point: "Let me make it quite clear that I have never objected to the condemnation of *acts*. I always insist that, e.g. religious persecution is wrong and murder is wrong — by which I mean that they are always wrong, they are absolutely wrong, no matter what allowances can be made for conditioning circumstances. . . . What I attack is not anything of this sort, but the moral judgment that is directed against *personalities* — the sort that Lord Acton once said he wanted: the verdict that this particular man is a *bad man*." He had forgotten *Whig Interpretation of History*, where the distinction between moral judgments against acts and those against personalities does not appear. In *Whig Interpretation* he condemns the intrusion of

moral judgments as such into historical writing, and his words appear equally
to forbid moral judgments against both people and their acts. Indeed, he particularly abhors the moral judgments that surreptitiously structure the story
and convert the actual history into a moral judgment against people and whole
sequences of acts and events over time. Only much later did he attempt to
distinguish between people and acts, and even then the object of his condemnation remained unclear. Ironically, his ad hoc paper in 1977, which does not
fail to cite Acton, probably constitutes the most precise writing he ever produced on moral judgments. He draws distinctions of various sorts which seem
to respond to the near-continuous barrage of complaints put forward by people who could never quite be sure what he meant to exclude. He most sharply
distinguishes between people and their acts. That he would feel strongly
enough to write the paper and speak so clearly on that point demonstrates in a
most existential manner just how crucial it is to him not to condemn people,
but to honour everyone as a personality before God in the universe.[91]

After Butterfield died, Adam Watson received Pamela Butterfield's approval
to edit the writings on the history of historiography for publication. *The
Origins of History* came out in New York in 1981, a volume of 250 pages,
Butterfield's twenty-second book, and yet another book based on lectures. The
editor supplied the name of the book with an obvious reference to *The Origins
of Modern Science,* forming a companion piece. He made the decision to limit
the edition to eight pieces instead of the ten of the original series. The first four,
on beginnings, Egypt and Mesopotamia, Israel, and Greece, publish Butterfield's writings almost exactly as he left them, and read as proper chapters. The
fifth, on China, reproduces Butterfield's typescript up to a long final section on
Ssù-ma Ch'ien. This Watson moved to the end of the book where it forms an
appendix on the man Butterfield treated as the Ranke of China, the most
influential classical Chinese historian.[92]

The editor created three additional pieces by placing together selected material from the typescripts of Butterfield's remaining five lectures. This required
numerous judgments about how to handle the available material, some of
which came in more than one rendition. The published version of these last
three chapters splices passages from the original Gifford Lectures with fragments of material which Butterfield later revised. Watson provided the titles
for piece six, "The Establishment of a Christian Historiography," and piece
seven, "The Development of Historical Criticism." The sixth published piece
joins passages on the New Testament with material on Eusebius, Augustine,
and Orosius taken from revised segments of lectures six and seven. Piece seven
presents a very short writing on the rise of historical criticism, a topic on which
longer, and arguably better, versions exist in his papers. Piece eight is a pas-

tiche, combining material on the secularization of the historical outlook from the original ninth lecture with some other reworked material and miscellaneous fragments. The title of the eighth piece, "The Great Secularisation," comes from lecture nine. At the end of piece eight is the curious addition of the entirely new fragment on Islam that Butterfield wrote up in the mid-1970s. The book contains no portions of the tenth lecture on Voltaire, Gibbon, and the nineteenth century. The editor also created all the subtitles; the original lectures contained only Roman numerals to mark breaks in the text. Overall, the first five chapters of the published volume offer accomplished writing which Butterfield carried well past the stage of the lecture. The last three pieces form something of an anthology of selected material of uneven quality. The result cannot quite be said to represent Butterfield's Gifford Lectures.[93]

The retirement project had remained unfinished, and Butterfield had not managed to transform the Gifford Lectures into his magnum opus. But in the first five chapters of *The Origins of History* he proceeded further than any historian before him to synthesize the historiography of Mesopotamia, Egypt, Israel, Greece, China, and early Christianity into an analysis of the emergence of historical writing and human consciousness of history. In spite of the patchwork and fragments, the reviewer in the *American Historical Review* remarked that the volume "does more than any other single work to explore the beginnings and the development of historiography." Even after death, Butterfield's voice spoke with originality.[94]

Conclusion

Looking at Butterfield's work over the long term of his career as historian, we cannot help but notice the versatility of his interests and projects. Yet, we detect a constant force pulling in one direction through all his work, no matter what the topic or theme ostensibly in view. In one way or another just about everything he treats becomes a question of general historical thinking. He is continuously engaged over the decades with the contemplation of the larger questions of human history and historical study, particularly those which induce him to ponder history and religion. When we consider what might be his most significant contributions overall, a clear answer emerges. His best gifts to the worlds he inhabited are his intellectual reconsiderations of history and historical study, and of the inter-suffusion of religion and history. He provided a lasting model of the benefits for historians and other scholars of general historical thinking.

The consequences of his engagement with historical thinking were enormous and tangible. He certainly affected the way other people thought about and did history. But more than that, he helped give shape to whole fields of study. His work had these results in Cambridge University, but also in the world beyond. We have seen his presence in quite a range of fields, and we come to realize the scale of his impact. In all these fields his works continued to be cited, quoted, rejected, and admired years after his studies on those topics appeared. He meets the definition of a seminal thinker.

It should not surprise us that Butterfield himself knew very well that historical reflections could have enduring consequences. By at least 1954, he had realized that Ranke and Acton were remembered by others, and important to him, not because of their actual results as research historians, but, as he put it, "because of their historical ideas, their principles of interpretation and their comments on the process of things in time." This is most certainly the case with Butterfield. Butterfield is important because of his historical thought.[1]

Butterfield's awareness of the lasting importance of general historical thinking only complicated his life. He held firmly to a doctrine about "scientific" history which belittled spending time on historical thinking. He resisted giving time to it. He repeatedly insisted that his real work, and indeed the only generator of real history, was highly detailed documentary research which collected "facts" and issued in "scientific" history. Such work ranked absolutely highest on his agenda for historical study, and he never relieved the pressure he placed on himself to produce that kind of history. This priority underlay his persistent self-assessment, which surfaced at least by the end of the 1930s, and which he repeated until the end of his life, that he was not productive as a scholar.

This is a man who published twenty-two books and scores upon scores of booklets, articles, and reviews, presented countless invited lectures, carried more than his share of the lecture load in the Cambridge History Faculty, and left behind a vast storehouse of unpublished writings. He belonged to a style of historian who wrote incessantly. He said he wanted to be a writer, and we can observe that he did indeed write. From his earliest adult days until his last, he thought by writing. He wrote out every classroom lecture. He wrote more than one draft of anything he published as well as the things he did not publish. If he sat down, he began to write. He most surely realized his youthful aspiration to be a writer.

But all that productivity did not satisfy him. What counted was books of "scientific" history. And he published only one book that met that standard, *The Peace Tactics of Napoleon, 1806–08*. He was twenty-nine. In the Cambridge system, where he never wrote a doctoral dissertation, this book was the substitute, the product of his apprenticeship under Temperley. It was a book of diplomatic history about the activity of a few elite figures over a microscopic period of time, and it depended largely on published documents, very little archival research, and the close correlation of chronologically arranged details. We have seen that the study took him years to complete, far longer than the actual events he studied, and he had Temperley's intense pressure on his back the whole time. It served as his model for "scientific" history. At the time of his retirement he called it his best book, not least because he liked his writing in it.[2]

For the rest, he spent nearly fifty years saying that he was writing a second book which would have met his "scientific" standard, the biography of Charles James Fox. He undertook the project in 1931, thanks to Trevelyan's generosity with the Fox papers, but he apparently had already nurtured from his youth the hope of writing a biography of Fox, which perhaps stretches the Fox desire to something like sixty-five years. That is a long time to talk about one project. He never wrote the biography, and mercilessly chastised himself for not doing so. Meanwhile a string of other people did write biographies of Fox. Not one of them came even close to approaching the standard of detail, thoroughness, and complexity that Butterfield had set for himself as befitting his version of "scientific" history.

The only other book of Butterfield's in the running as "scientific" history was *George III, Lord North, and the People, 1779–1780* (1949). It certainly contained many passages of carefully researched history, but it was such a miscellany, so apparently haphazard, that it did not meet his own standard for the genuine article. It did position his presence in the field of English eighteenth-century history, an area in which he carried on considerable work for decades. Beginning with that book and extending throughout the 1950s, notably in *George III and the Historians* (1957), he drew his own picture of the eighteenth century and especially the early years of George III. As we have seen, his rendering contrasted sharply with Namier's, and his debate with Namier became a celebrated case of the interplay of contempt, status, mistake, intellect, and insight in academic interchange. His position stood out as well against the influential neo-Marxist version of the eighteenth century produced by E. P. Thompson. Thompson's first statement appeared in 1963, followed by another in 1975, and Thompson's eighteenth century eclipsed both Butterfield's and Namier's as new trends in historiography turned away from narrow concentration on politics.[3]

By observing Butterfield at work the way we have, we see the personal cost of his theory of "scientific" history. He burdened himself with the impossible task of producing the final and detailed biography of Fox. He thus guaranteed the unlikelihood of the completion of the book. His theory and method of "scientific" history stopped him from doing "scientific" history.

Ironically, in contrast with the endless labour for few results in "scientific" history, virtually all of his publications attached to his general historical thinking came swiftly out of his pen. Some of these reflections represented years of pondering the topics or problems, but when it came to the actual writing he was quick. His greatest impact came from the least work.

His writings on historical thought are abundant. Altogether probably seventeen of his twenty-two books fit the description. It is probably also fair to say that most of his shorter writings and the preponderance of his unpublished materials belonged to the same territory. All these writings are also in some sense religious thought. His religious sensibilities continuously inform what he advocates for the course of human history, the approach to historical study, and the understanding of human relations. The published material generated by his historical and religious reflections created his reputation.

In two important cases he failed to keep his theory of "scientific" history away from his work on general historical thinking. In both cases he killed those projects with his theory the way he did the Fox biography. Neither the *Concise Cambridge Modern History* nor his Gifford Lectures reached publication from his hand.

Reviewing his career, we can say that at some point he himself made the practical decision to devote his most energetic efforts to the contemplation of history, rather than to the production of actual "scientific" history. He became the historian of ideas and the creator of ideas about history instead the "scientific" historian doing the things he professed he ought do. If we take his work on Fox as the sign, then we can say that he probably gave up the serious pursuit of researched history by the late 1930s, even though there were brief moments of the revival of his Fox drive now and then after he became Professor of Modern History in 1944.

The practical move towards a life of historical reflections may have come around 1938. One marker at that time is the preparation for his controversial tour of Hitler's Germany with the lecture on the history of the Whig interpretation of history. Another marker about the same time is the sidetracking from Fox onto Machiavelli's maxims. The first led into the wartime patriotism of *Englishman and His History* (1944), and the second to *The Statecraft of Machiavelli* (1940). This amoutned to the virtually intentional neglect of his publicly stated first priority of writing "scientific" history, and propelled him into his career of self-criticism. But it permitted him to accomplish extraordinarily creative work that flowed unimpeded from within him.

Perhaps he always preferred the road of historical reflections and historiography, long before 1938, even though his rhetoric said the opposite. His first book was about historical thought, *The Historical Novel* (1924), and then after *Peace Tactics of Napoleon* (1929) came the all-important *Whig Interpretation of History* (1931). Thereafter he kept producing books, articles, lectures, and notes on historical thought or on how to apply his historical thought or on the history of historical thought.

By far Butterfield's most far-reaching accomplishment in historical thinking was his simplest. He left his imprint on the basic terminology of the historical discipline as well as other fields. His creation of the odd term "Whiggish history" gave historians and students a way to recognize, admit to, and overcome the monumental faults of presentistic self-indulgence within historical study. Once Butterfield said it, people could see it "of course." Even those who had never read the book that produced the term could promote the attack on "Whiggish history."[4] In *The Whig Interpretation of History* he indicated the role of historical interpretation in the composition of whole societies, and indeed of whole areas of knowledge.

He went on to apply his historical thinking to several fields, notably the natural sciences, historical study itself, international politics, and religion. *The Origins of Modern Science* (1949) is a discussion of his own historical ideas and how to use them to reconceive the subject raised by the title. As an unexpected side effect, he thereby helped give definition and impetus to the history of science, a field of study taking shape in universities after the Second World War. The book stimulated rising historians to go into the field, and became mandatory reading in courses.

In a number of his writings he promoted historical thinking about the study of history itself, what he called the history of historiography. He was not the first to do so, by any means, but with *Man on His Past* (1955), *George III and the Historians,* and *Magna Carta in the Historiography of the Sixteenth and Seventeenth Centuries* (1968) he gave lasting impetus to the use of the history of historiography as a way of understanding any subject. His monumental article "Historiography" in the *Dictionary of the History of Ideas* (1973) is crucial. So also are his Gifford Lectures (1965, 1966) and the posthumous *Origins of History* (1981). He gave decisive inspiration to two important journals in the field, *Journal of the History of Ideas* and *History and Theory,* and provided incentive for the creation and maintenance of historiography courses in history departments and history faculties.

His reflections on history over the long term reached into the study of international politics. The combination of *Christianity, Diplomacy and War* (1953) with *International Conflict in the Twentieth Century* (1960) helped engender the historical study of international relations, and contributed to establishing the study of international relations as an independent field. His discourse on war, revolution, the nuclear bomb, and the conflict between world Communism and the capitalist "West" caught the attention of both liberal and conservative theorists as well as radical activists against the bomb.

Religion is a special case. We have seen how his Methodist religion animated his work as historian. His commitments to religion and historical understanding blend into each other. His religious thought is historical and his historical thought is religious. Our study of Butterfield has encountered a man whose daily interests and work concerned the basic matters of human history and religion, and who recommended to others what he came to believe was ultimately good and true and right.

Late in life Butterfield offered his self-perception about his work and motivation: "though I shudder at what must appear to be the priggishness of the confession, we must all have something to live for, and the desire to 'preach the Gospel', though it has been submerged on occasion, has perhaps been my most constant motor."[5] No sooner did he utter this admission, however, than in the next breath he recorded a contrary remark by Virginia Woolf to Clive Bell which no doubt reached into his heart: "I never meant to preach, and agree that like God, one shouldn't."[6]

Butterfield preached. He preached in his actual sermons on the Methodist circuit until his mid-thirties, and he preached in his explicitly religious lectures and writings, such as *Christianity and History* (1949), *History and Human Relations* (1951), and *Christianity, Diplomacy and War.* But, so too, he preached in the rest of his writings and lectures which convey his historical reflections. Indeed, all of his work is suffused with his religious sensibilities. Butterfield realized in this unexpected way his youthful aspiration to be a preacher.

His writings and lectures on the interconnections of religion and history allowed Butterfield to speak to the university world about understanding religons as historical phenomena. He introduced new readings of the historical character of Christianity. His work also let him cross over from academia to the general public. *Christianity and History* gave him by far his greatest outreach. Of all his books, that one was the most widely sold, most widely reviewed, most widely translated, and most widely remembered. His broadcasts of the lectures on BBC national radio put him into direct communication with a vast public. The rapport he established with the general public transmuted into frequent appearances in national and local public settings outside the university. Scholars and general readers alike found his message inspiring. Many responded like Eve Bogle, who testified, "He introduced me to the historical Jesus."[7]

Butterfield brought to the theme of Christianity and history the sensibilities and habits of the historian. It was an area of discourse dominated by theologians, and understood simply as a matter of theology. He took the discussion out of the realm of abstract ideas about theology and transferred it to the plane of human history and historical study. Particularly significant was his suggestion that certain beliefs held by Christian historians, especially those about human personality, human cupidity, and human action in conjunction with divine Providence, had, or ought to have, radical consequences for their study of human history. He articulated some of the intrinsic affinities between history and religion. His work on the theme contributed quite unexpectedly to the major revival of Christian interpretations of history among religious thinkers and historians after the Second World War.

The success that Butterfield enjoyed with his historical thinking was due in no small degree to his gift for making the arresting statement. Again and again we have heard the phrase or seen the example which evokes so vivid an image in our minds that we understand instantly what pages of involved logic could never convey. Here are three we have met along the way:

> On historical explanation: "in the case of two brothers brought up in very much the same way, we have the one who becomes a nonconformist minister because his father was a nonconformist minister, while his brother becomes a militant atheist because his father was a nonconformist minister."[8]

> The final line of *Christianity and History*: "We can do worse than remember a principle which both gives us a firm Rock and leaves us the maximum elasticity for our minds: the principle: Hold to Christ, and for the rest be totally uncommitted."[9]

> On the source of the greatest harm done in history: "The Moderate Cupidity of Everyman."[10]

These are the phrases, and countles others like them, which carry his message home, and which people can repeat even years later.

Our study of Butterfield's labours as historian has disclosed some vital features about his career. Nothing is more striking than the sheer continuity of his vocation, convictions, and interests. From the moment he came up to Peterhouse in 1919, indeed starting in his final years at Keighley, and extending throughout his career, he immersed himself almost entirely in the academic life and the work of being the historian, and he thrived. All of his cardinal religious and political tenets had direct connections with the world of his youth, and they were in place from his early years in Cambridge. They remained with him until he died. These include his Methodist identity, the contemplative spirituality, the preference for piety over doctrine, the individualism and personalism, and the noncommittal New Whig tendency in politics. It was during his undergraduate years that he stabilized his primary historical interests, some of which began to form in his mind before Cambridge, and he maintained the same chief interests thereafter until the end. Notable are the focus on elite political and diplomatic history, the attraction to Fox and eighteenth-century England, the fascination with historical reflections and historiography, the mystique of Germany, the affinity for narrative, the insistence on history as a certain type of science, and the attachment to Acton and Ranke. It is striking in retrospect how few thinkers he adds to his repertoire as he works out his discourse over the decades.

Equally striking was the enduring power of the small world of Cambridge in shaping his life. Once he completed the wrenching passage from the industrial village of Oxenhope to the highstanding milieu of Cambridge, his course became steady. Given his absolute commitment to the free will of discrete individuals and the lack of provision for community in his discourse, it is remarkable just how completely his membership in particular Cambridge communities determined his own career. Our study has shown the near total domination of his life after Oxenhope by the social, academic, and religious culture of Cambridge. Peterhouse, the prize system, undergraduate supervisions, courses of lectures, examinations, academic politics, patronage, professorships, the Fellows, the Faculty of History, Wesley Methodist Church, Peterhouse chapel, *Cambridge Historical Journal,* Cambridge University Press: all these presented him with tracks to ride on, and moved him through his career. A mere handful of people exercised constant and overwhelming influence upon him: Temperley and Vellacott in Peterhouse, and Acton and Ranke whom he encountered through Temperley and Peterhouse, and his father at home. When his fame spread beyond Cambridge, it travelled via precise channels made available to him because of his Cambridge status: the BBC, the London daily press, particular book publishers, invited lectureships, the Historical Association, outside visitors. The changes and innovations he negotiated during the course of his career were modifications within the boundaries set by his enduring beliefs and interests and his Cambridge small world.

We have tracked the subtle permutations of Butterfield's discourse, and noted as precisely as possible when something new appeared in his work. It becomes apparent that the books are products of long and complex processes. Sometimes they generate further creative processes, but frequently they represent sidetracking and the exhaustion of thought. The books are like the islands in the Mediterranean. Our observation of Butterfield's labour has permitted us to map the contours of the sea floor, so we can see the subaqueous geological structures of which the books are the visible land formations. We can see that he thought about history before he published. He jotted down notes, scribbled thought-essays, started drafts of papers, and wrote out his lectures. New discourse usually appeared first in these unpublished materials rather than in the drafts for the books. The published pieces become more intelligible when seen within the sequences of his labour. His intellectual impact, of course, proceeded largely from his publications, as well as from his university lectures and work with undergraduates and research students. But his intellectual creativity occurred chiefly before the writing of the publications. Some of the unpublished writings surpass in importance large quantities of what did get published. The prime case is the material for the *Concise Cambridge Modern History,* in which he writes general history and in some of which he demonstrates far better than in any of his published statements the merits of his approach to general history. Sometimes the unpublished essays reveal more about his approach than anything he did publish. For instance, we have seen how his unpublished essays, especially "In Defence of Diplomatic History" in 1963, and "The Nature of Political History" around 1972, illuminate a major tendency operating throughout his career and explain much of what we need to know about his rejection of new methods and approaches in historical study in the 1960s and 1970s.

If the successes of some of Butterfield's historical reflections were huge, certain of his major recommendations seemed to fall to the ground as soon as he uttered them, even if he repeated himself. Undoubtedly the least helpful of his primary proposals was, as we have seen, his relentless promotion of "scientific" history, which he also called "technical history." This became a mark of his approach. His repeated admonitions against moral judgments by historians depended on his idea of "technical history." Even sympathetic readers branded his views as amoral. At the same time, however, his own writings appeared to contain ample quantities of the very things he objected to.

Also unhelpful was his perennial reassertion of the priority of political and diplomatic history. He began his career by working in these fields in the 1920s. He then tied his understanding of "technical history" to the brand of method he used at that time. Meanwhile, within the historical profession at large, criticisms of traditional political and diplomatic history increased, rising to a crescendo in the 1960s, and the beginnings of new varieties of history became noticeable at the same time. At least by 1962, he was expressing his awareness that the new trends in historical study were leaving him behind with his attachment to "the school of Ranke." His unpublished lecture "In Defence of Diplomatic History" in 1963 put him deliberately and even vehemently in opposition to most of the new trends. He then gave over his inaugural address as Regius Professor of Modern History in 1964 to the vigorous promotion of old-style political history. He might have used the platform afforded by the Regius prestige to say something generative of the future course of the historical profession. But he did not. He chose rather to pronounce his objection to the new trends, and to announce his withdrawal into old-style history.

The third unhelpful item worth mentioning about his historical reflections was his unwavering intellectual dependence on the dualistic polarization of opposites. With nary a lapse, he remained the unflagging dualist. Once he emphasized one pole in his thought, he simply had to swing to the opposite. His presumption in favour of polarized pairs created intellectual inpediments to his analysis and depiction of things historical. The sets of oppositions he proliferated implanted confusion in virtually every one of his intellectual discussions.

His polarities were ubiquitous: individuals or society, detailed history or general history, moral or technical, scientific or religious, narrative or analysis, inner or outer, material or spiritual, souls as real or states as abstract nouns, neutral history or politicized history, and so on. With each of these oppositions, when he emphasized one pole, as was his habit, he would tend to neglect the other pole, and he could not perceive the living presence of what he took to be the other "pole" within the first "pole." For instance, when deeply engaged in stressing the polarities, he treated individuals as if they were not utterly social, he underrated the ways in which detailed history is saturated with general history, he left unacknowledged the moral character of the choices about technical things, he overlooked the religious impulses behind science, he missed the point that narrative requires analysis, he neglected the outer as the expression of the inner, he missed the spirituality of material life, and so on. The contradictions surge forward again and again as he swings from pole to pole. We encountered this process repeatedly throughout his career as he generated opposites. We did not feel relief from the force of these intellectual polarities until he finally sought the reconciliation of opposites at a higher level.

After all is said and done, there remains his pervasive commitment to sheer dissent. The effects of his version of Methodism are direct. As we contemplate the effects on himself and others of the polarities in his thought, we realize at another level that the oppositional tensions are not at all happenstantial. They form part of his intellectual equipment of dissent. They are simply intrinsic to his normal mode of discourse. His oppositional construction of history arises from his religious construal of the world. It derives as well from his enthusiastic embrace of the untidiness of historical processes which mere thinking cannot straighten up. He maximizes the effects of the polarities in his discourse by his reliance on metaphor and his rejection of carefully constructed concepts. And more than even all that, he may be the type of personality disinclined in any case to privilege logic and rational modes of knowing. In Butterfield we never met an appeal for orderly thinking or a worry about the contradictions. If I were to hazard a guess about his "personality type" in the terms of the Jungian Myers-Briggs Type Indicator, Butterfield would emerge INFP. If that is so, there is little point in waiting for him to produce precise and systematic thought.[11]

In the first instance his dissent was an intellectual strategy. Whatever barriers his polarization of opposites may have erected against intellectual understanding of things historical, the assertion of the oppositions served the strategy of intellectual dissent many times over. Butterfield wished for his thought to unsettle the thinking of others. He called this "picking up the other end of the stick," and "elasticity of mind." The mere mention of one thing evoked in him the opposite. This enabled him to ask the questions others did not think about, or want to think about. When others presented him a problem, he reconstructed it and gave it back to them in transmuted form. In his writing as well as in his teaching, his contradictory thinking destabilized thought.

The drive to unsettle was automatic. He utilized counterpoise, paradox, ambiguity, and metaphor, put there on purpose. The adversative style operated everywhere. The letters of reference he wrote on behalf of people's applications for lectureship and professorships exemplified candour in the way he gave praise in one paragraph and took away praise in the next. We have seen how some of his students and colleagues recalled his delight in keeping things loose by uttering the very thing that ran contrary to what they just said. This he did without letting on whether the position he presented was his own or not. People sometimes found him exasperating, hard to pin down, and, because of this, they would sometimes call him undercutting and they might not know when to believe him. He deliberately excavated the very things they most took for granted, and provoked them to think differently.

His impulse to dissent was also political. It is uncanny how he and E. P. Thompson, whose vision of the eighteenth century came to overwhelm his own, both derived their spirit of dissent from the Methodism of their youth. The one remained the Methodist, the other abandoned it, a neat instantiation of Butterfield's historical explanation seen above. Thompson lived outside the system running English academia. By contrast, Butterfield occupied just about every position of authority that was possible in his profession, and received just about every honour there was to receive. Yet, he too always felt the outsider, even as he rose in rank and fame and power. His dissenting politics, like his intellectual strategy, operated automatically, whatever the milieu, whether in historical studies, the university, society, government elections, and religion, or at high table with other Fellows, in the teaching of undergraduates in Peterhouse, and in his correspondence. He seemed almost congenitally unable to agree with what people said, whether they were his students, other historians, chief administrators, higher authorities, or leaders in religion and politics, especially when their views represented the dominant line. He sought to defeat the sureties of those who dominate.

Not the least of his acts of dissent was his admission of his religious convictions within the very process of conducting historical study. History and religion lived in tension throughout his discourse. To the historical establishment, this intrusion of religion into historical study was a problem. To him it was a matter of dissent. Among Christians, his appeal on behalf of Christ was not for the establishment of a presence in society or academia, not for peace, not for safety in the arms of Jesus, not for healing, not even for salvation. He incited people to an insurgent type of Christianity. His final line in *Christianity and History* preached only one certainty: "Hold to Christ, and for the rest be totally uncommitted."

Paradoxically, Butterfield seemed curiously drawn to the very things from which he wanted most to dissent. Throughout his entire adult life he locked himself to Lord Acton, the person who most personified the historian as judge and avenger, the dispenser of moral judgments in history. He spent all of his academic life studying the state, writing on Napoleon and wanting to write on Fox, exalting diplomatic and political history, assessing Machiavelli, focusing on George III, and developing the theory of international politics. Yet, the state is the very thing he insisted is unreal, nothing more than an abstract noun. He ranked the establishment of religion and the use of the atomic bomb, both actions executed by the ruling powers, as the two most unspeakable calamities in human history. During the last three decades of his life this Yorkshire Methodist drifted inexorably towards Anglican traditions. We then realize that the seeming contradictions in these cases, and in so many others, emerge as still more ways to unsettle the thinking of those who notice.

Faced with the diversification of histories in the sixties and seventies, and confronted with what he felt was the dissolution of the debate into sheer politics, Butterfield seemed to give up. Most of what he had to say about the character of historical study was completely out of touch with the debates about the future of history that then burst upon the profession.

The great exceptions were three points he raised which promised to contribute to the future configuration of the historical discipline. The first was his work in the 1960s for the Gifford Lectures on the history of historical study, where he took steps to expand his outlook to the horizon of global history. His revision of certain of these lectures, to be found in *The Origins of History*, suggested an alternative to the traditional long story of the progress, or rather the lack of progress, of the cultures of the past along the road to modern "scientific" history. His new treatment offered instead a glimpse of the beginnings of a unified global treatment of the history of historical consciousness which respected the radical multiplicity of the views and methods of history found throughout the ages and across the world. He opened a window onto general history embracing China, Islam, the Bible, Greece, Europe, and, by extension, all other cultures.

His suggestions in the Gifford Lectures renewed and expanded his campaign from the 1930s to broaden the scope of general modern history and to overthrow the hegemony within historical study of the political history of the powerful. The one thousand pages intended for his *Concise Cambridge Mod-*

ern History that never got put into print included, besides the ordinary, fresh hints of ways to reconstruct general history that passed beyond mere survey or the collection of national histories. He was in full stride towards developing inclusive studies of the many aspects of human societies, and he was beginning to employ multifactorial modes of historical explanation.

The second potential contribution to the future of historical study was epistemological. He frequently noted the significance of the primary convictions about life, politics, religion, and morality that historians bring to their study for the kind of history they produce. The point represented a reconciling unity that he constructed to overcome the debilitating effects of his original polarities. His observations suggested something extraordinarily relevant to the debates then getting underway about the significance of the historian's gender, social class, politics, nationality, economic position, race, and culture, indeed the historian's whole persona, for the configuration of historical studies. Historians' basic convictions inexorably steer their work even when, perhaps especially when, they do not realize it.

With the combination of these two points he possessed the wherewithal to keep on generating original thought, to lead rather than to disappear from the historical profession in the 1970s. After all, he was reading on China and Islam ahead of all the other historians of eighteenth-century England. And he was drawing the lines of a world-scale portrait of historical consciousness before most historians of European topics looked up from the page of their specialized reading. Both points promised to undermine the dominance of the "scientific" model for historical study.

On both points, instead, he worked against himself. In retreat, he admitted in the late 1970s that his theory of "scientific" history might account for "perhaps less than ten per cent" of what historians achieve. It was a severely undermined version of all he had said for decades. He was holding steadfastly to the theory nonetheless. Pursuing the two points together would have compelled him to reformulate his theory of historical study. They would have required him to refocus his attention upon the 90 percent of the historian's work untouched by his assertions. He would have had to deal with the rest of life beyond political history and beyond the elevation of European thought as the destination of history. Rather than follow out the implications of what he put forward, he defeated himself. He declined to consider that his advocacy of "technical history" left out too much. He simply repeated once again his claims for the 10 percent that he still insisted might be devoid of the effects of the profoundest human convictions. He could enjoy the irony that his views on technical history, when not ignored, stimulated others to overcome the defects in what he proposed about the character of historical study.

Butterfield's third potential contribution to the future shape of history was his most constructive. Since at least *The Whig Interpretation of History* he had articulated a reconciling method that enabled him to raise his handling of historical thinking to another level. The reconciliation of opposites, like dissent, operated intuitively. Once he perceived the barriers raised against intellectual understanding by the ubiquity of his polarities, he eventually, as we have seen, sought to find a higher unity. His stereoscopic vision allowed him to see the good on both sides of any opposing pair, or indeed, as he usually admitted in practice, on a multiplicity of sides on any matter. He revelled in difference, he preached tolerance, he rejected the moral judgment of others. His stereoscopic vision might have worked wonders on the new tendencies in historical study in the 1960s and 1970s. The initial achievements of the new histories offered him the opportunity to embrace something in all of them. He died before extending his reconciling method that far.

Paradoxically, even his reconciling move became a form of dissent. It put him at odds with others, especially those in power. It was as if his reconciling thrust presented a challenge to both sides of any of the oppositions he identified. In one stunning case above all, the reconciling move brought an avalanche of criticism on his head: his attempts to understand Hitler and withhold moral judgment from the perpetrator of Nazi Germany.

There was one brief moment when Butterfield's reconciling method promised to defeat the presence of polarities in his discourse entirely. It happened in 1951. He surprised us with a transcending image that relieves the perpetual tensions. As we saw, he unveiled the image before one thousand Christian youth in Wales in his address "God in History." He recalled the image briefly in *Man on His Past* in 1955. The image is of threes. With this image the things that seem like oppositions are really not. They are, rather, different ways to see the same thing. He dismisses his dualist discourse of the past, and speaks instead of threes. With his customary imprecision, he adds term to term which we learn to read as synonyms, or perhaps to extrapolate as multiple ways of seeing even threes. There are in historical thinking, he proposes, three ways of seeing the same thing, and they transmute into three levels of thinking, three types of analysis, three kinds of explanation. All three ways are true at once without contradiction: humans are makers of history, history operates in accordance with laws, and God acts in history. Why did such and such happen? Three answers come back from Butterfield: because those people acted to make it happen, because multiple laws of history converged, and because of the Providence of God. In one image of threes he surpasses his reliance on all those twos. He unveils the image, but then he puts it aside without further thought, and passes on. The image of the three ways exemplifies his reconciling method. It joins the lengthy list of arresting comments that unsettle our thought.[12]

Our study of Butterfield as historian has let us feel the compelling power of a candid man. We hear the new and the intriguing, as well as the repetitious and the sometimes unintelligible. No life is simply wonderful, and certainly not the academic life. When we think of the most significant historians of the twentieth century in the English-speaking world, we can understand why Butterfield comes immediately to mind. He made himself noticeable as he joined the long march of historians throughout the history of historiography.[13]

We now can fathom the nuances of comments made about him by two historians who later held positions he once held. One felt in sympathy with him, the other did not. Owen Chadwick, Butterfield's immediate successor as Regius Professor of Modern History at Cambridge, put his achievement succinctly: "[He] brought to an end an epoch of historical writing."[14] Hugh Trevor-Roper, one of Butterfield's successors as Master of Peterhouse, and one-time Regius Professor of Modern History at Oxford, spoke about Butterfield when questioned at High Table in Peterhouse:

Q. Did you ever meet Butterfield?
A. Yes.
Q. What did you think of him?
A. A likeable man.
Q. Did you read any of his books?
A. Not if I could help it.[15]

Abbreviations

HB	Herbert Butterfield
CTM	C. T. McIntire
ms	manuscript
typ	typescript
p	page or pages
ssp	single-spaced pages
ed./eds.	editor/editors
Jan, Feb	the months

Notes

Introduction

1. HB, *The Whig Interpretation of History* (London: Bell, 1931).

2. For the British Library chronology, see http://www.bl.uk/collections/british/modbrichron.html. The other histories on the list are by Lytton Strachey (1918), R. H. Tawney (1921 and 1926), Lewis Namier (1929), George Dangerfield (1935), and E. P. Thompson (1963).

3. Annabel Patterson, *Nobody's Perfect: A New Whig Interpretation of History* (New Haven: Yale University Press, 2002), 1, 17–19.

4. Denis Brogan, "Sir Herbert Butterfield as a Historian: An Appreciation," in J. H. Elliott and H. G. Koenigsberger, eds., *The Diversity of History: Essays in Honour of Sir Herbert Butterfield* (London: Routledge and Kegan Paul, 1970), 3.

5. Noel Annan, *The Dons: Mentors, Eccentrics, and Geniuses* (Chicago: University of Chicago Press, 1999), 265–266.

6. Among the historians with whom Butterfield mingled in Cambridge over the years, we may name the following: Adolphus Ward, J. B. Bury, Harold Temperley, G. M. Trevelyan, G. P. Gooch, G. M. Clark, Ernest Barker, J. H. Clapham, Eileen Power, M. M. Postan, C. W. Previté-Orton, G. G. Coulton, Z. N. Brooke, Denis Brogan, R. H. Tawney, David Knowles, Nicholas Pevsner, George Kitson Clark, Joseph Needham, Michael Oakeshott, C. R. Cheney, Owen Chadwick, E. H. Carr, Charles H. Wilson, F. H. Hinsley, J. H. Plumb, Walter Ullman, G. R. Elton, Gordon Rupp, Derek Beales, Maurice Cowling, and a remarkable stream of research students who went on to become historians of note.

7. See Maurice Cowling, *Religion and Public Doctrine in Modern England* (Cambridge: Cambridge University Press, 1980); see also C. H. Sisson's review of Cowling, in *Times Literary Supplement* (6 Feb 1981), 129.

8. Elliott and Koenigsberger, eds., *The Diversity of History.*

9. Noel Annan, *Our Age: Portrait of a Generation* (London: Weidenfeld and Nicholson, 1990), 3, 269–270, 392; Annan, *The Dons,* 264–265.

10. Owen Chadwick, "Sir Herbert Butterfield," *Cambridge Review* (16 Nov 1979), 7. Edward Norman, "Christian and Sceptic," *Times Higher Education Supplement* (9 Dec 1983), 15.

11. Annan, *the Dons,* 264; Patterson, *Nobody's Perfect,* 2, 11–13; Editorial, in *Radical Philosophy,* 37 (Summer 1984), 1.

12. Cowling, *Religion and Public Doctrine,* 195, 198–199, 229; J. C. D. Clark, *Revolution and Rebellion: State and Society in England in the Sixteenth and Seventeenth Centuries* (Cambridge: Cambridge University Press, 1986), 15.

13. HB to Acland, 27 Nov 1953.

14. Patrick Cosgrave, "An Englishman and His History," *Spectator* (18 July 1979), 22–23.

15. HB to Acland, 27 Nov 1953.

16. Butterfield made his declaration about not being Tory in his taped interviews with me, when he also told the story of the suggestion made by Charles Smyth, a staunch Tory, after reading *The Whig Interpretation of History.* Norman Cantor, quite on his own, suggested that in the context of English historiography Butterfield might be identified as a neo-Whig. See Cantor, *The English: A History of Politics and Society to 1760* (New York: Simon and Schuster, 1967), 291.

17. Jonathan Haslam, *The Vices of Integrity: E. H. Carr, 1892–1982* (London: Verso, 1999).

18. The fourth section of the bibliography lists writings about Butterfield arranged chronologically.

19. The first three sections of the bibliography list Butterfield's published works, his unpublished works, and works projected or invited.

20. C. T. McIntire, ed. with an Introduction: Herbert Butterfield, *Writings on Christianity and History* (New York: Oxford University Press, 1979).

21. Lady Butterfield presented the Butterfield papers in December 1979 through the Friends of Cambridge University Library; the library records the benefaction as January 1980. Lady Butterfield to CTM, 31 Dec 1979; Lady Butterfield to William Kenny, 15 Jan 1980; Memorandum by R. W. K. Hinton, 18 Feb 1980. The website for the Butterfield papers is: http://www.lib.cam.ac.uk/MSS/Butterf.html

22. HB to CTM, 24 May 1979.

Chapter 1 Aspirations

1. In general throughout this study I have not tried to identify the specific source of each piece of information about Butterfield's life. A large portion of such information comes from my own interviews with him at Peterhouse in 1975 and 1977 as well as my correspondence with him over several years. Other information derives from my inter-

views with Lady Butterfield between 1977 and 1986, with Mrs. Eve Bogle in 1986, and with colleagues, students, and friends over several years. The unpublished autobiographical writings in his papers include: "Personal: Early Youth, Father, Temperley, Vellacott" (ms, 67p, c1963); "My Early Life" (typ, 5p, 1978); and "My Literary Productions" (typ, 19p, 1978). The collection of his speeches delivered on various occasions around the time of his retirement appears as: "Miscellaneous Comments" (mss, talks and short speeches, 1960s).

2. Entry 59 in "Register of Marriages Solemnized at the Wesleyan Chapel, Lower Town, in the County of York." On the occasion of his fortieth wedding anniversary Herbert's father sent him one of the bell-shaped fold-out announcements for the wedding. It was apparently the one meant at the time for Mary Buckland's parents, who then lived at 16 Drapers Lane, Leominster, Herefordshire: Albert Butterfield to HB, 8 April 1938. See Herbert Butterfield (the uncle) to Herbert Butterfield, n.d. (c1956).

3. The register of baptisms records the baptism as follows: December 9th, 1900, Herbert, son of Albert and Ada Mary Butterfield, Upper Town, Oxenhope, born October 7th, 1900, William H. Bright, minister. I attended a service at the church on Sunday, 30 March 1980, when three baptisms occurred, completing the very same register book nearly 80 years and 397 baptisms later. The people in the church that day were very proud that the first name in the register book was Herbert Butterfield.

4. For information on the woolen mills of Oxenhope I have to thank Sidney Bancroft, former owner of Charles Mill, and a younger friend of Butterfield's. For information on the Dewhirst relationship I am indebted to Ian Dewhirst of Keighley, grandson of Amos Dewhirst, and author of *Yorkshire through the Years* (London: Batsford, 1975), who has the account books and other paraphernalia from the shop. Interview with Ian Dewhirst, March 1980; and Dewhirst to CTM, 4 April 1980.

5. HB to CTM, 9 July 1976.

6. HB, *The Remembrance of Things Past* (Southampton: University of Southampton, 1968), 3. See David Joy, *A Regional History of the Railways of Great Britain,* vol. 8, *South and West Yorkshire* (London: David and Charles, 1975), 71–72.

7. The Trade and Grammar School was located in part of the complex now occupied by Keighley Technical College at the corner of Cavendish and North Street. The grammar school, now known as Oakbank School, moved into new buildings away from the centre of town in the 1960s.

8. HB, "Crowe's Memorandum of Jan. 1, 1907" (typ, 21p, British Committee on the Theory of International Politics, July 1960), 12–13.

9. HB, *Whig Interpretation of History*; HB, *The Englishman and His History* (Cambridge: Cambridge University Press, 1944), 4–10, 33–36.

10. C. H. H. Parry, *The Evolution of the Art of Music,* 5th ed. (London: Kegan Paul, Trench, Trubner, 1909). The book is housed with the Butterfield collection in Ward Library in Peterhouse.

11. See HB, "Universal History and the Comparative Study of Civilization," in Noah Edward Fehl, ed., *Sir Herbert Butterfield, Cho Yun Hsu, and William H. McNeill on Chinese and World History* (Hong Kong: Chinese University of Hong Kong, 1971), 26–27.

12. HB, Diary, 1936.

13. I have not yet succeeded in locating the poem.

14. Owen M. Edwards and others, *A School History of England* (Oxford: Clarendon Press, 1901).

15. Butterfield gave these measurements to those who asked: Height: 5′7½″; Chest: 41″; Hat: 7⅛″.

16. Wesley Methodist Church, Haworth and Oakworth Circuit Plan and Directory. HB, Memoir, 1970s.

17. Wesley Methodist Church, Haworth and Oakworth Circuit Plan and Directory. See HB, "Sir Edward Grey in July 1914," *Historical Studies,* 5 (1965), 1–25; HB, "Revolution" (ms, 34p, Corpus Christi College, Cambridge, 1972).

18. For the details of Butterfield's relationship with Peterhouse between 1919 and 1939, see E. Ansell, comp., *Admissions to Peterhouse in the University of Cambridge, October 1911–December 1930* (Cambridge: Cambridge University Press, 1939), 331.

19. HB, "The Colleges and Halls of the University: Peterhouse," in J. P. C. Roach, ed., *A History of the County of Cambridge and the Isle of Ely,* 8, *The City and University of Cambridge* (London: Oxford University Press, 1959), 334–335.

20. See Appendix 1, "Fellows and Undergraduates of the Men's Colleges, 1869–1919," in Christopher N. L. Brooke, *A History of the University of Cambridge,* vol. 4, *1870–1990* (Cambridge: Cambridge University Press, 1993), 593–595.

21. See John D. Fair, *Harold Temperley: A Scholar and Romantic in the Public Realm* (Newark: University of Delaware Press, 1992), 53–54, 58–59. A. T. Bartholomew, *A Bibliography of Adolphus William Ward, 1837–1924,* with *A Memoir,* by T. F. Tout (Cambridge: Cambridge University Press, 1926); A. T. Bartholomew, "Sir A. W. Ward, a Great Cambridge Historian," *Times* (20 June 1924); Stanley Leathes, "The Editorial Methods of Sir Adolphus Ward, 1, The Cambridge Modern History," *Cambridge Historical Journal,* 1:2 (1924), 219–221. See Cowling, *Religion and Public Doctrine,* 205–212; Roland Hill, *Lord Acton* (New Haven: Yale University Press, 2000), 396–397; George Kitson Clark, "A Hundred Years of the Teaching of History at Cambridge, 1873–1973," *Historical Journal,* 16 (1973), 536–537; Brooke, *History of the University of Cambridge,* vol. 4: 52–54, 235–236.

22. See Clark, "History at Cambridge, 1873–1973," 540–545; T. A. Walker, *Biographical Register of Peterhouse,* vol. 1 (Cambridge: Peterhouse, 1927); and *Peterhouse* (Cambridge: Peterhouse, 1935). Fair, *Harold Temperley,* 15–17; Doris Goldstein, "The Professionalization of History in Britain in the Late Nineteenth and Early Twentieth Centuries," *History of Historiography,* 3 (1983), 3–26.

23. HB to Eleanor Millward Butterfield of Toronto, Canada, 6 Nov 1957.

24. See HB, Talk to the Cambridge History Faculty on the occasion of his retirement, Nov 1968, and HB, Talk to the Cambridgeshire Air Squadron, c1968, in: Miscellaneous Comments.

25. Butterfield left behind major unpublished writings on Temperley and Peterhouse: "Memoir of H. W. V. Temperley" (ms, 173p, c1962/1963); "Peterhouse in Temperley's Time" (ms, 60p, about 1956); and "Personal: Early Youth, Father, Temperley, Vellacott" (ms, 67p, c1962/1963). Also very useful is *The Sex,* the student magazine from the Peterhouse Sexcentenary Club, housed in Peterhouse Library. Butterfield also talked about his relationship with Temperley in my interviews with him. See Fair, *Harold Temperley,* especially chap. 8, "The Butterfield Connection," 167–189.

26. HB, "Paul Vellacott: Master of Peterhouse, 1939–1954," *The Sex*, 114 (June 1956), 1–4. Roger Lovatt, "David Knowles and Peterhouse," in Christopher Brooke, Roger Lovatt, David Luscombe, and Aelred Sillem, *David Knowles Remembered* (Cambridge: Cambridge University Press, 1991), 85–88. Cowling, *Religion and Public Doctrine*, 219–220.

27. No copy of the paper now exists, and we do not know what Butterfield said which so impressed everyone. See Fair, *Harold Temperley*, 168–169.

28. Temperley, *Life of Canning* (London: Finch, 1905); *Frederic the Great and Kaiser Joseph: An Episode of War & Diplomacy in the Eighteenth Century* (London: Duckworth, 1915); and *The Foreign Policy of Canning, 1822–1827: England, the Neo-Holy Alliance, and the New World* (London G. Bell 1925). Fair, *Harold Temperley*, chaps. 5 and 6.

29. Butterfield scattered references to Temperley's teaching throughout his writings and spoke freely about him in his interviews with me. There are notable references in the following: HB, "Personal: Early Youth, Father, Temperley, Vellacott"; HB's introductions to the second editions of Temperley's books on Canning and Frederick the Great; the speeches collected in the file "Miscellaneous Comments"; HB, *The Study of History: An Inaugural Lecture* (Cambridge: Cambridge University Press, 1944), 1–6. See Fair, *Harold Temperley*, 168–173.

30. HB, Talk to the Cambridgeshire Air Squadron, c1968, in: Miscellaneous Comments.

31. HB, "Universal History and the Comparative Study of Civilizations," in Fehl, ed., *Sir Herbert Butterfield, Cho Yun Hsu, William H. McNeill on Chinese and World History*, 26. See HB, *The Universities and Education Today* (London: Routledge and Kegan Paul, 1962). The theme appears repeatedly in his writings and speeches over the years.

32. Temperley to HB, 19 June 1920.

33. A. Lovejoy to HB, 6 May 1952: "Temperley would come around to all our rooms at any time to talk."

34. HB, "Harold Temperley and George Canning," in Temperley, *The Foreign Policy of Canning, 1822–1827: England, the Neo-Holy Alliance, and the New World*, 2d ed. (London: Frank Cass, 1966), vii. See Fair, *Harold Temperley*, 13–14, 16–18.

35. HB, "George Peabody Gooch," *Contemporary Review*, 200 (Jul–Dec 1961), 502 Frank Eyck, *G. P. Gooch: A Study in History and Politics* (London: Macmillan, 1982).

36. *The Sex*, 76 (Lent term 1923), 31.

37. *The Sex*, 70 (Lent term 1921), 47.

38. *The Sex*, 73 (Lent term 1922), with HB's "Editorial," 3–12.

39. Leathes, "The Editorial Methods of Sir Adolphus Ward: *The Cambridge Modern History*"; *The Sex*, 66 (Michaelmas term 1919), 49; *The Sex*, 69 (Michaelmas term 1920), 52.

40. Lord Acton, *Lectures on Modern History*, ed. J. N. Figgis and R. V. Laurence (London: Macmillan, 1906; rpt. 1918). See Owen Chadwick, "Acton and Butterfield," *Journal of Ecclesiastical History*, 38 (1987), 386–405.

41. See HB, "Temperley and Canning," xx–xxi; HB, "Introduction to the Second Edition," Temperley, *Frederic the Great and Kaiser Joseph: An Episode of War and Diplomacy in the Eighteenth Century*, 2d ed. (London: Frank Cass, 1968), xi–xiii; Temperley, *Research and Modern History: An Inaugural Lecture* (Cambridge: Cambridge

University Press, 1930). See Cowling, *Religion and Public Doctrine,* 212–219, and Doris S. Goldstein, "History at Oxford and Cambridge: Professionalization and the Influence of Ranke," in Georg G. Iggers and James M. Powell, eds., *Leopold von Ranke and the Shaping of the Historical Discipline* (Syracuse: Syracuse University Press, 1990), 141–53. See Hill, *Lord Acton,* 372 and Fair, *Harold Temperley,* 177–178.

42. G. P. Gooch, "Historical Novels," *Contemporary Review,* 117 (1920), 204–212. Temperley, "Maurus Jokai and the Historical Novel," *Contemporary Review,* 86 (July 1904), 107–110. Temperley, *Foreign Historical Novels* (London: Bell, 1929). See HB to Neville Masterman, 12 Oct 1966.

43. None of Butterfield's undergraduate essays appear to survive.

44. Samples of his poetry from 1919, 1920, and 1926 survive with his Diaries.

45. HB, Incomplete essay (ms, c1921/1922).

46. HB, "Editorial," *The Sex,* 73 (Lent term 1922), 3–12.

47. *The Sex,* 69 (Michaelmas term 1920), 62; *The Sex,* 70 (Lent term 1921), 60; *The Sex,* 72 (Michaelmas term 1921), 62; *The Sex,* 74 (Easter term 1922), 72.

48. HB, Diary, probably May 1922.

49. HB, Journal, Sunday, 23 Aug 1970.

50. "Herbert Butterfield," *The Sex,* 75 (Michaelmas term 1922), 8–10.

51. See W. H. Hughes, "Ten Years," *Wesley House Magazine,* no. 5 (Easter 1931).

Chapter 2 Art and Science

1. See Goldstein, "History at Oxford and Cambridge, 146–153.

2. Temperley's "special period" on Napoleon focused on the years 1813–1815. Butterfield tells of Temperley's interest in Tilsit in: HB, "Temperley and Canning," Temperley, *The Foreign Policy of Canning,* 2d edition, xvii–xviii. Temperley presented his views about research in a series of five lectures during Michaelmas term 1923, "Materials for Research in the Diplomatic Archives at Cambridge."

3. See HB, *The Study of History,* 5.

4. Temperley, *The Foreign Policy of Canning* (1925).

5. C. K. Webster, *The Foreign Policy of Castlereagh, 1815–1822: Britain and the European Alliance* (London: G. Bell, 1925).

6. HB, "Peterhouse in Temperley's Time" (ms, 60p, about 1956); HB. *The Study of History,* 3–4.

7. Temperley, ed., *A History of the Peace Conference of Paris,* 6 vols. (London: Oxford University Press, 1920–1924). Temperley invited G. P. Gooch to assist him with the British papers. Temperley and G. P. Gooch, eds., *British Documents on the Origins of the War, 1898–1914,* 11 vols. in 13 (London: His Majesty's Stationery Office, 1926–1938). See HB, *The Study of History,* 5.

8. See C. K. Webster, "The Study of International History," *History,* 18 (1933–1934), 97–114.

9. See HB, *The Study of History,* 2–3.

10. There is a manuscript in Butterfield's papers which may well be the draft of his Member's Prize essay: HB, "Charles Dickens," unpublished ms, 76p + iiip.

11. *The Sex,* 79 (Michaelmas term 1923), 37.

12. HB, no title, Essay on G. K. Chesterton (ms, 13p, early 1920s).

13. HB, *The Historical Novel: An Essay* (Cambridge: Cambridge University Press, 1924). For Tilsit, see 21–24.

14. *Historical Novel*, 2–5, 82–83. Ranke's phrase was "wie es eigentlich gewesen," commonly translated "what actually happened." Ranke, *Geschichten der romanischen und germanischen Volker von 1494 bis 1514*, 3d ed. (Leipzig: Duncker und Humblot, [1824] 1885), v–viii. See "Introduction to the *History of the Latin and Teutonic Nations*" [1824], in Rober Wines, ed. and trans., *Selected Writings [by Leopold von Ranke] on the Art and Science of History* (New York: Fordham University Press, 1981), 56–59.

15. *Historical Novel*, 2–3, 8–9, 11.

16. *Historical Novel*, 7–14.

17. *Historical Novel*, 14–18.

18. *Historical Novel*, 17–24.

19. *Historical Novel*, 33–39.

20. *Historical Novel*, 71, 74.

21. *Historical Novel*, 14–15, 24, 73–74, 111–113.

22. *Historical Novel*, 23.

23. *Historical Novel*, 24–29.

24. *Historical Novel*, 9–10.

25. See: J. C. Squire, *The Observer* (24 June 1924); *New Statesman* (19 July 1924), 446, 448; Florence M. G. Higham, *History*, 10 (1926), 362–363.

26. The two reprint editions: Folcroft, Pa.: Folcroft Library Editions, 1971; and Norwood, Pa.; Norwood Editions, 1975. Michael Bentley, "Butterfield at the Millennium: The 'Sir Herbert Butterfield Lecture,' 1999," *Storia della Storiografia*, 38 (2000), 17–32.

27. *The Sex*, 78 (Michaelmas term 1923), 7, and 79 (Lent term 1924), 37.

28. HB's *Onotto Diary*, 1924.

29. *The Sex*, no. 79 (Lent term 1924).

30. HB, Diary, 1 Oct 1924.

31. Fragments of this manuscript exist in his papers.

32. Butterfield wrote a brief unpublished memoir of Canon Gillett, who was Dean of the chapel until 1932, at the time of his death in 1957.

33. Butterfield would see Francis from time to time over the years and wrote an unpublished memoir for the author of Francis's biography: HB to L. B. Greaves, 17 May 1967. See Greaves, *Carey Francis of Kenya* (London: Rex Collings, 1969).

34. On Chalmers, see Harold Temperley, "Lord Chalmers," *Cambridge Review* (2 Dec 1938), 144–145.

35. HB, review of A. T. Bartholomew, *A Bibliography of Sir Adolphus William Ward, with A Memoir* by T. F. Tout (1926), in *Cambridge Review* (3 Sept 1926), 159.

36. Butterfield's notes on his American projects were transferred from a collapsed box into three unnamed boxes, the first of which contains a packet marked: USA Miscellaneous.

37. Diary, 9 Feb 1925.

38. Diary, 6 March and 8 March 1925.

39. Diary, 23–25 Jan 1925, and 21–22 March 1925, and various memoirs of Hart Crane, 1949.

40. Eight volumes of Butterfield's *Cambridge Pocket Diary* are extant for the sixteen years from 1928–1929 through 1943–1944. Thereafter, except for 1958–1959, the run of volumes is complete through the year of his death. His *Onotto Diary* for 1924 is the only other such daily book extant. He used these diaries for his academic, social, and special appointments such as outside lectures and lay preaching, although it is clear that they do not provide a complete record of all his appointments.

41. Diary, 4 Feb 1926.

42. Diary, 13 Feb 1926, and 4 Feb 1926.

43. Diary, 3 March 1926.

44. Diary, 9 March 1926.

45. See HB, *The Study of History,* 5.

46. HB, "Temperley and Canning," xvi–xx. HB, "Some Trends in Scholarship 1868–1968, in the Field of Modern History," *Transactions of the Royal Historical Society,* 5th series, 19 (1969), 168.

47. HB, *The Study of History,* 4.

48. The three titles: "Napoleon and the Peace of Europe, 1806–1808"; "The Problem of Peace in Europe, 1806–1808"; and "Napoleon and Europe, 1806–1808."

49. Many of Butterfield's notes for the study and various drafts remain scattered in his papers, in miscellaneous boxes of notes, and in boxes labelled: 1806; Fox, Foreign Secretary, 1806. See HB, "The Dangers of History," *History and Human Relations* (London: Collins, 1951), 175.

50. HB, "A French Minister at Vienna, 1806–1807," *Cambridge Historical Journal* (1927), 185–190.

51. HB, *The Peace Tactics of Napoleon, 1806–08* (Cambridge: Cambridge University Press, 1929). See Fair, *Harold Temperley,* 301.

52. *Peace Tactics,* vii–viii, 50.

53. *Peace Tactics,* 269–273.

54. *Peace Tactics,* 269–273, 250–252.

55. *Peace Tactics,* 251–260, 270–273.

56. *Peace Tactics,* 249.

57. *Peace Tactics,* viii, 357.

58. *Peace Tactics,* 265–268. Presumably these pages constitute Butterfield's essay on the inner life of Czar Alexander at Tilsit.

59. *Peace Tactics,* vii.

60. *Peace Tactics,* 231–232.

61. *Peace Tactics,* e.g., vii–viii, 266–267, and the many personality portraits throughout the book.

62. *Peace Tactics,* 266. Butterfield has identified the personality essays under each figure's name in the index.

63. See *Peace Tactics,* vii–vii, 50, 231–232, 249, 266–267, 273–275, 355, 357.

64. *Peace Tactics,* 260.

65. Hall, *American Historical Review,* 35 (1929–1930), 857–858; Reddaway, *Cambridge Review* (7 March 1930), 326; and H. M. Best, *English Historical Review,* 45 (1930), 658–659.

66. Ian F. D. Morrow, *History,* 18 (1933–1934), 179–181.

67. New York: Octogon Books, 1972, by arrangement with Cambridge University Press.

68. For example, Morrow, in *History,* and Reddaway, in *Cambridge Review.*

69. Savoie Lottinville, *The Rhetoric of History* (Norman: Oklahoma University Press, 1976).

70. HB, "Temperley and Canning," xx–xxi; HB, "Introduction to the Second Edition," Temperley, *Frederic the Great,* xi–xiii; Temperley, *Research and Modern History: An Inaugural Lecture* (Cambridge: Cambridge University Press, 1930). Butterfield refers extensively to Ranke, *Hardenberg und die Geschichte des preussischen Staates von 1793–1813,* in *Sämtliche Werke,* 46–48 (1879).

71. The inaugural address had been published in Acton's *Lectures on Modern History* in 1906 and reprinted in 1918.

72. I am referring to the thinking about Acton that led Butterfield into his next book, *The Whig Interpretation of History,* and Ranke figures there as well.

73. G. M. Trevelyan, "The Present Position of History: Inaugural Lecture" (1927), in *Clio, a Muse, and Other Essays* (London: Longmans, Green, 1930). See also "Clio, a Muse" in the same volume.

74. See HB, "History as a Branch of Literature," in *History and Human Relations.* Butterfield made his comments in the interviews with me.

Chapter 3 Reconciler

1. Butterfield's standing and activities in the Faculty of History over the years are reported in successive issues of *Cambridge University Reporter.* See Elisabeth Leedham-Green, *A Concise History of the University of Cambridge* (Cambridge: Cambridge University Press, 1996), 189–190.

2. For what follows, I rely chiefly on my interviews with Butterfield, and on the clues he gave in *The Whig Interpretation of History* to the thinking that led to the book.

3. Bury, "The Science of History: An Inaugural" (1903), and "Cleopatra's Nose" (1916), in Temperley, ed., *Selected Essays of J. B. Bury* (Cambridge: Cambridge University Press, 1930).

4. Bury, "The Science of History," and "Cleopatra's Nose."

5. G. M. Trevelyan, *Lord Grey of the Reformed Bill, being the Life of Charles, Second Earl Grey* (London: Longmans, Green, 1920).

6. Butterfield's paper from 1925 apparently is gone, but many jottings on Fox and 1792 remain. The problem of Fox and 1792 preoccupied him for years to come, and eventually he published an article on the subject: HB, "Charles James Fox and the Whig Opposition in 1792," *Cambridge Historical Journal,* 9 (1949), 293–330.

7. Acton, "The Study of History," in his *Lectures on Modern History,* ed. J. N. Figgis and R. V. Laurence (London: Macmillan, 1906).

8. Acton, "The Study of History."

9. Acton to Creighton, Cannes, 5 April 1887, in J. Rufus Fears, ed., *Selected Writings of Lord Acton,* 3 vols. (Indianapolis: Liberty Classics, 1985–1987), 2:384.

10. HB, *Whig Interpretation,* 109–120. HB, Diary, 1 Oct 1924.

11. Butterfield recounted how *Whig Interpretation* came about in his interviews with me.

12. *Whig Interpretation,* v–vi, 70–73.

13. These phrases come from *Whig Interpretation,* 109–110. The analytic philosophers apparently did not launch their usual criticism against *Whig Interpretation,* but one of them, Patrick Gardiner, did do so twenty years later against *Christianity and History.* See Patrick Gardiner, in *Mind,* 60 (1951), 133–134.

14. This passage runs on for two pages: *Whig Interpretation,* 52–54.

15. E. H. Carr, *What Is History?* (London: Macmillan, 1961), 33–36.

16. Patterson, *Nobody's Perfect,* 1. David Hackett Fischer, *Historian's Fallacies: Toward a Logic of Historical Thought* (New York: Harper and Row, 1970), 281.

17. *Whig Interpretation,* v.

18. *Whig Interpretation,* 3–4.

19. Michael Bentley, *Modern Historiography: An Introduction* (London: Routledge, 1999), 63–65.

20. Patterson, *Nobody's Perfect,* 1–17. See Nicholas Capaldi and Donald W. Livingston, eds., *Liberty in Hume's History of England* (Dortrecht: Kluwer, 1990). Hill, *Lord Acton,* 105.

21. Butterfield mentioned this story, without identifying Charles Smyth as the voice, in his review of Carr, *What Is History?,* in *Cambridge Review* (2 Dec 1961), 174–175. He also recounted the story in his interviews with me. He got the reversal of Burke's title right in the riposte to Carr. With me, however, he hesitated and then quoted Smyth as saying that his books should be entitled *An Appeal from the New Whigs to the Old.* Burke's essay is actually entitled *An Appeal from the New to the Old Whigs* (London: J. Dodsley, 1791). Burke thought that Fox, the New Whig of his day, was too sympathetic to the French Revolution of 1789, and called for a return to the ancient Whigs and their admiration for the fundamental principles informing the "laws, constitution, and usages of the kingdom." Compare Edmund Burke, *An Appeal from the New to the Old Whigs,* 2d ed., in *The Works of the Right Honourable Edmund Burke* (London: Thomas McLean, 1823), 6: 73–74, 261–264. Butterfield again mistook the wording of Smyth's suggestion in a list he drew up of corrections to the proofs of my essay introducing his *Writings on Christianity and History.* HB to CTM, 11 May 1979. See CTM, "Herbert Butterfield on Christianity and History," xxx–xxxii. On Smyth, see Cowling, *Religion and Public Doctrine,* 49–50, 72–95, 192, 197.

22. *Whig Interpretation,* 4. See Michael Stanford, *A Companion to the Study of History* (Oxford: Blackwell, 1994), 85–86.

23. *Whig Interpretation,* 109.

24. Lord Acton to Marie Acton, 10 July 1877, quoted in Hill, *Lord Acton,* 105.

25. *Whig Interpretation,* 120–125.

26. *Whig Interpretation,* 70–71.

27. *Whig Interpretation,* 11, 24, 16, 31.

28. William H. Dray, in *On History and Philosophers of History* (Leiden: E. J. Brill, 1989), chap. 10, reads the phrase to mean some such things.

29. *Whig Interpretation,* 72.

30. *Whig Interpretation,* 11, 92.

31. HB, *Magna Carta in the Historiography of the Sixteenth and Seventeenth Centuries* (Reading: University of Reading, 1969), 8.

32. *Whig Interpretation,* 11–12, 62–63. See Fischer, *Historian's Fallacies,* 139, 281; P. B. M. Blaas, *Continuity and Anachronism: Parliamentary and Constitutional Development in Whig Historiography and the Anti-Whig Reaction between 1890 and 1930* (The Hague: Nijhoff, 1978); and Marshall Poe, "Butterfield's Sociology of Whig History: A Contribution to the Study of Anachronism in Modern Historical Thought," *Clio: A Journal of Literature, History and the Philosophy of History,* 25 (1996), 345–363. Clark, *Revolution and Rebellion,* 10, 15. Kevin Sharpe, *Remapping Early Modern England: The Culture of Seventeenth Century Politics* (Cambridge: Cambridge University Press, 2000), 6.

33. *Whig Interpretation,* 9–12, 16–18, 34–39.

34. *Whig Interpretation,* 45.

35. *Whig Interpretation,* 53–58.

36. *Whig Interpretation,* 20–22, 39–47.

37. *Whig Interpretation,* 18–20. Butterfield refers once (129) to "laws" related to historical study, meaning that the kind of thinking that goes on in historical study has "rules" of its own.

38. *Whig Interpretation,* 19.

39. *Whig Interpretation,* 20–22, 73. See John Passmore, "The Objectivity of History," *Philosophy,* 33 (1958), 97–111.

40. *Whig Interpretation,* 14–16, 65–75, 90–96.

41. *Whig Interpretation,* 14–16, 69, 96–103.

42. Ranke, "Introduction to the *History of the Latin and Teutonic Nations,*" in Wines, ed. and trans., *The Secret of World History: Selected Writing [by Ranke],* 56–59; Ranke, *Geschichten der romanischen und germanischen Volker,* 3d ed., v–viii.

43. *Whig Interpretation,* 64–65.

44. *Whig Interpretation,* 107–108.

45. *Whig Interpretation,* 1–2, 107, 109–120.

46. *Whig Interpretation,* 73, 107–108, 104–106.

47. *Whig Interpretation,* 64–68. Butterfield uses the unusual term "judgments of value" rather than the more customary term "value judgments."

48. *Whig Interpretation,* 1–3, 107–109.

49. *Whig Interpretation,* 73–75.

50. *Whig Interpretation,* 104–106.

51. *Whig Interpretation,* 104–106.

52. *Whig Interpretation,* 125, but also passim.

53. *Whig Interpretation,* 79–89.

54. *Whig Interpretation,* 87–89, 77.

55. *Whig Interpretation,* 109–120.

56. See *Whig Interpretation,* 71–74.

57. Matthew 7:1–5.

58. See Keith C. Sewell, *Providence and Method: Herbert Butterfield and the Interpretation of History* (Sioux Center, Iowa: By the Author, 2001), 109.

59. Romans 8:28.

60. *Whig Interpretation*, 23, 45, 48–49, 77, 88–89.

61. HB, *Historical Novel*, 8, 81.

62. *Whig Interpretation*, especially 107–108, 115–118, 120, 130.

63. *Whig Interpretation*, 2–3, 130.

64. *Whig Interpretation*, 131–132.

65. See, for example, D. C. Somervell, in *History*, 32 (1932), 86; and B. H. Sumner, in *English Historical Review*, 48 (1933), 174.

66. Trevelyan, "Clio, a Muse," in *Clio, a Muse, and Other Essays*, 172. See David Cannadine, *G. M. Trevelyan: A Life in History* (London: HarperCollins, 1992), 209, and Fair, *Harold Temperley*, 16.

Chapter 4 General Horizons

1. Butterfield told this story about Vellacott and Trevelyan in his interviews with me. Some of it is caught in Ved Mehta, *The Fly and the Fly-Bottle: Encounters with British Intellectuals* (Boston: Little, Brown, 1963), 257–259. HB calls Trevelyan a Whig historian in "Historiography in England" (typ, 22p, late 1961 or early 1962). See Earl John Russell, *The Life and Times of Charles James Fox*, 3 vols. (London: Bentley, 1866); George Otto Trevelyan, *The Early Life of Charles James Fox* (London: Longmans, Green, 1880); and G. M. Trevelyan, *History of England* (London: Longmans, Green, 1926). See also Joseph M. Hernon, Jr., "The Last Whig Historian and Consensus History: George Macaulay Trevelyan, 1876–1962," *American Historical Review*, 81 (1976), 66–97.

2. HB, "Borrowed from Professor Trevelyan" (7 Dec 1931); and HB, "List of Professor G. M. Trevelyan's Fox Papers" (May 1951). In his biography of Trevelyan, David Cannadine placed Trevelyan's interaction with Butterfield on Fox a decade and a half late, and reversed the sequence. He had Butterfield taking on the project of writing "the definitive biography" of Fox in 1945, and Trevelyan making the Fox papers available to Butterfield after that, perhaps as late as 1949, instead of 1931. See Cannadine, *G. M. Trevelyan*, 211–212, including note 98.

3. HB, "Napoleon and the Peace of Europe, 1806–08" (typs, late 1920s), 29–30.

4. HB, Lecture on Fox, in his lectures entitled "George III and the Constitution, 1769–82" (ms, c1935–1937).

5. HB, Diary with various notes about Napoleon, 1922; HB, *Peace Tactics*, passim.

6. These were the judgments Butterfield brought against Napoleon in *Napoleon* (London: Duckworth, 1939).

7. This was Maurice Cowling's observation to me at Peterhouse, April 1986. Mehta, *Fly and the Fly-Bottle*, 259.

8. HB, Diary, 3 March 1926.

9. Haslam, *Vices of Integrity*, 58; Brian Porter, "E. H. Carr — the Aberystwyth Years, 1936–1947," in Michael Cox, ed., *E. H. Carr: A Critical Appraisal* (Basingstoke and New York: Palgrave, 2000), 41–42.

10. Lewis Namier, *The Structure of Politics at the Accession of George III* (London:

Macmillan, 1929); and *England in the Age of American Revolution* (London: Macmillan, 1930).

11. Some of Butterfield's request slips for Fox material in the British Museum are in his papers. The notes he took on Fox during the 1930s are in boxes marked "Fox," but some are scattered in other places, for instance, in two boxes marked "1806." Most of Butterfield's library is in the Ward Library of Peterhouse.

12. See HB, "George Peabody Gooch, 1873–1968," *Proceedings of the British Academy,* 55 (1969), 335.

13. The publishers were Edward Arnold and Bell.

14. HB, "Lord North and Mr Robinson, 1779," *Cambridge Historical Journal,* 5 (1937), 255–279.

15. HB, "Bolingbroke and the 'Patriot King,'" *Cambridge Review* (10 March 1933), 308–310.

16. HB, Lectures: "George III and the Constitution, 1769–82."

17. HB, *Whig Interpretation,* 80–81, 125.

18. HB, *Napoleon,* 99–100, 124–25.

19. Lord Acton, "Introduction," to Nicolò Machiavelli, *Il Principe,* ed. Laurence Arthur Burd (Oxford: Clarendon, 1891), xix–xl.

20. HB, *Cambridge Pocket Diary,* 1936–1937; HB, *The Statecraft of Machiavelli* (London: Bell, 1940).

21. *Statecraft of Machiavelli,* 155–58, 161.

22. *Statecraft of Machiavelli,* 162–165. See Namier, *England in the Age of the American Revolution.*

23. HB, "The Master," *The Sex,* no. 104 (May 1938), 10–11. Butterfield later wrote a memoir of Lord Birdwood in a letter to the author of the article on Birdwood in the *Dictionary of National Biography*: HB to R. V. Rhodes James, 4 Aug 1966. Birdwood published his own memoirs, which included his tenure at Peterhouse: *Khaki and Gown: An Autobiography* (London: Ward, Lock, 1941); and *In My Time: Recollections and Anecdotes* (London: Skeffington, n.d. [1945]). Butterfield recounted that Birdwood's name was put forward by a Fellow, probably the Senior Fellow, Professor W. E. Barnes, who was "an obvious candidate" himself but who was considered "unsuitable" by Butterfield and others.

24. Interview with Brian Wormald, 1980. Brian Wormald, "Brian Wormald Adds" [addendum on Sir Herbert Butterfield], in *Cambridge Review* (16 Nov 1979), 9. Fair, *Harold Temperley,* 186–187. See Cowling on Wormald, *Religion and Public Doctrine,* 192–194.

25. On Aydelotte, see Fair, *Harold Temperley,* 234–235, J. H. Plumb, "The Road to Professional History," in vol. 1, *The Collected Essays of J. H. Plumb, The Making of an Historian* (London: Harvester Wheatsheaf, 1988), 1: 6–7. Plumb's memory put his first meetings with Butterfield during 1935–1936, whereas Butterfield's *Cambridge Pocket Diary* records many meetings with Plumb starting in 1934–1935 and continuing in 1935–1936 (the diary for 1936–1937 is missing). See Fair, *Harold Temperley,* 219–220.

26. Many years later Butterfield still commented favourably on the tradition, in "In Defence of Diplomatic History" (ms, 23p, 1963).

27. HB, editor, *Select Documents of European History*, vol. 3, *1715–1920* (London: Methuen, 1931).

28. HB, *Man on His Past: The Study of the History of Historical Scholarship* (Cambridge: Cambridge University Press, 1955), 118.

29. Acton, "Preface," *The Cambridge Modern History*, vol. 1, *The Renaissance* (Cambridge: Cambridge University Press, 1902).

30. HB, "Arguments Pertaining to the Thesis: That the division of the Modern History Course at 1715 . . . is detrimental . . . " (ms, 6p, c1935).

31. HB, Diary, 9 Feb 1925.

32. HB, "Introduction," to Temperley, *Frederic the Great* (2d ed), xvi. Butterfield later reviewed favourably Trevelyan's *English Social History: A Survey of Six Centuries,* in HB, "English Social History," *Cambridge Review* (10 Feb 1945), 188–89. See HB, "Butterfield on Trevelyan," *Radio Times* (16 Feb 1976).

33. HB, "Historiography in England" (ms, 22p, 1962), 7–8. HB, "History and the Marxian Method," *Scrutiny*, 1 (1932–1933), 343. HB, "History in 1934," *Bookman*, 87 (Dec 1934), 141–142.

34. Marc Bloch, *The Historian's Craft* (New York: Knopf, 1953; Manchester: Manchester University Press, 1954). See "Introduction," *Past and Present: A Journal of Scientific History*, 1 (1952), 1; Carole Fink, *Marc Bloch: A Life in History* (Cambridge: Cambridge University Press, 1989), especially chaps. 7 and 10; Peter Burke, *The French Historical Revolution: The* Annales *School, 1929–89* (Stanford: Stanford University Press, 1990), 2; and François Dosse, *New History in France: The Triumph of the* Annales (Urabana: University of Illinois Press, 1987), chap. 1.

35. Jacob Burckhardt, *The Civilization of the Renaissance in Italy,* trans. S. G. S. Middlemore (London: Phaidon, 1926; Harrap, 1929).

36. In many of his writings Butterfield comments on the importance of Marxist influence on non-Marxists, including, "In Defence of Diplomatic History," 21–22.

37. Ronald Hayman, *Leavis* (London: Heinemann, 1976). See Georgi Plekhanov [1856–1918], *Fundamental Problems of Marxism* (London: Lawrence and Wishart, 1927); Maurice H. Dobb, *Capitalist Enterprise and Social Progress* (London: Routledge 1925). See Harvey J. Kaye, *The British Marxist Historians: An Introductory Analysis* (Cambridge: Polity Press, 1984).

38. HB, "History and the Marxian Method," *Scrutiny*, 1 (1932–1933), 339–355.

39. "History and the Marxian Method," 340–348.

40. "History and the Marxian Method," 350–53, 355. Cowling, *Religion and Public Doctrine*, 224.

41. Some of Butterfield's notes from c1935 on the history of science remain in his papers. He said in 1945–1946 that he had been promoting the history of science at Cambridge for fifteen years, but it cannot have been before he wrote *Whig Interpretation of History* since no sign of the notion of science in history shows up there.

42. HB, "The Philosopher as Historian," *Bookman*, 87 (1934), 194–195.

43. HB's draft of the text of the History Faculty regulation of 1938.

44. E.g., HB, "In Defence of Diplomatic History," 4–6.

45. About fifteen typescripts of his lectures from the 1930s exist, in boxes marked Cambridge Modern History or Cambridge Concise Modern History, and various lists of

titles of his lectures are found in his *Cambridge Pocket Diary* for 1935–1936, 1937–1938, and 1941–1942.

46. *Whig Interpretation*, 68.

47. "History and the Marxian Method," 352–354.

48. "History and the Marxian Method," 354–355.

49. "History and the Marxian Method," 339, 347, 352–353.

50. *Statecraft of Machiavelli*, 15–25.

51. *Statecraft of Machiavelli*, 16–20.

52. *Statecraft of Machiavelli*, 59–61, 76–83.

53. Nicolò Machiavelli, *The Discourses on the First Ten Books of Titus Livius*, trans. Christian E. Detmold (New York: Modern Library, 1950), Book 3, chap. 6, "Of conspiracies." See Machiavelli, *The Prince*, trans. Luigi Ricci, revised E. R. P. Vincent (New York: Modern Library, 1950), chap. 19, "That we must avoid being despised and hated."

54. *Statecraft of Machiavelli*, 82–83.

55. Butterfield discussed Machiavelli several times in later years, notably: HB, "Introduction," for Nicolò Machiavelli, *The Prince*, trans. W. K. Marriott (London: Everyman, 1958); HB, review of Felix Gilbert, *Machiavelli and Guicciardini: Politics and History in Sixteenth Century Florence*, in *New York Times Book Review* (21 Feb 1965), 6, 14; and HB, review of Nicolò Machiavelli, *Legazione, Commissarie, Scritti di Governo*, vol. 1, ed. Fredi Chiappelli, in *Renaissance Quarterly*, 26 (1973), 314–317.

56. Butterfield edited volume 5, number 2, in 1936, and then with volume 6, number 1, in 1938 he became permanent editor.

57. Memorandum of Agreement between HB and Cambridge University Press, 8 Dec 1939.

Chapter 5 Patriotic History

1. HB, Diary, 11 May 1933.

2. HB, Note on Socialism and Fascism, c1933. See Plumb, "The Road to Professional History," *Collected Essays*, 1:7.

3. HB, Diary, c1933.

4. Diary, 27 Aug 1932.

5. Diary, 1933.

6. Diary, possibly c1933.

7. *Cambridge Pocket Diary*, 1933–1934, 1934–1935, 1935–1936. *Wesley House Magazine*, June 1936, 86.

8. Diary and various notes, 1930s.

9. HB, "A King's Dilemma: The Fabulous History of Edward and Wally," a story for children, which includes the "Chorus of the Self-Righteous," in his Diary 1936.

10. Diary, 3 Oct 1936. See Haslam, *Vices of Integrity*, 228, 251. See also Annan, *The Dons*, 245–255, and the photo before 215.

11. Diary, c1936.

12. Diary, c1936.

13. Diary, c1936.

14. Butterfield discussed his attitude towards voting in his interviews with me, and

wrote a brief account in *Raison d'Etat: The Relations between Morality and Government* (Brighton: University of Sussex, 1975), 15.

15. HB, "George III and the Constitution," (ms), first lecture, p. 4.

16. HB, "George Peabody Gooch," *Proceedings of the American Philosophical Society* (1969), 125; Hernon, "The Last Whig Historian and Consensus History," 87.

17. HB to Arthur Salter, 24 June 1941, Folder Foreign Historians I.

18. Butterfield writes of his relationship with Galinsky in letters after the war: HB to H. K. Galinsky, 6 Nov 1946; Galinsky to HB, 27 Nov 1946; HB testimonial for Galinsky, 6 Dec 1946; HB testimonial for Galinsky, 16 April 1948; HB to Mr Birley, 16 April 1948, in folder Foreign Historians I.

19. At about the time of his retirement in 1968, Butterfield recalled that the German invasion of Prague in 1939 and the involvement of the United States in Vietnam in the 1960s were the two events in international politics during his life that angered him. See folder: Miscellaneous Comments.

20. HB to H. K. Galinsky, 6 Nov 1946; Galinsky to HB, 27 Nov 1946; HB testimonial for Galinsky, 6 Dec 1946; HB testimonial for Galinsky, 16 April 1948; HB to Mr Birley, 16 April 1948, in folder Foreign Historians I.

21. This he said in his interviews with me. See Annan, *The Dons,* 246; and Annan, *Our Age,* 392–393.

22. HB, *Napoleon,* 16–18, 102–08.

23. Trevelyan, "The Legacy of Napoleon," *Cambridge Review* (19 Jan 1940), 177.

24. HB, *Cambridge Pocket Diary,* 1941–1942.

25. HB, "Cambridge during the War: Peterhouse," *Cambridge Review* (1 Dec 1945), 140; HB, *Peterhouse, 1939–1943* (The Peterhouse Society); *The Sex,* 106 (1939–1940).

26. Probably HB, "Harold Temperley," *Cambridge Historical Journal,* 6 (1939), 123. G. P. Gooch, "Harold Temperley, 1879–1939," *Proceedings of the British Academy,* 25 (1939), 355–393.

27. Trevelyan to HB, 5 Dec 1939.

28. HB, *Statecraft of Machiavelli,* 102.

29. HB, Diary, 24 Sept 1940, and 12 Oct 1940; HB, "Napoleon and Hitler," *Cambridge Review* (6 June 1941), 474–475.

30. Annan published the gossip in *Our Age,* 392–393. HB, Diary, c1940; HB, "Napoleon and Hitler," 474–475. HB, *The Englishman and His History* (Cambridge: Cambridge University Press, 1944), v–vii.

31. *France,* 4 vols., B.R. 503–503C, *Geographical Handbook Series* (London: Great Britain, Admiralty, Naval Staff, Naval Intelligence Division, 1942). Butterfield's sections were "The Age of Napoleon" (with I. L. Foster), and "From Waterloo to Sedan," in vol. 2, B.R. 503A, *History and Administration,* 124–146, 147–165.

32. C. E. Carrington to HB, 5 March 1953, and HB to Carrington, 9 March 1953, in folder Cambridge University Press I—end of 1964. HB et al. *A Short History of France from Early Times to 1958,* ed. Hampden Jackson (Cambridge: Cambridge University Press, 1959); 2d ed., retitled *A Short History of France from Early Times to 1972* (1974).

33. HB to Helen Cam, 12 Nov 1941; HB to J. H. Clapham, 29 May 1942; HB to Clapham, 19 Feb 1943; HB to Cam, 16 Dec 1943; "Resolutions carried at the Informal Conference of Historians at Cambridge, on 23 Mach 1942"; "Interim Report on the

Work of the History Committee" (March 1948): in folder Foreign Historians I. See HB, "Tendencies in Historical Study in England," *Irish Historical Studies,* 4:15 (March 1945), 217.

34. Outline for a course, "The Historical Background for General Knowledge," in box Historical Geography.

35. "Historical Geography," (typ, 209p, plus ms, c125p, 1943); Brooke to HB, 22 Sept 1943, in box Historical Geography. After the war, Brooke succeeded Previté-Orton as Professor of Medieval History at Cambridge. See E. A. Freeman, *The Historical Geography of Europe,* ed. J. B. Bury, 3d ed. (London: Longmans, 1903).

36. HB, *Napoleon,* 17–18.

37. The edition most available to Butterfield at the time was: Edmund Burke, *Reflections on the French Revolution and Other Essays.* Everyman's Library, no. 460 (London: Dent, 1929).

38. HB, *The Englishman and His History* appeared as number 19 in the series "Current Problems" edited by his colleague at Peterhouse, Sir Ernest Barker, for Cambridge University Press.

39. *Englishman,* 1.

40. *Englishman,* v–vi.

41. Cowling, *Religion and Public Doctrine,* 230.

42. *Englishman,* 4, 16, 33–36.

43. HB, "Preface — 1970," *The Englishman and His History* (Hamden, Conn.: Archon, 1970), iii.

44. The text of Butterfield's address at the memorial service for Churchill in Great Saint Mary's Church, 31 Jan 1965, was published: HB, "In Memoriam Winston Churchill," *Cambridge Review* (6 Feb 1965), 234. See Cowling, *Religion and Public Doctrine,* 230, 233.

45. *Englishman,* 7 and vii.

46. *Englishman,* v–vii, and "Contents" on ix–x.

47. *Englishman,* vi–vii, 1–4, 78–82.

48. See, for example: *Times Literary Supplement* (8 July 1944), 331–332, 335; A. J. Woolford, "The Interpretation of History," *Scrutiny,* 13 (1945–1946), 2–11; G. Kitson Clark, "History and the English Tradition," *Cambridge Review* (4 Nov 1944), 60–61; and particularly Carr, *What Is History?,* 35–36. Cannadine, *G. M. Trevelyan,* 209–210. Patterson, *Nobody's Perfect,* 13–18, 255. A major exception is Keith Sewell, who stressed the continuities and offered a noteworthy solution of what he calls "The Herbert Butterfield Problem," compatible with my exegesis, in his book *Providence and Method,* 95–98.

49. *Englishman,* 73.

50. *Englishman,* 35, 52. See G. R. Elton, "Herbert Butterfield and the Study of History," *Historical Journal,* 28 (1984), 729–743; and Elton, *F. W. Maitland* (London: Weidenfeld and Nicholson, 1985), 34–36.

51. *Englishman,* vi–vii, 1–4, 78–82. See Hernon, "The Last Whig Historian and Consensus History," 86–87. Hernon did not notice that Butterfield himself had already expanded the location of the Whig interpretation from the writings of certain historians to the outlook of the whole of the English nation.

52. *Englishman*, 83–90.
53. Carr, *What Is History?*, 33–36.
54. HB, "What Is History?," *Cambridge Review* (2 Dec 1961), 172, 174–175.
55. Carr to HB, 12 Dec 1961; Carr to HB, 8 Jan 1963.
56. Mehta, *Fly and the Fly-Bottle*, 252–257. See Haslam, *Vices of Integrity*, 208–209, 217.
57. *Englishman*, 89–92, 94–98.
58. *Englishman*, 104–117, 127–135.
59. *Englishman*, vi, 10, 33–34, 81–82, 100, 106–108, 112–117, 127, 138.
60. *Englishman*, 137–139.
61. See HB, "Capitalism and the Rise of Protestantism," *Cambridge Review* (23 May 1942), 324–325.
62. *Englishman*, 118–121.
63. *Englishman*, 100–101, 126–127.
64. *Englishman*, 1.
65. *Englishman*, 138–139.
66. *Englishman*, 118–127.
67. *Englishman*, 122, 127–131.
68. *Englishman*, v–vii, 96–102, 116–117, 133–136.
69. *Englishman*, 127–128, 132–133.
70. *Englishman*, 124–127, 134.
71. E.g., *Times Literary Supplement* (8 July 1944), 331–332, 335; A. J. Woolford, "The Interpretation of History," *Scrutiny*, 13 (1945–1946), 2–11; G. Kitson Clark, "History and the English Tradition," 60–61. For acceptance by historians after the war, see, for instance, A. L. Rowse, *The Use of History*, Teach Yourself History Library (London: Hodder and Stoughton, 1946).
72. Cowling, *Religion and Public Doctrine*, 233.
73. Interview with HB, 1977. My interpretation of the relation of Butterfield's politics in relation to his history walks between Butterfield's views of himself and E. H. Carr's views of Butterfield. I think Butterfield is right to claim continuity between *Whig Interpretation* and *Englishman* and to lament that Carr missed his new distinction between Whig history and Whig politics. But Carr is right to point out that the patriotic needs of the war influenced Butterfield's interpretation of history. Butterfield changed from ambivalence towards the Whigs to clear favour for the Whigs politically, and he violated his admonition not to use the study of the past to serve present politics.

Chapter 6 Professor

1. Haslam, *Vices of Integrity*, 58, 111.
2. See, for instance, John Kenyon, *The History Men*, 161–162. Cannadine, *G. M. Trevelyan*, 210, 212.
3. Trevelyan to HB, 21 June 1944. HB to Dorothy Temperley, 9 Jan 1946; HB to Dorothy Temperley, 10 July 1946; Dorothy Temperley to HB, 13 July 1946; HB to Lillian Penson, 12 April 1946. Dorothy Temperley to HB, 2 June 1948. HB to the Editor, *Times Literary Supplement* (30 April 1949), 286. See Fair, *Harold Temperley*, 11–12.

4. Trevelyan to HB, 21 June 1944, and 26 June 1946; HB to Trevelyan, 2 July 1946; Trevelyan to HB, n.d. (July 1946).

5. HB, *Cambridge Pocket Diary*, from 1944–1945 to 1949–1950. From other references we know that he gave more lectures and attended more meetings than he recorded in his diary. HB to E. R. Adair, 12 Feb 1945.

6. HB, *Cambridge Pocket Diary* for 1945–1949; List of Papers Given (1945–1951).

7. See Brooke et al., *David Knowles Remembered,* especially Roger Lovatt's chapter "David Knowles and Peterhouse," 82–122.

8. The others (1947): G. N. Clark, then J. R. M. Butler (Regius), Norman Sykes (Dixie Ecclesiastical), F. E. Adcock (Ancient), E. A. Walker (Vere harmsworth Imperial and Naval), and the visiting chair (American). See Cowling, *Religion and Public Doctrine*, 147.

9. Brooke, *History of the University of Cambridge,* vol. 4: 207, 236–239.

10. HB, "The General Board's Prime Stipend," *Cambridge Review* (8 March 1947), 328.

11. HB, *The Study of Modern History: An Inaugural Lecture* (London: Bell, 1944).

12. *Study of Modern History,* 16–17, 31, 33.

13. *Study of Modern History,* 5–6.

14. *Study of Modern History,* 7–13, 21–22, 26–27.

15. *Study of Modern History,* 6–27.

16. *Study of Modern History,* 7, 25–26.

17. *Study of Modern History,* 29–34.

18. Interviews with Eve Bogle, Cambridge, June 1986. Butterfield's *Cambridge Pocket Diary* over the years records many of the things Butterfield and Bogle did together. Her name appears for the first time in his *Cambridge Pocket Diary* for 1944–1945. However, his diaries for 1942–1943 and 1943–1944 are missing. As an example of how he explained her role to archivists and librarians, see HB to M. Mackensie (Royal Archives), 17 Oct 1951.

19. Eve Bogle's *Cambridge Pocket Diary* for 1945–1946 records when she typed Butterfield's writings.

20. HB to Director, British Museum, 12 Oct 1945; HB to York City Librarian, 7 Dec 1945, plus similar letters to Nottingham, Bedford, Sheffield, Devize, Winchester, Salisbury; HB to Lord Stanhope, 28 Jan 1946.

21. HB, "The Yorkshire Association and the Crisis of 1779–80," *Transactions of the Royal Historical Society,* 4th series, 29 (1947), 69–91. He read the paper to the Royal Society on 16 March 1946.

22. HB, *Cambridge Pocket Diary* for 1945–1946 and 1946–1947. This is the activity Cannadine mistook as Butterfield's start on the biography of Fox, when, if anything, his new research diverted him from Fox, which he started in 1931. He also missed the connection between Butterfield's work on Fox and his big book which pleased Trevelyan so much, *George III, Lord North, and the People,* 1799–1780 (London: Bell, 1949). Cannadine, *G. M. Trevelyan,* 210–212.

23. See Namier, *The Structure of Politics,* and *England in the Age of the American Revolution.*

24. Butterfield's notes, handwritten drafts, typescripts, and much of his correspondence

about Fox are contained in various boxes and folders labelled with names like Fox, or 1780, or Ireland, or 1779; HB, *Cambridge Pocket Diary* for 1945–1946 and 1946–1947.

25. HB to E. M. Hampson, 15 Oct 1947; HB to J. Opochensky, 28 Jan 1948; HB to J. H. Watkin, 9 April 1953.

26. HB to Trevelyan, 7 July 1948; HB, *George III, Lord North, and the People*, vii, ix.

27. HB, "Charles James Fox and the Whig Opposition in 1792," *Cambridge Historical Journal*, 9 (1949), 293–330.

28. *George III, Lord North*. Trevelyan to HB, 8 July 1948; Trevelyan to HB, 10 Oct and 11 Oct 1949.

29. *George III, Lord North*, 7–10.

30. *George III, Lord North*, 281–283.

31. *George III, Lord North*, vii–viii, 5–6.

32. *George III, Lord North*, 75–76.

33. *George III, Lord North*, v–vi.

34. *George III, Lord North*, 379–382, and see 255–257.

35. *George III, Lord North*, 3–17, 138–139, 233–243.

36. Noteworthy reviews: *Times Literary Supplement* (6 Jan 1950), 841–842; Mark A. Thomson, in *History*, 38 (1953), 260–261; A. J. P. Taylor, in *New Statesman* (12 Nov 1949), 556, 558; *Listener* (10 Nov 1949), 821; J. M. Hone, in *Irish Times* (19 Nov 1949); R. R. Sedgwick, in *Cambridge Review* (22 April 1950), 449–450; W. T. Laprade, in *American Historical Review*, 56 (1951), 340–341. See G. Scott Bremner, "Two Notable Books by a Yorkshire Scholar," in *Yorkshire Post* (14 Oct 1949) — the other book was *Origins of Modern Science*.

37. J. H. Plumb, *England in the Eighteenth Century* (Harmondsworth: Penguin, 1950), 137, 216. Harold T. Parker, "Herbert Butterfield, 1900–," in William S. Halperin, ed., *Some Twentieth Century Historians: Essays on Eminent Europeans* (Chicago: University of Chicago Press, 1961), 75–101. John Derry, "Herbert Butterfield," in John Cannon, ed., *The Historian at Work* (London: George Allen and Unwin, 1980), 178. Elton, "Herbert Butterfield and the Study of History," 737–738. Clark, *Revolution and Rebellion*, 41–42.

38. The typescripts from the 1940s are in boxes marked Cambridge Modern History or Concise Cambridge Modern History. Typescripts of some of his lectures from the 1930s are also there, along with later revisions from the 1950s. R. J. L. Kingsford to HB, 15 Dec 1948, HB to Kingsford, 28 Dec 1948, and Kingsford to HB, 31 Jan 1949, in folder Cambridge University Press — to end 1964.

39. HB, "Tendencies in Historical Study in England," *Irish Historical Studies*, 4:15 (March 1945), 209–223. The paper was actually published before he delivered it on 10 April 1945.

40. "Tendencies in Historical Study," 210–217.

41. HB, Lectures on History of England, 1688–1792 (ms, 44p, 1944–46).

42. S. C. Roberts to HB, 14 Feb 1945, and 1 March 1945, in which he sends Butterfield copies of documents from the archives of the Press, in folder: Acton and the Cambridge Modern History.

43. G. N. Clark and HB, "Report on the *Cambridge Modern History*," 23 April 1945.

The report was drafted by Clark, the senior professor, but it incorporated sections on general history taken from two drafts written by Butterfield, in folder: Acton and the Cambridge Modern History.

44. HB's outlines are in folder: Acton and the Cambridge Modern History.

45. Roberts to Clark, 30 May 1945; Paul Vellacott to HB, 29 May 1945; Clark to HB, 6 June 1945; HB to Roberts, 6 June 1945.

46. HB to Roberts, 6 June 1945, postscript; Roberts to HB, 8 June 1945; Clark to HB, 20 Sept 1945. The advisory committee consisted of Clark, J. M. R. Butler, E. A. Banians, and J. P. T. Bury. The first volume appeared in 1957 and the final companion volume, a thirteenth volume, was published in 1979. See Jean Lindsay to HB, 21 Oct 1948, where she refers to efforts by Clark, Banians, and herself to persuade Butterfield to write for volume 5 on 1713–1763, perhaps writing on the Diplomatic Revolution, or the Enlightenment, or the history of science, or the rise of Prussia. See G. R. Potter to HB, 21 March 1951, and Potter to HB, 20 April 1951, where Potter asked him to write on "International Relations in the West" for volume 1 on the Renaissance.

47. F. Kessler to HB, 17 July 1945; HB to Kessler, 24 July 1945; Potter to HB, 5 Dec 1976. E. Bonjour, H. S. Offer, G. R. Potter, *A Short History of Switzerland* (Oxford: Clarendon Press, 1952). Butterfield had initially suggested that Geoffrey Barraclough, A. J. P. Taylor, and Potter divide the work in thirds.

48. Norman Sykes to HB, 14 Feb 1946, with a note by Vellacott in the margin. The first volume of the *Oxford History of the Christian Church* appeared in 1976, and the fourteenth in 2001.

49. Alfred Cobban to HB, 5 May 1947.

50. HB, "The History of Science," *Time and Tide* (5 Jan 1946), 6.

51. HB, "Tendencies in Historical Study," 213–214.

52. HB, "The History of Science," 6.

53. *Radio Times,* 23 Sept 1949, quoting a letter from HB to the BBC in fall 1945; HB, *Cambridge Pocket Diary,* 1945–1946.

54. HB, "The History of Science," 6. My interviews with Butterfield; my interview with Joseph Needham, Gonville and Caius College, Cambridge, 3 June 1986. HB, *Cambridge Pocket Diary,* 1947–1948 and 1948–1949.

55. Butterfield's interviews with me; interview with Joseph Needham. See Maurice Cowling, "Joseph Needham and the History of Chinese Science," *New Criterion* 11:6 (Feb 1993). See Anna-K. Mayer, "Setting Up a Discipline: Conflicting Agendas of the Cambridge History of Science Committee, 1936–1950," *Studies in History and Philosophy of Science,* Part A, 31 (2000), 665–689.

56. HB, Notebook on the history of science, in box: Misc. Notes. HB, *The Origins of Modern Science, 1300–1800* (London: Bell, 1949), 10. See George Sarton, *Introduction to the History of Science,* 2 vols. (Washington: Carnegie Institution, 1927–1931); the third volume appeared in 1948, too late for Butterfield's purposes. HB might have consulted, for instance, Philippe Lenard, *Great Men of Science: A History of Scientific Progress,* trans. H. Stafford Hatfield (London: Bell, 1933), or Grove Wilson, *Great Men of Science: Their Lives and Discoveries* (New York: New Home Library, 1942).

57. HB, Diary note, early 1949.

58. *Origins of Modern Science,* Introduction.

59. See I. Bernard Cohen, *Revolution in Science* (Cambridge: Belknap Press of Harvard University Press, 1985), 396–399.

60. *Origins of Modern Science,* Introduction.

61. HB, *Man on His Past,* 118. See as an example, Robert Fox, "The History of Science," in Harold Perkins, ed., *History: An Introduction for the Intending Student* (London: Routledge and Kegan Paul, 1970), 182–184.

62. *Origins of Modern Science,* 15, 129–133, 151–152, 171–172, 204.

63. *Origins of Modern Science,* 171–172, 187–192.

64. *Origins of Modern Science,* 191–202.

65. Arnold Toynbee, *A Study of History,* vol. 8 (Oxford: Oxford University Press, 1954), 118–119, 499–500.

66. *Origins of Modern Science,* Introduction.

67. *Origins of Modern Science,* 192.

68. *Origins of Modern Science,* 14–15, 100–101, 159, 190–191, 204–205, 210–212. Joseph Needham had recently published a lecture on his research, *Science and Society in Ancient China* (London: Watts, 1947), and was then at work on his extended study of science and civilization in China. Interview with Joseph Needham, June 1986.

69. E.g., Charles Singer, *Spectator* (16 Sept 1949), 362–364; *Times Educational Supplement* (7 Oct 1949); Henry Dale, *Sunday Times* (16 Oct 1949); J. Bronowski, *New Statesman* (19 Nov 1949), 586; *Times Literary Supplement* (25 Nov 1949), 761, 763; Philip P. Wiener, *New York Times Book Review* (26 Feb 1950); A. C. Crombie, *Cambridge Review* (20 May 1950), 537–538; A. R. Hall, *Cambridge Journal* (June 1950), 568–571.

70. William D. Stahlman, *Science* (12 Sept 1958), 589. See Carl Gustavson, *A Preface to History* (New York: McGraw-Hill, 1955), 148–150. Stephen Toulman and June Toulmin, *Observer* (1 Jan 1967). Thomas S. Kuhn, *The Structure of Scientific Revolutions,* vol. 2 (Chicago: University of Chicago Press, 1962): and Kuhn, *The Essential Tension: Selected Studies of Scientific Tradition and Change* (Chicago: University of Chicago Press, 1977), 35, 131–133. See Gerd Buchdahl, "A Revolution in the Historiography of Science," *History of Science: An Annual Review of Literature, Research and Teaching,* 4 (1965), 58.

71. Interview with Joseph Needham, June 1986. See Cohen, *Revolution in Science,* 396–399. A. Mark Smith, "Knowing Things Inside Out: The Scientific Revolution from a Medieval Perspective," *American Historical Review,* 95 (1990), 726.

72. HB, "Europe, History of," *Chambers Encyclopaedia,* vol. 5 (1950), 467–481; HB, "The Seventeenth Century," *Encyclopaedia Americana,* vol. 24 (1954), 613–618.

73. See *Radio Times* (23 Sept 1949). HB, "A Bridge between the Arts and the Sciences," *Listener* (15 July 1948), 95–96. HB (as *de facto* editor), *The History of Science: Origins and Results of the Scientific Revolution* (London: Cohen and West; Glencoe, Ill.: Free Press, 1951), containing HB, "Dante's View of the Universe" (15–24), and HB, "Newton and His Universe" (77–86). Other contributors included Sir Henry Tizard, Sir Lawrence Bragg, Sir Henry Dale, Charles E. Raven, then vice-chancellor of Cambridge University, and Prof. M. M. Postan. See HB, "The Historian and the History of Science," *Bulletin of the British Society for the History of Science,* 1:3 (April 1950), 49–58.

74. HB, *Essays on the History of Science,* ed. Karl W. Schweizer (Lewiston and London: Edwin, Mellen, 1998).

Chapter 7 Religion

1. HB, "Tendencies in Historical Study in England," 219–223.

2. HB, "Tendencies in Historical Study," 215–218. The essay by Meinecke is "Die Deutsche Geschichtswissenschaft und die modernen Bedürfnisse," in *Die Hilfe,* 6 April 1916, reprinted in Meinecke, *Preussen und Deutschland im 19. und 20. Jahrhundert: Historische und Politische Aufsätze* (Munich: Oldenbourg, 1918).

3. HB to John (Adam) Watson, 19 May 1948. See HB, "Official History: Its Pitfalls and Its Criteria," *Studies,* 38 (1949), 130–132, 142–143.

4. HB to M. D. O'Sullivan, 18 June 1945.

5. HB, Diary, August 1945.

6. HB, "German History Lectures" (typ, 89p, 1945–1947). There are a number of manuscript versions of these lectures.

7. See Butterfield's correspondence with the British Council, in box: British Council.

8. HB to Klaus Dockhorn, 9 March 1948, 2 June 1948, 18 June 1948, and 22 Feb 1949.

9. HB, "Die Gefahren der Geschichte," *Geschichte in Wissenschaft und Unterricht,* 1 (1950), 525–539. Butterfield published an English version in HB *History and Human Relations* (London: Bell, 1951), 158–181.

10. Grahame Clark to HB, 3 Feb 1945; Memorandum by HB, "Research Degrees for Work in Government Departments," 11 Feb 1945 (ms, 6p), in folder: Official History.

11. HB, "George Peabody Gooch, 1873–1968," *Proceedings of the British Academy,* 55 (1969), 323–338; W. N. Medlicott to HB, 3 Aug 1949.

12. HB to Vellacott, 10 July 1947; HB, *Cambridge Pocket Diary,* 1948–1949; various letters from Williams to HB in 1948.

13. HB, "Official History," 129–32; HB to P. J. Connolly, 16 Feb 1949 and 20 Feb 1949, in folder: Official History.

14. HB to Taylor, 2 Aug 1949.

15. Desmond Williams to HB, 24 March 1949, and HB to Williams, 1 April 1949; HB to Connolly, 25 July 1949; see the lists of names to whom Butterfield sent the article. Medlicott to HB, 3 Aug 1949, and 13 Aug 1949; HB to Medlicott, 5 Aug 1949; Woodward to HB, 28 July 1949, and 1 Aug 1949. HB to Connolly, 24 Aug 1949. See Eve Bogle to CTM, 26 Jan 1987. See also "Prof Desmond Williams," obituary in the *Daily Telegraph,* 21 Jan 1987. Interview with Edward Norman, 1987.

16. HB to Bragg, 14 June 1951.

17. Trevelyan to HB, 1 March 1946.

18. HB, review of David Mathew, *Acton: The Formative Years,* in *English Historical Review,* 61 (1946), 412–417.

19. Knowles to HB, 16 Sept 1947; Gooch to HB, 4 Feb 1947.

20. HB to G. N. Clark, 5 June 1946; HB to the Editor, *Fortnightly Review* (18 Feb 1947). HB, "The Journal of Lord Acton: Rome 1857," *Cambridge Historical Review,* 8 (1946), 186–204.

21. HB, *Lord Acton* (London: The Historical Association, 1948), 6–7, 10–13.

22. HB to Rupert Hart-Davis, 5 Nov 1948.

23. HB, *Lord Acton,* passim. Some years later he published another pamphlet on Acton in Italian which highlighted Acton's struggle with the Roman Catholic Church: HB, *Lord Acton* (Milan: Vità e Pensiero, 1962).

24. Watkin to HB, 11 July 1948; HB to Watkin, 14 July 1948. See F. A. Gasquet, ed., *Lord Acton and His Circle* (London: Burns and Oates, 1906). Aelred Watkin and HB, "Gasquet and the Acton-Simpson Correspondence," *Cambridge Historical Journal,* 10 (1950), 75–105. HB to Watkin, 31 May 1949; Watkin to HB, 17 June 1949. See Chadwick, "Acton and Butterfield," 395, where Butterfield tends to get the credit. George Kitson Clark, *The Critical Historian* (London: Heinemann, 1967), 117–118.

25. See HB, *Cambridge Pocket Diary* for 1944 to 1949; HB, "Antidote to Dogmatic History," *Time and Tide* (12 Jan 1946), 29–30; HB, "Limits of Historical Understanding," *Listener* (26 June 1947), 997–998; HB, "Reflections on the Predicament of Our Time," *Cambridge Journal,* 1:1 (Oct 1947), 5–13.

26. This and much of the information about the lectures which follows come from my interviews with Butterfield.

27. HB, notebooks named Notes and Extracts 1947–8, and Notes and Extracts 1948, and notebook with no name in box: Old Testament.

28. My interviews with HB.

29. Christopher Wright, in *John O'London's Weekly* (9 Dec 1949), 1. Interview with Kingsley Joblin, June 1987.

30. HB, *Christianity and History* (London: Bell, 1949), 35–39, 44–45, 60.

31. The Cambridge Faculty of Divinity, also excited about the response to Butterfield, mounted the special Saturday morning lectures during the Michaelmas terms of the next two years: in 1949, Alec Vidler on "Christian Belief," and in 1950, Basil Willey on "Christianity Past and Present." The need for the series seemed to lapse after that, perhaps a sign that the postwar era was over.

32. Peter Laslett, *Radio Times* (25 March 1949); Harman Grisewood, "The Third Programme and Its Audience," *World Review* (Dec 1949), 33–36; Martin Wight, "History's Theme," *Observer* (23 Oct 1949). Eve Bogle to CTM, 10 June 1986.

33. HB, "Christianity and History," *Listener* (7 April, 14 April, 21 April, 28 April, 5 May, 12, May 1949). The lectures were broadcast 2 April, 9 April, 16 April, 23 April, 30 April, and 7 May 1949.

34. HB, Diary note, early 1949; W. A. R. Collins to HB, 25 May 1949; HB to Collins, 30 May 1949; Collins to HB, 3 June 1949; HB to Collins, 3 June 1949.

35. From my interviews with Butterfield.

36. Both Thorp and Sewell discuss at length certain matters touched upon here. While both books deal with *Christianity and History,* they also range over a large portion of Butterfield's corpus in pursuing their themes. See Malcolm R. Thorp, *Herbert Butterfield and the Reinterpretation of the Christian Historical Perspective* (Lewiston and Queenstown: Edwin Mellen, 1997); and Sewell, *Providence and Method.*

37. *Christianity and History,* 22 and 146.

38. *Christianity and History,* 19–20.

39. *Christianity and History,* 12–14, 19–25.

40. *Christianity and History,* 14–15.

41. *Christianity and History,* 16–19.

42. *Christianity and History,* 19.

43. See Acton, "A Lecture on the Study of History," *Lectures on Modern History,* in Fears, ed., *Selected Writings of Lord Acton* 1: 530–532.

44. *Christianity and History,* 19–25.

45. *Christianity and History,* 46.

46. *Christianity and History,* 45–47.

47. See Arnold Toynbee, *A Study of History,* vol. 9 (Oxford: Oxford University Press, 1954), 194–210.

48. *Christianity and History,* 19–21.

49. *Christianity and History,* 26–28.

50. *Christianity and History,* 26–47.

51. *Christianity and History,* 26–29. See William A. Speck, "Herbert Butterfield on the Christian and Historical Study," *Fides et Historia,* 4 (1971), 51.

52. *Christianity and History,* 5–8.

53. *Christianity and History,* 36–39, 43–44, 64–65, 81–83, 93–97.

54. *Christianity and History,* 81–83, 108–109.

55. *Christianity and History,* 43–45.

56. *Christianity and History,* 44–45, 91.

57. *Christianity and History,* 48–53, 57–59.

58. *Christianity and History,* 52–58.

59. *Christianity and History,* 93–97. See Sewell's discussion of Providence in Butterfield's thinking, in *Providence and Method,* especially chap. 8.

60. *Christianity and History,* 97–99.

61. *Christianity and History,* 34–35, 98–99, 109.

62. *Christianity and History,* 98–99, 94–95.

63. *Christianity and History,* 99–111.

64. *Christianity and History,* 57–60, 111–112.

65. *Christianity and History,* 95–96. See Sidney Hook, *Philosophy and History* (New York: New York University Press, 1963), 265–266.

66. *Christianity and History,* 99–102.

67. *Christianity and History,* 23–25, 113.

68. *Christianity and History,* 2–3, 119–129.

69. *Christianity and History,* 23–24, 91–92, 98.

70. See, for instance, Philip Wright, Parish of Littlebury, in *Saffron Walden Deanery Parish Magazine* (Oct 1950); B. A. Y., in *Religion in Education* (Spring 1950); F. M. Powicke, in *History,* 35 (1950), 193–201; *Calcutta Statesman* (12 March 1950); Christopher Wood, in *Montreal Gazette* (7 Jan 1950); Roger Lloyd, "Herbert Butterfield," *Church Times* (11 Jan 1952), 24; Bishop of Lichfield, in *Church of England Newspaper* (17 Nov 1950); John J. O'Connor, in *America* (June 1950); Paul Ramsey, in *New York Times* (30 April 1950).

71. Martin Wight, "History and Judgment: Butterfield, Niebuhr, and the Technical Historian," *Frontier,* 1:8 (Aug), 301–314. Keith C. Sewell, "The Concept of Technical History in the Thought of Herbert Butterfield," *Fides et Historia,* 27 (1995), 52–76;

Sewell, *Providence and Method*, especially chap. 9. Sydney W. Jackman, in *ISIS,* 41 (1950), 326–327. See John Cannon, *Teaching History at University*, Teaching of History Series, 56 (London: The Historical Association, 1984), 9, 33. Patrick Gardiner, in *Mind*, 60 (1951), 133–134. See Annan, *Our Age,* 270; and Cannadine repeating Annan, in *G. M. Trevelyan,* 212. Ironically, Annan took an image which Ved Mehta had drawn, not of Butterfield, but of the *Times* and Lewis Namier, and transposed it unkindly onto Butterfield. See Mehta, *Fly and the Fly-Bottle,* 240.

72. Ranke, *Geschichten der romanischen und germanischen Volker,* 3d ed., v–viii. See Ranke, "Introduction to the *History of the Latin and Teutonic Nations [1494–1535],*" in Wines, ed., *The Secret of World History: Selected Writings [by Leopold von Ranke],* 56–59.

73. See CTM, ed., *God, History, and Historians: Modern Christian Views of History* (New York: Oxford University Press, 1977).

74. Butler to HB, 8 Oct 1949; Trevelyan to HB, 10 Oct 1949; *Times Educational Supplement* (27 Jan 1950). See Charles Smyth, in *Christendom* (June 1950).

Chapter 8 Public Figure

1. See HB to J. Robert Oppenheimer, 12 Oct 1963.

2. HB, Memoir, 6 and 7 Sept 1949, written aboard ship crossing the Atlantic.

3. J. R. M. Butler to HB, 30 Oct 1949.

4. HB, *Christianity and History,* 142–145.

5. HB, "Notes on: How far can and should the subject of International Relations be included in the curriculum for undergraduate students in History?", presented to the Fourth Conference on the University Teaching of International Relations, London School of Economics and Political Science, 6–7 Jan 1949 (typ, 4p). Possibly also discussed at the Royal Institute for International Affairs, Chatham House, London, April 1949.

6. HB, "The Tragic Element in Modern International Conflict," *Review of Politics,* 12 (April 1950), 147–164; also published in *The Wind and the Rain,* 7:1 (Autumn 1950), 8–21. See HB to Arnold Toynbee, 7 June 1950.

7. See HB, *Cambridge Pocket Diary* for these years.

8. Humphrey Sumner to HB, 21 Oct 1947.

9. HB to Trevelyan, 15 March 1951; HB to John Hope Franklin, 14 July 1969.

10. See HB to J. T. Saunders, 6 Jan 1953.

11. For examples of reviews: *Irish Times* (13 Jan 1951); *Economist* (17 Nov 1951); Malcolm Muggeridge, in *Daily Telegraph* (23 Dec 1951); L. T. Heron, in *Chicago Sunday Tribune* (1 July 1951); J. M. S. Careless, in *Canadian Forum* (Sept 1951); Boyd C. Shafer, in *American Historical Review,* 58 (1952–1953), 156. See Donald G. Creighton, *Towards the Discovery of Canada* (Toronto: Macmillan, 1972), 2–5, and J. W. Burrow, *A Liberal Descent: Victorian Historians and the English Past* (Cambridge: Cambridge University Press, 1981), 1–3. See Donald R. Kelley to HB, 7 July 1970, who remembers that *Whig Interpretation* and R. G. Collingwood's *Idea of History* were "the cornerstones for history and literature majors" at Harvard in the early 1950s.

12. David Watkin, *Morality and Architecture: The Development of a Theme in Architectural History and Theory from the Gothic Revival to the Modern Movement* (Oxford:

Clarendon, 1977), vii–viii. Donald R. Kelley, review in *Journal of the History of Ideas*, 40 (1979), 663. Peter R. H. Slee, *Learning and a Liberal Education: The Study of Modern History in the Universities of Oxford, Cambridge, and Manchester, 1800–1914* (Manchester: Manchester University Press, 1986), 4. J. C. D. Clark, *Revolution and Rebellion*, 11, 15, 164, and *English Society, 1688–1832* (Cambridge: Cambridge University Press, 1985), 1, 6. Bonnie G. Smith, "The Contribution of Women to Modern Historiography in Great Britain, France, and the United States, 1750–1940," *American Historical Review*, 89 (1984), 709–710. V. H. Galbraith, *An Introduction to the Study of History* (London: Watts, 1964), 5–6. Paul K. Conklin and Roland N. Stromberg, *The Heritage and Challenge of History* (New York: Dodd, Mead, 1975), 77–78, 99–100. David Thomson, *The Aims of History: Values of the Historical Attitude* (London: Thames and Hudson, 1969), 48–56. J. H. Plumb, *The Death of the Past* (London: Macmillan, 1969), 41–42. Elton, "Herbert Butterfield and the Study of History," 736.

13. Christopher Hill, *Reformation to Industrial Revolution* (London: Weidenfeld and Nicholson, 1967), 20. Patterson, *Nobody's Perfect*, 1.

14. HB to Woodcock, 6 April 1951. Bentley, *Modern Historiography*, 63–65. Eyck, *G. P. Gooch*, 268.

15. HB, *Cambridge Pocket Diary*, 1984–1949. HB, "The Christian and Academic History," "The Christian and the Biblical Interpretation of History," "The Christian and the Marxian Interpretation of History," and "The Christian and the Ecclesiastical Interpretation of History," *Christian News-Letter*, 333 (16 March 1949), 336 (27 April 1949), and 341 (6 July 1949).

16. HB, "The Predicament of Central Europe," and "The Predicament That Leads to War," *Time and Tide* (14 Jan and 21 Jan 1950).

17. HB, *Cambridge Pocket Diary*, 1949–1950, and 1950–1951. Lists of "Commitments" for 1950 and 1951, and "Promises of Visits" covering the same period.

18. HB, *Christianity in European History* (London: Oxford University Press, 1951), in an edition of only 800 copies as stipulated by agreement between Durham and OUP. It was republished by Collins in 1952.

19. HB, *The Reconstruction of an Historical Episode: The History of the Enquiry into the Origins of the Seven Years' War*, Glasgow University Publications, 91 (Glasgow: Jackson, 1951).

20. Wight's review of *Christianity and History*, in *Observer* (23 Oct 1949). HB, *Cambridge Pocket Diary*, 1949–1950, on the pages for 9–12 Nov 1949. Otherwise, the pages for the fall 1949, when he was in Princeton, are blank. See Trevelyan to HB, 23 Oct. 1951.

21. See for example, Toynbee to HB, 2 June 1950; Wight to HB, 2 Sept 1950; Geyl to HB, 8 Feb 1951.

22. Kingsford to HB, 26 April 1949; HB to Kingsford, 3 May 1949.

23. HB, *History and Human Relations* (London: Collins, 1951; New York: Macmillan, 1952). Memorandum of Agreement between HB and Collins, 25 Jan 1951. After *History and Human Relations* was published, in keeping with the advice of his agent, Butterfield rejected Oxford University Press's request to print more copies of *Christianity in European History* and turned again to Collins, who then brought the book out under its imprint in 1952.

24. The three published essays were: "The Tragic Element in Modern International Conflict," "The Dangers of History," and "Official History." The six beginning as lectures were: three of his standard lectures, given under various titles and revisions: "Marxist History" (since Jan 1948), "Moral Judgments in History" (since May 1945), "The Dangers of History" (since March 1947); and three lectures from particular occasions: "The Tragic Element in Modern International Conflict" (for Notre Dame University, fall 1949), "Official History" (for University College, Dublin, Dec 1948), and "History as a Branch of Literature" (for the Literary and Philosophical Society, Newcastle, March 1950). A seventh, "The Christian and Historical Study," was filially related to his essays in the *Christian News Letter* and possibly a compound of two or three lectures, including "How Christianity Affects the Teaching of History" (for the Popular Historical Association, Nov 1950). Even the eighth, "Christianity and Human Relationships," could have derived from his many lectures and sermons to church audiences.

25. Toynbee to HB, 2 June 1950; Wight to HB, 2 Sept 1950; Geyl to HB, 8 Feb 1951; Taylor, in *New Statesman and Nation* (24 Nov 1951), 594, 596; Barraclough, in *History Today,* 1 (1951), 70–71; Berlin to HB, 15 Sept 1953.

26. Taylor, in *New Statesman and Nation* (24 Nov 1951); Geoffrey Barraclough, *An Introduction to Contemporary History* (London: Watts, 1964), 11. Bryant, in *Sunday Times* (14 Oct 1951); "The Historian as Moralist," in *Times Literary Supplement* (17 August 1951). Trevelyan to HB, 29 July 1951.

27. The seven books were: in 1949, *George III, Lord North, and the People, Origins of Modern Science,* and *Christianity and History;* in 1951, *History and Human Relations, Christianity in European History,* and ed., *The History of Science: Origins and Results of the Scientific Revolution;* and in 1950, the reissue of *Whig Interpretation of History.*

28. HB to Maurice Powicke (Oxford), 2 Nov 1954.

29. HB to John (Adam) Watson, 25 August 1953. HB, *Christentum und Geschichte,* trans. Sylvia Erdmann (Stuttgart: Engelhornverlag, 1952).

30. HB, "Christianity and Human Relationships," *History and Human Relations,* 41.

31. "Christianity and Human Relationships," 43–43, 51–52, 62.

32. "Christianity and Human Relationships," 41–55, 63–65.

33. "Christianity and Historical Study," *History and Human Relations,* 152–154.

34. HB, *Christianity in European History,* 52–56.

35. See, for example, HB, *Christianity, Diplomacy and War* (London: Epworth, 1953; Nashville: Abington-Cokesbury, 1953), 17–18; and HB, *International Conflict in the Twentieth Century: A Christian View* (New York: Harper and Brothers, 1960), 23, 118–120.

36. *History and Human Relations,* 74, 101–103, 134–136, 146.

37. *History and Human Relations,* 145–146.

38. *History and Human Relations,* 101–102, 135, 146, 147; see *Christianity and History,* 17–18.

39. "Marxist History," *History and Human Relations,* 88–89 and 82. See HB, "History and the Marxian Method," *Scrutiny,* 1 (1932–1933), 339–355. See Sidney Hook, letter to *Times Literary Supplement* (29 April 1977).

40. "Marxist History," 83, 86; and see "Moral Judgments in History," *History and Human Relations,* 101–102; also *Whig Interpretation,* v–vi.

41. See *Christianity and History,* 46.

42. *Christianity and History,* 43–44.

43. "Marxist History," 66–67.

44. "Marxist History," 73, 77.

45. "Marxist History," 79–80.

46. "Marxist History," 69–71, 75.

47. *Whig Interpretation,* 20–22, 73; *Christianity and History,* 19–21.

48. "Marxist History," 68–70, and "Moral Judgments in History," 127.

49. "Marxist History," 69–70, 79–80, and see "Moral Judgments in History," 118–119 and 120.

50. *The Study of History,* and *Christianity and History,* 27.

51. "Marxist History," 74.

52. "Moral Judgments in History," 129. See Gordon Wright, "History as a Moral Science," *American Historical Review,* 81 (1979), 2, 11; Hans Meyerhoff, ed., *The Philosophy of History in Our Time* (Garden City, N.Y.: Doubleday, 1959); Gordon Leff, *History and Social Theory* (London: Merlin, 1969), 94–102; Howard Zinn, *The Politics of History* (Boston: Beacon, 1970), 284–285; C. Behan McCullagh, *Justifying Historical Descriptions* (Cambridge: Cambridge University Press, 1984), 222–225; and Adrian Oldfield, "Moral Judgments in History," *History and Theory,* 20 (1981), 260–277.

53. HB to Beloff, 19 Oct 1951.

54. HB to John (Adam) Watson, 25 August 1953.

55. "Moral Judgments in History," 103.

56. "Moral Judgments in History," 111.

57. "Moral Judgments in History," 103, 111.

58. "Moral Judgments in History," 112–113.

59. "Moral Judgments in History," 103, 108, 106, and see 116, 118, 123.

60. "Moral Judgments in History," 106–107.

61. "Moral Judgments in History," 120, 122, 123, 125.

62. "Moral Judgments in History," 120–127.

63. "Moral Judgments in History," 126–129, and see 104, 111.

64. "Moral Judgments in History," 103, 111.

65. HB, "The Christian and Academic History," *Christian News Letter,* 333, (16 March 1949).

66. "The Christian and Historical Study," 131–157.

67. "The Christian and Historical Study," 136–137, 139, 142–143.

68. "The Christian and Historical Study," 145–146.

69. "The Christian and Historical Study," 147–148.

70. E. Harris Harbison, reviewing *History and Human Relations,* was among those who noted at the time that Butterfield had identified his approach to history as Christian. Harbison, review in *William and Mary Quarterly,* 9 (1952), 414–416.

71. "The Christian and Historical Study," 148–152.

72. HB, *Christianity in European History,* 22, 24–25, 31–32, 55–56. HB to Van Doren, 20 Feb 1952. See review by Kenneth Scott Latourette, *American Historical Review,* 59 (1953–1954), 410–411.

73. HB, *Liberty in the Modern World* (Toronto: Ryerson, 1952), 29. William J.

McGill, "Herbert Butterfield and the Idea of Liberty," *South Atlantic Quarterly*, 70 (1971), 1–12. See George Watson, *Lord Acton's "History of Liberty": A Study of His Library, with an Edited Text of His "History of Liberty" Notes* (Aldershot: Scolar Press, 1994).

74. HB to Beloff, 19 Oct 1951.

75. See the report of a meeting on the Theory of International Relations at Columbia University which Butterfield attended, 12 June 1956, where he discussed his approach as a historian, in folder: Rockefeller Foundation.

76. "The Christian and Historical Study," 138–139, 144–145.

77. HB, "The Scientific versus the Moralistic Approach in International Affairs," *International Affairs*, 27 (1951), 411, 418.

78. Kenneth Slack, "Bangor 1951 — Discoveries and Tensions," *British Weekly* (6 Sept 1951); HB, *God in History*, Church of England Youth Council News-Letter Reprint, No. 2, 1952, 4–9.

79. *God in History*, 4–5, 7–9.

80. HB, *Cambridge Pocket Diary*, 1951–1952, and 1952–1953. See HB to Dr. Mc-Cracken (Regional Radium Institute, Bradford), 22 March 1950; HB to Aubrey Gwynn, 21 March 1950.

Chapter 9 On War and Historiography

1. HB to Paul Vellacott, 5 June 1951, and 25 Feb 1952; HB to Trevelyan, 15 March 1951.

2. See G. N. Clark to HB, 25 May 1952: after noting that the *CHJ* had only two editors in its then thirty-year history, Temperley and Butterfield, Clark wrote, "I must take this opportunity of saying that the *Journal* could not have been edited better than it has been by you, and that there is no living editor of a historical periodical who has upheld higher standards of scholarship." See HB to G. R. Elton, 3 Nov 1955; HB to J. P. T. Bury, 7 May 1956; HB to J. H. Plumb, 26 July 1956.

3. HB to M. Mackensie (Royal Archives), 17 Oct 1951; M. Mackensie to HB, 18 Oct 1951.

4. Trevelyan to HB, 9 March 1951; HB to Trevelyan, 15 March 1951.

5. Woodruff to HB, 8 Feb 1951; HB to Woodruff, 13 Feb 1951; Woodruff to HB, 4 June 1951; HB to Woodruff, 8 June 1951; Woodruff to HB, 11 June 1951, and 4 Jan 1952.

6. HB, "The Acton Correspondence" (typ, 14p n.d., cJan 1952), in folder: Acton, Correspondence About. HB to Vellacott, 5 Feb 1952; Vellacott to HB, 20 Feb 1952; HB to Vellacott, 25 Feb 1952; HB to Maurice Cowling, 18 July 1952.

7. HB to Vellacott, 25 Feb 1952.

8. Kendall (Collins) to HB, 23 Jan 1952. The Burke manuscripts are in the box: Burke. See Acton, Inaugural Lecture, in Fears, ed., *Selected Writings of Lord Acton*, 2: 551. See HB, *Man on His Past*, 18, 68–70.

9. R. J. L. Kingsford to HB, 21 May 1952.

10. Douglas Woodruff, ed., Acton, *Essays on Church and State* (London: Hollis and Carter, 1952).

11. HB to Vellacott, 29 Feb 1952. HB to R. F. Treharne (Editor, *History*), 9 July 1952; Treharne to HB, 14 July 1952. HB to Richard Pares (Editor, *English Historical Review*), 2 July 1952; Pares to HB, 7 July 1952; Duncan Forbes to HB, 11 July 1952. See HB to T. S. Gregory (BBC), 9 May 1951.

12. HB to Woodruff, 12 Sept 1952; T. F. Burns (Hollis and Carter) to HB, 24 Sept 1952, with Vellacott's remarks written on the letter; HB to Burns, 29 Sept 1952.

13. Woodruff to HB, 8 Oct 1952; HB to David Knowles, 20 Feb 1952.

14. HB to Woodruff, 13 Feb 1951; HB to T. S. Gregory, 9 May 1951; HB to Vellacott, 25 Feb 1952. See HB to H. R. Aldridge (British Museum), 31 May 1949. See Chadwick, "Acton and Butterfield," 394–397. Butterfield's and Eve Bogle's notes are spread in several files.

15. HB, "Lord Acton," *Cambridge Journal*, 6 (1952–1953), 475–485. He broadcast the BBC lecture on 19 June 1952.

16. HB, "Acton and the Massacre of St. Bartholomew," *Cambridge Historical Journal*, 11 (1953), 27–47; see "Lord Acton," 480.

17. "Lord Acton," 475–485. Acton, "The Study of History," in Fears, ed., *Selected Writings of Lord Acton*, 2: 513–514.

18. HB to Kingsford, 20 Jan 1953; HB to Vellacott, 3 Feb 1953; HB to Burns, 3 Feb 1953; Kingsford to HB, 6 Feb 1953.

19. HB to O. Evennett, 1 Feb 1956. Conzemius to HB, 3 June and 4 Dec 1956; HB to Conzemius, 30 Jan 1957. Victor Conzemius, ed., Ignaz von Döllinger, *Briefwechsel, 1820–1890*. 4 vols. (Munich: C. H. Beck, 1963–1981). Butterfield reviewed the first volume, the letters with Acton, 1850–1869: HB, "Lord Acton's Correspondence with Döllinger," *Historical Journal*, 9 (1966), 140–144.

20. *Letters and Diaries of John Henry Newman* [various editors], 31 vols. (Oxford: Clarendon Press; London and New York: Thomas Nelson, 1961–1977).

21. HB to R. W. David (CUP), 21 Oct 1965. Damian McElrath to HB, 26 June 1965, and 6 Oct 1965; HB to David, 21 Oct 1965; David Knowles to David, 25 Oct 1965. J. L. Altholz and Damian McElrath, eds., *The Correspondence of Lord Acton and Richard Simpson*, 3 vols. (Cambridge: Cambridge University Press, 1971–1975). See Chadwick, "Acton and Butterfield," 394–397.

22. See Gerald Humphrey (Headmaster, Leys School) to HB, 15 May 1950. My interviews with Eve Bogle and Butterfield.

23. HB to Director, Buckinghamshire County Record Office, 25 Sept 1953.

24. C. W. Previté-Orton, *The Shorter Cambridge Medieval History*, 2 vols. (Cambridge: Cambridge University Press, 1952). Previté-Orton's contract for this set apparently, like Butterfield's, dated from the 1930s.

25. Kingsford to HB, 3 April 1951.

26. HB to Vellacott, 25 Feb 1952.

27. HB to J. R. M. Butler, 18 Nov 1952; HB to R. C. Smail, 18 Nov 1952.

28. The extant typescripts in Butterfield's papers belonging to the revision of the 1950s are labelled "Modern European History Lectures." For Butterfield's commitment to the necessity of including the "material factors" within the interaction, see HB, "Marxist History," *History and Human Relations*, especially 66–86.

29. See HB to Isaiah Berlin, 16 May 1953; HB to Adolf Spemann, 3 Feb 1953.

30. See *Christianity and History*, chap. 7.

31. Butterfield's talk over the BBC entitled "Scientific Diplomacy" was not published, but he expanded it into his lecture "The Scientific versus the Moralistic Approach in International Affairs": HB to Michael Oakshott, 16 July 1951. See HB, *Cambridge Pocket Diary* for 1952–1953.

32. *Christianity, Diplomacy and War*, chaps. 1–3.

33. *Christianity, and History*, 137, 139; *Christianity, Diplomacy and War*, 5–6, 25–26, 34ff., 97, 111, 121–122.

34. *Christianity, Diplomacy and War*, 5–6, 35, 102–106; *Christianity and History*, 138–139.

35. "The Scientific versus the Moralistic Approach in International Affairs," *International Affairs*, 27 (1951), 411–422; "The Tragic Element in Modern Conflict," 17–29; *Christianity and History*, 142; *Christianity, Diplomacy and War*, 62–68, 74–77. HB to John (Adam) Watson, 2 May 1949.

36. "Tragic Element in Modern International Conflict," 18–23.

37. *Christianity, Diplomacy and War*, 37–40, 44, 52, 68, 85–86, 111.

38. "Tragic Element," 25–27, 30; *Christianity, Diplomacy and War*, 106–107, 115–116, 125–126. See HB to Beloff, 19 Oct 1951.

39. *Christianity, Diplomacy and War*, 5–6, 9–10, 20–21, 23–26, 83–84, 98–99.

40. *Christianity, Diplomacy and War*, 54–55, 81–86, 107, 114.

41. *Christianity, Diplomacy and War*, 82.

42. *Christianity, Diplomacy and War*, 23–24, 54–55, 93, 106–109.

43. *Christianity, Diplomacy and War*, 29–30, 57, 72, 101, 107–108, 111, 122.

44. Acton to Mandell Creighton, Cannes, 5 April 1887, in Fears, ed., *Selected Writings of Lord Acton*, 2: 383; "The Scientific versus the Moralistic Approach," 411, 418.

45. *Christianity, Diplomacy and War*, 9–10.

46. *Christianity, Diplomacy and War*, 29–30; the numbers in brackets are mine, not Butterfield's.

47. *Christianity, Diplomacy and War*, 84, 98.

48. *Christianity, Diplomacy and War*, 81, 84, 86–88.

49. *Christianity, Diplomacy and War*, 108ff.

50. *Christianity, Diplomacy and War*, 114–118.

51. Stuart Hampshire, in *New Statesman and Nation* (22 Aug 1953); H. G. Wood, in *Birmingham Post* (19 Jan 1954); Maurice B. Reckitt, in *Time and Tide* (29 Aug 1953); Martin Wight, in *Observer* (15 Aug 1953); Coulson to HB, 29 Sept 1951, and HB to Coulson, 4 Oct 1951, where he gives a long defense of his idea of "scientific diplomacy" and "technical diplomacy."

52. Editorial, *Life* (2 Nov 1953).

53. Charles Van Doren to HB, 20 Feb 1952; HB to Van Doren, 20 Feb 1952.

54. "The Highest Thing," *Times Literary Supplement* (21 Aug 1953); Charles Webster, "Lay Sermons," *Spectator* (21 Aug 1953), 204; A. R. Burns, in *History*, 40 (1955), 151–152.

55. HB, Thought-essay, 1953; HB to Reckett, 28 August 1953.

56. HB to Berlin, 16 May 1953, Berlin to HB, 1 Sept 1953, HB to Berlin, 21 Sept 1953, Berlin to HB, c25 Sept 1953.

57. HB to Acland, 27 Nov 1953. When Acland approached Butterfield, "Let's Start Waging Peace" already included as signatories G. D. H. Cole, Frida Laski, Charles Raven, Donald Soper, Mervyn Stockwood, and about twenty others inside and outside Parliament.

58. Thompson to HB, 12 April 1954; HB to Thompson, 26 April 1954; Thompson to HB, 30 April 1954 — in file: Rockefeller Foundation.

59. Eric Ashby (vice-chancellor, Queen's University, Belfast) to HB, 22 Oct 1952; Ashby to HB, 9 May 1953; Ashby to HB, 12 May 1953; HB to Ashby, 15 May 1953; HB to Janet D. Boyd (founder of the Wiles Trust), 15 May 1953; see *Man on His Past*, xi.

60. HB, "The Wiles Lectures at Queen's University, Belfast" (typs, 7p, Jan 1954). Vellacott to HB, 14 May 1953, and 29 Jan 1954. HB to Ashby, 15 May 1953.

61. HB, *Cambridge Pocket Diary*, 1954–1955. HB, "Man and His Past" (BBC, four scripts, typs, 89p, Nov and Dec 1954).

62. See HB to Kingsford, 18 March 1955; M. H. Black to HB, 29 April 1955. The contract for *Man on His Past* was part of the agreement between CUP and the Wiles Trust to publish the lectures annually, beginning with Butterfield's.

63. *Man on His Past*, xv; HB to Ashby, 6 Oct 1954.

64. *Man on His Past*, xii–xv, 103.

65. HB, "The Wiles Lectures at Queen's University, Belfast"; HB to Ashby, 6 Oct 1954; *Man on His Past*, xiii, 22–23.

66. See "Appendices" to *Man on His Past*, 205–232, where he displays his fascination with Acton's attachment to the history of historiography.

67. "Reconstruction of an Historical Episode," *Man on His Past*, 151, 154.

68. HB, *Cambridge Pocket Diary*, 1945–1946; Eve Bogle, *Cambridge Pocket Diary*, 1945–1946. See HB to Humphrey Sumner, 28 March 1947.

69. HB, review of Pieter Geyl, *Napoleon: For and Against*, in *Time and Tide* (22 Jan 1949), 80; *Man on His Past*, xv, 3–5.

70. *Christianity and History*, 12–25.

71. "Reconstruction of an Historical Episode," 142.

72. "Reconstruction of an Historical Episode," noting especially 143, 145, 152, 161–162. See the review of the little book *Reconstruction of an Historical Episode* published by the *English Historical Review*, 67 (1952), 447.

73. "Reconstruction of an Historical Episode," 143, 151, and passim; see also *Man on His Past*, xiii, 1–2, 103, 141.

74. "Reconstruction of an Historical Episode," 160–162, 169–170; see also *Man on His Past*, 15, 60–61, 100.

75. Butterfield's notes and lists on Acton's research appear in numerous files in his papers.

76. "Acton and the Massacre of St. Bartholomew," *Man on His Past*, 171–181, 186–195.

77. "Acton and the Massacre of St. Bartholomew," 67, 181–183, 186–187, 199–201. Hill, *Lord Acton*, 184–185.

78. "Acton and the Massacre of St. Bartholomew," 193–195, and the section called "Loose Ends," 195–201.

79. *Man on His Past*, 2–3, 14.

80. *Man on His Past,* 2–14, 39–61. On page 5, Butterfield writes at the start of his brief survey of the rise of the German school of the history of historiography, "The first of this series Göttingen history professors, J. C. Gatterer, wrote in 1760. . . . "

81. See the sections entitled "Its Subject-Matter and Its Scope" and "Its Utility for the Student of History," in *Man on His Past,* 14–26.

82. *Man on His Past,* xiii–ix, 17–18, 42.

83. *Man on His Past,* 22–25, 64.

84. "The Rise of the German Historical School," *Man on His Past,* 32–61, esp. 61; see also "Preface," xiv and xv.

85. *Man on His Past,* xvi.

86. *Man on His Past,* 15.

87. *Man on His Past,* 1, and see note 1.

88. "Acton and the Historical Movement," *Man on His Past,* 94.

89. *Man on His Past,* 139–140. See Sewell, "The Concept of Technical History in the Thought of Herbert Butterfield"; also Sewell, *Providence and Method,* chap. 9.

90. *Man on His Past,* 139, and compare 94, 95.

91. Pieter Geyl, in *Cambridge Historical Journal,* 12 (1956), 89–92; and Geyl, *Encounters in History* (London: Collins, 1963), 252–257.

92. *Man on His Past,* 140–141; see HB, *God in History,* Church of England Youth Council News-Letter Reprint, No. 2, 1952. See Michael Hobart, "History and Religion in the Thought of Herbert Butterfield," *Journal of the History of Ideas,* 32 (1971), 543–554; and Geyl, "Herbert Butterfield, or Thinking at Two Levels," in *Encounters in History,* 252–257.

93. *Man on His Past,* 141.

94. "Preface," *Man on His Past,* xi–xii.

95. "Ranke and the Conception of 'General History,'" *Man on His Past,* 104–109.

96. "Ranke and the Conception of 'General History,'" 114–116; and see the section "The Problem of Universal History," *Man on His Past,* 44–50.

97. "Preface," *Man on His Past,* xii–xiii, 21–21.

98. *Times Literary Supplement* (2 Dec 1955); Boyd C. Shafer, in *American Historical Review,* 61 (1956), 930–31; Eric John, in *History,* 41 (1956), 192–193; Duncan Forbes, in *Cambridge Review* (19 Nov 1955), 208–209; Arnold Toynbee, in *Observer* (3 Nov 1955); *Economist* (12 Nov 1955); Outram Evenette, in *Tablet* (31 Dec 1955); *Times Educational Supplement* (9 Dec 1955); G. M. Young, in *Sunday Times* (23 Oct 1955); Ernest Nagel, in *New York Nation* (3 March 1956). See Eric J. Sharpe, *Comparative Religion: A History* (London: Duckworth, 1975), 290–292.

99. Butterfield himself very kindly spoke with me about his son. Others who were willing to discuss the life of Giles Butterfield with me were Eve Bogle, Denis Mack Smith, Brian Wormald, and R. W. K. Hinton. Butterfield included news about his children in letters to various people from time to time.

100. Gerald Humphrey to HB, 15 May 1950.

101. HB to J. Opochensky, 2 Oct 1952; HB to Wolfgang von Tirpitz, 9 March 1954; HB to John Watson, 25 March 1954.

102. HB, *Cambridge Pocket Diary,* 1953–1954.

103. HB to Kenneth Thompson, 26 April 1954; HB to Desmond Williams, 14 July 1954. Butterfield, Eve Bogle, Denis Mack Smith, and Brian Wormald talked about these things in their interviews with me.

104. George Potter to HB, 15 June 1954; HB to Potter, 16 June 1954. See HB to Milton Waldman (Collins), 5 Nov 1957. See Adrian Morey, *David Knowles: A Memoir* (London: Darton, Longman and Todd, 1979).

105. HB, "Paul Vellacott," *Times*, 16 Nov 1954; HB, "Paul Vellacott: Master of Peterhouse," *The Sex*, 114 (June 1956), 1–4.

106. HB, *Cambridge Pocket Diary*, 1954–1955.

107. Knowles to HB, 7 Dec 1954.

108. HB to Governors, Birkbeck College, London, 4 Dec 1950. Lovatt, in *David Remembered*, 116–117.

Chapter 10 Master and Aggression

1. Butterfield himself compiled what is probably the most accurate list of the succession of Masters, in HB, "The Colleges and Halls of the University: Peterhouse," in Roach, ed., *A History of the County of Cambridge and the Isle of Ely*, 3:339–340. Maurice Cowling, "Raymond Williams in Retrospect," *New Criterion* (8 Feb 1990). See *Keighley News* (22 Jan 1955).

2. Interviews with various Peterhouse Fellows. Eve Bogle to CTM, 10 June 1986; Bogle to CTM, 13 Feb 1987. See Mehta, *Fly and the Fly-Bottle*, 245. HB to Mehta, 17 Jan 1963. Maya Jaggi, "Ved Mehta," *Guardian* (25 Aug 2001).

3. The others listed in the Faculty of History were (1955): Norman Sykes (Dixie Ecclesiastical), A. H. M. Jones (Ancient), E. E. Rich (Vere Harmsworth Imperial and Naval), C. R. Cheney (Medieval), P. N. S. Mansergh (Smuts British Commonwealth), and the annually changing chair (American).

4. Quoted in *The Sex*, 113 (1954), 13.

5. Tim Voelcker, "Peterhouse and the Fellows," *The Sex*, 113 (1954), 24–25.

6. Matriculation figures are in *The Historical Register of the University of Cambridge, Supplement 1951–1955*. Figures for distribution by fields are based on an enrolment of 154, as in *Peterhouse 1951–1953* (published by the college for the Peterhouse Society).

7. "Peterhouse Survey," *The Sex*, 111 (June 1952), 23–26. See *The Sex*, 114 (June 1956).

8. See HB, *Cambridge Pocket Diary*, from 1954 onwards. See Charles Walker, "The Chapel," *The Sex*, 114 (June 1956), 16–17; Maurice Cowling, "Butterfield, Sir Herbert (1900–1979)," *Dictionary of National Biography, 1971–1980*, 117.

9. HB, "Peterhouse in Temperley's Time" (ms, 60p, c1956).

10. HB, "Peterhouse," in Roach, ed., *A History of the County of Cambridge and the Isle of Ely*, 3:334–340. Butterfield's abundant notes for this history remain in the Peterhouse Archives.

11. *Peterhouse 1939–1943, Peterhouse 1949–1951, Peterhouse 1949–1951, Peterhouse 1951–1953, Peterhouse 1955–1968*: all published by the college for the

Peterhouse Society. See also HB, "Cambridge during the War: Peterhouse," *Cambridge Review* (1 Dec 1945), 140. Some of his speeches to the Peterhouse Society remain in his papers.

12. HB, "History in the Twentieth Century," in *Jubilee Addresses 1956* (London: Historical Association, 1956), 26. HB, "In Defence of History: Association of Teachers and Laymen," *Times Educational Supplement* (6 Jan 1956), 10.

13. Lists of Engagements for 1955 through 1958. HB, *Cambridge Pocket Diary* for those years.

14. HB, "Renaissance Art and Modern Science," *University Review,* 1:2 (1954), 25–34. Several versions of Butterfield's lecture on Leonardo are in his papers, and none was published.

15. HB, "The Historian and His Evidence" (typ, 22p, c1955).

16. HB, "The Role of the Individual in History," *History,* 40 (1955), 1–17; see HB, *Man on His Past,* xvi.

17. *The Historical Association, 1906–1956* (London: Historical Association, 1955). HB to Medlicott, 2 May 1955; HB to Geoffrey Barraclough, 2 May 1955; Stretton to HB, 18 June 1955. See also HB, "The History of the Historical Association," *History Today,* 6 (1956), 63–67.

18. HB (de facto editor), *Historical Writing,* a special issue of the *Times Literary Supplement* (6 Jan 1956), with introduction by Butterfield, i–xxvii. See HB to E. H. Carr, 12 Feb 1960, where he claims that he got the TLS to do the special number. HB, "Clio in Council," *Times Literary Supplement* (6 Jan 1956), 7. HB, "History in the Twentieth Century," 16–28.

19. "Clio in Council," 7; "History in the Twentieth Century," 23.

20. See for example, HB, review of Gordon Rupp, *The Righteousness of God: Luther Studies,* in *Cambridge Review* (13 Feb 1954), 300.

21. HB to Edward F. D'Arms (Rockefeller Foundation), 10 May 1956; HB to Wormald, 15 Nov 1956. Wormald prepared a description in November 1956 for a course entitled "European Historiography since the Renaissance," and the course was first offered in 1960–1961.

22. See *Man on His Past,* xvi. Research students producing theses on the history of historiography included: John Nurser on the idea of conscience in Lord Acton; Hedra Ben-Israel on English historiography of the French Revolution; and David W. L. Earl on Rapin de Thoyras and the English historiography of his time.

23. Felix Raab, *The English Face of Machiavelli: A Changing Interpretation, 1500–1700* (London: Routledge and Kegan Paul, 1964); Donald R. Kelley, *Foundations of Modern Historical Scholarship: Language, Law, and History in the French Renaissance* (New York: Columbia University Press, 1970), v; Joseph M. Levine, *Humanism and History: Origins of Modern English Historiography* (Ithaca: Cornell University Press, 1987), 214.

24. See Namier, *The Structure of Politics.* HB, plan for "The Wiles Lectures at Queen's University, Belfast" (Jan 1954). See G. R. Elton, *The Practice of History* (Sydney: Sydney University Press, and London: Methuen, 1967), 132. The first volumes of Namier's project appeared after his death in 1960: Lewis Namier and John Brooke, eds., *The History of Parliament: The House of Commons, 1754–1790,* 3 vols. (London: Published for History of Parliament Trust by H. M. Stationery Office, 1964); other volumes followed until 1983.

25. HB to Desmond Williams, 23 March 1955. Plumb, "The Road to Professional History," *Collected Essays,* 1: 9.

26. HB to Ross J. S. Hoffman (Fordham University), 29 May 1957.

27. HB to Vice-Chancellor, Cambridge University, and Master of Christ's College, 11 April 1957. See HB, "Historiography in England" (ms, 22p, late 1961 or early 1962), 14.

28. I have read many such letters in Butterfield's papers with his approval before they were deposited in Cambridge University Library, where most such correspondence is held under general restrictions of confidentiality until 2030! HB, "Historiography in England," 1, 3, 8. See C. H. Sisson, "The English Ideology," *Times Literary Supplement* (6 Feb 1981), 129.

29. HB, "George III and the Historians" (typ, 64p, March 1956). HB, "Historiography of George III" (typ, 16p, Anglo-American Historians Conference, July). The notes are in the file: History of the Historiography of George III. Some of the draft writings are in the file: Anglo-American Conference, July 1956.

30. HB, "George III and Historical Method," review of John Brooke, *The Chatham Administration, 1766–68,* in *Cambridge Review* (1 Dec 1956), 232–233. See HB to Milton Waldman (Collins), 5 Nov 1957.

31. HB, "The Originality of the Namier School," review of J. B. Owen, *The Rise of the Pelhams,* in *Cambridge Review* (25 May 1957), 614–616.

32. Kendall (Collins) to HB, 23 Jan 1952; HB to Waldman, 5 Nov 1957.

33. HB, "George III and the Namier School," *Encounter* (April 1957), 70–76. HB to Hoffman, 22 May 1957.

34. HB to Vice-Chancellor, Cambridge University, and Master of Christ's College, 11 April 1957.

35. HB, *George III and the Historians* (London: Collins, 1957). See HB to Waldman, 1 April 1957; Mark Bonham Carter (Collins) to HB, 9 April 1957; Carter to HB, 17 Sept 1957.

36. HB to Adrian House (Collins), 2 Nov 1957; HB to Waldman, 5 Nov 1957.

37. HB to Carter, 11 Sept 1957; HB to Waldman, 5 Nov 1957.

38. HB to Desmond Williams, 28 Jan 1958.

39. Lewis Namier, Foreword to John Brooke, *The Chatham Administration, 1766–68* (London: Macmillan, 1956); *George III and the Historians,* 285.

40. HB to Waldman, 5 Nov 1957.

41. *George III and the Historians,* Book 3, chaps. 3–7. See HB, "Bolingbroke and the 'Patriot King,'" *Cambridge Review* (10 March 1933), 308–310.

42. Namier, *The Structure of Politics at the Accession of George III* (2d ed.: London: Macmillan, 1957). See Cannon, *Teaching History at University,* 8.

43. Notable are: *Times Literary Supplement* (22 Nov 1957); *Times Educational Supplement* (27 Dec 1957); *Times* (London), (28 Nov 1957); C. L. Mowat, in *William and Mary Quarterly,* 16 (1959), 121–28.

44. Cobban to HB, 23 Oct 1957, and HB to Cobban, 25 Oct 1957; HB to the Editor, *Times Literary Supplement* (29 Nov 1957), 721. HB, "George III and the Constitution,' *History,* 43 (1958), 14–33. Ian R. Christie, "George III and the Historians — Thirty Years On," *History,* 71 (1986), 215.

45. Reviewers favourable to Butterfield's criticism of Namier included: Michael Oakeshott, in *Spectator* (22 Nov 1957); David Thomson, in *Time and Tide* (23 Nov 1957); A. J. P. Taylor, in *Observer* (7 Nov 1957); Arthur Schlesinger, in *Encounter* (March 1958), 73–77; W. T. Laprade, in *American Historical Review,* 63 (1958), 967–68; Derek Beales, "Sir Lewis Namier and the Party System," *Cambridge Review* (31 May 1958), 599, 601, and 603.

46. R. R. Sedgwick, in *Listener* (5 Dec 1957), and in *Daily Telegraph* (23 Nov 1957).

47. John B. Owen, "Professor Butterfield and the Namier School," *Cambridge Review* (10 May 1958), 528–531.

48. Lewis B. Namier to the Editor, *Times Literary Supplement* (6 Dec 1957); HB to the Editor, *Times Literary Supplement* (13 Dec 1957).

49. Namier to HB, 16 Dec 1957; HB to Namier, 18 Dec 1957, 13 Jan 1958, and 10 Dec 1958; Namier to HB, 11 Dec 1958. HB to Desmond Williams, 28 Jan 1958.

50. HB to Desmond Williams, 28 Jan 1958, and 19 May 1958. HB to the Editor, *Cambridge Review* (17 May 1958).

51. Elton, *The Practice of History,* 132–133. On Namier's religion, see Plumb, "The Road to Professional History," 10–12.

52. Christie, "George III and the Historians," 210–211, 214, 215–221. Plumb, "The Atomic Historian," *New Statesman* (1 August 1969), in *Collected Essays,* 1: 12–16.

53. Linda Colley, *Lewis Namier* (London: Weidenfeld and Nicholson, 1989), 108. See, for example, H. T. Dickinson, *Liberty and Prosperity: Political Ideology in Eighteenth Century Britain* (London: Weidenfeld and Nicholson, 1977), 3. G. R. Elton, *Political History: Principles and Practice* (London: Allen Lane, 1970), 106–107.

54. HB, "Sir Lewis Namier as Historian," *Listener* (18 May 1961), 873–876; HB, " 'The History of Parliament,' " *Listener* (8 Oct 1964), 535–537. Brooke to the Editor, *Listener* (15 Oct 1964), 591. See also HB, review of Namier and Brooke, eds., *The History of Parliament: The House of Commons,* in *English Historical Review,* 80 (1965), 801–805. See Mehta, *Fly and the Fly-Bottle,* 238–269, especially 243. HB to Mehta, 17 Jan 1963.

55. Boyd C. Schafer (Executive Secretary of the American Historical Association) to HB, 13 Sept 1962; HB to Schafer, 8 Oct 1962.

56. J. C. D. Clark, *The Dynamics of Change: The Crisis of the 1750s and English Party Systems* (Cambridge: Cambridge University Press, 1982), 448; Clark, *English Society, 1688–1832,* 8. Patterson, *Nobody's Perfect,* 1–3, 11–17.

57. HB, draft of *England and the French Revolution, 1792* (typs, 250p, c1957). See Felix Markham to HB, 30 April 1963; and HB to Markham, 14 May 1963.

Chapter 11 World Ideas, World Politics

1. HB, Jerusalem Lectures I and II (typ, c35p, Jerusalem, 1957); HB, Paper given to School of Oriental and African Studies (typ, 20p, London, Jan 1958).

2. HB, *History as the Emancipation from the Past* (London: London School of Economics and Political Science, 1956), a booklet of 18 pages.

3. HB, "Christianity in the Twentieth Century" (typ, four lectures, c100p, Bristol, Jan–Feb 1956).

4. HB to Editor, *Times* (10 Nov 1956), published 12 Nov 1956.

5. HB, review of Reinhold Niebuhr, *Faith and History: A Comparison of Christian and Modern Views of History*, in *Observer* (29 Jan 1950).

6. Editor of Longman's Publishers to HB, 29 March 1957.

7. Arnold Toynbee, *A Study of History*, vols. 7–10 (London: Oxford University Press, 1954). See C. T. McIntire and Marvin Perry, *Arnold J. Toynbee: Reappraisals* (Toronto: University of Toronto Press, 1989). See also HB, "The History of the Writing of History," *Rapports du Congrès International des Sciences Historiques, Stockholm, 21–28 août 1960* (Goteborg: Almquist and Wiksell, 1960), 1: 29.

8. Toynbee, *An Historian's Approach to Religion* (London: Oxford University Press, 1956).

9. Toynbee to HB, 2 June 1950; G. Cumberlege to HB, 6 Sept 1954. Toynbee, *A Study of History*, 8: 118–119, 170, 498–500, and 9: 46–47, 66–69, 191–196, 206–208. Toynbee, review of HB, *Man on His Past*, in *Observer* (3 Nov 1955). Toynbee, *Reconsiderations*, vol. 12 of *A Study of History* (London: Oxford University Press, 1961); HB, review of *Reconsiderations*, in *Sunday Telegraph* (7 May 1961).

10. See M. S. Khan to HB, 21 Oct 1957 and 25 Dec 1957.

11. See folder: Bibliography, which contains titles on the history of historiography.

12. See HB circular letter, 5 Dec 1958, sent to various people, including C. H. Phillips (Director, SOAS) and Peter Hardy (research student in Islamic Studies at SOAS).

13. HB, "Historiography," (typ, 150p), translated into Hebrew by his former doctoral student Hedra Ben-Israel, and published in *Encyclopedia Hebraica* (1960), 14: col. 259–318.

14. Barraclough to HB, 5 Feb 1960; HB to Barraclough, 12 Feb 1960, and 18 March 1960.

15. E.g.: HB, "The Christian and History," *Spectator* (29 April 1955), 540–543; HB, "Christianity and Humanism" (typ, 12p, Oct 1955, Christ's College, Cambridge).

16. HB, review of Rudolf Bultmann, *History and Eschatology*, in *Times Literary Supplement* (30 Aug 1957), 522. Butterfield's "thought-essays" about Bultmann are in the file: Bultmann.

17. The series in Bristol contained four lectures under the title "Christianity in the Twentieth Century" (typs, c100p, Bristol, Jan–Feb 1956). Three were published in CTM, ed., HB, *Writings on Christianity and History* (1979). They are: "The Challenge to Belief," "The Obstruction to Belief," and "The Prospect for Christianity." The remaining lecture, "Religion and the Problems of the World," was actually the third in the series, and is unpublished.

18. The Robert Waley Cohen Lecture for 1956, sponsored by the British Council of Christians and Jews, and published as HB, *Historical Development of the Principle of Toleration in British Life* (London: Epworth Press, 1957), a booklet of 17 pages.

19. HB, "The Prospect for Christianity," in *Writings on Christianity and History*, 253–254, 259–260.

20. HB, "Morality and Historical Process in International Affairs" (typ, 49p, New York, June 1956). A report of the discussion was kept: "Theory of International Relations Meeting, 2:00p.m., June 12, 1956, Men's Faculty Club, Columbia University" (typ, 9p). Those present, in addition to Butterfield, were: William T. R. Fox, Louis Halle,

Reinhold Niebuhr, Paul Nitze, Kenneth Thompson, Arnold Wolfers, and Kenneth Waltz (rapporteur); Hans Morgenthau could not come that day, but sent comments on the paper, which had been distributed to the participants in advance. George Kennan joined the group some time later. See HB to Martin Wight, 6 May 1958.

21. HB, "I ought not to talk about politics. . . . " (ms, 18p, 27 April 1956, Peterhouse Chapel Fellowship).

22. "Morality and Historical Process," 1–3, 15.

23. "Morality and Historical Process," 8.

24. "Morality and Historical Process," 18–21.

25. "Morality and Historical Process," 28–29.

26. "Morality and Historical Process," 32–35, 46–49.

27. "Theory of International Relations Meeting, June 12, 1956"; HB to Martin Wight, 6 May 1958.

28. Niebuhr and Bennett to HB, 20 Dec 1956; HB to Niebuhr, 1 Jan 1957; HB to Wayne Cowen, 17 Nov 1960; plus other letters in folder: Christianity and Crisis.

29. Watson to HB, 1 Nov 1955; HB to Watson, 10 Nov 1955.

30. Wayne Cowen to HB, 10 June 1965; HB to Cowen, 10 June 1965. HB, "Internationalism and the Defense of the Existing Status Quo." *Chrisitianity and Crisis* (10 June 1957), 75–77; and HB, "Western Policy and Colonialism," *Christianity and Crisis* (4 Aug 1958), 111–114. The 1957 article was included in Wayne Cowen, ed., *Witness to a Generation: Significant Writings from Christianity and Crisis, 1941–1966* (Indianapolis: Bobbs-Merrill, 1966), 79–83, with preface by HB, vii–ix.

31. "Theory of International Relations Meeting, 12 June 1956."

32. Butterfield recounted the beginnings of the committee in *Raison d'Etat,* 5–6. HB to Thompson, 17 Oct 1956; Thompson to HB, 14 Dec 1956; HB to Thompson, 1 Jan 1957.

33. HB to Wight, 6 May 1958; HB to Thompson, 6 May 1958; Wight to HB, 9 May 1958; HB to Thompson, 27 Dec 1958. See the memoir by Adam Watson, "The British Committee for the Theory of International Politics: Some Historical Notes (Nov 1998)," posted on this website: [www.ukc.ac.uk/politics/englishschool/watson98.doc].

34. HB to Williams, 1 July 1960; HB to Watson, 10 March 1959; Wight to HB, 3 Aug 1960; and various letters in folder: Rockefeller Committee, Personal Material. See Haslam, *Vices of Integrity,* 251–252.

35. HB, "Misgivings about the Western Attitude to World Affairs" (ms, 68p, Jan 1959, Peterhouse). The papers read are in two boxes: Rockefeller Committee Papers.

36. HB, "The Balance of Power," April 1959, published with revisions, in HB and Martin Wight, eds., *Diplomatic Investigations: Essays in the Theory of International Politics* (London: George Allen and Unwin, 1966), 132–148.

37. HB, *International Conflict in the Twentieth Century: A Christian View* (New York: Harper, 1960). See HB to Anshen, 7 Dec 1959. See also HB to Kenneth Thompson, 18 Feb 1960, where he acknowledges putting material from the New York paper in the book. See Alberto R. Coll, *The Wisdom of Statecraft: Sir Herbert Butterfield and the Philosophy of International Politics* (Durham: Duke University Press, 1985).

38. *International Conflict,* 15–19, 34, 83.

39. *International Conflict,* 41–57, esp. 48–49, 56–57.

40. Haslam, *Vices of Integrity,* 190–191.

41. *International Conflict,* 36–38, 54–55, 71–72, 91, 97–98, 104–106.

42. *International Conflict,* 63–65, 71–78.

43. "Human Nature and the Dominion of Fear," *International Conflict,* 81–98. HB to Kenneth Thompson, 9 Nov 1959.

44. *International Conflict,* 95–96.

45. HB, Diary, August 1945.

46. *International Conflict,* 95–98.

47. HB, Draft statement against nuclear weapons (typ, 5p, 1958). HB, paper to the Cambridge Christian Action Group, 1959.

48. "Christianity and Global Revolution," *International Conflict,* 101–120; *Writings on Christianity and History,* 254.

49. HB to Knowles, 3 March 1956.

50. Annan, *The Dons,* 266–267. Plumb, *Collected Essays,* 1: 7, 164–165, 374. HB to Knowles, 8 Oct 1955. Kitson Clark, "History at Cambridge, 1873–1973," 550–553.

51. Kitson Clark to HB, 15 Jan 1955; HB to G. K. Clark, 20 Jan 1955. HB to Knowles, 18 Oct 1954. HB to Kitson Clark, 12 Dec 1957; Kitson Clark to HB, 16 Dec 1957; Knowles to HB, 18 Dec 1957. See Kitson Clark to HB, 7 Oct 1951, a friendly letter in which Kitson Clark took the same view against team research in Namier's "History of Parliament" project that Butterfield latter expressed in public.

52. For two years, 1971–1973, I participated with pleasure in Kitson Clark's colloquium, which met in his rooms over the Great Gate of Trinity College. The courses, which ran between 1962 and 1966, were: "Materials of Modern History," with Butterfield, Kitson Clark, C. H. Wilson, F. H. Hinsley, and Peter Laslett; and "Classes on Select Topics in the Materials of Modern History," with Butterfield, Elton, C. B. A. Behrens, Peter Mathias, J. H. Elliott, C. W. Crawley, and J. P. T. Bury.

53. Those attending the meeting with Butterfield were: C. W. Crawley, O. Evennett, J. P. T. Bury, F. H. Hinsley, C. B. A. Behrens, Jean Lindsay, Denis Mack Smith, and Charles Wilson. HB to Knowles and Plumb, 21 Feb 1957; Knowles to HB, 22 Feb 1957; Plumb to HB, 25 Feb 1957. HB circular letter to Lecturers in European History, 27 Feb 1957; Behrens to HB, 8 March 1957; HB to Behrens, 12 March 1957; Behrens to HB, 14 March 1957; HB to Behrens, 15 March 1957. HB to Crawley, 30 Jan 1957.

54. Spear to HB, 20 July 1959. HB, Speech at the opening of an art exhibition at Keighley, summer 1961, in: Miscellaneous Comments. See Simba Vellacott to HB, 3 Dec 1959.

Chapter 12 *The Top and After the Top*

1. The archives of the University of Cambridge for Butterfield's time as vice-chancellor have not been open to me for research. Since my interest is, in any case, Butterfield as historian, I have been content to use the following principal sources: letters, speeches, documents, and other materials in Butterfield's papers; Butterfield's *Cambridge Pocket Diary*; interviews with Butterfield, Eve Bogle, Fellows of Peterhouse, and a few other people active at the time, including Owen Chadwick (Dixie Professor of Ecclesiastical History from 1958), C. R. Cheney (Professor of Medieval History from 1955), and Joseph Needham (History of Science); the publications of the university, notably the

Cambridge University Reporter; and comment on Butterfield in the public press and in the *Cambridge Review.*

2. HB to Eric Ashby, 30 Oct 1967.

3. HB to Wayne Cowen, 17 Nov 1960; HB to Harcourt Brown, 12 Aug 1960

4. HB to CTM, 24 May 1979.

5. See Butterfield's first official address as vice-chancellor, 1 Oct 1960, in *Cambridge University Reporter*, 91 (1960–1961), 256–261.

6. Many of Butterfield's speeches and talks remain scattered throughout his papers, but especially in a collection named: Miscellaneous Comments. See Butterfield's second official address as vice-chancellor, 2 Oct 1961, in *Cambridge University Reporter*, 92 (1961–1962), 253–258.

7. Owen Chadwick, "Sir Herbert Butterfield," *Cambridge Review* (16 Nov 1979), 8.

8. HB, "The American Student — A Visiting Professor's View: Is He Lacking in Intellectual 'Drive'?," *Saturday Review* (13 Sept 1958), 25. His visit to Wabash College came in March and early April 1958.

9. HB, *The Universities and Education Today* (London: Routledge and Kegan Paul, 1962), 8, 20–23. He gave the lectures over a period of three weeks in November 1961.

10. HB to Frank Cumbers (Epworth Press), 9 March 1960.

11. HB, "Why I Am a Non-Conformist" (typ, 23p, June 1959). See W. F. Flemington to Bernard Watson, 10 Nov 1959. Watson wrote three articles on Butterfield in *Vanguard* (Nov 1959, Dec 1959, Jan 1960), the periodical of the Salvation Army in England.

12. HB, "Reflections on Religion and Individualism," *Journal of the History of Ideas*, 22 (1961), 33–46. HB, No title: on Methodism, (ms, 6p, cSept 1961).

13. See many of his memoir notes from the 1970s. He stressed the differences emphatically in his interviews with me.

14. HB to P. E. Schramm, 24 Oct 1961; HB to Joseph Altholtz, 14 July 1961; HB to Eric Ashby (vice-chancellor, Cambridge University), 30 Oct 1967. HB, Speech at the opening of an art exhibition in Keighley, summer 1961.

15. See Butterfield's reports to the Peterhouse Society for 1960 and 1961. See also *Peterhouse 1968* (Published by the College for the Peterhouse Society, 1968), probably written by Butterfield, which covered the activities of the college during Butterfield's time as Master. It was the first such report since the series stopped with Butterfield's election as Master.

16. HB, "Historiography in England" (ms, 22p, late 1961 or early 1962).

17. H. N. V. Temperley to HB, 5 Nov 1961; HB to Temperley, 4 Dec 1961; HB to Dorothy Temperley, 13 Aug 1958.

18. HB, "Temperley" (ms, 173p, c1962/1963); HB, "Personal: Early Youth, Father, Temperley, Vellacott" (ms, 67p, c1962/1963). HB, "Temperley and Canning," in Temperley, *The Foreign Policy of Canning*, 2d ed.; HB, "Introduction to the Second Edition," in Temperley, *Frederic the Great and Kaiser Joseph*, 2d ed. See Fair, *Harold Temperley*, 12–13.

19. HB to Kenneth Thompson, draft ms, no date (late 1961 or early 1962), apparently not sent.

20. E.g., HB to Dean, New York University, 2 June 1967.

21. In the twentieth century, of the Regius Professors, only J. R. M. Butler seemed to make no impact on him, but to look up to him instead, embarrassingly so.

22. The other historians with professorships during Butterfield's time as Regius Professor were: Economic History: D. M. Joslin (succeeding Postan in 1965); Ancient: still Jones; British Commonwealth: still Mansergh; Imperial and Naval: still Rich; Political Science: Brogan; Political Economy: J. E. Meade. Special chairs were created: Modern English History (1966) for Plumb; Medieval Ecclesiastical History (1966) for Walter Ullman; English Constitutional History (1967) for Elton. J. R. Pole became a Reader in 1963; M. I. Finley in 1964; and F. H. Hinsley in 1965.

23. The first two chapters of *Whig Interpretation of History* appeared, without permission, as: HB, "L'interpretation 'progressiste' de l'Histoire," *La Table Ronde* (Feb 1967), 24–41. The various editions and reissues of Butterfield's books are listed in the bibliography following the original entry for each work.

24. See the file: America Invitations From (Accepted and Declined).

25. HB to Thompson, 27 April 1961.

26. Dean Rusk (Rockefeller Foundation) to HB, 18 Aug 1959; HB to John Marshall (Villa Serbelloni), 9 April 1960. HB to Thompson, 3 May 1962.

27. HB, *Charles James Fox: The Peace Negotiations of 1806* (London: University of London, The Athlone Press, 1962).

28. See Butterfield's handwritten statement at the top of the typescript of the lecture, in folder: 1806. See also folder: Additional 1806.

29. HB, "Reminiscences of an Enquiry into the Crisis of 1792" (typ, 19p, Peterhouse and Trinity College, 1963).

30. HB to Markham, 14 May 1963.

31. HB to F. H. Hinsley, 3 June 1962. See HB, "British Policy, 1762–1765," *Historical Journal*, 6 (1963), 131–140, a review of F. Spencer, ed., *The Fourth Earl of Sandwich: Diplomatic Correspondence, 1763–1765*.

32. The bulk of the lectures are in a bundle labelled: George III, 1760–1765. Three are in typescript from 1967, and the others are in manuscript from at least 1965 to 1968. Other lectures are in separate folders, including: George III; Education of George III; Party in the 18th Century.

33. HB, No title (the first lecture of the course on George III and the Politicians, 1760–1765), 2. See also Butterfield's diary notes about the discussions at the Conference of British Studies in New York in April 1963.

34. Brooke to HB, 26 Nov 1965.

35. Butterfield's public lectures included: "Some Controversial Issues of George III's Reign" (typ, 16p, Cambridge, 1963); "Earl of Bute and Frederick the Great" (Cambridge Historical Association, 1963); "The Early Years of George III" (various typ, c30p, Canterbury, Durham, York, 1968 and 1969). His published work included: HB, "Some Reflections on the Early Years of George III's Reign," *Journal of British Studies*, 4 (1965), 78–101; HB, "England in the Eighteenth Century," in Rupert Davies and Gordon Rupp, eds., *A History of the Methodist Church in Great Britain*, vol. 1 (London: Epworth Press, 1965), 3–33.

36. Gerard Emanuel Stearn (Prentice-Hall) to HB, 25 Nov 1966; HB to Stearn, 12 Jan 1967; HB to A. D. Peters, 12 April 1967; Peters to Peter C. Grenquist (Prentice-Hall), 2 May 1967; HB to Stearn, 14 June 1967; and see other letters in folder: George III: Great Lives Observed.

37. Barraclough to HB, 21 Aug 1963.

38. Blake to HB, 14 Dec 1968; HB to Blake, 2 Jan 1969.

39. Hamlyn to HB, 8 Aug 1967; HB to Hamlyn, 11 Aug 1967.

40. See Norman J. G. Pounds, *An Historical Geography of Europe,* 3 vols. (Cambridge: Cambridge University Press, 1973–1985).

41. HB to David, 10 Feb 1964; David to HB, 14 Feb 1964. See David to HB, 21 April 1966. See drafts of passages for the *Concise History* with 1964 written on them, in the bundle: The Enlightenment.

42. HB, "Acton: His Training, Methods, and Intellectual System," in A. O. Sarkissian, ed., *Studies in Honour of G. P. Gooch* (London: Longman's 1961), 169–198; HB, *Lord Acton* (20p in Italian; Milan: Vità e Pensiero, 1962).

Chapter 13 Going Global

1. HB, "The History of the Writing of History," *Rapports du XI Congrès International des Sciences Historiques,* 1: 25–39.

2. "The History of the Writing of History," 26–28, 35–38.

3. HB to Momigliano, Phillips, Schieder, 9 Aug 1960; HB to John Marshall (Villa Serbelloni), 31 Aug 1960; Marshall to HB, 6 Sept 1960.

4. HB to Marshall, 26 Sept 1960. HB, draft about a "Conference of those working on the History of Historiography" (after 26 Sept 1960).

5. Nadel to HB, n.d. (cAug/Sept 1960) — the letter probably was written after Butterfield's address at the Stockholm conference.

6. Minutes of the Organizational Meeting of the International Society for the History of Ideas, 30 Jan–1 Feb 1959, New York. See various letters in folder: History of Ideas (Society for the).

7. HB, *History and Man's Attitude to the Past: Their Role in the Story of Civilization* (London: University of London School of Oriental and African Studies, 1961). HB, "History and Man's Attitude to the Past," *Listener* (21 Sept 1961), 421–423.

8. Joseph Needham, ed., *Science and Civilisation in China* (Cambridge: Cambridge University Press, 1954–). My interviews with Butterfield; my interview with Needham.

9. HB, *History and Man's Attitude to the Past*; HB, "History and Man's Attitude to the Past," 421–423.

10. HB, review of Toynbee, *Reconsiderations,* vol. 12 of *A Study of History,* in *Sunday Telegraph* (7 May 1961).

11. HB, *Universities and Education Today,* 65–66, 104–05. E. G. Pulleyblank to the Editor, and Jane Hutchings to the Editor, *Listener* (28 Sept 1961), 473; HB to the Editor, *Listener* (5 Oct 1961), 503.

12. HB, "The History of the East," *History,* 47 (1962), 157–165, review of *Historical Writing on the Peoples of Asia,* vols. 1–3. He reviewed vol. 4 in *History,* 50 (1965), 396–397.

13. See folders: Development of Historical Criticism; and Dublin Lecture — Historical Criticism. The papers include the following: HB, "The Rise of Historical Criticism" (typ, 16p, 1962); HB, "The Use of Historical Materials" (typ, 7p, 1962); HB, no title (Second lecture on the Use of Materials, typ, 17p, 1962); HB, no title (on Development of Historical Criticism, typ, 41p, c1962/1963); "Criticism in the Pre-Critical Age" (typ, 20p,

Wesleyan University, 1965). His notes are collected in various folders (e.g., Thucydides, Latin Historiography) or unnamed boxes of notes.

14. HB, no title — on the Christian believer and the academic historian (typ, 10p, Rice University, 1963).

15. HB, *History and Man's Attitude to the Past,* 10–11; the remark about Augustine is from my interviews with Butterfield. Butterfield purchased books by these people for his own library, and his notes and the underlinings in the books indicate his readings. These books went to Peterhouse Library.

16. HB to Kenneth Thompson, 13 May 1964; HB to John Marshall, 9 Feb 1965; HB to Thompson, 14 July 1965.

17. HB, "Preface for Gifford Lectures" (typ, 3p, 1965). In what follows, I have used where possible Butterfield's texts labelled "GIFFORD LECTURES," which include his handwritten annotations.

18. The original texts of some, but not all, of his Gifford Lectures, with his handwritten additions, remain in his papers. These typescripts carry the heading "GIFFORD LECTURES."

19. No title (ms, 7p, c1964), in folder: Gifford, Old Testament.

20. Toynbee, review of HB, *Man on His Past,* in *Observer* (3 Nov 1955).

21. Butterfield summarized his new enterprise in the history of historiography in an address c1968, in Miscellaneous Comments.

22. HB, "History as the Organization of Man's Memory," in Paul H. Oehser, ed., *Knowledge among Men: Eleven Essays on Science, Culture, and Society Commemorating the 200th Anniversary of the Birth of James Smithson* (New York: Simon and Schuster, 1966), 33–42; HB, *The Remembrance of Things Past.*

23. HB to Michael Roberts, 21 Oct 1966; HB to R. W. David (CUP), 12 Oct 1966; HB to A. D. Peters, 10 April 1968; David to HB, 23 April 1968; HB to Secretary of the Syndic, Cambridge University Press, 6 May 1968; Peters to HB, 7 May 1968; HB to David, 20 May 1968; and other letters in folder: CUP and Wiles Trust.

24. HB, "Some Reflections on the Early Years of George III's Reign," *Journal of British Studies,* 4 (1965), 78–101; HB, "England in the Eighteenth Century," in Davies and Rupp, eds., *A History of the Methodist Church in Great Britain,* 1: 3–33.

25. HB to Martin Wight, 29 June 1966; HB, Remarks on international relations at the London School of Economics (ms, 15p, late 1960s).

26. HB, Memorandum of discussion in the British Committee on the Theory of International Politics, cApril 1961. See Leonard Liggio, "Herbert Butterfield: Christian Historian as Creative Critic," *New Individualist Review,* 1, 3 (Nov 1961), 29.

27. See HB, Talk, c1967, in: Miscellaneous Comments.

28. HB to A. J. Muste (Church Peace Commission, New York), 24 Nov 1960; HB to Tony Southall (Cambridge University Campaign for Nuclear Disarmament), 30 Nov 1961; HB to Eleanor Aitken (Petition for The Hague Peace Rally), 1 May 1964.

29. John Stacy (Methodist Peace Fellowship) to HB, 12 April 1963; HB to Stacy, 30 March 1964, and 11 April 1964.

30. HB, *Human Nature and the Dominion of Fear* (London: Christian CND Pamphlet No. 3, 1964).

31. HB, "Human Nature and the Dominion of Fear," in *Breakthrough to Peace* (Norfolk, Conn.: New Directions, 1962), 159–171.

32. HB, Journal, 12 Jan 1968; Journal, cJuly 1968.

33. See HB talks in: Miscellaneous Comments.

34. HB to Thompson, 18 Jan 1963.

35. The papers and notes are in two boxes: Rockefeller Committee Papers. See HB to Martin Wight, 7 April 1968.

36. HB to Thompson, draft letter c. early 1962; HB, "Notes for a Discussion on the Theory of International Politics" (typ, 8p, Jan 1964), 1; HB to Wight, 29 June 1966; HB to Wight, 7 April 1968; HB to Thompson, 24 July 1968.

37. HB, Remarks on International Relations at the London School of Economics (ms, 15p, late 1960s). Butterfield's notes and other materials are in a box: History of Diplomacy. See Adam Watson, "Introduction," in HB, *The Origins of History,* ed. Adam Watson (New York: Basic Books, 1981), 10–11.

38. HB and Wight, "Preface," *Diplomatic Investigations,* 12–13.

39. HB, "Notes for a Discussion on the Theory of International Politics" (typ, 8p, Jan 1964).

40. HB, "The Great Powers" (typ, 7p, July 1964).

41. HB, "The Historic 'States-Systems' " (typ, 6p, Jan 1965).

42. See HB, review of Arnold Toynbee, *Reconsiderations.*

43. Outline of contents for a volume on states-systems, April 1967; HB, No title, on the origins of the European states-system (typ, 10p, c1965); HB to Wight, 7 April 1968.

44. See HB to Boyd C. Schafer, 8 Oct 1962.

45. HB, "In Defence of Diplomatic History" (typ, 23p, Cambridge University History Club, Nov 1963).

46. "In Defence of Diplomatic History."

47. HB, *The Present State of Historical Scholarship: An Inaugural Lecture* (Cambridge: Cambridge University Press, 1965).

48. HB to T. S. Gregory, 8 May 1964.

49. See letters in files: German Visit May 1964; German Visit 1965.

50. See HB to P. E. Schramm (Göttingen), 8 March 1965; HB to the British Council, 7 Aug 1964.

51. HB, "Sir Edward Grey in July 1914," *Historical Studies,* 5 (1965), 1–25.

52. HB, Address (two drafts, ms, 8p, and ms, 9p, University of Bonn, July 1968); HB, "In Defense of Diplomatic History," 7.

53. HB, *Universities and Education Today,* 79. HB, talk to an American audience, c1967, in folder: Miscellaneous Comments.

54. See Butterfield's notes on Wesley in the file: Wesley. See also HB, Talk on Methodism, in: Miscellaneous Comments (ms, 6p, 1961). Butterfield's copy of John Wesley's *Sermons on Several Occasions,* 3 vols. (London: Wesleyan Conference Office, 1864) is well marked. HB, "The Springs of Intellectual Vitality," in Marjorie Reeves, ed., *Eighteen Plus: Unity and Diversity in Higher Education* (London: Faber and Faber, 1965), 196–199.

55. HB and R. Y. Jennings to the Editor, *Methodist Recorder,* 25 April 1964.

56. HB to C. K. Barrett, 18 Oct 1965, sending his signature of the statement circulated by the National Liaison Committee, and adding his marginal comments.

57. HB, "Basil Willey, A Tribute: The English Mind" (typ, 2p, 1964).

58. HB to Francis Rundall, 10 Aug 1967; HB to G. S. Windass, 2 March 1970.

59. HB statement to the *Cambridge News,* 6 June 1967; HB to Rundall, 10 Aug 1967; HB to D. W. L. Earl, 16 Feb 1968; HB to Windass, 2 March 1970.

60. HB to the Secretary to the Syndic, Cambridge University Press, 6 May 1968.

61. Cowling, "Butterfield," *Dictionary of National Biography, 1971–1980,* 116.

Chapter 14 Nothing but History and Religion

1. See e.g., HB to M. H. Varvill, 10 Oct 1969; HB to Peter J. Stanlis, 20 June 1969. Butterfield discussed his "retirement project" in my interviews with him.

2. HB, No title: On the Reformation (typ, 6p, BBC Television script, 1965). HB, "Evil in History" (typ, 5p, BBC Television, 1970). See Kathleen Burk, *Troublemaker: The Life and History of A. J. P. Taylor* (New Haven: Yale University Press, 2000). HB, Speech to a society of Cambridge Alumni, cOct/Nov 1968.

3. J. H. Elliott and H. G. Koenigsberger, eds., *The Diversity of History: Essays in Honour of Sir Herbert Butterfield* (London: Routledge and Kegan Paul; Ithaca: Cornell University Press, 1970).

4. Knowles to HB, 5 June 1974.

5. Many, but by no means all, of the sheets of his thoughts are in the files: Christianity; From July 1968; Memoirs. See Butterfield's talks and speeches in: Miscellaneous Comments; and in: Bonn, Honours Degree. His published writings around this time usually contained some autobiographical remarks.

6. HB, Memoir of G. P. Gooch (ms, c90p, c1969). HB, "George Peabody Gooch, 1873–1968," *Proceedings of the British Academy,* 55 (1969), 311–338; HB, "George Peabody Gooch, 1873–1968," *Year Book of the American Philosophical Society* (1969), 122–26. HB, "G. P. Gooch," *Contemporary Review,* 213 (Nov 1968), 226–228. See Eyck, *G. P. Gooch,* 4, 57.

7. "Sincerity and Insincerity in Charles James Fox," in *Proceedings of the British Academy,* 57 (1971), 3–27.

8. HB, *The Remembrance of Things Past,* 3.

9. HB, Journal, 12 Jan 1968; various, July 1968; 2 July 1970; and other entries c1970.

10. HB, Journal, cJuly 1968.

11. HB, Speech to Kingswood School, c1968. HB, Speech to a society of Cambridge graduates, HB to Brown. 24 June 1969; cOct/Nov 1968. HB, Journal, cJuly 1968, 23 Aug 1970.

12. HB to Black, 6 June 1969; Brown to HB, 20 June 1969; HB to Black, 24 June 1969; and other letters in file: Cornell. See HB, "Historiography," *Dictionary of the History of Ideas,* 2 (New York: Charles Scribner, 1973), 464–498.

13. HB, Talk to Peterhouse Society, cJune 1968. He referred to his interview with the undergraduate newspaper *Varsity* about the admission of women. Speech to a society of Cambridge graduates, cOct/Nov 1968.

14. HB, *The Discontinuities between the Generations in History: Their Effect on the Transmission of Political Experience* (Cambridge: Cambridge University Press, 1972), 17–23. HB, No title, on the nature of political history (ms, 34p, c1972), 33–34.

15. HB, "Revolution" (ms, 34p, Corpus Christi College, Cambridge, 1972), 1–2. He added to the text, but then removed, these words, after the phrase "encouraging the competitive spirit": "consigning us to the struggle for existence."

16. "Revolution," 1–2, 9–11, 20–23; *The Discontinuities between the Generations,* 26–27.

17. "Revolution," 29–32; HB to Henry Steele (Felix) Commager, 6 Sept 1968. Butterfield referred to the China case in my interviews with him.

18. HB to the Editor, *Times* (London), draft, c1972.

19. "Revolution," 32–33.

20. I attended Butterfield's Rede Lecture in November 1971.

21. *The Discontinuities between the Generations,* 8, 30–32. See HB, *The Remembrance of Things Past,* 7. HB, "Revolution," 9. HB to CTM, 24 May 1979.

22. *The Discontinuities between the Generations,* 17, 27–29.

23. *The Discontinuities between the Generations,* 12–13. HB, Journal, cApril 1968. See Butterfield's notes and letters in the file: International Politics, Theory of.

24. HB, thought-essay on English party politics (ms, 8p, 3 Oct 1969), in file: Christianity.

25. HB, Journal, 23 Aug 1970.

26. Journal, c1968/1969.

27. Journal, various, c1968, and 23 Aug 1970; HB to CTM, 9 July 1976.

28. Journal, various, July 1968.

29. What follows is based especially on: HB, Journal notebook on religion, cSept 1968 (ms, 47p; on one page the date for "yesterday" appears as 29 Sept 1968); and Journal writings in file; Christianity. In making quotations, I have written out all words which Butterfield abbreviated, e.g., Xn = Christian, and Xty = Christianity.

30. Journal, 1 Sept 1970.

31. Journal, 8 July 1973.

32. Journal, 11 June 1967.

33. HB to C. K. Barrett, 18 Oct 1965.

34. Journal, July 1968.

35. HB, Speech to the History Faculty, Cambridge, 12 Nov 1968, in: Miscellaneous Comments.

36. HB, *The Discontinuities between the Generations,* 28.

37. HB, *The Remembrance of Things Past,* 8.

38. HB, *The Discontinuities between the Generations,* 32.

39. HB, No title, Sermon-Address, St. Giles Cathedral, Edinburgh (mimeograph for distribution, 19 April 1970).

40. See particularly Butterfield's talks around the time of his retirement in: Miscellaneous Comments.

41. HB to Francis Rundall, 10 Aug 1967.

42. See file: American Academy of Arts and Sciences.

43. HB to Frank O'Gorman, 7 March 1966; HB to Felix Markham, 17 Feb 1960.

44. C. A. Williamson to HB, 18 Sept 1967; M. H. Varvill to HB, 3 Oct 1969; HB to Varvill, 10 Oct 1969.

45. HB, "Sincerity and Insincerity in Charles James Fox"; and HB, *Sincerity and Insincerity in Charles James Fox* (London: Oxford University Press, 1972).

46. *Sincerity and Insincerity,* 17–18.

47. *Sincerity and Insincerity,* 27.

48. HB to D. F. Allen (Secretary of the British Academy), 26 July 1972.

49. HB to Peter J. Stanlis, 20 June 1969; HB to M. H. Varvill, 10 Oct 1969.

50. HB, "The Early Years of George III" (various typ, c30p, Canterbury, Durham, York, 1968 and 1969).

51. "Early Years of George III," the opening pages for the version presented at Durham and York (ms, 4p, 1969).

52. R. W. David to HB, 9 June 1969; HB to David, 21 Oct 1969.

53. The old materials and new draft are in the folder: Acton and the Cambridge Modern History.

54. HB to Damian McElrath, 17 Aug 1966; HB to S. W. Jackson, 21 April 1967; HB to Knowles, 2 June 1967.

55. See the file: Acton Papers 1972. Chadwick, "Acton and Butterfield," 396–397.

56. HB, Remarks on International Relations at the London School of Economics (ms, 15p, c1968/1969). HB, "The Development of Diplomacy" (ms, 38p, c1969). Butterfield's materials are in a box: History of Diplomacy. See Watson, "Introduction," in HB, *The Origins of History,* 10–11.

57. HB, "Balance of Power," *Dictionary of the History of Ideas,* 1 (New York: Charles Scribner, 1973), 179–188.

58. HB, "The Moral Framework of International Relations" (Aberystwyth, 1969), in the file: The Moral Framework of International Relations. The section on the core ethical principles is in a draft version of his remarks, but was not placed in the printed version: HB, "Morality and an International Order," in Brian Porter, ed., *The Aberystwyth Papers: International Politics, 1919–1969* (London: Oxford University Press, 1972), 336–357.

59. HB, *Raison d'État.* He delivered the lecture on 23 April 1975.

60. HB to Neville Temperley, 4 May 1968; Neville Temperley to HB, 9 May 1968. Humphrey Temperley, Neville Temperley's son, Harold Temperley's grandson, was attending Peterhouse at the time.

61. Peters to HB, 7 May 1968; various letters and lists from 1970 in the folder: Publication of Essays.

62. HB, Speech, c1968, in: Miscellaneous Comments.

63. HB, "Some Trends in Scholarship, 1868–1968, in the Field of Modern History," *Transactions of the Royal Historical Society,* 5th series, 19 (1969), 159–184.

64. HB, "Narrative History and the Spade-Work behind It," *History,* 53 (1968), 165–180, esp. 165–167. The article started off as a review J. R. Hale, ed., *The Evolution of British Historiography from Bacon to Namier* (1967).

65. HB, *Magna Carta in the Historiography of the Sixteenth and Seventeenth Centuries* (Reading: University of Reading, 1969).

66. HB, "The Nature of Political History" (ms, 34p, c1972).

67. HB, "Universal History and the Comparative Study of Civilization," in Fehl, ed., *Sir Herbert Butterfield, Cho Yun Hsu, William H. McNeill on Chinese and World History,* 24–26.

68. See Arnold J. Toynbee with Jane Caplan, *A Study of History,* new edition in one volume (London: Oxford University Press, 1972). Contrast that with: Arnold Toynbee, *Mankind and Mother Earth: A Narrative History of the World* (London: Oxford University Press, 1976).

69. HB, "Universal History and the Comparative Study of Civilization," 24–25.

70. HB, "Historiography," *Dictionary of the History of Ideas,* 464–498. The original text is in the file: Dictionary Typescript. HB to Philip P. Wiener, 22 Aug 1969.

71. HB, "Universal History and the Comparative History of Civilization," 21–23; HB, "The Nature of Political History," 1–5.

72. HB, "Christianity in History," *Dictionary of the History of Ideas,* 373–412.

73. "Christianity in History," 396.

74. Butterfield's lectures at Duke (April 1969): "The Originality of the Old Testament," "The Development of a Christian View of History," "Christianity in a Secularized World," and "Christianity and Contemporary Affairs." His lectures at Chapel Hill (April 1969): "The Historian and Morality," "Moral Judgments in History," "Christianity and the Practising Historian," and "History as the Struggle of Good and Evil." The lectures at Northwestern (April 1974): "The Conflict between Right and Wrong in History," "The Originality of the Old Testament," "The Modern Historian and the New Testament," and "Does Belief in Christianity Validly Affect the Modern Historian?"

75. HB, "Global Good and Evil": part I, "The Moderate Cupidity of Everyman," *New York Times* (3 Jan 1973), 39, and part II, "Inward to Glory," *New York Times* (4 Jan 1973), 37.

76. HB, "Evil in History" (typ, 5p, BBC Television), March 1970.

77. HB, "Does Belief in Christianity Validly Affect the Modern Historian?" (typ, 19p), lecture 4 of the series The Secular Historian and the Christian Religion, Northwestern University, April 1974, as revised in 1977). See the file: "Can belief in Christianity validly affect the work of the modern technical historian?"

78. See "Does Belief in Christianity Validly Affect the Modern Historian?" Butterfield offered the figure of less than 10 percent in my interviews with him.

79. See HB folder: Egypt: New Material 1973.

80. HB, Journal, 5 April 1973.

81. HB, Journal at Villa Serbelloni, 1973. HB, "Villa Serbelloni under John Marshall," in John Burchard, ed., *Thoughts from the Lake of Time: A Group of Essays in Honor of the Villa Serbelloni and Especially John and Charlotte Marshall* (New York: Josiah Macy Junior Foundation), 269–275.

82. The original typescripts of the five chapters revised from the Gifford Lectures as well as the revised fragments for later chapters are in a box: History of Historiography — drafts used for "The Origins of History."

83. The new role for China and the failure of India are announced in his revised preface. HB, review of J. H. Plumb, *The Death of the Past,* in *Cambridge Review* (29 May 1970), 195.

84. Compare the original Gifford Lectures with the revisions. The original typescripts marked: "GIFFORD LECTURES"; the revisions in a box: History of Historiography — drafts used for "The Origins of History." See also HB, "Universal History and the Comparative Study of Civilization," 19, 24–26.

85. HB, "The History of Encyclopedias," *Times Literary Supplement* (17 May 1974), 531–533.

86. HB, "Address at the Memorial Service for Sir Denis Brogan," Great St. Mary's Church, 9 Feb 1974; HB, "Denis Brogan," *Encounter* (April 1974), 64–66. Butterfield sent a memoir of Knowles to Dom Adrian Morey for use in preparing Morey, *David Knowles: A Memoir* (London: Darton, Longman and Todd, 1979).

87. HB, Journal, 16 Jan 1975, 28 Jan 1975, and many other entries around the same period.

88. Pamela Butterfield to CTM, 3 June 1979; Peter Butterfield and Robin Butterfield to CTM, 15 June 1979; telephone conversation with Pamela Butterfield and Peter Butterfield, 29 June 1979; Peter Butterfield to CTM, 21 June 1979. See Maurice Cowling, "Butterfield, Sir Herbert," *Dictionary of National Biography, 1971–1980* (1986), 116–117.

89. Watson, "Introduction," in HB, *Origins of History*, 10–11.

90. Contrary to how the book is sometimes listed, it was not a posthumous work.

91. HB, "Moral Judgments" (ms, 11p, May 1977, written in response to an interview with me).

92. HB, *Origins of History*, passim.

93. Watson briefly describes the editorial process in "Introduction," *Origins of History*, 10–12. The texts which served as the basis of the book are in the box: History of Historiography—drafts used for "The Origins of History." The original Gifford Lectures and various other revised portions or versions are scattered in Butterfield's papers, including these folders: Untitled (Gifford lectures?); Beginnings of historical writing; Mesopotamia; Butterfield's essays; H. Butterfield's essays. Christianity; History of historical criticism.

94. Review by Lester D. Stephens, in *American Historical Review*, 87 (1982), 1041.

Conclusion

1. HB, *Man on His Past*, 21–22.

2. HB to the Secretary to the Syndics, Cambridge University Press, 6 May 1968.

3. E. P. Thompson, *The Making of the English Working Class* (London: Victor Gollancz, 1963). E. P. Thompson, *Whigs and Hunters: The Origins of the Black Act* (London: Allen Lane, 1975).

4. One day I came across a chat in progress on the Internet that somehow brought up "Whiggish History." The most self-assured of the participants clarified the issue: "The term 'Whig (or Whiggish) history' has its origin in Herbert Butterfield's book *The Whig Interpretation of History* (1931) which I haven't read, but as far as I know the term was used by Butterfield as meaning. . . . " Carsten Sestoft, accessed 7 April 1998.

5. HB, Memoir, 1970s.

6. HB, Note, 1970s, quoting Virginia Woolf to Clive Bell, Feb 1909, in HB 32, folder: E.

7. Interview with Eve Bogle, 1986.

8. HB, *The Discontinuities between the Generations*.

9. HB, *Christianity and History*, 146.

10. HB, "Global Good and Evil": part I, "The Moderate Cupidity of Everyman," *New York Times* (3 Jan 1973), 39.

11. INFP: Introvert⟨Extrovert⟩, iNtuitive⟨Sensing⟩, Feeling⟨Thinking⟩, Perceiving ⟨Judging⟩.

12. HB, "God in History," in CTM, ed., *God History, and Historians*, 192–204; and in CTM, ed., HB, *Writings on Christianity and History*, 3–16. HB, *Man on His Past*, 140–141.

13. See, for example, Ernst Breisach, *Historiography: Ancient, Medieval, and Modern,* 2d ed. (Chicago: University of Chicago Press, 1994).

14. Owen Chadwick, *Freedom and the Historian: An Inaugural Lecture,* delivered 27 Nov 1968 (Cambridge: Cambridge University Press, 1969). See Chadwick, "Sir Herbert Butterfield," *Cambridge Review* (16 Nov 1979), 6–8.

15. From my conversation with Lord Dacre, Peterhouse, 1986.

Bibliography

1. By Butterfield: Published Works

This list offers a chronological record of all of Butterfield's published books, booklets, chapters in books, and articles known to me. It does not list his writings that are simply book reviews, although it includes review articles, and it does not aim to include all reprintings of his writings. It is clear to me that Butterfield did not know everything that he had published. In July 1978, he sent me a list of his writings published since 1968, and I soon realized that he had left off a fair number of pieces.

This list is the result of a thorough search in Butterfield's papers as well as in the usual bibliographical resources. It adds to and extends three other bibliographies of his works. Eileen Partington compiled a record of his writings, including his reviews, to the year 1963, in "Bibliography of Works by and about Herbert Butterfield" (Project for Diploma, University of London School of Librarianship, 1963). R. W. K. Hinton, Fellow of Peterhouse, listed most of his scholarly works, and a few book reviews, to the year of his retirement, in "Bibliography of Sir Herbert Butterfield's Writings (to 1968)," in J. H. Elliott and H. G. Koenigsberger, eds., *The Diversity of History: Essays in Honour of Sir Herbert Butterfield* (London: Routledge and Kegan Paul, and Ithaca: Cornell University Press, 1970), 315–325. Keith C. Sewell published an extensive bibliography in *Providence and Method: Herbert Butterfield and the Intepretation of History* (Sioux Center, Iowa: By the Author, 2001), 224–254. His bibliography provides the fullest list to date of book reviews written by Butterfield as well as reviews of Butterfield's books written by others. I am aware of more reviews not listed there, but I have not sought to include reviews here.

I have marked with an *asterisk the twenty-two volumes which, for the purposes of this study, I have counted as a "book" by Butterfield. This includes three books that he edited or coedited, and two books of his writings edited by others with his approval. Two further books collecting some of his writings were edited by others after his death.

Within each year, books and booklets are placed first, followed by articles and chapters, listed alphabetically within those groupings.

c1917, a poem, possibly published at Keighley, not found.

"Editorial," *The Sex*, 73 (Lent 1922), 3–12.

*The Historical Novel: An Essay. Cambridge: Cambridge University Press, 1924. Folcroft: Folcroft Library Editions, 1971; Norwood: Norwood Editions, 1975; Philadelphia: R. West, 1977.

"A French Minister at Vienna, 1806–1807," *Cambridge Historical Journal* 2 (1927), 185–190.

*The Peace Tactics of Napoleon, 1806–08. Cambridge: Cambridge University Press, 1929. Reprint ed., with new preface: New York: Octagon, Hippocrene Books, 1972.

*Ed., Select Documents of European History, vol. 3, *1715–1920*. London: Methuen, 1931.

*The Whig Interpretation of History. London: Bell, 1931. London: Bell, 1950; New York: Charles Scribner, 1951; New York: Norton, 1965; Harmondsworth: Penguin, 1973; New York: AMS Press, 1978; eText: <http://www.eliohs.unifi.it/testi/900/butterfield>, 2002.

"Bolingbroke and the 'Patriot King,'" *Cambridge Review* (10 March 1933), 308–310.

"History and the Marxian Method," *Scrutiny*, 1 (1932–1933), 339–355.

"Wesley House Concert, March 3, 1933," *Wesley House Magazine* (June 1933), 4–5.

"History in 1934," *The Bookman*, 87 (1934), 141–143.

"The Philosopher as Historian," *The Bookman*, 87 (1934), 194–195.

"Lord North and Mr Robinson, 1779," *Cambridge Historical Journal*, 5 (1937), 255–279.

"The Master [Temperley]," *The Sex*, 104 (May 1938), 10–11.

*Napoleon. London: Duckworth, 1939. Revised ed., 1940, 1962. New York: Collier, 1962.

"Harold Temperley," *Cambridge Historical Journal*, 6 (1939), 123.

*The Statecraft of Machiavelli. London: Bell, 1940; republished, 1955. New York: Macmillan, 1956; London: Collier Macmillan, 1962; New York: Collier, 1962.

"Napoleon and Hitler," *Cambridge Review* (6 June 1941), 474–475.

"The Age of Napoleon" (with I. L. Foster), and "From Waterloo to Sedan," in *History and Administration*, vol. 2, B.R. 503A, in *France*, 4 vols., B.R. 503–503C, *Geographical Handbook Series*. London: Great Britain, Admiralty, Naval Staff, Naval Intelligence Division, 1942. 124–146, 147–165.

Peterhouse, 1939–1943. Cambridge: The Peterhouse Society, 1943.

"The History Teacher and Over-Specialisation," *Cambridge Review* (27 Nov 1943), 103–105.

*The Englishman and His History. Cambridge: Cambridge University Press, and New York: Macmillan, 1944. Reprint ed., with new preface: Hamden, Conn.: Archon, 1970.

The Study of History: An Inaugural Lecture. Cambridge: Cambridge University Press, 1944.

"Cambridge during the War: Peterhouse," *Cambridge Review* (1 Dec 1945), 140.

"Tendencies in Historical Study in England," *Irish Historical Studies,* 4: 15 (March 1945), 209–223.

"An Antidote to Dogmatic History," *Time and Tide* (12 Jan 1946), 29–30.

"The History of Science," *Time and Tide* (5 Jan 1946), 6–7.

"The Journal of Lord Acton: Rome 1857," *Cambridge Historical Journal,* 8 (1946), 186–204.

"The Master [Vellacott]," *The Sex,* 106 (1946), 5–6.

"Sir John Clapham, 1873–1946," *Cambridge Historical Journal,* 8 (1946), 115–116.

"The Birkbeck Lectures on Luther, Delivered by E. Gordon Rupp," *Cambridge Review* (24 May 1947), 490, 492.

"The General Board's Prime Stipend," *Cambridge Review* (8 March 1947), 328–330.

"Limits of Historical Understanding," *The Listener* (26 June 1947), 997–998.

"Reflections on the Predicament of Our Time," *Cambridge Journal,* 1 (1947), 5–13.

"The Yorkshire Association and the Crisis of 1779–80," *Transactions of the Royal Historical Society,* 4th series, 29 (1947), 69–91.

Lord Acton. London: The Historical Association, 1948.

Peterhouse, 1944–1948. Cambridge: The Peterhouse Society, 1948.

"A Bridge between the Arts and the Sciences," *The Listener* (15 July 1948), 95–96.

"The Protestant Church and the West," *The Listener* (24 June 1948), 1008–1009.

"The Teaching of English History," *Cambridge Journal,* 2 (1948), 3–10.

*Christianity and History. London: Bell, 1949. New York: Charles Scribner, 1950; London: Collins Fontana, 1957.

*George III, Lord North and the People, 1779–1780. London: Bell, 1949. New York: Russell and Russell, 1968.

*The Origins of Modern Science, 1300–1800, London: Bell, 1949. New York: Macmillan, 1951. Second ed., Bell, 1957; corrected 1970; New York: Macmillan, 1957; New York: Collier, 1962; New York: Free Press, 1965; Toronto: Clarke, 1968; London: Bell and Hyman, 1982.

"Charles James Fox and the Whig Opposition in 1792," *Cambridge Historical Journal,* 9 (1949), 293–330.

"The Christian and History," *The Christian News-Letter,* 4 parts: "The Christian and Academic History," Supplement to 333 (16 March 1949), 88–96; "The Christian and the Biblical Interpretation of History," Supplement to 336 (27 April 1949), 136–144; "The Christian and the Marxian Interpretation of History," and "The Christian and the Ecclesiastical Interpretation of History," Supplement to 341 (6 July 1945), 215–223, 224–232.

"Christianity and History," *The Listener,* 6 parts: "Christianity and the Historian" (7 April 1949), 559–560, 581–583; "Human Nature in History" (14 April 1949), 621–623, 626; "Judgment in History" (21 April 1949), 666–669, 672; "Cataclysm and Tragic Conflict" (29 April 1949), 711–713, 720; "Providence and Historical Process" (5 May 1949), 755–757, 760–761; and "Christianity as a Historical Religion" (12 May 1949), 794–796, 805–807.

"The History of Science," *Radio Times,* 76 (23 Sept 1949), 37.

"Official History: Its Pitfalls and Its Criteria," *Studies: An Irish Quarterly Review of Letters, Philosophy, and Science,* 38 (1949): 129–144.

"The Protestant View of Church and State," in *The Western Tradition*. London: Vox Mundi, 1949. Boston: Beacon Press, 1951, 45–50.

"The Christian Idea of God," *The Listener* (23 Nov 1950), 591, 594.

"Christianity and the Historian," *University of Chicago Round Table,* no. 661 (1950), 13–17.

"The Crucifixion in Human History," *British Weekly,* 127, 3308 (6 April 1950), 1–2.

"Europe, History of," *Chambers Encyclopedia,* 1950, 5: 467–481. New ed., 5: 442–454, including new passage "Post Second World War," 1966.

With Aelred Watkin, "Gasquet and the Acton-Simpson Correspondence," *Cambridge Historical Journal,* 10 (1950): 75–105.

"Die Gefahren der Geschichte," *Geschichte in Wissenschaft und Unterricht,* 1 (1950), 525–539.

"The Historian and the History of Science," *Bulletin of the British Society for the History of Science,* 1:3 (April 1950), 49–58.

"The Predicament of Central Europe," *Time and Tide* (14 Jan 1950), 31–32. German translation: "Das Mitteleuropaische Dilemma," *Die Bruecke,* 167: 405.

"The Predicament That Leads to War," *Time and Tide* (21 Jan 1950), 56.

"The Tragic Element in Modern International Conflict," *Review of Politics,* 12 (1950), 147–164; also published in *The Wind and the Rain,* 7:1 (Autumn 1950), 8–22.

*Christianity in European History, London: Oxford University Press; London: Collins, 1952.

*History and Human Relations. London: Collins, 1951. New York: Macmillan, 1952.

*De facto ed., The History of Science: Origins and Results of the Scientific Revolution. London: Cohen and West; Glencoe, Ill.: Free Press, 1951. Includes: "Dante's View of the Universe," 15–24, and "Newton and His Universe," 77–86. New ed. with new title, HB et al., *A Short History of Science: Origins and Results of the Scientific Revolution.* Garden City, N.Y.: Doubleday, Anchor Books, 1959.

Peterhouse, 1949–1951. Cambridge: The Peterhouse Society, 1951.

The Reconstruction of an Historical Episode: The History of the Enquiry into the Origins of the Seven Years' War, Glasgow University Publications, 91, Glasgow: Jackson, 1951.

"Broadcasting and History," *BBC Quarterly,* 6:3 (1951) 129–135.

"Christianity and Western Ideals," in *The Church and the Festival.* London: SPCK, 1951, 7–8, 10–11.

"The Contribution of Christianity to Our Civilization," in Festival of Britain Supplement, *Methodist Recorder* (3 May 1951), 1.

"Framework of the Future: By What Values?," *The Listener* (22 March 1951), 457–458. Reprinted in: *World Christian Digest* (July 1951), 24–26.

"Historical Perspective," *Britain Today,* 188 (Dec 1951), 6–10.

"A Historian Looks at the World We Live In," *Religion in Education,* 18 (1951), 43–49.

"The Natural Scientist," *Times Literary Supplement* (21 Sept 1951), 597.

"The Scientific versus the Moralistic Approach in International Affairs," *International Affairs,* 27 (1951), 411–422.

*_Liberty in the Modern World._ Toronto: Ryerson, 1952.

"God in History," _Church of England Youth Council News-Letter_ (July 1952). Also issued as booklet: _God in History,_ Church of England Youth Council News-Letter Reprint, No. 2, 1952. Reprinted in: R. J. W., ed., _Steps to Christian Understanding._ London: Oxford University Press, 1952. 105–121.

*_Christianity, Diplomacy and War._ London: Epworth; Nashville: Abington-Cokesbury, 1953.

Peterhouse, 1951–1953. Cambridge: The Peterhouse Society, 1953.

Acton and the Massacre of St. Bartholomew," _Cambridge Historical Journal,_ 11 (1953), 27–47.

"Lord Acton," _Cambridge Journal,_ 6 (1952–1953), 475–485.

"The Prospect for Christianity," _Religion in Life,_ 22 (1953) 271–379; _The Preacher's Quarterly,_ 1 (Dec 1954), 36–45.

"Foreword," in Edward Herbert Dance. _History without Bias? A Textbook Survey on Group Antagonisms._ London: Council of Christians and Jews, 1954, 7–11.

"Paul Vellacott," _Times_ (16 Nov 1954).

"Renaissance Art and Modern Science," _University Review,_ 1, 2 (1954), 25–34.

"The Seventeenth Century," _Encyclopedia Americana,_ 1954, 24: 613–618.

*_Man on His Past: The Study of the History of Historical Scholarship._ Cambridge: Cambridge University Press, 1955. Boston: Beacon Press, 1960, with a new preface.

De facto author, with "Foreword." _The Historical Association, 1906–1956._ London: Historical Association, 1955.

"The Christian and History," _Spectator_ (29 April 1955), 540–543.

"The Role of the Individual in History," _History,_ 40, 138–139 (Feb–June 1955), 1–17.

De facto ed., _Historical Writing,_ Special Issue, _Times Literary Supplement_ (6 Jan 1956), with "Introduction," i–xxvii.

History as the Emancipation from the Past. London: London School of Economics and Political Science, 1956.

"Clio in Council," _Times Literary Supplement_ (6 Jan 1956), 7.

"History in the Twentieth Century," in _Jubilee Addresses 1956._ London: Historical Association, 1956, 16–28.

"The History of the Historical Association," _History Today,_ 6 (Jan 1956), 63–67.

"In Defense of History: Association of Teachers and Laymen," _Times Educational Supplement_ (6 Jan 1956), 10.

"Paul Vellacott: Master of Peterhouse, 1939–1954," _The Sex,_ 114 (June 1956), 1–4.

"The Sense of the Past," _Times Literary Supplement_ (17 Aug 1956), x, xii.

*_George III and the Historians._ London: Collins, 1957. Revised ed., London: Cassell; New York: Macmillan, 1959.

Historical Development of the Principle of Toleration in British Life. London: Epworth, 1957.

"George III and the Namier School," _Encounter_ (April 1957), 70–76.

"History and Humanism," _Times Literary Supplement_ (20 Dec 1957), 773.

"Internationalism and the Defense of the Existing Status Quo," _Christianity and Crisis_ (10 June 1957), 75–77. With new title, "Christianity and the Status Quo," in Wayne Cowen, ed., _Witness to a Generation: Significant Writings from_ Christianity and Crisis,

1941–1966. Indianapolis: Bobbs-Merrill, 1966. 79–83. Internet: "Christianity and the Status Quo," *Religion Online* (http://www.religiononline.org), c2001.

"A Sense of the Past," *Times Literary Supplement* (27 Sept 1957), 577.

"The American Student—A Visiting Professor's View: Is He Lacking in Intellectual Drive?," *Saturday Review* (13 Sept 1958), 25.

"George III and the Constitution," *History,* 43 (1958), 14–33.

"Introduction to Machiavelli," in Nicolo Machiavelli, *The Prince,* trans. W. K. Marriott. London: Everyman, 1958. v–xi.

"Western Policy and Colonialism," *Christianity and Crisis* (4 Aug 1958), 111–114.

HB et al. *A Short History of France from Early Times to 1958.* Edited by Hampden Jackson. Cambridge: Cambridge University Press, 1959. Second ed., retitled, *A Short History of France from Early Times to 1972,* 1974.

"Christianity and the Global Revolution," *The Chaplain* (April 1959), 11–12.

"The Colleges and Halls of the University: Peterhouse," in J. P. C. Roach, ed., *A History of the County of Cambridge and the Isle of Ely,* 8, *The City and University of Cambridge.* London: Oxford University Press, 1959. 334–340.

"The Dominion of Fear," *Motive* (Jan 1959), 2–3.

"The History of Science and the Study of History," *Harvard Library Bulletin,* 13 (1959), 329–347.

"Introduction," in Arthur Koestler, *The Sleepwalkers: A History of Man's Changing Vision of the Universe.* London: Hutchinson; New York: Macmillan, 1959. 11–12. London: Penguin, 1964.

"Lord Acton," *Te Elfder Ure,* 9 (1959), 284–292.

"Macaulay as Historian: A Centenary Assessment," *Methodist Recorder* (31 Dec 1959), 9.

*International Conflict in the Twentieth Century: A Christian View. New York: Harper, 1960. Westport, Conn.: Greenwood, 1974.

"Historiography" (in Hebrew), *Encyclopedia Hebraica,* 1960, 14: col. 259–318.

"The History of the Writing of History," *Rapports du XI Congrès International des Sciences Historiques,* Stockholm, 21–28 août 1960. Goteborg: Almquist and Wiksell, 1960. 1:25–39.

"The Scientific Revolution," *Scientific American* (Sept 1960), 173–192.

History and Man's Attitude to the Past: Their Role in the Story of Civilization. London: University of London School of Oriental and African Studies, 1961.

"Acton: His Training, Methods, and Intellectual System," in A. O. Sarkissian, ed., *Studies in Diplomatic History and Historiography in Honour of G. P. Gooch.* London: Longman's, 1961. 169–198.

"George Peabody Gooch," *Contemporary Review,* 200 (July–Dec 1961), 501–505.

"History and Man's Attitude to the Past," *The Listener* (21 Sept 1961), 421–423.

"Portrait of a Turbulent Century," *Methodist Recorder* (6 April 1961), 3–4, 7.

"Reflections on Religion and Individualism," *Journal of the History of Ideas,* 22 (1961), 33–46. Reprinted in: Philip P. Wiener and Aaron Noland, eds., *Ideas in Cultural Perspective.* New Brunswick: Rutgers University Press, 1962. 725–738.

"Sir Lewis Namier as Historian," *The Listener* (18 May 1961), 873–876.

"The Springs of Discovery," *Observer Weekend Review* (9 July 1961), 17.

*The Universities and Education Today. London: Routledge and Kegan Paul, 1962.

Charles James Fox: The Peace Negotiations of 1806. London: University of London, The Athlone Press, 1962.

Lord Acton. Milan: Vità e Pensiero, 1962.

"Human Nature and the Dominion of Fear," in *Breakthrough to Peace.* Norfolk, Conn.: New Directions Books, 1962. 159–171.

"British Policy, 1762–1765," *Historical Journal,* 6 (1963), 131–140.

"Charlotte Brontë and Her Sisters in the Crucial Year," *Brontë Society Transactions,* 14 (1963), 3–17.

"Printing's Role in World Thought," *Times* (16 July 1963), 11.

[Untitled note on Trevelyan], *History,* 48 (1963), 44–45.

Human Nature and the Dominion of Fear. Pamphlet No. 3. London: Christian Campaign for Nuclear Disarmament, 1964.

"Additional Comments [on the Working Paper]," in *Report of the Seminar on Postgraduate Teaching and Research in History* [11–14 January 1964, Delhi University]. New Delhi: University Grants Commission, 1964. 22–24.

"Basil Willey: A Tribute," in Hugh Sykes Davies and George Watson, eds., *The English Mind: Studies in the English Moralists Presented to Basil Willey.* Cambridge: Cambridge University Press, 1964. 1–6.

"The History of Historiography and the History of Science," in *Mélanges Alexandre Koyré,* vol. 2, *L'aventure de l'esprit.* Paris: Hermann, 1964. 57–68.

" 'The History of Parliament,' " *The Listener* (8 Oct 1964), 535–537.

"The War That Shaped the World's Future," *Methodist Recorder* (30 July 1964), 10.

Moral Judgments in History. The Foundation Oration. London: Goldsmith College, 1965.

The Present State of Historical Scholarship: An Inaugural Lecture. Cambridge: Cambridge University Press, 1965.

"England in the Eighteenth Century," in Rupert Davies and Gordon Rupp, eds., *A History of the Methodist Church in Great Britain,* vol. 1. London: Epworth, 1965. 3–33.

"History as the Organisation of Man's Memory," *Nature* (11 Dec 1965), 1036–1039.

"Gooch, George Peabody," *Chambers World Survey 1965,* 1965, 208.

"In Memorian Winston Churchill," *Cambridge Review* (6 Feb 1965), 234.

"Sir Edward Grey in July 1914," *Historical Studies: Papers Read before the Sixth Conference of Irish Historians,* 5 (1965), 1–25.

"Some Reflections on the Early Years of George III's Reign," *Journal of British Studies,* 4 (1965), 78–101.

"The Springs of Intellectual Vitality," in Marjorie Reeves, ed., *Eighteen Plus: Unity and Diversity in Higher Education.* London: Faber and Faber, 1965. 186–199.

*With Martin Wight, eds., *Diplomatic Investigations: Essays in the Theory of International Politics.* London: George Allen and Unwin; Cambridge: Harvard University Press, 1966. Includes: "The Balance of Power," 132–148, and "The New Diplomacy and Historical Diplomacy," 181–192.

"Harold Temperley and George Canning," in Harold Temperley, *The Foreign Policy of Canning, 1822–1827: England, the Neo-Holy Alliance, and the New World.* London: Frank Cass, 1966. vii–xxvi.

"History as the Organization of Man's Memory," in Paul H. Oehser, ed., *Knowledge among Men: Eleven Essays on Science, Culture, and Society Commemorating the 200th Anniversary of the Birth of James Smithson.* New York: Simon and Schuster, 1966. 33–41.

"Preface," in Wayne Cowen, ed., *Witness to a Generation: Significant Writings from Christianity and Crisis, 1941–1966.* Indianapolis: Bobbs-Merrill, 1966. vii–ix.

"Christianity and Politics," *Orbis: A Quarterly Journal of World Affairs,* 10 (1967), 1233–1246.

"Delays and Paradoxes in the Development of Historiography," in Kenneth Bourne and D. C. Watt, eds., *Studies in International History: Essays Presented to W. N. Medlicott.* London: Longmans, Green, 1967. 1–15.

"L'interpretation 'progressiste' de l'histoire," *La Table Ronde* (Feb 1967), 24–41.

"Luther Opened a Wider Door Than He Knew: Issues Raised That Stand for All Time," *Methodist Recorder* (26 Oct 1967), 1–2.

"Professor Pieter Geyl: An Eminent Dutch Historian," *Times* (3 Jan 1967), 3.

"Thirty Years' Work in Irish History: The Eighteenth Century," *Irish Historical Studies,* 15 (1967), 376–390.

Peterhouse, 1968. Cambridge: The Peterhouse Society, 1968.

The Remembrance of Things Past. Southampton: University of Southampton, 1968.

"George Peabody Gooch," *Contemporary Review,* 213 (Nov 1968), 226–228.

"Introduction to the Second Edition," in Harold Temperley, *Frederic the Great and Kaiser Joseph: An Episode of War and Diplomacy in the Eighteenth Century,* 2d edition. London: Frank Cass, 1968. vii–xxii.

"Narrative History and the Spade-Work behind It," *History,* 53 (1968), 165–180.

Magna Carta in the Historiography of the Sixteenth and Seventeenth Centuries. Reading: University of Reading, 1969.

"George Peabody Gooch, 1873–1968," *Proceedings of the British Academy,* 55 (1969), 311–338. Reprinted as: *George Peabody Gooch, 1873–1968.* London: Oxford University Press, 1970.

"The Objectives of Society," *BACIE* [British Association for Commercial and Industrial Education] *Journal,* 23 (1969), 11–15.

"Some Trends in Scholarship, 1868–1968, in the Field of Modern History," *Transactions of the Royal Historical Society,* 5th series, 19 (1969), 159–184.

"Diplomacy," in R. Hatton and M. S. Anderson, eds., *Studies in Diplomatic History: Essays in Memory of David Bayne Horn.* London: Longmans, Green, 1970. 357–372.

"George Peabody Gooch, 1873–1968," *Year Book of the American Philosophical Society [1969],* 1970, 122–126.

Sermon-Address (19 April 1970). Edinburgh: St. Giles Cathedral.

"The Dangers of History," in Arthur N. Gilbert, ed., *In Search of a Meaningful Past.* Boston: Houghton Mifflin, 1971. 112–126.

"Eighteenth Century Ireland, 1702–1800," in T. W. Moody, ed., *Irish Historiography, 1936–1970.* Dublin: Irish Committee of Historical Science, 1971. 55–70.

"Frederich Crossfield Happold, 1893–1971," *Times* (19 July 1971), 13.

"Sincerity and Insincerity in Charles James Fox," *Proceedings of the British Academy,* 57 (1971), 3–27. Reprinted as: *Sincerity and Insincerity in Charles James Fox.* London: Oxford University Press, 1972.

"Universal History and the Comparative Study of Civilization," in Noah Edward Fehl, ed., *Sir Herbert Butterfield, Cho Yun Hsu, William H. McNeill on Chinese and World History*. Hong Kong: Chinese University of Hong Kong, 1971. 18–29

"Villa Serbelloni under John Marshall," in John Burchard, ed., *Thoughts from the Lake of Time: A Group of Essays in Honor of the Villa Serbelloni and Especially John and Charlotte Marshall*. New York: Josiah Macy Junior Foundation, 1971. 269–275.

The Discontinuities between the Generations: Their Effect on the Transmission of Historical Experience [Rede Lecture, 1971]. Cambridge: Cambridge University Press, 1972.

"Morality and an International Order," Brian Porter, ed., *The Aberystwyth Papers: International Politics, 1919–1969*. London: Oxford University Press, 1972. 336–357.

"Balance of Power," in *Dictionary of the History of Ideas*. New York: Charles Scribner, 1973. 1: 179–188.

"Christianity in History," in *Dictionary of the History of Ideas*. New York: Charles Scribner, 1973. 2: 373–412.

"Global Good and Evil": part I, "The Moderate Cupidity of Everyman," *New York Times* (3 Jan 1973), 39; and part II, "Inward to Glory," *New York Times* (4 Jan 1973), 37.

"Historiography: History of Historiography," in *Dictionary of the History of Ideas*. New York: Charles Scribner, 1973. 2: 464–498.

"Reflections on Macaulay," *The Listener* (13 Dec 1973), 826–827.

"Address by Sir Herbert Butterfield at the Memorial Service for Sir Denis Brogan, at the University Church of St. Mary's, Saturday, 9 February 1974," *Peterhouse*, 1974, 14–17.

"Denis Brogan," *Encounter* (April 1974), 64–66.

"The History of Encyclopedias," *Times Literary Supplement* (17 May 1974), 531–533.

"Sermon preached by Professor Sir Herbert Butterfield at the Commemoration of Benefactors in the College Chapel on 6 February 1974," *Peterhouse*, 1974, 3–7.

Raison d'État: The Relations between Morality and Government. Brighton: University of Sussex, 1975.

"Butterfield on Trevelyan," *Radio Times* (16 Feb 1976).

"Global Good and Evil," in Kenneth Thompson and Robert J. Myers, eds., *A Tribute to Hans Morgenthau*. Washington: New Republic Book Co., 1977. 199–203. Under new title, *Truth and Tragedy*. New Brunswick, N.J.: Transaction Books, 1984.

"A New Look at Jabez Bunting," *Methodist Recorder* (14 Sept 1978), 8–9.

* *Writings on Christianity and History*. Edited by C. T. McIntire. New York and London: Oxford University Press, 1979.

Toleration in Religion and Politics. Adam Watson on behalf of Sir Herbert Butterfield. New York: Council on Religion and International Affairs, 1980.

* *Origins of History*. Edited by Adam Watson. New York: Basic Books; London: Eyre Methuen, 1981.

Herbert Butterfield on History. Edited by Robin W. Winks. New York: Garland, 1985.

Essays on the History of Science. Edited by Karl W. Schweizer. Lewiston, New York, and London: Edwin Mellen, 1998.

2. By Butterfield: Unpublished Works

This section lists chronologically the writings which Butterfield left unpublished in his papers. It includes completed writings, lectures, unfinished writings, journals, diaries, pocket diaries, notes, and what I have called "thought-essays." Most of these materials are now collected in the Butterfield Papers in Cambridge University Library. The website of the Butterfield Papers is: <http://www.lib.cam.ac.uk/mss/butterf.html>. The papers may be accessed with the aid of an inventory, *A Catalogue of Papers of Sir Herbert Butterfield, 1900–1979*, 2 vols. (Cambridge University Library, 1994). The inventory is available in the Department of Manuscripts of Cambridge University Library as well as in the Bodleian Library in Oxford, and in the National Registry of Archives at Quality Court, Chancery Lane, in London.

However, certain of the materials listed below remained in the possession of the Butterfield family, and were not included in the inventory. One piece, entitled "Moral Judgments" (ms, 11p, May 1977), Butterfield wrote in response to my questions and gave to me. I have also included the tapes of my interviews with Butterfield, which remain with me. Another, on Cambridge University in the Renaissance and Reformation (ms, 18p, c1952), is in the Butterfield Papers in Peterhouse Library. Peterhouse Library also maintains a collection of about seven hundred books from Butterfield's personal library, many of which contain his annotations and marginalia.

Diaries: various cards and sheets; including samples of his poetry from 1919, 1920, and 1926.

"Charles Dickens" (typ, 76p + iiip, early 1920s).

"Chesterton" (ms, 13p, early 1920s).

"Napoleon and the Peace of Europe, 1806–1808" (typ, c170p, with fragments of other drafts, and with other titles: "The Problem of Peace in Europe, 1806–1808," and "Napoleon and Europe, 1806–1808," 1920s).

No title: Notebook on the history of science (ms, 14p, c1927).

"George the III and the Constitution, 1769–1782" (ms, c135p, c25 lectures, 1935–1937).

"Arguments pertaining to the thesis . . . That the division of the Modern History course at 1715 . . . is detrimental . . . " (ms, 5p, c1936, perhaps related to course on Modern European History, 1492–1715, given 1935–1937).

No title: On Modern European History (type, 169ssp, 16 lectures, late 1930s).

"The Historical Background of General Knowledge" (typ, 209p, + ms, c125p. 1943).

"History of England, 1688–1792" (typ, 44ssp, 6 lectures, 1944–1946).

"Factors in German History" (typ, 89p, lectures, 1944–1947).

"Notes on How Far Can and Should the Subject of International Relations Be Included in the Curriculum for Undergraduates of History?" (typ, 4ssp, 1949).

No title: On European History (typ, 30p, Dublin, May 1949).

"The Concise Cambridge Modern History/The Cambridge Shorter Modern History" (typ, c944p, c66 chapters, late 1940s).

"History of Historiography" (typ, 29p, Kingston, Ontario, Jan 1950).

"How Do We Know" (typ, 12p, BBC, 11 Oct 1950).

"Leonardo da Vinci" (typ, 10ssp, 1950).

No title: On Cambridge University in the Renaissance and Reformation (ms, 18p, c1952).

"Modern European History" (typ, c716p, c43 lectures, 1953–1957).

"Man and His Past" (typ, 89p, 4 lectures, BBC Script, 1954).

"Christianity and Humanism" (typ, 12p, 1955).

"The Historian and His Evidence" (typ, 22p, 1955).

"Morality and Historical Process in International Affairs" (typ, 49p, American Rockefeller Committee on International Relations, 1956).

"Peterhouse in Temperley's Time" (ms, 60p, 1956).

"Religion and the Problems of the World" (typ, c25p, Lecture 3 in the series "Christianity in the Twentieth Century," Bristol, 1956).

No title: On politics and the Christian (ms, 18p, Peterhouse Chapel Fellowship, 1956).

"England and the French Revolution, 1792" (typ, 250p, 1957).

"The Hebrew Scriptures and the Western Idea of History" (typ, 35p, 2 lectures, Jerusalem, 1957).

"Edmund Burke" (ms, 40p, 1958).

"The Old Testament and the Western Idea of History" (typ, 20p, London School of Oriental Studies, 1958).

"Misgivings about the Western Attitude to World Affairs" (ms, 57p, British Committee on the Theory of International Politics, 1959).

"Why I Am a Non-Conformist" (typ, 23p, June 1959).

Diary: kept while vice-chancellor of Cambridge University (ms, "very big," c1959–1961).

"The Christians and History" (typ, 8p, before 1955).

"Protestantism and the Rise of Capitalism" (typ, 11p, 1950s).

Notebooks on Peterhouse history (ms, many pages, late 1950s).

"Crowe's Memorandum of January 1907" (typ, 21p, British Committee on the Theory of International Politics, 1960).

"Historiography in England" (ms, 22p, late 1961 or early 1962).

No title: On Methodism (ms, 6p, 1961).

"Comments on Hedley Bull's Paper on the Grotian Conception of International Relations" (typ, 14p, British Committee on the Theory of International Relations, 1962).

"Personal: Early Youth, Father, Temperley, Vellacott" (ms, 67p, c1962/1963).

"2nd Lecture on the Use of Materials" (typ, 17p, 1962).

"Temperley" (ms, 173p, c1962/1963).

"The Use of Historical Materials" (typ, 7p, 1962, for a course with Kitson Clark).

"In Defence of Diplomatic History" (typ, 23p, Cambridge University History Club, Nov 1963).

"Reminicences of an Enquiry into the Crisis of 1792" (typ, 19p, Peterhouse and Trinity College, 1963).

No title: On the Christian believer and the academic historian (typ, 10p, Rice University, 1963).

No title: On the spiritual nature of Christianity (ms, 18p, University of London Methodist Society, 1963).

"George III and the Politicians, Oct 1760–Aug 1965" (typ, 41p, 3 lectures, plus ms, c300+ pages in various stages of revision, at least 17 lectures, 1963–1965).

"The Great Powers" (typ, 7p, British Committee on the Theory of International Relations, 1964).

"History Teaching in Schools and Universities" (typ, 20p, 1961).

"Notes for a Discussion on the Theory of International Relations" (typ, 8p, British Committee on the Theory of International Relations, 1964).

No title: On the causes of the outbreak of the war of 1914 (ms, 11p, 1964).

"Criticism in the Pre-Critical Age" (typ, 20p, Wesleyan University, 1965).

"The European States-System" (typ, 10p, British Committee on the Theory of International Relations, 1965).

"The Historic 'States-System'" (typ, 17p, British Committee on the Theory of International Relations, 1965).

No title: On the development of historical criticism (typ, 41p, c1965).

No title: On history in the curriculum (typ, 14p, July 1965).

No title: On the life of Carey Francis (typ, 4p, 1965).

No title: On the Reformation (typ, 6p, BBC Television script, 1965).

"Christians and Present-Day Problems" (ms, 18p, Duke University, Spring 1969).

"The Development of Diplomacy" (ms, 38p, c1969).

"The Early Years of George III" (various typ and mss, including 30p, for Canterbury, Durham, and York, c1968/1969).

"Historical Criticism" (typ, 41p, c1968).

"The Rise of a Christian Interpretation of History" (typ, 18p, Duke University, Spring 1969).

Journal-sheets: many, 1960s.

"The Flight from History" (typ, 31p, Eton, 1960s).

"The Function of Teacher and Student in a University History Department" (typ, 38p, Dublin, 1960s).

"The Rise of Historical Criticism" (typ, 16p, 1960s).

"The Use of Imagination in the Study of History" (typ, 42p, 1960s).

"Why Remember the Past?" (typ, 25p, 1960s).

"Why We Study History" (typ, 29p, 1960s).

Miscellaneous Comments: talks and short speeches, 1960s.

Thought-essays and notes, 1960s.

"Evil in History" (typ, 5p, BBC Television, 1970).

"The Role of the Historian in History" (typ, 31p, Public Record Office, Feb 1970).

No title: Memoirs (typ, 11p, 1970).

"The Nature of Political History" (ms, 34p, c1972).

"Revolution" (ms, 34p, Corpus Christi College, 1972).

"Macaulay the Historian" (typ, 6p, BBC Script, 1973).

Interviews with C. T. McIntire at Peterhouse (3 tape cassettes, c4½ hours, 17 June 1975).

Interviews with C. T. McIntire at Peterhouse (9 tape cassettes, c16½ hours, 11–24 May 1977).

"Moral Judgments" (ms, 11p, May 1977, written in response to interview with C. T. McIntire, Peterhouse).

No title: Memoirs: "My Early Life" and "My Literary Productions" (typ, 26p, for Kenneth Thompson, 1977).

No title: On religion and politics (typ, 13p, Council on Religion and International Affairs, 1977).

Journal-sheets and thought-essays (100s of pages), 1970s.

Pocket diaries: *The Onoto Diary,* for 1924; *Cambridge Pocket Diary,* for the following years: 1928–1929, 1929–1930, 1931–1932, 1933–1934, 1934–1935, 1935–1936, 1937–1938, 1941–1942, 1944–1945, 1945–1946, 1946–1947, 1947–1948, 1948–1949, 1949–1950, 1950–1951, 1951–1952, 1952–1953, 1953–1954, 1954–1955, 1955–1956, 1956–1957, 1957–1958, 1958–1959 with Eve Bogle, 1959–1960, 1960–1961, 1961–1962, 1962–1963, 1963–1964, 1964–1965, 1965–1966, 1966–1967, 1967–1968, 1968–1969, 1969–1970, 1970–1971, 1971–1972, 1972–1973, 1973–1974, 1974–1975, 1975–1976, 1976–1977, 1977–1978, 1978–1979; and Eve Bogle's *Cambridge Pocket Diary,* for 1945–1946.

3. By Butterfield: Works Projected

This section attempts to list chronologically all the books that Butterfield proposed, planned, or agreed to write or edit, but did not complete or, in some cases, begin. It also lists the books or other major publications which others invited him to write or edit or participate in, and which he declined. The projected works, plus the invitations declined to write or edit works, are arranged according to the year in which the work was conceived, or the invitation received.

Essays on American Relations with European States, 1848–1849: undertakes research in the United States, 1924–1925.

Fox Biography: decision to begin 1931.

The Concise Cambridge Modern History: contract 1939.

School Text-Book on Modern European History: proposed by Cambridge University Press; declines, 1930s.

Historical Geography of Europe: states intention to write, based on proposed course, with manuscript "The Historical Background of General Knowledge," 1943; renews proposal to Cambridge University Press in 1964, along with proposal for a series, *The Cambridge Historical Geography.*

New Cambridge Modern History: invited by Cambridge University Press to edit with G. N. Clark, 1945; agrees and begins to plan, but then withdraws when Clark declines.

Short History of Switzerland: invited by Societá Pro Helvetia to edit; declines, recommends G. R. Potter who co-authors the book, 1945.

Cambridge History of the Christian Church: invited by Norman Sykes to join planning group in Bishop Stephen Neill's rooms at Trinity, 1946; declines; project fails, but later carried out under different direction as the *Oxford History of the Christian Church.*

Temperley Memoir/Biography: pledges to Dorothy to write a memoir of Temperley, 1946; proposes to Temperley's son in 1965 to make it a short biography.

Acton Diaries, 1852–1859: intention to edit, 1947.

Burke's Correspondence: invited by Alfred Cobban to edit the correspondence on English Politics, Ireland, and America, 1947; declines.

Acton Essays: suggests edition to Bell Publishers, 1948.

New Cambridge Modern History: invited to contribute chapters in volumes 5 and 1, 1948 and 1951; declines.

UNESCO History: invited to participate, 1951; declines.

Burke: denies offer by Collins Publishers to write a volume for "Brief Lives Series," 1951.

New History of Europe in the Nineteenth and Twentieth Centuries: declines proposal by Cambridge University Press, 1951.

Acton Correspondence: proposes to edit for Cambridge University Press, 1952.

Acton Biography: considers with Cambridge University Press, 1953.

England and the French Revolution, 1792: extends section intended as part 4 of *George III and the Historians,* and tells Collins Publishers the book will be ready in about 18 months, 1957.

Volume on the Eighteenth Century or the Scientific Revolution: invited by Geoffrey Barraclough to write a volume for the Thames and Hudson series on European History, 1963; declines.

History of History. Gifford Lectures: intended for publication soon after delivery, 1965 and 1966.

George III: Great Lives Observed: contract with Prentice-Hall to edit, then withdraws in dispute over publisher's contract practice, c1967.

State-Systems: proposes project to edit a volume of papers from the British Committee on the Theory of International Relations, 1967.

World History Library, General Editorship: invited by Hamlyn Publishers to edit a 20-volume series, 1967.

British History, 1760–1865: invited by Robert Blake to write volume 8 for the Granada series on British history, 1968; declines.

The History of Diplomacy as Technique: suggests book around the time of his retirement, prepares initial notes and brief manuscript, c1968–1969.

The Early Reign of George III: plan to publish a book from his lectures, 1969.

The Language and Style of Historians: invited by Faber and Faber, 1969; declines.

Collected Essays, Essays on Namier, Essays on Christianity: proposes three volumes of collected writings to his agent A. D. Peters, 1970.

Political Biography of Fox, or Burke, or Pitt the Younger: invited by A. L. Rowse to write a short book for the series "Men and Their Times," to include a Penguin paperback edition, 1973; declines.

4. About Butterfield, Excluding Reviews

This list presents in alphabetical order books and articles devoted to, containing substantial passages about, or making significant reference to Butterfield. It makes no claim to be complete, and it does not include writings that are chiefly book reviews.

Anon. "Herbert Butterfield." *The Sex,* 75 (Michaelmas term, 1922), 8–10.

Beales, Derek. *History and Biography: An Inaugural Lecture.* Cambridge: Cambridge University Press, 1981.

Bentley, Michael. "Butterfield at the Millennium: The 'Sir Herbert Butterfield Lecture,' 1999." *Storia della Storiografia,* 38 (2000), 17–32.

Blaas, P. B. M. *Continuity and Anachronism: Parliamentary and Constitutional Development in Whig Historiography and the Anti-Whig Reaction between 1890 and 1930.* The Hague: Nijhoff, 1978.

Bradley, William L. "The Tragic View of History," *Theology and Life,* 4 (1961), 305–315.

Brent, Richard. "Butterfield's Tories: 'High Politics' and the Writing of British Political History." *Historical Journal,* 30 (1987), 943–954.

Brooke, Christopher N. L. *A History of the University of Cambridge,* vol. 4, *1870–1990.* Cambridge: Cambridge University Press, 1993.

Bultmann, Rudolf. *History and Eschatology.* Edinburgh: Edinburgh University Press, 1957.

Burke, Peter. "Butterfield, [Sir] Herbert," in Lucian Boia, ed.-in-chief, *Great Historians of the Modern Age: An International Dictionary.* Westport, Conn.: Greenwood, 1991.

Cabral, Regis. "Herbert Butterfield (1900–79) as a Christian Historian of Science." *Studies in History and Philosophy of Science,* Part A, 27 (1996), 547–564.

Cannadine, David. *G. M. Trevelyan: A Life in History.* London: HarperCollins, 1992. London: Penguin, 1997.

Cannon, John A. "Butterfield, Herbert," in Cannon et al., eds., *The Blackwell Dictionary of Historians.* New York: Blackwell, 1988. 61–62.

———. *Teaching History at University,* Teaching of History Series, 56. London: The Historical Association, 1984.

Carr, E. H. *What Is History?* London: Macmillan, 1961.

Chadwick, Owen. "Acton and Butterfield." *Journal of Ecclesiastical History,* 38 (1987), 386–405.

———. *Freedom and the Historian: An Inaugural Lecture.* Cambridge: Cambridge University Press, 1969.

———. "Sir Herbert Butterfield." *Cambridge Review* (16 Nov 1979), 6–8.

Christie, Ian. "George III and the Historians—Thirty Years On." *History,* 71 (1986), 205–221.

Clive, John. *Not by Fact Alone: Essays on the Writing and Reading of History.* New York: Knopf, 1989.

———. "The Prying Yorkshireman." *New Republic* (23 June 1982), 31–36.

Clouse, Robert. "Herbert Butterfield," in Michael Bauman and Martin Klauber, eds., *Historians of the Christian Tradition: Their Methodology and Influence on Western Thought.* Nashville: Broadman and Holman, 1995. 519–529.

Cohen, I. Bernard. *Revolution in Science.* Cambridge: Harvard University Press, 1985.

Coll, Alberto R. "The Wisdom of Statecraft: Sir Herbert Butterfield and the Philosophy of International Politics." Ph.D. diss., University of Virginia, 1983.

———. *The Wisdom of Statecraft: Sir Herbert Butterfield and the Philosophy of International Relations.* Durham: Duke University Press, 1985.

Conzemius, Victor. "Sir Herbert Butterfield: Ein Dissenter in englischen Geschichtsschreibung." *Neue Burcher Zeitung* (7 Oct 1975), 37.

Cosgrave, Patrick. "An Englishman and His History." *Spectator* (28 July 1979), 22–23.
——. "A Spectator's Notebook." *Spectator* (8 Nov 1975), 591.
Cowling, Maurice. "Butterfield, Sir Herbert." *Dictionary of National Biography, 1971–1980*, 1986. 116–117.
——. "Herbert Butterfield, 1900–1979." *Proceedings of the British Academy,* 65 (1979), 595–609.
[——]. "Professor Sir Herbert Butterfield: Sober Life and Wide Influence." *Times* (19 Nov 1979).
——. *Religion and Public Doctrine in England.* Cambridge: Cambridge University Press, 1980.
Cunningham, Andrew, and Perry Williams. "De-centering the 'Big Picture': *The Origins of Modern Science* and the Modern Origins of Science." *British Journal for the History of Science,* 26 (1993), 407–432.
Danielou, Jean. *The Lord of History: Reflections on the Inner Meaning of History.* London: Longmans, Green, 1958.
Derry, John. "Herbert Butterfield," in John Cannon, ed., *The Historian at Work.* London: George Allen and Unwin, 1980. 171 – 187.
——. "Whig Interpretation of History," in Cannon et al., eds., *The Blackwell Dictionary of Historians.* New York: Blackwell, 1988. 448–450.
Dukelow, Owen Warner. "Herbert Butterfield: The Epistemology of a Working Historian." Ph.D. diss., University of Minnesota, 1960.
Elliott, J. H., and H. G. Koenigsberger, eds. *The Diversity of History: Essays in Honour of Sir Herbert Butterfield.* London: Routledge and Kegan Paul, 1970.
Elton, G. R. "Herbert Butterfield and the Study of History." *Historical Journal,* 28 (1984), 729–743. Reprinted in: G. R. Elton, *Studies in Tudor and Stuart Politics and Government,* vol. 4, *Papers and Reviews, 1982–1990.* Cambridge: Cambridge University Press, 1992.
Epp, Roger. "The 'Augustinian Moment' in International Politics: Niebuhr, Butterfield, Wight, and the Reclaiming of a Tradition." *International Research Papers,* no. 10. Aberystwyth: Department of International Politics, University College of Wales, 1991.
Fair, John D. *Harold Temperley: A Scholar and Romantic in the Public Realm.* Newark: University of Delaware Press, 1992.
Fehl, Noah Edward. *History and Society.* Hong Kong: Chung Chi College, The Chinese University of Hong Kong, 1964.
Fox, Robert. "The History of Science," in Harold Perkins, ed., *History: An Introduction for the Intending Student.* London: Routledge and Kegan Paul, 1970. 173–186.
Fryer, Geoffry R. "English Politics in the Age of Burke: Herbert Butterfield's Achievement." *Studies in Burke and His Time,* 11 (1970), 1519–1542.
Gale, George. "Herbert Butterfield, Historian." *Encounter* (Nov 1979), 87–90.
Geyl, Pieter. *Encounters in History.* London: Collins, 1963.
Grafton, Anthony. "The Footnote from de Thou to Ranke." *History and Theory,* 33 (Theme Issue, 1994), 53–76.
Hall, A. Rupert. "On Whiggism." *History of Science,* 21 (1983), 45–59.
Harbison, E. H. *Christianity and History.* Princeton: Princeton University Press, 1963.

———. "The 'Meaning of History' and the Writing of History." *Church History,* 21 (1952), 97–107.

Hernon, Joseph M., Jr., "The Last Whig Historian and Consensus History: George Macaulay Trevelyan, 1876–1962." *American Historical Review,* 81 (1976), 66–97.

Hinsley, F. H. "A Obra do Historiador Herbert Butterfield." *Correio do Vouga* (28 Nov 1957).

Hobart, Michael. "History and Religion in the Thought of Herbert Butterfield." *Journal of the History of Ideas,* 32 (1971), 543–554.

Holmer, Paul L. "Historical Research and Christianity." *Encounter,* 20 (1959), 367–372.

Inoue, Hiroshi. "The Critique of Anthropology as Historical Study: Japanese, Cultural History, and Herbert Butterfield." Ph.D. diss., University of Oregon, 1990.

Jantzen, Kyle. "Herbert Butterfield," in Kelly Boyd, ed., *Encyclopedia of Historians and Historical Writing.* London: Fitzroy Dearborn, 1999.

Jones, A. "Where 'Governing Is the Use of Words,'" *Historical Journal,* 19 (1976), 253–254.

Kenyon, John. *The History Men: The Historical Profession in England since the Renaissance.* London: Weidenfeld and Nicolson, 1983.

Liggio, Leonard. "Herbert Butterfield: Christian Historian as Creative Critic." *New Individualist Review,* 1: 3 (Nov 1961), 26–32.

Lindberg, David C., and Robert S. Westman, eds. *Reappraisals of the Scientific Revolution.* Cambridge: Cambridge University Press, 1990.

Lindborg, Rolf. "Positivism Eller Humanism? Rupert Halls Kritik av Herbert Butterfields Ideer om en "Whig-Tolkning' av Historien." *Lychnos 1990,* 275–291.

Lloyd, Roger. "Herbert Butterfield." *Church Times* (11 Jan 1952), 24.

Lottinville, Savoie. *The Rhetoric of History.* Norman: Oklahoma University Press, 1976.

Marsden, George, and Frank Roberts, eds. *A Christian View of History?.* Grand Rapids, Mich.: Eerdmans, 1975.

Mayer, Anna-K. "Setting Up a Discipline: Conflicting Agendas of the Cambridge History of Science Committee, 1936–1950." *Studies in History and Philosophy of Science,* Part A, 31 (2000), 665–689.

Mayr, Ernst. "When Is Historiography Whiggish?" *Journal of the History of Ideas,* 51 (1990), 301–309.

McGee, Daniel Bennett. "The Meaning of History and Political Ethics in the Thought of Herbert Butterfield." Ph.D. diss., Duke University, 1966.

McGill, William J. "Herbert Butterfield and the Idea of Liberty." *South Atlantic Quarterly,* 70 (1971), 1–12.

McIntire, C. T. "Butterfield, Herbert," in *The Routledge Encyclopedia of Protestantism,* vol. 1. London: Routledge, 2003.

———. "Herbert Butterfield on Christianity and History," in Herbert Butterfield, *Writings on Christianity and History,* ed. C. T. McIntire. New York: Oxford University Press, 1979. xi–lviii.

———. "Herbert Butterfield, Scientific and Christian." *Christian History* 20: 4 (Nov 2001), 47–48.

———. "Moral Judgments in History: The Case of Herbert Butterfield." Colloquium Paper, Department of History, University of Toronto (21 Jan 1987).

———. *The Ongoing Task of Christian Historiography*. Toronto: Institute for Christian Studies, 1974.

———, ed. *God, History, and Historians: Modern Christian Views of History*. New York: Oxford University Press, 1977.

Mehta, Ved. *The Fly and the Fly-Bottle: Encounters with British Intellectuals*. Boston: Little, Brown, 1963.

———. "Onward and Upward with the Arts: The Flight of Crook-Taloned Birds, Part 2." *New Yorker* (15 Dec 1962), 47–129, especially 106–129.

Meyerhoff, Hans, ed. *The Philosophy of History in Our Time*. Garden City, N.Y.: Doubleday, 1959.

Montgomery, John Warwick, and James R. Moore, "The Speck in Butterfield's Eye: A Reply to William A. Speck." *Fides et Historia*, 4 (1971), 71–77.

Morton, Patricia M. "Life after Butterfield? John Burrow's *Liberal Descent* and the Recent Historiography of Victorian Historians." *Historical Reflections/Reflexions Historiques*, 10 (1983), 229–244.

Neatby, Hilda. "Christian Views of History: Toynbee and Butterfield." *Transactions of the Royal Society of Canada*, 52, section 2 (June 1958), 33–42.

Nixon, Mark. "Butterfield, Herbert, 1900–1979." *The Literary Encyclopedia and Literary Dictionary*, 2003. <http://www.litencyc.com>.

Norman, Edward. "Christian and Sceptic." *Times Higher Education Supplement* (9 Dec 1983), 15.

Oldfield, Adrian, "Moral Judgments in History." *History and Theory*, 20 (1981), 260–277.

Parker, Harold T. "Herbert Butterfield," in S. W. Halperin, ed., *Some Twentieth Century Historians: Essays on Eminent Europeans*. Chicago: University of Chicago Press, 1961. 75–103.

Partington, Eileen. "Bibliography of Works by and about Herbert Butterfield." Project for Diploma, University of London School of Librarianship, 1963.

Partner, Nancy. "Making Up Lost Time: Writing on the Writing of History." *Speculum*, 61 (1986), 90–117.

Patterson, Annabel. *Nobody's Perfect: A New Whig Interpretation of History*. New Haven: Yale University Press, 2002.

Plumb, J. H. "The Road to Professional History," in *The Collected Essays of J. H. Plumb*, vol. 1, *The Making of an Historian*. London: Harvester Wheatsheaf, 1988. 1–9.

Poe, Marshall. "Butterfield's Sociology of Whig History: A Contribution to the Study of Anachronism in Modern Historical Thought." *Clio: A Journal of Literature, History and the Philosophy of History*, 25 (1996), 345–363.

Price, Jacob M. "Party, Purpose, and Pattern: Sir Lewis Namier and His Critics." *Journal of British Studies*, 1 (1961), 71–93.

Reid, W. Stanford. "Professor Butterfield and a Christian Interpretation of History." *His*, 16 (May 1956), 23–25.

Rickman, H. P. "The Horizons of History." *Hibbert Journal*, 56 (1956), 167–176.

Roe, P. "The Intrastate Security Dilemma: Ethnic Conflict as a 'Tragedy.'" *Journal of Peace Research*, 36 (1998), 183–202.

Schweizer, Karl W. "Butterfield, Sir Herbert (1900–1979)." *A Global Encyclopedia of Historical Writing.* New York: Garland, 1998. 1: 126–127.

——. "Introduction." Herbert Butterfield, *Essays on the History of Science,* ed. Karl W. Schweizer. Lewiston and London: Edwin Mellen, 1998. iii–xi.

Sewell, Keith C. "The Concept of Technical History in the Thought of Herbert Butterfield." *Fides et Historia,* 27 (1995), 52–76.

——. "Herbert Butterfield as Historical Detective: British Policy and the Origins of the First World War." The History Institute of Victoria, Ninth Joyce Memorial Lecture, University of Melbourne, 28 July 1993.

——. "Leading Conceptions in the Theory and Historiography of Sir Herbert Butterfield." M.A. thesis, Victoria University of Wellington, 1978.

——. "Providence and Method: Herbert Butterfield and the Interpretation of History." Ph.D. diss., Deakin University, 1990.

——. *Providence and Method: Herbert Butterfield and the Interpretation of History.* Sioux Center, Iowa: By the Author, 2001.

Sharp, Paul. "The English School, Herbert Butterfield, and Diplomacy." *Discussion Papers in Diplomacy,* 83. The Hague: Netherlands Institute of International Relations Clingendael, Nov 2002.

——. "Herbert Butterfield, the English School, and the Civilizing Virtues of Diplomacy," *International Affairs,* 79 (2003), 855–878.

Soffer, Reba N. "The Conservative Historical Imagination in the Twentieth Century." *Albion,* 28 (1996), 1–17.

Speck, William A. "Herbert Butterfield on the Christian and Historical Study." *Fides et Historia,* 4 (1971), 50–70.

——. "The Role of the Christian Historian in the Twentieth Century as Seen in the Writings of Kenneth Scott Latourette, Christopher Dawson, and Herbert Butterfield." Ph.D. diss., Florida State University, 1965.

Thompson, Kenneth W. "Butterfield, Herbert," in David L. Shils, ed., *International Encyclopedia of Social Sciences,* 18, Biographical Supplement. New York: Free Press/Macmillan 1979. 91–97.

——. *Masters of International Thought.* Baton Rouge: Louisiana State University Press, 1980.

——, ed. *Herbert Butterfield: The Ethics of History and Politics.* Lanham, Md.: University Press of America, 1980.

Thomson, David. *The Aims of History: Values of the Historical Attitude.* London: Thames and Hudson, 1969.

Thorp, Malcolm R. *Herbert Butterfield and the Reinterpretation of the Christian Historical Perspective.* Lewiston, Queenston, Lampeter: Edwin Mellen, 1997.

——. "The 'Inescapable Predicament': Sir Herbert Butterfield's Reflections on the Human Dilemma." *Fides et Historia,* 14 (1983), 6–17.

Turner, J. Munsey. "The Christian and the Study of History: Sir Herbert Butterfield, 1900–1979." *Proceedings of the Wesley Historical Society,* 46 (1987), 1–12.

Tyson, Brady B. "Herbert Butterfield's Concept of International Relations: An Analysis and Comparison of a Christian Approach." Ph.D. diss., American University, 1963.

Vigezzi, Brunello. "Saggio introduttivo," in Hedley Bull and Adam Watson, eds., *L'espansione della società internazionale: L'Europa e il mondo dalla fine del Medioeva ai tempi nostri*. Milan: Jaca, 1994. 5–98.

Vincent, John. "The Whig Interpretation of History: Why Butterfield Matters," in Vincent, *An Intelligent Person's Guide to History*. London: Duckworth, 1995. 57–62.

Watson, Adam. "Introduction" Herbert Butterfield, *The Origins of History,* ed. Adam Watson. New York: Basic Books; London: Eyre and Methuen, 1981. 7–12.

Watson, Bernard. [Three articles on Butterfield], *Vanguard* [Salvation Army], (Nov and Dec 1959 and Jan 1960).

Watson, George. "The War against the Whigs: Butterfield's Victory . . . and Defeat." *Encounter* (Jan 1986), 19–25.

Wiener, Philip P. "Sir Herbert Butterfield, 1900–1979: In Memoriam." *Journal of the History of Ideas,* 41 (1980), 157–158.

Wight, Martin. "History and Judgment: Butterfield, Niebuhr, and the Technical Historian." *Frontier,* 1: 8 (Aug 1950), 301–314.

Wilson, Adrian, and T. G. Ashplant. "Whig History and Present-Centred History." *Historical Journal,* 31 (1988), 1–16.

Windsor, Mary P. "The Practitioner of Science: Everyone Her Own Historian." *Journal of the History of Biology,* 34 (2001), 229–245.

Winks, Robin W., ed. *Herbert Butterfield on History*. New York: Garland, 1985.

Wollheim, Richard. "The New Conservatism in Britain." *Partisan Review,* 24 (1957), 539–560.

Wormald, Brian. "Brian Wormald Adds" [addendum on Sir Herbert Butterfield]. *Cambridge Review* (16 Nov 1979), 9.

Wright, Esmond. "Professor Sir Herbert Butterfield." *Contemporary Review,* 253 (Dec 1979), 293–295.

Index

The index seeks to identify the principal people with whom Butterfield interacted, as well as the principal themes and subjects that occupied his attention. Not all people or themes mentioned in the text are cited here, and none of his book titles are included. The notes identify the principal places where his books are cited, and the bibliography names the people who wrote about him, most of whom are not included in the index.

Academic history. *See* Scientific history
Acland, Richard, 252–253
Acton, Lord, xi, 15–16, 94, 234, 366
    409–410; criticism of, 55–56, 60–61,
    67–69, 71–78, 258–259; impact of,
    22–23, 35, 48–49, 85, 109, 229; as
    model, 201, 238–239, 258, 260–261,
    324–325, 366, 404, 414; preoccupa-
    tion with, 100–101, 139, 151, 164,
    172, 328, 333, 380, 399; research on,
    141, 152, 170–173; writing on, 171–
    172, 235–240, 254–264, 383–384
American history, 38
Annales, Marc Bloch, Lucien Febvre, 89,
    91, 140, 217, 388
Ashton, T. H., 327

Barker, Ernest, 40, 84, 113, 272
Barraclough, Geoffrey, 209, 297
Beales, Derek, 285
Beloff, Max, 220
Berlin, Isaiah, 209, 251–252
Bogle, Eve, xix, 140–143, 170–171, 204,
    236, 240, 254, 266–267, 271–272,
    297, 366, 408
Brogan, Denis, x, 110, 113, 326, 361, 397
Brooke, Z. N., 115
Bull, Hedley, 307
Bultmann, Rudolf, 196
Burke, Edmund, 59, 61, 115, 144, 153–
    154, 237, 239, 291
Bury, J. B., 36, 52–55, 178
Butler, J. R. M, 134, 201, 267

Butterfield, Ada Mary, 3–4, 12–13, 26, 233–234

Butterfield, Albert, 2–6, 16, 39, 60, 104, 235, 328, 375, 423; influence, 11–14, 24–26, 104, 125–126, 135, 204, 233–234, 410

Butterfield family, xvi–xvii, 3, 233–234, 266–267, 366–367; sons, 86–87, 140–141, 202, 204, 240, 265–268, 366, 372

Butterfield, Pamela, Lady (Edith Joyce Crawshaw), xviii–xix, 49–50, 52, 204, 270–272, 340, 361–363, 400

Cambridge University, xi, 14–15, 76–77, 274, 409–410; and degrees, 26, 41–42; and Faculty of History, xii, 51, 87, 93, 100, 109, 133–134, 241, 315–318, 328–329, 377, 410, 421, 463; and vice-chancellor, xiii, 318–325, 376

Carr, E. H., 57, 80, 118–121, 134, 306–307, 430, 438

Chadwick, Owen, xviii–xix, 154, 322, 325, 328, 361, 384, 417

Chesterton, G. K., 29, 45

Christian historian, 20, 58–60, 208–209, 251–252, 262–263, 398–400, 415; Christian shaping of historical study, 67, 76, 195–201, 225–233, 242, 262–264, 393–395, 407–409; self-disclosure, 131–132, 174–178; credo, 73–76, 177–178, 297–300, 315, 347, 377–378, 414. *See* Dissent; Methodist

Christian interpretation of history, 126–132, 174–201, 207, 227, 296, 339, 393, 397–400, 408

Christianity in history, xiii, 196, 228–229, 392–392

Church history, 36, 40, 61, 94, 177, 228–229

Church of England, Anglican, 72, 86, 126–127, 273, 300, 315, 363; Peterhouse Chapel, 24, 36, 274, 398, 410;

relation with, 11, 54, 358–360, 373, 375–376, 414

Civilization, 55, 159, 178, 244–247, 260, 293; diffusion of, from higher to lower, 4–6, 38–40, 125–127, 305, 358, 374–375; as a unity, 90–91, 94, 151–152, 241, 317, 336, 388–392

Clark, G. N. 90, 133, 152–154, 280, 327–328, 450

Commager, Henry Steele, 136, 272

Communism, 102–103, 156, 220, 370–371; Soviet Union, 176, 202–203, 243–246, 251, 303–315, 354. *See* Marxist interpretation of history

Cowling, Maurice, xii, 80, 201, 237–238, 270, 326

Diplomatic history, xiv, 18, 27–28, 203, 350, 356–358, 384, 409; as model, 42, 88, 137–138, 242, 261, 275–278, 345–346, 353–358, 387–389, 411

Dissent, xiv–xv, xx, 39, 76, 176, 220–221, 228–229, 244–245, 267, 273, 412–417; insurgent Christianity as, 297–300, 315; intellectual, 25–26, 58, 97, 140, 242, 261, 302; political, social, 41, 79–80, 105–106, 112, 131, 170, 202–203, 313–315; religion as, xv, 38, 71–72, 126–128, 297–300, 314–315, 324–325, 346, 358–360, 363, 375–376; teaching as, 85–86; at the top, xv, 322. *See* Christian historian; Teetotaler

Dualism, 193–195, 208–209, 230–233, 262–266, 287, 301–302, 411–412; history-nature, 184; freedom-necessity, 284; morality-history, 74–76, 116, 213, 310; religious-material, 41, 197, 346, 391; spiritual-mundane, 213, 391; inner-outer, 43–45, 179–187, 213

Editor, of journal, 100, 110, 235–236; of books, 88–89, 171, 229, 236–240, 333, 386

English history, 19–21, 58–59, 71–72, 87, 121–132, 152, 229, 315–316; eighteenth century studies, 52, 60–61, 140–150, 204, 345, 409. *See* Fox, Charles James; George III; Whig interpretation of history

Fox, Charles James, xiii, 60, 409; impediments, 87, 132, 163, 217, 239–240, 265, 278, 338, 360; research on, 78–84, 140–143, 202, 210, 235–236, 240, 326–327, 432, 439; writing on, 143–144, 281, 290–291, 330–331, 379–381
Francis, Carey, 37, 135
French history, 112–113, 115, 282, 290, 331, 381. *See* Napoleon Bonapart

Galinsky, Hans K. 107–108, 137
General history, xii–xiii, 52, 66–67, 87–94, 138–140, 144–146, 335, 357, 410–411; European, 87, 93–94, 111, 150–154, 315–318; world, 140, 293–297, 389–392; writing on, 100–101, 136–137, 202, 235, 240–241, 254, 262–264, 276, 330–333, 338. *See* World history, global historiography
George III, 20, 142–150, 331–333, 360, 381, 414; early reign of, xiv, 82–84, 345, 381–383; historiography of, 278–291, 383
Germany, 6–7, 110–115, 188–189, 191, 224, 355, 396; against negative attitudes to, 137, 165–168, 171–176, 242–246, 256–257, 308, 337, 340–341, 349, 356, 409; visits to, 106–109, 168, 207, 330, 357. *See* Nazis
Geyl, Pieter, 209, 262–263
God in history, xiv, 184, 192–193, 207, 213, 294–295; experience of, 40–41, 103–104, 178; as final judge, 68–70, 167; and systematic theory, 230–233, 247, 263, 301, 416–417
God in nature, 184, 294

Gooch, G. P., 21, 23, 106, 110, 171, 206, 356, 366, 383

Hinton, R. W. K., 272
Historian, xvi–vii, 1, 8–10, 30–34, 394, 398, 409; becoming a, 19, 21–27, 35, 41, 49–50
Historical geography, 90, 94, 114–115, 167, 333, 384
Historical novel, xii, 2, 8, 23, 29–34, 60, 263
Historical process, 1, 29, 44–45, 54, 185–190, 230–233, 263; various understandings of, 32, 62–67, 73, 92, 185–186, 189–190, 217–218, 291. *See* Providence
Historical study, 30–33, 43, 61–62, 137–140, 178–182; limits of, 31, 72, 116, 173. *See* Scientific history; Technical history
Historical thinking, ix–x, 21, 29–30, 58, 106, 157–160, 292–293, 334–345; importance of, xii–xiii, 67, 76, 177, 210, 238–239, 265, 278, 306, 348, 362, 403–409; sources of, 166–167, 203, 306, 365–366; use of, 46–47, 61–62, 99–100, 253–254, 259–261. *See* History of historiography
History of historiography, xii, 106, 213, 241–242, 334–345; method, 255–256, 259–261, 278–279, 283–285, 334; as science, 257; as writing on, 253–265, 276, 296–297, 364, 391–392, 406–407. *See* George III; World history, global historiography
History of ideas, xiii, 384–385
History of science, xiii, 90–91, 94, 153–163, 204, 207, 400
Hitler, Adolf, 106–114, 127, 176, 187, 220–221, 225, 251, 354. *See* Nazis
Honours, xi–xii, 413; Festschrift, 365; honourary degrees, 254, 267, 301, 329–330, 357, 365; knighthood, 361–362; other awards, 37, 367–368, 379;

Honours (*continued*)
   prizes, 19–20, 28–29, 34, 36, 410;
   scholarships, 6, 9–10, 14

Idea(s) of history, 29–30, 292–297, 335
Imagination, imaginative sympathy, 31–
   33, 45, 66, 180, 185–187, 194, 213–
   214, 219, 226–227
Individual(s), xiv, 194, 212, 221, 263,
   348–349, 393; individualism as doctrine of, 3, 129, 197–199, 301–302,
   309, 324–325, 354–356, 409; as real,
   182–186, 216–217, 229–233, 246,
   299–300; writing on, 276–278
Intellectual biography, xv–xx
International theory, international relations, xi, xiii, 213, 253, 300–315, 331,
   345–353; balance of power, 308, 345,
   384–385; raison d'etat, 385; scientific
   approach to, 98, 203, 207, 230, 242–
   24, 306, 309–315, 357; states-system,
   246–250, 331, 345, 351–353; writing
   on 242–253, 301, 304–305, 309, 407.
   See War
Interpretation of history, 21, 66, 95, 195,
   207. *See* Christian interpretation of
   history; Marxist interpretation of
   history

Jews, Judaism, 177, 211–212, 223–224,
   273, 288, 294–295, 299, 393, 397

Keighley, Yorkshire, 2, 37, 233, 270,
   409; Keighley Trade and Grammar
   School, 6–10, 17, 86–87, 154, 423
Kitson Clark, George, 87, 315–318, 328
Knowles, David, 135–136, 272, 326,
   328, 361; as friend, 135, 171, 237,
   240, 267–269, 315–318, 365, 384,
   397

Languages, xii, 8, 258
Laski, Harold, 109
Laws in history, 53–54, 95, 230–233,

247–248, 301–304; and revolution,
   303–304, 311–312, 369–371. *See*
   Maxims
Lecturer, ix, 40, 204, 207–210, 235; on
   Christianity and history, 174–177, 298–
   300; on diplomacy and war, 241–242;
   on historiography, 253–254, 339–340;
   and lecture style, 51–52, 85–86, 156,
   177, 204, 210, 310, 331, 371; on modern science, 155–157; and publications,
   208; as public lecturer, 135, 137, 164,
   173, 275–276, 309, 329–330, 364,
   378–380; as university lecturer, 49, 51–
   52, 87–88, 93–94, 114, 137
Liberty, history of, 7, 9–10, 55, 63–64,
   71, 171, 212–213; as English liberty,
   7, 115–117, 122, 144–145, 229, 305,
   356, 373. *See* Acton, Lord; Whig interpretation of history
Lovatt, Roger, 326
Love, 211–213, 228–229, 377; as
   charitable-mindedness, 212, 221, 302

Machiavelli, Nicolo, xiii, 83–84, 98–
   101, 111–112, 137, 141, 146–147,
   306, 369, 414
Mack Smith, Denis, 135, 266–267, 272
Marxist interpretation of history, 91–93,
   102, 173, 176, 213–217; as example,
   95–98, 181; as influence, 123–124,
   230, 306, 369; and Marxism, 102, 205
Maxims, 71, 98–100, 112, 247–250,
   319, 357, 389, 393; as explanation,
   146–147, 248–249, 308, 346–347; as
   theory, 300–306, 349–353, 369–371.
   See Machiavelli
McKinnon, Donald, 306–307
Medlicott, W. M., 169–170, 276–277
Method, historical, xii, 145–146, 278–
   279, 348–349, 356–357, 410–411;
   and diversity of, 277–278, 288, 387–
   389, 394, 410–411, 414; and journal-
   sheets, 365–366, 377–378; as microscopic research, 42–43, 80–82, 141–

142, 145–146, 202, 238, 258; on modern science, 155–157; as reading, 175, 339–340, 344–345, 396; and thought-essays, 54–56, 104, 251, 366, 398. *See* Diplomatic history; Political history; Stereoscopic vision; Technical history

Methodist, xi, xv, 314–315, 347, 375–376, 407–409, 414; as chapel or church, 2–3, 10–14, 86, 363–364, 398; as identity, 16, 26, 37–38, 267, 298–300, 324–325, 358–360, 372. *See* Dissent; Preacher; Wesley House; Wesley Methodist

Moral judgments, xiv, 55–56, 67–73, 186–189, 208–209, 219–225, 399–400; and amorality, 209, 251–252, 411; and contemporary history, 104–109, 164–165, 171–172, 302–303; and historical study, 213, 411. *See* Acton, Lord

Namier, Lewis, 146, 149, 206, 217, 279–293, 326, 332, 386; and method, 80–83, 332, 335–336, 383. *See* George III

Napoleon Bonaparte, xii–xiii, 20, 70–71, 80–81, 134, 176, 243, 414; research on, 27–28, 41–43; writing on, 43–49, 60, 83–84, 101, 108–115, 127

Narrative, 45–47, 137–138, 143–145, 284, 291, 306, 409; and past and present, 61–66; and political history, 388–390; as story structure, 69–72, 157, 180, 277, 392–393. *See* Diplomatic history; Political history

Nazis, 102, 106–109, 127, 137, 165–168, 176, 220–225, 308, 348. *See* Hitler, Adolf

Needham, Joseph, 155, 161, 337

New Whig, xvi, 59–60, 76, 119–122, 131, 409, 422, 430; and historical study, 149, 287–288; and social change, 305, 322, 375. *See* Politics

Niebuhr, Reinhold, 175, 199, 207, 209, 253, 268, 301–312, 329

Oxenhope, Yorkshire, xi, xix, 2–14, 16, 26, 36–37, 39–40, 60, 356, 363, 375, 410, 423

Personality, 33, 39, 111, 177, 183–185; and Christianity, 128–129; and history, 45–47, 50, 64, 143, 299; and personalism, 103–106, 409; and personality type, 412. *See* Individual(s)

Peterhouse, ix, xi, 14–26, 37, 80, 154, 398, 409; and Fellow, 35, 40, 84, 109–110, 203, 272; and historians, 40, 84–85, 109–110, 135–136, 272–273, 325–326, 361; and Honourary Fellow, 361; and Master, xi, 268–275, 306–307, 315, 318, 325, 328, 360–362; as model, 368–369; and student, 2, 10, 14, 17–22, 26; and studentship, 26, 34–35

Plumb, J. H., 86, 150, 206, 279–280, 315–318, 325, 328, 397

Political history, xiii, 275–278, 353–358, 388–392, 409, 411, 414–415. *See* Diplomatic history

Politics, xv–xvi, 131, 314, 345–348, 358–360, 367–368, 373–375; and options, 10–11, 25, 102–106, 252–253, 304–305; and quietism, 102–106. *See* New Whig

Postan, M. M., 84, 110, 135, 272, 326, 361

Potter, G. R., 21, 154

Preacher, 23–24, 75–76, 178, 207, 210, 321–325, 335; aspiration to be, 2, 14–17, 21, 26, 41, 50; as lay preacher, 2, 13–14, 24, 36–37, 39–40, 103–104, 137; and preaching the Gospel, 174–175, 233, 298–300, 407–409. *See* Methodist

Predicament, 165, 173–174, 177, 185–186, 207; in world affairs, 203, 244–246, 310–315

Previte-Orton, 10, 100, 110, 240

Princeton, 37–39, 41, 202

Professor of Modern History, xi, 110, 133, 137–140, 163, 170, 203, 241, 270

Providence, xiv, 73–74, 127–128, 189–193; as constant, 1, 11, 39, 174, 177, 198, 207, 210. *See* God in history

Ranke, Leopold von, xi, 330, 404, 409–411; impact of, 22–23, 30, 48–49, 94, 170–172, 178, 200; as model, 42, 53, 68, 290, 353–355, 368, 400; writing on, 254–255, 263–264. *See* Scientific history

Reconciler, historian as, 75–75, 97, 146, 196–197, 372–373, 389, 416–417; and the reconciliation of opposites, 51–54, 195–197, 226. *See* Love; Stereoscopic vision

Regius Professor of Modern History, xi, 267–269, 315–318, 328–329, 331, 355, 360–361, 411, 417

Religion, the historian's, xiii–xiv, 61, 126–132, 172–177, 195, 415; and historical study, 181–182, 197–201. *See* Christian historian

Research students, 86, 135–136, 163, 204, 278, 325, 410, 456; and Festschrift, 365; and support, 86, 110, 135, 272, 285, 316–317, 321

Rockefeller Foundation, 253, 300; and the America Committee on the Theory of International Relations, 301–306, 309, 312; and the British Committee for the Theory of International Relations, 300–301, 306–309, 328, 345–353, 360–361, 384; and Villa Serbelloni, 330, 335, 340, 372, 375, 396. *See* International theory, international relations

Roman Catholic(s), 7, 11, 29, 228, 236, 239, 273, 300, 363; and family, friends, 267–269; in history, 71–72, 148, 258–259, 311–312, 392; and individualism, 324–325; as instances, 95–96, 181, 225, 262–263; and spir-

ituality, 376; and Whig interpretation, 60, 76, 119, 171–173. *See* Acton, Lord; Knowles, David

Sawston, Cambridgeshire, xi, xix, 363–364, 398

Scientific history, xiv, 32–33, 199, 207, 254–265, 354–355, 404–407, 409; and Christianity, 226–228; definition of, 179–182, 261–264; as final, 256–259, 264, 286, 343, 382–385; as induction, 98–100; as linked with laws, 53–54, 230–233; as model, 337–344, 352, 404–405, 415; as neutral to religion and politics, 37, 72, 94–100, 113–116, 165–166, 176, 180–181, 196–197, 200–201, 346, 394; as research and criticism, 53, 94. *See* History of historiography; Technical history

Sedgwick, R. R., 21, 282, 285–287, 291

Sin, 105–106, 129–131, 165, 187, 191, 211, 251, 302, 313; cupidity, 131, 173, 176–177, 185, 211, 370, 393

Smyth, Charles, 59–60, 120, 430

Social class, 41–42, 358, 374–375; as gentleman class, 17, 21, 24–25, 27, 86–87, 135, 270; and history, 123–126, 246–247; as working class, xi, 2–6, 16–17, 270, 361

Spirituality, 14, 24–25, 40–41, 299, 376–378, 393, 409

State, society, 197–198, 301–302, 314–315, 346–347, 354–355, 376, 391–393, 410; and nominalism, 183, 197–198; as provisionally 'real', 373–374; as 'unreal', 183–186, 212, 229, 246, 287, 309–310, 324–325, 414. *See* Individual(s)

Stereoscopic vision, 25–26, 53–54, 97, 146, 373–376, 416–417. *See* Reconciler, historian as

Tawney, R. H., 136, 272, 327

Taylor, A. J. P., 170, 209, 327, 364–365

Technical history, 116, 225, 252, 278, 294, 354–356, 411, 415; and Christianity, 193–197; definition of, 179–181, 213–219, 261–264; and historians, 167–170, 262, 328; as neutral to religion and politics, 198–199, 208–209, 213–219, 225–229, 262–263, 367–368, 394–395. *See* Scientific history

Teetotaler, 11, 16, 26, 35, 39, 49, 271, 274, 320–321, 375. *See* Dissent

Temperley, Harold, xi, 24–26, 327–328, 356, 383, 385–386, 424, 426; and biography, 134, 327–328; impact of, 15–22, 90, 178, 206, 353–355, 410; as Master, 109–110, 270; as Professor, 53, 87, 109–110, 133, 275; as supporter, 26, 35, 37–38, 40, 48, 100; as teacher, 17–19, 27–29, 41–43, 85

Thompson, Kenneth, 253, 301, 306

Toynbee, Arnold, 178, 206, 209, 230, 327, 329; as critic, 159–160, 182, 344; impact of, 89–91, 295–297, 338, 352–353

Trevelyan, George Macaulay, 76–77, 87, 106, 178, 280, 326–328; and history as literature, 52–55; impact of, 48–49, 90, 143; as supporter, 78–79, 109, 133–134, 170–171, 201, 210

Trevor-Roper, Hugh, 327, 417

Undergraduate teaching, 17–19, 85–86

University education, xiii–xiv, 319–325, 367–368

Vellacott, Paul, 17, 24, 37, 40, 84, 93; impact of, 17, 136, 268, 270, 318; as Master, 110, 136, 268, 270, 318; as supporter, 21, 78–79, 106, 154, 235, 237, 240, 254

War, 191, 242; and the bomb, 166–167, 312–315, 346–347, 350, 407; and bombs, 111; Great War of *1914–1919*, Seven Years' War, 256–258; Vietnam War, 347–348, 367; and wars for righteousness, 242–250; World War I, xi, xiv, 6–7, 14, 87, 165–166, 256, 356–358; World War II, 7, 101–102, 109–116, 132. *See* International theory

Ward, Adolphus, 15–16, 22, 24, 37–38, 270

Watson, Adam (John), 304, 307, 398, 400–401

Wesley House, 26, 36, 274, 315; teaching in, 36, 40, 61, 137

Wesley Methodist Church, 24, 36, 40, 104, 203–204, 274, 315

Whig historians, Whig politicians, 7, 59, 61–69, 78, 117–121, 305, 308, 317, 370

Whig interpretation of history, 95–97, 117–122, 205, 290; definition of, 58–59, 62; and Whiggish history, the Whiggish fallacy, ix–x, 63, 67, 108–109, 116, 145–146, 160–162, 205–206; writing on, 56–77. *See* New Whig

Wight, Martin, 177, 199, 208–209, 251, 306–307, 348–349, 353

Williams, Desmond, 169–170, 306, 348

Women's history, women, 15, 35, 368–369, 387, 389, 394

World Council of Churches, 314

World history, global historiography, xii, 140, 152, 200, 293–297, 304–315, 333; and China, xiii, 314, 336–338, 342–345, 390, 396–397, 400–401, 414–415; and historical writing, 334–353, 370–371, 389–391, 395–398; and India, 84–85, 199, 314, 336–339, 397; and Islam, 72, 200, 214, 228, 396, 401, 414–415

Wormald, Brian, 85–86, 110, 266–267, 278

Writer, 35, 50–52, 204, 404–407; aspiration to be, 1–2, 14, 21, 23; style, 33–34, 47–48, 56–57, 219, 226